MAR 1 6 1996

GW00949883

PACE
UNIVERSITY
SCHOOL OF LAW

TORT LIABILITY
FOR
PSYCHIATRIC
DAMAGE

SALES CENTRES AND AGENTS

HEAD OFFICE: 44-50 Waterloo Road NORTH RYDE NSW 2113
Tel: (02) 887 0177 Fax: (02) 888 2287

4th Floor 167 Phillip Street SYDNEY NSW 2000
Tel: (02) 235 0766 Fax: (02) 221 4004

568 Lonsdale Street MELBOURNE Vic 3000
Tel: (03) 670 7888 Fax: (03) 670 0138

1st Floor 40 Queen Street BRISBANE Qld 4000
Tel: (07) 221 6688 Fax: (07) 220 0084

9th Floor St George's Centre 81 St George's Terrace PERTH WA 6000
Tel: (09) 321 8583 Fax: (09) 324 1910

Sales Representative Keith Peterson GPO Box 384 ADELAIDE SA 5001
Tel/Fax: (08) 295 7644 mobile: 018 84 3052

Preferred Stockist The Bookworld 30 Smith Street DARWIN NT 0800
Tel: (089) 81 5277 Fax: (089) 411 226

Sales Representative Peter Stewart CPO Box 3139 AUCKLAND NZ
Tel: (09) 366 7204 Fax: (09) 309 5336

CANADA AND USA

The Carswell Company Ltd
Agincourt, Ontario

HONG KONG

Bloomsbury Books Ltd

MALAYSIA

Malayan Law Journal Pte Ltd
Kuala Lumpur

SINGAPORE

Malayan Law Journal Pte Ltd

UNITED KINGDOM

Sweet & Maxwell Ltd
London

USA

Wm W Gaunt & Sons, Inc
Holmes Beach, Florida

TORT LIABILITY FOR PSYCHIATRIC DAMAGE

The Law of "Nervous Shock"

by

NICHOLAS J MULLANY

LLB (Hons) (W Aust), BCL (Oxon)
Barrister and Solicitor of the Supreme Court of Western Australia

and

PETER R HANDFORD

LLB (Birm), LLM, PhD (Cantab)
Of the Middle Temple, Barrister
Barrister and Solicitor of the Supreme Courts of Western Australia and Victoria

Foreword by

THE RIGHT HON SIR THOMAS BINGHAM

Master of the Rolls

THE LAW BOOK COMPANY LIMITED   SWEET & MAXWELL
1993

KU
940
.M85
1993

Published in Sydney by

The Law Book Company Limited
  44-50 Waterloo Road, North Ryde, NSW
  568 Lonsdale Street, Melbourne, Victoria
  40 Queen Street, Brisbane, Queensland
  81 St George's Terrace, Perth, WA

National Library of Australia
  Cataloguing-in-Publication entry

Mullany, N J (Nicholas J).
  Tort liability for psychiatric damage.

  Bibliography.
  ISBN 0 455 21175 2.

  1. Torts—Australia. 2. Liability (Law)—Australia. 3. Stress
  (Psychology). I. Handford, Peter R. II. Title.

346.9403

British Library Cataloguing in Publication Data
  A CIP catalogue record for this book
  is available from the British Library.

  ISBN 0-455-21175-2

© The Law Book Company Limited 1993

This publication is copyright. Other than for the
purposes of and subject to the conditions prescribed under
the Copyright Act, no part of it may in any form or by
any means (electronic, mechanical, microcopying,
photocopying, recording or otherwise) be reproduced,
stored in a retrieval system or transmitted without prior
written permission. Inquiries should be addressed to
the publishers.

Designed and edited by Corina Brooks

Typeset in Times Roman, 10 on 11 point, by Mercier Typesetters Pty Ltd,
    Granville, NSW
  Printed by Ligare Pty Ltd, Riverwood, NSW.

For
Diane
and
Pauline

FOREWORD

THE RIGHT HON SIR THOMAS BINGHAM

Master of the Rolls

This book is greatly to be welcomed.

It addresses one of the most vexed and tantalising topics in the modern law of tort. For what kinds of mental damage will a claim lie? Who may claim? And in what circumstances? These deceptively simple questions have led to a welter of authority in a number of different jurisdictions. Underlying the cases has been the judges' concern that unless the limits of liability are tightly drawn the courts will be inundated with a flood of claims by plaintiffs ever more distant from the scene of the original mishap. So fine distinctions have been drawn and strict lines of demarcation established.

The field is, par excellence, one in which judges have much to learn from the insights and, it may be, errors of their colleagues in other jurisdictions, confronted by the same problems in different factual settings. It is a particular virtue of this book that it draws together threads of authority in the leading common law jurisdictions, particularly Australia, Canada and the United Kingdom, enabling both practitioners and judges to benefit from a pooling of experience in their search for solutions to these intractable problems. Incidentally, it is to be hoped that the book will hasten the interment of the label "nervous shock", which is not only misleading and inaccurate but, with its echoes of frail Victorian heroines, tends to disguise the very serious damage which is, in many cases, under discussion.

The authors have a point of view, which they express. They draw attention to the great advances which have been made in psychiatric medicine and believe that the barriers to recovery should be lowered and psychiatric damage treated like any other personal injury. This expression of opinion is also welcome. It adds bite to the narrative and the analysis and, whether readers agree with the authors' view or not, encourages them to test their own assumptions and question their own reservations. The forensic debate on this topic seems set to continue, in some jurisdictions at least: thanks to the authors it should be enlightened by a more comprehensive understanding of the subject and of what has been decided elsewhere.

Royal Courts of Justice, London
7 October 1992

PREFACE

The initial impetus for writing this book was provided by a series of decisions on psychiatric damage over the last few years, particularly in Australia. However both of us have a long-standing interest in the law of tort, and in particular in the law of what has traditionally been called "nervous shock". This complex and specialised aspect of tortious liability is, as Lord Macmillan observed, an area where "there are elements of greater subtlety than in the case of an ordinary physical injury".[1] Yet the space devoted to damage to the mind in the various torts texts (seldom more than a few token pages) did not, we believe, do this developing subject justice. The increase in attention being paid to this area as evidenced by recent judicial activity persuaded us that the time was ripe for an extended treatment of this branch of tort law, a decision confirmed by the advent of the litigation arising out of the Hillsborough soccer disaster, on which the House of Lords has now twice pronounced.[2] Our interest in the recent cases was also fired by the conviction that the ambit of liability could and should be extended, and that the courts were providing signs that this was beginning to happen. Regrettably, except in a few particular respects, the House of Lords now seems to have closed the door on further developments, at least in England, for some years to come. Plaintiffs in psychiatric damage cases are generally not out to make money: they seek some official recognition of the fact that the lives of themselves and their families have been shattered by events for which they were in no way to blame. This the House of Lords has conspicuously failed to provide, so far as the Hillsborough plaintiffs are concerned. This work therefore has a double aim: first, to analyse and expound the now considerable body of case law and the doctrinal ideas that are embedded in it, and secondly, to suggest how the law should move forward by expanding liability and removing unnecessary hurdles in the path of recovery. We have endeavoured to underline a principle that is in our view implicit in Lord Macmillan's statement quoted above—that psychiatric injury, like "ordinary physical injury", is a form of personal injury, and is just as deserving of proper redress, even granted the obvious truth that funds for accident compensation are limited. This is, we believe, the first occasion that a book has been devoted exclusively to liability for psychiatric damage.

This work has deliberately not been restricted to the law of any one particular jurisdiction. In the spirit of Professor John Fleming's *The Law of Torts*,[3] a treatise for which we both have the most profound admiration, it is written in the belief that no legal system has a monopoly on excellence, and that the courts in every common law country should be prepared to be outward-looking and receptive to developments elsewhere. We hope that it may encourage the citation, particularly in English courts,

---

1. *Bourhill v Young* [1943] AC 92 at 103.
2. *Alcock v Chief Constable of South Yorkshire Police* [1992] 1 AC 310; *Hicks v Chief Constable of the South Yorkshire Police* [1992] 2 All ER 65.
3. The current edition is the eighth, published in 1992.

of a wider variety of authority when next these matters arise for consideration. The highest tribunals in Australia and Canada seem to be much more prepared to benefit from the wisdom of a wide range of jurisdictions apart from their own.[4] Specifically, we have aimed to provide comprehensive coverage of the position in the three countries just mentioned, though there is also much material on the law in New Zealand (where despite the 1972 accident compensation legislation, common law development in this area may not have come to a halt[5]), Scotland, Ireland, the United States and South Africa.

Tort law provides plentiful illustration of the foibles of humankind, and so among the cases referred to will be found plaintiffs (not all of whom recovered damages) who claimed to suffer psychiatric harm or mental distress of some kind as a result of observing the coffin of a dead relative slip from its place on the hearse during a funeral procession,[6] viewing a circumcision on their son (performed as a family ceremony, in accordance with religious custom) which went horribly wrong,[7] seeing their truck loaded with plate glass run into by a streetcar,[8] learning of the death of a sister in a plane crash by "extra-sensory empathy",[9] being confronted by someone dressed up as a ghost,[10] seeing the negligent mutilation of their mother's picture,[11] being denied a make-up examination in Criminal Procedure,[12] and finding out that they had not after all won third prize in a lottery.[13] Cases involving animals seem to deserve a special mention in this regard: plaintiffs in such cases include those who were shocked at the death of the family dog,[14] and of a racehorse,[15] saw their pet cat shot,[16] had children who were infected by pet turtles,[17] found a dead mouse in a loaf of bread,[18] were chased by a bull,[19] mauled by a circus leopard

4. Compare, for example, the citation by Deane J in *Jaensch v Coffey* (1984) 155 CLR 549 of decisions not only from England, Scotland and Ireland but also from New Zealand and the United States, and the wide variety of English, Australian and American authority cited in *Rhodes v Canadian Pacific Railway* (1990) 75 DLR (4th) 248, with the small number of non-United Kingdom decisions referred to in *Alcock v Chief Constable of South Yorkshire Police* [1992] 1 AC 310. The cosmopolitan approach of the Canadian Supreme Court is well reflected in the recent seminal economic loss case of *Norsk Pacific Steamship Co v Canadian National Railway Co* (1992) 91 DLR (4th) 289. In stark contrast to the closeted British tradition, an encouragingly wide selection of comparative jurisprudence was seriously scrutinised by all seven members of the bench in the quest for the most appropriate doctrinal direction. The court's preparedness to entertain counsel's discussion of foreign law (and digestion of the relevant leading academic contributions) is indicative of the preferred style of judicial law-making.
5. See below, pp 8-9.
6. *Owens v Liverpool Corporation* [1939] 1 KB 394.
7. *Ibrahim (A Minor) v Muhammad* (unreported, QBD, 21 May 1984).
8. *Aronoff v Baltimore Transit Co* (1951) 80 A 2d 13 (Md).
9. *Burke v Pan-American World Airways Inc* (1980) 484 F Supp 850.
10. *Nelson v Crawford* (1899) 81 NW 335 (Mich).
11. *Furlam v Rayan Photo Works* (1939) 12 NYS 2d 921.
12. *McBeth v Dalhousie University* (1986) 173 APR 224 (NS).
13. *Sullivan v Atlantic Lottery Corporation* (1987) 205 APR 317 (NB).
14. *Campbell v Animal Quarantine Station* (1981) 632 P 2d 1066.
15. Cour de Cassation, chambre civile, 16 Jan 1962, D 1962, 199 (*L'affaire Lunus*).
16. *Davies v Bennison* (1927) 22 Tas LR 52.
17. *McMullin v F W Woolworth Co Ltd* (1974) 9 NBR (2d) 214.
18. *Vince v Cripps Bakery Pty Ltd* (1984) Aust Torts Rep 80-668.
19. *Bosley v Andrews* (1958) 142 A 2d 263 (Pa).

roaming at large,[20] attacked by an escaped chimpanzee,[21] defecated upon by a circus horse,[22] and injured as a result of the chaos caused by an escaping elephant.[23] Some cases defy belief. No one, other than perhaps a torts examiner, could have dreamed up the sequence of events that took place in *Masiba v Constantia Insurance Co Ltd*.[24] But it is most important that mention of such bizarre fact situations should not be allowed to obscure or trivialise the stark tragedy that underlies many of the decisions. No one could fail to be moved by the horror of the events which destroyed the families involved in *Hinz v Berry*,[25] or *Fenn v City of Peterborough*,[26] or *Kwok v British Columbia Ferry Corporation*,[27] to name but a few. The Hillsborough case, which evoked a national mourning, falls into the same category, but on a much vaster scale.

Though as this Preface is written we are on opposite sides of the world, much of the work was done by us together, first in Perth and then at Magdalen College, Oxford. Though one or the other produced initial drafts of particular chapters, we worked on every paragraph together and accept joint responsibility for the whole. Our thanks are due to a number of people, none of whom, of course, are responsible for any errors or omissions that there may be. Victor Kline and the production team at Law Book Co Ltd helped us in a variety of ways during the publication process. Dr Tony Hope, Leader of the Oxford Practice Skills Project, Honorary Consultant Psychiatrist, and Dr Hans Stampfer of the University of Western Australia Department of Psychiatry and Behavioural Science were kind enough to read and comment on parts of Chapter 2 in draft, and Harold Luntz, George Paton Professor of Law at the University of Melbourne, generously performed a similar office for Chapter 13. Basil Markesinis, Denning Professor of Comparative Law at the University of London, provided some assistance in relation to German authorities. Gregory Blue of the Law Reform Commission of British Columbia supplied us with information about Canadian statute law. Sue Blakey and Kaye Stacey typed much of the text from a manuscript which at one point incorporated so many glosses and highlights in different colours that it resembled the product of some mediaeval monastic institution. In particular, we owe a great deal to our families for the time we have stolen from them to write this book, and their patience with us while we did so— and the second-named author would like to make special mention of his parents, who by being strategically situated not too far away from Oxford provided an invaluable support base during that part of our work. But most of all, we owe an incalculable debt to two very special people without whose love, support, tolerance and forbearance this book could never have been written. We hope that this is in some measure reflected on the dedication page.

20. *Eyrich v Dam* (1984) 473 A 2d 539 (NJ).
21. *Lindley v Knowlton* (1918) 176 P 440 (Cal).
22. *Christy Bros Circus v Turnage* (1928) 144 SE 680 (Ga).
23. *Behrens v Bertram Mills Circus Ltd* [1957] 2 QB 1.
24. 1982 (4) SA 333 (C).
25. [1970] 2 QB 40.
26. (1976) 73 DLR (3d) 177.
27. (1987) 20 BCLR (2d) 318.

We have endeavoured to state the law as we understand it to be as at 30 August 1992, although it has been possible to make mention of a few later developments. Two which unfortunately came too late to permit their inclusion in the text of this work are the New South Wales Court of Appeal's decision in *Chiaverini v Hockey*[28] and the Canadian Supreme Court's contribution to the morass of law probing the appropriate limits on negligence liability through the formulation of the duty of care in *Norsk Pacific Steamship Co v Canadian National Railway Co*.[29]

The judgment delivered by Sheller JA, and concurred in by Meagher and Handley JJA, in the first of these cases touches on a number of the issues to which a chapter is devoted in this book. A wife claimed against two defendants who negligently injured her husband in two separate car accidents for mental illness allegedly associated with his injuries. She failed both at first instance and on appeal due to an inability to prove that her psychiatric complaint was attributable to an identifiable shock to her nervous system. The medical evidence indicated that it was caused not by stimuli which formed part of the accidents or their aftermath but by more remote consequences. The absence of a sudden perception of a shocking event and the fact the plaintiff's reactive depressive state stemmed instead from observing her husband's incapacitation, continuing disability, emotionally crippling dependence on her, and the inadequate settlement of his personal injuries claim were in the view of the Court of Appeal fatal to her claims both at common law and under s 4 of the *Law Reform (Miscellaneous Provisions) Act* 1944 (NSW). Five significant points can be distilled from the discussion of common law and statutory principles:

1. Gradually developing psychiatric injury was unfortunately confirmed as irrecoverable under the common law. A sudden impact on the psyche and shock-induced psychiatric illness remain central to the cause of action.[30]

2. Notwithstanding that the court confirmed that common law duty principles of reasonable foreseeability and proximity may not be relevant under s 4 of the *Law Reform (Miscellaneous Provisions) Act* 1944 (NSW),[31] it was considered to be "an inescapable conclusion" that the requirement that mental illness must be caused by shock is not eradicated by the statute. Some of the common law restrictions have, it would seem, survived to operate within Parliament's simplified scheme. With respect, it is submitted that the effect of the Act is not so clear cut. Whilst clearly there must be evidence of damage to the mind before statutory liability can be imposed, it contains nothing which indicates that psychiatric disorders attributable to other types of stimuli were intended to remain non-compensable, save for the retention of the inappropriate term "nervous shock" in the heading of Pt 3. It is suggested that even in 1944 this terminology was intended to convey psychiatric damage generally with little attention devoted by the drafters to whether compensable mental injury was caused solely by the sudden perception of trauma or brought on also by the

28. (Unreported, New South Wales CA, 16 Oct 1992, CA No 40654 of 1990).
29. (1992) 91 DLR (4th) 289. See J G Fleming, "Economic Loss in Canada" (1993) 1 Tort L Rev (forthcoming).
30. See below, Chapter 8.
31. See below, p 240.

accumulation of factors over a period of time. If the statute cannot be so interpreted, then for the same reasons that this antiquated and medically inaccurate requirement should be discarded under the common law, so should it be denied a licence to reduce the ambit of recovery under legislation implemented to overcome the hindrances introduced by the early authorities.

3. The rationale behind the introduction of the New South Wales legislation was, in line with previous indications, identified as a response to the harshness of the then prevailing common law.[32] Sheller JA considered it "plain that s 4 was introduced to overcome what were at the time seen as problems caused by the requirement of foreseeability and the application of a test of remoteness in the case of claims by members of the family of the person killed, injured or put in peril".

4. Some light has been shed on the limits of the aftermath doctrine.[33] The plaintiff appears to have learnt of both accidents when her husband was delivered to her at home hobbling on crutches and wearing a supportive collar. Although he did not elaborate on the issue, Sheller JA expressed "real doubt" as to whether these circumstances fell within the aftermath of the accident. This suggests that persons who come into contact with patched-up trauma victims for the first time at some place other than the hospital which treated them are outside the compensable range of claimants.

5. The court expressly confirmed, albeit by way of obiter dicta, that recovery is not precluded where psychiatric injury is sustained as a result of a combination of what is heard and seen.[34]

Although *Norsk Pacific Steamship Co v Canadian National Railway Co* does not deal with the specialised question of tort liability for psychiatric damage, the Canadian Supreme Court's comments impact on the general principles governing the recoverability for negligently caused harm discussed in Chapter 3. By a majority of 4:3 their Honours awarded damages to a railway which was the principal user (but not the owner) of a bridge damaged by a barge negligently towed in heavy fog by the defendant's tug, the basis of the claim being the interruption to the train routes while repairs were carried out. Although the judgments reflect divergent views on the vexed question of recoverability for pure economic loss,[35] all seven members were in agreement as to the lack of authoritativeness in Canada of the House of Lords pronouncement in *Murphy v Brentwood District Council*[36] that, save for certain exceptional categories of damage, recovery for non-consequential financial harm is automatically excluded. In line with its previous decisions,[37] the Supreme Court has sided with the Australian High Court[38] and the New Zealand Court of Appeal[39] in declining to rule out liability for pure financial loss as a matter of course.

32. See below, p 239, n 1.
33. See below, pp 137-140, 149-150, and particularly n 83.
34. See below, p 161, n 44.
35. Due to the uncertainty engendered by the decision an application for a rehearing before the Full Bench was made but dismissed: see (1992) 92 DLR (4th) 430.
36. [1991] 1 AC 398.
37. See eg *Rivtow Marine Ltd v Washington Iron Works* (1973) 40 DLR (3d) 530; *City of Kamloops v Nielsen* (1984) 10 DLR (4th) 641.
38. See *Caltex Oil (Australia) Pty Ltd v Dredge "Willemstad"* (1976) 136 CLR 529.
39. See eg *South Pacific Manufacturing Co Ltd v New Zealand Security Consultants & Investigations Ltd* [1992] 2 NZLR 282.

Importantly for present purposes, the court has in so holding confirmed that *Anns v Merton Borough Council*[40] still breathes across the Atlantic even if it has been smothered at home.[41] Significant also are the comments of Stevenson J who formed part of the majority concurring in a separate judgment. He has openly joined the band of appellate court judges who view proximity as a failed concept, expressing his agreement with the critical article by McHugh J[42] and Brennan J's well known concerns.[43] La Forest J in dissent can also be taken to have implicitly rejected the notion, agreeing with Stevenson J that proximity expresses a conclusion rather than a principle for limiting liability. Any evaluation of the utility of proximity is especially relevant for complex litigation such as that involving claims for psychiatric damage where the concept has a more significant role to play than in other personal injuries or property damage actions. One may venture the forecast that we have yet to hear the definitive word on the character of the duty to take care and this liability limitation device.

NICHOLAS MULLANY
Magdalen College, Oxford

PETER HANDFORD
Perth, Western Australia

20 October 1992

---

40. [1978] AC 728.
41. See below, pp 75-78.
42. See "Neighbourhood, Proximity and Reliance" in P D Finn (ed), *Essays on Torts* (1989), 5.
43. See below, p 80.

TABLE OF CONTENTS

TABLE OF CASES

TABLE OF STATUTES, ORDERS AND RULES

1

INTRODUCTION

"It is submitted, I think rightly, that this claim breaks new ground. No analogous claim has ever, to my knowledge, been upheld or even advanced. If, therefore, it were proper to erect a doctrinal boundary stone at the point which the onward march of recorded decisions has so far reached, we should answer the question of principle in the negative and dismiss the plaintiff's action. . . . But I should for my part erect the boundary stone with a strong presentiment that it would not be long before a case would arise so compelling on its facts as to cause the stone to be moved to a new and more distant resting place."[1]

Origins

Much has happened in the law of nervous shock since that fateful evening in May 1886 when James and Mary Coultas set out from Melbourne in their horse-drawn buggy to return home to Hawthorn. Through the negligence of a level crossing gatekeeper, they were allowed to proceed across a railway line when a train was approaching. James Coultas got the buggy across the line just in time to avoid a collision, but the near miss caused his wife to suffer fright and, as a consequence, a "severe nervous shock". When the case of *Victorian Railways Commissioner v Coultas* came before the Supreme Court of Victoria, the jury awarded damages for the shock, an award upheld on appeal to the Full Court.[2] However, on further appeal the Privy Council held that the damage was too remote.[3]

"Damages arising from mere sudden terror unaccompanied by any actual physical injury, but occasioning a nervous or mental shock, cannot under such circumstances . . . be considered a consequence which, in the ordinary course of things, would flow from the negligence of the gatekeeper."[4]

The defendant contended that there had to be "impact", in the shape of some contemporaneous physical injury, as a guarantee of the genuineness of the claim. The Privy Council refrained from saying that impact was necessary,[5] but subsequent authorities adopted the "impact rule" as a reason for denying recovery.[6]

1. *Attia v British Gas Plc* [1988] QB 304 per Bingham LJ at 320.
2. *Victorian Railways Commissioner v Coultas* (1886) 12 VLR 895.
3. *Victorian Railways Commissioner v Coultas* (1888) 13 App Cas 222.
4. Ibid at 225.
5. Ibid at 226.
6. Especially in the United States: see below, pp 10-12. Note also the Australian case of *Rea v Balmain New Ferry Co* (1896) 17 LR (NSW) 92 per Darley CJ at 98. Compare the earlier Canadian authority adopting *Coultas*: see *Henderson v Canada Atlantic Railway Co*

1

The reasoning in this case reflects the scepticism with which mental damage claims were initially greeted by the judiciary. Ignorance of the medical subtleties of the subject,[7] concerns of "opening the floodgates" to limitless liability and its ramifications for the insurance industry, the scope for feigned claims, inherent problems of establishing a causative link, and perceived administrative and practical difficulties of damages assessment combined to produce a long-time entrenched reluctance to protect mental tranquillity. This stance was in marked contrast to the early preparedness to compensate for actual physical harm, something viewed as far more important than the perceived trivialities of nervous stress.

Moving the boundaries

It was not long before the *Coultas* decision was challenged by courts in Ireland,[8] England,[9] Scotland,[10] South Africa,[11] New Zealand,[12] Canada[13] and Australia.[14] Ever since, in the light of steadily increasing knowledge

6. *Continued*
   (1898) 25 OAR 437, affirmed (1899) 29 SCR 632; *Geiger v Grand Trunk Railway Co* (1905) 10 OLR 511; *Miner v CPR* (1911) 3 Alta LR 408; *Lapointe v Champagne* (1921) 50 OR 477; *Penman v Winnipeg Electric Railway Co* [1925] 1 DLR 497. Note the slight "impact" in *Toronto Railway Co v Toms* (1911) 44 SCR 268 (damages awarded for mental suffering when plaintiff thrown against seat in streetcar) and *Negro v Pietro's Bread Co* [1933] 1 DLR 490 (relief granted when plaintiff's throat scratched by broken glass found in bread).

7. Note for example the story recounted in B Botein, *Trial Judge* (1952), reproduced in M Gilbert (ed), *The Oxford Book of Legal Anecdotes* (1986), 10-11, concerning an American case in which the plaintiff claimed to be suffering from neurasthenia (a state of nervous exhaustion: see below, p 273, n 51) as the result of a railway accident. A doctor testified that the main ground for his opinion that the plaintiff was suffering from neurasthenia was that he felt no pain when pricked with a pin on the top of his head. The defendant's lawyer convinced the jury that the plaintiff had suffered no injury by inserting a dozen or so needles into his head as they watched (the lawyer having previously anaesthetised his scalp by injecting it with cocaine). Needless to say, the evidence of the harm under discussion required in modern cases would be very different.

8. *Bell v Great Northern Railway Co of Ireland* (1890) 26 LR Ir 428, following *Byrne v Great Southern & Western Railway Co* (unreported, CA of Ireland, Feb 1884).

9. *Dulieu & White & Sons* [1901] 2 KB 669. *Coultas* had been questioned by Lord Esher MR in *Pugh v London, Brighton & South Coast Railway Co* [1896] 2 QB 248 at 250. Note also, in the context of workers' compensation, *Yates v South Kirby Collieries Ltd* [1910] 2 KB 538, where Farwell LJ said at 542: "In my opinion, nervous shock due to accident which causes personal incapacity to work is as much 'personal injury by accident' as a broken leg."

10. *Wallace v Kennedy* (1908) 16 SLT 485; *Campbell v Henderson Ltd*, 1915 1 SLT 419; *Brown v Watson* [1915] AC 1. *Cooper v Caledonian Railway* (1902) 4 F 880, *Gilligan v Robb*, 1910 SC 856 and *Fowler v North British Railway*, 1914 SC 866 have also been cited for this point, but it is not absolutely clear from the reports that such a step was taken because the courts involved decided that there was a relevant case for inquiry without investigating the points of law in any detail.

11. *Hauman v Malmesbury District Council*, 1916 CPD 216.

12. *Stevenson v Basham* [1922] NZLR 225.

13. *Negro v Pietro's Bread Co* [1933] 1 DLR 490; *Purdy v Woznesensky* [1937] 2 WWR 116; *Austin v Mascarin* [1942] OR 165; *Horne v New Glasgow* [1954] 1 DLR 832. The courts in *Toronto Railway Co v Toms* (1911) 44 SCR 268 and *Hogan v City of Regina* [1924] 2 DLR 1211 expressed the view that *Coultas* was confined to situations where there was evidence of pure mental injury unaccompanied by physical damage.

14. *Chester v Council of the Municipality of Waverley* (1939) 62 CLR 1. Burbury CJ in *Storm v Geeves* [1965] Tas SR 252 at 255 had no doubt that *Coultas* "has not been good law in Australia for many years". Note also *Daly v Commissioner of Railways* (1906) 8

of the effect on the human psyche of strong emotions such as fright, the courts have gradually widened the ambit of recovery—the law, in the words of Windeyer J, "marching with medicine but in the rear and limping a little".[15] At each stage they have overcome the traditional objections listed above.[16] As described by Bingham LJ, in a case in which it was recognised for the first time that liability might exist for nervous shock—or psychiatric damage, to use the modern terminology now preferred—caused by damage to property, rather than injury to the person,[17] on a number of occasions the boundary stone has been taken up and set down in a different place, only to be moved on once more. In the early 1980s, important decisions of the highest courts in England and Australia, *McLoughlin v O'Brian*[18] and *Jaensch v Coffey*,[19] set new limits, but these cases are now being scrutinised afresh in a series of recent decisions in both countries. In 1991, in only the third nervous shock case to reach the House of Lords, *Alcock v Chief Constable of South Yorkshire Police*[20] canvassed the need to expand the confines of liability for psychiatric damage still further. This litigation arose out of the tragic events which took place at the FA Cup semi-final between Liverpool and Nottingham Forest at Hillsborough in 1989. The recent pronouncement of the House of Lords in this case reconsiders some of the older authorities and once again reviews the proper limits of redress. It is the object of this work to examine the issues raised by this area of liability, particularly those exposed by the recent decisions, and explore the appropriateness of the current boundary marks.

In order to appreciate the restrictions currently placed on recovery, it is necessary to go briefly back over the successive extensions of the law.[21] In the earlier cases repudiating *Victorian Railways Commissioner v Coultas*[22] and the impact rule and granting recovery, liability was based on the principle that "the shock, in order to give a cause of action, must be one which arises from a fear of immediate personal injury to oneself"—to

14. *Continued*
    WALR 125 and *Sealy v Commissioner of Railways* [1915] QWN 1, where *Coultas* was distinguished on the ground that nervous injury was sustained through actual impact (respectively, a train collision with a horse and a slight cut by shattered glass) and not as the result of mere apprehended danger.
15. *Mount Isa Mines Ltd v Pusey* (1970) 125 CLR 383 at 395.
16. Note the discussion of these arguments in *McLoughlin v O'Brian* [1983] 1 AC 410 per Lord Wilberforce at 421 and per Lord Bridge at 441-442. Contrast the negative attitude of Griffiths LJ in the Court of Appeal [1981] QB 599 at 624: "Would it really be wise to introduce into this common experience of mankind [grief at the death of or injury to a relative or friend] the possibility of some monetary solatium for their suffering if they are able to persuade a judge that the suffering is due in part to shock, not grief. It will obviously be a very difficult question to decide and I venture to question how much good it will in most cases do for the sufferer. A modest sum of money may be recovered but I suspect the recovery of health may be seriously delayed by the litigation. . . . May we not by giving the remedy aggravate the illness? Surely health is better than money."
17. *Attia v British Gas Plc* [1988] QB 304 at 320, quoted above, p 1.
18. [1983] 1 AC 410, noted by A C Hutchinson & D Morgan (1982) 45 MLR 697; M Owen [1983] CLJ 41; H Street (1983) 34 NILQ 53.
19. (1984) 155 CLR 549, noted by A O'Connell & R Evans (1985) 15 Melb ULR 164; D Partlett (1985) 59 ALJ 44; F A Trindade (1985) 5 OJLS 305.
20. [1992] 1 AC 310.
21. Early analyses include D H Parry, "Nervous Shock as a Cause of Action in Tort" (1925) 41 LQR 297 and A Stirling, "Liability for Nervous Shock" (1928) 2 ALJ 46.
22. (1888) 13 App Cas 222.

quote Kennedy J in the leading case of *Dulieu v White & Sons*.[23] There a pregnant plaintiff recovered for nervous shock brought on by a fear for her safety when a horse-drawn van was negligently driven into a public house where she was standing behind the bar. She prematurely gave birth to a mentally defective child. To adopt a term commonly found in the American cases,[24] the plaintiff—like Mary Coultas—had to be within the "zone of danger", likely to suffer harm through physical impact. But it was not long before the courts were persuaded to overthrow this restriction.

It is generally recognised that *Hambrook v Stokes Bros*[25] was the first of a new wave of cases allowing recovery in a situation which has dominated the law of nervous shock ever since—the plaintiff, safely outside the area of possible impact, who suffers psychiatric damage through fear that another has been or may be killed, injured or put in peril.[26] Clearly, self-preservation is not the only natural human instinct. For some time, the key factors delineating the limits of liability were that the plaintiff should be present at the scene of the accident (or near-accident), and should suffer psychiatric injury as a result of experiencing the calamity through his or her own senses. Shock through being told of the accident by others was regarded as not giving rise to liability. In virtually all the cases, the plaintiff was a close relative—usually a parent or spouse—of the person injured or endangered by the defendant's negligence, and such a relationship was obviously an important factor in the finding that the psychiatric damage suffered was foreseeable, but some courts appear to have contemplated that even a mere bystander might have a cause of action. *Hambrook v Stokes Bros* is an important illustration of all these points. The English Court of Appeal granted recovery in a claim under the *Fatal Accidents Act* 1846 (UK) made on behalf of a mother who suffered psychiatric injury through seeing a driverless truck coming down a hill out of control, and the fear (which, as it turned out, was well-founded) that it might have injured her children who were further up the road out of sight. The majority said that the duty to avoid such injury was owed to persons such as the plaintiff who were not

---

23. [1901] 2 KB 669 at 675.

24. See below, p 12.

25. [1925] 1 KB 141, noted (1925) 41 LQR 132; D B Ross (1928) 2 ALJ 117. Kennedy J's limitation in *Dulieu v White & Sons* [1901] 2 KB 669 at 675 was criticised by Bankes LJ at 151, Atkin LJ at 157-158 (but note Sargant LJ's comments at 162); *Owens v Liverpool Corporation* [1939] 1 KB 394 per MacKinnon LJ at 399-400; *Bourhill v Young* [1943] AC 92 per Lord Wright at 110-112, per Lord Porter at 117, 120 (but note Lord Russell's comments at 103); *Dooley v Cammell Laird & Co Ltd* [1951] 1 Lloyd's Rep 271 per Donovan J at 276-277; *Storm v Geeves* [1965] Tas SR 252 per Burbury CJ at 265; *Chadwick v British Railways Board* [1967] 1 WLR 912 per Waller J at 919-920; *McLoughlin v O'Brian* [1983] 1 AC 410 per Lord Wilberforce at 418, per Lord Bridge at 435, 439. Note, however, the view of J Havard, "Reasonable Foresight of Nervous Shock" (1956) 19 MLR 478 at 488 that "it should have been unnecessary to have overruled Kennedy J's limitation as it could have been foreseen that Mrs Hambrook would be placed in immediate fear for her own personal safety".

26. Note, however, the earlier case of *Rickard v Plymouth Co-operative Society*, The Times, 4 Feb 1903, where Bigham J awarded damages to a plaintiff who feared for the safety of her children who were (as she thought) in her house when it fell down due to the defendant's excavation on adjoining land. They had in fact been moved to safety.

in personal danger[27] (indeed, Atkin LJ went so far as to include all bystanders, even those not related in any way to the accident victim[28]), provided that the shock was caused by the plaintiff's own unaided realisation of what had happened.[29] The same limitation was imposed by Evatt J in his important dissenting judgment in *Chester v Council of the Municipality of Waverley*,[30] in which the majority of the Australian High Court refused recovery where a mother suffered psychiatric damage when the body of her missing son was recovered from a water-filled trench. In fact, as the case law developed, the only non-relatives who recovered were rescuers[31] or workmates,[32] rather than mere bystanders, and plaintiffs (unlike Mrs Hambrook) usually saw the accident happen, though perception by seeing (as opposed, for example, to hearing[33]) was never essential. A typical example of the kind of case in which compensation was granted is *Hinz v Berry*,[34] where the plaintiff and her husband, four children and four foster children had stopped in a layby for a picnic tea after a day in the English countryside. The plaintiff, who was across the road with one child picking bluebells, heard a crash and turned round to see that the defendant in his Jaguar had mown down the rest of her family. She recovered damages for her resultant psychiatric illness.

In recent years *McLoughlin v O'Brian*[35] and *Jaensch v Coffey*[36] have once again moved the boundaries of recovery. The basis of this new extension of liability was the affirmation by the courts, in the cases described in the previous paragraph, that the determinant of liability was foreseeability of injury *by shock*.[37] On this reasoning, psychiatric damage, at least to close relatives, was foreseeable even where the relative was not present at the scene of the accident but arrived there shortly afterwards, often as a result of having been told of the disaster, and saw its

---

27. The defendants admitted that their servant had been negligent, and it is sometimes suggested that it is only on this basis that a duty of care was owed to the plaintiff. However, Atkin LJ [1925] 1 KB 141 at 156 said that apart from the admission the cause of action was complete. For discussion of this point see *King v Phillips* [1953] 1 QB 429 per Singleton LJ at 436-437, per Hodson LJ at 443-444.

28. [1925] 1 KB 141 at 156-159. Sargant LJ dissented, seeing the wide ambit of possible plaintiffs—relatives and others—as a reason against extending the law. Compare *King v Phillips* [1953] 1 QB 429 at 441 and *Hinz v Berry* [1970] 2 QB 40 at 42, in which Lord Denning made a distinction between relatives and others. In *Bourhill v Young* [1943] AC 92 shock to a mere bystander, unrelated to the accident victim, was held not to be foreseeable. This important issue is discussed in greater detail below, pp 128-133.

29. [1925] 1 KB 141 at 159, and see also per Bankes LJ at 152. For further discussion of this issue see below, pp 134-136, 153. A factually similar American case is *Bowman v Williams* (1933) 165 A 182 (Md).

30. (1939) 62 CLR 1. Note N Landau, "The Duty in Cases of Nervous Shock" (1940) 2 *Res Judicata* 129.

31. See eg *Chadwick v British Railways Board* [1967] 1 WLR 912; *Mount Isa Mines Ltd v Pusey* (1970) 125 CLR 383. See below, pp 108-111.

32. See eg *Dooley v Cammell, Laird & Co Ltd* [1951] 1 Lloyd's Rep 271; *Mount Isa Mines Ltd v Pusey* (1970) 125 CLR 383. See below, pp 111-113.

33. As in *Boardman v Sanderson* [1964] 1 WLR 1317, where the plaintiff's presence was known, rather than merely foreseeable, and *Mount Isa Mines Ltd v Pusey* (1970) 125 CLR 383, where the plaintiff came to the scene of the accident to rescue his injured workmates.

34. [1970] 2 QB 40, noted (1970) 86 LQR 457.

35. [1983] 1 AC 410.

36. (1984) 155 CLR 549.

37. See below, pp 69-70.

"aftermath".[38] In *McLoughlin v O'Brian* and *Jaensch v Coffey* the aftermath doctrine was ratified by the highest courts in England and Australia and extended to cases where the plaintiffs never arrived at the scene of the accident at all, but saw their loved ones lying injured in hospital.

This development has brought about important shifts in the balance between the various factors involved in such cases.[39] Presence, once essential, has been downgraded in importance, and learning of the accident through others is no longer fatal to recovery. In many cases the injury is caused by a combination of what plaintiffs see and what they are told,[40] and in some cases psychiatric damage caused purely through hearing of the accident from others has been held recoverable.[41] On the other hand, the element of relationship to the injured or endangered person became crucial. The English courts, if not those elsewhere, attempted to impose artificial restrictions on recovery, limiting it in the main to parents and spouses,[42] and the position of non-relatives, even when the accident happened in front of their eyes, seemed increasingly uncertain.

But in recent cases these principles are once again being subjected to close scrutiny. In particular, the facts of the latest House of Lords decision, *Alcock v Chief Constable of South Yorkshire Police*,[43] exposed the inadequacies of the present law in the face of a mass disaster in which hundreds of people were killed or injured in the sight of thousands present at the ground and millions watching on television. The action was brought by 16 plaintiffs, all of whom, it was alleged, had suffered psychiatric injury through the fear that loved ones had been killed or injured as a result of the negligence of police who had opened a gate at the Hillsborough soccer ground and allowed the Leppings Lane terraces to become seriously overcrowded. Sadly, in most cases their concerns turned out to be justified. Among the plaintiffs were a wife, a parent, a grandparent, a brother, a sister, an uncle, a brother-in-law, a fiancée and a friend. Some had been in the crowd, some saw it as it happened on television, others heard radio or television news broadcasts and some were told by third parties. These 16 plaintiffs were representative of some 150 others.[44] In each case it was admitted for the purposes of the proceedings that the Chief Constable was in breach of a tortious duty of care owed to the primary victim and that

---

38. See below, pp 136-152.
39. See H Teff, "Liability for Negligently Inflicted Nervous Shock" (1983) 99 LQR 100 at 100-104; F A Trindade, "The Principles Governing the Recovery of Damages for Negligently Caused Nervous Shock" [1986] CLJ 476.
40. See eg *Hambrook v Stokes Bros* [1925] 1 KB 141; *McLoughlin v O'Brian* [1983] 1 AC 410; *Jaensch v Coffey* (1984) 155 CLR 549. See the discussion below, p 161.
41. See *Petrie v Dowling* [1992] 1 Qd R 284 and other cases dealt with below, pp 161-165.
42. See eg *McLoughlin v O'Brian* [1983] 1 AC 410 per Lord Wilberforce at 422; *Alcock v Chief Constable of South Yorkshire Police* [1992] 1 AC 310 per Parker LJ at 359.
43. [1992] 1 AC 310.
44. Claims by some plaintiffs who were in the terraces, and "certain limited nervous shock cases", were settled without admission of liability, under an order by Steyn J made on 20 Dec 1989: see L Steel, "Hillsborough Blues" (1990) 134 SJ 1340 at 1341. Actions for pre-death pain and suffering brought on behalf of the estates of three other victims of the disaster were rejected by Hidden J, the Court of Appeal and the House of Lords: see *Hicks v Chief Constable of the South Yorkshire Police* (unreported, QBD, 31 July 1990); [1992] 1 All ER 690 (CA); [1992] 2 All ER 65 (HL), dealt with below, pp 50-51.

each plaintiff had suffered psychiatric illness, and a causal link between that illness and the circumstances in which he or she became aware of the death or injury of the primary victim was assumed. The sole question in issue was whether the defendant owed any duty in tort to the plaintiffs to avoid causing the type of injury complained of. Hidden J at first instance was prepared to consider extending the accepted limits of liability and held that ten of the plaintiffs (including some watching on television) had a good cause of action,[45] but the Court of Appeal adopted a more restrictive attitude, allowing the defendant's appeal in each case.[46] The House of Lords has recently confirmed the decision of the Court of Appeal,[47] although in certain respects its general attitude towards the expansion of liability is a little more encouraging. Other courts of final appeal, such as the High Court of Australia and the Supreme Court of Canada, will no doubt have to re-examine the problem before long. This work reviews the current principles of tortious liability for psychiatric damage in the light of these latest developments and suggests a more liberal direction which the law should take in the future.[48]

The range of reference

The importance of recent decisions of the highest appellate courts in Australia and England, together with the large number of other cases in those jurisdictions in the last few years, means that this work concentrates chiefly on the judicial output of these two countries.[49] However, it is our intention to cover as thoroughly as possible the law in all the major

45. *Alcock v Chief Constable of South Yorkshire Police* [1992] 1 AC 310, sub nom *Jones v Wright* [1991] 1 All ER 353, noted by S Hedley [1991] CLJ 229. See also M Napier, "The Medical and Legal Trauma of Disasters" [1991] *Medico-Legal Journal* 157.
46. [1992] 1 AC 310, sub nom *Jones v Wright* [1991] 3 All ER 88.
47. [1992] 1 AC 310, noted by B McDonald (1992) 66 ALJ 386; S Hedley [1992] CLJ 16; B Lynch (1992) 108 LQR 367. See also J Swanton, "Issues in Tort Liability for Nervous Shock" (1992) 66 ALJ 495; H Teff, "Liability for Psychiatric Illness after Hillsborough" (1992) 12 OJLS 440; K J Nasir, "Nervous Shock and Alcock: The Judicial Buck Stops Here" (1992) 55 MLR 705. Criminal charges against the officers involved were dropped: see "Disaster Charge Dropped", *The Times*, 14 Jan 1992, 3.
48. There have been very few judicial examinations of recovery for psychiatric damage in relation to occupiers' liability. It would appear, however, that if premises are maintained in a defective condition such that the occupier should have foreseen the possibility of shock-related injury to visitors, then an action could lie under occupiers' liability legislation, irrespective of any common law claim or common law restrictions on recovery: note *Lawrence v C J Evans (Properties) Ltd* (1965) 196 EG 407. Likewise the question of strict liability in relation to this particular loss has received almost no attention from the courts: for rare examples see *Creydt-Ridgeway v Hoppent*, 1930 TPD 664 (shock consequent on dog bite); *Behrens v Bertram Mills Circus Ltd* [1957] 2 QB 1 (shock consequent on injuries to wife from escaping elephant). Psychiatric damage cases in the sphere of nuisance are equally scarce: see *Pelmothe v Phillips* (1899) 20 LR (NSW) 58; *Evans v Finn* (1904) 4 SR (NSW) 297. It is not our intention to discuss the different issues raised in these contexts.
49. For Australian law see F A Trindade & P Cane, *The Law of Torts in Australia* (1985), 286-296; J G Fleming, *The Law of Torts* (8th ed, 1992), 159-165; R P Balkin, J L R Davis, *Law of Torts* (1991), 248-257. For English law see R F V Heuston & R A Buckley, *Salmond and Heuston on the Law of Torts* (20th ed, 1992), 219-223; M Brazier (ed), *Street on Torts* (8th ed, 1988), 177-181; W V H Rogers, *Winfield and Jolowicz on Tort* (13th ed, 1989), 106-110; R W M Dias et al (ed), *Clerk and Lindsell on Torts* (16th ed, 1989), paras 10.10-10.13; R W M Dias & B S Markesinis, *Tort Law* (2nd ed, 1989), 130-133.

countries influenced by the common law, and Canadian decisions in particular are fully dealt with.[50] There have been some important Canadian cases but, interestingly, developments in relation to some aspects of psychiatric damage law do not seem to have proceeded with the same speed as in Australia and England. In New Zealand, the evolution of the principles of recovery for shock-induced harm was brought to a halt by the *Accident Compensation Act* 1972, s 27 of which abolished the right to bring a common law action for personal injury, but prior New Zealand case law is referred to.[51] Recent legislative alterations to the coverage of the

50. See A M Linden, *Canadian Tort Law* (4th ed, 1988), 363-375; G H L Fridman, *The Law of Torts in Canada* (1989), Vol 1, 256-263; L Klar, *Tort Law* (1991), 279-282; J A Rendall, "Nervous Shock and Tortious Liability" (1962) 2 Osgoode Hall LJ 291; J S Williams, "Tort Liability for Nervous Shock in Canada" in A M Linden (ed), *Studies in Canadian Tort Law* (1968), 139-159.

51. See S M D Todd et al, *The Law of Torts in New Zealand* (1991), 129-131. Under the *Accident Compensation Act* 1972 (NZ) persons who suffer "personal injury by accident" may be awarded compensation, generally in the form of periodical payments, without any necessity to prove fault. The Act was consolidated and revised by the *Accident Compensation Act* 1982 (NZ). As to compensation for psychiatric injury under the Act see ibid, 46-52; R Tobin, "Personal Injury by Accident: Some Problems of Interpretation" [1991] NZLJ 239. In *ACC v E* [1991] NZAR 116 Greig J made it clear that "personal injury" extended to the mental as well as physical consequences of an accident, allowing recovery for a nervous breakdown sustained after a management course notwithstanding that there had not been any physical injury to the claimant giving rise to the emotional consequences. The decision was upheld by the New Zealand Court of Appeal, sub nom *Accident Compensation Corporation v E* [1992] 2 NZLR 426, the court stating at 433 that there could be "no other construction" of the statute. See also *King v ACC* [1992] NZAR 65 (woman recovered for the mental consequences of her smoke phobia attributable to the fire-bombing of her home even though she had suffered no physical injury in the fire); *Kennedy v ACC* [1992] NZAR 107 (man suffered mental effects as a result of having a shotgun pointed at him during armed robbery); *Re Chase* [1989] 1 NZLR 325 per Cooke P at 329 (gang member mistakenly shot and killed during police dawn raid); contrast *Accident Compensation Corporation v F* [1991] 1 NZLR 234 per Holland J at 240-241. As regards compensation for psychiatric harm suffered by secondary victims, a booklet issued by the Accident Compensation Corporation advised that "[a] claim may also stand for 'mental consequences' as a result of witnessing an accident, or as a result of being advised of the accident shortly thereafter": see *Unintentional Injury: New Zealand's Accident Compensation Scheme*, 16, cited by R Tobin, "Nervous Shock: The Common Law; Accident Compensation?" [1992] NZLJ 282 at 285. Moreover, the Claims Manual Instructions issued by the Corporation indicated that claims by persons who suffered mental harm as a result of being told of an accident and the resulting injuries were not ruled out. However, it has been held that the Act was not intended to cover consequential effects on the mental health of observers of accidents or persons associated with the victims of accidents: see *Accident Compensation Corporation v F* (reactive depression suffered by husband whose wife was unable to have sexual intercourse following medical misadventure); *Cochrane v ACC* (unreported, ACA 342/91) (recovery denied for emotional trauma suffered by mother as result of vigil at bed of son dying from gunshot wounds); and note the comments of Cooke P in *South Pacific Manufacturing Co Ltd v New Zealand Security Consultants & Investigations Ltd* [1992] 2 NZLR 282 at 297. "Personal injury by accident" is limited to physical and mental harm consequent on a mishap to the person and cannot include injuries to other interests such as financial or property damage or loss of reputation, even though the damages recoverable for that kind of harm include redress for injured feelings: see *Green v Matheson* [1989] 3 NZLR 564; *Willis v Attorney-General* [1989] 3 NZLR 574. According to the latter decision, physical and mental injuries caused by intentional assaults and batteries are "personal injury by accident" for the purpose of the *Accident Compensation Act* (note also *Re Chase*), but certain mental consequences of false imprisonment were excluded for policy reasons.

no-fault compensation scheme are such that common law claims for psychiatric damage may soon rise phoenix-like from the ashes.[52] Decisions from Scotland and South Africa, two countries in which the common law has been superimposed on a theoretical foundation of delictual liability based on Roman law, are also examined.[53] It is worthy of note that the law in these jurisdictions was much slower to abandon the requirement that the plaintiff, in order to recover, must fear for his or her own personal safety[54]—indeed, in this respect South African law "languished in the doldrums" until 1973.[55] The case law in Ireland is more limited, but has

52. Far-reaching changes to the accident compensation scheme have been effected by the *Accident Rehabilitation and Compensation Insurance Act* 1992 (NZ). In line with the restrictive decision of Holland J in *Accident Compensation Corporation v F* [1991] 1 NZLR 234, "personal injury" has been redefined to exclude most cases of mental injury not attendant on physical injury, a reform which reverses the New Zealand Court of Appeal's liberal interpretation in *Accident Compensation Corporation v E* [1992] 2 NZLR 426. The only exceptions reserved are very limited ones dealing with various sexual offences. This development raises the possibility that common law claims for psychiatric harm may once again be mounted both by traumatised but physically unharmed primary victims (eg "near miss" claimants) and secondary sufferers: see R Tobin, "Nervous Shock: The Common Law; Accident Compensation?" [1992] NZLJ 282; S Todd & J Black, "Accident Compensation and the Barring of Actions for Damages" (1993) 1 Tort L Rev (forthcoming).

53. See D M Walker, *The Law of Delict in Scotland* (2nd ed, 1981), 671-680 (Scotland); R G McKerron, *The Law of Delict* (7th ed, 1971), 154-157; J M Potgieter, "Emotional Shock" in W A Joubert (ed), *The Law of South Africa* (1979), Vol 9, §§1-13; P Q R Boberg, *The Law of Delict Vol 1: Aquilian Liability* (1984), 174-193 (South Africa).

54. In Scotland, the limitation was affirmed in *Wallace v Kennedy* (1908) 16 SLT 485; *Campbell v Henderson Ltd*, 1915 1 SLT 419; *Ross v Glasgow Corporation*, 1919 SC 174; *Brown v Glasgow Corporation*, 1922 SC 527. Other cases sometimes cited for this proposition (*Cooper v Caledonian Railway* (1902) 4 F 880; *Gilligan v Robb*, 1910 SC 856; *Fowler v North British Railway*, 1914 SC 866; *Cowie v London, Midland & Scottish Railway*, 1934 SC 433) do not make it clear on what basis the issue is allowed to go to proof, although on the facts the pursuers feared for their own safety. In *Currie v Wardrop*, 1927 SC 538, a woman walking arm-in-arm with her fiancé suffered shock when they were both knocked down by a bus. It appears that she was not physically struck. The court held that shock was caused both by fear for her own safety and for that of her fiancé, and the case is therefore not clear authority for the view that shock arising from apprehension for the safety of another is actionable in Scotland: see Walker, op cit, n 53 at 675. The first case to depart from the *Dulieu v White & Sons* limitation was *McLinden v Richardson*, 1962 SLT (Notes) 104, where Lord Wheatley at 105, in allowing proof before answer, said that he was not prepared to apply this limitation as an absolute proposition. More recent cases are consistent with the *Hambrook v Stokes Bros* approach: see eg *Bain v King & Co Ltd*, 1973 SLT 8; *Harvey v Cairns*, 1989 SLT 107.

55. See Boberg, op cit, n 53 at 176. The limitation was affirmed in *Waring & Gillow Ltd v Sherborne*, 1904 TS 340, *Sueltz v Bolttler*, 1914 EDL 176 and *Mulder v South British Insurance Co Ltd*, 1957 (2) SA 444 (W) (noted by M A Millner (1957) 74 SALJ 263), and abandoned only by the Appellate Division in *Bester v Commercial Union Versekeringsmaatskappy van SA Bpk*, 1973 (1) SA 769 (A) (noted by L Tager (1973) 90 SALJ 123; P Q R Boberg (1973) *Annual Survey of South African Law*, 136-139; J D van der Vyver (1973) 36 THRHR 169; J Neethling & J M Potgieter (1973) 36 THRHR 175; J M Potgieter (1973) 14 *Codicillus* 12). South African scholars had, in the main, disapproved of the conservative approach denying liability in the absence of fear for one's own safety: for criticism of *Bester* in the court below 1972 (3) SA 68 (D) see L Tager (1972) 89 SALJ 435 and D J McQuoid-Mason (1973) 36 THRHR 115. McKerron, op cit, n 53 at 156-157, (1953) 70 SALJ 74, 312 and (1957) *Annual Survey of South African Law*, 169-170, however, approved of the restriction. *Bester* is the leading authority on this topic in South Africa and there appear to have been no significant developments since it was decided.

nevertheless played an important part in the development of the law in this area.[56]

Reference is also made to United States decisions where appropriate, although no attempt has been made to provide a thorough analysis of the widely diverging developments found in the various States.[57] Again, it is interesting to note that the United States has generally been more reluctant to open up the gates of liability than Australia and England.[58] The United States courts adopted the *Coultas*[59] decision and erected a barrier to

56. Significantly, the first two cases awarding compensation for nervous shock were Irish: see *Byrne v Great Southern & Western Railway Co* (unreported, CA of Ireland, Feb 1884), where the plaintiff obtained the very considerable sum at that time of £325, and *Bell v Great Northern Railway Co of Ireland* (1890) 26 LR Ir 428, the first case repudiating *Victorian Railways Commissioner v Coultas* (1888) 13 App Cas 222. Note also *Hogg v Keane* [1956] IR 155; *State (Keegan) v Stardust Victims Compensation Tribunal* [1987] ILRM 202; *Hosford v Murphy* [1988] ILRM 300; *Mullally v Bus Eireann* (unreported, Irish HC, 13 June 1991). See generally B M E McMahon & W Binchy, *Irish Law of Torts* (2nd ed, 1990), 305-313. For Northern Ireland see *O'Dowd v Secretary of State for Northern Ireland* [1982] NI 210.

57. The literature on the law in the United States is immense. For a summary of the present position see W P Keeton, *Prosser and Keeton on the Law of Torts* (5th ed, 1984), 359-367; J Hwang, "Emotional Distress Law in Disarray" (1987) *Annual Survey of American Law* 475; D B Marlowe, "Negligent Infliction of Mental Distress: A Jurisdictional Survey of Existing Limitation Devices and Proposal Based on an Analysis of Objective versus Subjective Indices of Distress" (1988) 33 Villanova L Rev 781. The most important general discussions include R S Miller, "The Scope of Liability for Negligent Infliction of Emotional Distress: Making 'The Punishment Fit the Crime' " (1979) 1 U Haw L Rev 1; V E Nolan & E Ursin, "Negligent Infliction of Emotional Distress: Coherence Emerging from Chaos" (1982) 33 Hastings LJ 583; R A Chesley, "The Increasingly Disparate Standards of Recovery for Negligently Inflicted Emotional Injuries" (1983) 52 Cin L Rev 1017; P A Bell, "The Bell Tolls: Toward Full Tort Recovery for Psychic Injury" (1984) 36 U Fla L Rev 333; R N Pearson, "Liability for Negligently Inflicted Psychic Harm: A Response to Professor Bell" (1984) 36 U Fla L Rev 413; P A Bell, "Reply to a Generous Critic" (1984) 36 U Fla L Rev 437; W Winter, "A Tort in Transition: Negligent Infliction of Mental Distress" (1984) 70 ABAJ 62; C E Cantu, "Negligent Infliction of Emotional Distress: Expanding the Rule Evolved since Dillon" (1986) 17 Tex Tech L Rev 1557. For a historical perspective see F H Bohlen, "Right to Recover For Injury Resulting from Negligence Without Impact" (1902) 41 *American Law Register* (ns) 141, reprinted in F H Bohlen, *Studies on the Law of Tort* (1925), 252-290; F M Burdick, "Tort Liability for Mental Disturbance and Nervous Shock" (1905) 5 Col L Rev 179; A H Throckmorton, "Damages For Fright" (1921) 34 Harv L Rev 260; H F Goodrich, "Emotional Disturbance as Legal Damage" (1922) 20 Mich L Rev 497; L Green, " 'Fright' Cases" (1933) 27 Ill L Rev 761, 873; C Magruder, "Mental and Emotional Disturbance in the Law of Torts" (1936) 49 Harv L Rev 1033; F V Harper & M C McNeely, "A Re-examination of the Basis of Liability for Emotional Distress" [1938] Wis L Rev 426; M Chamallas & L K Kerber, "Women, Mothers and the Law of Fright: A History" (1990) 88 Mich L Rev 814.

58. See Comment, "Negligence and the Infliction of Emotional Harm: A Reappraisal of the Nervous Shock Cases" (1968) 35 U Chi L Rev 512; J K Golden, "The Development of Recovery for Negligently Inflicted Mental Distress Arising from Peril or Injury to Another: An Analysis of the American and Australian Approaches" (1977) 26 Emory LJ 647; P R Handford, "Intentional Infliction of Mental Suffering—Analysis of the Growth of a Tort" (1979) 8 Anglo-Am LR 1 at 3-13; A N Khan, "Liability for Nervous Shock by Negligence" (1983) 12 Anglo-Am LR 263; Comment, "The New English Approach to Emotional Distress: Should American Courts Declare Their Independence?" (1986) 19 Cornell International LJ 65.

59. *Victorian Railways Commissioner v Coultas* (1888) 13 App Cas 222.

recovery in the shape of the "impact rule".[60] The arguments against liability stated in *Coultas* were repeated over and over again.[61] However, the courts soon began to find that the impact rule was an inconvenient restriction on recovery. Some tried to get round it by finding that even the most trivial contact constituted impact.[62] Others went further and abolished the rule altogether.[63] The first State to do this was Texas in 1890,[64] and other jurisdictions gradually followed.[65] By 1990 the rule had

60. See eg *Lehman v Brooklyn City Rail Co* (1888) 47 Hun NY 355 (the first case); *Ewing v Pittsburg C C & St L Rail Co* (1892) 23 A 340 (Pa); *Mitchell v Rochester Rail Co* (1896) 45 NE 354 (NY); *Spade v Lynn & B Rail Co* (1897) 47 NE 88 (Mass). For a comprehensive list of cases, see *Restatement of Torts Second*, §436, Reporter's Note.

61. See the cases cited above, n 60. For more recent cases advocating these old-fashioned views, see *Morgan v Hightower's Administrator* (1942) 163 SW 2d 21 (Ky); *Bartow v Smith* (1948) 78 NE 2d 735 (Ohio); *Bosley v Andrews* (1958) 142 A 2d 263 (Pa) where an elderly lady who suffered a heart attack when chased by a bull escaping with a herd of cows was denied recovery because there was no impact—Musmanno J (dissenting) said at 280 "the policy of non-liability . . . is insupportable in law, logic and elementary justice—and I shall continue to dissent from it until the cows come home"; *Amaya v Home Ice, Fuel & Supply Co* (1963) 379 P 2d 513; 29 Cal Rptr 33 (a case upholding the "zone of danger" rule). See also W L Prosser, *The Law of Torts* (4th ed, 1971), 327; Handford, op cit, n 58 at 4-5.

62. For examples of instances held to satisfy this requirement see *Consolidated Traction Co v Lambertson* (1896) 36 A 100 (NJ) (a trivial jolt); *Spade v Lynn & B Rail Co* (1899) 52 NE 747 (Mass) (a slight blow) (this was the retrial—in the first hearing, (1897) 47 NE 88, it was held that no recovery could be granted in the absence of impact); *Homans v Boston Elevated Rail Co* (1902) 62 NE 737 (Mass) (a slight bump against a seat); *Porter v Delaware L & W Rail Co* (1906) 63 A 860 (NJ) (dust in the eye); *Driscoll v Gaffey* (1910) 92 NE 1010 (Mass) (a forcible seating on the floor); *Louisville & N Rail Co v Roberts* (1925) 269 SW 333 (Ky) (a trivial jolt); *Kentucky Traction Terminal Co v Roman's Guardian* (1929) 23 SW 2d 272 (Ky) (a trifling burn); *Morton v Stack* (1930) 170 NE 869 (Ohio) (inhaling smoke); *Comstock v Wilson* (1931) 177 NE 431 (NY) (a fall brought about by a faint after a collision); *Freedman v Eastern Massachusetts State Rail* (1938) 12 NE 2d 739 (Mass) (plaintiff wrenching her own shoulder in reaction to the fright); *Hess v Philadelphia Transportation Co* (1948) 56 A 2d 89 (Pa) (an electric shock); *Clark v Choctawhatchee Electric Co-op* (1958) 107 So 2d 609 (Fla) (an electric shock); *Zelinsky v Chimics* (1961) 175 A 2d 351 (Pa) (jarring and jolting); *Deutsch v Schein* (1980) 597 SW 2d 141 (Ky) (x-ray bombardment); *Eagle-Picher Industries v Cox* (1985) 481 So 2d 517 (Fla) (inhalation of asbestos fibres). The most absurd cases of this kind were *Kenney v Wong Len* (1925) 128 A 343 (NH) where there was held to be sufficient impact when a mouse hair in a spoonful of stew touched the roof of the plaintiff's mouth, and *Christy Bros Circus v Turnage* (1928) 144 SE 680 (Ga) in which the requirement was satisfied when a circus horse "evacuated its bowels" in the plaintiff's lap.

63. Among the factors which contributed to this development were the existence of special forms of liability involving purely mental injury—the liability of carriers to insulted passengers, and liability for interference with dead bodies: for leading cases see *Chamberlain v Chandler* (1823) 5 Fed Cas No 2,575; *Goddard v Grand Trunk Rail Co* (1869) 57 Me 202 (carriers); *Larson v Chase* (1891) 50 NW 238 (Minn) (bodies).

64. *Hill v Kimball* (1890) 13 SW 59 (Tex). See J E Hallen, "Hill v Kimball—A Milepost in the Law" (1933) 12 Tex L Rev 1.

65. Among the more prominent early decisions were *Purcell v St Paul City Rail Co* (1892) 50 NW 1034 (Minn); *Sloane v Southern California Rail Co* (1896) 44 P 320 (Cal); *Stewart v Arkansas S Rail Co* (1904) 36 So 676 (La); *Green v T A Shoemaker & Co* (1909) 73 A 688 (Md); *Alabama Fuel & Iron Co v Baladoni* (1916) 73 So 205 (Ala); *Hanford v Omaha & C B State Rail Co* (1925) 203 NW 643 (Neb); *Chiuchiolo v New England Wholesale Tailors* (1930) 150 A 540 (NH). After a lull, *Battalla v State* (1961) 176 NE 2d 729; 219 NYS 2d 34 (on which see T F Lambert, "Tort Liability for Psychic Injuries" (1961) 41 BUL Rev 584) provided the impetus for further change. Since then, the following jurisdictions have repudiated the impact rule: Delaware: see *Robb v Pennsylvania Rail Co* (1965) 210 A 2d 709; New Jersey: see *Falzone v Busch* (1965) 214 A 2d 12; Vermont: see

been abandoned in all except seven States.[66]

The jurisdictions which thus recognised liability for shock tended to do so on the basis of a requirement similar to that imposed by Kennedy J in *Dulieu v White & Sons*[67]—that the plaintiff must suffer shock through fear of injury to himself or herself.[68] This became known as the "zone of danger" rule, and is still adhered to by a substantial number of jurisdictions.[69] Not until 1968 was this barrier breached. Then, as is the case with subsequent developments in this area, California led the way. In *Dillon v Legg*,[70] a mother recovered damages for emotional distress suffered on witnessing the death of her infant daughter, who was run down by a negligent driver as she crossed the street, even though the mother was herself in no danger. The Californian Supreme Court held that liability should depend on whether harm was foreseeable by a reasonable person in all of the circumstances, taking into account the factors of the plaintiff's location, whether the shock resulted from a direct emotional impact on the plaintiff from sensory and contemporaneous observance, as contrasted with merely hearing about it later, and the plaintiff's relationship to the accident victim[71]—"nearness, hearness, and dearness", as one commentator has put it.[72] Thus did California recognise "bystander recovery".

65. *Continued*
    Savard v Cody Chevrolet Inc (1967) 234 A 2d 656; Arizona: see *City of Tucson v Wondergem* (1970) 466 P 2d 383; Hawaii: see *Rodrigues v State* (1970) 472 P 2d 509; Maine: see *Wallace v Coca-Cola Bottling Plants Inc* (1970) 269 A 2d 117; Michigan: see *Daly v La Croix* (1970) 179 NW 2d 390; Pennsylvania: see *Niedermann v Brodsky* (1970) 261 A 2d 84; New Mexico: see *Aragon v Speelman* (1971) 491 P 2d 173; North Dakota: see *Whetham v Bismarck Hospital* (1972) 197 NW 2d 678; Virginia: see *Hughes v Moore* (1973) 197 SE 2d 214; Mississippi: see *First National Bank v Langley* (1975) 314 So 2d 324; Colorado: see *Towns v Anderson* (1978) 579 P 2d 1163; Massachusetts: see *Dziokonski v Babineau* (1978) 380 NE 2d 1295; Illinois: see *Rickey v Chicago Transit Authority* (1983) 457 NE 2d 1; Missouri: see *Bass v Nooney Co* (1983) 646 SW 2d 765; Ohio: see *Schultz v Barberton Glass Co* (1983) 447 NE 2d 109; Wyoming: see *Gates v Richardson* (1986) 719 P 2d 193; Utah: see *Johnson v Rogers* (1988) 763 P 2d 771; District of Columbia: see *Williams v Baker* (1990) 572 A 2d 1062. It is worthy of note that the impact rule has been retained longest in jurisdictions with large urban areas and a consequent greater volume of traffic: see J McNeice, "Psychic Injury and Tort Liability in New York" (1949) 24 St Johns L Rev 1 at 32, the most conspicuous exceptions being California and Texas, which had settled their attitude to these cases before their cities started to grow.
66. Arkansas: see *Wood v National Computer Systems Inc* (1987) 814 F 2d 544; Florida: see *Williams v City of Minneola* (1991) 575 So 2d 683; Georgia: see *Dillman v Kahres* (1991) 411 SE 2d 43; Indiana: see *Shuamber v Henderson* (1990) 563 NE 2d 1314; Kansas: see *Bolin v Cessna Aircraft Co* (1991) 759 F Supp 692; Kentucky: see *Wilhoite v Cobb* (1989) 761 SW 2d 625; Oregon: see *Wilson v Tobiassen* (1989) 777 P 2d 1379.
67. [1901] 2 KB 669 at 675.
68. See particularly *Lindley v Knowlton* (1918) 176 P 440 (Cal) (family attacked by escaped chimpanzee); *Waube v Warrington* (1935) 258 NW 497 (Wis); *Resavage v Davies* (1952) 86 A 2d 879 (Md); *Amaya v Home Ice, Fuel & Supply Co* (1963) 379 P 2d 513; 29 Cal Rptr 33; *Tobin v Grossman* (1969) 249 NE 2d 419; 301 NYS 2d 554; *Whetham v Bismarck Hospital* (1972) 197 NW 2d 678 (ND) (mother saw nurse drop newborn baby on floor and heard skull crack).
69. Marlowe, op cit, n 57 at 796-799. Note also J A Davies, "Direct Actions for Emotional Harm: Is Compromise Possible?" (1992) 67 Wash L Rev 1.
70. (1968) 441 P 2d 912; 69 Cal Rptr 72.
71. Ibid at 920-921.
72. Comment, "Negligent Infliction of Emotional Distress: Formulating the Psychological Inquiry" (1984) 18 Suffolk L Rev 401 at 407.

A number of jurisdictions have followed California in recognising this extended liability, but the present picture is one of wide divergences,[73] not only as between jurisdictions but even within particular States. This is especially so in California itself. The intention behind the judgment in *Dillon v Legg* was that the three factors should not be prerequisites to recovery, but merely factors to assist in applying the foreseeability test. Some later cases so interpreted them[74]—thus, for example, recognising the aftermath doctrine[75]—but others did not. The subsequent pronouncement of the Californian Supreme Court in *Thing v La Chusa*[76] indicates a disenchantment with the uncertainty engendered by the *Dillon v Legg* approach. The court has ruled that the three factors are to be reinterpreted as strict rules. However, in an even more recent decision, *Burgess v Superior Court*,[77] the Californian Supreme Court has emphasised that these limitations apply only to "bystander" cases and not to "direct victim" situations, that is, cases where the plaintiff who suffers psychiatric injury is owed some pre-existing duty of care. Another important development is the abandonment by some jurisdictions of the requirement that the emotional distress must have physical or psychiatric results.[78] The law in the United States is a kaleidoscope in which the pattern is continually changing.

73. See Marlowe, op cit, n 57 at 806-817; J P Towey, "Negligent Infliction of Mental Distress: Reaction to Dillon v Legg in California and Other States" (1974) 25 Hastings LJ 1248; A J Simons, "Psychic Injury and the Bystander: The Transcontinental Dispute between California and New York" (1976) 51 St Johns L Rev 1; R N Pearson, "Liability to Bystanders for Negligently Inflicted Emotional Harm—A Comment on the Nature of Arbitrary Rules" (1982) 34 U Fla L Rev 477; J L Diamond, "Dillon v Legg Revisited: Toward a Unified Theory of Compensating Bystanders and Relatives for Intangible Injuries" (1984) 35 Hastings LJ 477.
74. In particular, *Ochoa v Superior Court (Santa Clara County)* (1985) 703 P 2d 1; 216 Cal Rptr 661.
75. See cases cited below, pp 145-146.
76. (1989) 771 P 2d 814; 257 Cal Rptr 98. See Comment, "Thing v La Chusa: Public Policy Demands a Limitation on the Bystander Recovery for Infliction of Emotional Distress" (1990) 17 W St U L Rev 499. See also below, pp 147-148. On the application of the principles of *Thing v La Chusa* to cases involving the negligent mishandling of human remains, see below, p 49, n 187.
77. (1992) 831 P 2d 1197; 9 Cal Rptr 2d 615.
78. See below, pp 48-49. The first case to take this step was *Rodrigues v State* (1970) 472 P 2d 509 (Haw). California did likewise in *Molien v Kaiser Foundation Hospitals* (1980) 616 P 2d 813; 167 Cal Rptr 831.

2

RECOGNISABLE PSYCHIATRIC DAMAGE

The need for recognisable psychiatric damage

"Nervous shock" is the "hallowed expression"[1] which the courts have traditionally used to describe the form of personal harm with which this work is concerned. If ever it had any real significance in medical terms, that time is long since past, and the retention by lawyers of such "quaint" language has often been criticised.[2] Its use "indicates a scant acquaintance with the subtleties of psychiatric medicine".[3] The chief objection is that it is entirely inappropriate to describe the harm for which relief may be had. Transient shock does not attract damages, rather it is the mental and physical consequences which flow from it which may be compensable.[4] Some judges have gone so far as to stigmatise the use of such terminology as "misleading and inaccurate",[5] though a few have retained "nervous shock" as a convenient label, on the proviso that it is understood to refer to the psychiatric illnesses that result from emotional stress and not the emotional stress itself.[6] Outdated terminology can only operate to confuse. Moreover, it hinders the evolution of desirable doctrine, for example serving as a constant reminder that according to the present (and we will argue unsatisfactory) law compensable damage under this type of negligence claim must arise by way of a reaction to a particular and sudden

1. *McLoughlin v O'Brian* [1983] 1 AC 410 per Lord Wilberforce at 418.
2. See eg *McLoughlin v O'Brian* [1983] 1 AC 410 per Lord Bridge at 432; *De Franceschi v Storrier* (1988) 85 ACTR 1 per Miles CJ at 6; *Campbelltown City Council v Mackay* (1989) 15 NSWLR 501 per Kirby P at 503 ("It is highly artificial to imprison the legal cause of action for psychiatric injury in an outmoded scientific view about the nature of its origins.").
3. *Swan v Williams (Demolition) Pty Ltd* (1987) 9 NSWLR 172 per Samuels JA at 185.
4. In *Behrens v Bertram Mills Circus Ltd* [1957] 2 QB 1 at 27-28 Devlin J said when referring to a case of fright caused by an elephant: "I am satisfied that the shock must have been considerable. I should like to award [the plaintiff] a most substantial sum under this head but I am satisfied that I cannot do so except to the extremely limited extent that the shock resulted in physical and mental harm. I think that is clearly the effect of the authorities. When the word 'shock' is used in them it is not in the sense of a mental reaction but in a medical sense as the equivalent of nervous shock." His Lordship went on to refer to MacKinnon LJ in *Owens v Liverpool Corporation* [1939] 1 KB 394 at 400 who spoke of this as a "form of ill-health" which is "ascertainable by the physician". The same sentiments were expressed in *Applicant v Larkin, Withnell and Wilkinson* [1976] WAR 199 per Wickham J at 201 and *F v H* (unreported, Western Australian SC, 3 Sept 1992, No 45 of 1992) per Nicholson J at 7.
5. *Attia v British Gas Plc* [1988] QB 304 per Bingham LJ at 317. See also *Ravenscroft v Rederiaktiebφlaget Transatlantic* [1991] 3 All ER 73 per Ward J at 76.
6. See eg *Mount Isa Mines Ltd v Pusey* (1970) 125 CLR 383 per Windeyer J at 394-395; *Jaensch v Coffey* (1984) 155 CLR 549 per Brennan J at 560; *Brice v Brown* [1984] 1 All ER 997 per Stuart-Smith J at 1006; *Attia v British Gas Plc* [1988] QB 304 per Dillon LJ at 311, per Woolf LJ at 313; *Alcock v Chief Constable of South Yorkshire Police* [1992] 1 AC 310 per Parker LJ at 351.

isolated event.[7] The first step to developing a modern body of coherent principle governing the law in this area is to sever all links with the past and to adopt language which is consistent with modern medical practice and accurately reflects the injury which the plaintiff seeks to redress. In the last 20 years many, but unfortunately not all, judges have appreciated this, electing to refer, in more medically appropriate terms, to a "recognisable psychiatric illness".[8] We will adopt such expressions throughout our analysis, retaining the term "nervous shock" only when referring to the pre-1970 case law in order to reflect the language utilised by the courts in those authorities.

Modern cases rest on the principle that the plaintiff must suffer legally recognised harm—some recognisable psychiatric injury or illness resulting from the infliction of traumatic shock—rather than mere mental or emotional distress or suffering such as grief, sorrow, distress, worry, anxiety, disappointment, anger, outrage and the like. The genesis of contemporary thought can be traced to the leading expression by Lord Denning MR in *Hinz v Berry*:[9]

> "In English law no damages are awarded for grief and sorrow caused by a person's death. No damages are to be given for the worry about the children, or for the financial strain or stress, or the difficulties of adjusting to a new life. Damages are however recoverable for nervous shock, or, to put it in medical terms, for any recognisable psychiatric illness caused by the breach of duty by the defendant."

Equally important is Windeyer J's statement in *Mount Isa Mines Ltd v Pusey*:[10]

> "Sorrow does not sound in damages. A plaintiff in an action of negligence cannot recover damages for a 'shock', however grievous, which was no more than an immediate emotional response to a

7. See below, Chapter 8.
8. See eg *Hinz v Berry* [1970] 2 QB 40 per Lord Denning MR at 42; *Mount Isa Mines Ltd v Pusey* (1970) 125 CLR 383 per Windeyer J at 394; *McLoughlin v O'Brian* [1983] 1 AC 410 per Lord Bridge at 431; *Jaensch v Coffey* (1984) 155 CLR 549 per Brennan J at 559-560, per Deane J at 593; *Attia v British Gas Plc* [1988] QB 304 per Bingham LJ at 317; *Swan v Williams (Demolition) Pty Ltd* (1987) 9 NSWLR 172 per Samuels JA at 184-185; *Beecham v Hughes* (1988) 52 DLR (4th) 625 per Taggart JA at 638; *Petrie v Dowling* [1992] 1 Qd R 284 per Kneipp J at 286; *Spence v Percy* (1990) Aust Torts Rep 81-039 per Derrington J at 68,036; (1991) Aust Torts Rep 81-116 per Shepherdson J at 69,081, per Williams J at 69,086-7, per de Jersey J at 69,088-9; *Ravenscroft v Rederiaktiebølaget Transatlantic* [1991] 3 All ER 73 per Ward J at 76; *Alcock v Chief Constable of South Yorkshire Police* [1992] 1 AC 310 per Stocker LJ at 365, per Nolan LJ at 382, per Lord Keith at 393, per Lord Ackner at 399, per Lord Oliver at 406; *Mullally v Bus Eireann* (unreported, Irish HC, 13 June 1991) per Denham J; *Miller v Royal Derwent Hospital Board of Management* (unreported, Tasmanian SC, 29 May 1992, No 282 of 1988) per Zeeman J at 17. Note also the adoption of the term "psychological or psychiatric injury" in s 77 of the *Motor Accidents Act* 1988 (NSW): see below, p 244. However, antiquated terminology still persists even in some of the most recent decisions: see eg *Jaensch v Coffey* (1984) 155 CLR 549 per Dawson J at 611; *Kralj v McGrath* [1986] 1 All ER 54 per Woolf J at 61-62; *Rowe Estate v Hanna* (1989) 71 Alta LR (2d) 136 per Forsyth J at 140; *Wilks v Haines* (1991) Aust Torts Rep 81-078 per Loveday J at 68,657; *Hevican v Ruane* [1991] 3 All ER 65 per Mantell J at 67; *Alcock v Chief Constable of South Yorkshire Police* [1992] 1 AC 310 per Lord Jauncey at 419.
9. [1970] 2 QB 40 at 42-43.
10. (1970) 125 CLR 383 at 394.

distressing experience sudden, severe and saddening. It is, however, today a known medical fact that severe emotional distress can be the starting point of a lasting disorder of mind or body, some form of psycho-neurosis or a psychosomatic illness. For that, if it be the result of a tortious act, damages may be had.''

Another salient dictum appears in the judgment of Lord Bridge in *McLoughlin v O'Brian*:[11]

"The common law gives no damages for the emotional distress which any normal person experiences when someone he loves is killed or injured. Anxiety and depression are normal human emotions. Yet an anxiety neurosis or a reactive depression may be recognisable psychiatric illnesses, with or without psychosomatic symptoms. So, the first hurdle which a plaintiff claiming damages of the kind in question must surmount is to establish that he is suffering, not merely grief, distress or any other normal emotion, but a positive psychiatric illness."

These sentiments are echoed in the case law in Australia,[12] England,[13]

11. [1983] 1 AC 410 at 431.
12. *Chester v Council of the Municipality of Waverley* (1939) 62 CLR 1 per Latham CJ at 6; *Benson v Lee* [1972] VR 879 per Lush J at 880; *Richters v Motor Tyre Service Pty Ltd* [1972] Qd R 9 per Wanstall ACJ at 17-18; *Diakogiorgic v Anastasas* (unreported, Queensland SC, 4 Nov 1974, No 179 of 1972), noted (1975) 49 ALJ 188; *Tsanaktsidis v Oulianoff* (1980) 24 SASR 500 per Mitchell J at 501; *Bassanese v Martin* (1982) 31 SASR 461 per Zelling J at 464; *Vince v Cripps Bakery Pty Ltd* (1984) Aust Torts Rep 80-668 per Underwood J at 68,814; *Jaensch v Coffey* (1984) 155 CLR 549 per Brennan J at 559-560, per Deane J at 587; *Mellor v Moran* (1985) 2 MVR 461 per Vasta J at 462; *Stergiou v Stergiou* (1987) Aust Torts Rep 80-082 per Gallop J at 68,437; *Andrewartha v Andrewartha* (1987) 44 SASR 1 per White J at 4; *Swan v Williams (Demolition) Pty Ltd* (1987) 9 NSWLR 172 per Samuels JA at 185, per Priestley JA at 195; *Chapman v Lear* (unreported, Queensland SC, 8 Apr 1988, No 3732 of 1984) per Williams J at 10; *De Franceschi v Storrier* (1988) 85 ACTR 1 per Miles CJ at 6; *Barrett v Short* (unreported, New South Wales SC, 12 April 1989, No 14685 of 1984) per Calloway J at 13; *Anderson v Smith* (1990) 101 FLR 34 per Nader J at 49-50; *Orman v Harrington* (unreported, South Australian SC, 30 Apr 1990, No 296 of 1990) per Mulligan J at 10; *Gibson v Trueba* (unreported, New South Wales SC, 2 Nov 1990, No 19749 of 1986) per Master Greenwood at 4-5; *Spence v Percy* (1990) Aust Torts Rep 81-039 per Derrington J at 68,035, 68,039; *Klug v Motor Accidents Insurance Board* (1991) Aust Torts Rep 81-134 per Zeeman J at 69,271; *Petrie v Dowling* [1992] 1 Qd R 284 per Kneipp J at 286; *Miller v Royal Derwent Hospital Board of Management* (unreported, Tasmanian SC, 29 May 1992, No 282 of 1988) per Zeeman J at 15.
13. *Dulieu v White & Sons* [1901] 2 KB 669 per Kennedy J at 673; *Cook v Swinfen* [1967] 1 WLR 457 per Lord Denning MR at 461; *McLoughlin v O'Brian* [1981] QB 599 per Stephenson LJ at 614, per Griffiths LJ at 624; [1983] 1 AC 410 per Lord Wilberforce at 418; *Brice v Brown* [1984] 1 All ER 997 per Stuart-Smith J at 1006; *Bagley v North Herts Health Authority* (1986) 136 NLJ 1014 per Simon Brown J at 1015; *Kralj v McGrath* [1986] 1 All ER 54 per Woolf J at 61-62; *Attia v British Gas Plc* [1988] QB 304 per Dillon LJ at 311, per Bingham LJ at 320; *Al-Kandari v J R Brown & Co* [1987] QB 514 per French J at 526; [1988] QB 665 per Lord Donaldson MR at 675; *Hevican v Ruane* [1991] 3 All ER 65 per Mantell J at 68; *Ravenscroft v Rederiaktiebφlaget Transatlantic* [1991] 3 All ER 73 per Ward J at 76; *Calveley v Chief Constable of the Merseyside Police* [1989] AC 1228 per Lord Bridge at 1238; *Alcock v Chief Constable of South Yorkshire Police* [1992] 1 AC 310 per Hidden J at 318, per Parker LJ at 355-356, per Stocker LJ at 365, per Lord Ackner at 401, per Lord Oliver at 416; *Nicholls v Rushton, The Times,* 19 June 1992, per Parker LJ.

Canada[14] and elsewhere.[15] The courts have repeatedly emphasised that the initial obstacle to a successful claim of this kind is to provide evidence that there is a recognisable psychiatric illness, and that there can be no recovery for emotions which, while distressing, fall short of that standard. It does not matter, on the better view, that this damage has healed before proceedings commenced[16] or will eventually respond to treatment.[17]

14. *Alaffe v Kennedy* (1973) 40 DLR (3d) 429 per Gillis J at 432; *McMullin v F W Woolworth Co Ltd* (1974) 9 NBR (2d) 214 per Cormier CJQBD at 216; *Fenn v City of Peterborough* (1976) 73 DLR (3d) 177 per Holland J at 208; *Cameron v Marcaccini* (1978) 87 DLR (3d) 442 per Macdonald J at 445; *Duwyn v Kaprielian* (1978) 94 DLR (3d) 424 per Morden J at 438; *Kernested v Desorcy* [1978] 3 WWR 623 per Dewar CJQB at 626-628; *Griffiths v Canadian Pacific Railways* (1978) 6 BCLR 115 per Taggart JA at 121; *Montgomery v Murphy* (1982) 136 DLR (3d) 525 per Galligan J at 529; *Mathison v Hofer* (1984) 28 CCLT 196 per Morse J at 199; *Beaulieu v Sutherland* (1986) 35 CCLT 237 per Legg J at 247; *Kwok v British Columbia Ferry Corporation* (1987) 20 BCLR (2d) 318 per Cumming J at 373; *Sullivan v Atlantic Lottery Corporation* (1987) 205 APR 317 (NB) per McLellan J at 323; *Heighington v The Queen* (1987) 41 DLR (4th) 208 per Holland J at 223-225; *Norberg v Wynrib* (1988) 44 CCLT 184 per Oppal J at 190; *Frank v Cox* (1988) 213 APR 370 (NS) per Kelly J at 379; *McDermott v Ramadanovic Estate* (1988) 27 BCLR (2d) 45 per Southin J at 52; *Morrell-Curry v Burke* (1989) 237 APR 402 (NS) per Hallett J at 410; *Rowe Estate v Hanna* (1989) 71 Alta LR (2d) 136 per Forsyth J at 139; *Rhodes v Canadian National Railway* (1990) 75 DLR (4th) 248 per Wallace JA at 264; *Campbell v Varanese* (1991) 279 APR 104 (NS) per Chipman JA at 118-119.

15. For example, Scotland: see *Simpson v Imperial Chemical Industries Ltd*, 1983 SLT 601 per Lord Wheatley at 605, per Lord Grieve at 609; *Mallon v Monklands District Council*, 1986 SLT 347 per Lord Jauncey at 349; *Harvey v Cairns*, 1989 SLT 107 per Lord Murray at 109; Ireland: see *State (Keegan) v Stardust Victims Compensation Tribunal* [1987] ILRM 202 per Finlay CJ at 212, per Henchy J at 217; *Hosford v Murphy* [1988] ILRM 300 per Costello J at 303; *Mullally v Bus Eireann* (unreported, Irish HC, 13 June 1991) per Denham J.

16. See eg *Regan v Harper* [1971] Qd R 191; *Mathison v Hofer* (1984) 28 CCLT 196; *Swan v Williams (Demolition) Pty Ltd* (1989) 9 NSWLR 172 per Priestley JA at 199; *Petrie v Dowling* [1992] 1 Qd R 284; *Wheatley v Cunningham* (unreported, QBD, 11 Dec 1991).

17. See eg *Regan v Harper* [1971] Qd R 191; *Vince v Cripps Bakery Pty Ltd* (1984) Aust Torts Rep 80-668; *De Franceschi v Storrier* (1988) 85 ACTR 1. Note also *Chapman v Lear* (unreported, Queensland SC, 8 Apr 1988, No 3732 of 1984) where damages were awarded for the aggravation of a pre-existing post-traumatic stress disorder over a three-year period, the aggravation having tapered off in the last 18 months. There has been some suggestion in Canada that the impact of the trauma in question on the mind of the claimant must be permanent: see *Rhodes v Canadian National Railway* (1990) 75 DLR (4th) 248 per Macfarlane JA at 251, per Southin JA at 272, 285. See also *Muzik v Canzone del Mare*, 1980 (3) SA 470 (C) where recovery was denied for anxiety resulting from food poisoning through eating contaminated mussels. Broeksma J stressed that, even if this amounted to nervous shock or psychiatric damage, it had been of short duration (six days) and had not caused mental or physical impairment or affected bodily well-being. In *Harvey v Cairns*, 1989 SLT 107 Lord Murray attached significance to the fact that an accident to the plaintiff's sister had not caused him "continuing mental effects". R Kelly & B N Smith, "Post-Traumatic Syndrome: Another Myth Discredited" (1981) 74 *Journal of the Royal Society of Medicine* 275 show that, contrary to earlier hypotheses, patients do recover and return to full-time work before litigation is settled; see also below, p 39, n 121. Note also that very few traumatic injuries are capable of producing permanent pain: see H W Smith, "Problems of Proof in Psychic Injury Cases" (1963) 14 Syr L Rev 586 at 610. However, there is no reason why the duration of the psychiatric harm should bear on the question of recoverability (although it may influence the quantum of damages awarded: see below, pp 266, n 16, 277). Whether transitory or enduring in nature, once the psychiatric damage threshold is reached, relief must be forthcoming on proof of negligence.

What is important is that the plaintiff had to contend with it at some stage. [18]

It is not uncommon for claimants to fall at this first hurdle. The basic principle prevented the plaintiff recovering damages in *Orman v Harrington*, [19] where she was summoned by telephone to hospital to be informed that her daughter had suffered serious injuries in a car accident. After a detailed review of the medical evidence Mullighan J concluded that it did not disclose that the plaintiff, though clearly distressed and anxious at the plight of her daughter, had suffered a recognisable psychiatric illness or any other injury or complaint which could sound in damages. [20] *Beaulieu v Sutherland* [21] provides further illustration that unless such harm is established an action will be doomed to failure. There the court turned down a claim for compensation following an accident in which the plaintiff's friend, while walking along the road beside her, was struck by a vehicle and killed. It was held that the plaintiff's reactions suggested anxiety and grief, not mental illness of any kind, and that this was fatal to her claim. [22]

It should be noted that *physical* symptoms resulting from shock, such as strokes, miscarriages, peptic ulcerations or increased blood pressure, will fall outside the category of recognisable psychiatric illness. This does not mean that such harm is not compensable, merely that it is conceptually distinct from damage to the mind. Where physical harm of the kind referred to results from a negligent breach of duty, redress will be available without proof of a recognisable psychiatric illness, or indeed any interference with peace of mind.

There have been a few controversial cases where the courts appear to have awarded damages for something less than recognisable psychiatric injury. In what is perhaps the most problematic decision, Comyn J in *Whitmore v Euroways Express Coaches Ltd* [23] drew a distinction between "ordinary" shock, which he considered does not need to be proved by medical evidence,

18. It is also immaterial that the psychiatric damage in question was not of a particularly serious nature although, again, it will be taken into account in the assessment of compensation: see eg *Mallon v Monklands District Council*, 1986 SLT 347 where Lord Jauncey spoke of the plaintiff's "minor psychiatric illness", assessing damages at £100.
19. (Unreported, South Australian SC, 30 Apr 1990, No 296 of 1990).
20. For other Australian examples see *Mitchell v Clancy* [1960] Qd R 62, affirmed by the High Court [1960] Qd R 532; *Diakogiorgic v Anastasas* (unreported, Queensland SC, 4 Nov 1974, No 179 of 1972), noted (1975) 49 ALJ 188; *Stergiou v Stergiou* (1987) Aust Torts Rep 80-082.
21. (1986) 35 CCLT 237.
22. For other Canadian examples see *Alaffe v Kennedy* (1973) 40 DLR (3d) 429; *McMullin v F W Woolworth Co Ltd* (1974) 9 NBR (2d) 214; *Cameron v Marcaccini* (1978) 87 DLR(3d) 442; *Duwyn v Kaprielian* (1978) 94 DLR (3d) 424 (the mother's claim); *Kernested v Desorcy* [1978] 3 WWR 623; *Griffiths v Canadian Pacific Railways* (1978) 6 BCLR 115; *Montgomery v Murphy* (1982) 136 DLR (3d) 525; *Norberg v Wynrib* (1988) 44 CCLT 184; *Rowe Estate v Hanna* (1989) 71 Alta LR (2d) 136. In *Sullivan v Atlantic Lottery Corporation* (1987) 205 APR 317 (NB) no compensation was available to the plaintiff for disappointment caused by being erroneously led to believe through an inaccurate brochure that she had won third prize in a lottery, though the court suggested that the result might be different had the prize been a million dollars rather than the $1272 in question.
23. *The Times*, 4 May 1984. See M A Jones, " 'Ordinary Shock'—Thin Skull Rules OK?" (1985) 4 *Litigation* 114.

and "psychiatric shock", where such evidence is necessary. In this case the plaintiff and her husband were injured in a coach accident in France, the husband suffering very grave injuries. The plaintiff's claim for physical injuries included a plea for relief both for the trauma and shock in respect of her own experiences and the immediate and continuing shock suffered as a consequence of her husband's injuries. What is of interest is not that the court distinguished between the "profound shock" occasioned to the plaintiff by the injured husband's state, for which damages were recoverable, and the worry, strain and distress suffered as a result of those injuries and their continuing debilitating effects, for which damages were not recoverable,[24] but what it was prepared to include within the compensable category. The shock in question was not psychiatric in nature, but "shock in the ordinary, general, everyday meaning of the word and not in any medical or psychiatric sense".[25] No reference having been made to *McLoughlin v O'Brian*,[26] the not insignificant sum of £2,000 was awarded for something which we are told amounts to more than emotional upset but less than medical incapacitation.[27] We are not informed how this "ordinary shock" differs, for example, from grief or distress, merely that it is "a concept known to all of us" which is to be measured by reference to the evidence of the particular sufferer. It is not susceptible to medical proof and must be decided by the judge himself or herself using common sense. The decision in this case was no doubt influenced by Comyn J's expressed wish to judge damages claims in an ordinary, "down-to-earth" and realistic manner rather than subject them to legal technicalities, in an attempt to make litigation comprehensible to ordinary people who have suffered ordinary accidents. The reasoning behind it cannot be explained as an unconscious slip on Comyn J's part, for his Lordship clearly appreciated the case's uniqueness in involving "a shock, not psychiatric in character, which endured beyond the moment of impact".[28]

It might have been possible to dismiss this case as an aberration were it not for the existence of some similarly questionable Australian authority and a Canadian judge's recent decision which goes so far as to reject outright Lord Denning MR's insistence in *Hinz v Berry*[29] on a recognisable psychiatric illness. In South Australia in *Brown v Mount*

24. Although he did express the view that the law is harsh in categorically excluding such emotions as recoverable as a head of damages. On this issue see below, pp 43-51, 56-58.
25. Note also *Lutzkie v S A R and H*, 1974 (4) SA 396 (W) where, in an action for personal injuries, the plaintiff claimed, inter alia, for "surgical shock". Trengove J rejected this, ruling that it was no different from that generally associated with the type of surgical treatment the plaintiff had received and that it was compensable, not as a separate item, but as part of the pain and suffering associated with the operation.
26. [1983] 1 AC 410.
27. Separate damages were awarded for the shock suffered in relation to her own experiences. These were subsumed in the £4,500 compensation for general damages.
28. Note *Kralj v McGrath* [1986] 1 All ER 54 where Woolf J analysed the plaintiff's claim by utilising the traditional language of "nervous shock". His Lordship makes no reference to "psychiatric illness" per se and it is not absolutely clear from the report that the plaintiff suffered such damage. In all probability, however, this was the case. It seems that, unlike Comyn J, Woolf J was not consciously expanding recovery in this context (although he clearly was in other respects, on which see below, pp 203-204) and that, like so many other judges, he merely found it easier to talk in "nervous shock" terms.
29. [1970] 2 QB 40 at 42-43, quoted above, p 15.

Barker Soldiers' Hospital,[30] a mother recovered for "shock, discomfort and inconvenience" consequent on being told of an accident in which her newborn baby had been burnt. It seems, however, very doubtful on the facts whether the plaintiff suffered a recognisable psychiatric illness in the sense required for actionable nervous shock.[31] In *Swan v Williams (Demolition) Pty Ltd*[32] the majority of the New South Wales Court of Appeal accepted medical reports that the plaintiff had not suffered any psychiatric illness, yet granted relief on the basis that he had suffered more than ordinary grief.[33] Southin JA of the British Columbia Court of Appeal has been the most explicit of those who have recognised additional levels of mental disturbance as satisfying the damage requirement of this particular tort action. The question before Southin J at first instance in *McDermott v Ramadanovic Estate*[34] was whether a young girl who saw her parents die in the front seat of their car had a right to recovery for the impact that scene left on her mind. Notwithstanding that there was no evidence of a recognisable psychiatric illness, her Honour ruled that the emotional pain, as distinct from grief, was sufficient to ground a claim, awarding her $20,000 compensation.[35] Southin J queried:

> "[W]hat is the logical difference between a scar on the flesh and a scar on the mind? If a scar on the flesh is compensable although it causes no pecuniary loss, why should a scar on the mind be any the less compensable? In both cases, there are serious difficulties of assessment. That has not been allowed to stand in the way of the courts making awards for non-pecuniary losses. Nor has it prevented awards for pain caused by physical injury which is . . . a 'bad memory'.
>
> And, too, pain from a physical injury is not the result of a 'recognisable psychiatric illness'. It is the result of the interplay of tissue, nerves and brain. But to the sufferer, what is the difference between physical pain and emotional pain? Indeed, the former may be easier to bear, especially with modern analgesics, than the latter.
>
> Therefore, with the greatest of respect, I reject Lord Denning's limitation (if he intended it as a limitation of law) of recovery to cases of 'recognisable psychiatric illness'."[36]

30. [1934] SASR 128. Note Millhouse J's comments in *Pibworth v Bevan M Roberts Pty Ltd* (unreported, South Australian SC, 28 May 1992, No 770 of 1986).
31. See P G Heffey, "The Negligent Infliction of Nervous Shock in Road and Industrial Accidents" (1974) 48 ALJ 196, 240 at 208 n 29. Significantly, the hospital already owed the plaintiff a duty by reason of accepting her into its care.
32. (1987) 9 NSWLR 172. Strictly the case may be authority only in relation to the *Law Reform (Miscellaneous Provisions) Act* 1944 (NSW) (as to which see below, pp 239-243) but the court discusses the point by reference to the standard common law authorities.
33. Note also that, interestingly, in the arbitrations pursuant to the Zeebrugge disaster settlement "pathological grief" (ie grief the extent and duration of which is in excess of the normal emotional reaction to trauma) was accepted as legal damage: see *A v P & O Ferries (Dover) Ltd, The Independent*, 5 May 1989; "Zeebrugge Ten Share £645,000", *The Times*, 29 Apr 1989. See also M Napier, "The Medical and Legal Trauma of Disasters" [1991] *Medico-Legal Journal* 157.
34. (1988) 27 BCLR (2d) 45.
35. Compare this with the $5,000 damages given for her physical injuries. Although counsel had agreed on an award of $5,000 as general damages it was open to the court to consider its appropriateness since the plaintiff was still an infant and $20,000 was accordingly added for the emotional scar.
36. (1988) 27 BCLR (2d) 45 at 53.

Her Honour reiterated these views in the Court of Appeal in *Rhodes v Canadian National Railway*:[37]

"An argument can be made for the proposition that to award damages as I did in [*McDermott v Ramadanovic Estate*], is, as a matter of policy, wrong. There are all sorts of people throughout the world who have gone through the horrors of war and somehow got on with their lives without compensation for the terrible memories with which they have to live. In my opinion, the question of policy is better answered not by saying that scars on the flesh are compensable but scars on the mind are not, but by making all awards for scars on the mind, including scars said to lead to 'psychiatric illness', conventional, even as damages for pain and suffering have been made conventional."

Interestingly, in none of the above judgments was any allusion made to the other cases where deviation from the traditional rule is detectable. Rather, they reveal a cross-jurisdictional dissatisfaction with what is arguably an unnecessarily severe limitation on the range of permissible claims and show different courts independently feeling their way forward to what may be a more sensible stopping point. Certainly, insistence on a recognisable psychiatric injury may exclude some deserving claimants such as those in *Whitmore v Euroways Express Coaches Ltd* and *Swan v Williams (Demolition) Pty Ltd* where something was suffered which, while short of medically proved psychiatric harm, was considerably more serious and impacting than commonplace grief or sorrow. Broken minds have always been greeted with a scepticism which contrasts sharply with the sympathy generated by broken bones. To many, the fact that an injury does not manifest itself overtly or exhibit outward signs of its effects casts serious doubts on its existence. Demanding that there be damage of a recognisable psychiatric nature is one way in which the law has erected safeguards perceived to be necessary against unauthentic and illegitimate claims. One wonders, however, how many of the pre-1970 plaintiffs actually suffered recognisable psychiatric illnesses. Excluding Mrs Hambrook[38] who died as a result of her shock, it is open to question whether, for example, Mrs Dulieu[39] or Mrs King[40] would have satisfied the threshold test had they brought their claims today. Courts, in all probability, have simply tightened things up, maybe unfairly so, since those days. Whether or not additional levels of compensable harm are desirable or merely introduce unwanted complications in an already complex and difficult area of the law, the line of authority discussed above does represent a significant variation from the conventional position and may well influence future development, particularly in the light of the diagnostic difficulties that may arise in assessing some post-traumatic responses.[41]

If the first essential prerequisite of a successful psychiatric damage claim is proof of a recognisable psychiatric illness resulting from mental or emotional distress or suffering, the exact nature of that distress or suffering

37. (1990) 75 DLR (4th) 248 at 289.
38. *Hambrook v Stokes Bros* [1925] 1 KB 141, discussed above, pp 4-5, below, pp 134-136, 153.
39. *Dulieu v White* [1901] 2 KB 669, discussed above, pp 3-4, below, pp 106, 230.
40. *King v Phillips* [1953] 1 KB 429, discussed below, pp 66-67, 135, 153-154.
41. See below, pp 39-40.

would seem to be of secondary importance. Yet there is some authority which suggests that the root of mental damage is material and that where recognisable psychiatric harm results from grief, rather than from emotions such as fright or horror, there can be no recovery. Galligan J in *Montgomery v Murphy*[42] refused to compensate a husband for that part of his serious clinical depression which resulted from grief and sorrow over the loss of his wife, who had been run over by a car in front of him. His Honour's approach makes it necessary to attempt the often near-impossible task of analysing the many potential distinct and interlocking causes of psychiatric illnesses in a particular individual merely so that the law can artificially separate out those portions of mental damage deemed compensable from those which are not, thereby distracting attention from the central established fact—that a recognised psychiatric illness has been caused to the plaintiff by the defendant's negligence. The sorts of sentiments expressed in this case threaten to disadvantage recovery for all psychiatric conditions in that such conditions do not suddenly appear out of thin air, but follow emotional imbalance triggered by some external stressor—thus, in a sense, inevitably "resulting from" or "attributable to" natural feelings. The situation where psychiatric damage is attributed wholly rather than partially to grief arose in the Irish case of *State (Keegan) v Stardust Victims Compensation Tribunal*.[43] Finlay CJ took a similar line, remarking that "grief even so extreme as to cause psychiatric disorder as distinct from nervous shock may not give rise to liability for damages".[44] Similarly, Henchy J in the same proceedings stated:

> "[T]he [applicant's] claim in essence is that his grief at the deaths of the two daughters who died in the fire developed into severe psychiatric illness. That, I fear, is not, according to Lord Wilberforce's speech [in *McLoughlin v O'Brian*[45]], a ground for compensation, for it ignores the test of shock by sight or sound."[46]

It is only by linking Lord Wilberforce's general comments on grief with those on the physical perception of trauma that such a conclusion about *McLoughlin v O'Brian* can be reached. His Lordship was not moved to discuss this slightly different situation when canvassing the issue of no recovery for grief or the need for recognisable psychiatric harm. It is not clear why grief should be distinguished from other emotions in this way if such harm has resulted. There has been some support for recovery for worry-induced psychiatric conditions.[47] In the United States courts have indicated that in certain circumstances they are prepared to grant relief to plaintiffs who fear the development of cancer (cancerophobia) as a result

---

42. (1982) 136 DLR (3d) 525 at 529-530.
43. [1987] ILRM 202.
44. Ibid at 212.
45. [1983] 1 AC 410.
46. [1987] ILRM 202 at 217.
47. See eg *Mitchell v Clancy* [1960] Qd R 62 and *Palamara v Fragameni* (unreported, Western Australian SC, 13 Oct 1983, No 89 of 1983), discussed below, pp 234-235. These cases involved worry over ability to support a family financially after a physically debilitating accident, but the same conclusion would apply to psychiatric illness caused by worry or anxiety that physical harm *may* eventuate following the tortiously caused event.

of exposure to toxic materials[48] or based on other factors,[49] or for fear of other illnesses or conditions.[50] Another example where there seems no good reason why recovery should not be granted if psychiatric injury through fear or worry does result is where someone has a sexual liaison with another who, unbeknown to them at the time, was infected with the AIDS virus, or is otherwise in fear of catching AIDS, as for example through being bitten, or stabbed with an infected syringe.[51] Recovery has even been granted for the mental anguish a plaintiff *might* suffer if she worried in later life about the effects of physical injuries sustained as a child.[52] It is submitted that, providing a causal connection can be established, any

48. See eg *Laxton v Orkin Exterminating Co Inc* (1982) 639 SW 2d 431 (Tenn); *Wetherill v University of Chicago* (1983) 565 F Supp 1553; *Gideon v Johns-Manville Sales Corporation* (1985) 761 F 2d 1129; *Devlin v Johns-Manville Corporation* (1985) 495 A 2d 495 (NJ); *Jackson v John-Manville Sales Corporation* (1986) 781 F 2d 394; *Herber v Johns-Manville Corporation* (1986) 785 F 2d 79; *Hagerty v L & L Marine Services Inc* (1986) 788 F 2d 315; *Anderson v W R Grace & Co* (1986) 628 F Supp 1219; *Re Hawaii Federal Asbestos Cases* (1990) 734 F Supp 1563; *Gerardi v Nuclear Utility Services Inc* (1991) 566 NYS 2d 1002. For discussion see T M Dworkin, "Fear of Disease and Delayed Manifestation Injuries: A Solution or a Pandora's Box?" (1984) 53 Fordham L Rev 527; F J Gale & J L Goyer, "Recovery for Cancerphobia and Increased Risk of Cancer" (1985) 15 Cumb L Rev 723; F L Edwards & A H Ringleb, "Exposure to Hazard and the Mental Distress Torts: Trends, Applications and a Proposed Reform" (1986) 11 Col J Environ L 119; Comment, "Toxic Emotional Distress Claims: The Emerging Trend for Recovery Absent Physical Injury" (1991) 20 Cap U L Rev 995.
49. See eg *Ferrara v Galluchio* (1958) 152 NE 2d 249 (NY) (recovery allowed for fear of cancer based on plaintiff's x-ray burns); *Lorenc v Chemirad Corporation* (1962) 179 A 2d 401 (NJ) (recovery allowed for fear of cancer based on severe chemical burns to hands).
50. See eg *Hayes v New York Central Rail Co* (1962) 311 F 2d 198 (fear of amputation after frostbite); *Baylor v Tyrrell* (1964) 131 NW 2d 393 (fear of bone deterioration after car accident); *Kapuschinsky v United States* (1966) 259 F Supp 1 (anxiety over possible development of arthritis after malpractice by doctor); *Plummer v United States* (1978) 580 F 2d 72 (fear of sickness after exposure to active tuberculosis); *Martin v City of New Orleans* (1982) 678 F 2d 1321 (fear of paralysis and circulatory system problems from bullet wound); *Davis v Graviss* (1984) 672 SW 2d 928 (Ky) (fear of future neurological, eye and speech problems resulting from skull injury).
51. See eg *Doe v Doe* (1987) 519 NYS 2d 595 (wife claimed for "AIDS-phobia" after husband disclosed his homosexual activities, but claim failed because there was no allegation that either the husband or the wife herself had contracted the disease); *Hare v State of New York* (1989) 570 NYS 2d 125 (plaintiff claimed psychiatric injury including "AIDS-phobia" as a result of a bite by a prison inmate, suffered while attempting to prevent him committing suicide by repeatedly stabbing his throat with a fork, but after tests for the virus proved negative the claim was dismissed, the court holding inter alia that the plaintiff's fears were unfounded); *Johnson v West Virginia University Hospitals Inc* (1991) 413 SE 2d 889 (WVa) (security officer bitten by patient he was attempting to subdue, patient having first bitten himself so his own blood was in his mouth at time of bite); *Castro v New York Life Insurance Co, New York Law Journal*, 5 August 1991, 23; *Ordway v County of Suffolk* (1992) 583 NYS 2d 1014; see however *Petri v Bank of New York Co Inc* (1992) 582 NYS 2d 608 (action by homosexual plaintiff against lover could not succeed unless there was evidence that lover had AIDS). See D P Brigham, "You Never Told Me . . . You Never Asked: Tort Liability for the Sexual Transmission of AIDS" (1986) 91 Dickinson L Rev 529; D H J Herrman, "Liability Related to Diagnosis and Transmission of AIDS" (1987) 15 *Law, Medicine & Health Care* 36; J Schwartz, "Liability for the Transmission of AIDS and Herpes" (1987) *Annual Survey of American Law* 523; J P Darby, "Tort Liability for the Transmission of the AIDS Virus—Damages for Fear of AIDS and Prospective AIDS" (1988) 45 Wash & Lee L Rev 185; R O'Dair, "Liability in Tort for the Transmission of AIDS: Some Lessons from Afar and Prospects for the Future" (1990) 43 CLP 219; Intergovernmental Committee on AIDS Working Party, *Civil Liability for Transmission of HIV/AIDS* (1992), 17-26.
52. See *Tamplin v Star Lumber & Supply Co* (1991) 824 P 2d 219 (Kan).

emotional or mental suffering which develops into damage of a psychiatric nature should be compensable whether it stems from fear or horror, or worry, anxiety, anger, disappointment, distress, sorrow or grief. If the courts intend to persist with the requirement of a recognised psychiatric illness, then the existence of this damage and not the way which it was brought about or the catalyst behind its development is what should really matter. This would be especially so if the present requirement of direct physical perception were dismantled and recovery for oral or written communication permitted.[53] It is interesting to note that there is Australian authority granting relief for grief-based psychiatric damage. In *Mellor v Moran*[54] it was held that a child's grief at the death of her mother in a car accident had developed into a depressive condition amounting to a compensable psychiatric illness. Significantly also, Lord Oliver in *Alcock v Chief Constable of South Yorkshire Police*[55] spoke of the "cases in which, as in the instant appeals, the injury complained of is attributable to the grief and distress of witnessing the misfortune of another person". It is too early to say, however, that this isolated statement heralds some liberalisation in England in this respect.[56]

A medical perspective

It is important to define what we mean by "recognisable psychiatric illness or injury" and to endeavour to contrast it with "mental or emotional" "distress or suffering", since the antithesis between the two has had much influence on the development of this area of the law. By way of preliminary discussion, there is in general medicine an important distinction between "disease" and "illness". "Disease" refers to a definite morbid process having a characteristic train of symptoms or, to put it another way, refers to objective physical pathology. "Illness" denotes the subjective appreciation dimension of a medical condition or, in other words, the subjective awareness of distress or limitation of function. Although the two often coexist, they are mutually exclusive concepts. One may be diseased without being ill (as, for example, in well-controlled diabetes) or ill without having a disease (as, for example, where a person loses a limb as a result of an industrial mishap). The majority of psychiatric conditions which are potentially the subject of tort claims are best regarded as illnesses.[57] The terms "illness" and "mental illness" are both bandied around in everyday speech without much precision. The composition of appropriate definitions has proved notoriously difficult. Reference to states marked by a pronounced deviation from a normal healthy condition merely compounds the problem because "health" is even more difficult to define. The World Health Organisation defined it as "a state of complete physical, mental and social well-being, and not merely the absence of disease or infirmity"[58]—a

53. On this issue see below, pp 153-170.
54. (1985) 2 MVR 461.
55. [1992] 1 AC 310 at 408.
56. Note that anguish and grief resulting from an illness due to shock are compensable: see *Macpherson v Commissioner for Government Transport* (1959) 76 WN (NSW) 352.
57. See M Gelder et al, *Oxford Textbook of Psychiatry* (2nd ed, 1989), 76.
58. World Health Organisation, *Current State of Diagnosis and Classification in the Mental Health Field* (1981).

definition labelled as one that "could hardly be more comprehensive . . . or more meaningless".[59] Nor do definitions of "illness" based on the presence of suffering or pathological processes greatly assist.[60] In practice, rather than struggle to find a global definition for "mental illness", most psychiatrists allocate various psychiatric disorders to diagnostic categories designed to represent distinct entities, grouping them collectively under the umbrella of "mental illness".[61]

It should also be noted from the outset that, as is the case with "recognisable psychiatric illness or injury", expressions such as "mental distress" and "emotional suffering" are not terms of art: there is no universally accepted language to characterise these states of the human mind. One often finds "mental suffering", "mental anguish", "emotional distress"[62] and the like both in the case law and the literature and there does not appear to be any discernible difference between them. Objections can be raised to the use of both "mental" and "emotional" in this context. The term "mental" to some may convey a psychological or psychiatric condition, thereby making distinction between the two identified categories more difficult than need be. It may also be said that the use of the word "emotional" to describe a person's mood or spirits is better avoided because it is often used to indicate a state of agitation or excitement, perhaps with unfavourable overtones. However, no better terms appear to be available, and they are sanctioned by long usage. As there is no clear reason for preferring one term to the other we have therefore chosen to use them throughout this work interchangeably to characterise states of the human mind which lack objective symptoms, other than the primary instinctive reactions outlined below.

The foregoing paragraph should be read subject to the major qualification that in recent years the United States courts have adopted a practice of using the term "emotional distress" (and occasionally, "mental distress") to cover both initial emotional responses to stimuli and the later more serious physical and mental consequences which may flow from them. This has caused confusion between psychiatric and psychological conditions and normal mental suffering. It is frequently unclear from the judgments what the precise nature of the plaintiff's complaint is. This imprecision can be explained, but perhaps not excused, by the fact that both types of effect on human well-being are compensable in many jurisdictions in that country. In Commonwealth countries, however, the distinction between the two remains, at present, a crucial one, for failure to at least attempt to separate these states of mind has profound medico-legal implications. This work, therefore, avoids using the terms "emotional distress" or "mental distress" to refer to a recognisable psychiatric illness, except when it is necessary in discussing particular American decisions to reflect the language used in those cases.

59. A J Lewis, "Health as a Social Concept" (1953) 4 Brit J Sociology 109 at 110, reprinted in A J Lewis, *The State of Psychiatry* (1967), 179-194. Note also B Wootton, *Social Science and Social Pathology* (1959), 203-226.
60. See Gelder et al, op cit, n 57 at 76-77.
61. See below, pp 30-40. Problems may arise with certain abnormalities of behaviour such as sexual deviance, sexual preference or drug abuse. These behaviours are not usually regarded as mental illnesses notwithstanding that they are considered suitable for medical treatment. See generally M Roth & J Kroll, *The Reality of Mental Illness* (1987).
62. *Restatement of Torts Second*, §§46-48 consistently uses this term.

· The best way to appreciate the ambit of what is recoverable under the current law is to examine from a medical perspective the "mental distress" or "emotional suffering" which most common law systems have viewed as unworthy of compensation. Mental distress has been described as any "disagreeable disturbance of emotional or mental tranquillity"[63] or "traumatically induced reaction which is medically detrimental to the individual".[64] It is thus best understood as a comprehensive label covering a variety of unpleasant emotional reactions. There does not appear to be any universally accepted classification of human emotions.[65] They may be pleasant (such as love, joy, elation, companionship, excitement, happiness, contentment and so on) or unpleasant. The mental distress which is the origin of the harm suffered in the cases we will be considering usually consists of a combination of the following unpleasant emotions:

1. Fear or apprehension.

2. Horror.

3. Grief, sorrow and loneliness.

4. Shame, humiliation and embarrassment.

5. Anger, annoyance and vexation.

6. Disappointment and frustration.

7. Worry and anxiety.[66]

For a proper understanding of what follows it is important first to have some knowledge of the human nervous system. This consists of the central nervous system and the peripheral nervous system. It may be further subdivided functionally into the somatic and autonomic nervous systems. These various systems are anatomically and physiologically distinct. The central nervous system comprises the cerebral hemispheres, the rest of the forebrain, the midbrain, the brain stem and the spinal cord, which are the main centres where correlation and integration of nervous information occurs. Injury to this system, particularly trauma to the brain, is a matter for the neurologist. The peripheral system consists of the nerves emerging from the brain (cranial nerves) and from the spinal cord (spinal nerves) which convey neural messages from the sense organs and sensory receptors inward to the central nervous system and from the central nervous system outward to the muscles and glands of the body. The somatic nervous system comprises those neural structures of the central and peripheral systems responsible for

---

63. Smith, op cit, n 17 at 610.

64. Comment, "Negligently Inflicted Mental Distress: The Case for an Independent Tort" (1971) 59 Geo LJ 1237 at 1255.

65. S Cobb, *Emotions and Clinical Medicine* (1950), 25 says of the term "emotion": "The term 'emotion' designates a multidimensional referent: (1) the private, consciously felt effect; (2) the complex set of biochemical processes which constitute the internal milieu in which a multitude of reactions take place at various 'levels' of physiological integration, as well as the functioning of various neurological mechanisms, notably the 'visceral brain' and the autonomic nervous system, which are more directly concerned with the somatic expression of emotion; and (3) the more or less typical overt patterns of behaviour which may be said to 'express' the felt effect and to be manifestations of the stirred-up internal state."

66. For slightly different classifications see Cobb, op cit, n 65 at 108; H W Smith, "Relation of Emotions to Injury and Disease: Legal Liability for Psychic Stimuli" (1944) 30 Va L Rev 193 at 214; *Restatement of Torts Second*, §46 comment (j).

conveying and processing conscious and unconscious sensory information (such as vision, touch, pain and unconscious muscle sense) from the head, body wall and extremities to the central nervous system, and the motor control of the voluntary muscles. In other words, it innervates the body (for example, the skin and skeletal muscles) but not the viscera[67] or blood vessels. We are here chiefly concerned with the remaining category—the autonomic nervous system, which involves the innervation of involuntary structures within the body. It operates independently of the volition on these structures and is responsible for conveying and processing sensory input from the visceral organs (for example, the digestive and cardiovascular systems), and the motor control of the involuntary (smooth) and cardiac muscles and of glands of the viscera (for example, the large internal organs found in the abdominal cavity or "guts").

In 1902 Gillett J in *Kline v Kline*,[68] attempting to describe mental or emotional distress, said that there was "a touching of the mind, if not of the body". However, from the scientific point of view, it is incorrect to think of any sort of emotional response as purely *mental* suffering. A considerable amount of medical evidence has been assembled during the present century to demonstrate that all emotions have physical effects.[69] The basis of our knowledge of this subject remains the pioneering work of Dr Walter B Cannon of the Harvard Medical School who, during the early years of the 20th century, conducted extensive investigations into the physical effects of various emotions and produced very convincing evidence that emotions bring about important bodily changes.[70] Although more is

67. A term applied to the larger internal organs of the body which are closely related to, or contained within, one of the three great cavities of the body: the thorax (ie chest, containing the heart and lungs), pelvic cavity, and abdominal cavity. The term applies particularly to the organs of the abdominal cavity. "Viscus" is also applied individually to these organs.
68. (1902) 64 NE 9 (Ind) at 10.
69. For accounts in legal journals of this research see F V W Tibbits, "Neurasthenia, the Result of Nervous Shock, as a Ground for Damages" (1904) 59 Cent LJ 83; H F Goodrich, "Emotional Disturbance as Legal Damage" (1922) 20 Mich L Rev 497; L Vold, "Tort Recovery for Intentional Infliction of Emotional Distress" (1939) 18 Neb L Bull 222 at 222-228; H W Smith & H C Solomon, "Traumatic Neuroses in Court" (1943) 30 Va L Rev 87; Smith, op cit, n 66; M Keschner, "Simulation of Nervous and Mental Disease" (1946) 44 Mich L Rev 715; J Havard, "Reasonable Foresight of Nervous Shock" (1956) 19 MLR 478; P D Cantor, "Psychosomatic Injury, Traumatic Psychoneurosis, and Law" (1957) 6 Clev Mar L Rev 428; C E Wasmuth, "Psychosomatic Disease and the Law" (1958) 7 Clev Mar L Rev 34; Smith, op cit, n 17; D I Sindell, "The Terror Neurosis" (1966) 15 Clev Mar L Rev 41; E Tanay, "Psychic Trauma and the Law" (1969) 15 Wayne L Rev 1033 at 1033-45; R I Gordon, "Mental Distress in Psychological Research" (1969) 21 Baylor L Rev 520; M L Selzer, "Psychological Stress and Legal Concepts of Disease Causation" (1971) 56 Cornell L Rev 951; Comment, op cit, n 64 at 1248-62; D J Leibson, "Recovery of Damages for Emotional Distress caused by Physical Injury to Another" (1976-1977) 15 *Journal of Family Law* 163 at 190-211; J T Smith, "Post Traumatic Stress Disorder: An Often Overlooked Element of Trauma" (1984) 20 *Trial* 92; M M Duran, "Nothing New: Unwrapping the Packaging of Post-Traumatic Stress Disorder" (1988) 33 Loyola L Rev 1076; R J Bragg, "Post-Traumatic Stress Disorder" (1992) 136 SJ 674.
70. See *Bodily Changes in Pain, Hunger, Fear and Rage* (1915); *The Wisdom of the Body* (1932). Dr George W Crile also made important contributions to the subject: see *The Origin and Nature of the Emotions* (1915); *Man—An Adaptive Mechanism* (1916). Note, however, that as Vold, op cit, n 69 at 222, n 3 points out, Crile was a surgeon rather than a physiologist or a psychologist and so on the matters under discussion may be less authoritative.

now known about physiology, modern research has done nothing to invalidate his thesis.[71] But even before his study there was significant scientific opinion which supported such a contention. William Harvey in the 17th century recognised that affections of the mind were accompanied by bodily responses,[72] and in the 19th century what was probably the first serious study of the physical effects of fright was carried out by Charles Darwin.[73] Much of the scientific evidence deals with the bodily effects of fear. Fear may be of many types but it inevitably involves the threat of loss or damage to something which the individual greatly values and to which he or she is strongly attached. It may be for one's own personal safety or that of another, for loss of a prized possession or even an abstract ideal such as honour, reputation or a political or religious canon.[74] Fear causes various bodily changes: it affects the digestive processes, making the mouth dry and checking the flow of pancreatic juices and bile, and the bladder, increasing the frequency of urination; peristaltic movements of the stomach and intestines are stopped, hair may stand on end and skin may "goosebump" or perspire. It also affects the organs of the body which can aid it in its attempts to combat or escape the cause of the fear. Blood flows at an increased rate and pressure from the internal organs into the skeletal muscles, the supply of blood sugar rises, and the adrenal glands respond by secreting adrenalin to restore tired muscles which become more tense and less liable to fatigue. The spleen is contracted so that its content of concentrated corpuscles is squeezed out into the bloodstream. Blood vessels of the skin are constricted to guard against excessive bleeding from possible lesions, the rate of breathing is accelerated and the thyroid gland is triggered into action. Fear is thus very much a physical thing—it puts the whole body in a state of readiness for fight or flight.[75] This bodily reaction which aided primitive humans survives in us today. What is true of fear is true of all other emotions—horror, anger, shame, disappointment, worry, anxiety and so on have all been demonstrated to have complex physical effects, which vary according to the individual and the length and intensity of the emotional response. In the words of Goodrich, "[a]n emotion as a purely mental thing does not exist".[76]

These bodily reactions are short-term in duration, subjective in nature and in themselves are not harmful. In fact, such reactions may even be beneficial in the short term, because of the restorative effect on adrenalin secretion caused by emotional stimulation.[77] In the long term, however, these bodily changes may cause serious and permanent damage. Crile points out[78] that, when nature developed the physical reactions following fear, fear usually meant fight or flight, but today it seldom means either. Such consequential action would use up the products of emotional stimulation,

---

71. See A Storr, *Human Aggression* (1970), 28; Cobb, op cit, n 65 at 89-90.
72. W Harvey, *On the Motion of the Heart and Blood in Animals* (1628), Ch 15.
73. C Darwin, *Expression of the Emotions in Man and Animals* (1872).
74. See Havard, op cit, n 69 at 481-482. For discussion of the causation of fear see R R Grinker & J P Spiegel, *Men Under Stress* (1945).
75. "Fear hath torment": 1 John 4:18.
76. Op cit, n 69 at 501.
77. Ibid at 502, quoting W B Cannon, *Bodily Changes in Pain, Hunger, Fear and Rage* (1915).
78. G W Crile, *The Origin and Nature of the Emotions* (1915), 93, 139.

such as adrenalin and sugar, but if no action follows these products must be eliminated as waste; and there is a limit to the amount to which the body can withstand this process. The body is like a car with the accelerator pressed down when the clutch is let out.[79] No adverse consequences will result after the first couple of times this is done but there is a limit to the number of occasions it can be repeated before serious and possibly lasting damage occurs. So with the body: the infliction of emotional distress, if serious or intense enough or repeated often enough, may cause debilitating and permanent harm.

There is thus a primary, automatic and instinctive reaction to traumatic stimuli, which may be seen as the body's attempt to combat and protect the individual from the stress associated with the situation in question, and this may be followed by a secondary, longer-term reaction, which occurs when the body can no longer overcome the problem of emotional stress or adequately cope with the traumatic event.[80] Despite the undeniable progress that has been made in psychiatric medicine, the line between "normal" initial emotional responses to trauma and "abnormal" secondary psychiatric reactions remains, in some cases, a hazy one. Certain psychiatric disorders are simply extreme versions of commonplace human frames of mind. For example, reactions diagnosed as mild clinical anxiety[81] or depressive states[82] may merge imperceptibly with normal and natural anxiety and despondency.[83] The distinction is more readily made in relation to the more severe disorders (such as manic depressive disorder and schizophrenia[84]) which can be characterised as autonomous "categorical" illnesses beyond voluntary control or influence. One either exhibits or does not exhibit evidence of these sorts of illnesses. Greater difficulty arises in relation to the milder "dimensional" disorders which may overlap with the ordinary feelings experienced in everyday life. In contrast to the "all or nothing" nature of "categorical" illness, a person

79. Ibid at 61, 139-140, 161.
80. Trauma can be understood as a sudden extreme discontinuity in a person's experience. It commonly brings about extensive alterations of emotional, cognitive, and volitional processes which may ultimately threaten the self as a coherent whole: see D Spiegel & E Cardena, "Dissociative Mechanisms in Posttraumatic Stress Disorder", in M E Wolf & A D Mosnaim (eds), *Posttraumatic Stress Disorder: Etiology, Phenomenology, and Treatment* (1990), 23. Freud argued that traumatic neuroses result when the ego is overwhelmed as a consequence of an extensive breach made in its "protective shield" against stimuli; by this he meant a sort of psychic skin necessary for the crucial daily function of keeping at bay external stimuli that might otherwise swamp the ego. "Ego" refers to one of the three major divisions of the personality—the id, ego, and superego. The ego is the "executive branch" of the personality, mediating between the needs of the self and reality. When the "shield" is penetrated or the "skin" pierced the individual's normal adaptive capabilities are disturbed and he or she reverts to the primitive form of defence known as repetition compulsion which involves mentally repeating the distressing happening over and over, most commonly in dreams. The active re-creation of the event in this manner rather than the passive experience of it as in the original situation allows the trauma victim to overcome it: see S Freud, *Introduction to Psycho-Analysis and the War Neuroses* (1919); S Freud, *Beyond the Pleasure Principle* (1920).
81. See below, p 31.
82. See below, p 32.
83. Note *Hudson v Mutual of Omaha Insurance Co* (1974) 51 DLR (3d) 115 where it was held (for the purposes of a question in an insurance proposal) that depression, without more, was not a mental disorder.
84. See below, p 32.

can, for example, be more or less anxious or depressed than the next person. Although it is clear that anxiety and depression pose a risk to health, the fundamental problem in a mildly anxious or depressed individual and a grossly or "abnormally" anxious or depressed individual is identical. It is the consequences of the two forms of condition which are statistically different. Persons who are in a heightened anxiety state or suffering from grossly reactive or manic depression will experience a more serious, effective, rapid and longer-lasting decline in mental well-being than moderately anxious or depressed people. True it is that statistical group differences will necessarily be evident between any two individuals who are mildly and grossly anxious or depressed but the root problem is the same. Commonly, it is less severe forms of psychiatric illness such as these which are under consideration in litigation, complicating the determination of the issue of compensability and bringing into question the wisdom of the courts' forced division between normal and abnormal mental conditioning.

Not only does the prevailing law insist that this secondary damage be distinguished from transitory or momentary human response, it must be separated from any direct physical injury sustained as a result of immediate reaction, for example, to being startled, taken by surprise or frightened. Damage of this kind was suffered in *Brook v Cook*[85] when an African monkey suddenly appeared on top of the plaintiff's garden wall, frightening her so that she fell breaking her wrist trying to turn away quickly. Similarly, in *Slatter v British Railways Board*[86] the plaintiff was startled by a loud bang caused by the violent shunting of goods wagons into a stationary wagon which he was examining. He fell and his hand was cut off by the wagon.[87] Whilst recovery was allowed for this instantaneous injury the case cannot be regarded as one involving recognisable psychiatric harm. It is the secondary injuries or illnesses which manifest themselves subsequent to initial responses to exposure to trauma (and consequent and immediate physical injury sustained by falling, tripping and so on) which may be classified under that rubric. What we (and the courts) are concerned with when discussing compensable damage are those injuries or illnesses which can be categorised as acknowledged medical conditions. Medical science has now built up a great deal of knowledge about these secondary states which include both somatic damage such as miscarriages, heart attacks and peptic ulcerations and psychic (mental) damage such as various "traumatic neuroses",[88] psychoses[89] and psycho-neuroses[90] although in relation to the

85. (1961) 105 SJ 684. Note that the plaintiff failed on the facts, her injury being unforeseeable because it had not resulted from an attack of any kind by the animal.
86. [1966] 2 Lloyd's Rep 395.
87. See also *Cohn v Ansonia Realty* (1914) 148 NYS 39 (fright caused plaintiff to fall down elevator shaft); *Brandon v Osborne, Garrett & Co Ltd* [1924] 1 KB 548 (husband injured by falling glass in shop, wife instinctively pulled him out of danger and strained her leg); *Devine v Colvilles Ltd*, 1969 SC 67 (fear and panic after explosion caused steelworker to jump from high platform).
88. The word "neurosis" is a collective term for psychiatric disorders which have three things in common: (1) They are functional in nature, ie they are unaccompanied by organic brain disease; (2) They are not psychoses, ie the sufferer does not lose touch with external reality however severe the condition; (3) They differ from personality disorders in that they have a discrete onset rather than a continuous development from early adult life: see Gelder et al, op cit, n 57 at 154. Neuroses are less severe forms of mental illness than psychoses and are characterised by symptoms closer to normal experiences. The term is less than

latter three categories comprehensive understanding of the etiology,[91] pathology[92] and pathological physiology[93] remains elusive.

A common trauma-induced neurosis is the anxiety reaction where sufferers are tortured by the dread that all is not well and that something terrible is about to happen to them or to those they love. Because persons so afflicted do not know where the danger is going to come from, their happiness and efficiency is constantly curtailed by the perceived need to worry. The emotional stress produces severe tension resulting in symptoms such as nervousness and timidness, nausea, cardiac palpitations, shortness of breath, loss of weight, persistent headaches and backaches, stomach pains, weakness and so on. Another not uncommonly observed post-traumatic neurosis is the conversion reaction where the individual converts impulses which he or she consciously disavows into various physiological symptoms such as pain, muscular spasms, paralysis, and loss of hearing or sight. The effects of trauma manifest themselves not as anxiety but in terms of physical injury—though there is of course no physical cause. Other secondary reactions to trauma have been identified: hypochondria,

88. *Continued*
satisfactory as a formal component of a system of classification. It is difficult to define, the conditions it embraces have little in common, and increased information can be conveyed by using a more specific diagnosis. Moreover, neurosis has sometimes been misused to denote etiology (see below, n 91, pp 38-39) rather than used in its historically correct sense to designate disorder: see Gelder et al, op cit, n 57 at 79. For these reasons the term does not appear in the United States system of classification DSM-III-R, although it has been retained in ICD (revised 10th ed); for discussion of both systems see below, pp 33-34. Nevertheless "neurosis" continues to be used in everyday clinical practice and will be adopted in this work in its global sense. See generally M A Schwartz, *Neuroses Following Trauma* (1959); S Furst (ed), *Psychic Trauma* (1967); L Keiser, *The Traumatic Neurosis* (1968); R Culpan & C Taylor, "Psychiatric Disorders following Road Traffic and Industrial Injuries" (1973) 7 Aust NZ J Psych 32; M R Trimble, *Post Traumatic Neurosis: From Railway Spine to the Whiplash* (1981); M J Horowitz, *Stress Response Syndromes* (2nd ed, 1986); L Michelson & L M Ascher (eds), *Anxiety and Stress Disorders: Cognitive-Behavioral Assessment and Treatment* (1987); G Mendelson, *Psychiatric Aspects of Personal Injury Claims* (1988); J P Wilson et al (eds), *Human Adaptation to Extreme Stress: From the Holocaust to Vietnam* (1988). For a clear explanation of the medical terms see A Mann, *Medical Aspects of Injuries for Legal Purposes* (4th ed, 1985), Chs 3-4.

89. Broadly speaking, "psychosis" refers to the more severe forms of mental illness. However, reference to greater severity is not particularly helpful as the disorders which fall under this head occur in mild as well as severe forms. Unsuccessful attempts have been made to define the term more precisely: eg, insight is often suggested as a criterion for psychosis but this concept is itself difficult to define. The best criterion is perhaps the inability to distinguish between subjective experience and reality as evidenced by hallucinations and delusions—but again these criteria are not easily applied. As with the term "neurosis", "psychosis" is undesirable in that, apart from difficulties of definition, the conditions covered by the term have little in common and it is insufficiently informative. Once again, it is nevertheless widely used in practice as a convenient term for disorders which cannot be given a more precise diagnosis due to insufficient data: see Gelder et al, op cit, n 57 at 79.

90. These are intermediate types of disorder displaying characteristics of both neurosis and psychosis.

91. Etiology is the study or theory of the causation of any disorder; the sum total of knowledge of causes.

92. Pathology is that branch of medical science which deals with the essential nature of disorders, in particular the structural and functional alterations caused by them.

93. Pathological physiology concerns those deviations from normal functioning of particular organs or bodily processes which are produced by disorder or abnormal interference.

characterised by fears of illness and excessive concern with health; phobias, which cause the trauma victim to avoid contact with other people, places or situations; obsessive-compulsive disorders, where there is a continued appearance of unwelcome ideas in the mind or a repeated urge to carry out certain acts and rituals; depressive reactions, which may cause sleeplessness, loss of appetite, impaired initiative and fatigue; and hysteria, which affects the sensory and motor systems leading to possible loss of sensory capacity and part paralysis (particularly in the extremities) and may also result in epileptic-like convulsions.

Of the secondary afflictions which are psychotic in nature the most serious is schizophrenia, an extremely complex disorder involving delusions, hallucinations, and disturbance in the affect and form of thought. There have long been, and continue to be, widely diverging concepts of the condition, making it the most difficult "recognisable psychiatric illness" to define and describe. The disorder can be viewed as having three stages: in chronological order, the prodromal, active and residual phases.[94] The first and third of these are characterised by social isolation or withdrawal, clear deterioration from a previous level of role functioning (for example, as a wage earner, student or homemaker), peculiar behaviour (such as talking to oneself in public or collecting refuse), odd beliefs or thinking (for example, that others can "feel my feelings", telepathy), unusual perceptual experiences (for example, sensing the presence of a force or of absent persons), speech and communicative deterioration, marked decline in personal hygiene and grooming, and a lack of initiative, interests or energy. During the active phase the sufferer will experience bizarre delusions (for example, that he or she is controlled by a dead person or can broadcast thoughts) and vivid hallucinations throughout the day for several days or several times a week for several weeks. Such hallucinatory experiences are not limited to a few brief moments and may take the form of voices keeping a running commentary on the person's behaviour or thoughts, or two or more voices conversing with each other. There may, in addition, be a loosening of association, incoherence, and flat or grossly inappropriate affect. In flat affect there are virtually no signs of affective expression—the voice is monotonous and the face immobile. In inappropriate affect the affect is clearly discordant with the content of the person's speech or thoughts (for example, when discussing being tortured by electric shock the sufferer may laugh or smile). Active schizophrenic patients also engage in catatonic behaviour which is characterised by negativistic reactions, phases of stupor, immobility with muscle rigidity or inflexibility and outbreaks of excitement. Associated features of the syndrome include psychomotor abnormalities (such as pacing, rocking or apathetic immobility), memory impairment, disorientation, dysphoric moods which may take the form of depression, anxiety, anger or a mixture of these, eccentric grooming or dressing, dishevelment, and depersonalisation.

94. This is the approach adopted in DSM-III-R. It stipulates that there are five different subtypes of schizophrenia; catatonic, disorganised, paranoid, undifferentiated, and residual. Although the description and categorisation in ICD (revised 10th ed) are more complicated, there are broad similarities between the two major schemes of classification. For discussion of these schemes in this context see Gelder et al, op cit, n 57 at 282-286 and generally below, pp 33-34.

Of all the "recognisable psychiatric illnesses" of particular significance for our purposes is the very considerable interest focused in the last decade or so on Post-Traumatic Stress Disorder ("PTSD")[95] and it is on this neurotic condition that we will concentrate our discussion. Although the clinical features of PTSD have been observed for hundreds of years[96] the psychiatric nomenclature is of recent vintage. It was only in 1980 that American psychiatrists introduced this new diagnostic category into the *Diagnostic and Statistical Manual of Mental Disorders*—the standardised diagnostic psychiatric text in the United States.[97] Previously what is really a relatively common human post-trauma problem had been known under a variety of different names such as "post-traumatic neurosis" or "post-accident syndrome". One catalyst for its inclusion was the results of growing research being carried out on combat veterans and in particular

95. This disorder has generated a voluminous body of literature. A selection of the more general discussions includes J I Walker, "Posttraumatic Stress Disorder after a Car Accident" (1968) 69 *Postgraduate Medicine* 82; Kelly & Smith, op cit, n 17; M J Horowitz, "Postraumatic Stress Disorder" (1983) 1 Behav Sci Law 9; C B Scrignar, *Postraumatic Stress Disorder: Diagnosis, Treatment and Legal Issues* (1984); T Van Putten & J Yager, "Posttraumatic Stress Disorder" (1984) 41 Arch Gen Psy 411; C R Figley (ed), *Trauma and its Wake: The Study and Treatment of Posttraumatic Stress Disorder* (1985); R J McCaffrey & J A Fairbank, "Behavioral Assessment and Treatment of Accident-Related Posttraumatic Stress Disorder: Two Case Studies" (1985) 16 *Behavior Therapy* 406; B L Green et al, "Post Traumatic Stress Disorder: Toward DSM-IV" (1985) 173 J Nerv Ment Dis 406; J E Helzer et al, "Post Traumatic Stress Disorder in the General Population" (1987) 317 New Eng J Med 1630; M J Horowitz et al, "Diagnosis of Post-Traumatic Stress Disorder: Commentary" (1987) 175 J Nerv Ment Dis 267; C R Marmar & M J Horowitz, "Diagnosis and Phase-Oriented Treatment of Post-Traumatic Stress Disorder" in Wilson et al, op cit, n 88 at 81; G Mendelson, "The Concept of Posttraumatic Stress Disorder: A Review" (1987) 10 Int J Law & Psy 45; T M Keane & W E Penk, "The Prevalence of Post Traumatic Stress Disorder" (1988) 318 New Eng J Med 1690; J P Wilson, *Trauma, Transformation, and Healing: An Integrative Approach to Theory, Research, and Post Traumatic Therapy* (1989); A Burstein, "Posttraumatic Stress Disorder in Victims of Motor Vehicle Accidents" (1989) 40 Hosp Comm Psy 295; R S Epstein, "Postraumatic Stress Disorder: A Review of Diagnostic and Treatment Issues" (1989) 19 Psychiatry Ann 556; L C Kolb, "Chronic Post-Traumatic Stress Disorder: Implications of Recent Epidemiological and Neuropsychological Studies" (1989) 19 *Psychological Medicine* 821; J D Kinzie, "Post-Traumatic Stress Disorder" in H I Kaplan & B J Sadock (eds), *Comprehensive Textbook of Psychiatry* (5th ed, 1989), Vol 1, 1000; R Ramsay, "Invited Review: Post-Traumatic Stress Disorder: A New Clinical Entity?" (1990) 34 *Journal of Psychosomatic Research* 355; H G Stampfer, " 'Negative Symptoms': A Cumulative Trauma Stress Disorder?" (1990) 24 Aust NZ J Psych 516; Wolf & Mosnaim, op cit, n 80; E L Giller (ed), *Biological Assessment and Treatment of Post-Traumatic Stress Disorder* (1990); K C Peterson et al, *Post-Traumatic Stress Disorder: A Clinician's Guide* (1991). For treatment of the legal implications of PTSD see L F Sparr & J K Boehnlein, "Posttraumatic Stress Disorder in Tort Actions: Forensic Minefield" (1990) 18 Bull Am Acad Psy Law 283; L F Sparr, "Legal Aspects of Posttraumatic Stress Disorder: Uses and Abuses" in Wolf & Mosnaim, op cit, n 80 at 238.

96. See generally Trimble, op cit, n 88; Mendelson, op cit, n 88. Note also M R Trimble, "Post-Traumatic Stress Disorder: History of a Concept" in Figley, op cit, n 95 at 5-14; E Hare, "The History of 'Nervous Disorders' from 1600 to 1840, and a Comparison with Modern Views" (1991) 159 Br J Psy 37.

97. See generally R L Spitzer & J B W Williams, "Classification in Psychiatry" in H I Kaplan & B J Sadock (eds), *Comprehensive Textbook of Psychiatry* (4th ed, 1985), 591; G L Tischler (ed), *Diagnosis and Classification in Psychiatry* (1987); J B W Williams, "Psychiatric Classification" in J A Talbott et al (eds), *Textbook of Psychiatry* (1988), 201; H S Akiskal, "The Classification of Mental Disorders" in Kaplan & Sadock, op cit, n 95 at 583.

into the catastrophic effects of the Vietnam war.[98] Some continue to debate the validity of this syndrome but the vast majority of the scientific community accept it as a psychiatric entity, pointing to repeated observation and description of identical sets of symptoms following traumatic events.[99] Although it was not included in the ninth edition of the World Health Organisation's *International Classification of Diseases*[100]—the standard psychiatric classification used in the United Kingdom—its clinical validity looks assured given its incorporation in the revised tenth edition which has been recommended to come into effect from 1 January 1993. Although courts have been somewhat hesitant to utilise the benefits of the latest developments in this field, there are signs that this is changing. In a few recent cases the sufferings of plaintiffs have been identified as PTSD,[101] and in one remarkable Irish decision the court expressly adopted the DSM-III-R criteria.[102]

98. The first edition, DSM-I (1952), which coincided with the Korean War, had referred to gross stress reaction, a transient response to severe physical or emotional stress capable of developing into chronic neurotic reaction in accordance with predisposing character traits. The second edition, DSM-II (1968), developed during a period without war, eliminated the diagnostic category of gross stress reaction. It categorised the effects of traumatic stress under the diagnosis "transient situational disturbance" if the symptoms were short-lived and used the category "anxiety neurosis" for more enduring symptoms. See Ramsay, op cit, n 95 at 356. It has been estimated that there are between 500,000 and 1.5 million Vietnam veterans suffering PTSD: see P Thiens-Honthos et al, "Stress Disorder Symptoms in Vietnam and Korean War Veterans" (1982) 50 *Journal of Consulting & Clinical Psychology* 558.

99. Previously controversy arose as to the "legitimacy" of the disorder and its true discriminability from other disturbances: see eg N Breslau & G Davis, "Posttraumatic Stress Disorder: The Stressor Criterion" (1987) 175 J Nerv Ment Dis 255. It was questioned whether PTSD constituted a verifiable disorder or whether it should be alternatively recategorised as a variant or subset of other major syndromes such as major depression: see eg D W Goodwin & S B Guze, *Psychiatric Diagnosis* (4th ed, 1989), 93-94. However, an increasing number of studies have generated a substantial amount of factual data about PTSD and its distinctive symptomatology. This has assisted greatly in the resolution of earlier questions about diagnostic validity and taxonomy. Research conducted from about 1979 to 1983 provided the empirical support for this and work continues today to build on that foundation: see J Wolfe & T M Keane, "Diagnostic Validity of Posttraumatic Stress Disorder" in Wolf & Mosnaim, op cit, n 80, 49 at 50.

100. The closest equivalent category in ICD (9th ed) was "acute reaction to stress" which is defined as: "[V]ery transient disorders of any severity in nature which occur in individuals without any apparent mental disorder, in response to exceptional physical or mental stress, such as natural catastrophe or battle, and which usually subside within hours or days". See now "Acute stress reaction" in ICD (revised 10th ed). This is conceptually very different from PTSD as defined in DSM-III-R, a fact reflected in the proposal to add the disorder to the forthcoming revised American manual: see below, p 40. It is significant that until the 6th ed published in 1948 mental disorders were not included in ICD.

101. For example *Chapman v Lear* (unreported, Queensland SC, 8 Apr 1988, No 3732 of 1984); *A v P & O Ferries (Dover) Ltd, The Independent*, 5 May 1989; *Ross v Bowbelle and Marchioness* (unreported, Admiralty Registrar, 18 June 1991); *Clark v Commonwealth* (unreported, Victorian SC, 24 Feb 1992, No 31 of 1985); *Re Kelley and Criminal Code of Queensland* (unreported, Queensland SC, 26 Feb 1992, No 363 of 1991); *Pibworth v Bevan M Roberts Pty Ltd* (unreported, South Australian SC, 28 May 1992, No 770 of 1986); *Miller v Royal Derwent Hospital Board of Management* (unreported, Tasmanian SC, 29 May 1992, No 282 of 1988); *Reditt v Williamson* (unreported, South Australian SC, 7 July 1992, No 180 of 1991). According to the expert evidence given in *Alcock v Chief Constable of South Yorkshire Police* [1992] 1 AC 310 at 317, "[t]he most common diagnosis made was post-traumatic stress disorder".

102. *Mullally v Bus Eireann* (unreported, Irish HC, 13 June 1991). Denham J commented that PTSD was "a very psychiatric disease".

The American literature[103] currently defines PTSD as requiring exposure to a psychologically distressing external event that is outside the range of usual human experience (so common experiences such as simple bereavement, serious illness, business or financial losses and marital conflict will not suffice).[104] The definition recognises that not all trauma victims are necessarily normal individuals, although the stressor must be of sufficient severity to invoke the symptoms in normal persons. Consequently, PTSD may be diagnosed in those who have had previous psychiatric problems. Importantly, it is also recognised that the trauma may be experienced through direct physical perception or on learning of it through third parties,[105] alone or in the company of others. Stressors capable of producing the condition include military combat, natural disasters, intentionally caused disasters (such as confinement in concentration camps, subjection to torture or presence at bombing sites), and the situation with which we are concerned, accidental disasters.[106]

103. See generally M J Horowitz, "Stress of Post-Traumatic Stress Disorder: Commentary" (1987) 175 J Nerv Ment Dis 267; R M Scurfield, "Post-Trauma Stress Assessment and Treatment: Overview and Formulations" in Figley, op cit, n 95 at 219; E A Brett, "DSM-III-R Criteria for Post-Traumatic Stress Disorder" (1988) 145 Am J Psych 1232. DSM-IV was originally scheduled to appear by the end of 1992 (see (1988) *Psychiatric News*, 15 Jan, 1), a move which met with some disapproval on the basis that the five-year interval between DSM-III-R and DSM-IV was insufficient time for the accumulation of adequate data to guide the developers of the new manual: see M Zimmermann, "Why Are We Rushing to Publish DSM-IV?" (1988) 45 Arch Gen Psy 1135; Kaplan & Sadock, op cit, n 95 at x. However, the Task Force on DSM-IV appointed in 1988 by the Board of Trustees of the American Psychiatric Association to commence revision of the existing manual does not now expect to finalise DSM-IV before 1994. It has published its work in progress in the form of an Options Book identifying the major diagnostic issues and options for change that may be included in the new manual: see American Psychiatric Association, *DSM-IV Options Book: Work in Progress* (1991). A DSM-IV Sourcebook summarising the literature reviews should be available shortly.

104. The DSM-III-R stressor criterion has been criticised in some quarters as being vague and unreliable. Three options have been put forward by the Task Force on DSM-IV for an amended definition of the stressor: see American Psychiatric Association, op cit, n 103 at H:15-17. The first provides a more specific and narrower description of the allowable stressor, ie that the victim has "experienced, witnessed, or been confronted with an event or events that involve actual or threatened death or injury, or a threat to the physical integrity of oneself or others". The second option adds a subjective component by stipulating that the stressor must also provoke a response in the person which involved "intense fear, helplessness, or horror". The third option, which has been taken from ICD (revised 10th ed), is the most similar to the existing definition stating that there must have been "exposure to an exceptional mental or physical stressor, either brief or prolonged".

105. For discussion of the means of communication of trauma see below, Ch 7.

106. As the case law illustrates such happenings may have detrimental effects on those injured, their loved ones and others, and rescue workers. After a devastating disaster it is not uncommon for as many as 50-80% of the survivors to develop PTSD: see H I Kaplan & B J Sadock, *Synopsis of Psychiatry* (6th ed, 1991), 409. For discussion in psychiatric terms of the rescue worker's responses see M R Hersheiser & E L Quarantelli, "The Handling of the Dead in a Disaster" (1976) 7 *Journal of Death and Dying* 195; P Short, "Victims and Helpers" in R L Heathcote & B G Thom (eds), *Natural Hazards in Australia* (1979); B Raphael et al, "Disaster: The Helper's Perspective" (1980) 2 Med J Aust 445; D C J Frazer & A J W Taylor, "The Stress of Post-Disaster Body Handling and Victim Identification Work" (1982) 8 *Human Stress* 5; C B Wilkinson, "Aftermath of a Disaster: The Collapse of the Hyatt Regency Hotel Skywalls" (1983) 140 Am J Psy 134; B Raphael, "Rescue Workers: Stress and their Management" (1984) 1 *Emergency Response* 27; B Raphael, "Who Helps The Helpers? The Effects of a Disaster on the

Exposure to such phenomena must lead to a characteristic collection of symptoms involving mental re-experience of the traumatic event, numbing of responsiveness to the external world, the avoidance of stimuli associated with the trauma and increased arousal.[107] These states do not always occur in a prescribed pattern, there being variations in the oscillations between them. All four criteria must, however, be present in order to make the diagnosis. They assume relative homogeneity of response, but do utilise an approach which accommodates individual differences in response by identifying multiple items for the re-experience, numbing and avoidance and arousal components. An individual is required to demonstrate a specified number, but not all, of the items within each criterion in order to qualify for diagnosis.

PTSD thus focuses on specific psychological responses to an extreme environmental condition which would evoke distress symptoms in almost everyone. It consists of a combination of "tonic" features (those that the victim manifests all or most of the time) and "phasic" features (those that are manifested intermittently). Although comprised of the trilogy of intrusion (phasic), avoidance (tonic) and arousal (a mixture of phasic and tonic) symptoms, it is the first of these which is the characteristic feature of the disorder. Unwelcomed memories of the traumatic event may manifest themselves in recurrent and distressing recollections (in young children, in the form of repeated engagement in play in which themes or aspects of the trauma are expressed), nightmares, sudden acting or feeling as if the event were recurring in the form of a sense of reliving the experience, illusions, hallucinations and dissociative states (visual and auditory flashbacks not unlike those experienced by LSD users) lasting from a few seconds to several hours or even days[108] (including those that

106. *Continued*
    Rescue Workers" (1983-1984) 14 *Omega* 9; A C McFarlane, "Ash Wednesday and the CFS Firefighters" (1984) 1 *Emergency Response* 34; D R Jones, "Secondary Disaster Victims: The Emotional Effects of Recovering and Identifying Human Remains" (1985) 142 Am J Psy 303; T W Durham et al, "The Psychological Impact of Disaster on Rescue Personnel" (1985) 14 *Annals of Emergency Medicine* 664; D H Duckworth, "Psychological Problems Arising From Disaster Work" (1986) 2 *Stress Medicine* 315; P Bartone et al, "The Impact of a Military Air Disaster on the Health of Assistance Workers: A Prospective Study" (1989) 177 J Nerv Ment Dis 317; A J W Taylor, *Disasters and Disaster Stress* (1989); D A Alexander, "Psychological Intervention For Victims and Helpers After Disasters" (1990) 40 Br J General Practice 345; D A Alexander, "The Piper Alpha Oil Rig Disaster" in J P Wilson & B Raphael (eds), *The International Handbook of Traumatic Stress Syndromes* (1990); K M Wright et al, "The Shared Experience of Catastrophe: An Expanded Classification of the Disaster Community" (1990) 60 Am J Orthopsychiatry 35; Napier, op cit, n 33.
107. For discussion of the treatment of PTSD see J B Frank et al, "Anti-depressants in the Treatment of Posttraumatic Stress Disorder", S Lipper, "Carbamazepine in the Treatment of Posttraumatic Stress Disorder: Implications for the Kindling Hypothesis", M J Friedman, "Interrelationships Between Biological Mechanisms and Pharmacotherapy of Posttraumatic Stress Disorder", C K Embry, "Psychotherapeutic Interventions in Chronic Posttraumatic Stress Disorder" in Wolf & Mosnaim, op cit, n 80 at 170, 184, 204, 226 and the references cited therein; Peterson, op cit, n 95, Part IV.
108. See eg A Burstein, "Posttraumatic Flashbacks, Dream Disturbances and Mental Imagery" (1985) 46 J Clin Psychiatry 374; D Spiegel, "Dissociation and Hypnosis in Post-Traumatic Stress Disorders" (1988) 1 *Journal of Traumatic Stress* 17; D Spiegel & E Cardena, "Dissociative Mechanisms in Post-Traumatic Stress Disorder" in Wolf & Mosnaim, op cit, n 80 at 23.

occur on waking or when intoxicated), and intense distress at exposure to events that symbolise or resemble an aspect of the trauma (such as anniversaries of the trauma). [109]

The unconscious defence mechanisms of general non-responsiveness and avoidance strategy may manifest themselves in deliberate efforts to avoid thoughts or feelings about the event in question and activities or situations that arouse recollections of it. PTSD victims may even experience memory fragmentation, developing psychogenic amnesia for an important aspect of the trauma. Commonly there is a markedly diminished interest in significant activities which in the case of children may result in the loss of recently acquired developmental skills such as toilet training or improvement in language. Feelings of detachment or estrangement from others, "emotional blunting", inability to express loving feelings and a sense of a life without future (for example, empty of marriage, children or career) are also signs of the existence of these components of the disorder. [110]

Persistent symptoms of increased arousal that were not present prior to the trauma include difficulty in falling or staying asleep, hypervigilance and exaggerated startle response. Sufferers may also experience problems in concentrating or completing tasks and display irregular aggressive behaviour ranging from irritability, with fears of losing control, to unpredictable explosions of anger, to inability to express anger at all. Additionally, physiological reactivity on exposure to situations or activities that resemble or symbolise the trauma (as, for example, when a mother whose child was killed in a bus accident breaks out in a sweat when boarding any bus) is likely. [111]

The original definition of PTSD drew a distinction between three subtypes: an acute disorder which began within six months of the trauma and lasted less than six months; a chronic disorder lasting six months or longer; and delayed PTSD which had its onset at least six months after the event in question. The literature reveals that most researchers conceptualise PTSD as a syndromal progression of clinical features from the acute to the chronic stage, although it is certainly true that this progression may be affected by secondary "symptoms" such as involvement in continuing or prospective litigation. The revised 1987 definition in DSM-III-R stipulates that the symptoms outlined above must be present for at least one month before the diagnosis of PTSD will be made, although it is silent on the question of the time of the disturbance's onset. [112] The capacity of PTSD

109. A number of minor additions and deletions to the list of items within the re-experience criterion have been advanced in the DSM-IV Options Book: see American Psychiatric Association, op cit, n 103 at H:17.
110. Minor amendments to the components of the numbing and avoidance criterion have been proposed. It has also been suggested that the threshold for this criterion be reduced from the display of three to two items: see American Psychiatric Association, op cit, n 103 at H:18.
111. Physiologic reactivity has been transferred from the increased arousal criterion to the list of items within the re-experience criterion in the DSM-IV Options Book: see American Psychiatric Association, op cit, n 103 at H:17.
112. The Task Force on DSM-IV has suggested that there is a case for setting a higher threshold by requiring a three-month duration of symptomatology. If this option was adopted those patients with symptoms lasting less than three months would not be

to occur with a delayed start—it can be as little as a week or as long as 30 years[113]—remains one of the puzzling aspects of the condition.

The etiological factors of PTSD have not yet been fully determined. There is a consensus that the nature and intensity of the stressor is the primary etiological factor determining the symptoms that people develop in the face of extreme adversity. The role of the stressor can be compared to the role of force in breaking a leg. It is normal for a leg to break if enough force is applied. Individual legs vary, however, in the amount of force required to produce a break, the amount of time required for healing to occur and the degree of residual pathology that may remain.[114] In most PTSD cases although the stressor is a necessary cause, it is not a sufficient one because even the most severe stressors do not produce PTSD in every individual experiencing them. Whilst the disorder is both age and sex indiscriminate, it is true that in general the very young and very old have greater difficulty coping with trauma than do persons experiencing it in mid life.[115] A variety of psychological,[116] physical,[117] genetic and social[118] factors may contribute to the onset, effect and duration of the disorder. However, the different contributions made, for example, by personality and other premorbid characteristics remain unclear. A minor trauma might be an important cause of the onset of PTSD in a highly vulnerable individual, where the same trauma would be an unlikely trigger in a less predisposed person.[119] The degree of impairment also varies between

112. *Continued*
     classified as suffering from a mental disorder. Another possibility which has been identified is to set no minimum duration requirement but to exclude those whose symptomatology resolves within one month of the onset of the stressor. A subtyping scheme complements this latter proposal, classifying a condition as acute if the duration of symptoms lasts less than three months, as chronic if it is three months or longer and with delayed onset if the onset of the symptoms takes place six (or alternatively three) months after exposure to the stressor: see American Psychiatric Association, op cit, n 103 at H:18-19.

113. Note C Van Dyke et al, "Posttraumatic Stress Disorder: A Thirty-Year Delay in a World War II Veteran" (1985) 142 Am J Psy 1070.

114. See N C Andreasen, "Posttraumatic Stress Disorder" in Kaplan & Sadock, op cit, n 97 at 919.

115. The body's coping mechanisms designed to deal with the emotional and physical impact of traumatic stimuli are not fully developed in children of tender years. The elderly are likely to have more rigid mechanisms and diminished capacity to develop flexible approaches to coping with the effects of trauma: see ibid at 919.

116. For example, it is widely, although not universally, believed that the more previous trauma experienced by an individual the more likely he or she is to develop symptoms following a stressful event.

117. Often PTSD victims will have also suffered physical injuries due to the traumatic event (eg in a car accident) and this may increase the likelihood of a prolonged psychiatric reaction, particularly if the injury is to the head.

118. For example, there is some evidence that PTSD is more likely to occur in those who are single, divorced, widowed, economically handicapped or socially deprived: see Andreasen, op cit, n 114 at 920.

119. See A C McFarlane, "Vulnerability to Posttraumatic Stress Disorder", F Flach, "The Resilience Hypothesis and Posttraumatic Stress Disorder", J H Reich, "Personality Disorders and Posttraumatic Stress Disorder" in Wolf & Mosnaim, op cit, n 80 at 3, 37, 65. Although the evidence suggesting personality can predispose an individual to PTSD is fragmented, the best-designed studies do show some link: see eg Helzer et al, op cit, n 95; A C McFarlane, "The Aetiology of Posttraumatic Stress Disorders Following a Natural Disaster" (1988) 152 Br J Psy 116.

PTSD victims ranging from slight to severe. Not every individual suffers the same degree of impairment in response to the same traumatic situation—as with the leg, everyone has their own mental breaking point. As a general rule those with normal intelligence, healthy premorbid personality, adequate social supports and sufficient adaptive capabilities are likely to suffer only minimal impairment and recover quickly. Persons with less psychological stamina and fewer social supports may develop more serious symptoms for a longer period.[120] When the stressor is intense or the individual has little resilience the disorder may potentially affect almost every aspect of daily life and may become quite refractory to treatment.[121]

Despite the original recognition of PTSD in DSM-III, the revised entry in DSM-III-R designed, inter alia, to minimise false-positive and false-negative diagnoses, and the sophistication of psychology and psychiatry over the years, a number of PTSD cases go unrecognised by experts in both disciplines. The disorder's symptoms are similar to other complaints and it is sometimes confused with other anxiety conditions, anti-social personality disorders, paranoid schizophrenia, alcoholism and other substance abuse, and depressive reactions. The identification difficulties are compounded by the fact that PTSD may coexist with any of these and with other psychiatric disorders. One reason for diagnostic inaccuracy stems from the nature of the psychopathology.[122] Where an x-ray clearly reveals evidence of fracture, or laboratory testing denotes abnormal growth hormone levels in atypically short or tall patients, there can be no doubt as to the nature of the particular complaint. Such unequivocal and reliable evidence is not always ascertainable when assessing mental disturbance. Current psychiatric assessment and evaluation procedure still primarily consists of descriptive interview with the possible additional use of questionnaires to gather further information.[123] Reported experience and observed behaviour (by clinicians, family, friends, and so on) is measured against clinical concepts of the "normal" and the "abnormal" accumulated over time. However, most trauma victims will not readily respond to inquiries about their distressing experiences; they will very rarely provide information unprompted by clinicians and when asked directly often respond evasively with generalities or denial. There may be genuine difficulty in recalling past happenings, resulting in retrospective fabrication. Other methodological hurdles include the inability to plan prospective studies of PTSD due to the fact that by definition the disorder involves the subject experiencing trauma beyond the normal realm of experience. Researchers are forced to wait until such a situation arises and then examine the impact, and, in the context of survivors of accidents or disasters involving large groups of people, to obtain a suitable control

120. See Andreasen, op cit, n 114 at 923.
121. Approximately 30% of sufferers recover, 40% have mild symptoms, 20% have moderate symptoms while 10% do not respond to treatment or become worse: see Kaplan & Sadock, op cit, n 106 at 411.
122. Psychopathology is the study of abnormal states of mind.
123. Although there have been advances in psychometric instruments, there are few standardised examiner-administered interview formats for PTSD. Rating scales include the Impact of Event Scale (IES) which assesses the degree of subjective stress experienced as a result of a particular event: see M J Horowitz et al, "Impact of Event Scale: A Measure of Subjective Stress" (1979) 43 *Psychosomatic Medicine* 209.

group. It must be pointed out, however, that whilst these types of factors may make life more difficult for those investigating this disorder, for the trained and experienced eye they do not present insurmountable obstacles to accurate diagnosis. Efforts to develop new detection and diagnosis validation techniques continue. Use has been made, for example, of epidemiological approaches which examine disease distributions across population, [124] and focused biologic and physiologic approaches which involve the search for intrinsic biologic or centrally mediated "markers" such as biochemical and neuroendocrine [125] alterations and heart rate reactivity. [126]

Whilst much space has been devoted to outlining the psychiatric disorder with which lawyers and the general public are probably most familiar, it is significant, particularly for those concerned with the legal implications of trauma, that a related but conceptually distinct new diagnosis has recently been included in the revised tenth edition of the ICD (as acute stress reaction) and proposed by the American Psychiatric Association for consideration for inclusion in DSM-IV. [127] This diagnosis, as yet unplaced and unnamed by the Task Force on DSM-IV (possible labels include acute stress disorder and brief reactive dissociative disorder), is designed to assist in the categorisation of trauma-induced conditions which do not meet the criteria for diagnosis as PTSD because of differences in onset, duration and symptom presentation. If incorporated it is proposed that the stressor criterion will be identical to that in PTSD but that there will be a different blend and composition of other criteria for diagnosis. Some combination of identified dissociative, anxiety and other symptoms is to be selected at a later date based on data reanalysis. Apart from causing reactions of this nature, the disturbance, an episode of which lasts less than four weeks, causes significant impairment or distress manifested by marked interference with social or occupational functioning or the prevention of the pursuit of some necessary task such as obtaining necessary medical or legal assistance. Once researchers have identified the best selection of items and most appropriate threshold for this proposed disorder lawyers and courts are likely to find themselves confronted with an even broader cross-section of mental damage claimants beyond those afflicted with the more publicised members of the family of psychiatric illnesses such as PTSD.

124. One study examining the prevalence of PTSD in the United States established a rate of 1% for this disorder: see Helzer, op cit, n 95 (and note the comments by Keane & Penk, op cit, n 95). This is comparable to the incidence of schizophrenia in that country. Kaplan & Sadock, op cit, n 106 at 409 state the prevalence of PTSD in the general US population to be 0.5% in men and 1.2% in women.

125. Relating or belonging to the effect produced on the organism by the nerves and the action of the ductless (endocrine) glands.

126. See eg P Malloy et al, "Validation of a Multimethod Assessment of Post-Traumatic Stress Disorders in Vietnam Veterans" (1983) 51 J Consult Clin Psychol 488; T Kosten et al, "Sustained Urinary Norepinephrine and Epinephrine Elevation in Post-Traumatic Stress Disorder" (1987) 12 Psychoneuroendocrinology 13; E Blanchard, "Cardiac Response to Relevant Stimuli as an Adjunctive Tool for Diagnosing Post-Traumatic Stress Disorder in Vietnam Veterans" (1986) 17 Behavior Therapy 592; R Pitman et al, "Psychophysiologic Assessment of Post-Traumatic Stress Disorder Imagery in Vietnam Veterans" (1987) 44 Arch Gen Psy 970.

127. See World Health Organisation, International Classification of Diseases (rev 10th ed, 1992); American Psychiatric Association, op cit, n 103 at K:5-6.

Other disciplines have contributed to the understanding of the etiology of psychiatric complaints. The social sciences, most notably sociology, which is the science concerned with the development, constitution and laws of human society, emphasise the social dimension of mental illness. Of particular importance is the sociological research which has examined the social and cultural determinates of psychiatric disorder and the harmful effects on physical and mental health of stressful "life events" and crises. A number of studies using epidemiological methods[128] show a causal association between life events and mental illness and physical ailments, suggesting that the risk to health is greater at a period of change in a person's life than at an uneventful time. For example, researchers have identified a correlation between specific life changes and psychotic breakdown in schizophrenics.[129] Earlier more general research which observed the morbidity of several hundred people over many years found that episodes of illness clustered at transitional stages rather than periods of stability in human existence.[130] Evidence was adduced that stressful events by stimulating psychophysiologic reactions were important causative agents in the development of many illnesses. The foundation work in this area, however, was that of Holmes and Rahe who in the 1960s attempted to improve on the highly subjective measures adopted in previous research.[131] They developed a "social readjustment scale" according to which various life events necessitating adaptation or change were quantified by formulating the "life stress unit". "Stress" is not used here in the

128. Epidemiology is the study of the distribution of disease in space and time within the population and of the factors that influence this distribution. It is concerned with illness among groups of persons, not the individual.

129. One study has shown that in the three weeks prior to the onset of schizophrenic episode, 60% of patients experienced events which impinged directly on themselves or on close relatives. The comparable figure for a control group was only 19%: see J L T Birley & G W Brown, "Crisis and Life Changes Preceding the Onset or Relapse of Acute Schizophrenia: Clinical Aspects" (1970) 116 Br J Psy 327. See also G W Brown & J L T Birley, "Crisis and Life Changes and the Onset of Schizophrenia" (1968) 9 *Journal of Health & Social Behavior* 203; G W Brown et al, "Life Events and Psychiatric Disorders: Part 2: Nature of Causal Links" (1973) 3 *Psychological Medicine* 159; S Jacobs & J Myers, "Recent Life Events and Acute Schizophrenic Psychosis: A Controlled Study" (1976) 162 J Nerv Ment Dis 75.

130. See H G Wolff, "A Concept of Disease in Man" (1962) 24 *Psychosomatic Medicine* 25. Note also H G Wolff et al (eds), *Life Stress and Bodily Disease* (1950). This type of research evolved from the work of Meyer: see A Lief (ed), *The Commonsense Psychiatry of Dr Adolf Meyer* (1948).

131. T H Holmes & R H Rahe, "The Social Readjustment Rating Scale" (1967) 11 *Journal of Psychosomatic Research* 213. See also eg C M Parkes, "Recent Bereavement as a Cause of Mental Illness" (1964) 110 Br J Psy 198; A Antonovsky & R Kats, "The Life Crisis History as a Tool in Epidemiologic Research" (1967) 8 *Journal of Health & Social Behavior* 15; R Rahe et al, "Demographic and Psychological Factors in Acute Illness Reporting" (1970) 23 J Chronic Dis 245; C M Parkes & R J Brown, "Health after Bereavement: A Controlled Study of Young Boston Widows and Widowers" (1972) 34 *Psychosomatic Medicine* 449; E S Paykel, "Recent Life Events and Clinical Depression" in E G Gunderson & R H Rahe (eds), *Life Stress and Illness* (1974), 134; B S Dohrenwend & B P Dohrenwend (eds), *Stressful Life Events: Their Nature and Effects* (1974); E S Paykel, "Contribution of Life Events to Causation of Psychiatric Illness" (1978) 8 *Psychological Medicine* 245; T K J Craig & G W Brown, "Life Events, Meaning and Physical Illness: A Review" in A Steptoe & A Matthews (eds), *Health Care and Human Behaviour* (1984), 7-39; C Tennant, "Psychosocial Causes of Duodenal Ulcer" (1988) 22 Aust NZ J Psych 195.

conventional negative sense, but to connote the requirement of some accommodative or coping behaviour on the part of the affected individual. Thus the scale included both socially desirable and undesirable events, for change for the better and for the worse both produce stress in this context—indeed good news may be more stressful than some bad news or unfortunate events—as well as changes within and outside the individual's control. Forty-three different varieties of life changes (for example, those concerning work, residence, finance, family and marital relationships, pregnancy, injury and illness) were identified and assigned a value depending on their apparent severity and the degree of stress they commonly evoke. The death of a spouse was found to be the greatest stressor and assigned a unit value of 100. At the other end of the spectrum was the taking of a vacation with a relative stress value of 13 and a minor violation of the law with 11. If a certain tally of points was accumulated by a person within the preceding year he or she was found to be at an increased risk for developing some type of medical or psychiatric illness in the following months. More recent research suggests that external events may in some circumstances, although not acting as stressors in themselves, render a person more vulnerable to later stressful life events. [132] Whilst the methodology, results and significance of life event research have been questioned, [133] it does provide a complementary insight into the genesis of psychiatric illness.

It is thus indisputable that emotional and mental distress brought on by exposure to trauma may often have serious long-term physical and psychiatric effects. Adequate proof that such secondary damage has in fact been suffered is currently a prerequisite to any detailed legal inquiry as to the compensability of the particular harm in question—but psychology and psychiatry are now equal to this task. Some assessment and classification confusion will surface as long as the courts demand that a delineation between normal initial and abnormal subsequent responses to stressors be made. But if there are to be any allegations of inadequacy they ought to be directed at the law and not at these disciplines. Medical science can with an acceptable degree of certainty establish the existence of the various types of recognised psychiatric complaints, their degree and effects and very often isolate their causes. Although the courts have gradually recognised the fruits of advances in these disciplines and that they allow them to jettison many of the original requirements thought necessary as guarantees of genuineness (for example, the need for physical harm or the likelihood of it), in many respects the common law has either clung to outdated and historical notions or merely tinkered with principles that are fundamentally unsound. It is to this unpreparedness to deviate from the past and to provide a more extensive remedy for tortiously caused mental harm that we now turn.

132. See eg G W Brown & T O Harris, *Social Origins of Depression* (1978).
133. See eg E S Paykel et al, "Life Events and Depression: A Controlled Study" (1969) 21 Arch Gen Psy 753; Paykel, op cit, n 131; S Henderson et al, *Neurosis and the Social Environment* (1982); E S Paykel, "Methodological Aspects of Life Event Research" (1983) 27 *Journal of Psychosomatic Research* 341; Gelder et al, op cit, n 57 at 107-108. Note also G W Brown et al, "Life Events and Psychiatric Disorders: Part 1: Some Methodological Issues" (1973) 3 *Psychological Medicine* 74.

Mere mental or emotional distress or suffering

In general

Although it may be expected that relatives and others may experience severe emotional turmoil at the death or injury of a loved one, the common law does not seek to provide compensation. As Lord Wensleydale said well over a century ago in *Lynch v Knight*:[134] "mental pain and anxiety the law cannot value, and does not pretend to redress, when the unlawful act complained of causes that alone". This principle has been repeated so often that it is generally accepted without question. It is frequently stated as a truism without explanation of any kind, most recently by Lord Ackner in *Alcock v Chief Constable of South Yorkshire Police*[135] who said simply: "Mere mental suffering, although reasonably foreseeable, if unaccompanied by physical injury, is not a basis for a claim for damages."

Repetition without elucidation is intellectually unsatisfying. It is important to ask *why* the law gives no damages for "mere" mental or emotional distress or suffering. The statement of Lord Wensleydale suggests the reason that the law is unable to value such injury, but, as we have already seen, more is now known about the effects of emotions on the body and doctors can with a considerable degree of precision identify various forms of emotional distress and their effects.[136] Moreover, difficulty of valuation and assessment is a poor rationale for denial when one considers that awards for the non-pecuniary components of personal injury damages, such as pain and suffering, are routinely made but, by their very nature, are also incapable of valuation.[137] Other traditional arguments, such as the problems of proof, that the damage is too remote and the danger of false claims succeeding,[138] are also much more difficult to sustain in the light of developments in medical knowledge: psychiatry may arguably not be "an exact science",[139] but it is capable of uncovering simulation.[140] Some judges have suggested that such emotional damage is not compensable because it is something experienced by any normal person when someone they love is killed or injured,[141] but it is not easy to see why

---

134. (1861) 9 HL Cas 577; 11 ER 854 at 855; see also *Mitchell v Rochester Rail Co* (1896) 45 NE 354 (NY).
135. [1992] 1 AC 310 at 401.
136. See the discussion above, pp 24-42.
137. See *McDermott v Ramadanovic Estate* (1988) 27 BCLR (2d) 45 per Southin JA at 53, quoted above, p 20. Note also *Naylor v Yorkshire Electricity Board* [1968] AC 529 per Lord Devlin at 548 who stated: "In the law of damages . . . difficulty in calculation is not ordinarily taken as a ground either for reducing or for increasing the award."
138. These were among the arguments put forward for denying liability in *Victorian Railways Commissioner v Coultas* (1888) 13 App Cas 222 at 225-226.
139. *Rhodes v Canadian National Railway* (1990) 75 DLR (4th) 248 per Southin JA at 285.
140. See *Hevican v Ruane* [1991] 3 All ER 65 per Mantell J at 71. Note L Sparr & L D Pankratz, "Factitious Posttraumatic Stress Disorder" (1983) 140 Am J Psy 1016; P R Tobias et al, "Recognising Shammed and Genuine Posttraumatic Stress Disorder" (1987) V A Practitioner 37.
141. See eg *Richters v Motor Tyre Service Pty Ltd* [1972] Qd R 9 per Wanstall ACJ at 17; *McMullin v F W Woolworth Co Ltd* (1974) 9 NBR (2d) 214 per Cormier CJQBD at 216; *Hewitt v Bernhardt* (1979) 21 SASR 510 per Mitchell J at 511; *McLoughlin v O'Brian* [1983] 1 AC 410 per Lord Bridge at 431; *Sullivan v Atlantic Lottery Corporation* (1987) 205 APR 317 (NB) per McLellan J at 323; *Kwok v British Columbia Ferry Corporation* (1987) 20 BCLR (2d) 318 per Cumming J at 373; *De Franceschi v Storrier* (1988) 85

the fact that it is commonly experienced is of itself a reason for denying recovery. This logic has not affected recoverability for the universally experienced sensation of physical (as opposed to emotional) pain. It may simply be another way of expressing the traditional floodgates argument,[142] which in other contexts has, in the main, been eventually repudiated.[143] Closely related to this argument is the suggestion that the rule acts as a deterrent to trivial claims. The courts seem to have been motivated by the belief that requiring physical consequences will verify the reality of trauma and make it easier to distinguish cases deserving of compensation.

Perhaps the best reason for refusing recovery for mere emotional distress is that, if one looks at the priorities for compensation, emotional distress ranks lower down the list than physical harm caused by impact and the recognised psychiatric damage that is the subject of "nervous shock" cases. In 1915 Roscoe Pound, discussing the interest in the physical person, suggested that immunity of the mind and the nervous system from injury, and freedom from annoyance interfering with mental poise and comfort, were interests which had become more important with the progress of civilisation, as opposed to more basic interests such as immunity of the body from direct and indirect injury.[144] Lush J probably had such considerations in mind in *Benson v Lee* when he said that the law's policy not to give damages for grief or other emotional distress had to be maintained for practical reasons.[145] This philosophy is apparent also in Lord Oliver's statement in *Alcock v Chief Constable of South Yorkshire Police* that the law will not compensate a person for mental anguish flowing from the loss of a relative or from being compelled to look after an invalid.[146] His Lordship's judgment was founded on the well-entrenched common law principle that, save for exceptional circumstances, the law compensates only the primary victim.[147] Mental distress suffered by a secondary party does not have a high enough priority to warrant legal recognition. It is these considerations, coupled with the fact that emotional distress is often of relatively short-lived duration,[148] rather than the

141. *Continued*
   ACTR 1 per Miles CJ at 6; *Orman v Harrington* (unreported, South Australian SC, 30 Apr 1990, No 296 of 1990); *Spence v Percy* (1990) Aust Torts Rep 81-039 per Derrington J at 68,037.
142. Another argument put forward in *Victorian Railways Commissioner v Coultas* (1888) 13 App Cas 222: see above, pp 1-2, 43, n 138. For this argument in other contexts, see eg *Simpson & Co v Thomson, Burrell* (1877) 3 App Cas 279 per Lord Penzance at 289-290; *Weller & Co v Foot and Mouth Disease Research Institute* [1966] 1 QB 569 per Widgery J at 585; *Spartan Steel & Alloys Ltd v Martin & Co (Contractors) Ltd* [1973] QB 27 per Lord Denning MR at 38 (economic loss); *Walker v Great Northern Railway Co of Ireland* (1890) 28 LR Ir 69 (unborn plaintiffs).
143. For example, in Australia in economic loss cases: see *Caltex Oil (Australia) Pty Ltd v Dredge 'Willemstad'* (1976) 136 CLR 529, and in cases involving liability to unborn plaintiffs: see *Watt v Rama* [1972] VR 353 per Gillard J at 379-380; *X and Y v Pal* (1991) 23 NSWLR 26 per Clarke JA at 37-45.
144. R Pound, "Interests of Personality" (1915) 28 Harv L Rev 343, 445 at 355-356.
145. [1972] VR 879 at 880. On this case see below, p 137.
146. [1992] 1 AC 310 at 409.
147. See below, pp 90-99.
148. See eg *Stergiou v Stergiou* (1987) Aust Torts Rep 80-082; *Ravenscroft v Rederiaktiebφlaget Transatlantic* [1991] 3 All ER 73, reversed by the English Court of Appeal [1992] 2 All ER 470n.

longer-lasting psychiatric illness to which it may give rise, which provide the most plausible explanation why the law has remained firm in not giving compensation for mere mental distress.[149] What has so far gone unappreciated is that there may potentially be genuine cases worthy of compensation where the loss in question falls short of the higher standard[150] and that the process of filtering out undeserving claims carries with it the undesirable consequence that some which are sound may also be excluded. The fact, for example, that a reaction is relatively short-lived does not necessarily mean it is less worthy of redress. Temporary imbalances can be both very intense and damaging, something most courts have recognised in relation to harm of a psychiatric nature.[151]

Damages for mental distress in tort

Though damages are not awarded in tort for mental distress standing alone, the law has always been content to award damages for such loss consequent upon the commission of some other wrong.[152] Such damages are sometimes referred to as "parasitic damages", because they are awardable only where they can be attached to some recognised wrong.[153] Some judges have expressed dislike of the term "parasitic damages". To Lord Denning MR, for example, it conveys "the idea of damages which ought not in justice to be awarded, but which somehow or other have been allowed to get through by hanging on to others".[154] However, the awarding of such damages is a well-established practice, the origins of which are somewhat obscure, but can probably be ascribed to the fact that the assessment of damages was for a long period in the hands of juries,[155] who looked at the real and not the legal injury.[156]

149. See generally H Teff, "Liability for Negligently Inflicted Nervous Shock" (1983) 99 LQR 100 at 105-106.
150. Note the discussion above, pp 18-21.
151. See above, pp 17-18.
152. See generally P R Handford "Damages for Injured Feelings in Australia" (1982) 5 UNSWLJ 291 at 296-298, 301-302.
153. See H McGregor, *Damages* (15th ed, 1988), para 213.
154. *Spartan Steel & Alloys Ltd v Martin & Co (Contractors) Ltd* [1973] QB 27 at 35. See also *French Knit Sales Pty Ltd v N Gold & Sons Pty Ltd* [1972] 2 NSWLR 132; but contrast *Seaway Hotels Ltd v Cragg (Canada) Ltd* (1960) 21 DLR (2d) 264.
155. In Victoria, juries are still quite widely used in such cases: see *Supreme Court Rules* (Vic) r 47.02, and they are also used in New South Wales (though not generally in motor accident cases): see *Supreme Court Act* 1970 (NSW), ss 86-87, but in other Australian States and Territories personal injury cases are virtually never tried by jury. Juries are no longer used in personal injury cases in England: see *Ward v James* [1966] 1 QB 273; *H v Ministry of Defence* [1991] 2 QB 103. They are still in use in the Scottish Court of Session, but have been abolished in Northern Ireland: see *Judicature (Northern Ireland) Act* 1980 (UK), as amended by the *Jury Trial (Amendment) (Northern Ireland) Order* 1987, and, save for a few exceptional instances, in the Republic of Ireland: see *Courts Act* 1988 (Ire). Civil jury trials are still relatively common in Ontario and British Columbia, but in other Canadian provinces they are becoming increasingly rare: see A M Linden, *Canadian Tort Law* (4th ed, 1988), 209.
156. See F H Bohlen, "Right to Recover for Injury Resulting from Negligence without Impact" (1902) 41 *American Law Register* (ns) 141, reprinted in F H Bohlen, *Studies in the Law of Torts* (1925), 252-290.

Such damages may be awarded in most torts. Thus, though assault, battery and false imprisonment in the main protect dignitary interests,[157] there are cases where substantial physical harm or inconvenience results and damages for mental distress are tacked onto the main award.[158] Consequential damages for mental distress are also available in actions for trespass to land[159]—though not, it seems, in nuisance,[160] or in torts involving interference with goods.[161] Damages for emotional suffering may be awarded in defamation, at least in those cases (libel and slander actionable per se) where defamation is actionable without proof of damage.[162] Where proof of damage is required, there is dispute: some authorities hold that the damages recoverable are limited to the actual damage suffered,[163] others take a wider view and allow damages for

157. Assault, since its essence is causing an apprehension of imminent hostile or offensive contact, protects a purely dignitary interest. Battery, though it may involve substantial personal injury, also extends to protect purely dignitary interests, since "the least touching of another in anger is a battery": *Cole v Turner* (1704) Holt KB 108; 90 ER 958. Thus spitting in a person's face, cutting their hair or kissing them without consent are all batteries of this kind. It seems that a battery could even be committed where the plaintiff is ignorant of it at the time, because the injury to feelings is just as real when the plaintiff does not discover what happened until later. False imprisonment, similarly, can protect a purely dignitary interest. As long as the restraint is total, it may cause the plaintiff no harm except the indignity of being unable to exercise freedom of movement. Again, despite the old case of *Herring v Boyle* (1834) 1 Cr M & R 377; 149 ER 1126, it seems that the tort may be committed even though the plaintiff is not conscious of it at the time, because of the injury to feelings element involved in the later discovery of what took place: see *Meering v Grahame-White Aviation Co* (1919) 122 LT 44; *Murray v Ministry of Defence* [1988] 1 WLR 692. See generally Handford, op cit, n 152 at 294-296; P R Handford, "Tort Liability for Threatening or Insulting Words" (1976) 54 Can BR 563.

158. For example, *Hurst v Picture Theatres Ltd* [1915] 1 KB 1 (battery and false imprisonment); *Forde v Skinner* (1830) 4 C & P 239; 172 ER 687; *Kohan v Stanbridge* (1916) 16 SR (NSW) 576; *Costi v Minister of Education* (1973) 5 SASR 328; *Fogg v McKnight* [1968] NZLR 330; *L v Commonwealth* (1976) 10 ALR 269; *W v Meah* [1986] 1 All ER 935 (battery); note also *Lane v Holloway* [1968] 1 QB 379 (battery, though on the facts no damages for mental distress were awarded because of provocation); *Warwick v Foulkes* (1844) 12 M & W 507; 152 ER 1298; *Childs v Lewis* (1924) 40 TLR 870; *Hook v Cunard SS Co Ltd* [1953] 1 WLR 682 (false imprisonment); note also *Walter v Alltools Ltd* (1944) 61 TLR 39 (damages awarded in false imprisonment for loss of reputation).

159. For example, *Bruce v Rawlins* (1770) 3 Wils KB 61; 95 ER 934; *Bennett v Allcott* (1787) 2 TR 166; 100 ER 90; *Waters v Maynard* (1924) 24 SR (NSW) 618.

160. See *Thompson-Schwab v Costaki* [1956] 1 WLR 335.

161. See *Graham v Voight* (1989) 89 ACTR 11 (in action for conversion of stamp collection, plaintiff compensated for loss of his hobby). Note also *Thurston v Charles* (1905) 21 TLR 659, where damages were awarded in conversion for lost reputation.

162. See eg *Goslin v Corry* (1844) 7 Man & G 342; 135 ER 143; *Ley v Hamilton* (1935) 153 LT 384 per Lord Atkin at 386; *McCarey v Associated Newspapers* [1965] 2 QB 86 per Pearson LJ at 104; *Fielding v Variety Inc* [1967] 2 QB 841 per Salmon LJ at 855. Note that in Australia it has been held that in defamation mental distress amounts to actual damage: see *Rigby v Mirror Newspapers Ltd* (1963) 64 SR (NSW) 34. This case rejects as out of date the old English case of *Allsop v Allsop* (1860) 5 H & N 534; 157 ER 1292 which was influenced by the same kind of thinking as *Victorian Railway Commissioners v Coultas* (1888) 13 App Cas 222. Note also *Wilkinson v Downton* [1897] 2 QB 57 per Wright J at 60-61. In New South Wales, Queensland, Tasmania and the Australian Capital Territory, the distinction between libel and slander has been abolished and all defamation is actionable per se.

163. *Brown v Smith* (1855) 13 CB 596; 138 ER 1333 per Williams J at 1334-5; *Ratcliffe v Evans* [1892] 2 QB 524 per Bowen LJ at 530-532; *Albrecht v Patterson* (1886) 12 VLR 821.

mental suffering. [164] The position in injurious falsehood remains uncertain. [165] Damages for injured feelings are also available in torts affecting domestic relations [166] (in jurisdictions where such torts still exist [167]) and in most torts involving pure economic loss. [168]

Most of the torts mentioned in the previous paragraph are intentional torts. However, damages for injured feelings can also be awarded in certain negligence cases. In personal injury cases, damages for mental suffering are commonly awarded as part of the overall compensation—the damages award includes non-pecuniary elements such as damages for pain and suffering and loss of amenities, which incorporate elements of mental anguish which would not be compensable if it stood alone. [169] It is also generally recognised that compensation can be given for mental distress consequent on damage to property. In *Attia v British Gas Plc*, [170] the English Court of Appeal refused to rule out a cause of action for psychiatric damage caused by the destruction of the plaintiff's home, and the court made it clear that had the claim for property damage not been settled compensation for shock and mental distress could have been granted consequent on the property damage. In a later Australian case, *Campbelltown City Council v Mackay*, [171] the New South Wales Court of Appeal awarded damages to the plaintiff for grief and mental anguish consequent on the collapse of her "dream home". Similarly, in New Zealand damages have been awarded for ill-health resulting from the subsidence of a house [172] and for anxiety affecting health following the receipt of negligent advice from a health inspector that a coffee lounge, milk bar and confectionery business had a "clean bill of health" but which was subsequently found to be heavily infested with cockroaches. [173]

164. *Dixon v Smith* (1860) 5 H & N 450; 157 ER 1257 per Martin B at 1258; *Lynch v Knight* (1861) 9 HL Cas 577; 11 ER 854 per Lord Wensleydale at 864.
165. *Joyce v Sengupta* (1992) 142 NLJ 1306.
166. *Lough v Ward* [1945] 2 All ER 338 (enticement and harbouring); *Murray v Kerr* [1918] VLR 409 per Irvine CJ at 412 (seduction); *Butterworth v Butterworth* [1920] P 126 (adultery).
167. These torts have now been abolished in many jurisdictions: see below, p 98, and also P B Kutner, "Law Reform in Tort: Abolition of Liability for 'Intentional' Interference with Family Relationships" (1987) 17 UWALR 25.
168. *Doyle v Olby (Ironmongers) Ltd* [1969] 2 QB 158; *Mafo v Adams* [1970] 1 QB 548; *Shelley v Paddock* [1979] QB 120; *Archer v Brown* [1985] QB 401 (deceit); *Quinn v Leathem* [1901] AC 495; *Huntley v Thornton* [1957] 1 WLR 321 (conspiracy); *Pratt v British Medical Association* [1919] 1 KB 244 (interference with contract); *Moore v News of the World* [1972] 1 QB 441 (infringement of copyright). Contrast *Fielding v Variety Inc* [1967] 2 QB 841 per Lord Denning MR at 850 (injurious falsehood).
169. The various heads of damage were first distinguished in *Phillips v London & South Western Railway Co* (1879) 5 CPD 280.
170. [1988] QB 304, discussed below, pp 208-209. See also *Batty v Metropolitan Property Realisations* [1978] QB 554 (damages for injury to peace of mind due to imminent collapse of defective house); *Perry v Sidney Phillips & Son* [1982] 1 WLR 1297.
171. (1989) 15 NSWLR 501, discussed below, pp 199-202, 209-210. See also *Brickhill v Cooke* [1984] 3 NSWLR 396; *Clarke v Shire of Gisborne* [1984] VR 971; *Delaney v F S Evans & Sons Pty Ltd* (1984) 58 LGRA 395; *Rentokil Pty Ltd v Channon* (1990) 19 NSWLR 417.
172. *Gabolinscy v Hamilton City Corporation* [1975] 1 NZLR 150. See also *Young v Tomlinson* [1979] 2 NZLR 441; *Callaghan v Robert Ronayne Ltd* (unreported, Auckland SC, 17 Sept 1979, No A1112 of 1976); *Stieller v Porirua City Council* [1986] 1 NZLR 84.
173. *R A & T J Carll Ltd v Berry* [1981] 2 NZLR 76.

Long ago, an American writer, Thomas Atkins Street, suggested that the treatment of an element of damages as parasitic was merely the precursor to its recognition as an independent basis of liability.[174] Such sentiments were unconsciously echoed by Nader J in *Anderson v Smith*,[175] commenting on *Campbelltown City Council v Mackay*, when he suggested that if the law gave damages for mental anguish consequent on damage to property and not for mental anguish caused by caring for a young child who suffered brain damage in an accident, it was time for the law to take another "cautious step".[176]

In the United States, Street's prophecy has been fulfilled: grief, worry, anxiety and the like can now, in certain circumstances, be the subject of a damages award.[177] This happened first in the area of mental suffering caused intentionally: the intentional infliction of severe emotional distress by extreme and outrageous conduct is now an actionable tort.[178] In negligence, until quite recently, the law retained the requirement that injury to feelings must result in bodily harm or illness.[179] However in 1970 a Hawaiian decision, *Rodrigues v State*,[180] suggested that the time had come to recognise a general duty not to cause mental distress by negligence. In this case the plaintiffs, husband and wife, recovered against the State of Hawaii for their negligence in failing to attend to a drainage system, resulting in a flood which destroyed their recently completed home, for which they had saved for 15 years. There was of course property damage to which the damages for emotional distress might have been attached—this was the approach suggested in the later Australian case of *Campbelltown City Council v Mackay*,[181] the facts of which are strikingly similar. However, the Hawaii Supreme Court was firm in its opinion that it was time to recognise an independent duty not to inflict mental distress by negligence. Other jurisdictions have begun to follow this initiative, notably California in *Molien v Kaiser Foundation Hospitals*[182] where a wife recovered damages in respect of a negligent misdiagnosis that she was

---

174. T A Street, *Foundations of Legal Liability* (1906), Vol 1, 470.
175. (1990) 101 FLR 34 at 50-51, discussed below, pp 193-194, 202.
176. A reference to *Jaensch v Coffey* (1984) 155 CLR 549 per Gibbs CJ at 555: "The law must continue to proceed in this area step by cautious step." Windeyer J in *Mount Isa Mines v Pusey* (1970) 125 CLR 383 at 403 also refers to the courts proceeding "cautious step by cautious step".
177. See W P Keeton, *Prosser and Keeton on the Law of Torts* (5th ed, 1984), 364-365; D B Marlowe, "Negligent Infliction of Mental Distress: A Jurisdictional Survey of Existing Limitation Devices and Proposal Based on an Analysis of Objective versus Subjective Indices of Distress" (1988) 33 Villanova L Rev 781 at 801-802.
178. See below, pp 297-304.
179. According to the *Restatement of Torts Second*, §313 (published in 1965) a person was liable for "illness or bodily harm" resulting from emotional distress if he or she realised that there was an unreasonable risk of such harm occurring. The Comment states: "The rule . . . does not give protection to mental and emotional tranquillity in itself."
180. (1970) 472 P 2d 509 (Haw).
181. (1989) 15 NSWLR 501.
182. (1980) 616 P 2d 813; 167 Cal Rptr 831. See W S Blackmer, "Molien v Kaiser Foundation Hospitals: Negligence Actions for Emotional Distress and Loss of Consortium without Physical Injury" (1981) 69 Cal L Rev 1142; E Finneran, "The Death of the Ensuing Physical Injury Rule: Validating Claims for Negligent Infliction of Emotional Harm" (1981) 10 Hofstra L Rev 213; C J Spector, "Negligent Infliction of Emotional Distress Absent Physical Impact or Subsequent Injury" (1982) 47 Mo L Rev 124.

suffering from syphilis, which caused her severe emotional suffering and wrecked her marriage.[183] By 1988, at least 15 jurisdictions recognised a cause of action for the negligent infliction of emotional distress,[184] and consequential issues which had surfaced in cases concerned with classified psychiatric disorder had also begun to emerge in this area, such as whether bystanders could recover for emotional distress caused by seeing an accident to a loved one,[185] and whether emotional distress caused by hearing of an accident to relatives, rather than seeing it with one's own eyes, was sufficient.[186] This development of negligence liability for pure emotional distress was foreshadowed by a recognition of liability for negligently caused mental distress in two particular instances: the negligent transmission of telegraph messages and the negligent mishandling of corpses.[187]

183. See also *Wallace v Coca-Cola Bottling Plants Inc* (1970) 269 A 2d 117 (Me); *Whetham v Bismarck Hospital* (1972) 197 NW 2d 678 (ND); *Hunsley v Giard* (1976) 553 P 2d 1096 (Wash); *Montinieri v Southern New England Telephone Co* (1978) 398 A 2d 1180 (Conn); *Sinn v Burd* (1979) 404 A 2d 672 (Pa); *Portee v Jaffee* (1980) 417 A 2d 521 (NJ); *Taylor v Baptist Medical Center Inc* (1981) 400 So 2d 369 (Ala); *Barnhill v Davis* (1981) 300 NW 2d 104 (Ia); *Chappetta v Bowman Transport Inc* (1982) 415 So 2d 1019 (La); *Schultz v Barberton Glass Co* (1983) 447 NE 2d 109 (Ohio); *Bass v Nooney Co* (1983) 646 SW 2d 765 (Mo); *Johnson v Supersave Markets Inc* (1984) 686 P 2d 209 (Mont); *James v Lieb* (1985) 375 NW 2d 109 (Neb); *Gates v Richardson* (1986) 719 P 2d 193 (Wyo); *St Elizabeth Hospital v Garrard* (1987) 730 SW 2d 649 (Tex); *Corgan v Muehling* (1991) 574 NE 2d 602 (Ill). For discussion of the current uncertainty as to the position in New York see J M Mega, "Negligent Infliction of Emotional Distress: Confusion in New York and a Proposed Standard" (1990) 56 Brooklyn L Rev 379.
184. See J E Rooney, "Maine Recognizes the Independent Tort of Negligent Infliction of Emotional Distress" (1989) 41 Me L Rev 181 at 182 n 10.
185. See eg *Culbert v Sampson's Supermarket Inc* (1982) 444 A 2d 433 (Me) (allowing recovery to a bystander); *Starrett v Iberia Airlines of Spain* (1989) 756 F Supp 292 (possibility of bystander action recognised, but no liability on facts).
186. Contrast *Kelley v Kokua Sales & Supply Ltd* (1975) 532 P 2d 673 (Haw) and *Campbell v Animal Quarantine Station* (1981) 632 P 2d 1066 (Haw), dealt with below, p 182.
187. See Keeton, op cit, n 177 at 362. On negligent telegraph messages see eg *So Relle v Western Union Telegraph Co* (1881) 55 Tex 308; *Western Union Telegraph Co v Redding* (1930) 129 So 743 (Fla); *Russ v Western Union Telegraph Co* (1943) 23 SE 2d 681 (NC); on negligent mishandling of corpses see eg *Louisville & N Rail Co v Hull* (1902) 68 SW 433 (Ky); *Missouri K & T Rail Co v Hawkins* (1908) 109 SW 221 (Tex) (negligent shipment); *St Louis South Western Rail Co v White* (1936) 91 SW 2d 277 (Ark) (running over body); *Chelini v Nieri* (1948) 196 P 2d 915 (Cal) (negligent embalming); *Gonzalez v Sacramento Memorial Lawn* (1982) 25 ATLA L Rep 348 (female mortuary employee committed 20-40 acts of necrophilia on corpse before driving away stolen hearse and coffin); *Wargelin v Sisters of Mercy Health Corporation* (1986) 385 NW 2d 732 (intern failed to recognise newborn infant's signs of lifelessness and presented corpse to mother "in a manner reserved for successful deliveries"); *Christensen v Superior Court* (1991) 820 P 2d 181; 2 Cal Rptr 2d 79, which is of particular importance for its ruling that the principles of *Thing v La Chusa* (1989) 771 P 2d 814; 257 Cal Rptr 98 do not necessarily apply in cases involving the negligent handling of human remains. Note also *Strachan v John F Kennedy Memorial Hospital* (1988) 538 A 2d 346 (NJ) (body of brain-dead son maintained on life-support system even after parents demanded that system be removed; damages granted for their emotional distress, despite lack of resulting psychiatric illness, by applying dead body cases); *Corso v Crawford Dog & Cat Hospital Inc* (1979) 415 NYS 2d 182 (plaintiff who had arranged elaborate funeral for pet poodle recovered for mental anguish on learning that cat remains had been substituted for it in casket). Contrast the attitude of Canadian courts: see *Miner v CPR* (1911) 3 Alta LR 408 (no damages for mental suffering against carrier for negligently delaying delivery of dead body).

Other common law jurisdictions have not yet trodden the same path as the United States. The requirement of recognisable psychiatric damage remains an important prerequisite to the recovery of tortious damages for shock-induced harm, and not only in negligence. Even intentionally caused emotional distress must result in some form of significant physical or psychiatric harm before liability will exist.[188]

A special problem that has arisen in recent years, both in the United States and elsewhere, is that of "pre-impact emotional distress": the problem of whether plaintiffs, or their estates, can recover for the mental anguish of knowing, before there is any impact, that an accident is inevitable and that they will die or be seriously injured. This issue has arisen in a number of cases concerning air crashes[189] or near-crashes[190] and is also illustrated by the fate of the astronauts in the 1986 Challenger space shuttle tragedy, who for at least some seconds or minutes were aware that the malfunction of their rocket had sealed their fate.[191] A somewhat similar problem arose out of the Hillsborough soccer disaster. In *Hicks v Chief Constable of the South Yorkshire Police*[192] actions for damages for pain and suffering prior to death were brought on behalf of the estates of three young people who were crushed to death on the Leppings Lane terraces. Hidden J, the Court of Appeal and the House of Lords all rejected the claim. It was accepted that a person who through negligence was caused injuries which resulted in pain and suffering and loss of amenities had a cause of action which would survive for the benefit of that person's estate.[193] In the circumstances of this case, however, during the 30 minutes or so in which the deceased persons were crushed together before asphyxia resulted in death, they suffered fear, horror and acute mental anguish but no physical or psychiatric injury. If there was pain and suffering, it occurred only in the last few seconds before unconsciousness and death, and was really part of the dying process. In the words of Parker LJ in the Court of Appeal:

"Apprehension and fear are of themselves not compensatable, nor in my view are discomfort or shortness of breath by themselves. Anyone

188. See below, pp 283-289, 304-307.
189. See eg *Re Paris Aircrash on March 3 1974* (1975) 399 F Supp 732; *Sanchez v Schindler* (1983) 651 SW 2d 249 (Tex); *Re Eastern Airlines Inc, Engine Failure, Miami International Airport on May 5, 1983* (1986) 629 F Supp 307; *Re Aircrash Disaster Near New Orleans* (1986) 789 F 2d 1092; *Fogarty v Campbell* (1986) 640 F Supp 953. See also G N Woods, "Texas Bystander Recovery: In the Aftermath of Sanchez v Schindler" (1983) 35 Baylor L Rev 883; N R McGilchrist, "Mental Anguish—Before and After the Crash" [1984] LMCLQ 311.
190. See *Eastern Airlines Inc v Floyd* (1991) 111 S Ct 1489, where passengers claimed damages for emotional distress as a result of an aircraft losing power on a flight from Miami to the Bahamas. Liability was denied under art 17 of the Warsaw Convention, under which an air carrier is liable for the death or injury of a passenger only if the event which caused the death or injury took place on board or during the course of embarking or disembarking.
191. See K M Turezyn, "When Circumstances Provide a Guarantee of Genuineness: Permitting Recovery for Pre-Impact Emotional Distress" (1987) 28 BCL Rev 881.
192. (Unreported, QBD, 31 July 1990) (Hidden J); [1992] 1 All ER 690 (CA); [1992] 2 All ER 65 (HL). See A Unger, "Pain and Anger" (1992) 142 NLJ 394.
193. Under the provisions of the *Law Reform (Miscellaneous Provisions) Act* 1934 (UK), s 1(1).

who regularly travels on the London Underground frequently suffers discomfort and shortness of breath from the press of bodies in overcrowded trains."[194]

Similar sentiments were expressed by Lord Bridge in the House of Lords:

"It is perfectly clear law that fear by itself, of whatever degree, is a normal humane motion [sic] for which no damages can be awarded. Those trapped in the crush at Hillsborough who were fortunate enough to escape without injury have no claim in respect of the distress they suffered in what must have been a truly terrifying experience. It follows that fear of impending death felt by the victim of a fatal injury before that injury is inflicted cannot by itself give rise to a cause of action which survives for the benefit of the victim's estate."[195]

The logic of this approach rests on the conclusion that the victims of the disaster suffered only mental distress, rather than some recognised injury for which they could be compensated. Putting aside the question of the defensibility of a rule that denies recovery for the sheer all-consuming terror caused by an appreciation of the impending end of one's life, it is hard to see how, when many persons are negligently herded into a confined space and crushed to death, there is no actionable physical injury. Duration of discomfort has been afforded an undeserved prominence. One wonders how long such an agonising ordeal would have to be endured before it is characterised as separate and compensable harm. Is one minute, five minutes, an hour or an even longer period of pain and suffering necessary before a court would be prepared to see it as something antecedent to death, rather than an inextricably integral part of it? The decision seems to pay scant regard to the victims of the tragedy and their families.

Damages for mental distress in contract

Outside the law of tort, the awarding of damages for mental suffering is much more widespread than may at first be supposed. In contract, it is now generally recognised that damages may be awarded for mental distress.[196] Formerly, damages for injured feelings were not recoverable,[197] with the exception of breach of promise of marriage (which, though in form an

---

194. [1992] 1 All ER 690 at 693.
195. [1992] 2 All ER 65 at 69.
196. See generally D W Greig and J L R Davis, *The Law of Contract* (1987), 1411-4; H McGregor, op cit, n 153, paras 91-102; G H Treitel, *The Law of Contract* (8th ed, 1991), 876-879; G H L Fridman, *The Law of Contract in Canada* (2nd ed, 1986), 673-681; H Hahlo, "Contractual Damages for Mental Distress" (1973) 51 Can BR 507; E Veitch, "Sentimental Damages in Contract" (1977) 16 UWOLR 227; F D Rose, "Injured Feelings and Disappointment" (1977) 55 Can BR 333; B S Jackson, "Injured Feelings Resulting from Breach of Contract" (1977) 26 ICLQ 502; P H Clarke, "Damages in Contract for Mental Distress" (1978) 52 ALJ 626; F Dawson, "General Damages in Contract for Non-Pecuniary Loss" (1983) 10 NZULR 232; M G Bridge, "Contractual Damages for Intangible Loss: A Comparative Study" (1984) 67 Can BR 323; A S Burrows, "Mental Distress Damages in Contract—A Decade of Change" [1984] LMCLQ 119. For the position in the United States see C K Goldberg, "Emotional Distress Damages and Breach of Contract: A New Approach (1986) 20 UCDL Rev 57.
197. *Hamlin v Great Northern Railway Co* (1856) 1 H & N 408; 156 ER 1261; *Addis v Gramophone Co* [1909] AC 488; *Groom v Crocker* [1939] 1 KB 194. Note *Rae v Yorkshire Bank Plc* [1988] BTLC 35.

action for breach of contract, was really much more like a tort action).[198] The law of contract, like the law of tort, awarded damages for physical injury,[199] psychiatric injury[200] and physical inconvenience,[201] but went no further. Since 1973, however, there has been a fundamental revolution in contract damages, and as a result injured feelings are now recognised as worthy of redress in actions for breach of certain contracts. The start of this development was *Jarvis v Swan's Tours*,[202] in which a solicitor recovered damages for injured feelings resulting from a disappointing holiday. This case has been followed in other holiday cases, not only in England[203] but also in Australia,[204] Canada[205] and elsewhere. A closely analogous situation occurred in Scotland in *Diesen v Samson*,[206] where damages for

198. So, eg, the measure of damages was totally unlike any other action for beach of contract, including not only the loss of the material advantage which would have been gained (which would be consistent with the then accepted rules as to contract damages) but also injured feelings: see *Quirk v Thomas* [1916] 1 KB 516. Other factors might also be at work in the assessment process: "The average jury, proverbially generous with the money of other people, recognises only two bases of computation, ie the plaintiff's beauty and the defendant's ability to pay": H F Wright, "The Action for Breach of the Marriage Promise" (1914) 10 Va L Rev 361 at 374. For another example, see W S Gilbert, *Trial by Jury* (1875), in which the plaintiff emphasises her love for the defendant, and the defendant his bad qualities, as factors to be borne in mind by the jury when they "are assessing/The damages Edwin must pay". The action has now been abolished in some jurisdictions: see eg *Marriage Act Amendment Act* 1977 (Cth), s 21; *Law Reform (Miscellaneous Provisions) Act* 1970 (UK).

199. For example, *Godley v Perry* [1960] 1 WLR 9. Awards for pain and suffering take account of mental anguish: see eg *H West & Son Ltd v Shephard* [1964] AC 326.

200. *Cook v Swinfen* [1967] 1 WLR 457. The woman in this case suffered a nervous "breakdown in mental health" when, due to the carelessness of her solicitors, a divorce suit did not turn out as planned: see Lord Denning MR at 461-462 who spoke in terms of "nervous shock".

201. *Burton v Pinkerton* (1867) LR 2 Ex 340; *Hobbs v London & South Western Railway Co* (1875) LR 10 QB 111 (having to walk five miles home because train failed to stop at station); *Bailey v Bullock* [1950] 2 All ER 1167 (having to live in overcrowded house); *Stedman v Swan's Tours* (1951) 95 SJ 727; *Piper v Daybell, Court-Cooper & Co* (1969) 210 EG 1047; *Athens-MacDonald Travel Service Pty Ltd v Kazis* [1970] SASR 264; *Mafo v Adams* [1970] 1 QB 548; *Dunn v Disc Jockey Unlimited Co Ltd* (1978) 87 DLR (3d) 408; *Wilkins v Bower* [1987] CLY 1133; *Lubren v London Borough of Lambeth* (1987) 20 HLR 165. Note also *McCall v Abelesz* [1976] QB 585 where "mental upset and distress" appears to have been regarded as analogous to "inconvenience".

202. [1973] QB 233, noted by D Yates (1973) 36 MLR 535. There were earlier authorities but the basis on which damages were awarded in these cases is not clear: see *Sharples v Informal Tours* [1958] CLY 556; *Trackman v New Vistas* [1959] CLY 527; *Cook v Spanish Holiday Tours Ltd* [1960] CLY 525.

203. *Jackson v Horizon Holidays* [1975] 1 WLR 1468; *Adcock v Blue Sky Holidays* (unreported, English CA, 13 May 1980); *Wings Ltd v Ellis* [1985] AC 272 per Lord Hailsham LC at 287; *Spencer v Cosmos Air Holidays Ltd, The Times*, 6 Dec 1989. Note also *Ichard v Frangoulis* [1977] 1 WLR 556 where compensation for the loss of a holiday was awarded in a personal injury damages case; *Kemp v Intasun Holidays Ltd* [1987] BTLC 353 per Kerr LJ at 357.

204. *Baltic Shipping Co v Dillon* (1991) 22 NSWLR 1. *Athens-MacDonald Travel Service Pty Ltd v Kazis* [1970] SASR 264 was an Australian holiday case prior to *Jarvis v Swan's Tours* [1973] QB 233. The South Australian Supreme Court allowed damages for physical inconvenience, but not for mental distress as such, though it admitted that all inconvenience has some mental element.

205. *Keks v Esquire Pleasure Tours Ltd* [1974] 3 WWR 406; *Elder v Koppe Pleasure Tours* (1975) 53 DLR (3d) 705; *Fuller v Healey Transportation Ltd* (1978) 92 DLR (3d) 277; *Pitzel v Saskatchewan Motor Club Travel Agency Ltd* (1983) 149 DLR (3d) 122; *Cameron v Maritime Travel (Halifax) Ltd* (1983) 123 APR 379 (NS).

206. 1971 SLT 49.

mental distress were awarded when a photographer failed to turn up to take photographs of the pursuer's wedding. [207]

Since the major benefit to be expected from these types of contracts is non-pecuniary in nature, the situation in cases like *Jarvis v Swan's Tours* cannot be regarded as typical of the majority of commercial contracts. The possibility of recovery being confined to these exceptional cases was hinted at by the English Court of Appeal which suggested that mental distress damages would be recoverable in a "proper case", [208] such as a contract to provide entertainment and enjoyment. However, in *Cox v Philips Industries Ltd*, [209] an employee received damages for non-pecuniary loss caused by breach of his contract of employment—surely not, as the court in that case admitted, a contract to provide entertainment and enjoyment. Lawson J, relying on the judgment of Lord Denning MR in *Jarvis v Swan's Tours*, said:

> "I can see no reason in principle why, if a situation arises which within the contemplation of the parties would have given rise to vexation, distress and general disappointment and frustration, the person who is injured by a contractual breach should not be compensated for that breach." [210]

Later cases have not endorsed the views of Lawson J. In *Heywood v Wellers* [211] the defendant firm of solicitors failed to gain an injunction to stop molestation of their client by an ex-boyfriend. An unsupervised trainee lawyer's errors—he went to the wrong court, asked for the wrong remedy, paid the wrong fees and failed to enforce the remedy once granted—were held to have caused the plaintiff considerable upset and distress. In granting damages to her for mental distress caused by breach of the defendant's contractual duty of care, Lord Denning MR said that *Cox v Philips Industries Ltd* might require reconsideration. In *Bliss v South East Thames Regional Health Authority*, [212] where the defendant health authority had

---

207. Note also *Chande v East African Airways Corporation* [1964] EA 78 (chartered plane carrying bride and groom failed to stop over at two airports where wedding breakfasts had been arranged for family and guests); *Dunn v Disc Jockey Unlimited Co Ltd* (1978) 87 DLR (3d) 408 (disc jockey failed to arrive at wedding reception); *Wilson v Sooter Studios Ltd* (1988) 55 DLR (4th) 303 (photographer failed to supply satisfactory wedding photographs). For analogous United States authority see eg *Lewis v Holmes* (1903) 34 So 2d 66 (La) (milliner failed to deliver wedding dress in time for wedding); *Browning v Fies* (1912) 58 So 931 (Ala) (livery stable failed to furnish carriage and horses at agreed time and place to carry groom, his family and friends to wedding, forcing them to take a public street car to the church); *Seidenbuchs Inc v Williams* (1961) 361 P 2d 185 (Okl) (department store failed to deliver wedding gown and veil in time for wedding).
208. [1973] QB 223 per Lord Denning MR at 237-238.
209. [1976] 1 WLR 638.
210. Ibid at 644.
211. [1976] QB 446. See also *Buckley v Lane Herdman & Co* [1977] CLY 3143; *P A Wournell Contracting Ltd v Allen* (1979) 100 DLR (3d) 62; *Webber v Gasquet Metcalfe & Welton* (unreported, QBD, 7 April 1982); *Dickinson v James Alexander & Co* (1989) 20 Fam Law 137. Compare *Malyon v Lawrance Messer & Co* [1968] 2 Lloyd's Rep 539. Note also the Californian case *Jarchow v Transamerica Title Insurance Co* (1975) 122 Cal Rptr 470 where two small entrepreneurs learned that their modest investment had failed due to the negligence of the defendant title insurer to discover, disclose or eliminate a recorded easement over land they had purchased. See generally J Murdoch, "Professional Negligence and Damages for Distress" (1989) 5 PN 52.
212. [1987] ICR 700, noted by H Carty (1986) 49 MLR 240.

suspended the plaintiff consultant surgeon on the unfounded ground that he was mentally unsuitable for the job, the English Court of Appeal said that Lawson J's views were incorrect. The exceptional cases were rationalised by Dillon LJ as examples where "the contract which [had] been broken was itself a contract to provide peace of mind or freedom from distress".[213] In this situation mental damage awards are considered justifiable. Recovery for mental distress has been allowed on this basis against a surveyor who negligently failed to mention to a home buyer that a house had significant defects,[214] against the seller of a faulty car,[215] against the developer of photographs which were delivered into the wrong hands with resultant embarrassment,[216] against a builder for delay and defects in the renovation of a house,[217] against a landlord for breach of his covenant to repair which left a flat so damp as to make it uninhabitable[218] and for breach of the covenant for quiet enjoyment where he abused, frightened and intimidated the tenants resulting in them leaving the premises,[219] and against a cemetery for breach of a contract to grant exclusive burial rights.[220] Where relief of this type is forthcoming the authorities reveal that it will be of modest proportions.[221]

Australian cases support these principles. In *Falko v James McEwan & Co*[222] the court affirmed that in a proper case damages could be awarded

213. Ibid at 718. Note also *Shove v Downs Surgical Plc* [1984] ICR 532. Specifically there can be no recovery for mental distress or anxiety for breach of a contract made in the course of or in connection with a business and resulting in the failure of that business: see *Hayes v James & Charles Dodd* [1990] 2 All ER 815, noted by K B Soh (1989) 105 LQR 43. See also *Hutchinson v Harris* (1978) 10 BLR 19; *Reed v Madon* [1989] Ch 408.

214. *Perry v Sidney Phillips & Son* [1982] 1 WLR 1297, noted by A S Burrows (1983) 46 MLR 357; *Fryer v Bunney* (1982) 263 EG 158; *Wilson v Baxter Payne & Lepper* [1985] 1 EGLR 141; *Hooberman v Salter Rex (a firm)* [1985] 1 EGLR 144; *Westlake v Bracknell District Council* [1987] 1 EGLR 161; *Jowitt v Woolwich Building Society* (unreported, QBD, 14 Dec 1987); *Syrett v Carr & Neave* (1990) 48 EG 118. See also *Watts v Morrow* [1991] 4 All ER 937, where on the facts no damages were awarded.

215. *Bernstein v Pamson Motors (Golders Green) Ltd* [1987] 2 All ER 220.

216. *Dunn v Moto Photo Inc* (1991) 828 SW 2d 747 (Tenn).

217. *Franks & Collingwood (a firm) v Gates* (1983) 1 Con LR 21; *McKinnon v County Metropolitan Development Ltd* (1985) 9 Con LR 61; *Thomas v T A Phillips (Builders) Ltd* (1985) 9 Con LR 72; *Lowe v R J Haddock Ltd* [1985] 2 EGLR 247; *Fry & Pym v Robert A Jackson (Builder & Contractor) Ltd* (1986) 7 Con LR 97; *Inglis v Cant* [1987] CLY 1132; *Wilkins v Bower* [1987] CLY 1133; *Corrigan v Paffitas* (unreported, Official Referee, 21 May 1987).

218. *Calabar Properties Ltd v Sticher* [1984] 1 WLR 287; *Elmcroft Developments Ltd v Tankersley-Sawyer* (1984) 15 HLR 67; *Stockley v Knowsley Metropolitan Borough Council* [1986] 2 EGLR 141. See also *Chiodi v De Marney* [1988] 2 EGLR 64 where damages were awarded for breach of a statutory covenant to repair.

219. *Sampson v Floyd* [1989] 2 EGLR 49. See also *McCall v Abelesz* [1976] QB 585.

220. *Reed v Madon* [1989] Ch 408. Contrast *McNeil v Forest Lawn Memorial Services Ltd* (1976) 72 DLR (3d) 556 (funeral home cremated daughter's body without giving parents opportunity to view it).

221. Only in the United States have awards for mental distress gone beyond this: see eg *Jarchow v Transamerica Title Insurance Co* (1975) 122 Cal Rptr 470 where in relation to a $10,000 land transaction $200,000 damages were awarded for emotional distress. This sum, however, clearly included a punitive component. Note K Franklin, "Damages for Heartache: The Award of General Damages for Inconvenience and Distress in Building Cases" (1988) 4 Const LJ 264, arguing that the misery caused by being in an unsatisfactory home is more serious than the distress caused by ruined holidays, and that comparison with pain and suffering awards in personal injury cases would be a more appropriate basis for the assessment of compensation.

222. [1977] VR 447.

in contract for mental distress, but that although the list of contract cases where relief of this nature was granted had grown, they were still an exception to the general rule applying to ordinary commercial contracts. In such contracts, of which the case itself was an example, the ordinary purchaser or customer could not expect to recover damages for injury to feelings. It appears that this view has the support of the High Court of Australia. *Burns v MAN Automotive (Australia) Pty Ltd*[223] concerned an action for a breach of a warranty that a prime mover had been fitted with air-conditioning. Damages for nervous stress awarded at first instance were disallowed by the Queensland Full Court, a decision upheld on appeal to the High Court. The Supreme Court of Canada has adopted similar views, recognising that, subject to the rules of remoteness, damages for mental distress can in appropriate circumstances be awarded.[224] Recovery for such harm has been granted in that country to bereaved animal lovers whose dogs were carried by an airline under unsuitable conditions, as a result of which one died,[225] where defendants failed to honour their obligations under a contract to sell a house[226] or a car,[227] and would have been afforded in a case where the plaintiffs returned from sabbatical leave to find their house, which they had leased out, in a dilapidated condition, had mental distress been shown to have been suffered.[228] Some Canadian courts have in addition recognised that such damages may be granted in an action for wrongful dismissal,[229] a development which in England would

223. (1986) 161 CLR 653.
224. *Vorvis v Insurance Corporation of British Columbia* (1989) 58 DLR (4th) 193, noted by B Feldthusen (1990) 69 Can BR 169. Note, however, the refusal of the courts in Nova Scotia to depart too far from the traditional rule denying damages for mental distress in contract: see *McBeth v Dalhousie University* (1986) 173 APR 224 (NS) (law student denied relief for mental distress consequent on university's breach of contract in failing to provide a make-up examination in Criminal Procedure when scheduled one missed through illness, and resultant failure and inability to proceed with studies); *Newfoundland Capital Corporation v Mettam* (1986) 189 APR 189 (NS) (damages for upset denied against architect who grossly underestimated renovation costs).
225. *Newell v Canadian Pacific Airlines* (1977) 74 DLR (3d) 574.
226. *Widdrington v Dickinson* (1982) 133 DLR (3d) 472; *Taylor v Gill* [1991] 3 WWR 727. Note also *Marko v Perry* (1980) 18 BCLR 263 (foreclosure of mortgage).
227. *Zuker v Paul* (1982) 135 DLR (3d) 481.
228. *Turner v Jatko* (1978) 93 DLR (3d) 314.
229. *Pilon v Peugeot Canada Ltd* (1980) 114 DLR (3d) 378; *Cringle v Northern Union Insurance Co Ltd* (1981) 124 DLR (3d) 22; *Brown v Waterloo Regional Board of Commissioners of Police* (1982) 37 OR (2d) 277; *Bohemier v Storwal International Inc* (1982) 142 DLR (3d) 8 (reversed on other grounds (1983) 4 DLR (4th) 383); *Grant v MacMillan Bloedel Industries Ltd* (1982) 16 ACWS (2d) 91; *Speck v Greater Niagara General Hospital* (1983) 2 DLR (4th) 84; *Pilato v Hamilton Place Convention Centre Inc* (1984) 7 DLR (4th) 342; *McOnie v River Pub Ltd* (1987) 196 APR 379 (NS). See also *Tippett v International Typographical Union Local 226* (1977) 71 DLR (3d) 146 where damages were awarded, inter alia, for mental distress caused by a groundless expulsion from a union for "ratting". Contrast, however, *Vorvis v Insurance Corporation of British Columbia* (1989) 58 DLR (4th) 193 where a majority of the Supreme Court of Canada refused to extend recovery for mental distress to actions for wrongful dismissal. See I F Ivankovich, "Mental Distress in Wrongful Dismissals: Towards a More Rationalized Approach" (1989) 18 Man LJ 277. See also *Abouna v Foothills Provincial General Hospital Board (No 2)* (1978) 83 DLR (3d) 333; *McMinn v Town of Oakville* (1978) 85 DLR (3d) 131. Note *Peso Silver Mines Ltd (NPL) v Cropper* (1966) 58 DLR (2d) 1.

be contrary to older authority.[230] Similarly, New Zealand courts have indicated that they are prepared to recognise a wide-ranging principle of liability in contract for causing mental distress. In *Rowlands v Collow*,[231] for example, the three plaintiffs were awarded substantial sums in damages for the mental suffering resulting from an engineer's negligent performance of a contract to construct a driveway to their houses, a contract which clearly could not be construed as one in which the object was to provide the plaintiffs with peace of mind or freedom from distress. Thomas J suggested that it was unnecessary and unwise to limit damages for mental distress to certain classes of case.[232] In *Mouat v Clarke Boyce*[233] an elderly widow was confronted with the threat of losing her home when a mortgage given to her son as security for a loan was called in. A substantial damages award was upheld by the New Zealand Court of Appeal.[234]

Comparisons and conclusions

The common law, other than in the United States, therefore affords no general recognition to a protected interest in freedom from mental distress. Its attitude to this issue is perhaps understandable, although the justifiability of this stance is not completely free from doubt. Moreover, the wisdom of the current approach must be questioned when the potential difficulties associated with distinguishing between certain emotional and psychiatric states are borne in mind.[235] Comyn J in *Whitmore v Euroways Express Coaches Ltd*[236] was strongly of the view that the law was harsh in making worry, strain and distress occasioned by the continuing effects of injury to a spouse irrecoverable in damages. Even some members of the House of Lords have acknowledged that there is "no readily discernible logical reason" why those who negligently inflict an injury upon another should not be held accountable for its inevitable consequences to persons other than the primary victim who suffer as a result.[237] So too Southin J of the British Columbia Court of Appeal has confessed to having some difficulty with the fact that this type of loss is presently non-compensable, stating in *McDermott v Ramadanovic Estate*[238] that she could "not see

230. *Addis v Gramophone Co* [1909] AC 488. See also *Shove v Downs Surgical Plc* [1984] ICR 532; *Bliss v South East Thames Regional Health Authority* [1987] ICR 700 overruling *Cox v Philips Industries Ltd* [1976] 1 WLR 638; *O'Laoire v Jackel International Ltd* [1991] IRLR 170.
231. [1992] 1 NZLR 178.
232. Ibid at 207.
233. [1992] 2 NZLR 559.
234. See also *Horsburgh v New Zealand Meat Processors Industrial Union of Workers* [1988] 1 NZLR 698, a case concerning the expulsion of a trade union member, where Cooke P indicated that the question of the application of *Addis v Gramophone Co* [1909] AC 488 in New Zealand would have to be given full consideration; *Whelan v Waitaki Meats Ltd* [1991] 2 NZLR 74, where the case was not followed. Prior to 1988 New Zealand authorities on the point were scarce, though note *Byrne v Auckland Irish Society Inc* [1979] 1 NZLR 351 (damages for loss of enjoyment of club amenities by member wrongfully expelled from club).
235. See above, pp 29-30.
236. *The Times*, 4 May 1984.
237. *Alcock v Chief Constable of South Yorkshire Police* [1992] 1 AC 310 per Lord Oliver at 410.
238. (1988) 27 BCLR (2d) 45 at 52.

why, in theory, if A causes B's death, B's widow or child does not have an independent cause of action for the suffering caused by that death", a view she reiterated in *Rhodes v Canadian National Railway*.[239]

Many legal systems outside the common law tradition readily admit mental or emotional suffering as something worthy of compensation, seemingly unconcerned with what Lord Oliver has identified as the "impracticability or unreasonableness of entertaining claims to the ultimate limits of the consequences of human activity".[240] In France, for example, where art 1382 of the *Code civil* provides that anyone who by fault causes damage to another is liable to pay compensation, the most basic distinction in the law of damage is that between dommage materiél and dommage moral—injuries to interests of substance and injury to the feelings.[241] Many other civil law systems with civil codes based on the French model have a similar general principle and admit claims for injury to the feelings.[242] Turning to uncodified civil law systems, there is a similar basic division in South Africa. Two of the old Roman law delicts, injuria and the action on the lex Aquilia, have become the twin foundations of the law of delict, the Aquilian action forming the basis for all interests of substance, such as personal injury and damage to property, and the actio injuriarum the general principle governing all remedies for injury to the feelings.[243] Though there has been considerable English influence, the Roman law origins remain clear.[244] Scottish law, also much influenced by Roman law, has a similar conceptual basis, though now much obscured by English law.[245]

Not all legal systems adopted such an attitude to claims for mental distress, however. The civil codes of the former Soviet states excluded claims for emotional suffering,[246] and recovery for such harm is rather more limited in German law than in most other civil law countries. The German *Bürgerliches Gesetzbuch*, which was enacted nearly a hundred years later than the French Code and had a rather different genesis,[247] does not have a general principle of liability similar to the French art 1382 and does not recognise any general protected interest in freedom from

239. (1990) 75 DLR (4th) 248 at 287.
240. *Alcock v Chief Constable of South Yorkshire Police* [1992] 1 AC 310 at 410.
241. See eg F H Lawson et al, *Amos and Walton's Introduction to French Law* (3rd ed, 1967), 209; H & L Mazeaud & A Tunc, *Responsabilité Civile* (6th ed, 1965), Vol 1, Ch 3; B Starck, *Droit Civil—Obligations* (1972), 45-63; G Viney, *Traité de Droit Civil: Les Obligations—La Responsabilité: Conditions* (1982), 307-333. Apart from injury to feelings, moral damage, as recognised in France, covers injury to honour, reputation, invasion of privacy and interferences with family and similar relationships.
242. See generally H McGregor, *Damages for Personal Injuries and Death (International Encyclopedia of Comparative Law*, Vol 11, Torts, Ch 9), 15-20.
243. See R G McKerron, *The Law of Delict* (7th ed, 1971), 53-57; P Q R Boberg, *The Law of Delict Vol 1: Aquilian Liability* (1984), 18-21.
244. For example, Boberg, op cit, n 243 is divided into two volumes, the first dealing with the Aquilian action and the second principally with the actio injuriarum. On the latter action see also C F Amerasinghe, *Aspects of the Actio Injuriarum* (1966); C F Amerasinghe, *Defamation and Other Aspects of the Actio Injuriarum* (1968).
245. See D M Walker, *The Law of Delict in Scotland* (2nd ed, 1981), 17-31.
246. See McGregor, op cit, n 242 at 15-17.
247. See F P Walton, "The New German Code" (1904) 16 JR 148; O F Robinson et al, *An Introduction to European Legal History* (1985), 465-480.

emotional injury.[248] It is true that German law recognises claims for injury to the Persönlichkeit, closely analogous to the right of privacy,[249] but other kinds of mental suffering do not generally give rise to a right to redress. As in the common law, some kind of physical or mental injury or illness is required before there is any liability for the infliction of shock.[250]

Thus there are mixed messages from other common law areas, and from legal systems outside the common law, about the justifiability of damages claims for purely mental or emotional distress or suffering. But in Commonwealth tort law, the requirement of recognisable psychiatric damage remains an important prerequisite to recovery.

---

248. "It runs counter to the most profound German sensibilities to assess the most sacred emotions in terms of base mammon and to compensate every culpable interference with those feelings by means of a money payment": Hartmann, "Der Civilgesetzentwurf, Das Aequitätsprincip und Die Richterstellung" (1888) AcP 73, 309 at 364 cited in H Stoll, *Consequences of Liability: Remedies (International Encyclopedia of Comparative Law*, Vol 11, Torts, Ch 8), 37.
249. See P R Handford, "Moral Damage in Germany" (1978) 27 ICLQ 849; B S Markesinis, *A Comparative Introduction to the German Law of Torts* (2nd ed, 1990), 55-58.
250. See Handford, op cit, n 249 at 852-855, 871-875. In some cases, eg (1931) 133 RGZ 270; (1938) 157 RGZ 111; (1971) BGHZ, NJW 1883 (as to which see J G Fleming, "Distant Shock in Germany (And Elsewhere)" (1972) 20 AJCL 485), mothers have recovered for a nervous collapse suffered on the death of a child, but they recovered under art 823 for a wrong done to them personally and there would have been no liability if they had not suffered physical or psychiatric illness. (1971) 56 BGHZ 163 confirms that mere mental distress is not compensable in Germany and that transient shock and normal grief reactions must have such manifestations before recovery may be had.

3

FUNDAMENTALS OF LIABILITY

Introduction

It is occasionally suggested that there is a separate tort of causing "nervous shock". Indeed, the Canadian case of *Abramzik v Brenner*[1] affirms this proposition.[2] There is no discernible logic in the process by which particular forms of liability have become identified as "nominate torts",[3] nor in the end-results of that process. So it is by virtue of accident of phraseology and frequency of occurrence that there have developed various individual torts involving intentional harm to the person (such as assault, battery, false imprisonment and *Wilkinson v Downton*[4] liability) and property (such as trespass to land and goods, and conversion) but one tort of negligence covering all forms of harm unintentionally but carelessly inflicted.[5] This said, it is clear that the *Abramzik v Brenner* view is wrong and that "nervous shock" is not a tort in itself, but an application of the tort of negligence to a particular kind of personal damage. This has often been judicially stated,[6] not least in Canada where the view taken in *Abramzik v Brenner* has met with a uniformly critical response.[7] Legal

1. (1967) 65 DLR (2d) 651 per Culliton CJS at 654.
2. See also *Radovskis v Tomm* (1957) 9 DLR (2d) 751 per Williams CJQB at 755.
3. See W V H Rogers, *Winfield and Jolowicz on Tort* (13th ed, 1989), 50-52.
4. [1897] 2 QB 57.
5. J G Fleming, *The Law of Torts* (8th ed, 1992), 102 however says: "Despite widespread current usage, it is misleading to speak of *a* tort of negligence. Negligence is a basis of liability rather than a single nominate tort." S F C Milsom, *Historical Foundations of the Common Law* (2nd ed, 1981), 398-399 suggests that negligence, because of its more modern development, is a different kind of tort from the old traditional torts.
6. See eg *Chester v Council of the Municipality of Waverley* (1939) 62 CLR 1 per Rich J at 11 (citing P H Winfield, *Law of Tort* (1937), 85); *King v Phillips* [1953] 1 QB 429 per Denning LJ at 440 ("There are [not] two different torts—one tort when [one] can foresee physical injury, and another tort when [one] can foresee emotional injury. . . . There is one wrong only, the wrong of negligence."); *Mount Isa Mines Ltd v Pusey* (1970) 125 CLR 383 per Windeyer J at 385 ("[N]ervous shock cases are not a new tort: they turn simply on the circumstances in which damages are recoverable for a particular kind of harm caused by a tort."); *Attia v British Gas Plc* [1988] QB 304 per Dillon LJ at 311 ("[D]amage for 'nervous shock', ie for psychiatric illness occasioned by shock, is regarded as a separate head of damage, distinct, for example, from damage for personal injury"); *Alcock v Chief Constable of South Yorkshire Police* [1992] 1 AC 310 per Lord Ackner at 400 ("Shock is no longer a variant of physical injury but a separate kind of damage."). Note also the emphasis in recent Californian cases that negligent infliction of emotional distress is not a tort in itself, but a species of negligence: see eg *Christensen v Superior Court* (1991) 820 P 2d 181; 2 Cal Rptr 2d 79; *Akins v Sacramento Municipal Utility District* (1992) 8 Cal Rptr 2d 785; *Nahrstedt v Lakeside Village Condominium Association Inc* (1992) 11 Cal Rptr 2d 299.
7. See *Marshall v Lionel Enterprises Inc* (1971) 25 DLR (3d) 141 per Haines J at 149; *Anderson v St Pierre* (1987) 46 DLR (4th) 754 per Jewers J at 757-758; *Turton v Buttler* (1987) 42 CCLT 74. See also J S Williams (1968) 46 Can BR 515; H J Glasbeek (1969) 47 Can BR 96.

responsibility for psychiatric damage, then, is an aspect of negligence liability, and this chapter discusses the general principles of liability in negligence as they apply to such loss.

The conventional analysis of the tort of negligence suggests that three elements must be satisfied as a condition of liability: there must be a duty of care owed by the defendant to the plaintiff, breach of that duty, and resulting damage. Over the past one hundred years, as the law of liability for psychiatric damage has developed through the progressive removal of artificial barriers erected by the courts in order to place limits on the scope of recovery, it has not always been certain whether these barriers were properly classified as issues of duty of care or remoteness of damage. The initial case which denied liability, *Victorian Railway Commissioners v Coultas*,[8] did so on the basis that physical injury or illness caused by fright was too remote a consequence of negligent conduct to be actionable. Even when, a few years later, in cases such as *Dulieu v White & Sons*[9] the courts abandoned this attitude and held that there could be liability for shock if it was caused by fear of physical injury to the plaintiff, there was still considerable doubt whether this requirement related to duty or remoteness. The defendant's plea was that the damage was too remote, and the judgment of Kennedy J suggests that the objection to be overcome is one of remoteness and not duty:

> "In regard to the existence of the duty here, there can, I think, be no question. The driver of a van and horses in a highway owes a duty to use reasonable and proper care and skill so as to not to injure either persons lawfully using the highway or property adjoining the highway, or persons who, like the plaintiff, are lawfully occupying that property."[10]

However Phillimore J saw the difficulty as one of duty rather than remoteness.[11] When we come to the next extension of liability in *Hambrook v Stokes Bros*,[12] allowing a person outside the area of potential danger to recover for shock caused by an accident or near-accident to another, there is still substantial uncertainty, perhaps as a result of the defendant's admission of negligence, which Atkin LJ, at least, seemed to regard as disposing of the duty question.[13] Nonetheless, at the end of the day, for his Lordship "the question appears to be as to the extent of the duty, and not as to remoteness of damage",[14] and it seems that the other judges were in agreement.[15] But it was not until the early 1940s, when in *Bourhill v Young*[16] the question of nervous shock liability reached the House of Lords for the first time, that the matter was authoritatively put to rest. The Law Lords had no doubt that the core issue was one of duty

8. (1888) 13 App Cas 222.
9. [1901] 2 KB 669.
10. Ibid at 671-672. Kennedy J also referred to *Smith v Johnson* (unreported, QBD, Jan 1897, cited in *Wilkinson v Downton* [1897] 2 QB 57 per Wright J at 61), where liability for shock suffered by a bystander was denied, as turning on remoteness.
11. [1901] 2 KB 669 at 685.
12. [1925] 1 KB 141.
13. Ibid at 156.
14. Ibid at 158.
15. Ibid per Bankes LJ at 151, per Sargant LJ at 162-163.
16. [1943] AC 92, noted by C A Wright (1943) 21 Can BR 65; A L Goodhart (1944) 8 CLJ 265.

of care,[17] and practically all cases since that time have seen the essential issue as one of duty.

However, there may still be some scope for confusion. Some cases suggest that the duty and remoteness concepts are interchangeable, at least in certain circumstances. If there should be an initial breach of duty to the plaintiff, as in cases where he or she is involved in an accident and later suffers shock and psychiatric damage through learning of injuries to others in the same accident,[18] the question of liability for mental harm caused by this means is treated as a remoteness issue whereas in other circumstances it is a matter of duty. Another example is furnished by *Attia v British Gas Plc*,[19] where the English Court of Appeal held that there was no rule that psychiatric injury caused by witnessing damage to property (in that case, the burning down of the plaintiff's house) could never be actionable. Woolf and Bingham LJJ considered that because the defendants clearly owed the plaintiff a duty of care not to cause damage to her home the important issue in this context was one of remoteness and not duty.[20] Dillon LJ would have agreed if the plaintiff had claimed for the property damage[21]—in fact, this issue had been settled. But all three judgments deal with foreseeability and policy issues which are normally analysed under the heading of duty. In *King v Phillips*,[22] the English Court of Appeal had to examine the case of a mother who suffered shock when she heard her son scream and looked out of the window of her home to see a taxi reversing over his tricycle. Denning LJ found difficulty in dealing with the case by applying the duty concept, stating that the driver's duty should not differ according to whether the injury suffered was physical harm or nervous shock. He suggested that the reason why the mother should not recover was not because of lack of a duty owed to her, but because the damage was too remote.[23] The other judges did not, however, share this view.[24]

Lord Denning's approach as revealed by his judgment in this case may seem like a relic of a bygone era; alternatively, together with the cases in which an existing breach of duty compelled the court to resort to remoteness, it may be evidence of dissatisfaction with the duty-breach-damage analysis. Such dissatisfaction is in fact not confined to psychiatric harm cases. General analyses of the law of negligence have often found the tripartite division of negligence liability to be a straitjacket into which the various issues do not always fit satisfactorily. The modern duty of care, for example, is a complex concept in which notions of foreseeability, proximity and policy all play a part. A proper analysis of duty requires an examination

---

17. Ibid per Lord Thankerton at 98, per Lord Russell at 101, per Lord Macmillan at 104, per Lord Wright at 106, per Lord Porter at 113.

18. As eg in *Schneider v Eisovitch* [1960] 2 QB 430 and *Andrews v Williams* [1967] VR 831. This situation is discussed in more detail below, pp 156-159.

19. [1988] QB 304.

20. Ibid per Woolf LJ at 314, per Bingham LJ at 319 who said: "[I]t seems to me to be preferable, where *a* duty of care undeniably exists, to treat the question as one of remoteness and ask whether the plaintiff's psychiatric damage is too remote to be recoverable because not reasonably foreseeable as a consequence of the defendant's careless conduct."

21. Ibid at 312.

22. [1953] 1 QB 429.

23. Ibid at 440.

24. Ibid per Singleton LJ at 435-436, per Hodson LJ at 443-444.

of a number of variables, such as the kind of harm suffered (is it, for example, personal or property, physical or mental, economic or non-economic?), the manner of its infliction (for example, was it by way of act or omission?), and various other disparate factors which may affect both the plaintiff's and the defendant's positions. The damage issue encompasses not only establishing that a recognised kind of damage was suffered by the plaintiff, but also that there was a causal link between that damage and the tortfeasor's negligent conduct, and that it was not too remote a consequence of that negligence to be recoverable. In addition, there is the often complicated question of assessing the measure of damages to be awarded.

The most preferable approach is therefore to abandon the threefold classification in favour of a more comprehensive and revealing analysis of the issues involved.[25] No fewer than six requirements can be identified, the first four of which are necessary to establish liability and the remaining two of which govern the damages awarded. The first four requirements have been described as follows:

> "(1) The existence in law of a duty of care situation, that is, one in which the law attaches liability to carelessness. There has to be recognition by law that the careless infliction of the kind of damage in suit on the type of person to which the plaintiff belongs by the type of person to which the defendant belongs is actionable.
>
> (2) Careless behaviour by the defendant, that is, that it fails to measure up to the standard and scope set by law.
>
> (3) A causal connection between the defendant's careless conduct and the damage.
>
> (4) Foreseeability that such conduct would have inflicted on the particular plaintiff the particular kind of damage of which he complains."[26]

The third and fourth requirements have not infrequently been referred to respectively as the questions of "cause in fact" and "cause in law",[27] but this terminology serves only as a source of confusion between what are, in truth, two distinct criteria which perform two distinct functions relying on two different tests. The former ascribes causal responsibility to the *defendant*, whereas the latter is designed to limit actionability by the *plaintiff* by determining whether he or she should have a claim against the defendant in respect of a certain type of damage. The remaining requirements, which become relevant only once liability has been established, are:

> "(5) The extent of the damage attributable to the defendant; and
>
> (6) The monetary estimate of that extent of damage."

The compilation of this "list" of prerequisites to legal accountability in negligence is not to be taken as suggesting that every criterion will be in issue

---

25. See R W M Dias (ed), *Clerk and Lindsell on Torts* (16th ed, 1989), para 10.02; R W M Dias & B S Markesinis, *Tort Law* (2nd ed, 1988), 54-60; Fleming, op cit, n 5 at 103; A M Linden, *Canadian Tort Law* (4th ed, 1987), 88-89.
26. See Dias, op cit, n 25, para 10.02.
27. The remoteness of damage issue is usually referred to in United States jurisprudence as the inquiry whether the want of care was the "proximate cause" of the plaintiff's loss.

in every case—in fact, this will rarely be so, as is illustrated by the psychiatric damage authorities where, more often than not, duty of care has almost exclusively occupied the courts' attention. Most commonly, the existence of one or more of the requirements will not even be the subject of argument. Judges do not trudge robot-like through every stage but confine themselves to the contentious aspects of the liability equation raised by the particular circumstances of the action before them.

Although theoretically distinct, the ingredients of liability are not always clearly separated from one another. Indeed, it is sometimes suggested that they are all aspects of one and the same question. Thus, for example, in a psychiatric damage case, *Beecham v Hughes*, Lambert JA stated:

> "The questions of foreseeability, proximity, causation and remoteness are interlocked. They are not four answers to four questions, but one composite answer to one composite question." [28]

In a similar vein Denning LJ in *Roe v Minister of Health* [29] again revealed his difficulties with the standard categories by saying: "In all these cases you will find that the three questions, duty, causation and remoteness, run continually into one another." [30] Nonetheless, for informed analysis it is essential to have a clear picture of the various elements of negligence. It is in relation especially to cases dealing with damage to the mind that the above analysis proves its usefulness, on two counts. First, it gathers together two important issues of foreseeability—foreseeability of the plaintiff and foreseeability of the kind of damage in suit. The conventional analysis of the first of these as a part of the concept of duty and the second as a matter of remoteness of damage [31] obscures the important connection between the two, especially in psychiatric injury claims—a connection which is probably at least partially responsible for the confusion between duty and remoteness in the early cases. Further, consigning the second

28. (1988) 52 DLR (4th) 625 at 665.
29. [1954] 2 QB 66 at 85.
30. See also *Home Office v Dorset Yacht Co Ltd* [1970] AC 1004 per Lord Pearson at 1052 who said it may be "artificial and unhelpful" to consider the question of the existence of a duty of care in isolation from the other criteria of liability, and spoke of possible "illuminati[on]" by starting with the damage suffered and working back through the cause of it to the possible duty which may have been broken; *Spartan Steel & Alloys Ltd v Martin & Co (Contractors) Ltd* [1973] QB 27 per Lord Denning MR at 37 who said: "The more I think about these cases, the more difficult I find it to put each into its proper pigeon-hole. Sometimes I say: 'There was no duty.' In others I say: 'The damage was too remote.' So much so that I think the time has come to discard those tests which have proved so elusive. It seems to me to be better to consider the particular relationship in hand." For other examples of difficulties and confusion caused by the terminology of negligence see *Glasgow Corporation v Muir* [1943] AC 448; *Woods v Duncan* [1946] AC 401 where an action failed for want of foreseeability, three Law Lords viewing this as denoting the absence of causation, two others viewing it as meaning that there was no breach; *Caledonian Collieries Ltd v Speirs* (1957) 97 CLR 202 where questions of duty and breach appear to merge; *King v Liverpool City Council* [1986] 1 WLR 890 where "duty of care" was used as an analogy for "breach of duty" in that it was said that the absence of breach by the defendant meant the absence of a duty owed to the plaintiff; *Skuse v Commonwealth* (1986) 62 ALR 108. Note also *SCM (United Kingdom) Ltd v W J Whittall & Son Ltd* [1970] 1 WLR 1017 per Thesiger J at 1031; *Al-Kandari v J R Brown & Co* [1987] QB 514 per French J at 525.
31. Something labelled by Fleming, op cit, n 5 at 144 as reflecting merely "an inconsequential and largely accidental choice".

foreseeability issue to the category of remoteness may be misleading if it suggests that it is merely a matter relating to the *extent* of liability, rather than its existence. Foreseeability has a dual relevance—crucial in two respects to the establishment of a duty of care, it also operates as a limiting mechanism by testing its scope once established. The second advantage of the analysis outlined is that it makes a clear separation between the issue of foreseeability and the other elements involved in the duty of care component. Much of the law of psychiatric damage involves a study of particular duty requirements which have been developed by the courts. Such limitations are examined below in Chapters 5 to 10. As liability has been expanded many of these requirements have been stripped away—and it is our thesis that this process should go much further. Putting aside the possibility of rational and well-founded policy arguments which mandate a denial of liability in certain special circumstances, the logical end-point of such a process would be a recognition that if psychiatric damage was foreseeable in the circumstances there is no other duty requirement. Indeed, this was the argument of the plaintiff in two of the leading cases at the highest level—*Jaensch v Coffey*[32] in the High Court of Australia and *Alcock v Chief Constable of South Yorkshire Police*[33] in the House of Lords in England. In each case the courts rejected that argument. In each case they affirmed that apart from foreseeability there are other considerations which limit liability.[34] However, the identification of that extra element requires questions of foreseeability to be separated and put to one side.

The analysis that follows assumes that recognisable psychiatric damage has been medically proved to exist—the issue dealt with above in Chapter 2. Adopting the argument advanced in the foregoing paragraphs, it deals first with the foreseeability issues, secondly with other questions of duty and thirdly with the remaining requirements—breach, causation and remoteness (which in this context means the extent of liability once psychiatric damage is foreseeable).

Foreseeability

No study of the elements of liability in negligence can proceed far without encountering Lord Atkin's famous neighbour principle as enunciated in *Donoghue v Stevenson*.[35] Taking his cue from the lawyer's question which led to the telling of the parable of the good Samaritan,[36] Lord Atkin stated:

32. (1984) 155 CLR 549.
33. [1992] 1 AC 310.
34. *Jaensch v Coffey* (1984) 155 CLR 549 per Gibbs CJ at 554, per Deane J at 583-587, though see per Brennan J at 577, per Dawson J at 611-612; *Alcock v Chief Constable of South Yorkshire Police* [1992] 1 AC 310 per Lord Keith at 396, per Lord Ackner at 402, per Lord Oliver at 406, per Lord Jauncey at 419. See also *McLoughlin v O'Brian* [1983] 1 AC 410 per Lord Wilberforce at 420, though see per Lord Bridge at 433; *Beecham v Hughes* (1988) 52 DLR (4th) 625 per Taggart JA at 664; *Rhodes v Canadian National Railway* (1990) 75 DLR (4th) 248 per Macfarlane JA at 250, per Wallace JA at 254; *Thing v La Chusa* (1989) 771 P 2d 814; 257 Cal Rptr 98, per Eagleson J at 826-827.
35. [1932] AC 562.
36. See Luke 10: 25-37.

"The rule that you are to love your neighbour becomes in law, you must not injure your neighbour; and the lawyer's question, who is my neighbour? receives a restricted reply. You must take reasonable care to avoid acts or omissions which you can reasonably foresee would be likely to injure your neighbour. Who, then, in law is my neighbour? The answer seems to be—persons who are so closely and directly affected by my act that I ought reasonably to have them in contemplation as being so affected when I am directing my mind to the acts or omissions which are called in question."[37]

In the 60 years since this statement was uttered it has been viewed in many different ways. Pockets of initial resistance can be found,[38] but its seminal nature and influence on the modern law of negligence was soon recognised. Sometimes it has been seen as a self-sufficient general test of duty in negligence,[39] at other times merely a general philosophy which does not avoid the need for looking to particular rules governing individual situations.[40] Clearly, foreseeability lies at the heart of Lord Atkin's statement, but current thinking emphasises that Lord Atkin did not advocate a test of foreseeability alone, his use of the word "reasonably" indicating the essentiality of other requirements.[41] Foreseeability, then, is clearly a necessary, if not a sufficient, criterion of liability. What is it that must be foreseen?

The plaintiff must be foreseeable

It is clear, first of all, that the plaintiff must be foreseeable. The plaintiff cannot build on a duty owed to someone else, but must establish that it was

37. [1932] AC 562 at 580.
38. See eg Farr v Butters Bros & Co [1932] 2 KB 606 per Scrutton LJ at 613-614; Haynes v G Harwood & Sons [1935] 1 KB 146 per Roche LJ at 167-168; Old Gate Estates Ltd v Toplis & Harding & Russell [1939] 3 All ER 209 (where the neighbourhood principle was confined to carelessness resulting in physical damage to life, limb or health); Barnett v H & J Packer Co Ltd [1940] 3 All ER 575 per Singleton LJ at 597; Deyong v Shenburn [1946] KB 227 per du Parcq LJ at 233. His Lordship's words were, during this early stage, relegated to the status of obiter dictum, the ratio of the case being restricted to the liability of manufacturers of goods to the ultimate consumer.
39. See particularly Home Office v Dorset Yacht Co Ltd [1970] AC 1004, in which Lords Reid at 1027, Morris at 1034 and Pearson at 1054 thought that the neighbour principle had the status of a rule of law, subject only to exceptions based on particular justifications or policy grounds. As examples of this approach see Clay v A J Crump & Sons Ltd [1964] 1 QB 533; Lee Cooper Ltd v C H Jeakins & Sons Ltd [1967] 2 QB 1.
40. See Hedley Byrne & Co v Heller & Partners [1964] AC 465 per Lord Devlin at 524-525; Home Office v Dorset Yacht Co Ltd [1970] AC 1004 per Lord Diplock at 1060; Governors of the Peabody Donation Fund v Sir Lindsay Parkinson & Co Ltd [1985] AC 210 per Lord Keith at 239-240.
41. For this view expressed in psychiatric damage cases see McLoughlin v O'Brian [1983] 1 AC 410 per Lord Wilberforce at 420; Jaensch v Coffey (1984) 155 CLR 549 per Gibbs CJ at 553, per Deane J at 580; Rhodes v Canadian National Railway (1990) 75 DLR (4th) 248 per Macfarlane JA at 250, per Wallace JA at 252-253, per Taylor JA (Wood JA concurring) at 295-296; Alcock v Chief Constable of South Yorkshire Police [1992] 1 AC 310 per Lord Keith at 396-397, per Lord Ackner at 402, per Lord Oliver at 410. In other cases see Sutherland Shire Council v Heyman (1985) 157 CLR 424 per Deane J at 495-496; Stevens v Brodribb Sawmilling Co Pty Ltd (1986) 160 CLR 16 per Deane J at 51; San Sebastian Pty Ltd v Minister Administering the Environmental Planning and Assessment Act 1979 (1986) 162 CLR 340 per Brennan J at 368-369; Yuen Kun Yeu v Attorney-General of Hong Kong [1988] AC 175 per Lord Keith at 710-711.

"owed to" him or her—either individually, or as a member of a class.[42] Unless the plaintiff comes within this umbrella of foreseeability, no action can lie.

This rule owes its origin to the United States case of *Palsgraf v Long Island Rail Co*[43] where the defendant's servants, in attempting to bundle two late passengers into a train, caused one of them to drop a parcel, which exploded and caused a weighing machine at the other end of the station to topple over and injure the plaintiff. It was held that though the defendant may have been in breach of a duty to the passengers, no duty was owed to the plaintiff. She could not build on a duty owed to someone else and no duty was owed to her because she was outside the range of foreseeable harm. Older cases which overlooked this requirement[44] are no longer authoritative.

In the context of this rule, *Bourhill v Young*[45] has a twofold importance. First, at a general level, it adopted the *Palsgraf* principle for English and Scottish law—no doubt influenced by the neighbour principle in which the concept of the plaintiff being foreseeable is deeply embedded. Secondly, it applied the principle to cases of psychiatric damage. The plaintiff, "doomed to celebrity, in the pages of the Law Reports, in language thought acceptable in another era, as the pregnant 'fishwife' ",[46] had just got off a tram and had gone round to the driver's platform on the far side to collect her fish basket. A motor cyclist passed between the near side of the tram and the pavement and was killed in a collision with a car at a nearby intersection, about 15 yards away from Mrs Bourhill. She could not see the impact, but heard it, and later saw blood on the road. The plaintiff claimed that as a result she suffered a severe shock to her nervous system and one month later gave birth to a stillborn child. She sued the estate of the deceased motorcyclist. The Scottish courts concerned themselves with the issue, still at that time unresolved in Scots law, whether it was a necessary condition of recovery that the plaintiff suffer shock through fear for her own safety.[47] The House of Lords held that it was unnecessary to resolve this issue. The plaintiff's claim could be rejected on the logically prior ground that she was not a foreseeable victim. The motorcyclist owed a duty only to such persons as he could foresee might be injured by his failure to exercise care, and this did not include the plaintiff, who was not within the area of potential danger.[48]

Another important case where the plaintiff failed on this ground was *King v Phillips*.[49] As already related, a mother in her house heard the

---

42. See *Farrugia v Great Western Railway Co* [1947] 2 All ER 565 per Lord Greene MR at 567. As an example, in *Home Office v Dorset Yacht Co Ltd* [1970] AC 1004, it was held that the defendants should have foreseen that permitting Borstal boys to escape might result in damage to the property of persons in the vicinity.
43. (1928) 162 NE 99 (NY). See W L Prosser, "Palsgraf Revisited" (1953) 52 Mich L Rev 1.
44. For example, *Smith v London & South Western Railway Co* (1870) LR 6 CP 14.
45. [1943] AC 92.
46. *Jaensch v Coffey* (1984) 155 CLR 549 per Deane J at 594.
47. See *Bourhill v Young's Executor*, 1941 SC 395.
48. [1943] AC 92 per Lord Thankerton at 98, per Lord Russell at 102, per Lord Macmillan at 105, per Lord Wright at 111, per Lord Porter at 119. Compare *John Mill & Co Ltd v Public Trustee* [1945] NZLR 347.
49. [1953] 1 QB 429.

screams of her toddler, who was playing outside, and looked out of an upstairs window to see his tricycle beneath the wheels of a reversing taxi, sustaining psychiatric injury as a result. Singleton and Hodson LJJ applied the principle of *Bourhill v Young* and held that the taxi driver could not reasonably have contemplated that as a result of his negligence in reversing his taxi without looking where he was going he would cause psychiatric injury to the mother 70 yards away.[50] It has been suggested that the result of the case would be different if it were to be litigated at the present day, and that a court would not have difficulty in viewing the mother's presence as foreseeable,[51] and significantly in a Scottish case with almost identical facts the defendant was held liable.[52] However, even if its application in particular cases can be called into question, the principle is clear: it must be established that the defendant owed a duty to a foreseeable plaintiff.

The same principle was applied in the important Australian case of *Chester v Council of the Municipality of Waverley*[53] to defeat the claim of a mother who suffered shock when she saw the body of her son recovered from a water-filled trench, and in Canadian cases, to rule out an action by a father who went to the scene of an accident in which his daughter had been badly injured,[54] and a claim by the mother of children who contracted a salmonella infection from pet turtles.[55] By contrast, there are cases in which courts have specifically pointed out that plaintiffs have overcome this first foreseeability hurdle.[56] A bizarre illustration of the principle is *Ibrahim (A Minor) v Muhammad*.[57] In accordance with Moslem custom, Tayfun, a five year old Turkish Cypriot, was to be circumcised in the presence of his family (and the event was being recorded for posterity on cine-film by his uncle). Lamentably, the pride and joy of his mother and father turned to horror when the local general practitioner, who held himself out as an expert in such matters, cut off not just the foreskin but about half of Tayfun's penis, causing blood to spout out of what remained of that organ and Tayfun to scream with pain and shock. Actions were brought by Tayfun and his mother and father—in the case of the parents, for psychiatric harm caused by the shock of what happened. Taylor J held that shock to the parents was within the bounds of foresight. In assessing what was reasonably foreseeable, it was necessary to have in mind a Moslem parent of reasonable fortitude viewing the particular type of injury inflicted in the festive circumstances in which it was witnessed.

These cases all involve the now typical psychiatric damage scenario where the plaintiff suffers such harm as the result of an accident or near-accident

50. Ibid per Singleton LJ at 435, per Hodson LJ at 443.
51. *Alcock v Chief Constable of South Yorkshire Police* [1992] 1 AC 310 per Lord Oliver at 412.
52. *McLinden v Richardson*, 1962 SLT (Notes) 104.
53. (1939) 62 CLR 1. Evatt J at 33 referred to the *Palsgraf* rule as a "truism". See also the earlier decision in *Bunyan v Jordan* (1937) 57 CLR 1.
54. *Brown v Hubar* (1974) 45 DLR (3rd) 664.
55. *McMullin v F W Woolworth Co Ltd* (1974) 9 NBR (2d) 214.
56. See eg *Owens v Liverpool Corporation* [1939] 1 KB 394 (although the discussion on this point is very brief); *Dooley v Cammell Laird & Co Ltd* [1951] 1 Lloyd's Rep 271; *Boardman v Sanderson* [1964] 1 WLR 1317; *Anderson v Smith* (1990) 101 FLR 34; *Bechard v Haliburton Estate* (1991) 84 DLR (4th) 668.
57. (Unreported, QBD, 21 May 1984).

to someone else. They show the importance, in such a situation, of establishing that the plaintiff was foreseeable and that a duty was owed to him or her.[58] A Canadian judge has expressly recognised that it is easier to satisfy this test where plaintiffs are directly involved than where they are merely observers.[59]

The kind of damage must be foreseeable

It is now clear that foreseeability is required not only of the plaintiff but also of the kind of damage suffered or, if more than one type of damage is inflicted, of each kind of damage. This may have been a general requirement in negligence a long time ago,[60] but after the decision in *Re Polemis and Furness, Withy & Co*[61] it appeared to have been superseded by a rule that the defendant was responsible for all direct consequences of his or her negligence, however unforeseeable. Such a rule seemed to leave no room for any proposition based on foresight of the kind of damage in suit.[62] *Re Polemis* in its turn, however, was rejected. In *The Wagon Mound (No 1)*,[63] the Privy Council restored the foreseeability test and held that there would be no liability for a negligent breach of duty unless the damage suffered was of a foreseeable kind. This begged the question how foreseeable the damage had to be, for the range of probability stretches from "infinitely remote" through "possible" and "probable" and all the other variant shades of likelihood to "almost certain". The degree of foreseeability which would satisfy the new test was articulated in a second action arising out of the same circumstances, Lord Reid identifying a foreseeable risk as a "real risk", that is, "one which would

---

58. The role of this principle in the more general context of compensating the victims of negligence is dealt with in more detail below, pp 90-99.
59. See *Duwyn v Kaprielian* (1978) 94 DLR (3d) 424 per Morden JA at 437-438 (Brooke JA concurring). Psychiatric injury to a baby boy severely shocked when a car backed into his mother's car in which he and his grandmother were sitting was reasonably foreseeable, but such injury to the mother who returned from a nearby building to see the commotion was not. Note also *Jaensch v Coffey* (1984) 155 CLR 549 per Brennan J at 570.
60. See *Rigby v Hewitt* (1850) 5 Exch 240; 155 ER 103 per Pollock CB at 104; *Greenland v Chaplin* (1850) 5 Exch 243; 155 ER 104 per Pollock CB at 106.
61. [1921] 3 KB 560. See M Davies, "The Road from Morocco: Polemis through Donoghue to No-Fault" (1982) 45 MLR 534.
62. See however Dias, op cit, n 25, para 10.151 for an alternative interpretation of the *Polemis* principle which recognises the need for a foreseeable kind of damage.
63. *Overseas Tankship (UK) Ltd v Morts Dock & Engineering Co* [1961] AC 388: see especially per Viscount Simonds at 425-426. Notes include those by A L Goodhart (1961) 77 LQR 175; A M Honoré (1961) 39 Can BR 267; R W M Dias [1961] CLJ 28. See J G Fleming, "The Passing of Polemis" (1961) 39 Can BR 489; W L Morison, "The Victory of Reasonable Foresight" (1961) 34 ALJ 317; L Green, "Foreseeability in Negligence Law" (1961) 61 Col L Rev 1401; D Payne, "Foresight and Remoteness of Damage in Negligence" (1962) 25 MLR 1; R W M Dias, "Remoteness of Liability and Legal Policy" [1962] CLJ 178 (fn 2 listing some of the vast literature that has accumulated on this topic); D Jackson, "A Kind of Damage—Foreseeability, Probability and Causation" (1965) 39 ALJ 3; J C Smith, "Requiem for Polemis" (1965) 2 UBCLR 159. It must be remembered that this discussion is concerned only with responsibility for unintended consequences. The consequences which flow from an intention to injure the plaintiff are never too remote: see *Quinn v Leathem* [1901] AC 495 per Lord Lindley at 537; *Bettel v Yim* (1978) 88 DLR (3d) 543 per Borins J at 552-554; *Allan v New Mount Sinai Hospital* (1980) 109 DLR (3d) 634 per Linden J at 643; H McGregor, *Damages* (16th ed, 1988), para 157.

occur to the mind of a reasonable man in the position of the defendant's servant and which he would not brush aside as far-fetched".[64] His Lordship summarised the two *Wagon Mound* cases as having decided that "the defendant will be liable for any type of damage which is reasonably foreseeable as liable to happen even in the most unusual case, unless the risk is so small that a reasonable man would in the whole circumstances feel justified in neglecting it".[65]

In the conventional threefold analysis of negligence this aspect of foreseeability belongs to the area of remoteness, not duty, but in fact it, like the rule that the plaintiff must be foreseeable just considered, is a rule that limits actionability by the plaintiff. The affinity between the two rules is particularly evident in psychiatric damage cases, which played an important part in bringing about the first *Wagon Mound* decision. Viscount Simonds noted that test of liability for nervous shock was foreseeability of injury by shock. He substituted fire for shock and applied it to the facts of *The Wagon Mound (No 1)*[66] which, as is well known, involved the ignition through welding operations of oil carelessly discharged into Sydney Harbour and the consequent damage to the plaintiff's wharf and two vessels moored there. While damage by fouling was clearly foreseeable, damage by fire was not. The prior utilisation of these principles in mental damage suits led Haines J in *Marshall v Lionel Enterprises Inc*[67] to say that the *Wagon Mound* decision had made little change in the law governing liability for psychiatric injury.

In the early shock cases the need for foreseeability of injury by shock was not made clear. The courts were most hesitant to recognise shock as a kind of damage in its own right, and even after repudiating the need for contemporaneous physical impact retained, for a time, the requirement that the plaintiff must be within the area of possible injury by impact and must suffer shock through fear for his or her own safety.[68] In these conditions what is required is foreseeability of injury by impact rather than by shock—a theory that has been labelled the "impact theory".[69] The distinction between the two theories is clearly stated in *Abramzik v Brenner* where Culliton CJS asked:

> "Is the duty which a plaintiff must establish in seeking to recover damages for nervous shock only that the defendant ought, as a reasonable man, to have foreseen injury to the plaintiff as a result of his conduct, or must the plaintiff establish that the defendant ought, as a reasonable man, to have foreseen nervous shock (as opposed to other physical injury) to the plaintiff as a result of his conduct?"[70]

---

64. *Overseas Tankship (UK) Ltd v Miller Steamship Co Pty (The Wagon Mound (No 2))* [1967] 1 AC 617 at 643. See R W M Dias, "Trouble on Oiled Waters: Problems of The Wagon Mound (No 2)" [1967] CLJ 62.
65. *Koufos v C Czarnikow Ltd (The Heron II)* [1969] 1 AC 350 at 385-386.
66. [1961] AC 388 at 426.
67. (1971) 25 DLR (3d) 141 at 147.
68. *Dulieu v White & Sons* [1901] 2 KB 669.
69. See Dias, op cit, n 25, para 10.07.
70. (1967) 65 DLR (2d) 651 at 656.

Many of the older cases are consistent with the "impact theory" approach. [71]

However, the courts gradually began to appreciate that shock was a distinct kind of damage in itself, different from conventional cases of personal injury. [72] This process was assisted by the recognition, in *Hambrook v Stokes Bros* [73] and subsequent cases, that persons outside the zone of physical danger were owed a duty of care, because injury by shock was the only kind of injury that was foreseeable in such circumstances. *Bourhill v Young* [74] is instructive in this respect. Though the judgments are not always clear on this issue, Lords Russell, Macmillan and Porter, at least, appear to ratify a test that the defendant must foresee injury *by shock*. [75] A few years later in *King v Phillips* [76] the judgment of Denning LJ states clearly that the test of liability for nervous shock is foreseeability of injury by nervous shock [77] and this influential judgment was expressly affirmed in *The Wagon Mound (No 1)*. [78] The "shock theory" has thus replaced the "impact theory", and all the modern psychiatric damage cases affirm that the test is whether injury by shock was foreseeable. [79]

71. For example, *Dulieu v White & Sons* [1901] 2 KB 669 per Kennedy J at 675; *Hambrook v Stokes Bros* [1925] 1 KB 141 per Sargant LJ (dissenting) at 162; *King v Phillips* [1953] 1 QB 429 per Singleton LJ at 435, per Hodson LJ at 443.
72. Note also above, pp 14-18.
73. [1925] 1 KB 141.
74. [1943] AC 92.
75. Ibid per Lord Russell at 102, per Lord Macmillan at 105, per Lord Porter at 117—though there is room for differences of interpretation of the judgments in this case: see eg Dias, op cit, n 25, para 10.07. In *King v Phillips* [1953] 1 QB 429, Denning LJ at 438 suggested that all five judges had supported this test, but this seems an overstatement. Other older cases which appear to indorse the view that what is required is foreseeability of injury by shock are *Bunyan v Jordan* (1937) 57 CLR 1 per Dixon J at 16; *Chester v Council of the Municipality of Waverley* (1939) 62 CLR 1 per Latham CJ at 7, per Rich J at 11, per Starke J at 13-14; *Dooley v Cammell Laird & Co Ltd* [1951] 1 Lloyd's Rep 271 per Donovan J at 276-277; *Pollard v Macarchuk* (1959) 16 DLR (2d) 225 per Johnson JA at 229.
76. [1953] 1 QB 429.
77. Ibid at 441.
78. [1961] AC 388 at 426.
79. See eg *Boardman v Sanderson* [1964] 1 WLR 1317 per Danckwerts LJ at 1322; *Storm v Geeves* [1965] Tas SR 252 per Burbury CJ at 255-256; *Chadwick v British Railways Board* [1967] 1 WLR 912 per Waller J at 920; *Mount Isa Mines Ltd v Pusey* (1970) 125 CLR 383 per Windeyer J at 395, per Walsh J at 410-411; *Marshall v Lionel Enterprises Inc* (1971) 25 DLR (3d) 141 per Haines J at 149; *Cameron v Marcaccini* (1978) 87 DLR (3d) 442 per Macdonald J at 444; *Duwyn v Kaprielian* (1978) 94 DLR (3d) 424 per Morden JA at 435; *Young v Burgoyne* (1981) 122 DLR (3d) 330 per Hallett J at 336; *McLoughlin v O'Brian* [1983] 1 AC 410 per Lord Wilberforce at 417-418, per Lord Edmund-Davies at 423, per Lord Bridge at 432; *Jaensch v Coffey* (1984) 155 CLR 549 per Gibbs CJ at 552-553, per Brennan J at 560-562, per Deane J at 581, 591, per Dawson J at 611; *Brice v Brown* [1984] 1 All ER 997 per Stuart-Smith J at 1007; *Vince v Cripps Bakery Pty Ltd* (1984) Aust Torts Rep 80-668 per Underwood J at 68,814; *Harrison v State Government Insurance Office* (1985) Aust Torts Rep 80-273 per Vasta J at 69,175; *Mellor v Moran* (1985) 2 MVR 461 per Vasta J at 462; *Stergiou v Stergiou* (1987) Aust Torts Rep 80-082 per Gallop J at 68,436; *Attia v British Gas Plc* [1988] QB 304 per Dillon LJ at 310-312, per Woolf LJ at 315, per Bingham LJ at 319-320; *Beecham v Hughes* (1988) 52 DLR (4th) 625 per Taggart JA at 647; *Spence v Percy* (1990) Aust Torts Rep 81-039 per Derrington J at 68,037; *Rhodes v Canadian National Railway* (1990) 75 DLR (4th) 248 per Macfarlane JA at 250, per Wallace JA at 264, 266; *Ravenscroft v Rederiaktiebφlaget Transatlantic* [1991] 3 All ER 73 per Ward J at 84; *Alcock v Chief Constable of South Yorkshire Police* [1992]

It is not always clear what is meant by the *Wagon Mound* requirement that the *kind* of damage must be foreseeable.[80] On at least one occasion it has been held that damage falling under the umbrella description "mental illness" or "nervous shock" or "psychiatric damage" will not satisfy the "kind of damage" criterion in all cases. In *Rowe v McCartney*[81] although the causing of "nervous shock" to a friend was considered to have been a reasonably foreseeable consequence of the defendant's negligence in ramming a telegraph pole in the friend's car, thereby rendering himself a quadriplegic, the friend failed in her claim for damages, inter alia,[82] because the *type* of mental disorder she sustained was not foreseeable. Two judges of the New South Wales Court of Appeal proceeded on the basis that it was proper to define the type of injury more narrowly. Although the plaintiff (who had been a passenger) was physically uninjured in the accident, she developed a psychiatric illness unassociated with the experience of involvement in a car crash, but stemming from guilt at having agreed to allow the defendant to drive her car which was too powerful for him and with which he was unfamiliar, and aggravated by the fact that his injuries were non-compensable. Perceiving a need to "penetrate" the category of "mental illness" more closely, Moffitt P and Samuels JA found the neurotic guilt-based disorder an injury that no reasonable driver could have regarded as a likely consequence of his or her carelessness.[83] However, in the context of psychiatric damage it is usually accepted that what is required is foreseeability of shock generally—of some kind of psychiatric damage—and that the precise nature of that damage need not be foreseeable. This issue was specifically raised in *Mount Isa Mines Ltd v Pusey*[84] where the plaintiff's efforts to rescue workmates who had been badly burnt by an electric arc when testing a switchboard caused him to develop schizophrenia. The trial judge held that although this particular manifestation of psychiatric injury could not have been foreseen, it was within the broad category of psychiatric damage which was foreseeable. On appeal to the High Court the defendant contended that this was wrong, but the High Court disagreed, affirming the proposition that what the defendant had to foresee was the occurrence of the class of injury, mental disorder, rather than the particular illness.[85] This approach was reaffirmed

79. *Continued*
   1 AC 310 per Lord Keith at 396, per Lord Ackner at 400, per Lord Oliver at 406; *Miller v Royal Derwent Hospital Board of Management* (unreported, Tasmanian SC, 29 May 1992, No 282 of 1988) per Zeeman J at 15, 17.
80. See Jackson, op cit, n 63. Windeyer J in *Mount Isa Mines Ltd v Pusey* (1970) 125 CLR 383 at 402 referred to this requirement as a "comfortable latitudinarian doctrine".
81. [1976] 2 NSWLR 72.
82. A causal connection between the plaintiff's neurosis and the defendant's negligent conduct was also lacking. The mental damage was considered to have been caused by the plaintiff's own antecedent decision to allow the defendant to drive her car.
83. [1976] 2 NSWLR 72 per Moffitt P at 75-76, per Samuels JA at 89-90. Moffitt P took the view that "psychiatric damage arising from circumstances external to the trauma caused by the negligent act can . . . be classified according to the kind of chain that links the damage with the negligent act". Glass JA dissented, refusing to qualify the "kind of damage" criterion in this manner.
84. (1970) 125 CLR 383.
85. See particularly per Barwick CJ at 390, per McTiernan J at 392, per Menzies J at 393, per Windeyer J at 402, per Walsh J at 410-412, 414.

by Brennan J in *Jaensch v Coffey*.[86] Once the plaintiff has sustained the kind of injury which could reasonably have been foreseen as the result of the trauma caused by the tortfeasor (namely, damage to the mind), not only is it immaterial that the precise medical category of psychiatric injury was unforeseeable, but also foresight of the precise mental or psychological process that *led* to the condition in question is unnecessary.[87]

Lord Bridge in *McLoughlin v O'Brian* suggested that there were at least two theoretically possible approaches to establishing that the kind of damage suffered by the plaintiff was foreseeable:

"The first is that the judge should receive the evidence of psychiatrists as to the degree of probability that the particular cause would produce the particular effect, and apply to that the appropriate legal test of reasonable foreseeability as the criterion of the defendant's duty of care. The second is that the judge, relying on his own opinion of the operation of cause and effect in psychiatric medicine, as fairly representative of that of the educated layman, should treat himself as the reasonable man and form his own view from the primary facts whether the proven chain of cause and effect was reasonably foreseeable. In principle, I think there is much to be said for the first approach. Foreseeability, in any given set of circumstances, is ultimately a question of fact. If a claim in negligence depends on whether some defect in a complicated piece of machinery was foreseeably a cause of injury, I apprehend that the judge will decide that question on the basis of the expert evidence of engineers. But the authorities give no support to this approach in relation to the foreseeability of psychiatric illness. The judges, in all the decisions we have been referred to, have assumed that it lay within their own competence to determine whether the plaintiff's 'nervous shock' (as lawyers quaintly persist in calling it) was in any given circumstances a sufficiently foreseeable consequence of the defendant's act or omission relied on as negligent to bring the plaintiff within the scope of those to whom the defendant owed a duty of care. To depart from this practice and treat the question of foreseeable causation in this field, and hence the scope of the defendant's duty, as a question of fact to be determined in the light of the expert evidence adduced in each case would, no doubt, be too large an innovation in the law to be regarded as properly within the competence, even since the liberating 1966 practice direction . . . of your Lordships' House. Moreover, psychiatric medicine is far from being an exact science. The opinions of its practitioners may differ widely. Clearly it is desirable in this, as any other, field that the law should achieve such a measure of certainty as is consistent with the demands of justice. It would seem that the consensus of informed judicial opinion is probably the best yardstick available to determine whether, in any given circumstances, the

---

86. (1984) 155 CLR 549 at 563. See also *Brice v Brown* [1984] 1 All ER 997 per Stuart-Smith J at 1007; *Attia v British Gas Plc* [1988] QB 304 per Dillon LJ at 312; *Hevican v Ruane* [1991] 3 All ER 65 per Mantell J at 70. Note also *Ostrowski v Lotto* (1968) 2 DLR (3d) 440 where it was held that mental illness was not a kind of damage that was foreseeable as a consequence of negligence in the performance of an operation.
87. *Brice v Brown* [1984] 1 All ER 997 per Stuart-Smith J at 1007.

emotional trauma resulting from the death or injury of third parties, or indeed the threat of such death or injury, ex hypothesi attributable to the defendant's negligence, was a foreseeable cause in law, as well as the actual cause in fact, of the plaintiff's psychiatric or psychosomatic illness. But the word I would emphasise in the foregoing sentence is 'informed'. For too long earlier generations of judges have regarded psychiatry and psychiatrists with suspicion, if not hostility. Now, I venture to hope, that attitude has quite disappeared. No judge who has spent any length of time trying personal injury claims in recent years would doubt that physical injuries can give rise not only to organic but also to psychiatric disorders. The sufferings of the patient from the latter are no less real and frequently no less painful and disabling than from the former. Likewise, I would suppose that the legal profession well understands that an acute emotional trauma, like a physical trauma, can well cause a psychiatric illness in a wide range of circumstances and in a wide range of individuals whom it would be wrong to regard as having any abnormal psychological make-up. It is in comparatively recent times that these insights have come to be generally accepted by the judiciary. It is only by giving effect to these insights and the developing law of negligence that we can do justice to an important, though no doubt small, class of plaintiffs whose genuine psychiatric illnesses are caused by negligent defendants."[88]

According to Lord Bridge, then, the foreseeability of psychiatric damage is not purely and simply a question of fact, but is an issue to be decided by the judge, approaching the matter from a commonsense point of view, enlightened by progressive awareness of mental illness.[89] In this manner the judge reaches a decision as to whether the mental harm suffered was the kind of harm which the defendant should have foreseen might befall a foreseeable plaintiff. However, even if both the foreseeability questions are satisfied, it is clear that establishing a duty of care involves additional elements, now to be considered.

The other general duty requirements

When, in the first half of the 19th century, negligence was finally recognised as an independent tort,[90] the need for limitations on liability quickly became apparent. It is in this context that the duty of care element originated.[91] Its earlier history is shrouded in obscurity, but it seems clear that it was recognised at least by 1842, when the privity requirement was

88. [1983] 1 AC 410 at 432.
89. Ibid at 443. Note also *Mullally v Bus Eireann* (unreported, Irish HC, 13 June 1991) where Denham J referred to "our ever advancing awareness of medical knowledge of mental illness".
90. On the history of negligence see P H Winfield, "The History of Negligence in the Law of Torts" (1926) 42 LQR 184. It is probable that negligence only became an independent tort with the decision in *Williams v Holland* (1833) 10 Bing 112; 131 ER 848 which allowed an action for unintentional harm to be brought either in trespass or in case: see M J Prichard, "Trespass, Case and the Rule in Williams v Holland" [1964] CLJ 234; S F C Milsom, op cit, n 5 at 392-400; J H Baker, *Introduction to English Legal History* (3rd ed, 1990), 464-467.
91. The most well-known historical account of duty is P H Winfield, "Duty in Tortious Negligence" (1934) 34 Col L Rev 41.

imposed to limit the tort liability of manufacturers and the like to persons to whom they were in a contractual relationship.[92] Policy considerations, and in particular the need to keep negligence liability within proper bounds, have thus always been the most important raison d'être of the duty concept.

In the 19th and early 20th centuries the duty requirement was essentially a collection of particular rules governing particular negligence situations, not reducible to any kind of general principle. Indeed, today, after a number of theories have come and gone, the idea that "the law should develop novel categories of negligence incrementally and by analogy with established categories",[93] rather than by reference to a general principle, is still strongly supported.[94] Nevertheless, over the past one hundred years, a number of attempts have been made to find some general principle of duty which would either explain or supersede all the particular rules. The first such attempt, that of Brett MR in *Heaven v Pender*,[95] suggested that a duty would arise whenever a person was by circumstances placed in such a position with regard to another that everyone of ordinary sense who did think would recognise that a failure to use ordinary care and skill would cause danger of injury to the other's person or property. This proposition, which in essence reduced duty to no more than "a simple test of attributed foresight",[96] was quickly recognised as too wide, not least by Brett MR himself. In *Le Lievre v Gould*,[97] he said that his statement had to be limited to situations where there was a degree of physical proximity between the defendant and the persons or property affected. However, 50 years later, Lord Atkin in *Donoghue v Stevenson*[98] returned to the problem.

92. *Winterbottom v Wright* (1842) 10 M & W 109; 152 ER 402. The case was concerned with a defective mail coach which, owing to negligence in its construction, broke down injuring a third party (a mail coachman) who was held to have no cause of action in tort or contract. Alderson B stated emphatically at 405: "The only safe rule is to confine the right to recover to those who enter into the contract; if we go one step beyond that there is no reason why we should not go 50." Similarly Lord Abinger CB said at 405: "Unless we confine the operation of [contracts of repair] to the parties who entered into them, the most absurd and outrageous consequences, to which I can see no limit, would ensue." Contracts were, it was thought, liable to be "ripped open" by tort actions if such a restriction was not imposed. In *Donoghue v Stevenson* [1932] AC 562 at 588 Lord Buckmaster (dissenting) referred to *Winterbottom v Wright* and concluded: "This case seems to me to show that the manufacturer of any article is not liable to a third party injured by negligent construction for there can be nothing in the character of a coach to place it in a special category." See C E Labatt, "Negligence in Relation to Privity of Contract" (1900) 16 LQR 168; V Palmer, "Why Privity Entered Tort—An Historical Re-examination of Winterbottom v Wright" (1983) 27 Am J Leg Hist 85.
93. *Sutherland Shire Council v Heyman* (1985) 157 CLR 424 per Brennan J at 481.
94. See eg *Curran v Northern Ireland Co-ownership Housing Association* [1987] AC 718 per Lord Bridge at 726; *Yuen Kun Yeu v Attorney-General of Hong Kong* [1988] AC 175 per Lord Keith at 191; *Caparo Industries Plc v Dickman* [1990] 2 AC 605 per Lord Bridge at 618, per Lord Roskill at 626, per Lord Oliver at 633-634; *Murphy v Brentwood District Council* [1991] 1 AC 398 per Lord Keith at 461.
95. (1883) 11 QBD 503 at 509. The plaintiff, a ship's painter, was injured when scaffolding supplied by the defendant dock owner collapsed. His claim was allowed by Cotton and Bowen LJJ based on established rules of occupiers' liability.
96. *Alcock v Chief Constable of South Yorkshire Police* [1992] 1 AC 310 per Lord Oliver at 410.
97. *Le Lievre v Gould* [1893] 1 QB 491 per Lord Esher MR (formerly Sir Baliol Brett MR) at 497, per Bowen LJ at 502, per A L Smith LJ at 504. See also *Heaven v Pender* (1883) 11 QBD 503 per Cotton LJ at 516, per Bowen LJ at 517.
98. [1932] AC 562.

Echoing the sentiments of Brett MR, he said: "There must be, and is, some general conception of relations giving rise to a duty of care, of which the particular cases found in the books are but instances."[99] He found this principle in the well known proposition already quoted[100] that a person must take reasonable care to avoid acts or omissions which he or she can reasonably foresee would be likely to injure his or her neighbour—anyone so closely and directly affected that the person ought reasonably to have them in contemplation when directing his or her mind to the acts or omissions in question.

This remains the most enduring of all the attempts to state a general test of duty, but it has had a chequered career.[101] For many years the predominant judicial attitude was that it was too wide to serve as anything but a general yardstick against which potential new duties could be measured, and that the real importance of *Donoghue v Stevenson* was in the recognition that a manufacturer of products owed a duty to the ultimate consumer and the rejection of the privity of contract fallacy adopted 90 years before.[102] However, in the 1970s the neighbour principle became the basis of new attempts to generalise a test of duty. In *Home Office v Dorset Yacht Co Ltd*[103] Lord Reid suggested that the time had come to recognise that the neighbour principle ought to apply unless there was some justification or valid explanation for its exclusion. This statement led Lord Wilberforce in *Anns v Merton London Borough Council*[104] to formulate a two-stage test of duty. He suggested that one should first ask whether, as between the defendant and the plaintiff, there was a "sufficient relationship of proximity or neighbourhood, such that, in the reasonable contemplation of the former, carelessness on his part may be likely to cause damage to the latter". If so, there would be a prima facie duty of care. It was then necessary to consider whether there were "any considerations which ought to negative, or to reduce or limit the scope of the duty or the class of person to whom it is owed or the damages to which a breach of it may give rise".[105]

For a few years, the *"Anns* two-step"[106] was much in vogue as a general test of duty, and was the catalyst for significant expansions of liability in

---

99. Ibid at 580.
100. See above, p 65.
101. See R F V Heuston, "Donoghue v Stevenson in Retrospect" (1957) 20 MLR 1; R F V Heuston, "Donoghue v Stevenson: A Fresh Appraisal" [1971] CLP 37; A C Hutchinson & D Morgan, "Snail Tales—A Golden Trail" (1982) 132 NLJ 502; J C Smith & P Burns, "Donoghue v Stevenson: The Not-So-Golden Anniversary" (1983) 46 MLR 147; A M Linden, "The Good Neighbour on Trial: A Fountain of Sparkling Wisdom" (1983) 17 UBCLR 67; J C Smith & P Burns, "The Good Neighbour on Trial: Good Neighbours Make Bad Law" (1983) 17 UBCLR 93. Note also A Rodger, "Lord MacMillan's speech in Donoghue v Stevenson" (1992) 108 LQR 236.
102. See especially *Hedley Byrne & Co v Heller & Partners* [1964] AC 465 per Lord Devlin at 524-525; *Home Office v Dorset Yacht Co Ltd* [1970] AC 1004 per Lord Diplock at 1060.
103. *Home Office v Dorset Yacht Co Ltd* [1970] AC 1004 at 1027.
104. [1978] AC 728.
105. Ibid at 751-752.
106. See M Davies, "Negligently Caused Economic Loss" (1985) 16 UWALR 209 at 216.

a number of directions, [107] not least in *Anns* itself, which confirmed that
local authorities could be held liable for negligent building approvals which
allowed defective buildings to be constructed. *Anns* was utilised not only by
English courts [108] but also those in Australia, [109] Canada, [110] New Zealand [111]
and Ireland. [112] However, it was not long before cracks began to appear in
the *Anns* general principle, just as they had done in the dwellings which
were the subject of the proceedings in that case. Starting with the High
Court of Australia in *Sutherland Shire Council v Heyman*, [113] the courts
began to question the idea of a duty that applied unless there was some valid
reason for its exclusion, particularly if it was founded solely on

107. In particular *Ross v Caunters* [1980] Ch 297 (liability of solicitors to persons other than
their clients); *Schiffahrt & Kohlen GmbH v Chelsea Maritime Ltd* [1982] QB 481; *The
Nea Tyhi* [1982] 1 Lloyd's Rep 606 (liability to buyer under cif contract before property
passes—a doctrine now repudiated by *Leigh & Sillivan Ltd v Aliakmon Shipping Co Ltd*
[1986] AC 785); *Junior Books Ltd v Veitchi Co Ltd* [1983] AC 520 (liability of
manufacturers for financial loss suffered by consumers—a decison now virtually
distinguished out of existence: see eg *Tate & Lyle Food and Distribution Ltd v Greater
London Council* [1983] 2 AC 509; *Candlewood Navigation Corporation Ltd v Mitsui
OSK Lines Ltd* [1986] AC 1; *Muirhead v Industrial Tank Specialities Ltd* [1986] QB 507;
Simaan General Contracting Co v Pilkington Glass Ltd (No 2) [1988] QB 758; *Greater
Nottingham Co-operative Society Ltd v Cementation Piling & Foundations Ltd* [1989]
QB 71; *D & F Estates Ltd v Church Commissioners for England* [1989] AC 177; *Murphy
v Brentwood District Council* [1991] 1 AC 398; *Department of the Environment v
Thomas Bates & Son* [1991] 1 AC 499).
108. *Batty v Metropolitan Property Realisations* [1978] QB 554; *McLoughlin v O'Brian* [1981]
1 QB 599; *Latchford v Beirne* [1981] 3 All ER 705; *Yianni v Edwin Evans & Sons* [1982]
QB 438; *Acrecrest Ltd v W S Hattrell & Partners* [1983] QB 260; *McLoughlin v O'Brian*
[1983] 1 AC 410; *Tate & Lyle Food and Distribution Ltd v Greater London Council*
[1983] 2 AC 509; *P Perl (Exporters) Ltd v Camden London Borough Council* [1984] QB
342; *Inland Revenue Commissioners v Hoogstraten* [1985] QB 1077; *Lawton v BOC
Transhield* [1987] ICR 7; *Hill v Chief Constable of West Yorkshire* [1988] QB 60.
109. *L Shaddock & Associates Pty Ltd v Parramatta City Council* (1978) 38 LGRA 23;
Wyong Shire Council v Shirt (1980) 146 CLR 40 per Mason J at 44; *Sutherland Shire
Council v Heyman* [1982] 2 NSWLR 618; *Minister Administering the Environmental
Planning and Assessment Act 1979 v San Sebastian Pty Ltd* [1983] 2 NSWLR 268; *Clarke
v Shire of Gisborne* [1984] VR 971; *Hackshaw v Shaw* (1984) 155 CLR 614; *Travis v
Vanderloos* (1984) 54 LGRA 268; *Delaney v F S Evans & Sons Pty Ltd* (1984) 58 LGRA
395; *Sasin v Commonwealth* (1984) 52 ALR 299; *Robertson v Swincer* (1989) 52 SASR
356.
110. *Pugliese v National Capital Commission* (1977) 79 DLR (3d) 592; *Ordog v District of
Mission* (1980) 110 DLR (3d) 718; *Barratt v District of North Vancouver* (1980) 114 DLR
(3d) 577; *Diversified Holdings v The Queen in Right of the Province of British Columbia*
(1982) 143 DLR (3d) 529; *Nicholls v Township of Richmond* (1983) 145 DLR (3d) 362;
Baird v The Queen (1983) 148 DLR (3d) 1; *City of Kamloops v Nielsen* (1984) 10 DLR
(4th) 641; *BDC Ltd v Hofstrand Farms Ltd* (1986) 26 DLR (4th) 1; *Rothfield v
Manolakos* (1989) 63 DLR (4th) 449; *Just v British Columbia* (1989) 64 DLR (4th) 689.
111. *Scott Group v McFarlane* [1978] 1 NZLR 553; *Takaro Properties Ltd v Rowling* [1978]
2 NZLR 314; *J & J C Abrams Ltd v Ancliffe* [1978] 2 NZLR 420; *Mount Albert Borough
Council v Johnson* [1979] 2 NZLR 234; *R A & T J Carll Ltd v Berry* [1981] 2 NZLR
76; *Port Underwood Forests v Marlborough County Council* [1982] 1 NZLR 343; *Bruce
v Housing Corporation of New Zealand* [1982] 2 NZLR 28; *Allied Finance &
Investments Ltd v Haddow & Co* [1983] NZLR 22; *Gartside v Sheffield, Young & Ellis*
[1983] NZLR 37; *Meates v Attorney-General* [1983] NZLR 308; *Morton v Douglas
Homes Ltd* [1984] 2 NZLR 548; *New Zealand Forest Products v Attorney-General* [1986]
NZLR 14; *Brown v Heathcote County Council* [1986] 1 NZLR 76; *Stieller v Porirua City
Council* [1986] 1 NZLR 84; *Craig v East Coast Bays City Council* [1986] 1 NZLR 99.
112. *Siney v Dublin Corporation* [1980] IR 400; *Ward v McMaster* [1988] IR 337.
113. (1985) 157 CLR 424.

foreseeability—though whether issues other than this were relevant at the first stage of the inquiry remained the subject of dispute.[114] In *Sutherland Shire Council v Heyman*, where the facts were similar to *Anns*, the High Court rejected the idea that local authorities, and thus ultimately ratepayers, should be held responsible for defective building.[115] Subsequent decisions likewise dissented from the *Anns* general principle.[116] The English courts, too, have put *Anns* to rout. The first case to call the *Anns* test into question was *Governors of the Peabody Donation Fund v Sir Lindsay Parkinson & Co Ltd*,[117] where Lord Keith cautioned against treating Lord Wilberforce's words as definitive.[118] Subsequent decisions of the House of Lords[119] and the Privy Council[120] took up the view that no single general principle could provide a practical test applicable to every situation, a process completed by the decision of the House of Lords in *Caparo Industries Plc v Dickman*[121] which seems to mark the final rejection of Lord Wilberforce's test. *Murphy v Brentwood District Council*[122] completed the demise of *Anns* by overruling the decision itself and all subsequent decisions which had imposed liability based on the

114. For a range of differing interpretations see *Sutherland Shire Council v Heyman* (1985) 157 CLR 424 per Gibbs CJ at 440, per Brennan J at 477, per Deane J at 506; *Leigh & Sillivan Ltd v Aliakmon Shipping Co Ltd* [1986] AC 785 per Lord Brandon at 815-816; *Takaro Properties Ltd v Rowling* [1986] 1 NZLR 22 per Woodhouse J at 57, per Somers J at 73; *Yuen Kun Yeu v Attorney-General of Hong Kong* [1988] AC 175 per Lord Keith at 191-192. See generally J A Smillie, "Principle, Policy and Negligence" (1984) 11 NZULR 111.

115. *Sutherland Shire Council v Heyman* (1985) 157 CLR 424 per Gibbs CJ at 440, per Brennan J at 477, per Deane J at 506-508.

116. *San Sebastian Pty Ltd v Minister Administering the Environmental Planning and Assessment Act 1979* (1986) 162 CLR 340 per Brennan J at 367; *Gala v Preston* (1991) 172 CLR 243 per Brennan J at 262. For decisions of State courts adopting the *Sutherland Shire Council v Heyman* approach see eg *Parker v Housing Trust* (1986) 41 SASR 493; *Parramatta City Council v Lutz* (1988) 12 NSWLR 293; *Casley-Smith v F S Evans* (1989) Aust Torts Rep 80-227; *Opat v National Mutual Life Association of Australia Ltd* [1992] 1 VR 283; *Curran v Greater Taree City Council* (1992) Aust Torts Rep 81-152.

117. [1985] AC 210.

118. Ibid at 240-241.

119. *Leigh & Sillivan Ltd v Aliakmon Shipping Co Ltd* [1986] AC 785; *Curran v Northern Ireland Housing Co-ownership Association Ltd* [1987] AC 718; *CBS Songs v Amstrad Plc* [1988] AC 1013; *Hill v Chief Constable of West Yorkshire* [1989] AC 53. Note also the English Court of Appeal decisions in *Investors in Industry Commercial Properties Ltd v South Bedfordshire District Council* [1986] QB 1034; *Muirhead v Industrial Tank Ltd* [1986] QB 507; *Jones v Stroud District Council* [1986] 1 WLR 1141; *Jones v Department of Employment* [1989] QB 1.

120. *Candlewood Navigation Corporation Ltd v Mitsui OSK Lines Ltd* [1986] AC 1; *Yuen Kun Yeu v Attorney-General of Hong Kong* [1986] AC 175; *Tai Hing Cotton Mill Ltd v Liu Chong Hing Bank* [1986] AC 80; *Rowling v Takaro Properties Ltd* [1988] AC 473; *Davis v Radcliffe* [1990] 1 WLR 821.

121. [1990] 2 AC 605.

122. [1991] 1 AC 398, noted by J G Fleming (1990) 106 LQR 525; T Weir [1991] CLJ 24. See also *Department of the Environment v Thomas Bates & Son* [1991] 1 AC 499. On these developments see R Cooke, "An Impossible Distinction" (1991) 107 LQR 46; I N D Wallace, "Anns Beyond Repair" (1991) 107 LQR 228; J Stapleton, "Duty of Care and Economic Loss: A Wider Agenda" (1991) 107 LQR 249; D Howarth, "Negligence after Murphy: Time to Rethink" [1991] CLJ 58; M Giles & E Szyszczak, "Negligence and Defective Buildings: Demolishing the Foundations of Anns?" (1991) 11 Leg Stud 85; *Negligence after Murphy v Brentwood District Council* (Papers presented at a seminar held by the Legal Research Foundation at the University of Auckland, 7 Mar 1991).

reasoning in that case.[123] Though the latest decisions in New Zealand show no signs of dissatisfaction with *Anns*,[124] those in Canada are more equivocal.[125] The English and Australian decisions cannot but have some influence in these jurisdictions.[126]

What, then, is the current thinking of the courts on duty issues? In Australia an expanded concept of "proximity" has well and truly taken root.[127] Its current status is essentially attributable to Deane J. The contemporary formulation of the notion was first outlined by him in *Jaensch v Coffey*[128] as a response to the proposition that reasonable foreseeability could be a sufficient test of duty. His Honour found this concept present in Lord Atkin's neighbour principle and saw it as the factor which unified all the particular rules which had been laid down across the wide range of individual duty situations. Proximity was a flexible concept:

"It involves the notion of nearness or closeness and embraces physical proximity (in the sense of space and time) between the person or property of the plaintiff and the person or property of the defendant, circumstantial proximity such as an overriding relationship of employer and employee or of a professional man and his client and

123. *Dutton v Bognor Regis Urban District Council* [1972] 1 QB 373, the precursor to *Anns*, was also overruled.
124. See S M D Todd et al, *The Law of Torts in New Zealand* (1991), 121-123; Cooke, op cit, n 122; *Deloitte Haskins & Sells v National Mutual Life Nominees Ltd* (1991) 3 NZLBC 102,259; *South Pacific Manufacturing Co Ltd v New Zealand Security Consultants & Investigations Ltd* [1992] 2 NZLR 282, noted by S Todd (1992) 108 LQR 360; *Lester v White* [1992] 2 NZLR 483, commented upon by Smellie J, "Murphy—A Response from the High Court of New Zealand" [1992] ICLR 237. Prior to these cases, in *Williams v Attorney-General* [1990] 1 NZLR 646, noted by S Todd (1990) 14 NZULR 172, the court relied on post-*Anns* authorities limiting Lord Wilberforce's general principle, particularly *Leigh & Sillivan Ltd v Aliakmon Shipping Co Ltd* [1986] AC 785, and in *Balfour v Attorney-General* [1991] 1 NZLR 519 Hardie Boys J said at 528 that he did not have to decide how the demise of *Anns* was to be viewed in New Zealand. See also *Mainguard Packaging Ltd v Hilton Haulage Ltd* [1990] 1 NZLR 360.
125. In *Birchard v Alberta Securities Commission* (1987) 54 Alta LR (2d) 302 Agrios J elected to follow the decisions expressing doubts about *Anns*. Lord Wilberforce's test was critically reviewed in *Romaniuk v The Queen in Right of Alberta* (1988) 44 CCLT 148 per Miller ACJQB at 175-177 and in *Canadian National Railway Co v Norsk Pacific Steamship Co* (1990) 65 DLR (4th) 321 per Stone JA at 327-328. Cases decided after *Murphy* suggest that the law is unclear: see *Brewer Bros v Attorney-General of Canada* (1991) 80 DLR (4th) 321 per Stone JA at 340; *Oakville Storage & Forwarders Ltd v Canadian National Railway* (1991) 80 DLR (4th) 675 per Carthy JA at 696; *Abramovic v Canadian Pacific Ltd* (1991) 85 DLR (4th) 587 per Carthy JA at 595; *Armak Chemicals Ltd v Canadian National Railway* (1991) 3 OR (3d) 1 per Carthy JA at 23. Contrast *University of Regina v Pettick* (1991) 77 DLR (4th) 615 per Sherstobitoff JA (Vancise JA concurring) at 643, not following *Murphy*, and *Lake v Callison Outfitters Ltd* (1991) 58 BCLR (2d) 99 per Melnick J at 129 and *Privest Properties Ltd v Foundation Co of Canada* (1991) 61 BCLR (2d) 201 per Drost J at 211, assuming that *Anns* still applies.
126. See G H L Fridman, *The Law of Torts in Canada* (1989), Vol 1, 236 who suggests that in the light of the way Canadian courts have followed English precedents in this area the status of Lord Wilberforce's remarks may need to be reviewed; L Klar, *Tort Law* (1991), 125; contrast W S Schlosser, "What Has Become of Anns?" (1991) 29 Alta LR 673, especially at 696-700, suggesting that the Canadian position, for the most part, will not be affected by the demise of *Anns*; E A Cherniak & K F Stevens, "Two Steps Forward or One Step Back? Anns at the Crossroads in Canada" (1992) 20 Can Bus LJ 164; L A Reynolds & D A Hicks, "New Directions for the Civil Liability of Public Authorities in Canada" (1992) 71 Can BR 1.
127. This term has a long history. Its birth can probably be attributed to the judgment of Lord Esher MR in *Thomas v Quartermaine* (1887) 18 QBD 685 at 688.
128. (1984) 155 CLR 549.

causal proximity in the sense of the closeness or directness of the relationship of the particular act or cause of action and the injury sustained. . . . The identity and relative importance of the considerations relevant to an issue of proximity would obviously vary in different classes of case and the question whether the relationship is '*so*' close '*that*' the common law should recognise a duty of care in a new area or class of case is, as Lord Atkin foresaw, likely to be 'difficult' of resolution in that it may involve value judgments on matters of policy and degree. . . . The requirement of a 'relationship of proximity' is a touchstone and a control of the *categories* of case in which the common law will admit the existence of a duty of care and, given the general circumstances of a case in a new or developing area of the law of negligence, the question whether the relationship between plaintiff and defendant with reference to the allegedly negligent act possessed the requisite degree of proximity is a question of law to be resolved by the processes of legal reasoning by induction and deduction. The identification of the content of the criteria or rules which reflect that requirement in developing areas of the law should not, however, be either ostensibly or actually divorced from the considerations of public policy which underlie and enlighten it." [129]

In *Jaensch v Coffey* itself the other members of the court, with the possible exception of Gibbs CJ, [130] did not express themselves in these terms. In a series of subsequent decisions, however, nearly all the members of the High Court have come to tread the path of proximity. [131]

The problem with the proximity criterion is that it conceals more than it reveals. [132] Eight years have passed since Deane J's description of its chameleon-like nature and yet we are, in truth, no closer to an appreciation of its constitution or modus operandi. Asking whether a relationship is "proximate" is a very uncertain guide to whether a duty will be found to exist because the notion's inherent imprecision makes it possible for the

---

129. Ibid at 584-585.
130. Ibid at 553.
131. *Hackshaw v Shaw* (1984) 155 CLR 614 (Deane J); *Papatonakis v Australian Telecommunications Commission* (1985) 156 CLR 7 (Deane J); *Sutherland Shire Council v Heyman* (1985) 157 CLR 424 (Gibbs CJ, Wilson and Deane JJ); *Stevens v Brodribb Sawmilling Co Pty Ltd* (1986) 160 CLR 16 (Mason and Deane JJ); *San Sebastian Pty Ltd v Minister Administering the Environmental Planning and Assessment Act 1979* (1986) 162 CLR 340 (joint judgment of Gibbs CJ, Mason, Wilson and Dawson JJ); *Cook v Cook* (1986) 162 CLR 376 (joint judgment of Mason, Wilson, Deane and Dawson JJ); *Australian Safeways Stores Pty Ltd v Zaluzna* (1987) 162 CLR 479 (joint judgment of Mason, Wilson, Deane and Dawson JJ); *Hawkins v Clayton* (1988) 164 CLR 539 (Mason CJ; joint judgment of Wilson, Deane and Gaudron JJ); *Gala v Preston* (1991) 172 CLR 243 (joint judgment of Mason CJ, Deane, Gaudron and McHugh JJ).
132. See N J Mullany, "Proximity, Policy and Procrastination" (1992) 9 Aust Bar Rev 80; J Stone, *Precedent and Law* (1985), 254-255. See also Smillie, op cit, n 114; D Gardiner, "Jaensch v Coffey: Foresight, Proximity and Policy in the Duty of Care for Nervous Shock" (1985) 1 QITLJ 69; R Kidner, "Resiling from the Anns Principle: The Variable Nature of Proximity in Negligence" (1987) 7 Leg Stud 319; S Quinlan & D Gardiner, "New Developments with Respect to the Duty of Care in Tort" (1988) 62 ALJ 347; J A Smillie, "The Foundation of a Duty of Care in Negligence" (1989) 15 Mon ULR 302; J F Keeler, "The Proximity of Past and Future: Australian and British Approaches to Analysing the Duty of Care" (1989) 12 Adel LR 93.

word to mean whatever one wants it to mean. [133] As Goff LJ pointed out in *Leigh & Sillivan Ltd v Aliakmon Shipping Co Ltd*, as soon as "proximity is no longer treated as expressing a relationship founded simply on foreseeability of damage, it ceases to have an ascertainable meaning; and it cannot therefore provide a criterion for liability". [134] The core proximity notions of "nearness" and "closeness" provide illusory assistance to courts, for a duty to take care may arise despite great distances between parties or be absent notwithstanding the presence of a very close and direct relationship. Its nebulous and shapeless character is apt to camouflage the true basis of judicial decision making, allowing a curtain to be drawn across the process of determining whether a duty exists. This is a process in which policy considerations are inevitably at work, and which would be much better understood if those considerations were brought out in the open. This was appreciated by at least one Canadian judge in the 1950s [135] and by other judges, [136] not least Lord Denning, [137] in the 1960s and 1970s. The true influence of administrative, economic, social, ethical, moral, philosophical, justice and public interest factors must be articulated, rather than subsumed within such an ill-equipped and impoverished doctrinal housing. On the Australian High Court, Brennan J has consistently refused to indorse the proximity approach, preferring to identify the considerations which affirm or negate a duty of care rather than simply to assert the presence or absence of proximity. [138] But at present he remains a voice crying in the wilderness. [139]

133. " 'When *I* use a word,' Humpty Dumpty said, in rather a scornful tone, 'it means just what I choose it to mean—neither more nor less' ": L Carroll, *Through the Looking Glass and What Alice Found There* (1871), Ch 6.
134. [1985] QB 350 at 395.
135. *Nova Mink Ltd v Trans-Canada Airlines* [1951] 2 DLR 241 per MacDonald J at 254. On the relevance of policy considerations in Canada see Linden, op cit, n 25 at 258-260; Fridman, op cit, n 126 at 245-247; Klar, op cit, n 126 at 120-125.
136. See eg *Hedley Byrne & Co v Heller & Partners* [1964] AC 465; *Weller & Co v Foot and Mouth Disease Research Institute* [1966] 1 QB 569; *McCarthy v Wellington City* [1966] NZLR 481; *Rondel v Worsley* [1969] AC 191; *Smith v Jenkins* (1970) 119 CLR 397; *Home Office v Dorset Yacht Co Ltd* [1970] AC 1004; *Morgans v Launchbury* [1973] AC 127; *Caltex Oil (Australia) Pty Ltd v Dredge 'Willemstad'* (1976) 136 CLR 529; *Saif Ali v Sydney Mitchell & Co* [1980] AC 198; *McKay v Essex Area Health Authority* [1982] QB 1166; *Tai Hing Cotton Mill v Liu Chong Hing Bank* [1986] AC 80.
137. See his judgments in *Dorset Yacht Co Ltd v Home Office* [1969] 2 QB 412; *SCM (United Kingdom) Ltd v W J Whittall & Son Ltd* [1971] 1 QB 337; *Launchbury v Morgans* [1971] 2 QB 245; *Nettleship v Weston* [1971] 2 QB 691; *Dutton v Bognor Regis Urban District Council* [1972] 1 QB 373; *Spartan Steel & Alloys Ltd v Martin & Co (Contractors) Ltd* [1973] QB 27.
138. See his judgments in *Sutherland Shire Council v Heyman* (1985) 157 CLR 424; *Stevens v Brodribb Sawmilling Co Pty Ltd* (1986) 160 CLR 16; *San Sebastian Pty Ltd v Minister Administering the Environmental Planning and Assessment Act 1979* (1986) 162 CLR 340; *Cook v Cook* (1986) 162 CLR 376; *Australian Safeways Stores Pty Ltd v Zaluzna* (1987) 162 CLR 479; *Hawkins v Clayton* (1988) 164 CLR 539; *Gala v Preston* (1991) 172 CLR 243.
139. But see *Gala v Preston* (1991) 172 CLR 243 where three judges focused directly on policy considerations rather than principle in order to deny relief to a drunken teenage joyrider injured when the driver of the stolen car in which he was a passenger lost control of the vehicle, colliding with a tree. Brennan, Dawson and Toohey JJ openly based their decisions to differing degrees on public policy, deriving minimal assistance from proximity. Their reasoning in this case reflects an encouraging recognition that the proximity concept will not always be a "touchstone" in the determination of a duty of

The English courts, in their retreat from *Anns* and search for an alternative, have also ratified the notion of proximity, not so much as an all-embracing test but as one of a number of considerations to be taken into account. The leading statement of the current English position is that of Lord Bridge in *Caparo Industries Plc v Dickman*:

> "What emerges is that, in addition to the foreseeability of damage, necessary ingredients in any situation giving rise to a duty of care are that there should exist between the party owing the duty and the party to whom it is owed a relationship characterised by the law as one of 'proximity' or 'neighbourhood' and that the situation should be one in which the court considers it fair, just and reasonable that the law should impose a duty of a given scope upon the one party for the benefit of the other. But it is implicit in the passages referred to that the concepts of proximity and fairness embodied in these additional ingredients are not susceptible of any such precise definition as would be necessary to give them utility as practical tests, but amount in effect to little more than convenient labels to attach to the features of different specific situations which, on a detailed examination of all the circumstances, the law recognises pragmatically as giving rise to a duty of care of a given scope. Whilst recognising, of course, the importance of the underlying general principles common to the whole field of negligence, I think the law has now moved in the direction of attaching greater significance to the more traditional categorisation of distinct and recognisable situations as guides to the existence, the scope and limits of the varied duties of care which the law imposes."[140]

Though the influence of the Australian jurisprudence is clear, proximity has not taken over as completely. Not only foreseeability, but also ideas of fairness, justice and reasonableness, openly play their part in the determination of duty—and the latter ideas make it easier for policy issues to come to the surface. Policy considerations were clearly discernible in, for example, *Hill v Chief Constable of West Yorkshire*[141] where the House of Lords dismissed an action against the police for alleged negligence in failing to apprehend the Yorkshire Ripper sooner than they did, and in *Murphy v Brentwood District Council*[142] in which the House of Lords departed from *Anns* and held that local councils should not be liable for pure economic loss suffered as a result of bad building, merely through failure to ensure compliance with building regulations and by-laws.

139. *Continued*
     care: see Mullany, op cit, n 132. The extra-curial comments and criticisms of McHugh J in "Neighbourhood, Proximity and Reliance" in P D Finn (ed), *Essays on Torts* (1989), 5 at 36-42 are also significant for the future of proximity in Australia.
140. [1990] 2 AC 605 at 617-618. Other statements include *Governors of the Peabody Donation Fund v Sir Lindsay Parkinson & Co Ltd* [1985] AC 210 per Lord Keith at 240-241; *Hill v Chief Constable of West Yorkshire* [1988] QB 60 per Fox LJ at 68; *Caparo Industries Plc v Dickman* [1989] QB 653 per Bingham LJ at 678-679, per Taylor LJ at 697; *Murphy v Brentwood District Council* [1991] 1 AC 398 per Lord Oliver at 487; *Punjab National Bank v de Boinville* [1992] 3 All ER 104 per Staughton LJ at 116-117. Note *Smith v Eric S Bush* [1990] 1 AC 831 where the House of Lords employed the "fair and reasonable" standard of the *Unfair Contract Terms Act* 1977 (UK), s 2(2).
141. [1989] 1 AC 53.
142. [1991] 1 AC 398.

How are these principles applied in psychiatric damage cases? What, in addition to foreseeability, must be shown in such cases to establish a duty not to inflict damage to the psyche? Recent decisions of high authority in Australia, England and Canada are of considerable assistance in answering this question.

It should first be noted that there are straightforward cases of negligence—cases of physical injury suffered in road and work accidents—where it now seems to be accepted without question that once the requirements of foreseeability are satisfied no further duty issue exists. [143] This had led plaintiffs in recent cases before the highest courts in Australia and England to argue that foreseeability, without more, gives rise to a duty not to cause psychiatric damage. [144]

The major foundation for this argument was *McLoughlin v O'Brian* [145] where the House of Lords unanimously allowed the appeal of a plaintiff who never went to the scene of an accident but suffered psychiatric damage through seeing wounded members of her family in hospital. In coming to this decision, Lord Bridge [146] and Lord Scarman [147] appear to have rejected considerations of policy as irrelevant and held that liability should be determined purely on questions of principle. Lord Bridge, in particular, can perhaps be regarded as suggesting that foreseeability without more was sufficient. Their approach was roundly criticised by a third member of the court, Lord Edmund-Davies. [148] But the most important judgment in this case, that of Lord Wilberforce, clearly regards foreseeability alone as an insufficient criterion of liability, and policy considerations as highly relevant [149]—and this may suggest that Lord Wilberforce never intended the first of his two stages in *Anns* [150] to be limited to the issue of foreseeability. It was as part of the policy element of liability that Lord Wilberforce identified the three elements that were inherent in any psychiatric injury claim, [151] elements which have often provided the

---

143. See eg *Alcock v Chief Constable of South Yorkshire Police* [1992] 1 AC 310 per Lord Keith at 396, per Lord Jauncey at 419. One of the first to make this point was P S Atiyah, *Accidents, Compensation and the Law* (1970), 48 (see now P Cane, *Atiyah's Accidents, Compensation and the Law* (4th ed, 1987), 63-65). Note also the suggestion of Lord Reid in *Home Office v Dorset Yacht Co Ltd* [1970] AC 1004 at 1027 that the neighbour principle should apply unless there was some justification or explanation for its exclusion: see above, p 75. See however Deane J in *Jaensch v Coffey* (1984) 155 CLR 549 at 581-582, suggesting that proximity is an essential element in such cases also, even if not separately identified.

144. *Jaensch v Coffey* (1984) 155 CLR 549; *Alcock v Chief Constable of South Yorkshire Police* [1992] 1 AC 310.

145. [1983] 1 AC 410.

146. Ibid at 441-443. But quaere whether Lord Bridge is totally rejecting the relevance of policy: see P Handford, "Shock and Policy: McLoughlin v O'Brian" (1983) 15 UWALR 398 at 409-410. His later judgment in *Caparo Industries Plc v Dickman* [1990] 2 AC 605, quoted above, p 81, clearly affirms the relevance of policy.

147. [1983] 1 AC 410 at 429-431.

148. Ibid at 426-428.

149. Ibid at 421-423. Lord Russell also regarded policy as a relevant consideration: ibid at 429.

150. [1978] AC 728 at 751-752.

151. [1983] 1 AC 410 at 422. These three factors appear to have been drawn from the judgment of Tobriner J in the leading United States case of *Dillon v Legg* (1968) 441 P 2d 912; 69 Cal Rptr 72.

framework for discussion in more recent cases[152] and which have influenced the structure of this book. Those three elements are:

1. the class of persons whose claims should be recognised;

2. the physical proximity of such person to the accident;

3. the means by which the shock is caused.

In *Jaensch v Coffey*,[153] a case very similar on its facts to *McLoughlin v O'Brian*, the plaintiff argued before the High Court of Australia that to prove a duty of care it was sufficient to show foreseeability of psychiatric illness to a person in that position. The court however held that foreseeability was not the only test of duty. This appears most clearly in the judgments of Gibbs CJ[154] and Deane J[155]—Deane J outlining the additional factor of proximity which, as already explained,[156] represents the current approach of the majority of the High Court to duty issues. The other judges were less definite. Brennan J was against the recognition of new criteria of liability[157] and his judgment can be read as suggesting that foreseeability is a sufficient criterion. Dawson J found it unnecessary to resolve this issue.[158] Murphy J, in a short and rather offbeat judgment dealing mainly with accident compensation and social security, merely said that there were no acceptable reasons of public policy for limiting recovery.[159] In spite of the equivocation of some of the judges in this case, in later cases on psychiatric damage in State courts Australian judges, as one would expect, have adopted the approved doctrine of the High Court and viewed the duty issue in terms of proximity.[160]

In *Alcock v Chief Constable of South Yorkshire Police*,[161] the plaintiffs before the House of Lords once again argued that foreseeability was a sufficient test of duty, in spite of the rejection of this argument in the leading judgments in *Jaensch v Coffey*. The contention did not succeed. All four judgments specifically indorsed the view that duty was not just a matter of foreseeability. Lords Keith and Ackner simply referred to the extra element as "proximity", without going into any detail[162]—which may suggest that Deane J's approach is gaining ground in the House of Lords. Lord Oliver, who discussed the issue at greater length, also indorsed the notion of proximity,[163] dealing with it mainly from the perspective that

---

152. For example in *Alcock v Chief Constable of South Yorkshire Police* [1992] 1 AC 310, the judgments of Hidden J at first instance, Nolan LJ in the English Court of Appeal and Lord Ackner in the House of Lords.
153. (1984) 155 CLR 549.
154. Ibid at 552-554.
155. Ibid at 578-585.
156. Above, pp 78-80.
157. (1984) 155 CLR 549 at 571-573.
158. Ibid at 612.
159. Ibid at 558.
160. Note in particular the attempt of Derrington J in *Spence v Percy* (1990) Aust Torts Rep 81-039 to apply the test of causal proximity to hold the defendants liable for psychiatric damage to a mother caused as the result of her daughter's death, three years after the initial accident, and the rejection of this approach to proximity by the Full Court (1991) Aust Torts Rep 81-116.
161. [1992] 1 AC 310.
162. Ibid per Lord Keith at 396, per Lord Ackner at 402.
163. Ibid at 410-413.

in most psychiatric damage cases the plaintiff is not the primary victim. [164] However, his reference to the judgment of Lord Bridge in *Caparo Industries Plc v Dickman* [165] confirms that the basic requirements of duty in psychiatric damage cases are the same as for other areas of negligence law. These issues aside, it does seem clear that *Alcock v Chief Constable of South Yorkshire Police* is, in the ultimate analysis, a decision in which the incidence of duties of care was limited for policy reasons. [166]

The highest tribunal in Canada, the Supreme Court, has not yet had to consider these issues in the context of psychiatric injury. However, the British Columbia Court of Appeal decision in *Rhodes v Canadian National Railway* [167] shows that the latest Australian and English cases will be persuasive. The court rejected a claim by a mother who suffered psychiatric damage as the result of the death of her son in a train crash and the unco-operative conduct of the railway authorities during her struggle over the next few days to find out about his fate. It was clearly stated by a majority of the court that foreseeability alone was insufficient. Informed by a detailed consideration of the latest Australian, English and American authorities, the court affirmed the need for proximity (which was recognised to encompass policy elements). Taylor JA, with whom Wood JA agreed, held that, because the plaintiff's injury had been an indirect consequence of the railway's negligence, causal proximity was lacking. [168] Wallace JA also pointed to a lack of proximity, although he did not include causal proximity among the kinds of proximity that went to make up the overall concept. [169]

It seems likely that in psychiatric damage cases most courts will continue to concentrate on the three specific areas identified by Lord Wilberforce in *McLoughlin v O'Brian*. [170] Questions of proximity have not featured prominently, except at the highest level—for example, there is little on this in the *Alcock v Chief Constable of South Yorkshire Police* [171] judgments either of Hidden J or of the English Court of Appeal. In our view, many of the detailed limitations imposed in psychiatric damage cases should be rejected, and foreseeability should be the key issue, limited only by sound policy notions where appropriate. Whilst it is undeniable that the inclusion of the expansive concept of proximity in the liability equation currently

164. See below, pp 99-101.
165. [1990] 2 AC 605.
166. *Mouat v Clarke Boyce* [1992] 2 NZLR 559 per Cooke P at 569. See also *South Pacific Manufacturing Co Ltd v New Zealand Security Consultants & Investigations Ltd* [1992] 2 NZLR 282, where Cooke P at 295, commenting on the statement of Stocker LJ in the English Court of Appeal in *Alcock v Chief Constable of South Yorkshire Police* [1992] 1 AC 310 at 377 that "some limitations must be put upon what is reasonably foreseeable if a duty of care is not to be owed to the whole world at large", suggested that in statements such as this the English courts are coming to speak of reasonable foresight in a deliberately artificial sense. "There could be no objection to this usage, provided that it is acknowledged to be a special usage and is not employed to conceal the fact that the decision is one of policy rather than one as to what was reasonably foreseeable in fact."
167. (1991) 75 DLR (4th) 248.
168. Ibid at 296-298.
169. Ibid at 265.
170. [1983] 1 AC 410 at 422, outlined above, pp 82-83.
171. [1992] 1 AC 310.

represents the law both in Australia and in England, it is significant that, in addition to Brennan J's consistent stand on this issue, another of the present justices of the High Court has expressed doubt whether it will become a permanent feature of the law of negligence.[172] The sooner the proximity smokescreen clears to allow the truly important issues to be clearly seen the better.

Breach, causation and remoteness

Since psychiatric damage cases mainly involve duty issues, the other elements of negligence are usually comparatively straightforward.

Breach

Breach occasions no special difficulties. The plaintiff must establish that the defendant was negligent, that is, that the defendant failed to live up to the standard set by a reasonable person in his or her position.[173] In the words of Alderson B in *Blyth v Birmingham Waterworks Co*:

"Negligence is the omission to do something which a reasonable man, guided upon those considerations which ordinarily regulate the conduct of human affairs, would do, or doing something which a prudent and reasonable man would not do."[174]

Various factors, such as age, intelligence and experience, are taken into account in setting this standard,[175] though of course there are cases where it is not appropriate, pre-eminently when the defendant professes some special skill, in which case he or she must be judged by the standard not of the ordinary person but of a reasonable member of that profession.[176] Whatever the standard, various factors are applied in determining how the reasonable person would act in the situation in question—for example, the likelihood of harm,[177] its potential seriousness,[178] the cost of taking precautions,[179] and the benefits of the activity in which the defendant was

172. See McHugh, op cit, n 139 at 36.
173. The requirement was first stated by Tindal CJ in *Vaughan v Menlove* (1837) 3 Bing NC 468; 132 ER 490 at 493.
174. (1856) 11 Exch 781; 156 ER 1047 at 1049.
175. See eg Fleming, op cit, n 5 at 107-108, 112-114.
176. See *Bolam v Friern Hospital Management Committee* [1957] 1 WLR 582 per McNair J at 586; *Saif Ali v Sydney Mitchell & Co* [1980] AC 198; *Whitehouse v Jordan* [1981] 1 WLR 246; *Maynard v West Midlands Regional Health Authority* [1984] 1 WLR 634; *Sidaway v Governors of Bethlem Royal Hospital* [1985] AC 871; Fleming, op cit, n 5 at 108-112.
177. See eg *Bolton v Stone* [1951] AC 850 (compare *Miller v Jackson* [1977] QB 966); *Haley v London Electricity Board* [1965] AC 778; *Wyong Shire Council v Shirt* (1980) 146 CLR 40.
178. See eg *Paris v Stepney Borough Council* [1951] AC 367; *Bryden v Chief General Manager of the Health Department* (1987) Aust Torts Rep 80-075.
179. See eg *Ware's Taxi Ltd v Gilliham* [1949] 3 DLR 721; *Latimer v AEC Ltd* [1953] AC 643; *Caledonian Collieries Ltd v Speirs* (1957) 97 CLR 202; *Goldman v Hargrave* [1967] 1 AC 645; *Leakey v National Trust* [1980] QB 485; *Smith v Littlewoods Organisation Ltd* [1987] AC 241; *Ogwo v Taylor* [1988] AC 431. Note Judge Learned Hand's famous formula expressed in *United States v Carroll Towing Co* (1947) 159 F 2d 169 at 173: "The duty . . . is a function of three variables: (1) the probability that [the defendant's ship] will break away; (2) the gravity of the resulting injury if she does; (3) the burden of the adequate precautions. Possibly it serves to bring this notion into relief to state it

involved.[180]

It should be stressed that the relevant standard is the reasonable person in the defendant's position. Lord Russell in *McLoughlin v O'Brian*[181] pointed out that there was a tendency in the cases to talk of the reasonable *bystander*, an error which probably originated with Lord Wright in *Bourhill v Young*[182] who talked of the reasonable observer, a phrase echoed by Denning LJ in *King v Phillips*[183] and the English Court of Appeal in *McLoughlin v O'Brian*.[184] Lord Russell is of course correct. Questions of breach of the duty to prevent causing psychiatric injury must be assessed from the point of view of a reasonable person in the shoes of the tortfeasor.

Causation

There must be a causal link between the defendant's negligence and the psychiatric harm suffered by the plaintiff. Even where an admission of negligence has been made the plaintiff's right to judgment will hinge on it being shown that his or her loss was caused by the defendant's conduct.[185] This issue has generally been decided by asking if the latter would not have occurred but for the former.[186] The "but-for" test never resolved all causation issues, particularly the more complex ones such as those involving multiple causes or successive injuries,[187] and cases where some other factor (whether the intervention of a third party or the plaintiff, or some natural event)[188] came between the negligence and the damage were always more difficult, involving as they did not just pure causation questions but also issues of foreseeability and reasonableness.[189] Now, however, the

179. *Continued*

in algebraic terms: if the probability be called P; the injury L; and the burden B; liability depends on whether B is less than L multiplied by P; ie whether B<PL." This was one of the catalysts which inspired the development of the economic analysis of negligence law: see R A Posner, "A Theory of Negligence" (1972) 1 J Leg Stud 29 at 32; R A Posner, *Economic Analysis of Law* (4th ed, 1992), 163-167.

180. See eg *Daborn v Bath Tramways Motor Co* [1946] 2 All ER 333; *South Australian Ambulance Transport Inc v Wahlheim* (1948) 77 CLR 215 per Dixon J at 228; *Watt v Hertfordshire County Council* [1954] 1 WLR 835, especially per Denning LJ at 838; *Priestman v Colangelo and Smythson* (1959) 19 DLR (2d) 1.

181. [1983] 1 AC 410 at 429.

182. [1943] AC 92 at 111.

183. [1943] 1 QB 429 at 441.

184. [1981] QB 599 per Stephenson LJ at 613.

185. See *Rankine v Garton Sons & Co Ltd* [1979] 2 All ER 1185.

186. See eg *Barnett v Chelsea & Kensington Hospital Management Committee* [1969] 1 QB 428. For examples in psychiatric damage cases see *Griffiths v Canadian Pacific Railways* (1978) 6 BCLR 115 where it was held that the plaintiff's emotional injuries (which in any case probably did not amount to psychiatric damage) were not caused by viewing the accident; *Tash v Nicholas* (1981) 132 NLJ 989 where the plaintiff was unable to establish a causal link between the accident and a later depressive attack, one of a series of such attacks to which the plaintiff was susceptible.

187. See eg Fleming, op cit, n 5 at 196-199; R J Peaslee, "Multiple Causation and Damage" (1934) 47 Harv L Rev 1127; D M A Strachan, "The Scope and Application of the 'But-For' Causal Test" (1970) 33 MLR 386; H McGregor, "Successive Causes of Personal Injury" (1970) 33 MLR 378; U Wagner, "Successive Causes and the Quantum of Damages in Personal Injury Cases" (1972) 10 Osgoode Hall LJ 369.

188. For example, the ineffective response of the child's parents following the initial traumatic experience in *Duwyn v Kaprielian* (1978) 94 DLR (3d) 424, which on the facts did not sever the chain of causation.

189. See eg Fleming, op cit, n 5 at 216-224.

Australian High Court in *March v E & M H Stramare Pty Ltd*[190] has rejected the "but-for" test as the exclusive determinant of causation in favour of applying the principles of common sense. The criterion for determining whether a breach of duty to take care caused damage is to be based on general considerations including the drawing of inferences from established facts and the assessment of alleged causative factors from the standpoint of material contribution. Ultimately this will necessitate a value judgment involving ordinary notions of language and common sense. The "causa sine qua non" test applied as a negative criterion of causation may still play an important role in the resolution of disputes, but the role traditionally afforded to it has been significantly downplayed. Australian courts are already applying these principles in psychiatric damage cases. In *Miller v Royal Derwent Hospital Board of Management*[191] Zeeman J used the *March* approach to reject a claim by a nurse that the psychiatric illness she suffered following the death by strangulation of a young epileptic she had strapped to a chair in an emergency was due to the hospital's failure to provide post-trauma psychiatric counselling.

Whilst English courts have also espoused such views,[192] the latest indications are that, in contrast to the Australian position, English law has realigned itself with the "but-for" test as the primary causation test. The House of Lords in *Hotson v East Berkshire Area Health Authority*[193] and *Wilsher v Essex Area Health Authority*[194] quelled any suggestion that following the controversial decision in *McGhee v National Coal Board*[195] (which deviated from the traditional approach by employing a fictional equation of the material increase of risk of damage with the material contribution to it) English courts could now be seen as entertaining a general "benevolent" principle of causation which allows the bridging of "evidential gaps" where factual uncertainty makes a decision about cause and effect impossible on the balance of probabilities. "But-for" has been reinvigorated, in that cases which do not satisfy the test are unlikely to be seen as material contributors to damage because they will seldom clear the "de minimis" hurdle.[196] The Canadian Supreme Court has also recently

190. (1991) 171 CLR 506. See N J Mullany, "Common Sense Causation—An Australian View" (1992) 12 OJLS 431. The decision was applied by the court in *Bennett v Minister of Community Welfare* (1992) 66 ALJR 550.
191. (Unreported, Tasmanian SC, 29 May 1992, No 282 of 1988).
192. See Mullany, op cit, n 190 at fns 6-7.
193. [1987] AC 750.
194. [1988] AC 1074.
195. [1973] 1 WLR 1. The defendant was required to pay for injuries to the plaintiff which he had not been shown on the balance of probabilities to have caused. Due to the absence of adequate washing facilities at the defendant's brickworks, the plaintiff employee had to wait until he got home from work to wash, cycling there sweating and caked in dust. Although unable to prove that the supply of washing facilities would have prevented the onset of dermatitis, the plaintiff could show that the defendant's breach of duty had materially increased the risk of injury and this, it was said, could not for practical purposes be differentiated from material contribution to the injury itself. Note also the earlier decision in *Bonnington Castings Ltd v Wardlaw* [1956] AC 613 where a factory owner was held accountable for the plaintiff's lung condition which resulted from the combined effect of workplace dust from two sources, for only one of which the defendant was responsible. Liability was imposed, notwithstanding that the precise mechanism of the inception of the disease remained unclear.
196. As discussed in *Bonnington Castings Ltd v Wardlaw* [1956] AC 613 per Lord Reid at 621.

declined to follow *McGhee v National Coal Board* and, although making reference to "common sense", confirmed that the traditional "but-for" test occupies centre stage.[197]

In practice, a causal relationship may be assumed (as it was in *Alcock v Chief Constable of South Yorkshire Police*[198]), thus allowing the court to concentrate on other issues of liability. In other cases it falls to be established on the evidence, and in such situations the court may be particularly dependent on the evidence of professionals such as psychiatrists and psychologists.[199] As Lord Bridge has remarked, "psychiatric medicine is far from being an exact science"[200] but nonetheless psychiatrists are experienced in separating truth from falsehood.[201]

Remoteness

Liability having been established by showing that some damage of the kind that happened was foreseeable,[202] a plaintiff who can show that the defendant is in breach of a duty of care can recover for all damage of that kind which flows from the breach,[203] even though it is only the general kind of damage which was foreseeable and not its particular nature, its extent or the manner of its infliction. These rules are confirmed by decisions[204] which elaborate upon the general rule requiring foreseeability of the kind of damage laid down by *The Wagon Mound (No 1)*.[205]

In some psychiatric injury cases, these principles have resulted in holdings that particular items of damage are too remote because they are not of a foreseeable kind. In *Antonatos v Dunlop, Allsop & Transport & General Insurance Co Ltd*,[206] for example, the plaintiff's mental condition following a car accident caused the break-up of his marriage and led him to dispose of his share in a partnership at a substantial under-value. The court held that though these losses were consequences which ensued from

197. *Snell v Farrell* (1990) 72 DLR (4th) 289. For discussion of the developments in both England and Canada see J G Fleming, "Probabilistic Causation in Tort Law" (1989) 68 Can BR 661; J G Fleming, "Probabilistic Causation in Tort Law—A Postscript" (1991) 70 Can BR 136. See also S M Waddams, "Causation in Canada and Australia" (1993) 1 Tort L Rev (forthcoming).
198. [1992] 1 AC 310.
199. On refusal to submit to a psychiatric examination see eg *Lane v Willis* [1972] 1 WLR 326.
200. *McLoughlin v O'Brian* [1983] 1 AC 410 at 432.
201. See *Hevican v Ruane* [1991] 3 All ER 65 per Mantell J at 71.
202. See above, pp 68-73.
203. For a case where particular items of damage claimed by the plaintiff were held not to have resulted from the anxiety condition suffered by him as a result of the defendant's negligence see *Keys v British Gas Plc* (unreported, English CA, 10 July 1991).
204. See eg *Chapman v Hearse* (1961) 106 CLR 112 at 120-121; *Smith v Leech Brain & Co Ltd* [1961] 2 QB 405; *Hughes v Lord Advocate* [1963] AC 837; *Doughty v Turner* [1964] 1 QB 518; *Sayers v Perrin (No 3)* [1966] Qd R 89; *McCarthy v Wellington City* [1966] NZLR 481 per McCarthy J at 522; *Bradford v Robinson Rentals Ltd* [1967] 1 WLR 337; *Tremain v Pike* [1969] 1 WLR 1556; *Wieland v Cyril Lord Carpets Ltd* [1969] 3 All ER 1006; *R v Coté* (1974) 51 DLR (3d) 244 per Dickson J at 252; *Taupo Borough Council v Birnie* [1978] 2 NZLR 397; *Brice v Brown* [1984] 1 All ER 997; *Mihaljevic v Longyear (Australia) Pty Ltd* (1985) 3 NSWLR 1; *Attorney-General v Geothermal Produce New Zealand Ltd* [1987] 2 NZLR 348. Note also the talem qualem rule that the defendant must take the plaintiff as he or she finds him or her, dealt with below, pp 229-238.
205. [1961] AC 388.
206. [1968] Qd R 114.

the defendant's tort, the *Wagon Mound* principle did not entitle him to be compensated for the losses sustained as the result of the sale of the business or losing his wife's affection and companionship. They were not foreseeable, and they were different in kind from those losses which were foreseeable. Again, in *Jinks v Cardwell*,[207] though the wife of a mental patient who drowned in a bath due to the defendant's negligence recovered for the shock she suffered when told by a doctor that he had committed suicide, the legal costs of clearing his name were adjudged different in kind and too remote.[208] By contrast, in *Duwyn v Kaprielian*[209] and also in *Nader v Urban Transit Authority*,[210] children recovered for recognisable psychiatric injury because the damage was of a foreseeable kind even though its extent was not foreseeable. In each case, the injury had been exacerbated as a result of the over-protective response of the child's parents. Nonetheless, such a reaction was not outside the bounds of foreseeability. Morden JA in *Duwyn v Kaprielian*[211] added that, quite apart from foreseeability, the conduct of the parents could not be considered to be a new intervening force which actively operated to produce the harm after the defendant's negligent act had taken place.[212]

207. (1987) 39 CCLT 168, reversed in part on other grounds, sub nom *Jinks v Abraham* (unreported, Ontario CA, 23 June 1989, Doc Nos CA 181/87, 195/87).
208. A more debatable decision is *Shewan v Sellars (No 1)* [1963] QWN 19 where the plaintiff was held unable to recover for the anxiety neurosis suffered on learning of the severity of the injuries to his wife and child in a car accident in which he was also involved or for the loss of his employment consequent on his ability to cope. The court's decision was influenced by *Chester v Council of the Municipality of Waverley* (1939) 62 CLR 1. Under current law it is probable that the anxiety neurosis, at least, would not be regarded as too remote.
209. (1978) 94 DLR (3d) 424.
210. (1985) 2 NSWLR 501.
211. (1978) 94 DLR (3d) 424 at 441.
212. Note also *Government Insurance Office of New South Wales v Maroulis* (unreported, New South Wales CA, 6 April 1990, CA No 274 and 275 of 1988) where the court rejected an argument that the domestic discord between husband and wife after the husband's accident had obliterated the effects of the wife's initial psychiatric injury.

4

PSYCHIATRIC DAMAGE AND GENERAL PRINCIPLES OF COMPENSATION IN NEGLIGENCE

It is important to see the issue of liability for psychiatric damage in the context of the general principles which underlie the common law system of compensating the victims of negligence. Of particular significance is that, in the main, the law compensates only the primary victim, and does not give redress to secondary parties who suffer some kind of loss consequent on the primary victim's injury.[1] Negligent conduct may affect persons other than the primary victim in various ways.[2] They may suffer financially. The most obvious case of financial loss is where the secondary party is supported by the primary victim, but a secondary party may also suffer financially as the result of an accident through having to pay for medical treatment to the victim, giving up a job to perform nursing services, having to travel to visit the victim in hospital, or having to employ someone to perform domestic services that the victim can no longer render. In addition there are other losses which though material are not overtly financial, such as the companionship or guidance which a family member obtains from a spouse or parent. Finally, secondary parties may suffer mental distress and emotional strain as a result of the accident—grief, sorrow, anxiety, worry and the like. In some cases, these may take a particularly heavy toll on the mind and develop into or trigger a recognisable psychiatric illness.

Liability limited to the primary victim

The general rule

The general attitude of the law is to prevent a secondary party from recovering damages from the tortfeasor for injuries or losses such as those referred to above. It has been well expressed by Fleming:

"Generally, the law has considered itself fully extended by affording compensation only to persons immediately injured, such as the accident victim himself, without going to the length of compensating also third persons who, secondarily (par ricochet), incur expenses or

---

1. See generally P Handford, "Relatives' Rights and Best v Samuel Fox" (1979) 14 UWALR 79.
2. Consideration of cases where one person suffers loss as the result of an accident to another because there is a *commercial* relationship between them (see eg *Cattle v Stockton Waterworks Co* (1875) LR 10 QB 453; *Société Anonyme Remorquage a Hélice v Bennett* [1911] 1 KB 243; *Weller & Co v Foot and Mouth Disease Research Institute* [1966] 1 QB 569; *French Knit Sales Pty Ltd v N Gold & Sons Pty Ltd* [1972] 2 NSWLR 132) are beyond the scope of this chapter.

lose their livelihood, support or expected benefits from their association with him. . . . [T]he burden of compensating anyone besides the primary casualty is feared to be unduly oppressive because most accidents are bound to entail repercussions, great or small, upon all with whom he had family, business or other valuable relations.''[3]

The law, then, compensates the primary victim, and the primary victim alone. The secondary party is not completely ignored, because the damages payable to the victim will be assessed with relatives in mind. The primary victim whose ability to earn a living in the future is impaired or destroyed will recover a sum in respect of lost future earning capacity, and this is obviously to be used to support his or her family in lieu of former earnings.[4] Likewise, where the primary victim has become obliged to reimburse secondary parties for services provided or expenses incurred on his or her behalf, these sums are usually included in the victim's damages award.[5] But the general policy is that secondary parties have no rights separate from that of the victim—they can be compensated only through the victim, and only in so far as it is appropriate so to compensate them.

One means by which this policy can be put into effect is the rule that a duty of care is owed only to a foreseeable plaintiff.[6] However, it is clear that apart from reliance upon notions of foreseeability, the responsibility of a tortfeasor is limited to compensating the primary victim, and not others who suffer loss in consequence. In *Kirkham v Boughey*[7] a wife was injured in a road accident due to the defendant's negligence. Her husband decided not to return to his employment in Africa, from which at the time of the accident he was on leave, because of anxiety about his wife and the problem of caring for their two small children. He claimed damages in respect of loss of earnings for the period during which it was reasonable for him to remain in England on the ground of his wife's health. It was argued, in the words of Diplock J, that:

3. J G Fleming, *The Law of Torts* (8th ed, 1992), 179.
4. In *Lim v Camden & Islington Area Health Authority* [1980] AC 174 it was argued (unsuccessfully) that damages for future lost earning capacity should not be awarded to persons without dependants.
5. Older cases debated whether a legal obligation to pay was required: see *Gage v King* [1961] 1 QB 188; *Haggar v De Placido* [1972] 1 WLR 716; or whether a moral obligation was sufficient: see *Roach v Yates* [1938] 1 KB 256; *Wattson v Port of London Authority* [1969] 1 Lloyd's Rep 95. In *Schneider v Eisovitch* [1960] 2 QB 430 Paull J held that even a moral obligation was unnecessary and all that was required was an undertaking to pay. For similar debate in Australia see *McGregor v Rowley* [1928] SASR 67; *Blundell v Musgrave* (1956) 96 CLR 73; *Groves v Lingston* [1965] WAR 186 (legal obligation necessary); *Nicholls v Jack* [1963] Qd R 1; *Renner v Orchard* [1967] QWN 3; *Gaydon v Public Transport Commission* [1976] 2 NSWLR 44 (legal obligation not necessary); and in Canada see *Greenaway v Pacific Rail Co* [1925] 1 DLR 992; *Stewart v Lepages Inc* [1955] OR 957; *Hamilton v Hayes* (1962) 36 DLR (2d) 657 (legal obligation necessary); *Sunston v Russell* (1921) 21 OWN 160 (legal obligation not necessary). The present position is discussed below, pp 92-93.
6. See above, pp 65-68. The leading cases on this doctrine make it clear that it can be applied to defeat the claim of a relative: see *Palsgraf v Long Island Rail Co* (1928) 162 NE 99 per Cardozo J at 100: "What the plaintiff must show is 'a wrong' to herself, ie a violation of her own right, and not merely a wrong to someone else"; *Bourhill v Young* [1943] AC 92 per Lord Wright at 108: "If however the appellant has a cause of action it is because of a wrong to herself. She cannot build on a wrong to someone else."
7. [1958] 2 QB 338.

"The circle which encloses those to whom the driver owes a duty to take care is not a mere geographical circle, but extends to the family circle of those who find themselves within the geographical circle."[8]

Diplock J rejected this contention and held that the husband could not recover, affirming the desirability of compensating only the primary victim and not his relatives.

His Lordship mentioned that the position of a husband might be different from the position of others, because of the action for loss of consortium.[9] As the law then stood,

"The husband can . . . recover damages against the driver even though the husband was a hundred miles away from the highway when the accident took place."[10]

In *Best v Samuel Fox & Co*[11] the House of Lords recognised this action as an anomalous survival of mediaeval times, and refused to extend it to a wife. Lords Morton and Goddard rested this refusal on the desirability of compensating only the accident victim, and not family members consequentially affected by the injury.[12] In *Kirkham v Boughey*, the action was expressly said *not* to be based on loss of consortium,[13] but Diplock J nonetheless held that any extension of the rights of the husband of an injured wife would be in conflict with the principles of *Best v Samuel Fox*.

Another context in which the traditional principle of compensating only the primary victim has been indorsed is the question of recovery for services rendered to the victim by others. Compensation for such services is normally given in the damages awarded to the accident victim, and courts have ruled out the possibility of a direct action by the provider of the services. In *Donnelly v Joyce*,[14] an action brought on behalf of a child injured in an accident to recover for the services of his mother who gave up her job to nurse him, the defendants argued that the loss was one suffered by the provider of the services rather than the primary victim, and conceded that the provider would have a direct right of action against them, safe in the knowledge that the mother could not now be joined as a plaintiff because of the expiry of the limitation period. The English Court of Appeal,

---

8. Ibid at 341.
9. Dealt with in more detail below, pp 97-99.
10. [1958] 2 QB 338 at 342.
11. [1952] AC 716.
12. Ibid at 731 and 734 respectively.
13. Counsel placed much reliance on the decision of Devlin J in *Behrens v Bertram Mills Circus* [1957] 2 QB 1, where the immediate accident victim was a 3-foot high circus performer injured by an elephant. Her 2-foot 6-inch husband, also a circus performer, recovered damages for the fact that while his wife was injured he had refrained from going on tour with the circus because she would be unable to perform with him and give him society and domestic help. Diplock J said that if *Behrens v Bertram Mills Circus* was to be read as extending the rights of the husband of an injured wife, then it was in conflict with the principles of *Best v Samuel Fox & Co* [1952] AC 716 and was insupportable. However, he thought that the decision could perhaps be justified within the framework of the action for loss of consortium, the husband's action in staying at home being a proper step to take in mitigation of damages—a view of the case which was confirmed by Devlin J himself in *McNeill v Johnstone* [1958] 1 WLR 888. See also *Hunter v Scott* [1963] Qd R 77.
14. [1974] QB 454.

however, held that the loss was not the expenditure itself, but the creation of the need for that expenditure, and the appropriate compensation was the proper and reasonable cost of supplying that need. This loss was the victim's loss because his injuries had created a need for nursing services, and the provider of such services had no direct right of action.[15] The relationship between the primary victim and the secondary party who had borne the cost was irrelevant—there was no need to establish either a legal or a moral obligation, or an undertaking to reimburse. Three years afterwards, in *Griffiths v Kerkemeyer*,[16] the Australian High Court adopted the principles stated in *Donnelly v Joyce*,[17] Stephen J making it clear that a direct action by the provider of the services would seldom, if ever, be recognised.[18] Canadian courts have taken a similar approach.[19]

Three other decisions, one from New Zealand and two from Australia, have repulsed direct assaults on the principle that no duty of care is owed to relatives.[20] In *Marx v Attorney-General*,[21] the husband was severely injured in an accident at work and suffered brain damage. This caused him to suffer a personality change and affected relations between him and his wife—he began to display a hypersexual attitude towards her and repeatedly assaulted her physically and sexually. The wife alleged that the husband's

15. In the companion case of *Cunningham v Harrison* [1973] QB 942, decided by a different division of the English Court of Appeal on the day before *Donnelly v Joyce*, Lord Denning MR held that the wife of an injured husband who had nursed him likewise had no direct action against the defendant.

16. (1977) 139 CLR 161. See now the Court's comments in *Van Gervan v Fenton* (1992) 66 ALJR 828.

17. Gibbs J however imposed the qualification that the need must be productive of financial loss. This was done in order to accommodate *Blundell v Musgrave* (1956) 96 CLR 73 where the issue was whether the defendant should reimburse the plaintiff for free medical treatment provided by the Navy. The High Court held, by a majority, that a legal obligation to pay was necessary before such sums could be included in a damages award. An earlier case taking a similar approach to *Griffiths v Kerkemeyer* is *Wilson v McLeay* (1961) 106 CLR 523, in which the plaintiff, a 22-year-old girl injured in an accident while on holiday in Queensland, recovered damages in respect of the travelling expenses incurred by her parents who came from New South Wales to visit her. The damages were awarded on the basis that the expenditure helped to alleviate her condition, and was incurred with that purpose in mind. It seems that Taylor J viewed the loss as one suffered by the accident victim herself.

18. (1977) 139 CLR 161 at 171, 176-178. Stephen J did not entirely rule out the possibility of a direct action. He quoted Fullagar J in *Blundell v Musgrave* (1956) 96 CLR 73 and *Commissioner of Railways (NSW) v Scott* (1959) 102 CLR 392 as contemplating a direct action where the provider was under a *legal* obligation to provide or pay for services to the injured person, and also suggested that an action by the provider for economic loss might be distilled from *Caltex Oil (Australia) Pty Ltd v Dredge 'Willemstad'* (1976) 136 CLR 529—but in the ordinary case of nursing services rendered by relatives he thought a direct action incongruous and that the principle in *Donnelly v Joyce* [1974] QB 454 was the one most likely to provide a satisfactory remedy. The other judges did not discuss the possibility of a direct action.

19. See eg *Thornton v Board of School Trustees of School District No 57 (Prince George)* (1976) 73 DLR (3d) 35; *Hasson v Hamel* (1977) 78 DLR (3d) 573; *Urbanski v Patel* (1978) 84 DLR (3d) 650.

20. Note also the application of *Kirkham v Boughey* [1958] 2 QB 338 in Canada in *Jones v Taylor* (1983) 27 Sask LR 161, where a husband claimed damages for loss of consortium as a result of injury to his wife and its consequent effect on their bee-keeping business. In denying the claim, Walker J said at 177 that "It is clear that because an injury to one merely affects another does not give that other a cause of action in damages against the wrongdoer."

21. [1974] 1 NZLR 164.

employer owed her a duty of care, on the basis that she was a person whom it was reasonably foreseeable might be ill-treated by the husband as a consequence of the injury. The court rejected the wife's claim, stressing the need for the plaintiff to found her claim on a breach of a duty owed to herself,[22] and the desirability of compensating only the primary victim.[23]

A similar duty to a secondary party was alleged to exist in *Pratt and Goldsmith v Pratt*.[24] A wife was injured by a husband's negligent driving, and actions were brought against the husband by the wife and also by her mother, who had arrived to care for her injured daughter. The mother's claim was for services provided to her daughter, for shock caused by viewing her post-accident state, and for financial loss in the shape of travelling expenses and lost earnings. The Victorian Full Court held that the mother's claim disclosed no cause of action. The second and third claims were ruled out by the application of accepted principles as to liability for shock-related mental illness and economic loss respectively,[25] and as to the first claim the court again excluded the possibility of a direct action.[26] Once more, the court pointed out that the plaintiff had to establish a duty owed to herself and that only the primary victim could recover.

Again, in *Andrewartha v Andrewartha*[27] the husband of a quadriplegic victim of a road accident who brought an action for loss of consortium sought to claim not only damages for material losses and loss of his wife's society and services, but also general damages for pain and suffering and other mental, emotional and spiritual harm suffered in the course of his efforts to care for her at home. He argued that he was a person within the contemplation of the defendant who was likely to be injured as a result of his negligence and that therefore a direct duty of care was owed to him. The Full Court of the Supreme Court of South Australia rejected this argument and held that the losses under the general claim were not compensable. According to White J, if this contention were correct, all defendants who caused harm to plaintiffs who lived with others in a close loving relationship should contemplate that those others might suffer distress and even psychiatric illness as a result of caring for the victim. In his Honour's words, this "would open up avenues of compensation unknown to the law".[28]

Exceptions

The cases, then, reveal a consistent refusal to recognise the right of anyone other than the primary victim to mount a direct action against the tortfeasor in respect of any loss that they may have suffered. There are,

22. Ibid per McCarthy P at 168, per Beattie J at 173.
23. Ibid per McCarthy P at 169-170, per Beattie J at 175, 177. The court affirmed *Kirkham v Boughey* [1958] 2 QB 338.
24. [1975] VR 378.
25. As to the nervous shock claim, see below, p 193.
26. [1975] VR 378 per Adam and Crockett JJ at 386, per Starke J at 390. The court affirmed *Kirkham v Boughey* [1958] 2 QB 338.
27. (1987) 44 SASR 1.
28. Ibid at 4. Note also the older Australian case of *Johnson v Commonwealth* (1927) 27 SR (NSW) 133. For Scottish examples see *Soutar v Mulhern*, 1907 SC 723; *Robertson v Turnbull*, 1982 SC 1. For a United States example see *Bailey v Wilson* (1959) 111 SE 2d 106 (Ga).

however, some exceptions to this principle. None of them have been deliberately created; rather they have resulted, in the main, from the development of other types of liability.

The chief exception is the right of relatives to recover in wrongful death cases. At common law, wrongfully causing the death of another did not give rise to any civil liability, either to the victim's estate[29] or to his or her relatives.[30] However, as regards relatives, the position was altered by statute in England in 1846, the growth of railways and the consequent increase in fatal accidents having made the position intolerable. The *Fatal Accidents Act* provided that where death was caused by a wrongful act, neglect or default, which, if death had not ensued, would have involved the actor in liability to the victim, an action would lie against the actor[31] at the suit of various listed relatives.[32] The English example was speedily copied in Australia and other common law jurisdictions.[33]

The Fatal Accidents Acts are a clear exception to the general rule of no recovery by relatives in respect of losses suffered consequent on the death of or injury to another. The policy of compensating only the primary victim is simply not adhered to in this case. Nor is it necessary to show that a duty of care was owed to the relatives. The statute merely requires that the defendant should have owed a duty to the deceased—it provides that the

29. Because the victim's cause of action died with him: actio personalis moritur cum persona.
30. *Baker v Bolton* (1808) 1 Camp 493; 170 ER 1033 where a husband recovered damages for the loss of his wife's consortium during the month which she survived after a stagecoach accident, but nothing further consequent upon her death. This rule survives in cases not affected by wrongful death statutes: see eg *Osborne v Gillett* (1873) LR 8 Ex 88; *Admiralty Commissioners v S S Amerika* [1917] AC 38. For a recent discussion of the rule see *Swan v Williams (Demolition) Pty Ltd* (1987) 9 NSWLR 172 per Samuels JA at 175-184, per Priestley JA at 190-191.
31. *Fatal Accidents Act* 1846 (UK), s 1. This Act is often referred to as *Lord Campbell's Act* after its sponsor. See now *Fatal Accidents Act* 1976 (UK), s 1(1).
32. *Fatal Accidents Act* 1846 (UK), ss 2-3. See now *Fatal Accidents Act* 1976 (UK), s 1(2)-(3), under which the action lies for the benefit of the deceased's dependants, who are defined as the wife or husband or a former wife or husband of the deceased, any person living with the deceased as husband or wife in the same household who had been so living throughout a period of two years immediately preceding the death, a parent or other ascendant of the deceased, any person who was treated by the deceased as his or her parent, any child or other descendant of the deceased, any person treated by the deceased as a child of the family, and any person who is, or is the issue of, a brother, sister, uncle or aunt of the deceased. Relationships by affinity are treated as relationships by consanguinity, relationships of the half blood as relationships of the whole blood, the stepchild of a person as his or her child, and an illegitimate person as the legitimate child of his or her mother and reputed father: s 1(5).
33. In Australia, see *Compensation (Fatal Injuries) Act* 1968 (ACT); *Compensation to Relatives Act* 1897 (NSW); *Compensation (Fatal Injuries) Act* 1974 (NT); *Common Law Practice Act* 1867 (Qld), ss 12-15c; *Wrongs Act* 1936 (SA), Pt II; *Fatal Accidents Act* 1934 (Tas); *Wrongs Act* 1958 (Vic), Pt III; *Fatal Accidents Act* 1959 (WA). In Canada, see *Fatal Accidents Act*, RSA 1980, c F-5; *Family Compensation Act*, RSBC 1979, c 120; *Fatal Accidents Act*, RSM 1987, c F-50; *Fatal Accidents Act*, RSNB 1973, c F-7; *Fatal Accidents Act*, RSN 1990, c F-6; *Fatal Accidents Ordinance*, RONWT 1974, c F-3; *Fatal Injuries Act*, RSNS 1989, c 163; *Family Law Act*, RSO 1990, c F-3, ss 61-63; *Fatal Accidents Act*, RSPEI 1988, c F-5; *Fatal Accidents Act*, RSS 1978, c F-11; *Fatal Accidents Act*, RSYT 1986, c 64. See generally H Luntz, *Assessment of Damages for Personal Injury and Death* (3rd ed, 1990), 386-448; H McGregor, *Damages* (15th ed, 1988), paras 1534-1600; K D Cooper-Stevenson & I B Saunders, *Personal Injury Damages in Canada* (1981), 403-464.

relatives will have a right of recovery if the tortfeasor would have been liable to the deceased accident victim had he or she survived.[34]

The existence of such a wide-ranging departure from the general principle of no recovery is probably due to the fact that the Fatal Accidents Acts made their appearance at a time when the tort of negligence was at a very early stage of development.[35] The idea of duty of care was still in the process of formulation,[36] and certainly there was then no requirement that plaintiffs had to rely on duties owed to them personally.[37] In the words of Atiyah, the right of recovery under the Fatal Accidents Acts "predates the present conceptual structure of the law of negligence".[38] Moreover, in 1846 there was no alternative for relatives in the form of an action by the victim's estate, the proceeds of which might come to them under the will or on intestacy, because tort claims did not survive the death of either the victim or the tortfeasor. When survival of actions was introduced a century later,[39] it was necessary to ensure that appropriate deductions for Fatal Accidents Acts damages were made so as to prevent double recovery,[40] and ultimately to prevent the survival to the estate of claims for lost earnings in the lost years.[40a] The resulting complications perhaps show that

34. See eg *Fatal Accidents Act* 1976 (UK), s 1(1).
35. See above, pp 73-75.
36. This requirement may not have been completely established until *Winterbottom v Wright* (1842) 10 M & W 109; 152 ER 402.
37. As is made clear by *Smith v London & South Western Railway Co* (1870) LR 6 CP 14.
38. See P Cane, *Atiyah's Accidents, Compensation and the Law* (4th ed, 1987), 79.
39. Originally by the *Law Reform (Miscellaneous Provisions) Act* 1934 (UK), s 1. This Act was introduced in order to allow persons injured in motor vehicle accidents to claim against the estates of defendants killed in the accident. Similar provisions were introduced in other Commonwealth jurisdictions. In Australia, see *Law Reform (Miscellaneous Provisions) Act* 1955 (ACT), Pt II; *Law Reform (Miscellaneous Provisions) Act* 1944 (NSW), s 2; *Law Reform (Miscellaneous Provisions) Act* 1956 (NT), Pt II; *Common Law Practice Act* 1867 (Qld), s 15D; *Survival of Causes of Action Act* 1940 (SA); *Administration and Probate Act* 1935 (Tas), s 27; *Administration and Probate Act* 1958 (Vic), s 29; *Law Reform (Miscellaneous Provisions) Act* 1941 (WA), s 4. In Canada, see *Survival of Actions Act*, RSA 1980, c S-30; *Estate Administration Act*, RSBC 1979, c 114, s 66; *Trustee Act*, RSM 1987, c T-160, s 53(1); *Survival of Actions Act*, RSNB 1973, c S-18; *Survival of Actions Act*, RSN 1990, c S-32; *Trustee Ordinance*, RONWT 1974, c T-8, s 33; *Survival of Actions Act*, RSNS 1989, c 453; *Trustee Act*, RSO 1990, c T-3, s 38; *Survival of Actions Act*, RSPEI 1988, c S-11; *Trustee Act*, RSS 1978, c T-23, s 58; *Survival of Actions Act*, RSYT 1986, c 166.
40. Thus, although the *Law Reform (Miscellaneous Provisions) Act* 1934 (UK), s 1(5), and similar provisions in the legislation of other jurisdictions, provided that the rights under that Act should be in addition to and not in derogation of any rights conferred on the deceased's dependants by the *Fatal Accidents Act*, it is clear that if a claimant under the *Fatal Accidents Act* has received, or is likely to receive, damages under the *Law Reform (Miscellaneous Provisions) Act*, then the amount of benefit must be deducted from the *Fatal Accidents Act* damages: see eg *Davies v Powell Duffryn Associated Collieries* [1942] AC 601; *Murray v Shuter* [1976] QB 972.
40a. This problem arose as a result of holdings that living plaintiffs whose life expectancy had been shortened as a result of their injuries could recover for this loss: see *Skelton v Collins* (1966) 115 CLR 94; *Andrews v Grand & Toy Alberta Ltd* (1978) 83 DLR (3d) 452; *Pickett v British Rail Engineering* [1980] AC 136 (reversing the rule in *Oliver v Ashman* [1962] 2 QB 210 that damages for lost earnings were to be assessed on the basis of the post-accident life expectancy). Courts then held that such claims survived for the benefit of the estate. In Australia, following a decision to this effect by the High Court in *Fitch v Hyde-Cates* (1982) 150 CLR 482, all jurisdictions passed legislation preventing the survival of such claims: see Fleming, op cit, n 3 at 234, 678; Luntz, op cit, n 33 at 380-384. In England the similar decisions in *Kandalla v British European Airways Corporation* [1981]

if all claims which may be made by living plaintiffs survive for the benefit of the estate, the direct action by the relatives under the Fatal Accidents Acts may not be necessary.[41]

Fatal Accidents Acts do not generally give guidance on the kinds of damages that may be awarded. Though the Scottish law on which the legislation was based did not limit the relatives' right of recovery to economic losses, but also allowed compensation (solatium) for grief and suffering,[42] the English courts immediately limited recovery to financial loss,[43] and developed a general requirement that relatives show a reasonable expectation of pecuniary benefit.[44] Recovery for non-pecuniary losses is possible only in jurisdictions where the statute has been amended to permit the award of such damages. South Australia led the way in 1936,[45] and a few other jurisdictions have gradually followed.[46] Those jurisdictions which allow such a claim impose strict limitations. In England, for example, which first permitted damages for "bereavement" in 1982, there are limits both on the relatives who may claim and on the amount that may be recovered.[47]

If we turn to cases where the primary victim is not killed but merely injured, the common law again recognised that in limited circumstances some relatives had a right of action. This was the effect of the ancient actions for loss of consortium and services. Mediaeval law recognised that a man had a kind of proprietary right in his wife, his children and his

40a. *Continued*

QB 158 and *Gammell v Wilson* [1982] AC 27 led to the insertion of s 1(2)(a)(ii) in the *Law Reform (Miscellaneous Provisions) Act* 1934 (UK) by s 4(2) of the *Administration of Justice Act* 1982 (UK) barring estates from claiming damages for lost earnings. The position is analogous in Canada: see Cooper-Stevenson & Saunders, op cit, n 33 at 387-401.

41. It has even been suggested that the *Fatal Accidents Act* should be repealed: see S M Waddams, "Damages for Wrongful Death: Has Lord Campbell's Act Outlived its Usefulness?" (1984) 47 MLR 437.

42. See D M Walker, *The Law of Delict in Scotland* (2nd ed, 1981), 718-820. The action was limited to spouses, parents and children of the deceased: see *Eisten v North British Railway Co* (1870) 8 M 980.

43. *Gillard v Lancashire & Yorkshire Railway Co* (1848) 12 LT 356; *Blake v Midland Railway Co* (1852) 18 QB 93; 118 ER 35. The same development took place in the United States: see S M Speiser & S S Malawer, "An American Tragedy: Damages for Mental Anguish of Bereaved Relatives in Wrongful Death Actions" (1976) 51 Tul L Rev 1.

44. The requirement was first stated by Pollock CB in *Franklin v South Eastern Railway Co* (1858) 3 H & N 211; 157 ER 448 at 449.

45. *Wrongs Act* 1936 (SA), ss 23a-23c, added in 1940.

46. *Civil Liability Act* 1961 (Ire), s 49; *Compensation (Fatal Injuries) Act* 1974 (NT), s 10; *Fatal Accidents Act* 1976 (UK), s 1A (added in 1982); *Fatal Accidents Act*, RSA 1980, c F-5, s 8(1) (note Alberta Law Reform Institute, *Non-Pecuniary Damages in Wrongful Death Actions—A Review of Section 8 of the Fatal Accidents Act* (Report for Discussion No 12, 1992)). For the present Scots law, see the *Damages (Scotland) Act* 1976 (UK), s 1(4), replacing the relatives' action for solatium with damages acknowledging the non-pecuniary loss suffered by a husband, wife, parent or child of the deceased.

47. *Fatal Accidents Act* 1976 (UK), s 1A. "Bereavement" is not defined by the statute. According to Simon Brown J in *Bagley v North Herts Health Authority* (1986) 136 NLJ 1014 at 1015: "[I]t clearly encompasses both consolation of grief and sorrow and compensation for loss of society." A claim may be made only by the deceased's wife or husband or, if the deceased was a minor who had never married, by the parents if the deceased was legitimate or by the mother if he or she was illegitimate. The sum to be awarded is fixed by statute. Originally £3,500, it was raised to £7,500 in 1990: see *Damages for Bereavement (Variation of Sum) (England and Wales) Order* 1990 (UK).

servants, and enforced this right by giving him an action against anyone who interfered with it.[48] The action was a variety of trespass in which damage had to be proved: in the case of the child or the servant, the damage was the deprivation of the services to which the parent or master was entitled, and in the case of the wife the damage was the interference with consortium—the benefits of the married state, such as companionship and sexual relations. Intentional interference was redressed by the torts of enticement, harbouring, seduction of a female child and adultery with a wife. By the 19th century, at latest, it was clear that an action would also lie for interference with consortium or services committed negligently.[49] In the latter case the effect of this was that the law was compensating not only the primary victim, but also someone consequentially affected by the accident, if that secondary party was a husband, parent or employer.[50] In modern times, the existence of these actions was seen as anomalous. The loss of services which had to be proved, at least in relation to young children living with their parents, was really a fiction[51]—in reality these actions provided compensation for a wider variety of losses, including non-pecuniary loss. The refusal to extend the husband's action to a wife[52] was, in 20th century conditions, an obvious injustice. Many jurisdictions, therefore, have now abolished these actions by statute.[53] Others have

48. For the history of these actions, see P Brett, "Consortium and Servitium: A History and Some Proposals" (1955) 29 ALJ 321, 389, 428; G H Jones, "Per Quod Servitium Amisit" (1958) 74 LQR 39.
49. In the case of the husband's loss of consortium, this was recognised by *Baker v Bolton* (1808) 1 Camp 493; 170 ER 1033. See also *Martinez v Gerber* (1841) 3 M & G 88; 133 ER 1069; *Brockbank v Whitehaven Junction Railway Co* (1862) 7 H & N 834; 158 ER 706.
50. In form, these actions do not breach the principle that a plaintiff must show a duty owing to himself or herself personally, because the actions for loss of consortium and services are completely independent of the victim's action, as is shown by cases which hold that the contributory negligence of the accident victim does not operate to reduce the damages under the consortium action: see *Mallett v Dunn* [1949] 2 KB 180; *Curran v Young* (1965) 112 CLR 99; *Cook v Wright* [1967] NZLR 1034—though contrast the position under statute in three Australian jurisdictions: see *Wrongs Act 1936* (SA), s 27a(9); *Law Reform (Miscellaneous Provisions) Act 1955* (ACT), s 17; *Law Reform (Miscellaneous Provisions) Act 1956* (NT), s 18. This is an important contrast to the position under the Fatal Accidents Acts, where the contributory negligence of the accident victim reduces the damages that can be awarded to the dependants: see *Fatal Accidents Act 1976* (UK), s 5, but note the different practice in New South Wales (in cases other than road and work accidents) and Victoria, where the deceased's contributory negligence does not reduce the damages payable to dependants: see *Law Reform (Miscellaneous Provisions) Act 1965* (NSW), s 10(4); *Wrongs Act 1958* (Vic), s 26(4).
51. If a child is under the age of majority, a mere right to services is sufficient; if the child is of full age, proof of actual services is required, but the most trivial acts suffice, see eg *Carr v Clarke* (1818) 2 Chit 260 (making a cup of tea).
52. *Best v Samuel Fox & Co* [1952] AC 716. See Handford, op cit, n 1 at 113-132. In England the employer's action has been limited to cases involving domestic live-in servants, taking the action out of the commercial sphere: see *Inland Revenue Commissioners v Hambrook* [1956] 2 QB 641. A different view has been taken by courts in Australia: see *Commissioner for Railways (NSW) v Scott* (1959) 102 CLR 392; *Marinovski v Zutti* [1984] 2 NSWLR 571; New Zealand: see *Attorney-General of New Zealand v Wilson & Horton Ltd* [1973] 2 NZLR 238, and Canada: see *Genereux v Peterson* (1972) 34 DLR (3d) 614; *R v Buchinsky* (1983) 145 DLR (3d) 1. In *Swan v Williams (Demolition) Pty Ltd* (1987) 9 NSWLR 172 a claim by the employer company failed for lack of evidence that its operations were affected by the mental damage suffered by Mr Swan: see per Priestley JA at 199.
53. The action has been abolished in the Australian Capital Territory, New South Wales, Tasmania, Western Australia, England, New Zealand, British Columbia, Manitoba, Ontario and Saskatchewan: see *Law Reform (Miscellaneous Provisions) Act 1955* (ACT), s 32; *Law Reform (Marital Consortium) Act 1984* (NSW), s 3(1); *Common Law (Miscellaneous Amendments) Act 1986* (Tas), s 3; *Law Reform (Miscellaneous Provisions) Act 1941* (WA),

sought to rationalise them.[54] Where they still exist, they represent another exception to the principle that the law compensates only the primary victim.

Secondary victims and psychiatric damage

How do the psychiatric damage cases fit into this general pattern? Though the early cases allowing recovery did so on the basis that the plaintiff was within the zone of physical danger and suffered shock through fear of injury to him or herself,[55] in time it became accepted that nervous shock claims were not limited to such cases, and that persons could recover for shock-induced psychiatric illness suffered consequent on a physical injury to someone else, providing certain conditions were met[56]— conditions which are still the subject of controversy and which will be discussed in detail in later chapters. On one interpretation, it can be said that these cases are not really exceptions to the general principle under discussion, because of the rule that in order to recover for psychiatric damage a plaintiff must prove a duty owed to himself or herself.[57] In this sense, the plaintiff is not merely a secondary victim of the accident. However, the fact remains that the typical psychiatric damage case involving a bystander who witnesses an accident to a relative has many features in common with other cases involving secondary victims discussed earlier.

In this context the judgment of Lord Oliver in *Alcock v Chief Constable of South Yorkshire Police*[58] is an original and stimulating contribution to the psychiatric injury jurisprudence. Lord Oliver, like the other judges in the House of Lords, faced with the plaintiff's argument that liability for psychiatric damage was purely an issue of foreseeability, took the view that liability in negligence was not purely a question of foreseeability but also involved the general requirement of proximity. What is interesting about his discussion of the application of proximity in shock cases is that he sets it in the context of the general principle outlined above.[59]

This leads him to the conclusion that the psychiatric damage cases are not all of one kind.

> "It is customary to classify cases in which damages are claimed for injury occasioned in this way under a single generic label as cases of

53. *Continued*
   s 3; *Administration of Justice Act* 1982 (UK), s 2; *Accident Compensation Act* 1972 (NZ), s 5(2); *Family Relations Act*, RSBC 1979, c 121, s 75; *Equality of Status Act*, RSM 1987, c E-130, s 1(1); *Family Law Reform Act*, SO 1978, c 2, s 69(3); *Equality of Status of Married Persons Act*, SS 1984-85-86, c E-10.3, s 6. In Nova Scotia it has been held that the discriminatory nature of the rule is contrary to the Canadian Charter of Rights and Freedoms: see *Blotnicky and Blotnicky v Oliver* (1988) 213 APR 14 (NS).
54. In Queensland, South Australia and Alberta the action has been extended to a wife: see *Law Reform (Husband and Wife) Act* 1968 (Qld), s 3; *Wrongs Act* 1936 (SA), s 33; *Domestic Relations Act*, RSA 1980, c D-37, s 43. Note, however, the recent affirmation of *Best v Samuel Fox & Co* [1952] AC 716 by the Queensland Supreme Court in *Harris v Grigg* [1988] 1 Qd R 514.
55. *Dulieu v White & Sons* [1901] 2 KB 669, above, pp 3-4.
56. *Hambrook v Stokes Bros* [1925] 1 KB 141, above, pp 4-5.
57. See above, pp 65-68.
58. [1992] 1 AC 310 at 406-411.
59. Lord Keith, ibid at 396, also remarked that the present case was "a secondary sort of injury brought about by the infliction of physical injury, or the risk of physical injury, upon another person".

'liability for nervous shock'. This may be convenient but in fact the label is misleading if and to the extent that it is assumed to lead to a conclusion that they have more in common than the factual similarity of the medium through which the injury is sustained—that of an assault upon the nervous system of the plaintiff through witnessing or taking part in an event—and that they will, on account of this factor, provide a single common test for the circumstances which give rise to a duty of care. Broadly they divide into two categories, that is to say, those cases in which the injured plaintiff was involved, either mediately or immediately, as a participant, and those in which the plaintiff was no more than the passive and unwilling witness of injury caused to others. In the context of the instant appeals the cases of the former type are not particularly helpful, except to the extent that they yield a number of illuminating dicta, for they illustrate only a directness of relationship (and thus a duty) which is almost self-evident from a mere recital of the facts."[60]

The older variety of nervous shock case, in which the plaintiff suffers shock through fear for his or her own safety,[61] obviously belongs in the first category. The plaintiff is the primary victim and no other party is involved. Interestingly, however, Lord Oliver also places in this category cases where a person suffers shock on learning of the death of or an injury to another in an accident, where that person was directly involved in that accident as a victim.[62] The rescue cases,[63] according to Lord Oliver, also belong in this category, because:

"It is well established that the defendant owes a duty of care not only to those who are directly threatened or injured by his careless acts but also to those who, as a result, are induced to go to their rescue and suffer injury in so doing."[64]

Cases on liability to workmates[65] also fall into this group, because "the defendant's negligent conduct has foreseeably put the plaintiff in the position of being an unwilling participant in the event."[66]

Other psychiatric damage cases, according to Lord Oliver, are to be seen in a very different light:

"In those cases in which, as in the instant appeals, the injury complained of is attributable to the grief and distress of witnessing the misfortune of another person in an event by which the plaintiff is not

---

60. Ibid at 407. Note also the similar language adopted by Evatt J in *Chester v Council of the Municipality of Waverley* (1939) 62 CLR 1 at 44-45.
61. For example, *Dulieu v White & Sons* [1901] 2 KB 669.
62. For example, *Schneider v Eisovitch* [1960] 2 QB 430, discussed below, pp 156-157.
63. For example, *Chadwick v British Railways Board* [1967] 1 WLR 912, discussed below, p 108.
64. *Alcock v Chief Constable of South Yorkshire Police* [1992] 1 AC 310 at 408.
65. For example, *Dooley v Cammell Laird & Co* [1951] 1 Lloyd's Rep 271, discussed below, pp 111-112.
66. *Alcock v Chief Constable of South Yorkshire Police* [1992] 1 AC 310 at 408. Although his Lordship does not mention the group of miscellaneous cases illustrating that shock can be suffered in circumstances not involving a near-accident to the plaintiff or an accident or anticipated accident to another, he would presumably classify them as within his first category: see below, pp 212-215.

personally threatened or in which he is not directly involved as an actor, the analysis becomes more complex. The infliction of injury on an individual, whether through carelessness or deliberation, necessarily produces consequences beyond those to the immediate victim. Inevitably the impact of the event and its aftermath, whether immediate or prolonged, is going to be felt in greater or lesser degree by those with whom the victim is connected whether by ties of affection, of blood relationship, of duty or simply of business. In many cases those persons may suffer not only injured feelings or inconvenience but adverse financial consequences as, for instance, by the need to care for the victim or the interruption or non-performance of his contractual obligations to third parties. Nevertheless, except in those cases which were based upon some ancient and now outmoded concepts of the quasi-proprietorial rights of husbands over their wives, parents over their children or employers over their menial servants, the common law has, in general, declined to entertain claims for such consequential injuries from third parties save possibly where loss has arisen from the necessary performance of a legal duty imposed on such party by the injury to the victim."[67]

What factors, then, mark out the cases in which secondary victims who suffer psychiatric damage should be granted a right of action? Lord Oliver rejects appeals to logic. He says there is no readily discernible logical reason why a careless tortfeasor should not be responsible for the consequences not only to the immediate victim but also to others who suffer as a result. Nor can it be viewed as a matter of foreseeability, since the consequences for secondary victims are not beyond the bounds of foresight. In Lord Oliver's view, such persons are not, in contemplation of law, in a relationship of sufficient proximity or directness with the tortfeasor to give rise to a duty of care.[68] As his Lordship says, it is more difficult to account for the fact that, when the law in general declines to compensate anyone other than the primary victim, it should make an exception in cases where the plaintiff suffers a particular kind of injury (that is, psychiatric injury arising from sudden shock) through witnessing the injury to the primary victim or its immediate aftermath. He is driven to conclude that:

"The answer has, as it seems to me, to be found in the existence of a combination of circumstances from which the necessary degree of 'proximity' between the plaintiff and the defendant can be deduced. And, in the end, it has to be accepted that the concept of 'proximity' is an artificial one which depends more upon the court's perception of what is the reasonable area for the imposition of liability than upon any logical process of analogical deduction."[69]

He suggests that the present state of the law is not satisfactory or logically defensible.[70] On these grounds at least, Lord Oliver must be taken to have serious doubts about the justification of recovery for second category plaintiffs.

67. Ibid at 408-409.
68. Ibid at 410.
69. Ibid at 411.
70. Ibid at 418.

Comparisons and conclusions

If the present state of the common law is not satisfactory, two solutions are possible. One would be to go back to the position before *Hambrook v Stokes Bros*[71] and compensate those who suffer psychiatric damage only in cases where they are the primary victims, allowing them to recover as part of their damages whatever sums in respect of expenditure by third parties are thought proper, and leaving the Fatal Accidents Acts to operate as a special case. But, as Lord Oliver recognised,[72] such a radical about-turn is not now possible, and it would leave uncompensated many plaintiffs with a just cause for relief.

A possible alternative would be to re-examine the principle that the law compensates only the primary victim. The adoption of this principle is certainly not the only position which the law could take. A number of legal systems which are not part of the common law tradition adopt an entirely different approach. France is a notable example. There, within the ambit of the general principle of liability for fault,[73] anyone who suffers any sort of loss, whether pecuniary in nature or consisting merely of injury to the feelings, consequent on the death of another may recover damages.[74] This includes not only lawful spouses and legitimate children but also those in relationships outside marriage and their children, indeed anyone who can prove the existence of a sufficient degree of grief.[75] In cases where the primary victim is merely injured, relatives, although admittedly a more limited class, and others such as fiancés have similar rights.[76] Analogous principles operate in some other legal systems with a similar general principle.[77]

However, not all legal systems outside the common law go so far. According to Fleming:[78]

71. [1925] 1 KB 141.
72. *Alcock v Chief Constable of South Yorkshire Police* [1992] 1 AC 310 at 410.
73. *Code civil*, art 1382, discussed above, p 57.
74. See eg H & L Mazeaud & A Tunc, *Responsabilité Civile* (6th ed, 1965), Vol 1, ch 3; B Starck, *Droit Civile—Obligations* (1972), 75-79; G Viney, *Traité de Droit Civil: Les Obligations—La Responsabilité: Conditions* (1982), 310-333.
75. See the decision of the Cour de Cassation, chambre mixte, 27 February 1970, D 1970, 100 ('L'arrêt Dangereux'), which confirmed the line of cases in the chambre civile allowing recovery to a mistress, and Cour de Cassation, chambre criminelle, 19 June 1975, D 1975, 679, allowing such recovery even where the relationship was adulterous. In an extreme case, Cour de Cassation, chambre civile, 16 Jan 1962, D 1962, 199 ('L'affaire Lunus') the owner and trainer of a racehorse recovered damages for their grief consequent on the horse being electrocuted.
76. See Cour de Cassation, chambre civile, 22 October 1946, D 1947, J 49 (the first case recognising this right of recovery—damages were awarded to the parents of the injured person); Cour d'appel de Lyon, 26 May 1966, D 1967, somm 9 (in which a fiancée recovered damages); Cour de Cassation, chambre civile, 23 May 1977, D 1977, I R 441 and 1 Mar 1978, JCP 1978, IV 145 (removing the requirement that the harm suffered had to be of an exceptional gravity).
77. For example, Belgium: see H McGregor, *Damages for Personal Injuries and Death (International Encyclopedia of Comparative Law*, Vol 11, Torts, ch 9), 16; Spain, where art 1902 of the *Código civil* is to be interpreted in the same way as the French art 1382: see Sentencia 6 December 1912, cited McGregor, ibid at 17 n 123; Italy, where the rights of relatives are also widely protected: see P Catala and J A Weir, "Delict and Torts—A Study in Parallel (Part III)" (1964) 38 Tul L Rev 663 at 689, n 113.
78. J G Fleming, "Distant Shock in Germany (And Elsewhere)" (1972) 20 AJCL 485 at 487-488.

"Most legal systems, especially the German and Anglo-American, though less so the French, tend to disqualify claims by persons only consequentially or (in more common continental parlance) 'mediately' injured, except in such carefully controlled and special situations as fatal injuries where the risk of double liability is virtually ruled out. The underlying policy is clear: to reduce the tortfeasor's burden in view of the fact that most accidents are apt to entail injurious consequences to the accident victim's family and other associates."

Even in some countries which have adopted the French general principle of liability for fault, relatives have more limited rights,[79] and there are some civil law countries, such as Germany, which have no such general principle and where the position is similar to the common law.[80] In Germany payments may be made to relatives on the death of another, but they are limited to losses of a pecuniary nature.[81] In any other case, a person claiming to have suffered injury, whether by shock or otherwise, consequent on harm to another must prove a wrong done to himself or herself,[82] and show resulting injury to health.[83] Turning to uncodified civil law countries, though Roman law recognised that when a family member was injured this constituted an injury to the feelings of the head of the family, the paterfamilias,[84] in the modern systems in which the law of delict is founded on Roman law principles this right has for all intents and purposes died, and the position is very close to that of the common law.[85]

79. In Quebec, though the *Code civil* incorporates a general principle of liability (art 1053) similar to art 1382 of the French *Code civil*, relatives' rights of recovery are limited to those available under another section of the Code equivalent to the Fatal Accidents Acts (art 1056): see *Canadian Pacific Railway Co v Robinson* (1887) 14 Can SCR 105; *Driver v Coca Cola Ltd* (1961) 27 DLR (2d) 20 per Taschereau J at 26-27. A new Civil Code was adopted in Quebec in December 1991 but is not yet in force. In the Netherlands, relatives have no right to recover except for financial loss: see McGregor, op cit, n 77 at 17-18. The position is similar in the Scandinavian countries: ibid at 17.

80. See B S Markesinis, *A Comparative Introduction to the German Law of Torts* (2nd ed, 1990), 33-35, 101-103, 684-687; P R Handford, "Moral Damage in Germany" (1978) 27 ICLQ 849 at 872-873. The position is similar in Switzerland: see *Obligationenrecht*, arts 28(2) and 47.

81. *Bürgerliches Gesetzbuch*, arts 844-845.

82. By claiming under art 823(I) of the *Bürgerliches Gesetzbuch*.

83. See the cases cited above, p 58, n 250, where mothers recovered for psychiatric injury consequent on the death of a child. German law emphasises the seriousness and extraordinary nature of the shock, and the need for it to be an appropriate and understandable consequence of the accident. Recovery is not always restricted to relatives: see eg (1968) LG Tubingen, NJW 1187; (1969) LG Frankfurt, NJW 2286; (1973) LG Stuttgart, VersR 648.

84. D.47.10.1.3. A similar action was available to a master in respect of an injury to his slave: D.47.10.13.

85. In South Africa the only survival appears to be the right of a husband to sue in respect of an injury to his wife: see *Banks v Ayres* (1888) 9 NLR 34; *Jacobs v Macdonald* (1909) TS 442. There is no decision on whether a wife has a similar right of action in respect of an injury to her husband. In Scotland, the old Roman law action has been cut down even more, and only in one special case, in which a husband is allowed an action in respect of the rape of his wife: see *Black v Duncan*, 1924 SC 738, is any action by a relative allowed. However, in cases involving death, Scots law did recognise the right of the relatives to recover not only for financial losses but also for solatium: see above, p 97. South Africa also allows relatives an action in death cases, but only for pecuniary loss: see *Union Government v Warneke*, 1911 AD 657, rejecting a claim by a husband for the loss through her death of his wife's comfort and society.

It seems unlikely that the common law would ever approach the French position where a wide range of relatives and others can recover for emotional suffering (and not merely for psychiatric damage) on the sole basis of their relationship to the primary victim, whether or not they were anywhere near the scene of the accident and however they became aware of it. But recent developments in the case law do provide some evidence of a growing acceptance of the idea that relatives, qua relatives, may be expected to suffer psychiatric injury as the result of an accident to someone else. This was particularly evident in the judgment of Deane J in *Jaensch v Coffey*.[86] His Honour referred to a current body of modern medical opinion that the most important explanation of shock-induced psychiatric damage resulting from injury to another is the existence of a close, constructive and loving relationship with that person, and that it is largely immaterial whether the close relative is at the scene of the accident or how he or she learns of it.[87] Lord Scarman in *McLoughlin v O'Brian* was broadly of the same opinion.[88] Deane J also noted medical evidence that genuine nervous shock and mental damage can be caused to a person caught up in a disaster in which neither that person nor anyone in a pre-existing relationship with him or her is physically injured or threatened.[89] He concluded:

"While it must now be accepted that any realistic assessment of the reasonably foreseeable consequences of an accident involving actual or threatened serious bodily injury must, in an appropriate case, include the possibility of injury in the form of nervous shock being sustained by a wide range of persons not physically injured in the accident, the outer limits of reasonable foreseeability of mere psychiatric injury cannot be identified in the abstract or in advance."[90]

His Honour went on to say that, on an unqualified test of reasonable foreseeability, there would be no rational basis for excluding liability to a close relative or friend who has no contact with the accident or its immediate aftermath but who suffers reasonably foreseeable nervous shock and consequent psychiatric damage by reason of constant social contact, as nurse or companion, with the injured victim, and suggested that the law in Australia might eventually come to recognise liability in some or all of these cases—subject, however, to the importance of policy considerations, which are likely to continue to place limits on recovery.[91]

There are some Australian jurisdictions where the common law is supplemented by statutory provisions.[92] These show even more clearly an acceptance of the position that close relatives of the accident victim, merely because of their status as relatives, have a right to be compensated if they

86. (1984) 155 CLR 549 at 600-601.
87. Note in particular D J Leibson, "Recovery of Damages for Emotional Distress Caused by Physical Injury to Another" (1976-1977) 15 *Journal of Family Law* 163 at 196.
88. [1983] 1 AC 410 at 431. His Lordship was obviously conscious of this when he said that he foresaw social and financial problems if damages for "nervous shock" should be made available to persons *other* than parents and children who without seeing or hearing the accident, or being present at the immediate aftermath, suffer "nervous shock" in consequence.
89. Citing B Raphael et al, "Disaster: The Helper's Perspective" (1980) 2 Med J Aust 445.
90. (1984) 155 CLR 549 at 601.
91. Ibid at 602-604. For a more in-depth discussion see below, Chapter 8.
92. See the discussion below, pp 239-243.

suffer "mental or nervous shock". Parents and spouses are given a right to recover damages which is not dependent on any other factor. Foreseeability and policy considerations have been excluded in this context.

Both common law and statute, however, continue to impose important limitations on the ambit of recovery which will ensure that the common law is unlikely to get too close to the French position and too far away from the general principle of compensating only the primary victim. The cardinal limitation is the requirement that the plaintiff suffer shock, or, more accurately, a recognised psychiatric injury, rather than mere grief or sorrow. This has already been dealt with.[93] The others are analysed in the following chapters.

93. See above, Chapter 2.

5

RELATIONSHIP TO ACCIDENT VICTIM

Introduction

The oft-lamented limitation imposed on liability for nervous shock in 1901 by Kennedy J in *Dulieu v White & Sons*[1] meant that during the embryonic stages of the action's development the issue of relationship never arose. As compensable shock had to arise "from a reasonable fear of immediate personal injury to oneself",[2] there was no role for any third party to play.[3] With the demise of this restriction,[4] judicial focus was redirected to search for new methods to reduce the potentiality for liability and the scope for manufactured claims. This took the form of a stringent examination of the bonds between the parties involved.

Conventional doctrine has long dictated that in order to recover for psychiatric damage the plaintiff and the person killed, injured or put in peril by the negligent defendant must be in a special kind of relationship, one that is close or intimate. The prevailing judicial attitude accepts that in these circumstances "it is readily defensible on grounds of policy to allow recovery".[5] Traditionally both Australian and English courts have focused only on immediate familial ties, restricting recovery to those within the special relationships of spouses[6] and child and

---

1. [1901] 2 KB 669.
2. Ibid at 675.
3. Thus in cases where shock and psychiatric illness have been induced through actual physical injury to, or fear of physical injury to, or the death of, the claimant there is no relationship for the courts to scrutinise: see eg *Victorian Railways Commissioner v Coultas* (1883) 13 App Cas 222; *Bell v Great Northern Railway Co of Ireland* (1890) 26 LR Ir 428; *Dulieu v White & Sons* [1901] 2 KB 669; *Vince v Cripps Bakery Pty Ltd* (1984) Aust Torts Rep 80-668; *Al-Kandari v J R Brown & Co* [1988] QB 665. Note also *Bradfield v British Railways Board, The Times*, 10 Mar 1955 (plaintiff in railway carriage which was suddenly turned on its side, spent 20 minutes under a pile of passengers who were unable to get out of the carriage). A recent Australian example is furnished by the compensation claim by naval personnel on board the destroyer HMAS Voyager who required medical and psychiatric treatment for 20 years after it was sliced in two as a result of the negligent operation of the aircraft carrier HMAS Melbourne. In February 1992 Coldrey J of the Victorian Supreme Court gave leave for the action to proceed, even though the limitation period had expired: see *Clark v Commonwealth* (unreported, Victorian SC, 24 Feb 1992, No 31 of 1985). Analagous to situations involving personal injury are the cases where compensable injury has resulted from damage to property: see eg *Owens v Liverpool Corporation* [1939] 1 KB 394; *Attia v British Gas Plc* [1988] QB 304; *Campbelltown City Council v Mackay* (1989) 15 NSWLR 501, discussed below, pp 208-212.
4. See above, pp 4-5.
5. *Jaensch v Coffey* (1984) 155 CLR 549 per Gibbs CJ at 555. See eg *Regan v Harper* [1971] Qd R 191.
6. This approach has resulted in a reluctance to pursue claims relating to persons outside these categories. This is illustrated by *Swan v Williams (Demolition) Pty Ltd* (1987) 9 NSWLR 172, where a husband suffered psychiatric damage when a large sandstone block crushed a car containing his wife and her parents. He confined his claim to loss consequent on the death of his wife, no action being brought in respect of his in-laws.

parent.[7] The common law's concentration on these two particular categories of relatives was confirmed by the House of Lords in *Alcock v Chief Constable of South Yorkshire Police*,[8] the latest pronouncement on this issue. The question arises whether nowadays the existence of such a limited species of relationship is or should be a prerequisite to recovery and whether public policy and/or logic sanctions or demands the imposition of liability beyond the traditional links. The latest indications are that strict adherence to historic convention is unjustifiable, and that rather than adopt a policy of exclusion based on blind categorisation, the expansion of potential claimants is warranted in particular circumstances.

Although not determinative of a claim for shock-related injury,[9] the relationship between the parties will bear on the question of the existence of a duty of care: specifically, it is of crucial importance to the issue of reasonable foreseeability of the injury suffered (and arguably also that of proximity).[10] On one view, the "closer the tie"[11] the more likely this criterion will be satisfied, although it cannot be automatically assumed that the absence of any recognised relationship will inevitably render psychiatric injury unforeseeable. True, it may be more difficult to establish, but it does not necessarily doom a claim to failure. This is reflected in the common law's development over the last quarter of a century so as to widen the ambit of the categories of persons able to recover for shock-induced mental harm.

7. Stephenson LJ in *McLoughlin v O'Brian* [1981] 1 QB 599 at 606 raised the question whether adoptive and illegitimate relationships ought to be included within these categories. The issue of illegitimate children has never been analysed. Presumably, however, today there would be no barrier to recovery on the ground that a relationship was an illegitimate one rather than a legitimate blood relationship. In *McLinden v Richardson*, 1962 SLT (Notes) 104 a mother of an adopted child brought an action against the driver of a van which had run over the child. In allowing proof before answer Lord Wheatley made no mention of the fact that the child was adopted and proceeded on the basis that it made no difference to the actionability of the claim. Foster children are certainly regarded as being within the recognised categories: see *Hinz v Berry* [1970] 2 QB 40; *Alcock v Chief Constable of South Yorkshire Police* [1992] 1 AC 310 per Nolan LJ at 385. Note that one of the plaintiffs in the Hillsborough litigation, Denise Hough, had fostered her young brother who died in the tragedy, but this fact was assumed at all stages not to prejudice her claim. That the relationship between a foster parent and a foster child is sufficiently close to allow either to maintain an action for emotional distress is accepted also by United States courts: see eg *Mobaldi v Regents of the University of California* (1976) 127 Cal Rptr 720; *Leong v Takasaki* (1974) 520 P 2d 758 (Haw) (ten-year-old boy recovered after witnessing the death of his "foster grandmother" (stepfather's mother)). Compare *Ramirez v Armstrong* (1983) 673 P 2d 822 (NM) (claim of girl living with deceased's family rejected, there being no evidence that the deceased occupied a legitimate position in loco parentis). There is authority in Texas and Washington affording the same rights to those within step relationships: see *Grandstaff v Borger* (1985) 767 F 2d 161 (police officers mistakenly shot and killed claimant's stepfather); *Freeman v City of Pasadena* (1988) 744 SW 2d 923 (Tex); *Meredith v Hanson* (1985) 697 P 2d 602 (Wash); *Strickland v Deaconess Hospital* (1987) 735 P 2d 74 (Wash). Note also the Australian statutes dealt with below, pp 239-245.
8. *Alcock v Chief Constable of South Yorkshire Police* [1992] 1 AC 310. See particularly per Lord Ackner at 399, per Lord Oliver at 411, per Lord Jauncey at 420.
9. *Mount Isa Mines Ltd v Pusey* (1970) 125 CLR 383 per Windeyer J at 404.
10. *Jaensch v Coffey* (1984) 155 CLR 549 per Deane J at 605-606, per Brennan J at 569-570 (foreseeability), per Gibbs CJ at 555 (proximity); *Alcock v Chief Constable of South Yorkshire Police* [1992] 1 AC 310 per Lord Keith at 397, per Lord Oliver at 415-416 (foreseeability). See above, pp 68-85.
11. *McLoughlin v O'Brian* [1983] 1 AC 410 per Lord Wilberforce at 422.

Non-relatives: rescuers and fellow-workers

The need for a special type of familial relationship has never been absolute. The Australian, English and Canadian courts have indicated a preparedness to extend relief beyond these ties to include those plaintiffs claiming for nervous shock and psychiatric illness in their capacity as rescuers or work colleagues. The circumstances surrounding rescue or employment are viewed by the courts as giving rise to a sufficiently close relationship to warrant deviation from a strict insistence on family membership.

Motivated by altruism and commitment various courageous and dedicated groups of professionals (such as the police and fire services, emergency workers, army personnel, doctors and nurses) and ordinary untrained people not infrequently become deeply involved in the demanding and dangerous tasks generated by accidents, unselfishly exposing themselves to the risk of adverse physical and psychiatric repercussions. The ability of a rescuer to recover in negligence for physical injury generally which is sustained in the course of attempting to assist others in peril has been recognised since the early part of this century. Cardozo J, the great American jurist, in *Wagner v International Rail Co*,[12] stated in a celebrated dictum:

> "Danger invites rescue. The cry of distress is the summons to relief. The law does not ignore these reactions of the mind in tracing conduct to its consequences. It recognises them as normal. It places their effects within the range of the natural and probable. The wrong that imperils life is a wrong to the imperilled victim; it is a wrong also to his rescuer."[13]

That shock-induced psychiatric harm suffered by a rescuer constituted an exception to the "immediate relative rule" was first recognised in *Chadwick v British Railways Board*[14] where the plaintiff assisted in rescue operations at the scene of the Lewisham train disaster, witnessing grotesque injuries (for example, bodies impaled on girders) causing him shock and permanent mental injury. Waller J held that a duty of care was owed to rescuers, it being foreseeable that they might intervene to aid victims of the defendant's carelessness. It followed that they could recover for damage, including psychiatric illness, sustained as a result of their efforts, irrespective of whether operations had been successful or they had voluntarily assisted.[15] This reasoning was indorsed by the House of Lords in *McLoughlin v O'Brian*.[16] Tucker J adopted the same principle in *Wigg v British Railways Board*[17] where a railway guard who negligently gave the signal to start a train was held liable for psychiatric illness sustained by the driver,

---

12. (1921) 133 NE 437 (NY). For the earliest English statement of this principle, see *Haynes v G Harwood & Sons* [1935] 1 KB 146. See also *Baker v T E Hopkins & Son Ltd* [1959] 1 WLR 966; *Videan v British Transport Commission* [1963] 2 QB 650.
13. (1921) 133 NE 437 (NY) at 437.
14. [1967] 1 WLR 912, noted (1967) 83 LQR 474; J Tiley [1967] CLJ 157; C J Miller (1968) 31 MLR 92. Note, however, *Pugh v London, Brighton & South Coast Railway Co* [1896] 2 QB 248, below, p 110, n 27.
15. [1967] 1 WLR 912 at 920-921.
16. [1983] 1 AC 410 per Lord Wilberforce at 419, per Lord Bridge at 437-438.
17. *The Times*, 4 Feb 1986.

who went to the assistance of a person struck by the train.[18] It is not only that those responsible for accidents should foresee the arrival of rescuers who may be shocked by what they see. The common law considers it appropriate from a policy perspective that they should owe such Samaritans a duty of care.[19] It is in the interests of all community members that rescue operations be encouraged by the courts, and this necessitates the granting of relief for loss sustained in the process.

The leading Australian case in this context is *Mount Isa Mines Ltd v Pusey*.[20] While at work in a powerhouse the plaintiff engineer heard a loud explosion and went upstairs to discover a workmate severely burnt. He aided the injured man and helped carry him to a waiting ambulance but he died nine days later. The fact that the plaintiff was unacquainted with the accident victim did not operate to bar his compensation claim for a schizophrenic condition which developed approximately four weeks later due to the shock of seeing the consequences of the accident. Windeyer J was emphatic that relationships will not serve as a limit on recovery. Following the lead of Waller J, his Honour said:

> "There seems to be no sound ground of policy, and there certainly is no sound reason in logic, for putting some persons who suffer mental damage from seeing or hearing the happening of an accident in a different category from others who suffer similar damage in the same way from the same occurrence. The supposed rule that only relatives can be heard to complain is apparently a transposition of what was originally a humane and ameliorating exception to the general denial that damages could be had for nervous shock. Close relatives were put in an exceptional class. This allowed compassion and human sympathy to override the older doctrine, draconic and arbitrary, which recognised only bodily ills as compensable by damages and made a rigid difference between ills of the mind and hurts to the body. What began as an exception in favour of relatives to a doctrine now largely abandoned has now been seen as a restriction, seemingly illogical, of the class of persons who can today have damages for mental ills caused by careless conduct."[21]

Perhaps of even more significance was Windeyer J's unwillingness to rule out the possibility of other types of claimants. His Honour opined that where a duty of care arose solely from foreseeability of harm to a neighbour (as distinct from a relationship of status or of contract such as master and servant) it will not always follow that recovery for psychiatric damage will be confined to family members or rescuers. Walsh J was the only other

18. See also *Ross v Bowbelle and Marchioness* (unreported, Admiralty Registrar, 18 June 1991) where a passenger on the Marchioness riverboat which sank in the Thames made unsuccessful attempts to rescue another passenger and suffered moderate depression and post-traumatic stress disorder.
19. See *Alcock v Chief Constable of South Yorkshire Police* [1992] 1 AC 310 per Lord Jauncey at 421.
20. (1970) 125 CLR 383, noted by C S Phegan (1971) 45 ALJ 428; C D Gilbert (1971) 45 ALJ 431.
21. (1970) 125 CLR 383 at 404. See also *Smith v State Government Insurance Commission* (unreported, South Australian SC, 5 June 1990, No 2018 of 1988) where a truck driver who was not in any way responsible for a collision between his vehicle and a car went to assist the occupants of the car and suffered psychiatric injury as a result of the experience.

member of the court who alluded to the relationship issue. Importantly, while acknowledging that the existence of a family relationship may be very relevant to the question of foreseeability of the injury sustained, he too could discern no rule of law which categorically denied relief to claimants who were not in a close natural bond with the impact victim. His Honour considered that:

> "[T]here is no warrant for holding that [the question whether or not mental injury to the plaintiff was reasonably foreseeable], which is a question of fact, must always receive a negative answer unless the plaintiff be a close relative." [22]

This was recognised also in Ontario in the tragic case of *Fenn v City of Peterborough* [23] where a father attempted to search through the rubble of his home, destroyed by a gas explosion, for two of his children. He had arrived a few minutes after the catastrophe to see his grotesquely injured wife (her legs had been burnt off) and the body of another child being loaded into an ambulance, and immediately ran to the wreckage but was restrained. In assessing liability for shock-related psychiatric injury, Holland J clearly acknowledged the existence of the rescuer principle, although recovery was not based solely on the fact that Mr Fenn had attempted to rescue his children. [24]

The most recent Canadian authority has applied the rescue principle to found recovery in a more unusual fact situation than that normally encountered in "pure" rescue cases. In *Bechard v Haliburton Estate*, [25] as the result of colliding with a car in which the plaintiff was a passenger, a motorcyclist was injured and thrown into the middle of the road. Seeing the defendant's car approaching, the plaintiff attempted to warn him to stop by screaming and waving her arms. The defendant paid no heed and drove over the injured motorcyclist, killing him. The sight and sound of this tragic happening caused the plaintiff to suffer amnesia and a post-traumatic stress reaction. Though there are statements in the judgment of Griffiths JA referring to liability to bystanders generally, [26] the defendant's liability to the plaintiff was grounded on the rescue principle, in that she was attempting to save the motorcyclist from further injury, so performing a function analogous to that of a rescuer. [27]

The limits of the rescue principle were made apparent by the English Court of Appeal in *Rapley v P & O European Ferries (Dover) Ltd* [28] in reversing an order for summary judgment made by the trial judge and granting unconditional leave to defend. The plaintiff was a member of one

22. Ibid at 417.
23. (1976) 73 DLR (3d) 177.
24. Ibid at 208-209. See also *Brown v Hubar* (1974) 45 DLR (3d) 664 per Grant J at 673; *Rhodes v Canadian National Railway* (1990) 75 DLR (4th) 248 per Wallace JA at 259, per Southin JA at 281-282.
25. (1991) 84 DLR (4th) 668.
26. See below, p 129.
27. Note also *Pugh v London, Brighton & South Coast Railway Co* [1896] 2 QB 248 where a signalman suffered nervous shock as a result of the excitement and fright caused by endeavouring to prevent an accident to a train by signalling to the driver. The English Court of Appeal decided that the plaintiff had been incapacitated "by reason of accident" under the terms of an insurance policy.
28. (Unreported, English CA, 21 Feb 1991).

of the crews of the Herald of Free Enterprise but was not on board when she sank in a Zeebrugge harbour. He made two trips to the scene: going as a volunteer three days afterwards to help with relatives and then having to identify the bodies of two colleagues, and returning later to repeat the identification process in relation to a large number of crew members' bodies which had by then been lying underwater for some time. His claim for psychiatric injury was based on the rescuer principle, but the Court of Appeal distinguished the case from *Chadwick v British Railways Board*,[29] saying that the plaintiff could not in ordinary terms be described as a rescuer, since he did not help the injured involved in the accident.

Can the "rescuer" exception be utilised to extend recovery to those relatives outside the traditional spousal or parental categories (or indeed to any other person)? Does the common perception of rescuers plucking climbers off cliff faces or pulling dying adolescents from twisted car wrecks permit the inclusion of a person who visits the injured in hospital to comfort and care? Lord Edmund-Davies thought so in *McLoughlin v O'Brian*,[30] although in that case the plaintiff was in any event within the immediate familial nucleus. The "quasi-rescuer" extension was however expressly rejected by Griffiths LJ in the English Court of Appeal[31] and the other Law Lords were silent on the issue. No Australian or Canadian judge has followed his Lordship's path, leaving the future and scope of this particular extension uncertain in all three jurisdictions.[32] Significantly, however, in *Alcock v Chief Constable of South Yorkshire Police*[33] Lord Jauncey, speaking at a more general level, expressed the view that neither the rescuer nor the employee category could be utilised so as to justify the further expansion of liability for shock-induced psychiatric damage. Any deviation from the orthodox position would need to be based on other grounds.

That recovery can be had for psychiatric damage caused through the perception of the death, injury or peril of workmates is clear from *Dooley v Cammell Laird & Co Ltd*.[34] There, a crane driver was lowering heavy containers into a ship's hold when the rope holding one of them snapped. As a consequence of the fear that his colleagues working below would be crushed by the falling load, the plaintiff sustained shock and psychiatric damage. Notwithstanding that no one was in fact harmed, that he was susceptible to injury by shock and that he was unrelated to any of the shiphands, the plaintiff succeeded in his claim. Donovan J, ruling that the company which owned the containers was negligent, was of the view that

29. [1967] 1 WLR 912.
30. [1983] 1 AC 410 at 424.
31. [1981] 1 QB 599 at 622-623.
32. See, however, *Chester v Council of the Municipality of Waverley* (1939) 62 CLR 1 per Evatt J at 39. Note also Cardozo J's comments in *Wagner v International Rail Co* (1921) 133 NE 437 (NY) at 437, quoted above, p 108.
33. [1992] 1 AC 310 at 421. Could a person applying a tourniquet or searching for a severed limb be a rescuer?
34. [1951] 1 Lloyds Rep 271. Compare the position in the United States: see eg *Beanland v Chicago R I & P Rail Co* (1973) 480 F 2d 109; *Dierker v Gypsum Transport Ltd* (1985) 606 F Supp 566; *Hinojosa v South Texas & Drilling Exploration Inc* (1987) 787 SW 2d 320 (Tex). Note *Gillman v Burlington Northern Rail Co* (1989) 878 F 2d 1020 where a railway foreman was denied recovery for emotional distress arising from an accident in which a co-worker was dragged under a train and killed, not on the basis of his relationship to the deceased, but because he could not show a contemporaneous fear for his own safety.

it was reasonably foreseeable that an employee might suffer nervous shock and incur psychiatric injury if he feared the death of or injury to fellow workers due to a load which he was lifting being precipitated from a great height into a ship's hold.[35] In a like case, *Carlin v Helical Bar Ltd*,[36] the plaintiff was compensated by his employer for a shock-related personality change when a man was crushed by a crane he was operating. Similarly in *Galt v British Railways Board*[37] a train driver rounded a bend at about 65 mph in conditions of restricted visibility to find himself confronted by two fellow railwaymen on the track only a short distance in front of him. It was impossible for him to stop and he feared that he had hit and killed the men (who had in fact managed to jump out of the way in time). He recovered for myocardial infarction (a heart attack) brought on by nervous shock notwithstanding that he was predisposed to such injury.[38] In these cases the careless act of the defendant put the plaintiff in the position of believing that he was about to become, or had been, the involuntary cause of a colleague's death or injury and the mental illness complained of stemmed from the shock of becoming conscious of this supposed fact. The fact that the negligent conduct has foreseeably put the plaintiff in the position of being an unwilling participant in the events establishes of itself a sufficiently proximate relationship between the parties, and the principal question is whether, in the circumstances, injury of that type to the particular plaintiff was reasonably foreseeable.[39] In *Galt v British Railways Board* Tudor Evans J held that shock-induced injury was a reasonably foreseeable result of the defendant Board's failure to take care not to expose the driver to such damage.

Rescuers and workmates, then, are recognised as categories of plaintiff who may foreseeably suffer psychiatric harm if the defendant fails to take due care.[40] A dramatic illustration of both situations was furnished by a

---

35. [1951] 1 Lloyd's Rep 271 at 277. Note that in this case the inference was drawn that the men in the hold were friends of the plaintiff. See also *Mount Isa Mines Ltd v Pusey* (1970) 125 CLR 383, where the persons assisted by the plaintiff were fellow-workers. Note *Wilks v Haines* (1991) Aust Torts Rep 81-078 where it was held that an employee who suffers psychiatric illness does not have a reasonable cause of action for damages against the employer if: (1) the psychiatric illness is the result of learning of the death of or injury to another employee at the workplace; (2) the death or injury is due to the negligence of the employer; (3) the employee suffering the psychiatric illness is not at the workplace when the death or injury occurs; and (4) there is no family relationship between the employees.

36. (1970) 9 KIR 154. Note *Yates v South Kirby Collieries Ltd* [1910] 2 KB 538, a workers' compensation case, where the English Court of Appeal granted recovery to a worker who became alarmed and suffered neurasthenia on seeing a fellow-worker fatally injured.

37. (1983) 133 NLJ 870. Note that there is no evidence from the report of any contributory negligence by the plaintiff.

38. The plaintiff would have recovered for the physical manifestations of his fright regardless of whether it led to a psychiatric complaint: see above, p 18. Note also *Meek v British Railways Board* (unreported, QBD, 15 Dec 1983) where a train driver suffered psychiatric injury after hitting, killing and viewing the dismembered remains of a railwayman who was on the line at night. Park J would have followed the reasoning of Tudor Evans J in *Galt v British Railways Board* (1983) 133 NLJ 870 but for the fact that the dead railwayman was not acting in the course of his employment.

39. See *Alcock v Chief Constable of South Yorkshire Police* [1992] 1 AC 310 per Lord Oliver at 408. Note also Hidden J at 347.

40. In *Rapley v P & O European Ferries (Dover) Ltd* (unreported, English CA, 21 Feb 1991), dealt with above, pp 110-111, the plaintiff's claim would probably have been better based on the fellow-worker principle, rather than the rescue cases.

recent instance in which the pilot of a BAC 1-11 passenger aircraft was prevented from being sucked out of his cockpit when a defective windscreen blew out only through the efforts of other crew members, who hung onto his legs until the aircraft could be landed by the co-pilot. Not only the rescuers, but also other crew members, suffered trauma-related mental conditions as a result.[41]

Relatives

As noted, save for the special exceptions discussed above, the courts have traditionally viewed the existence of marital or filial bonds between the victim of shock-induced psychiatric harm and the person killed, injured or imperilled by the defendant's carelessness as an essential pre-condition to compensation.[42] When one turns to examine the long-standing focus of the common law on those within the relationships of spouses and parent-child, it becomes clear that the rationale advanced for this conservative restriction on liability is unsound. The reasons have been expressed as follows:

> "It is only in cases where the relationship is of the closest known to man that it is reasonably foreseeable that the doing of physical harm to the one may cause mental harm amounting to true psychiatric illness to the other. It has . . . been considered that in the spectrum of human relationships ranging from the closest of ties known to man, through all degrees of relationship to that of the mere bystander, it is only in the former in which it is reasonably foreseeable that such damage may follow. For all other relationships it is reasonably foreseeable that the possession of 'reasonable phlegm', as the law puts it, will prevent the onset of a psychiatric illness."[43]

> "[N]ormally, the parent-child and the husband-wife relationship can be presumed to be so close that fear for the child or spouse can be reasonably foreseen by the wrongdoer as likely to result in nervous shock to a parent or spouse of ordinary phlegm who witnesses or comes upon the immediate aftermath of catastrophe involving, or which appears likely to involve, the child or other spouse."[44]

41. Damages are being claimed against the employer airline: see "BA Sued by Crew who Saved Pilot", *The Times*, 25 Apr 1992, 5.
42. United States jurisdictions have not always focused on the *immediate* familial nucleus to the same extent as Commonwealth courts. However, in some States the problem of mishaps during the birth process has been approached by requiring the existence of a bond between mother and foetus as a condition of recovery, instead of regarding the medical negligence as causing emotional harm directly to the mother: see eg *Justus v Atchison* (1977) 565 P 2d 122; 139 Cal Rptr 97; *Vaccaro v Squibb Corporation* (1978) 412 NYS 2d 722; *Austin v Regents of the University of California* (1979) 152 Cal Rptr 420; *Sesma v Cueto* (1982) 181 Cal Rptr 12; *Kahn v Hip Hospital Inc* (1985) 487 NYS 2d 700; *Tebbutt v Virostek* (1985) 483 NE 2d 1142; 493 NYS 2d 1010; *Crenshaw v Sarasota County Public Hospital Board* (1985) 466 So 2d 427 (Fla); *Johnson v Ruark Obstetrics & Gynecology Association* (1990) 395 SE 2d 85 (NC); *Wideman v DeKalb County* (1991) 409 SE 2d 537 (Ga); *Giualdo v Allen* (1991) 567 NYS 2d 255; *Ferrara v Bernstein* (1992) 582 NYS 2d 673. In California this approach has now been firmly repudiated by the Supreme Court in *Burgess v Superior Court* (1992) 831 P 2d 1197; 9 Cal Rptr 2d 615, holding that the mother is the "direct victim" of negligence because of the pre-existing duty owed to her.
43. *Alcock v Chief Constable of South Yorkshire Police* [1992] 1 AC 310 per Hidden J at 337.
44. Ibid per Parker LJ at 359. See also *McLoughlin v O'Brian* [1983] 1 AC 410 per Lord Wilberforce at 422.

"The underlying logic of allowing claims of parents and spouses is that it can readily be foreseen by the tortfeasor that if they saw or were involved in the immediate aftermath of a serious accident or disaster they would, because of their close relationship of love and affection with the victim be likely to suffer nervous shock."[45]

There are considerable difficulties with an approach which arbitrarily demarcates between different categories of relationship thereby condemning the suits of remoter claimants to failure without consideration of their individual merits. Such rigidity is illogical, unconvincing and produces intolerable injustice. In what is perhaps the most encouraging development in psychiatric damage law in recent years, the House of Lords in *Alcock v Chief Constable of South Yorkshire Police*[46] has recognised the irrationality of the early common law approach, ruling that it ought no longer to prevail (if it ever should have) in the light of "modern knowledge and modern circumstances".[47] It is hoped that other Commonwealth courts will follow their Lordships' lead.

By way of preliminary discussion, three points should be made. First, and with respect we would say correctly, members of both the High Court of Australia[48] and the House of Lords[49] had always maintained that the categories of claimants were not closed. Lord Wilberforce, for example, in *McLoughlin v O'Brian*[50] said:

"As regards the class of persons [whose claim should be recognised], the possible range is between the closest of family ties—of parent and child, or husband and wife—and ordinary bystander. Existing law recognises the claims of the first; it denies that of the second. . . . In my opinion, these positions are justifiable, and since the present case falls within the first class, it is strictly unnecessary to say more. I think, however, that it should follow that other cases involving less close relationships must be very carefully scrutinised. I cannot say that they should never be admitted. The closer the tie (not merely in relationship, but in care) the greater the claim for consideration. The claim, in any case, has to be judged in the light of the other factors, such as proximity to the scene in time and place, and the nature of the accident."[51]

Certainly, the courts were not indelibly locked into the continued arbitrary exclusion of worthy claimants.

Secondly, although the predominant strategy of Commonwealth courts has been to search for an immediate familial nucleus, not all courts have always adhered to this religiously. In addition to the special rescuer and workmate exceptions, isolated deviations have occurred, creating precedent for a more radical and long overdue change in tack. An early example is

45. *Alcock v Chief Constable of South Yorkshire Police* [1992] 1 AC 310 per Lord Jauncey at 422.
46. [1992] 1 AC 310.
47. Ibid per Hidden J at 337.
48. *Mount Isa Mines Ltd v Pusey* (1970) 125 CLR 383 per Windeyer J at 404-405, per Walsh J at 416-417 and *Jaensch v Coffey* (1984) 155 CLR 549 per Brennan J at 571.
49. *McLoughlin v O'Brian* [1983] 1 AC 410 per Lord Wilberforce at 422.
50. [1983] 1 AC 410.
51. Ibid at 422.

Owens v Liverpool Corporation,[52] in which the English Court of Appeal awarded compensation to the mother, uncle, cousin and husband of the cousin of a deceased person whose coffin was overturned during a funeral possession and nearly ejected from the hearse. The court did not question the appropriateness of allowing each of these relatives to recover.[53] More recently, in the Tasmanian case of *Storm v Geeves*,[54] Burbury CJ was prepared on principle to widen the categories of relationship where damages for nervous shock are recoverable to include brothers and sisters. The plaintiff's three children were waiting for a school bus when one daughter was hit and killed by a negligently driven truck. The remaining daughter and son were physically unharmed and the boy ran home to fetch his mother who returned to find the first daughter pinned helplessly beneath the wheels of the vehicle. The mother, brother and living sister claimed compensation for psychiatric illness. Damages were awarded to both the mother and brother and, while on the facts Burbury CJ was unconvinced that the girl had suffered a recognisable and therefore compensable psychiatric illness, his Honour was willing to include the sister within the categories of claimants potentially able to recover.[55] Similar decisions have been given in several English cases. In *Mortiboys v Skinner*[56] four elderly women claimed compensation, inter alia, for nervous disorders stemming from a collision between the Devonshire Maid, a motor boat on which they had been travelling, and a paddle steamship. Two other passengers were drowned and in both cases they were sisters of one or other of the surviving plaintiffs. Thus, in addition to the shock of the collision, immersion in the water off Brixham Harbour, and their own escape from drowning, the surviving plaintiffs had, as Willmer J expressly noted, experienced the shock of being present at the death of a sister. Damages were awarded for their overall shock and consequent psychiatric disabilities, no distinction being drawn between that suffered as a result of a sister's death and the accident itself.[57] In *Shaw v Mills*[58] a young girl was awarded damages for psychiatric injury caused by the shock of seeing her mother and youngest sister killed before her eyes by a motorcycle combination when all three were walking together along the footpath. Significant also is *Turbyfield v Great Western Railway Co*[59] where the twin sister of a girl who was

52. [1939] 1 KB 394, noted by C A Wright (1939) 17 Can BR 56.
53. The case was criticised by the House of Lords in *Bourhill v Young* [1943] AC 92, but in the light of the subsequent development of the law of psychiatric damage this criticism may not be justified. Compare the Californian case of *Trapp v Schuyler Construction* (1983) 197 Cal Rptr 411 where two children who witnessed their first cousin drown in a swimming pool were denied relief for emotional distress notwithstanding that they enjoyed a relationship akin to that of siblings.
54. [1965] Tas SR 252.
55. Ibid at 266-267.
56. [1952] 2 Lloyd's Rep 95.
57. Note also *Moores v Dixon* (unreported, Manchester County Ct, 26 September 1991) where a sister and twin brothers all suffered psychiatric damage through concern for each other's safety when a car crashed into the sitting room of their house while they were watching television. Though they all received slight physical injuries, the principal claim was for "nervous shock".
58. (Unreported, English CA, 7 Mar 1961).
59. (1937) 54 TLR 221. Note, however, that these and other "peculiar" damages (eg £21 for funeral expenses) had been agreed upon prior to the proceedings, the only question for Greaves LJ being one of liability.

injured (and who died nine days later) due to the negligent driving of a horse and dray by a servant in the employment of the defendant recovered £25 for the shock of witnessing the accident. Similarly, the British Columbia Supreme Court in *Cameron v Marcaccini*[60] was not moved to question a young woman's right to claim for shock incurred from witnessing her sister's death and injury to her niece in a road accident in which she also suffered physical injury. In Scotland, although Lord Murray of the Outer House in *Harvey v Cairns*[61] rejected the claim of a brother for the shock and emotional effect of witnessing the death of his sister who had stepped in front of an oncoming vehicle, he did not do so on the basis of the pursuer's connection with the primary victim. A decision of the South African Appellate Division, *Bester v Commercial Union Versekeringsmaatskappy van SA Bpk*,[62] also recognises the rights of siblings to redress, allowing a young boy to recover for an anxiety neurosis stemming from the sight of his younger brother's death under the wheels of a carelessly driven car. As *Dillon v Legg*[63] itself shows, it is clear that in the United States also brothers and sisters are considered to be within the type of relationship justifying a right to litigate.

So too, some courts have been prepared to grant recovery to claimants who sustain mental damage on the death, injury or imperilment of a close friend. In *Kohn v State Government Insurance Commission*[64] Bray CJ of the South Australian Supreme Court felt no compulsion to bar the psychiatric damage claim of the seriously injured girlfriend of a young man killed in a road accident. Although the evidence reveals that she hoped to marry the deceased, they were not formally engaged and thus the case can only be viewed as authority for extension of the relationship criterion in respect of friends, albeit extremely close ones, rather than fiancés. It is noteworthy also that in *Rowe v McCartney*[65] although the plaintiff failed in her claim for shock induced by guilt at having granted a friend permission to drive her high powered car which he negligently crashed, thereby rendering himself a quadriplegic, the New South Wales Court of Appeal gave no indication that she faced any barrier to compensation due to the fact that her relationship with the defendant was not a familial one. She was unsuccessful not because he was her friend, but on grounds of absence of reasonable foreseeability of injury and the damage suffered

60. (1978) 87 DLR (3d) 442. The case concerned the assessment of damages, liability having been admitted.
61. 1989 SLT 107. Three reasons were given: absence of a causal link, an inability to distinguish the symptoms experienced by the boy from those appropriate to a loss of society award, and lack of a factual basis for the claim.
62. 1973 (1) SA 769 (A).
63. (1968) 441 P 2d 912; 69 Cal Rptr 72. See also eg *Shepard v Superior Court of Alameda County* (1977) 142 Cal Rptr 612; *Landreth v Reed* (1978) 570 SW 2d 486 (Tex); *Burke v Pan American World Airways Inc* (1980) 484 F Supp 850; *Rickey v Chicago Transit Authority* (1981) 457 NE 2d 1 (Ill); *Goncalvez v Patuto* (1983) 458 A 2d 146 (NJ); *Bovsun v Sanperi* (1984) 461 NE 2d 843 (NY); *James v Lieb* (1985) 375 NW 2d 109 (Neb); *Garrett v City of New Berlin* (1985) 362 NW 2d 137 (Wis); *Ebarb v Woodbridge Park Association* (1985) 210 Cal Rptr 751; *Gates v Richardson* (1986) 719 P 2d 193 (Wyo); *Wright v City of Los Angeles* (1990) 268 Cal Rptr 309. Relationships of the half blood are similarly treated: see *Gaston v Flowers Transportation* (1987) 675 F Supp 1036.
64. (1976) 15 SASR 255. For a similar United States case see *Binns v Fredendall* (1987) 513 NE 2d 278 (Ohio).
65. [1976] 2 NSWLR 72.

being too remote.[66] There is some Scottish authority for the proposition that fiancés may recover for shock-related injuries in certain circumstances, at least where there is evidence also of psychiatric damage through fear for personal safety. In *Currie v Wardrop*[67] a young woman and her fiancé were walking on a grass verge of the roadway arm-in-arm when they were both knocked down from behind by an omnibus. The man was severely injured and the plaintiff, although not physically struck, was shocked, both through apprehension for her own safety and that of her companion, to the extent that she developed tachycardia[68] and tremors. The majority of the Court of Session concluded that once it is established that there is a good ground of action for nervous shock sustained in consequence of apprehension as to one's own well-being, it is immaterial whether this was aggravated by alarm about the safety of a fiancé involved in the traumatic incident in question. Recovery may be had for shock stemming from both sources.[69] In addition, the focus on the husband/wife bond has, on occasion, been extended to include de facto spouses. The Tasmanian Supreme Court in *Klug v Motor Accidents Insurance Board*,[70] for example, did not resort to the issue of relationship to defeat a claim for shock and a pathological grief disorder suffered on the death of the plaintiff's de facto wife. Canadian judges also have not been averse to

66. Note also *Beaulieu v Sutherland* (1986) 35 CCLT 237 where Legg J did not have to consider whether the relationship between two workmates who were "good" but not "close" friends was sufficient to give rise to liability because he held that the plaintiff did not suffer a recognisable psychiatric illness; *Marshall v Lionel Enterprises Inc* (1971) 25 DLR (3d) 141 per Haines J at 151. Compare *Newby v General Lighterage Co Ltd* [1954] 2 Lloyd's Rep 625, affirmed [1955] 1 Lloyd's Rep 273, where a barge adrift on a river at night collided with a rowing eight, and the plaintiff, one of the members of the crew, suffered nervous injury due principally to the death of another crew member; *Ross v Bowbelle and Marchioness* (unreported, Admiralty Registrar, 18 June 1991) where a passenger on a riverboat which sank suffered depression and post-traumatic stress disorder due in part to loss of a friend but also due to her own involvement and unsuccessful attempt to rescue another passenger. In the United States it appears that friends are unable to recover for emotional distress: see eg *Beanland v Chicago R I & P Rail Co* (1973) 480 F 2d 109; *Kately v Wilkinson* (1983) 195 Cal Rptr 902; *Trapp v Schuyler Construction* (1983) 197 Cal Rptr 411 (court held at 412 that a "close relationship" "does not include friends, housemates or those standing in a 'meaningful relationship' "). Note, however, *Eyrich v Dam* (1984) 473 A 2d 539 (NJ) where a man recovered for emotional distress sustained in an attempt to rescue a neighbour's child from an escaped circus leopard.

67. 1927 SC 538.

68. Rapid heart beat (more than 100 beats per minute); racing of the heart, increased pulse rate.

69. Subsequent developments in Scotland indicate that the *Dulieu v White & Sons* [1901] 2 KB 669 limitation which troubled the court no longer restricts recovery in that jurisdiction: see *McLinden v Richardson*, 1962 SLT(Notes) 104; *Bain v King & Co Ltd*, 1973 SLT 8; *Harvey v Cairns*, 1989 SLT 107; above, p 9, n 54. Consequently *Currie v Wardrop* may be stronger authority in favour of fiancés' rights to sue than may be apparent at first glance. For a Canadian case see *Brown v Matheson and von Kintzel* (1990) 258 APR 428 (NS) where damages for shock and consequent serious psychiatric injury stemming from the death of her fiancé in a car accident were subsumed within the plaintiff's personal injury award, no reference being made to the relationship between her and the deceased for the purposes of the actionability of the psychiatric component. Note also *Marshall v Lionel Enterprises Inc* (1971) 25 DLR (3d) 141 per Haines J at 151. American courts have also allowed recovery: see eg *Pieters v B-Right Trucking Inc* (1987) 669 F Supp 1463.

70. (1991) Aust Torts Rep 81-134.

diluting the conventional insistence on the "closest of human ties" as a prerequisite to recovery for shock-induced psychiatric injury. In *Beecham v Hughes*[71] the plaintiff's claim for psychiatric illness in the form of reactive depression arising out of his de facto wife's injuries sustained in a car crash was not ruled out by the British Columbia Court of Appeal on the basis that the parties were not in lawful wedlock.[72]

The third preliminary point is that those jurisdictions which have enacted legislation governing the recoverability of compensation for psychiatric damage have expanded considerably the range of potential plaintiffs. Nearly 50 years ago the New South Wales legislature decided that it was appropriate to redefine the traditional categories of permissible claimants. The Australian Capital Territory and Northern Territory Parliaments followed suit a few years later. By way of illustration, s 4(5) of the *Law Reform (Miscellaneous Provisions) Act* 1944 (NSW) provides:

> " 'Member of the family' means the husband, wife, parent, child, brother, sister, half-brother or half-sister of the person in relation to whom the expression is used.
>
> 'Parent' includes father, mother, grandfather, grandmother, stepfather, stepmother and any person standing in loco parentis to another.
>
> 'Child' includes son, daughter, grandson, granddaughter, stepson, stepdaughter and any person to whom another stands in loco parentis."[73]

Clearly, the orthodox common law restrictions have not always been enthusiastically embraced by either the courts or legislatures.

As Stephenson LJ perceptively observed over a decade ago, the question of how close the tie between the person injured by impact and the person injured by shock has to be before a cause of action lies had to be definitively answered "sooner or later".[74] The test litigation spawned by the

71. (1988) 52 DLR (4th) 625.
72. For a similar United States decision see *Ledger v Tippitt* (1985) 210 Cal Rptr 814 where an unmarried cohabitant who had been sitting next to her lover (the father of her child) in a car when he was stabbed to death recovered for her emotional distress. The position on this issue in the American States, and even within particular States, varies widely, but it is fair to say that, generally speaking, there is discernible a recent backlash against recovery by de facto spouses: see eg *Drew v Drake* (1980) 168 Cal Rptr 65 (but note the strong dissent by Poche J at 66-67 rejecting the majority's "adherence to an older morality as the key to the courtroom"); *Hastie v Rodriguez* (1986) 716 SW 2d 675 (Tex); *Ferretti v Weber* (1987) 519 So 2d 986 (Fla); *Elden v Sheldon* (1988) 758 P 2d 582; 250 Cal Rptr 254, on which see T M Cavenaugh, "A New Tort in California: Negligent Infliction of Emotional Distress (For Married Couples Only)" (1990) 41 Hastings LJ 447; *Sollars v City of Albuquerque* (1992) 794 F Supp 360. Almost certainly the reluctance to recognise the legitimacy of heterosexual cohabitee relationships in this context would also be evident (perhaps even more strongly) with respect to homosexual and lesbian cohabitees who attempt to sue for shock and psychiatric harm consequent on death, injury or imperilment to their partners, but this situation has not arisen for discussion in the case law.
73. Similar provisions can be found in the *Law Reform (Miscellaneous Provisions) Act* 1955 (ACT), s 22 and the *Law Reform (Miscellaneous Provisions) Act* 1956 (NT), s 23. A 1986 addition to the *Wrongs Act* 1936 (SA) providing for compensation for "mental or nervous shock" in the limited context of road accidents also relies on an equivalently worded definition section: see ss 3a, 35a(1)(c), though there are no such definitions applying to s 77 of the *Motor Accidents Act* 1988 (NSW). For a more detailed discussion of the statute law in these jurisdictions, see below, pp 239-245.
74. *McLoughlin v O'Brian* [1981] 1 QB 599 at 606.

Hillsborough soccer disaster[75] has brought the relationship issue to the forefront of the judicial mind again and, it is submitted, highlights the totally unsatisfactory nature of the conventional state of affairs and the urgent need for the implementation of an entirely different strategy. Varying degrees of judicial dissatisfaction with the restrictive approach are discernible at all three levels of the proceedings, and the judgments reveal subtle differences in the extent to which the judges were prepared to abandon the restraints of the past. It is informative therefore to consider in detail the varying attitudes of and methods adopted by each of the courts which considered these claims.

Hidden J at first instance took a significant, but nevertheless small, step forward, a step which was unfortunately retraced by an English Court of Appeal apparently still under the influence of much derided floodgates arguments. The 16 carefully chosen plaintiffs represented a wide cross-section of those suffering the ill-effects of the actual or feared loss or injury of others close to them. They included spouses, parents, brothers, sisters, uncles, grandfathers, brothers-in-law, fiancées and friends most of whom, genuine loss or not, were according to current law beyond the bounds of assistance. Confirming that injury by shock to parents and spouses has long been recognised as foreseeable, Hidden J went further: in contrast to the handful of previous decisions which had allowed recovery outside these groups, glossing over the relationship issue, his Lordship in a landmark decision (in England at least) considered that the common law was ready to cast the net a little wider to embrace brothers and sisters of those killed, injured or imperilled through negligent acts or omissions. Duties of care were owed to these claimants also, it being reasonably foreseeable by the defendant police that mental injury could be caused to siblings of those within the ground by their carelessness. The rationale behind this extension seems to have been twofold: a desire to make it possible for all those within the immediate familial nucleus to sue and a belief that siblings are somehow closer than other relatives (or even spouses!) based predominantly on the time spent together. His Lordship stated:

> "I can see no basis in logic, or in law, why [the relationship of brother and sister] should be excluded. If we take, as an example, a family of four consisting of a mother, father, son and daughter, each of the four is already within the line for certain purposes. The mother and father are within that line downward towards their children. They are also within that line in their relationship as husband and wife. The son and daughter are, again, within that line in that their relationship upwards to their parents entitles their parents to come within the line. Although no case was cited to me where a child had succeeded in a claim for psychiatric illness occasioned by the injury or death of a parent caused by the defendant's negligence, the mirror image of claims by a parent for such damage to a child, I cannot think that the principle would be different. . . .[76]

75. *Alcock v Chief Constable of South Yorkshire Police* [1992] 1 AC 310.
76. No reference was made to *Shaw v Mills* (unreported, English CA, 7 Mar 1961) where a young girl recovered damages for psychiatric injury caused when her mother was killed before her eyes. Nor was the Queensland case of *Mellor v Moran* (1985) 2 MVR 461 cited by his Lordship or referred to by counsel. The case concerned a young girl who recovered

Once there are two or more children of a family it is the normal and hoped for . . . course of events, that they grow up together through their years as tiny tots on into their teens, and further on into adulthood. . . . It is the normal instance of family life as to which any defendant is properly fixed with reasonable foreseeability, that the relationships between mothers and fathers, sons and daughters are of the closest known to mankind. Further, when children have grown up together and have got to their late teens or early twenties, their brothers and sisters will usually be the very people with whom they have spent virtually their entire lives; the human beings they know best apart from their parents. That is a general remark which can be applied to all groups. . . .

Those young [married men who were at the game] will have known their wives a far shorter length of time than they have known their brothers or sisters. All those young men will be at the stage in their lives when their ties to their family—their original family—not just to their fathers and mothers, but also to their brothers and sisters, will be of the strongest. They will have had the longest number of years to grow into adulthood, and the least number of years to go their separate ways." [77]

The net would be cast no further, however; the inclusion of brothers and sisters within the class of persons able to recover for psychiatric damage meant that the common law had "reached the margin of what the process of logical progression would allow". [78] Thus, whilst prepared to deviate to some degree from the traditional position, in the final analysis Hidden J resorted to a strategy of arbitrary and irrational demarcation. His Lordship felt compelled to bar the claims of grandfathers, uncles, brothers-in-law, fiancées and friends notwithstanding that "nobody doubts the love of the latter group" [79] and his appreciation of "the closeness, the fondness, the love and affection which can flow in all of [these] other relationships". [80] Surprisingly, his Lordship stated:

"Such love can be strong and compelling, but the various relationships are not so immediate, in my view, as to make it reasonably foreseeable to a defendant that psychiatric illness, rather than grief and sorrow, would follow death or damage to the loved one." [81]

76. *Continued*
   for shock-induced mental damage after the death of her mother in a car accident and indicates that his Lordship's view is consistent with the Australian position. Note also *Gregory v Government Insurance Office of New South Wales* (unreported, New South Wales SC, 1 Mar 1991, No 13756 of 1985) where a son recovered damages for shock and consequent psychiatric harm caused by viewing the horrific injuries suffered by his father under the wheels of a large truck.
77. *Alcock v Chief Constable of South Yorkshire Police* [1992] 1 AC 310 at 337-338.
78. Ibid at 338.
79. Ibid at 339.
80. Ibid at 338.
81. Ibid at 338-339. On Hidden J's reasoning the uncle who was filming the circumcision in *Ibrahim (A Minor) v Muhammad* (unreported, QBD, 21 May 1984), discussed above, p 67, and a theatre nurse who assisted when the operation went wrong, could not have recovered if they had suffered psychiatric damage. Compare *Lafferty v Manhasset Medical Center Hospital* (1980) 425 NYS 2d 244 (woman allowed recovery for emotional distress caused by witnessing the death of her mother-in-law from the transfusion of mismatched blood); *Genzer v City of Mission* (1983) 666 SW 2d 116 (damages for mental

With respect, one can only wonder at the logic behind both the limited extension made and the refusal to carry it through to its rational end. Why does the common law persist in taking small and hesitant steps forward, frequently tottering backwards before stumbling on again? Is this behaviour thought to make new doctrine somehow more palatable? In truth, it serves only to frustrate and stunt the development of sensible law. While Hidden J's innovation, albeit confined, was welcome, surely it cannot be accepted that the common law is unable to foresee recognisable psychiatric harm to other admittedly loving and caring relatives and friends through the defendant's failure to take care? Moreover, it cannot be assumed as a matter of law that siblings are inevitably more intimately linked than those within the remaining categories. Focus must be on the individual claimant rather than making class presumptions. Brothers and sisters separated at an early age or even those together for years who simply do not get on can hardly be said to enjoy the bond that, for example, young lovers do. Intimacy must be regarded as a question of fact in every circumstance, something which, as we will see, the House of Lords has now insisted upon.

This was also recognised by the Court of Appeal which in contrast to Hidden J opined that inquiry into the closeness, in terms of love and affection, of relationships is an appropriate and essential judicial exercise. However, any advance which Hidden J had achieved was substantially nullified by their Lordships' return to conservatism and limitation of the categories of those entitled to recover to the traditional classes in almost all cases. Persons outside the categories of spouse or parent were excluded on the basis advanced by Lord Wilberforce in *McLoughlin v O'Brian*,[82] namely that in relation to claimants with marital or filial ties the presumption was that the love and affection normally exhibited within such relationships was of such a degree that psychiatric injury by shock was reasonably foreseeable to members of ordinary fortitude, but persons in more remote relationships should be expected to withstand shock without injury. With respect, this rationale is simply inaccurate. Persons in more remote relationships are equally likely to be mentally affected by seeing their loved ones involved in trauma. Significantly, none of the cases outlined above where courts have shifted the traditional focus on spouses and parents, save for *Storm v Geeves*,[83] were cited in argument before either Hidden J or the Court of Appeal.

All three of their Lordships considered the presumption of love and affection to be rebuttable by evidence that the particular parent or spouse exhibited no such emotion towards the impact victim. Thus, status as a biological parent or being in lawful wedlock does not now guarantee a shock victim a day in court. As Parker LJ observed:

81. *Continued*
    distress awarded to the grandparents of a girl killed in a fireworks mishap); *Kriventsov v San Rafael Taxicabs Inc* (1986) 229 Cal Rptr 768 (uncle recovered in relation to the hit and run death of his nephew); *Cameron v Marcaccini* (1978) 87 DLR (3d) 442 (aunt recovered for viewing injury to her niece).
82. [1983] 1 AC 410 at 422.
83. [1965] Tas SR 252.

"What, for example, of the mother who has handed over her 16-year-old child to foster parents shortly after its birth, has never seen it or communicated with it or inquired after it ever since? It is submitted that these matters need not and cannot be canvassed. If a mother in fact suffers nervous shock from witnessing the death of her child the very fact, it is said, establishes the correctness of the presumption. I do not accept this. The mother may witness the death of a child without even knowing it is hers and may suffer nervous shock, not because it was her child but because she was not possessed of ordinary phlegm. What also of the husband and wife who are still legally married but have been parted for years and are well known to hate each other?"[84]

Similarly, Nolan LJ stated:

"There is no support in law or in logic for the proposition that an uncaring parent or spouse should stand in any different position from a stranger. It follows that in so far as the defendants' appeals are based upon the judge's inclusion of all brothers and sisters within the requisite proximity of relationship I would feel bound to allow them."[85]

Although it will be a rare case where, for example, a mother whose child is an accident victim but who has not had contact with the child since birth claims for shock-related injury,[86] there is force in the argument that should such a claim ever be made she should stand in no better position than a stranger. Her biological relationship when viewed in the light of such enduring remoteness rightly entitles her to no greater (or lesser) claim to compensation than any other member of the public. Of course, it must be open to her to prove the existence of an affectionate (if distant) bond but such emotional ties cannot and should not be assumed. This "negative" development can thus be rationally justified, though its articulation does reflect the Court of Appeal's willingness to formulate methods for cutting down even further the categories of claimants able to recover, rather than extending them.

There were, however, some encouraging signs in some of the judgments. And this is where their Lordships diverged in opinion. In contrast to Stocker and Nolan LJJ who adopted a more liberal attitude, Parker LJ remained steadfastly loyal to the past, refusing to canvass the possibility of additional species of claimant. His Lordship would not extend the presumption made in relation to spouses and parents to other plaintiffs, opining that defendants should not reasonably be expected to contemplate that there will or may be amongst those affected by their acts or omissions persons other than those within recognised categories or exceptions who are likely to suffer psychiatric harm. Thus, although Parker LJ conceded that a godfather or friend who has taken on the care and custody of a small baby on the death of its parents and has brought it up as his own would appear to be "every bit as deserving as the parent", and that it was logical that one of two people who had lived together as man and wife for 30 years but who

---

84. *Alcock v Chief Constable of South Yorkshire Police* [1992] 1 AC 310 at 359-360.
85. Ibid at 385. See also per Stocker LJ at 376.
86. Indeed Stocker LJ at 376 referred to it as "such an unlikely situation that it need hardly be considered".

had remained unmarried due to legal, religious, moral or philosophical impediments should be treated in the same manner as a legal spouse, he was not prepared, in the perceived absence of some legal justification, to allow common sense to prevail in these types of fact situations.[87] Stocker and Nolan LJJ were less staid. The retention of a degree of flexibility in Lord Wilberforce's obiter dictum in *McLoughlin v O'Brian*[88] led their Lordships to rule that in the most exceptional cases the categories of those entitled to recover could be extended on evidence that a similar degree of love, care and affection for the victim to that exhibited by a spouse or parent was shown by the non-traditional claimant in question. In such circumstances the plaintiff will be treated as being in the same position vis-à-vis the victim as members of the conventional classes. The potentially protracted evidence-gathering investigations and the possible resultant delay and complication of already difficult cases was acknowledged but not considered a sufficient reason to abandon this strategy.[89]

Both judges decided that as Hidden J had not scrutinised the brothers' and sisters' feelings they could not be automatically entitled to recover, falling as they did outside the traditional categories. Had he done so, the facts may have justified an extension and entitled them to recover in accordance with the principle outlined above. However, their Lordships differed on the question of the scope of the extension of the categories entitled to recover on proof of care, love and affection similar to that of a parent or spouse. Stocker LJ confined it on policy bases to those within some familial relationship:

"[C]onsider the case where the victim's parents are dead and the victim himself was brought up by grandparents who have fulfilled the parental role since early infancy. A careful scrutiny might, in such a case, involve no more than the assertion and proof of those facts. The same position might be established without difficulty in the case of other relationships. . . .

In my view, foreseeability of psychiatric illness through shock to persons should not be extended to persons who do not have any family relationships, even if such persons did as a fact entertain feelings of love and affection towards the victim. If such persons . . . are included within the ambit of those to whom a duty is owed, then a duty might be owed to the whole world and thus impose a duty which would place an intolerable burden on a tortfeasor."[90]

Nolan LJ, in the most liberal judgment delivered, could identify no impediment in principle to going even further and including friends whose love and care for the impact victim is akin to that of the normal parent or spouse. Uninfluenced by the indeterminate liability concerns which had restrained Stocker LJ, his Lordship stated:

"I see no difficulty in principle in requiring a defendant to contemplate that the person physically injured or threatened by his negligence may

87. Ibid at 360.
88. [1983] 1 AC 410 at 422, quoted above, p 114.
89. *Alcock v Chief Constable of South Yorkshire Police* [1992] 1 AC 310 per Stocker LJ at 375, per Nolan LJ at 385.
90. Ibid at 375-378.

have relatives or friends whose love for him is like that of a normal parent or spouse, and who in consequence may similarly be closely and directly affected by nervous shock. . . . The identification of the particular individuals who come within that category, like that of the parents and spouses themselves, could only be carried out ex post facto, and would depend upon evidence of the 'relationship' in the broad sense which gave rise to the love and affection. . . . I see no reason in principle why identification should not be possible on a case by case basis. I have in mind such examples as the grandparents or uncles and aunts who, upon the premature death of the parents, bring up the children as their own; or Mrs Hinz (see *Hinz v Berry* [1970] 2 QB 40) whose feelings for her foster children were assumed without question to be the same as those for her natural children. I have in mind also the judgment of Burbury CJ in *Storm v Geeves* [1965] Tas SR 252 at 266 in which he felt able to identify the brother and sister as well as the mother as coming within the scope of the duty of care, and was further able to find on the evidence that whereas the mother and the brother had suffered nervous shock caused by the defendant's acts or omissions, the sister had not. . . . I have no means of knowing whether [a certain grandmother who reared her grandson as a son] satisfies the conditions for bringing her within the scope of the duty of care, but in so far as the extent of the duty depends upon proximity in terms of personal relationship I can see no reason in principle why she should be excluded. . . .

I cannot agree with [Hidden J] that the line should be drawn around what is called the nuclear family. The criterion is loving care, not blood relationship, still less legal relationship. Unfortunately, people within those relationships do not always care for each other. Fortunately people outside those relationships often care for each other very much.''[91]

Of all the positions taken to this point, that of Nolan LJ is the most preferable, serving as the springboard to the total abandonment of a limitation on liability imposed during an era of medical ignorance and scepticism.

Nolan LJ's philosophy found favour with the House of Lords,[92] which adopted a practical approach to complete the dissolution of the logically indefensible conventional stance. Rather than retreat to the conformity of the past, their Lordships recognised (at least in the context of the relationship issue) that "good sense"[93] dictates that the scope of the cause of action be expanded considerably. Nor did they view public policy as demanding the existence of a marital or filial relationship as a pre-condition to liability. There was a unanimous refusal to limit the class of claimants by reference to these specific bonds, focus being directed instead on the factual question of the closeness of the particular parties in terms of love and affection. Their Lordships agreed with the Court of Appeal that the

91. Ibid at 384-385.
92. Per Lords Keith, Ackner, Oliver and Jauncey (Lord Lowry concurring).
93. *Bourhill v Young* [1943] AC 92 per Lord Wright at 110; *Jaensch v Coffey* (1984) 155 CLR 549 per Brennan J at 572.

presumed existence of strong emotional ties between spouses and parents and their issue must, in practice, be rebuttable.[94] More importantly, they indorsed the suggestion advanced by Stocker and Nolan LJJ that where the "primary" (accident) victim and "secondary" (shock) victim share an intimacy comparable to that normally (but not always) found within marital or blood relationships they should be treated in the same manner. Lord Oliver stated that he could:

> "see no logic and no virtue in seeking to lay down as a matter of 'policy' categories of relationship within which claims may succeed and without which they are doomed to failure in limine. So rigid an approach would, I think, work great injustice and cannot be rationally justified. Obviously a claim for damages for psychiatric injury by a remote relative of the primary victim will factually require most cautious scrutiny and faces considerable evidentiary problems. Equally obviously, the foreseeability of such injury to such a person will be more difficult to establish than similar injury to a spouse or parent of the primary victim. But these are factual difficulties and I can see no logic and no policy reason for excluding claims by more remote relatives. Suppose, for instance, that the primary victim has lived with the plaintiff for 40 years, both being under the belief that they are lawfully married. Does she suffer less shock or grief because it is subsequently discovered that their marriage was invalid? The source of the shock and distress in all these cases is the affectionate relationship which existed between the plaintiff and the victim and the traumatic effect of the negligence is equally foreseeable, given that relationship, however the relationship arises."[95]

Significantly, the hesitancy expressed by Stocker LJ to carry the "love and affection" analysis through to its logical conclusion was not shared by the House of Lords. Their Lordships emphasised that, outside the traditional categories, sufficiently strong emotional bonds may not only exist between remote relatives but also friends and lovers. As Lord Keith pointed out, closer and stronger ties may be found, for example, in the case of engaged couples than between persons who have been married for years.[96] Thus, it is clear that the search for proof of love and affection is not to be confined, as Stocker LJ would have it, to those with some familial link to the accident victim, but in appropriate circumstances will operate, as Nolan LJ postulated, to assist a much wider sphere of associates. Ultimately, arbitrary categorisation and exclusion has been replaced by an insistence on the investigation of the nature of every relationship before the

---

94. See especially *Alcock v Chief Constable of South Yorkshire Police* [1992] 1 AC 310 per Lord Keith at 397, per Lord Ackner at 403. Would the likelihood of rebuttal be any greater where there are several children in a family, as opposed to a case where the accident victim is an only child? Their Lordships did not allude to this issue, but there may be scope for argument that slightly stronger evidence would be required to rebut the presumption in the latter situation. Note *Morton v Wiseman*, 1989 SCLR 365 at 370 where "the whole of the pursuer's case was implicitly based on the fact that she had no other child".

95. *Alcock v Chief Constable of South Yorkshire Police* [1992] 1 AC 310 at 415-416. Note also *Champion v Gray* (1985) 478 So 2d 17 (Fla) where it was said that the right to recover depends on the relationship and the circumstances.

96. [1992] 1 AC 310 at 397.

court. The remoter the tie between the parties the closer the attention required. The merits of individual claimants, rather than their particular status, now determine whether compensation will be forthcoming. Lord Jauncey stated:

"I would respectfully agree with Lord Wilberforce [in *McLoughlin v O'Brian*[97]] that cases involving less close relatives should be very carefully scrutinised. That, however, is not to say they must necessarily be excluded. . . . There may . . . be others whose ties of relationship are as strong [as parents and spouses]. I do not consider that it would be profitable to try and define who such others might be or to draw any dividing line between one degree of relationship and another. To draw such a line would necessarily be arbitrary and lacking in logic. In my view the proper approach is to examine each case on its own facts in order to see whether the claimant has established so close a relationship of love and affection to the victim as might reasonably be expected in the case of spouses or parents and children. If the claimant has so established and all other requirements of the claim are satisfied he or she will succeed since the shock to him or her will be within the reasonable contemplation of the tortfeasor. If such relationship is not established the claim will fail."[98]

Similarly, Lord Ackner emphasised that:

"Whether the degree of love and affection in any given relationship, be it that of relative or friend, is such that the defendant, in the light of the plaintiff's proximity to the scene of the accident in time and space and its nature, should reasonably have foreseen the shock-induced psychiatric illness, has to be decided on a case by case basis."[99]

The House of Lords referred, as the Court of Appeal had done, to the inevitable evidentiary difficulties associated with this process of scrutinisation but apparently did not view them as insurmountable.[100] The precise methodology to be utilised to establish the requisite tie of relationship in the case of remoter relatives and friends was not articulated, the only guidance offered being that of Lord Ackner who spoke of comparing the love and affection between these claimants and the tort victim to "that of the normal parent, spouse or child of the victim",[101] and Lord Jauncey who made a similar reference.[101a] The wisdom of the use of the concept of normality as a yardstick to establish "sufficiently close" ties of love and affection is open to question. For example, does the "normal" family in 1993 comprise both a mother and a father, and do they have to be married to each other and reside under the same roof? Perhaps more importantly, it is not clear why the bond between friends or cousins, for example, should be assessed by reference to the most formal relationships.

97. [1983] 1 AC 410 at 422.
98. *Alcock v Chief Constable of South Yorkshire Police* [1992] 1 AC 310 at 422.
99. Ibid at 404.
100. Ibid per Lord Oliver at 415.
101. Ibid at 403.
101a. Ibid at 422, quoted above, p 114.

Those appellants outside the traditional relational categories who were present at the soccer ground and thus satisfied this aspect of the proximity requirement (Brian Harrison, who lost two brothers, and Robert Alcock, who lost a brother-in-law), failed in their actions due to the absence of any evidence of an especially close tie of love and affection with the relevant primary victims. Nor did such bonds exist in relation to the plaintiffs whose brothers and grandsons were killed but who were not at the ground (and whose claims would thus have failed on other grounds in any event). The mere fact of these particular relationships (brother, brother-in-law, grandson) did not suffice to ground recovery. Apparently, a "normal" degree of brotherly love for an accident victim will not entitle a psychiatrically damaged sibling to recover from the tortfeasor. An "abnormal" tie (missing in Brian Harrison's case) is required in order to render this type of loss reasonably foreseeable and recoverable. True it is that the "quality of brotherly love is well known to differ widely—from Cain and Abel to David and Jonathan", [102] but we would question whether shock-induced psychiatric injury can be regarded as unforeseeable in all but the most unusual cases. Certainly, we do not advocate the imposition of an irrebuttable presumption that such damage is always reasonably foreseeable as between siblings, for it is a sad fact that some have a closer rapport with strangers than each other. What we do suggest is that the typical bond in this situation makes the suffering of shock-related illness to one reasonably foreseeable if the other is killed, injured or imperilled. It is submitted therefore that relationships between children within the immediate familial nucleus should be elevated to the status afforded to spousal and parental links; [103] namely the presumed existence of love and affection, always rebuttable by evidence to the contrary. It is clear from Lord Keith's judgment that the category of the "presumptive relationship" is not closed. His Lordship held that the mere presence of the bond of engagement was sufficient to attract the presumption of intimacy. Thus, Alexandra Penks, the appellant who lost her fiancé, was viewed as having had the closest feelings of love and affection for the deceased (there being no evidence to rebut this presumption [104]), failing in her claim only because of the way news of his death was communicated to her. [105] No change in approach should be made in relation to in-laws (both brothers and sisters-in-law, and mothers and fathers-in-law) or to grandchildren where evidence of a unique and especially close tie should continue to be required to be shown.

The comments of both Nolan LJ and the House of Lords on the issue of relationship are particularly significant in that it is only a short step from acknowledging a friend's right to sue in appropriate circumstances to the recognition of the same right in relation to an ordinary bystander.

102. Ibid per Lord Ackner at 406. Contrary to Lord Ackner's assumption, David and Jonathan were not brothers, but their relationship displayed the characteristics identified by Lord Ackner. Jonathan was the son of King Saul. He made a pact with David to love him as his own soul: see 1 Samuel 18: 3.
103. Note Hidden J's comments [1992] 1 AC 310 at 337-338, quoted above, pp 119-120.
104. Ibid at 398.
105. That is, by way of live television: on this issue see below, pp 170-179.

"Mere bystanders"

Until very recently, save for isolated exceptional cases,[106] persons lacking the requisite natural or social link with the person killed, injured or imperilled through the defendant's negligence were automatically relegated to the category of accident victim to whom no duty is owed. Traditional doctrine dictated that defendants were not required to go about their business in such a way as to avoid shocking such "mere bystanders". As Lord Porter stated obiter, disapproving of the suggested inclusion of the stranger:

"It is not every emotional disturbance or every shock which should have been foreseen. The driver of a car or vehicle, even though careless, is entitled to assume that the ordinary frequenter of the streets has sufficient fortitude to endure such incidents as may from time to time be expected to occur in them, including the noise of a collision and the sight of injury to others, and is not to be considered negligent towards one who does not possess the customary phlegm."[107]

Similarly Lord Wilberforce in *McLoughlin v O'Brian* was moved to exclude ordinary bystanders on the basis that either:

"such persons must be assumed to be possessed of fortitude sufficient to enable them to endure the calamities of modern life, or that defendants cannot be expected to compensate the world at large."[108]

This reasoning was indorsed by the English Court of Appeal in *Alcock v Chief Constable of South Yorkshire Police*[109] which, although prepared to canvass the possibility that non-spouses and non-parents might recover in unusual circumstances, expressly rejected counsel's submission that any person can recover if the scene is sufficiently horrific.[110] With respect, this view is unconvincing. The approach of courts to psychiatric damage suits must be uniform regardless of the identity of the particular claimant. The question of recovery must be answered having regard to normal standards of susceptibility, causation, foreseeability and proximity issues and not pre-empted on the basis of the status of individual victims. As one learned commentator lamented almost 40 years ago:

106. See the discussion of rescuers and employees above, pp 108-113.
107. *Bourhill v Young* [1943] AC 92 at 117. Note that although the pregnant fishwife in this case was unrelated to the deceased motorcyclist and did not know him the rejection of her claim turned on questions of reasonable foreseeability: see above, p 66.
108. [1983] 1 AC 410 at 422.
109. [1992] 1 AC 310 per Parker LJ at 359-361, per Stocker LJ at 377-379 and per Nolan LJ at 384-385.
110. For example, the pursuer in *Bourhill v Young* [1943] AC 92 would fall into the uncompensable class of non-rescuer or non-employee stranger. Note also *Smith v Johnson* (unreported, QBD, Jan 1897, cited in *Wilkinson v Downton* [1897] 2 QB 57 per Wright J at 61) where a man who saw another killed by the defendant's negligence and incurred psychiatric damage not from fear of self-harm but from witnessing the trauma was denied compensation on the ground that that species of injury was too remote a consequence of the negligence. For a United States perspective see *Devereux v Allstate Insurance Co* (1990) 557 So 2d 1091 (La) where a driver who struck and killed a pedestrian could not recover for the emotional distress of witnessing his body come through the windshield because the relationship between them was too distant; *Covello v Weis Markets Inc* (1992) 610 A 2d 50 (Pa) where a police officer who saw someone being crushed to death in an industrial compactor failed to recover.

"[T]he answer . . . must depend on the nature of the accident, and it is contrary to human experience to say that in no circumstances is it reasonably foreseeable that one who sees a violent accident will receive a dangerous shock. If the person threatened is a husband, wife or child of the person receiving the shock, the foreseeability is, of course, greater than in other circumstances, but it is a gloomy view of human nature which suggests that the sight of the death or injury of someone else cannot create such a shock. It must always be a question of reasonable foresight, and this cannot depend on arbitrary categories." [111]

The latest indications reveal an appreciation of the illogicality of an absolute and arbitrary bar. Confessing to having difficulties with the classification theory, Lords Keith, Ackner, Oliver and Jauncey in *Alcock v Chief Constable of South Yorkshire Police*[112] could distil no reason in principle for the common law's long-standing refusal to sanction bystander relief in any circumstances. In an encouraging liberalisation, their Lordships declined categorically to rule out potential bystander claims, envisaging situations where the circumstances of catastrophe would be particularly emotionally agitating even to innocent strangers.[113] Nor has this possibility been overlooked by Australian courts. Brennan J was alive to it in *Jaensch v Coffey*,[114] observing that the categories of claimant are not closed and pointing out that the prerequisite criteria to a cause of action, while more easily satisfied in the case of parent and child or husband and wife, also:

"furnish the framework of principle within which the courts determine whether a particular claim by a bystander or by a plaintiff in 'a less close relationship' with a physically injured victim is to be allowed." [115]

In a recent case a Canadian judge has also adverted to the possibility that, in appropriate cases, bystanders witnessing accidents to strangers might be owed a duty of care. Griffiths JA, giving the judgment of the Ontario Court of Appeal in *Bechard v Haliburton Estate*, suggested that "it is reasonably foreseeable that witnessing a horrifying or gruesome accident . . . might well upset the average sensitive bystander".[116] However, in ruling on the existence of a duty, the court relied principally on the fact that the defendant had indirectly performed a role analogous to that of a rescuer.

Contentions that bystanders must be automatically ruled out for fear that their inclusion would place an intolerable burden on tortfeasors are exaggerated. When pleas for compensation are decided on ordinary foreseeability principles it is likely that recovery will be relatively rare rather

111. A L Goodhart, "The Shock Cases and Area of Risk" (1953) 16 MLR 14 at 25. But see J Havard, "Reasonable Foresight of Nervous Shock" (1956) 19 MLR 478 at 496, n 13 who argues that this approach is not consistent with medical experience.
112. [1992] 1 AC 310.
113. Ibid per Lord Keith at 397, per Lord Ackner at 403, per Lord Oliver at 416, per Lord Jauncey at 421-422. Note also *Currie v Wardrop*, 1927 SC 538 per Lord Murray at 555.
114. (1984) 155 CLR 549 at 571. See also *Mount Isa Mines Ltd v Pusey* (1970) 125 CLR 383 per Windeyer J at 404-405 and per Walsh J at 416-417.
115. (1984) 155 CLR 549 at 571.
116. (1991) 84 DLR (4th) 668 at 681.

than lead to a flood of actions.[117] Arguably, at least according to one Australian judge, there are two reasons for this. Apart from satisfying the requirement of foreseeability of injury by shock, Brennan J in *Jaensch v Coffey* attached significance to the tortfeasor's role in how the bystander came to be at the scene of the trauma:

"It would be an exceptional case if it could be found that the attendance of other persons at the scene of an accident is the result of the defendant's negligence. However foreseeable it may be that passers-by will stop or that morbid curiosity will bring others to the scene, it is difficult to envisage a case where their attendance at the scene and their perception of it could fairly be regarded as a result of the defendant's conduct. Unless their attendance at and perception of the scene is shown to be a result, and a reasonably foreseeable result, of the defendant's conduct, they are not entitled to recover damages for psychiatric illness induced by sudden perception of it. That is, however, a question of fact."[118]

With respect, it is hard to see why liability in the case of strangers should hinge on whether the defendant is responsible for the bystander's presence at and perception of the incident in question. Significantly, their Lordships in *Alcock v Chief Constable of South Yorkshire Police* did not focus on this as an explanation for the potential rarity of bystander recovery. While refusing to close the door on these claimants, they too viewed it as likely to be unusual, but for the reason that psychiatric injury to such persons would not, they forecast, ordinarily be within the range of reasonable foreseeability. Clearly the closeness of the relationship between the plaintiff and the primary victim will continue to be of relevance in determining this question. If, on ordinary principles, strangers can be accommodated within the framework of negligence they must be afforded the privileges that come with this.

Hitherto, there appears to be no Commonwealth decision permitting ordinary onlookers who perceive (let alone those who hear of) traumatic and distressing events to recover.[119] This is a most disturbing fact. However, there are important dicta in favour of bystander recovery. Almost 70 years ago Atkin LJ expressed a preference for assessing every claim on its merits:

"Personally I see no reason for excluding the bystander in the highway who receives injury in the same way from apprehension of or the actual sight of injury to a third party. There may well be cases where the sight of suffering will directly and immediately physically shock the most obdurate heart."[120]

117. See H Teff, "Liability for Negligently Inflicted Nervous Shock" (1983) 99 LQR 100 at 104-105.
118. (1984) 155 CLR 549 at 570.
119. Note, however, the recent settlement of a claim arising out of the 1977 Granville train disaster in New South Wales, where the plaintiff, a passenger on the train, suffered from manic depressive psychosis after seeing fellow passengers crushed to death when the carriage ceiling collapsed "like a deck of cards" under the weight of a falling overhead bridge: see "Granville Deal", *The Australian*, 18 Feb 1992, 6.
120. *Hambrook v Stokes Bros* [1925] 1 KB 141 at 157-158.

It seems also that Lord Bridge in *McLoughlin v O'Brian*[121] was more open to the notion of stranger relief than Lord Wilberforce and the English Court of Appeal in *Alcock v Chief Constable of South Yorkshire Police*,[122] as he denounced attempts to petrify principle: the courts "should resist the temptation to try yet once more to freeze the law in a rigid posture which would deny justice to some who . . . ought to succeed".[123] It is significant that his Lordship expressed difficulty in distinguishing in principle the position of a rescuer who, as noted earlier, would not be automatically prevented from suing, from that of a mere spectator, citing the example of an uninjured or slightly injured accident victim who takes no part in any rescue operations that unfold but is present at the scene for some time observing the goings on around him or her while waiting for transport home. After prolonged criticism Atkin LJ's words have found favour. His sentiments were expressly indorsed by Lord Ackner in *Alcock v Chief Constable of South Yorkshire Police* who, striking a resonant note, queried:

> "[H]ow do you explain why the duty is confined to the case of parent or guardian and child and does not extend to other relations of life also involving intimate associations; and why does it not eventually extend to bystanders? As regards the latter category, while it may be very difficult to envisage a case of a stranger, who is not actively and foreseeably involved in a disaster or its aftermath, other than in the role of rescuer, suffering shock-induced psychiatric injury by the mere observation of apprehended or actual injury of a third person in circumstances that could be considered reasonably foreseeable, I see no reason in principle why he should not, if in the circumstances, a reasonably strong-nerved person would have been so shocked."[124]

Lord Ackner postulated one vivid example where he would not be prepared to rule out a claim by a passer-by shocked and mentally injured by the distressing scene: where he or she witnesses a petrol tanker careering out of control into a school in session and bursting into flames.[125] If his Lordship was willing to consider relief to bystanders in this unusual situation, presumably on the basis that it was reasonably foreseeable that shock-related harm would be suffered if care was not taken, it would seem to follow that, contrary to his prediction, a similar conclusion must logically be reached in a vast number of other fact situations. It may well be, therefore, that the likelihood of stranger recovery is greater than the court envisaged. Other scenarios likely to traumatise the most "phlegmatic spectator" come to mind. For example, should beachgoers on Bondi Beach who witness a young child drown just beyond their rescuable distance due to the failure of lifesavers to watch over swimmers be denied relief for genuine shock caused by perceiving this frantic and desperate scene simply because there is no tie between the parties? What of a grotesque shark attack close enough to shore for onlookers to appreciate the savagery involved, if its presence was due to the negligent maintenance of shark

121. *McLoughlin v O'Brian* [1983] 1 AC 410 at 442-443.
122. [1992] 1 AC 310.
123. [1983] 1 AC 410 at 443.
124. [1992] 1 AC 310 at 403.
125. Ibid.

protection nets? How can it be logically maintained that a couple whose picnic in the English countryside is shattered by the sight of a Rottweiler which, due to the negligence of its owner, is allowed to maul another's toddler, and the hideous consequences of the attack, are somehow unworthy of compensation for resultant psychiatric harm just because the victim is not their child? Can it be right to assert that nature walkers enjoying a Sunday stroll in a national park who see an abseiler plummet to his death due to faulty equipment or his own failure to take care would not suffer shock or psychiatric illness? Are airshow spectators who watch in horror as a parachute fails to open owing to the carelessness of the parachutist, see his desperate struggle as panic consumes him, hear the sickening thud as he impacts with the ground and perhaps even see the gruesome aftermath, expected in all seriousness to endure this calamity[126] without any ill-effects merely because they do not know the man? And why, despite Lord Robertson's assertions to the contrary in *Bourhill v Young's Executor*,[127] should a window cleaner (or his estate) who, due to his own negligence, falls from a height and impales himself upon spiked railings not be held liable for the shock-induced psychiatric harm caused to a pregnant woman who witnesses the incident from the window of her house on the opposite side of the street? Less unusual, but still distressingly dramatic, are pedestrians who see a speeding driver skittle a young girl or old lady right before their eyes really any less deserving of compensation if they suffer a recognisable psychiatric illness than a parent or spouse? In each of these examples, we would argue that, providing all the normal pre-requisites to a successful negligence claim exist, recovery is unquestionably justified. Finally, an interesting conundrum is whether a stranger who mistakenly believes that the person who has been killed, injured or endangered in an accident is someone known or dear to them is entitled to redress for resultant psychiatric harm. A Massachusetts court has seen fit to turn down a plaintiff's claim in such circumstances on foreseeability grounds.[128] It is submitted that liability should not categorically be excluded and that the right to compensation must hinge on both foreseeability of damage and reasonableness and genuineness of belief.

In a considerable improvement on the previous state of affairs, the Law Lords have finally removed some of the arbitrary barriers to relief for shock-induced injury, denounced illogical distinctions and unambiguously declared that, in appropriate circumstances, defendants will be held responsible for all the legally recognised emotional consequences of their negligence to all persons who suffer harm as a result. Although these

---

126. As Lord Wilberforce in *McLoughlin v O'Brian* [1983] 1 AC 410 at 422 would have them do.

127. 1941 SC 395 at 399. Note also F A Trindade, "The Principles Governing the Recovery of Damages for Negligently Caused Nervous Shock" [1986] CLJ 476 at 489. This example also raises the question of recovery for psychiatric damage occasioned by the self-inflicted death, injury or imperilment of the tortfeasor, a traditional limitation on liability which is discussed below, pp 215-220.

128. *Barnes v Geiger* (1983) 446 NE 2d 78 (Mass). A mother saw a car strike a young male pedestrian and toss him in the air near an area where her 13-year-old son and ten-year-old daughter had gone ice skating. Convinced that the accident victim was her son she ran to the scene only to discover her mistake. The next day she died of a cerebral vascular haemorrhage allegedly triggered by the elevation of her blood pressure as a result of the prior trauma. Recovery could not be had against the driver.

"MERE BYSTANDERS" 133

advances did not actually benefit any of the claimants before the House of Lords they will assist other plaintiffs, including some who suffered as a result of the Hillsborough disaster and whose cases were dependent on the outcome of the decision. Regrettably these developments with respect to the issue of relationship did not extend to other aspects of the law governing psychiatric damage urgently in need of reform.

6

PROXIMITY OF TIME AND SPACE

The presence requirement

As already related, cases such as *Hambrook v Stokes Bros*,[1] which overruled the "Kennedy limitation"[2] and held that a plaintiff outside the zone of danger could recover for shock caused by fear for the safety of others, stressed the elements of *presence* at the scene of the accident and *perception* of it with one's own unaided senses (as opposed to being informed by someone else).[3] It may well be that modern cases do not place quite the same degree of emphasis on these twin requirements as did the court in *Hambrook v Stokes Bros*. Hidden J in *Alcock v Chief Constable of South Yorkshire Police*[4] summarised this development as follows:

"From the review of the various authorities which I have sought to make, it can be seen that, once it was established that a claim for damages lay for nervous shock resulting from a fear not for one's own safety, but for that of someone else, the courts originally demanded of

1. [1925] 1 KB 141.
2. *Dulieu v White & Sons* [1901] 2 KB 669 per Kennedy J at 675.
3. Note also the use of the concept of presence in the Australian statutory provisions on liability for psychiatric damage: see below, pp 239-245.
4. [1992] 1 AC 310 at 340. For examples of cases where the plaintiff was present at the scene but did not directly witness the traumatic event in question see *Owens v Liverpool Corporation* [1939] 1 KB 394 (only one of the four claimants actually saw the collision between the tram and the hearse which upset the coffin); *Vana v Tosta* (1967) 66 DLR (2d) 97 (driver did not see his wife ejected from their vehicle upon impact with another car, but discovered her badly injured and bleeding on the ground a short while later); *Diakogiorgic v Anastasas* (unreported, Queensland SC, 4 Nov 1974, No 179 of 1972), noted (1975) 49 ALJ 188 (mother on opposite side of the road to her husband and two children became aware that they had been struck by an oncoming vehicle only after hearing her daughter scream); *Kralj v McGrath* [1986] 1 All ER 54, discussed below, pp 142-143; *Whitty v Hackney Borough Council* (unreported, QBD, 5 Feb 1987) (woman heard 21 month-old son shriek, turned round to see him lying prostrate in a pall of smoke, having been electrocuted by touching broken illuminated sign). That one may be present without perceiving an incident is evidenced also by United States case law: see eg *Jansen v Children's Hospital Medical Center of East Bay* (1973) 106 Cal Rptr 883 (recovery denied to a mother who witnessed her child's painful death because she could not have sensorily perceived the negligent misdiagnosis, but only the result); *Krouse v Graham* (1977) 562 P 2d 1022; 137 Cal Rptr 863; *Justus v Atchison* (1977) 565 P 2d 122; 139 Cal Rptr 97; *Bliss v Allentown Public Library* (1980) 497 F Supp 487 (mother turned to see child lying underneath fallen statue); *Neff v Lasso* (1989) 555 A 2d 1304 (Pa); *Wright v City of Los Angeles* (1990) 268 Cal Rptr 309 (brother observed negligent treatment by paramedic but was not aware deceased was being injured); *Golstein v Superior Court* (1990) 273 Cal Rptr 270 (negligent overdose of radiation given to cancer victim incapable of being sensorily perceived); *Gonzalez v New York City Housing Authority* (1992) 580 NYS 2d 760 (mother fainted as lift doors opened between floors and did not see daughter fall to her death).

the plaintiff both presence at the scene and sight of the event. Gradually those rigid requirements were relaxed to extend to presence near the scene without any actual sight of the accident.''

But, as Hidden J went on to point out, in recent years the presence limitation has increasingly been called into question. As Lord Bridge said in *McLoughlin v O'Brian*, once the zone of danger limitation is crossed there is no logical reason for limiting the defendant's duty to persons in physical proximity to the place where the accident occurred.[5] Moreover, persons who are not actually present at the accident to see or hear it with their own eyes or ears, unless they happen on the scene shortly afterwards by chance, are going to learn of it by being told by someone else. Given that the emphasis in the cases now seems to be on the *relationship* between the plaintiff and the primary accident victim as the key factor in determining whether psychiatric injury is foreseeable in the circumstances, are any other limits to recovery appropriate, and if so how are they to be drawn? These questions have exercised the attention of the courts in many of the recent cases.

The requirement that the plaintiff be present at the accident and perceive it through his or her own unaided senses caused difficulty right from the start. In *Hambrook v Stokes Bros*, Mrs Hambrook's personal representative recovered on the basis that, as the truck went past her and crashed into a house, she suffered shock and injury through fear for the safety of her children. But that fear was that an accident *had already happened*, an accident which she was not there to see. She went to the scene, discovered that there had been an accident, and that a little girl had been injured. She went to the hospital, and found that the injured girl was indeed her daughter. No doubt all this contributed to the injury she suffered, but liability to her was based on her perception at the moment the truck went by her. In other cases plaintiffs were unable to recover because they were not present at the crucial moment. In *Chester v Council of the Municipality of Waverley*,[6] a mother suffered psychiatric harm through seeing the body of her son recovered from a water-filled trench, but it was held that the council, which had left the trench unprotected, owed her no duty of care to prevent causing such injury. It would have been different if she had been there to see him fall in. In *King v Phillips*,[7] a mother who heard a scream, looked out of her window and saw her son, as she thought, disappear under the wheels of a taxi was not given damages because it was not foreseeable that she might be watching from such a position and suffer emotional injury. But of course her response to the occurrence was to get to the scene of the accident as fast as she could, and on the way there she met her son running towards her and discovered that he had escaped physically unscathed.[8]

5. [1983] 1 AC 410 at 439. See also *Ravenscroft v Rederiaktiebφlaget Transatlantic* [1991] 3 All ER 73 per Ward J at 87, though note the reversal of this decision by the English Court of Appeal [1992] 2 All ER 470n in the light of the disapproval expressed by the House of Lords in *Alcock v Chief Constable of South Yorkshire Police* [1992] 1 AC 310.
6. (1939) 62 CLR 1.
7. [1953] 1 KB 429.
8. The Scottish case of *McLinden v Richardson*, 1962 SLT (Notes) 104 is very similar, the only distinction being that the vehicle had in fact injured the child.

What cases like these show is that relatives who do not happen to be present when the accident occurs are likely to arrive there shortly afterwards, and the whole experience may well result in distressing consequences in the form of shock and psychiatric illness. It seems artificial to make presence at a particular point in time the crucial factor in determining whether any duty is owed to them.

The aftermath doctrine

It is in response to such problems that the law has developed what is now known as the "aftermath" doctrine—a plaintiff whose relationship with the accident victim satisfies the criteria laid down by the law, and who suffers psychiatric injury from direct perception of the accident or its immediate aftermath, is within the boundaries of foreseeability and may recover. In the words of Lord Lowry, the need for presence at the accident scene in psychiatric damage cases "has been consigned to the lumber room of rejected legal fallacies".[9] The aftermath doctrine might well have been applied in the cases dealt with above if they were to have occurred today.

The aftermath doctrine originated in a series of cases in which the courts held that it was foreseeable that a plaintiff not present at the scene of the accident would arrive shortly afterwards. Perhaps the first case was *Boardman v Sanderson*[10] in 1964, where a father and his son had accompanied a friend to a garage to collect his car. The father went into the garage office, leaving his son outside. The friend, in backing the car out of the garage, negligently ran over the son's foot. The father heard his screams and immediately ran to his son. These events caused the father to suffer nervous shock. The court said that the defendant knew the father was only a few yards away and could foresee that in such circumstances he would immediately come to the scene. The next year in an Australian case, *Storm v Geeves*,[11] the potential of this idea was extended: a child was run over by a truck and killed while waiting for a bus close to her home, and her brother rushed inside the house to fetch his mother, who suffered shock and consequent emotional injury due to the sight of her daughter's crushed body. The court held that she could recover, because, as in *Boardman v Sanderson*, it was foreseeable that the circumstances would bring her to the site of the accident. In *Mount Isa Mines Ltd v Pusey*[12] the plaintiff was quite close to where the accident took place, and heard the explosion which caused it; in *Chadwick v British Railways Board*[13] the plaintiff was at his home 200 yards away from the scene of a train crash. Both went to the

9. *O'Dowd v Secretary of State for Northern Ireland* [1982] NI 210 at 214.
10. [1964] 1 WLR 1317, noted by G Dworkin (1962) 25 MLR 353; (1965) 81 LQR 3. Note also two recent Australian cases with very similar facts: *Government Insurance Office of New South Wales v Maroulis* (unreported, New South Wales CA, 6 April 1990, CA Nos 274 and 275 of 1988) (plaintiff and husband crossing street to visit nephew, plaintiff had gone ahead and entered house, heard loud noise and rushed outside to find husband lying unconscious in gutter after being hit by car); *Gregory v Government Insurance Office of New South Wales* (unreported, New South Wales SC, 1 Mar 1991, No 13756 of 1985) (plaintiff, whose father was at other side of their caravan, heard sound of breaking glass as truck passed by and went round to find his father lying in the road, badly injured).
11. [1965] Tas SR 252.
12. (1970) 125 CLR 383.
13. [1967] 1 WLR 912.

rescue and recovered damages for the psychiatric injury they suffered as a result. In each case it was accepted that the arrival of rescuers was entirely foreseeable.

By the early 1970s some courts were beginning to use the word "aftermath" to describe the basis of the defendant's liability. In Canada in *Marshall v Lionel Enterprises Inc*,[14] a wife recovered damages when she came upon her husband who had been injured in a snowmobile accident. The court rejected a submission that the shock she suffered was the result of viewing the aftermath rather than the accident itself. In Australia in *Benson v Lee*,[15] a mother at home 100 yards away was summoned to the scene of the accident where she saw her unconscious son, and was later informed at the hospital that he was dead. Lush J formulated liability in the following terms:

> "[W]hat is, at the present time, required, is, I think, a direct perception of some of the events which go to make up the accident as an entire event, and this includes seeing the *immediate aftermath* of the accident, even if, for example, the impact or explosion is neither seen nor heard."[16]

Other courts were utilising the aftermath concept in all but name. In *Fenn v City of Peterborough*,[17] for example, a man who arrived home minutes after a gas explosion destroyed his house, killed his three children and seriously injured his wife was held entitled to recover for shock-induced psychiatric damage.[18]

The doctrine received the indorsement of the House of Lords in *McLoughlin v O'Brian*,[19] in which it was extended to a case in which the plaintiff did not go to the scene of the accident, but to the hospital, where she saw the injured members of her family still covered in mud and oil, and crying and screaming. The leading statement of the principles approved by their Lordships appears in the judgment of Lord Wilberforce:

> "As regards proximity to the accident, it is obvious that this must be close in both time and space. It is after all, the fact and consequence of the defendant's negligence that must be proved to have caused the 'nervous shock'. Experience has shown that to insist on direct and immediate sight or hearing would be impractical and unjust and that under what might be called the 'aftermath' doctrine, one who, from

14. (1971) 25 DLR (3d) 141.
15. [1972] VR 879, noted (1973) 47 ALJ 206.
16. Ibid at 880 (emphasis added).
17. (1976) 73 DLR (3d) 177.
18. For cases where the claimant came to the aftermath of the accident but was denied compensation on other grounds see *Brown v Hubar* (1974) 45 DLR (3d) 664 (criticised by A M Linden, *Canadian Tort Law* (4th ed, 1988), 371; W Binchy, "Annual Survey of Canadian Law, Part 2, Torts—II" (1977) 9 Ottawa LR 339 at 350-351) (plaintiff, having been requested by phone to come and pick up his daughter who had been involved in an accident, arrived to find her lying lifeless under a blanket); *Duwyn v Kaprielian* (1978) 94 DLR (3d) 424 (woman returned to her car, which contained her baby and mother, and found it had been smashed into and a general commotion); *Young v Burgoyne* (1981) 122 DLR (3d) 330 where Hallett J said at 336: "There is no logical reason to require as a condition of obtaining an award that the plaintiff be present at the time the [primary] victim sustains the injury."
19. [1983] 1 AC 410.

close proximity, comes very soon on the scene, should not be excluded."[20]

Two years later this doctrine was adopted, and indeed extended, by the High Court of Australia in *Jaensch v Coffey*.[21] In this case also, the plaintiff went not to the scene of the accident but to the hospital, where her seriously injured husband had undergone major surgery and was still on the danger list. The facts were not quite like those of *McLoughlin v O'Brian* where the plaintiff arrived within about two hours of the accident and saw her family before they had been treated and cleaned up. Mrs Coffey saw the extent of her husband's injuries on the day of the accident and was there for a long period the following day. Some days later it became apparent that she had suffered psychiatric illness. The High Court was willing to accept the aftermath doctrine. In the words of Deane J:

"The facts constituting a road accident and its aftermath are not, however, necessarily confined to the immediate point of impact. They may extend to wherever sound may carry and to wherever flying debris may land. The aftermath of an accident encompasses events at the scene after its occurrence, including the extraction and treatment of the injured. In a modern society, the aftermath also extends to the ambulance taking an injured person to hospital for treatment and to the hospital itself during the period of immediate post-accident treatment."[22]

Their Honours, however, were not prepared to indorse all of the limitations placed on the concept by Lord Wilberforce. Gibbs CJ reserved his opinion as to the correctness of Lord Wilberforce's comment to the effect that there must be close proximity in space as well as in time, and that the shock must come through sight or hearing of the event or its immediate aftermath.[23] Brennan J suggested that these considerations were relevant but were not principles limiting liability.[24] Deane J in an important passage saw two possible rationales for the distinction between cases where psychiatric injury was sustained as a result of direct observation at the scene of the accident and its aftermath and cases where the psychiatric injury was sustained from subsequent contact, away from the scene of the accident and its aftermath, with a person suffering from the effects of the accident:

"One such rationale lies in considerations of physical proximity, in the sense of space and time, between the accident and its immediate aftermath on the one hand and the injury on the other. The other lies in considerations of causal proximity in that in the one class of case the psychiatric injury results from the impact of matters which themselves formed part of the accident and its aftermath, such as the actual occurrence of death or injury in the course of it, whereas, in the other

20. Ibid at 422.
21. (1984) 155 CLR 549.
22. Ibid at 607-608. Note also the earlier case of *White v Butcher* (unreported, New South Wales SC, 13 Oct 1982, Nos 9576, 9577 and 9578 of 1981) where parents of a teenage girl rendered unconscious in an accident recovered damages for psychiatric injury caused by a combination of being told of the accident and seeing her in hospital, where she lay unconscious for four days. On the problems of this case see below, p 162.
23. (1984) 155 CLR 549 at 555.
24. Ibid at 572.

class of case, the psychiatric injury has resulted from contact with more remote consequences such as the subsequent effect of the accident upon an injured person. The choice between one or other or a combination of these two distinct rationales may obviously be of importance in the more precise identification of any essential criteria of the existence of the requisite duty relationship. On balance, I have come to the conclusion that the second, which justifies the line of demarcation by a reference to considerations of causal proximity, is to be preferred as being the less arbitrary and the better attuned both to legal principle and considerations of public policy."[25]

The limits of the High Court's approach have recently been put to the test in a decision of the Queensland Supreme Court. In *Spence v Percy*[26] the plaintiff's daughter (who was blind) suffered serious injuries in an accident caused by the defendant's negligence. She remained in a pitiable vegetative state for the next three years, and death was inevitable, though when it did occur it was somewhat unexpected. The plaintiff, who saw her daughter on the day following the accident and spent much time in the hospital during the ensuing years, maintained an unreasonable expectation that she would recover. When she died, the plaintiff suffered shock which produced a psychiatric illness. The trial judge, adopting the principles laid down by the High Court in *Jaensch v Coffey*,[27] was prepared to accept that the aftermath had no temporal connotation, and held that "because the plaintiff has established that she suffered a psychiatric illness directly caused by shock of the death of her daughter as the inevitable aftermath of her injury she should succeed".[28]

The Full Court allowed the appeal and said that the injury suffered here was not part of the aftermath. Shepherdson J interpreted Deane J's judgment as holding that the aftermath extended no further than the conclusion of "immediate post-accident treatment",[29] but he did not offer an explanation of the ambit of this concept. Williams J said that the High Court did not define aftermath, but the context of the case indicated that it had a temporal connotation, and the proximity test would not be satisfied where there was a "significant time lapse",[30] a term on which his Honour did not elaborate. De Jersey J agreed that the aftermath could not be regarded as extending to this situation three years later.[31] It is clear that the Full Court were most reluctant to extend the aftermath doctrine to events which happened at a time long removed from the initial injury

25. Ibid at 606-607.
26. (1990) Aust Torts Rep 81-039 (Derrington J); (1991) Aust Torts Rep 81-116 (FC). An application for special leave to appeal to the High Court was subsequently refused: see (unreported, Aust HC, 13 Dec 1991, No B27 of 1991). Note J Meredith, "Step by Cautious Step—A Recent Finding on Nervous Shock" (1991) 21 QLSJ 427.
27. (1984) 155 CLR 549.
28. (1990) Aust Torts Rep 81-039 at 68,041.
29. (1991) Aust Torts Rep 81-116 at 69,081. Would it, for example, extend beyond the initial cleaning and bandaging of the wounded in *McLoughlin v O'Brian* [1983] 1 AC 410?
30. Ibid at 69,087.
31. Ibid at 69,089. Note also *Pratt and Goldsmith v Pratt* [1975] VR 378, a case decided before *McLoughlin v O'Brian* [1983] 1 AC 410 and *Jaensch v Coffey* (1984) 155 CLR 549, where a mother suffered psychiatric harm some weeks after seeing the extent of her daughter's injuries and was held unable to recover.

suffered by the daughter. It is interesting, however, to note that
"aftermath" is defined in the *Oxford English Dictionary* without any
temporal connotation (apart from implying subsequence to the causal
event) but only one of consequence.[32] Though Derrington J at first
instance gave some weight to this,[33] Williams J was not swayed by the
dictionary meaning.[34] But if the aftermath problem is put aside the logic
of the trial judge's decision cannot be refuted. Given the nature of the
injuries suffered, the daughter's eventual death was inevitable. That the
mother might suffer psychiatric injury as a result of that death, after years
of watching and hoping for a recovery, was entirely foreseeable.

   Spence v Percy is a case like *McLoughlin v O'Brian*[35] and *Jaensch v
Coffey*[36] in that the plaintiff arrived at the hospital as soon as she could,
but unlike those decisions in that this was the commencement of a long
period of anxiety and uncertainty as to the ultimate outcome of the
tortfeasor's negligence, culminating in the daughter's eventual death. The
aftermath doctrine does not seem to be able to accommodate this kind of
case, as two other recent decisions illustrate.[37]

   The first of these is *Rhodes v Canadian National Railway*,[38] in which
the British Columbia Court of Appeal again gave a narrow construction to
Deane J's theory of causal proximity, one judge going so far as to doubt
its utility in determining either foreseeability or causation. The plaintiff's
son was killed in a train crash in Alberta. She first heard of the crash on
radio[39] in British Columbia, and endured many hours of extreme anxiety
before learning that her son was among the victims. By the time she was
able to see the scene of the accident, eight days had elapsed. The horror of
the situation was compounded by being denied access to the crash site,
being directed to the wrong memorial service and so missing the official
ceremony in remembrance of the dead. Her son's remains were sent to her
unannounced, by ordinary mail, in an unmarked cardboard box. All this
caused the plaintiff to suffer severe depression and other signs of mental

32. The *Oxford English Dictionary* (2nd ed, 1989) defines the term as "a state or condition
    left by a (usu[ally] unpleasant) event or some further occurrence arising from it".
33. *Spence v Percy* (1990) Aust Torts Rep 81-039 at 68,041.
34. (1991) Aust Torts Rep 81-116 at 69,087.
35. [1983] 1 AC 410.
36. (1984) 155 CLR 549.
37. Note also two recent English cases involving major disasters. In *Singh v London
    Underground Ltd* (unreported, QBD, 24 Apr 1990) the plaintiff learnt on television of the
    fire at the King's Cross underground station in London, knowing that the route home
    taken by three members of her family would have brought them through the station at
    the time of the fire. Her anxiety mounted as the hours passed and they did not return,
    until she was told next day of their deaths. As a result she suffered a psychiatric illness.
    Refusing an application for trial by jury, the court recognised that to hold the defendant
    liable would require an extension of the principles laid down by *McLoughlin v O'Brian*
    [1983] 1 AC 410. In *Crocker v P & O European Ferries (Dover) Ltd* (unreported, QBD,
    3 Dec 1990), an action was brought by 64 relatives of passengers and crew members on
    the Herald of Free Enterprise which sank with tragic loss of life at Zeebrugge. The
    plaintiffs claimed damages for alleged psychiatric illness suffered as a result of the shock
    sustained on learning of the disaster and the death of loved ones. The court allowed a lead
    action involving a few plaintiffs to enable the determination of common issues of law,
    including the question of proximity, and fact.
38. (1990) 75 DLR (4th) 248.
39. Means of communication of bad news is discussed below, pp 183-191.

and emotional disturbance. Maczko J in the court below held that it was appropriate to award damages based on Deane J's doctrine of causal proximity, even though she had not directly perceived the accident or its immediate aftermath. The Court of Appeal, however, allowed the defendant's appeal. Taylor JA (Wood JA concurring) said that the concept of causal proximity ought to be taken to exclude indirect injury such as that caused by visiting the scene some days later. Wallace JA questioned the usefulness of the notion, rejecting the plaintiff's claim on different proximity and policy considerations. [40] Thus where, for various good reasons, a substantial period of time elapses before the claimant arrives at the accident site (for example, the fact that it only gradually becomes clear that a relative was a victim, misinformation or misdirection by the relevant authorities or the time taken to travel), the aftermath doctrine will not assist.

The latest English decision, *Alcock v Chief Constable of South Yorkshire Police*, [41] examines the limits of the aftermath problem in a situation which has some affinity with *Rhodes v Canadian National Railway*. Some of the plaintiffs were at the ground where the tragedy took place. Others went there to try and find out what had become of missing relatives, and in some cases visited the temporary mortuary which had been set up. Some went to local hospitals in search of loved ones. Others simply waited at home for news. In all these cases, it was simply the scale of the disaster which prevented immediate contact with the dead and injured. It was the strain of searching, and the agony of waiting and not knowing, which caused the psychiatric injury alleged to have been suffered by the plaintiffs.

Of the plaintiffs who originally learnt of the sad happenings at Hillsborough on television or radio, there can be no suggestion that those who could do no more than wait for news of the fate of their loved ones in any real sense came to the aftermath of the accident. Others, however, travelled to Sheffield to search for friends and relatives. Robert Spearrit went there late on the evening of the day in question, and found his brother in the intensive care unit in hospital and his nephew's body in the temporary mortuary at Hillsborough. Stephen Jones also went to the temporary mortuary, and found his parents there in tears because his brother was dead. Yet others, having undergone a period of waiting and then being informed of the death of their relative, had to go to the ground to identify the dead body. In addition, those plaintiffs who were at the ground had to go through the same process of searching and then waiting for news. One made an unsuccessful search among the dead bodies, and another had to identify a victim late that night. The prevailing law necessitated an attempt to apply the aftermath doctrine to such varying circumstances.

Hidden J at first instance, because he was prepared to find that those plaintiffs who watched on simultaneous television were, in a sense, present at the match and were thus within the ambit of foreseeability and owed a duty of care, [42] did not have to pronounce on this issue and in fact expressly refrained from doing so. [43]

40. (1990) 75 DLR (4th) 248 at 265. Macfarlane JA agreed with both Taylor and Wallace JJA. Southin JA concurred in the result on different grounds.
41. [1992] 1 AC 310.
42. This issue is discussed below, pp 170-179.
43. [1992] 1 AC 310 at 344.

The English Court of Appeal, who took a different attitude to the television issue, were forced to examine this problem. They were not prepared to regard cases where plaintiffs had had the responsibility of identifying the body at the mortuary as part of the aftermath.[44] In this respect they cast some doubt on the decision of *Hevican v Ruane*[45] a few months earlier. In that case, the plaintiff was caused to suffer psychiatric injury by, inter alia, seeing the body of his dead son in the mortuary approximately three hours after he was killed along with other members of his school soccer team in a bus accident. Mantell J had held that this damage was recoverable even though it was stretching language to say that the condition was caused by coming upon the immediate aftermath. For Parker LJ in the Hillsborough case, however, there would be liability only if the plaintiff had to identify the body as part of the immediate aftermath of the accident.[46] In the case before him, according to the evidence the earliest identification took place at about midnight, nearly nine hours after the start of the match and ten or more after the gates were opened, and so this requirement was not met. Still less, it seems, were the Court of Appeal prepared to countenance the process of searching and waiting as bringing plaintiffs within the aftermath. Even the aftermath at the hospital, as in *McLoughlin v O'Brian*[47] itself, is, it seems, to be interpreted narrowly. Parker LJ stressed that this was to be regarded as part of the catastrophe because none of the victims had been cleaned up or attended to.[48] Is his Lordship suggesting that if victims have received preliminary treatment they can no longer be said to be within the aftermath of an accident, but while they remain "begrimed with dirt and oil"[49] relatives or others shocked by viewing their condition are not excluded from a potential cause of action? If so, this is impossible to justify. What if a hospital is particularly well organised and has a trauma victim bathed, bandaged and bedded with unusual speed? Are relatives to be denied recovery simply because of this efficiency? What of the hospital emergency room inundated with accident victims on a busy Saturday night which cannot deal with an injured person immediately, leaving him or her, bloody and bruised, unattended for a lengthy period? Is the ambit of psychiatric damage claims greater in such circumstances? Moreover, where injuries are sustained not as a result of an external accident but through medical negligence, especially those which occur behind closed doors within a hospital, relatives are unlikely ever to view the victim before he or she has been properly attended to. The right to sue should not hinge on such extraneous considerations. That the aftermath at the hospital may be considerably longer than the hour or two suggested by *McLoughlin v O'Brian* is arguably supported by *Kralj v McGrath*[50] where a baby was injured at birth through an obstetrician's negligence. The mother recovered for shock damage sustained through watching over the baby for a period of eight weeks as it gradually weakened and died. The plaintiff in this case was actually present "at the scene" of

44. Ibid per Parker LJ at 363, per Nolan LJ at 387.
45. [1991] 3 All ER 65.
46. *Alcock v Chief Constable of South Yorkshire Police* [1992] 1 AC 310 at 363.
47. [1983] 1 AC 410.
48. *Alcock v Chief Constable of South Yorkshire Police* [1992] 1 AC 310 at 358.
49. *McLoughlin v O'Brian* [1983] 1 AC 410 per Lord Wilberforce at 417.
50. [1986] 1 All ER 54.

the negligent event, but she was unaware of the injury to the child at the time because it was delivered by caesarian section.

The House of Lords in *Alcock v Chief Constable of South Yorkshire Police*[51] in dealing with this problem have almost certainly limited the aftermath doctrine to a narrower scope than that allowed by the High Court in *Jaensch v Coffey*.[52] In contrast to the reservations expressed in that case as to the correctness of Lord Wilberforce's statements in *McLoughlin v O'Brian*[53] that there must be close proximity in space as well as in time, and that shock must come through sight or hearing of the event or its immediate aftermath,[54] the House of Lords indorsed these limitations. Lord Ackner,[55] for example, repeated the words of Lord Wilberforce[56] and emphasised his statement that the facts in *McLoughlin v O'Brian*, where the plaintiff first viewed the primary victims about two hours after the accident, were on the margin of what the process of logical progression from case to case would allow. Similarly, Lord Oliver expressed the view that the case represented an extension not "wholly free from difficulty",[57] and arguably his Lordship may have restricted the aftermath doctrine still further. He stressed the need for the plaintiff to be present at the scene or in the "more or less immediate vicinity", and for a "close temporal connection" between the event and the plaintiff's perception of it[58]— criteria which he did not define. Later in his judgment he said:

"No case prior to the hearing before Hidden J from which these appeals arise has countenanced an award of damages for injuries suffered where there was not at the time of the event a degree of physical propinquity between the plaintiff and the event caused by the defendant's breach of duty to the primary victim nor where the shock sustained by the plaintiff was not either contemporaneous with the event or separated from it by a relatively short interval of time. The necessary element of proximity between plaintiff and defendant is furnished, at least in part, by both physical and temporal proximity and also by the sudden and direct visual impression on the plaintiff's mind of actually witnessing the event or its immediate aftermath. . . . In my opinion, the necessary proximity cannot be said to exist where the elements of immediacy, closeness of time and space, and direct visual or aural perception are absent."[59]

The specific question of the plaintiffs who had to identify the dead body of a relative was dealt with by Lord Ackner and Lord Jauncey. Lord Ackner said that it was clear from *McLoughlin v O'Brian*[60] that the subsequent identification of a dead body could be part of the immediate aftermath, but the earliest identification in the instant case took place some

51. [1992] 1 AC 310.
52. (1984) 155 CLR 549.
53. [1983] 1 AC 410 at 422.
54. See above, pp 138-139.
55. *Alcock v Chief Constable of South Yorkshire Police* [1992] 1 AC 310 at 404-405.
56. *McLoughlin v O'Brian* [1983] 1 AC 410 at 419.
57. *Alcock v Chief Constable of South Yorkshire Police* [1992] 1 AC 310 at 417.
58. Ibid at 411.
59. Ibid at 416-417.
60. [1983] 1 AC 410.

eight hours after the accident and this could not be described as part of the *immediate* aftermath.[61] But to focus on hours and minutes in this type of situation is fallacious. It cannot be asserted that the trauma of viewing a dead child is any less horrific after eight or nine hours than two. Anguish of this gravity does not dissipate as rapidly as this. Consider, for example, a parent on holiday overseas who receives a phone call that his or her son has been killed and returns on the next available flight to view the body a week later. Providing all the other prerequisites of liability are satisfied, recovery should be no more difficult to come by than if the parent had been able to call at the mortuary within a couple of hours of the death. Lord Jauncey, having labelled attempts to define "the immediate aftermath" as a "fruitless exercise", took an even narrower view of the identification issue:

> "In these appeals the visits to the mortuary were made no earlier than nine hours after the disaster and were made not for the purpose of rescuing or giving comfort to the victim but purely for the purpose of identification. This seems to me to be a very different situation from that in which a relative goes within a short time after an accident to rescue or comfort a victim. I consider that not only the purpose of the visits to the mortuary but also the times at which they were made take them outside the immediate aftermath of this disaster."[62]

It seems that in addition to concentrating on the time lapse between death and viewing a body his Lordship is introducing a further restriction on recovery. His allusion to the purpose of identification is regrettable. Is he suggesting that the reason for coming to the scene will affect the closeness in time required for relief? The implication of this seems to be that the courts consider the viewing of a body as somehow less emotionally disturbing than seeing an injured person who is still alive, albeit possibly seriously injured. Why should rescuers or comforters have up to nine hours, perhaps even longer, to get to their loved ones before a potential shock claim lapses, whereas, on one interpretation of Lord Jauncey's words, those who have to go to the morgue to identify a body have, at best, two hours to arrive there? In addition, his Lordship overlooks the distinction between those who go to a mortuary knowing for a fact that a loved one has died to go through the formality of identifying the body, and those who have the distressing task of searching through rows of corpses not knowing whether the one they seek is alive but hoping and praying that they will not find that person's body. Clearly this latter exercise, whatever its outcome, is every bit as likely to cause psychiatric harm as viewing the less serious after-effects of physical injury.

Interestingly, some of their Lordships even viewed the cases of the four plaintiffs who were in the West Stand and saw the events with their own eyes as cases raising aftermath issues. Lords Keith and Jauncey accept these cases as falling into the presence category,[63] but Lord Oliver said:

> "In the case of both Brian Harrison and Robert Alcock, although both were present at the ground and saw scenes which were obviously

61. *Alcock v Chief Constable of South Yorkshire Police* [1992] 1 AC 310 at 404-405.
62. Ibid at 424.
63. Ibid per Lord Keith at 404, per Lord Jauncey at 421, 424.

distressing and such as to cause grave worry and concern, their perception of the actual consequences of the disaster to those to whom they were related was again gradual. In my judgment, the necessary proximity was lacking in their cases too."[64]

His Lordship seems to be suggesting a return on policy grounds to the strict requirements of presence and perception as originally outlined in *Hambrook v Stokes Bros.*[65] Regression rather than progression seems to be the order of the day. Lord Ackner's view of these cases is difficult to ascertain. He says that "[o]nly two of the plaintiffs before us were at the ground", but then discusses the case of Robert Alcock as turning on the proximity of identification in time and space.[66] Later, however, he admits that Alcock was present at the ground and suggests that his case turns on the point of relationship to the accident victim.[67]

Another interesting problem in the Hillsborough case concerns William Pemberton, the plaintiff who had travelled with his son to Hillsborough by coach, intending to stay in the coach while it was parked at the ground during the match. As a result of what he was told about the chaos unfolding inside, he watched the live coverage on the coach television. He later searched for his son and eventually identified his body in the mortuary very late in the evening. Hidden J held that he had a cause of action on the basis that he was within the proximity of time and space.[68] It is noteworthy that he was the one plaintiff against whom no appeal was taken, but it seems most unlikely that the Court of Appeal or the House of Lords would have agreed with Hidden J's view of this claim for relief.

If the House of Lords has shown signs of a preparedness to keep the aftermath doctrine within check, a recent United States case has suggested total repudiation. It will be recalled that the leading case of *Dillon v Legg*,[69] in which the Californian Supreme Court recognised the possibility of recovery for emotional injury by plaintiffs who were not themselves within the zone of physical danger, identified contemporaneous observance as one of the factors involved in a decision whether emotional harm was foreseeable. There has been an enormous disparity in the treatment this particular consideration has received in the various American jurisdictions. Some succeeding cases held that this first *Dillon* guideline did not prevent recovery where plaintiffs saw only the aftermath of the accident,[70]

64. Ibid at 417.
65. [1925] 1 KB 141.
66. *Alcock v Chief Constable of South Yorkshire Police* [1992] 1 AC 310 at 404-405.
67. Ibid at 405-406.
68. Ibid at 339.
69. (1968) 441 P 2d 912; 69 Cal Rptr 72.
70. See eg *Gustafson v Faris* (1976) 241 NW 2d 208 (Mich); *Dziokonski v Babineau* (1978) 380 NE 2d 1295 (Mass); *Portee v Jaffee* (1980) 417 A 2d 521 (NJ); *Ferriter v Daniel O'Connell's Sons* (1980) 413 NE 2d 690 (Mass) (visit to hospital rather than accident site is within aftermath); *General Motors Corporation v Grizzle* (1982) 642 SW 2d 837 (Tex) (mother came on accident scene "moments" after collision); *Henley v Department of State Highways & Transportation* (1983) 340 NW 2d 72 (Mich) (recovery denied where parents went to hospital five hours after accident); *Pearsall v Emhart Industries Inc* (1984) 599 F Supp 207 (plaintiff arrived home to find house ablaze and bodies of her husband and children); *Champion v Gray* (1985) 478 So 2d 17 (Fla) (mother saw daughter's body at accident scene, collapsed and died on the spot. The Supreme Court noted obiter at 20 that seeing the injured person in the hospital shortly after the event "reaches the outer

contemporaneous observance being only a factor in determining foreseeability and not an inflexible requirement. Other States have placed great emphasis on direct perception of the shock-inducing event.[71] The extremes of interpretation are no better illustrated than in California itself, where the pendulum has swung sharply back and forth.[72] Recently, the

70. *Continued*
   limits of the required involvement"); *City of Austin v Davis* (1985) 693 SW 2d 31 (Tex) (father found body of his missing son at bottom of air shaft in mental hospital where son had been inmate); *James v Lieb* (1985) 375 NW 2d 109 (Neb); *Gates v Richardson* (1986) 719 P 2d 193 (Wyo); *Tommy's Elbow Room Inc v Kavorkian* (1986) 727 P 2d 1038 (Alaska) (parents arrived at accident scene and saw dying daughter being dragged by her hair from wrecked car); *Croft v Wicker* (1987) 737 P 2d 789; *Masaki v General Motors Corporation* (1989) 780 P 2d 566 (Haw).

71. See eg *Tobin v Grossman* (1969) 249 NE 2d 419; 301 NYS 2d 554; *Perlmutter v Whitney* (1975) 230 NW 2d 390 (Mich); *Cabone v Melba Ice Cream Co* (1982) 423 So 2d 739 (La) (husband arrived home to find family choking, frothing at mouth from escaping ammonia); *Schmeck v City of Shawnee* (1982) 647 P 2d 1263 (Kan) (mother learnt of daughter's injuries an hour after accident and went immediately to hospital); *Marzolf v Hoover* (1984) 596 F Supp 596; *Oberreuter v Orion Industries Inc* (1984) 342 NW 2d 492 (Ia) (plaintiff did not observe her husband and son severely burned when antenna they were holding touched electrical line); *Nutter v Frisbie Memorial Hospital* (1984) 474 A 2d 584 (NH) (parents arrived at hospital shortly after their infant's death and were immediately informed of it); *Baas v Hoye* (1985) 766 F 2d 1190 (parent did not see child ingest improperly bottled medication); *Tebbutt v Virostek* (1985) 483 NE 2d 1142; 493 NYS 2d 1010 (claim that amniocentisis caused stillbirth of child, no recovery since observation of death by mother was not contemporaneous with allegedly negligent acts); *McClellan v Bohmer* (1985) 700 SW 2d 687 (Tex); *Crenshaw v Sarasota County Public Hospital Board* (1985) 466 So 2d 427 (Fla) (recovery denied to parent of stillborn child who did not see body which was mutilated after it was placed with hospital laundry); *Brooks v Decker* (1986) 516 A 2d 1380 (Pa) (no recovery even though father overtook ambulance and arrived at scene of his son's accident before it); *Halliday v Beltz* (1986) 514 A 2d 906 (Pa) (mother did not view actual negligent surgery on daughter); *Mazzagatti v Everingham* (1986) 516 A 2d 672 (Pa) (mother was one mile from the scene of her child's accident); *Roberts v Burns* (1986) 387 NW 2d 140 (Ia); *Detroit Automobile Inter-Insurance Exchange v McMillan* (1987) 406 NW 2d 232 (Mich) (mother arrived one hour after daughter was removed from her damaged vehicle); *Pate v Children's Hospital* (1987) 404 NW 2d 632 (Mich) (deceased died in sister's arms two days after negligent failure to admit to hospital); *Freeman v City of Pasadena* (1988) 744 SW 2d 923 (Tex) (stepfather first saw his injured stepson in an ambulance); *Hewitt v Chadwick* (1988) 760 SW 2d 333 (Tex); *McCarthy v City of Cleveland Heights* (1989) 583 NE 2d 981 (Ohio) (mother and brother of arrested person who committed suicide in jail could not recover because not present when suicide occurred); *McKethean v WMATA* (1991) 588 A 2d 708 (DC) (father was one block away when car hit daughter, granddaughter and friends); *Bloom v Dubois* (1991) 597 A 2d 671 (Pa) (husband who found wife hanged in hospital denied recovery as he had not witnessed death); *Cameron v Pepin* (1992) 610 A 2d 279 (Me) (parents arrived at hospital soon after accident to son to see him "cut, bloody and battered").

72. The aftermath principle was adopted in eg *Archibald v Braverman* (1969) 79 Cal Rptr 723 (mother arrived moments after an explosion which injured her son); *Krouse v Graham* (1977) 562 P 2d 1022; 137 Cal Rptr 863; *Nazaroff v Superior Court* (1978) 145 Cal Rptr 657 (mother who heard neighbour scream rushed to defendant's yard to see her son being pulled from swimming pool and participated in unsuccessful resuscitation attempts); *Nevels v Yeager* (1984) 199 Cal Rptr 300; *Ochoa v Superior Court (Santa Clara County)* (1985) 703 P 2d 1; 216 Cal Rptr 661 (parents of boy who died from pneumonia in juvenile hall through lack of adequate medical treatment, medical personnel ignoring his worsening illness, did not see his death). It was rejected in eg *Deboe v Horn* (1971) 94 Cal Rptr 77 (wife did not see her injured husband until she arrived at hospital); *Powers v Sissoev* (1974) 114 Cal Rptr 868 (mother saw daughter 30-60 minutes after she was struck by truck); *Hair v County of Monterey* (1975) 119 Cal Rptr 639 (plaintiffs denied recovery for emotional distress stemming from damage suffered by their son following oral surgery, notwithstanding that mother had accompanied him to hospital, had been in

liberal approach has been called into question in that State. In *Thing v La Chusa*[73] the Supreme Court of California took the opportunity to review the law in this area in the light of what it saw as the uncertainty created by the cases following *Dillon v Legg* and concern with the social cost of liability for emotional injury. It held, by a majority, that the three factors identified in *Dillon v Legg* should be strictly reinterpreted as limitations on the scope of recovery, since "the societal benefits of certainty in the law, as well as traditional concepts of tort law, dictate limitation of bystander recovery of damages for emotional distress".[74] In particular, the court held that the plaintiff must be present at the scene of an injury-producing event at the time it occurs. It therefore denied recovery to a mother who was close by the scene of an accident to her son but who did not see or hear it, even though, when told of the accident, she had rushed to the scene, where she saw her son's bloody and unconscious body. Given the influence of Californian law on American jurisprudence, this decision seems likely to retard the further development of liability for psychiatric harm in the United States. This process seems to have already begun. The hardline approach now being taken by Californian courts is illustrated by *Fife v Astenius*[75] where the argument that "contemporaneous" perception of the injury-producing event does not mean "simultaneous" perception but rather perception within a short period of time was rejected—parents and brothers of the accident victim heard the impact and were on the scene within seconds but could not recover because their perception of the accident was not simultaneous and they did not know at the moment of impact that a member of their family was being injured. Another graphic example is *Martin By and Through Martin v United States*[76] where

72. *Continued*
   waiting room when surgery performed and had seen him afterwards, because neither plaintiff observed injury-producing event, ie the surgery itself); *Vanguard Insurance Co v Schabatka* (1975) 120 Cal Rptr 614; *Arauz v Gerhardt* (1977) 137 Cal Rptr 619 (mother arrived at scene within five minutes of collision); *Hoyem v Manhattan Beach City School District* (1978) 585 P 2d 851; 150 Cal Rptr 1 (plaintiff saw son in hospital a few hours after accident); *Parsons v Superior Court* (1978) 146 Cal Rptr 495 (parents arrived at scene of accident in which their daughters were killed "before the dust had settled"); *Hathaway v Superior Court* (1980) 169 Cal Rptr 435 (parents found their electrocuted six-year-old son lying in puddle of water within minutes of the accident); *Madigan v City of Santa Ana* (1983) 193 Cal Rptr 593 (plaintiffs arrived at automobile collision scene 15 minutes afterwards and before victim's body was removed); *Ebarb v Woodbridge Park Association* (1985) 210 Cal Rptr 751; *Hurlbut v Sonora Community Hospital* (1989) 254 Cal Rptr 840; *Ortiz v HPM Corporation* (1991) 285 Cal Rptr 728 (liability would exist only if accident considered still to have been happening when trapped body discovered); *Breazeal v Henry Mays Newhall Memorial Hospital* (1991) 286 Cal Rptr 207.
73. (1989) 771 P 2d 814; 257 Cal Rptr 98. See Comment, "Thing v La Chusa: Public Policy Demands a Limitation on the Bystander Recovery for Infliction of Emotional Distress" (1990) 17 W St U L Rev 499.
74. (1989) 771 P 2d 814; 257 Cal Rptr 98, at 815. However the decision is limited to the "bystander" problem, and has no application to cases in which the plaintiff is independently owed a duty of care: see *Burgess v Superior Court* (1992) 831 P 2d 1197; 9 Cal Rptr 2d 615, noted above, p 13.
75. (1991) 284 Cal Rptr 16. See also *Wright v City of Los Angeles* (1990) 268 Cal Rptr 309.
76. (1991) 779 F Supp 1242. See also *Evan F v Hughson United Methodist Church* (1992) 10 Cal Rptr 2d 748 (sister of child sexually molested by pastor could not recover because she did not appreciate that his actions caused injury to her brother); compare *Wilks v Hom* (1992) 3 Cal Rptr 2d 803 (mother present at explosion, instantly knew of likely severe damage to child, even though she did not see or hear her being injured).

negligent supervision allowed six-year-old Jennifer Martin to be abducted from a day care centre outing and raped. A federal court applying Californian law held that neither her mother nor her sister could recover for emotional distress. The mother (who was of course not present) was not the direct victim of negligence since the supervision was not conduct directed at her, and the sister, who was also on the outing, did not know what was happening at the time the abduction took place. It seems that not only are the courts insisting that plaintiffs be on the scene at the crucial time, but also that they appreciate what is going on.[77] In *Golstein v Superior Court*[77a] the requirement of contemporaneous observance was insisted upon notwithstanding that the tortious act in question was, as the court acknowledged, incapable of being sensorily perceived. The parents of a boy with curable cancer were denied relief for emotional distress caused by his death from an overdose of radiation treatment because they did not, and could not, witness the injury-inducing event. However, despite the current trend, one decision has taken a more enlightened view. In *Re Air Crash Disaster near Cerritos, California, on August 31, 1986*,[77b] the United States Court of Appeals for the Ninth Circuit granted recovery to a plaintiff who returned home to see it engulfed in flames minutes after a plane had crashed into it. She did not see the crash, but knew instantly that her family were being burned, and it was on this basis that the court felt itself able to distinguish *Thing v La Chusa* and *Fife v Astenius*.

On a more encouraging note, a recent decision of the Irish High Court takes a much more positive attitude to the aftermath problem than either the Supreme Court of California or the House of Lords. *Mullally v Bus Eireann*[78] arose out of a bus accident in which three people were killed and 49 injured. The plaintiff, whose husband and three sons had gone to a soccer match and were on the bus, was telephoned and told to come to Limerick straight away. The situation was complicated by the fact that two of her boys were in one hospital and her husband in another. It was nearly four hours before the plaintiff reached the hospital her sons were in, and when she arrived there it "looked like a hospital out of a war film, like a field hospital. There were bodies everywhere, people moaning and groaning, and many distressed relatives milling around." Her son Paul had bad head injuries and she was told that he was dying. She then had to look for her son Francis and did not recognise him because of his injuries. She then went to the other hospital to find her husband receiving the last rites, although in fact he eventually recovered. Paul was not so lucky. His head had been opened in the accident and his brain exposed. The inside of his head had to be cleaned every day, and he would allow no one but the plaintiff or her sister to hold his head while this was done. He lingered on for nine months before he died. He was the plaintiff's favourite son.

Denham J, having satisfied herself that the plaintiff had suffered psychiatric damage, held that it was foreseeable in the circumstances, and that it was caused by the accident and its aftermath. She said that the case was within the parameters set by Lord Wilberforce in *McLoughlin v*

77. See above, p 134, n 4.
77a. (1990) 273 Cal Rptr 270.
77b. (1992) 967 F 2d 1421.
78. (Unreported, Irish HC, 13 June 1991).

O'Brian,[79] though she was assisted more by Lord Bridge's speech. That the time lapse between accident and perception of aftermath was twice that taken by Mrs McLoughlin to reach and view her family was inconsequential. There is no sense from Denham J's judgment of the case being at the margin of recovery, no concern with counting the hours that had elapsed since the accident. The tragic nature of the case was a compelling factor in the ultimate decision that it was appropriate to impose liability, but her Ladyship does this, without allowing emotion to displace principle, by adopting a commonsense attitude to the situation in the spirit of earlier Irish decisions[80] rather than being preoccupied with the problem of limiting liability.

It thus appears that courts in different parts of the common law world have not adopted a uniform attitude to the aftermath problem. Leaving aside the situation in the United States in the light of *Thing v La Chusa*, it is necessary to try and draw some conclusions on the scope of the aftermath doctrine as developed by courts in Australia, England, Canada and elsewhere. Those who come to the scene of the accident soon afterwards and suffer shock are generally within the aftermath,[81] at least if there is still something to see.[82] The same applies where the primary victim comes to the plaintiff.[83] Those who instead go to the hospital are also within the aftermath. This must be correct—as Brennan J has said, liability "cannot rationally be made to depend upon a race between a spouse and an ambulance".[84] However, it is not clear whether the aftermath at the hospital is limited to cases such as *McLoughlin v O'Brian*[85] where the plaintiff sees the victim before immediate treatment is carried out or whether it is sufficient to view the effects of the accident as the victim lies in a hospital bed after treatment or surgery. Even if the first instance decision in *Spence v Percy*[86] is disregarded, the Australian courts[87] seem prepared to take a more expansive attitude in such cases, as

---

79. [1983] 1 AC 410.
80. *Byrne v Great Southern & Western Railway Co* (unreported, CA of Ireland, Feb 1884) and *Bell v Great Northern Railway Co of Ireland* (1890) 26 LR Ir 428, both of which were cited. See above, p 10, n 51.
81. See the cases cited above, pp 136-137. For a more recent example see *Hartmann v Nominal Defendant* (unreported, New South Wales SC, 20 Fed 1987, No CLD 15634 of 1985).
82. See eg *Anderson v Smith* (1990) 101 FLR 34, where the plaintiff arrived at the pool in which her daughter had almost drowned to find it empty, the daughter having been taken to hospital.
83. *Bain v King & Co Ltd*, 1973 SLT (Notes) 8 is illustrative. There a young boy covered in tar after an explosion, who "resembled a black bundle", ran home to his mother who suffered a nervous reaction. Instead of the shock victim "coming to the aftermath" the aftermath came to the shock victim. Note also *Cote v Litawa* (1950) 71 A 2d 792 (NH) where the defendant, whose car struck a little girl, carried the child to her house and handed her to her mother. Recovery was denied because, adopting the principle of *Palsgraf v Long Island Rail Co* (1928) 162 NE 99 (NY), no duty to the mother had been established.
84. *Jaensch v Coffey* (1984) 155 CLR 549 at 578.
85. [1983] 1 AC 410.
86. (1990) Aust Torts Rep 81-039.
87. See eg *Orman v Harrington* (unreported, South Australian SC, 30 Apr 1990, No 296 of 1990), where the plaintiff did not visit her daughter until the next day but recovered damages. There was no dispute about proximity at the trial. Note also *Mellor v Moran* (1985) 2 MVR 461, in which it appears that the plaintiff was not present at any time and yet was awarded damages; Vasta J plainly overlooked the requirements of *Jaensch v Coffey* (1984) 155 CLR 549. Again, in *Swan v Williams (Demolition) Ltd* (1987) 9

do those of Ireland.[88] No Australian or Canadian case raises the issue of identification of a dead body, but the English courts again are taking a rather narrow attitude, saying that, by analogy with *McLoughlin v O'Brian*, identification must be part of the immediate aftermath if recovery is to be allowed. Lord Jauncey in *Alcock v Chief Constable of South Yorkshire Police*[89] would not even go this far: we are now told that even the purpose of being present at the aftermath may be crucial. Courts in Australia might be prepared to be more generous. In *Butcher v Motor Accidents Board*[90] the plaintiff suffered psychiatric illness after seeing the body of her dead son in hospital. She had already been told of his death, and the body had been identified by the doctor for whom she worked as a secretary. It was held that compensation was recoverable. Canadian courts may well adopt a similar approach.

Nor do the problems of the aftermath doctrine end here. It seems that the courts are ready to accept that the plaintiffs in such cases suffer psychiatric harm as a combination of what they see and what they are told, but the balance of these two elements may make all the difference. What of the plaintiff who goes to the scene but cannot get close enough to see what is happening and is told later that a relative has been killed or injured?[91] Consider, for example, a train crash on a bridge or a fire in a London underground station[92] around which police have erected barriers, where people race frantically to the scene to find out what has happened to those they know were on board or at the station, can see the emergency services at work but are unable to get any closer or find out any further information. Are they to be denied recovery? What about a plaintiff who is informed that a relative has been injured in an accident and is too overcome with shock and grief to go to the scene at all,[93] or who due to a pre-existing disability (for example, one which confines him or her to a bed or a wheelchair) is physically incapable of doing so? What of the plaintiff who goes to hospital but cannot see the accident victim because he or she

---

87. *Continued*
   NSWLR 172, the plaintiff was not present at any time and yet liability was admitted. For an English case where a more liberal approach was taken see *Kralj v McGrath* [1986] 1 All ER 54, discussed above, pp 142-143.
88. *Mullally v Bus Eireann* (unreported, Irish HC, 13 June 1991).
89. [1992] 1 AC 310 at 424, quoted above, p 144.
90. (1984) *Victorian Motor Accidents Cases* 72-026 (CCH). In the words of the Motor Accidents Tribunal, "[t]o say that the personal injury was not caused by the driving of a motor vehicle but by being told about an accident and visiting a child in the hospital, etc, is to introduce subtleties rather than apply broad and practical conceptions". The Tribunal refused to follow the earlier case of *Reid v Motor Accidents Board* (1982) *Victorian Motor Accidents Cases* 74-135 (CCH) (mother told that child severely injured, went to hospital, saw him on life support system; no recovery for depressive illness on ground that the injuries did not arise out of the use of a motor vehicle, but were caused by her being told of the accident and subsequently seeing her son).
91. See eg *De Franceschi v Storrier* (1988) 85 ACTR 1. The plaintiff recovered damages, probably because she saw her son in intensive care after being told the extent of his injuries.
92. For a psychiatric damage case arising out of the fire at King's Cross London underground station in 1987 see *Singh v London Underground Ltd* (unreported, QBD, 24 Apr 1990), dealt with above, p 140, n 37.
93. An instance put by Deane J in *Jaensch v Coffey* (1984) 155 CLR 549 at 608-609. See also F A Trindade, "The Principles Governing the Recovery of Damages for Negligently Caused Nervous Shock" [1986] CLJ 476 at 494.

is undergoing surgery, and is then told that they have died?[94] Further problems can be postulated. What if there is no opportunity to be involved before the death occurs, for example where parents wake to find that their baby has succumbed to cot death, due to the negligence of the manufacturer or supplier of an infant distress warning device? Suppose the circumstances of the negligence are such that there will be a long delay before anyone can arrive at the accident site, as for example where a plane crashes in the wilds of Northern Canada in the middle of winter in frozen conditions and weeks or months pass before bodies can be retrieved from beneath the ice and snow. Are those shocked and psychologically disturbed by what they find really any less worthy of relief simply because of the unavoidable time lapse between the crash and the discovery? Fact situations like these show how difficult it is to set rational limits to the aftermath doctrine. Moreover, it is ill-equipped to deal with cases where the full consequences of a tortfeasor's wrongdoing take a while to become apparent. Cases such as *Spence v Percy*,[95] *Rhodes v Canadian National Railway*[96] and *Alcock v Chief Constable of South Yorkshire Police*,[97] the essence of which is ignorance of events and uncertainty of outcome, seem to penalise the family, friends and others of those who linger, rather than die immediately as a result of the defendant's carelessness, or who are caught up in the chaos and confusion of large-scale catastrophes where it is inevitable that a clear picture of the true facts will not emerge for some time. There will be, in addition, many cases where there is simply no aftermath to perceive. Reference to the concept in these situations is futile.[98]

Much depends on whether the courts are now willing to accept that plaintiffs who suffer psychiatric injury through being told of the accident, without having seen something of the aftermath, may recover—an issue considered below in Chapter 7. If the limitation barring recovery in such cases is removed—and it is our view that it should be—this compels the law to recognise that the aftermath doctrine is an inappropriate limiting mechanism and should also be abandoned. One halfway house that has been suggested is to dispense with the aftermath requirement for those who have a close tie of relationship or care with the accident victim, but retain it for other plaintiffs.[99] This seems illogical. Relationship is certainly the

---

94. In *Chapman v Lear* (unreported, Queensland SC, 8 Apr 1988, No 3732 of 1984), the plaintiff was unable to see his son before an operation was performed, but the court accepted that the defendant owed him a duty. In *Anderson v Smith* (1990) 101 FLR 34 the plaintiff could not see her daughter in hospital straight away because efforts were being made to revive her following a near drowning. The court said that there was no less proximity in time and space than in *Jaensch v Coffey* (1984) 155 CLR 549. In *Petrie v Dowling* [1992] 1 Qd R 284, the plaintiff was told at hospital that her daughter was dead. The defendant did not argue that the plaintiff was outside the aftermath. See also *Rowe Estate v Hanna* (1989) 71 Alta LR (2d) 136; *Ravenscroft v Rederiaktiebølaget Transatlantic* [1991] 3 All ER 73, reversed by the English Court of Appeal [1992] 2 All ER 470n, where a mother was summoned to hospital by her husband to be told that their son had been crushed to death in an industrial accident and due to the state of the body was not permitted by him to view it.
95. (1991) Aust Torts Rep 81-116.
96. (1990) 75 DLR (4th) 248.
97. [1992] 1 AC 310.
98. See below, pp 167-168.
99. Trindade, op cit, n 93 at 499-500.

factor which is most likely to produce a conclusion that the harm suffered was foreseeable, [100] but there are cases where harm to persons unrelated to the accident victim is just as foreseeable. It is as artificial to restrict recovery in such situations by the use of devices such as the aftermath doctrine as it is in cases where there are close family or other ties.

100. See above, p 107.

7

MEANS OF COMMUNICATION

Being told of a traumatic event

The traditional rule

What strikes one immediately on a survey of the psychiatric damage cases is that in the overwhelming number of successful claims shock was suffered either as a result of the plaintiff's direct and unaided perception of the traumatic event or of the combined effect of what he or she perceived and what was communicated at the scene or its aftermath.[1] Traditionally, the absence of personal perception, even where there is an intimate relationship between the parties, has doomed a shock-related claim based on a communication of bad news (whether orally or in writing) by a third party to failure. This conservative attitude towards "distant shock"[2] is reflected in a number of older English authorities but is perhaps best illustrated by *Hambrook v Stokes Bros.*[3] There, the pregnant plaintiff saw the defendant's unattended truck rolling out of control down a hill and around a corner. Her three children had just walked up the same street in the direction from which the truck had come. Although she could not see what happened to them she feared the worst, immediately rushing to the scene, where bystanders informed her that a child answering to her daughter's description had been struck. This shocked her to such an extent that she haemorrhaged and died. Her husband brought a fatal accident claim. The English Court of Appeal considered that even if she had lived the plaintiff could only have maintained a successful action if the shock resulted from what she herself had sensed and not from something told to her.[4]

Likewise in *King v Phillips*,[5] where a mother suffered shock after hearing her child scream and looking out of a window to see a taxi reversing and her child's tricycle underneath it, Denning LJ stated:

> "Some cases seem plain enough. A wife or mother who suffers shock on being told of an accident to a loved one cannot recover damages from the negligent party on that account. . . . But . . . a mother who

---

1. Recovery for psychiatric illness in this situation is to be distinguished from claims against the bearer or creator of bad tidings: see below, pp 183-191.
2. The term used by J G Fleming, *The Law of Torts* (8th ed, 1992), 165.
3. [1925] 1 KB 141.
4. Ibid per Bankes LJ at 152, per Atkin LJ at 159 and per Sargant LJ at 165. See also *Bourhill v Young* [1943] AC 92 per Lord Macmillan at 103. For a more in-depth discussion see A L Goodhart, "The Shock Cases and Area of Risk" (1953) 16 MLR 14 at 18-19; J Havard, "Reasonable Foresight of Nervous Shock" (1956) 19 MLR 478 at 486-490; P G Heffey, "The Negligent Infliction of Nervous Shock in Road and Industrial Accidents" (1974) 48 ALJ 196, 240 at 204-205.
5. [1953] 1 QB 429.

suffers from shock by hearing or seeing, with her own unaided senses, that her child is in peril . . . may be able to recover."[6]

Although there was some equivocation amongst the majority, it was reaffirmed, at least by Lord Wilberforce, in *McLoughlin v O'Brian*[7] that shock by third party communication as opposed to direct visual or aural appreciation of a distressing event or its aftermath does not give rise to liability. In that case although Mrs McLoughlin heard of the accident involving her family before she saw its results in hospital, her shock stemmed only from that later perception and it was on that basis that the House of Lords ruled that a duty of care was owed to her. In the most recent English case, *Alcock v Chief Constable of South Yorkshire Police*,[8] their Lordships have again indorsed the traditional attitude to shock-related damage claims, this time unanimously ruling out liability for communication-induced shock and related psychiatric harm.

The extreme caution with which the courts have proceeded in this area can also be seen in Canadian cases. That psychiatric damage claims will not be actionable when shock stems solely from bad news given by a third party is supported by the Canadian case of *Abramzik v Brenner*.[9] There the husband of the plaintiff told his wife that two of their children (as well as two of the defendant's children) had been killed by a freight train at a level crossing when the defendant, who had been driving the children to church, negligently drove in front of it. In refusing the wife's claim for nervous shock on the basis of an absence of reasonable foreseeability,[10] the Saskatchewan Court of Appeal[11] stressed that unlike the husband (who did not suffer psychiatric injury and therefore made no claim), the wife never went to the scene or saw the bodies of her children. Liability cannot arise, it was said, in these circumstances.

Australian courts also have, until recently, been reluctant to allow recovery in situations where there is no personal perception, doubting whether shock sustained merely upon hearing distressing news is sufficient to ground a claim. Although the case did not require excursion into the "told" issue, Windeyer J in *Mount Isa Mines Ltd v Pusey*[12] took the opportunity to state:

> "I repeat that in this case we are concerned with only one kind of occurrence causing nervous shock—a plaintiff employee in a factory

6. Ibid at 441. See further A L Goodhart, "Emotional Shock and the Unimaginative Taxicab Driver" (1953) 69 LQR 347. See also Lord Denning MR's comments in *Hinz v Berry* [1970] 2 QB 40 at 42.
7. [1983] 1 AC 410 per Lord Wilberforce at 422-423. Contrast Lord Bridge at 442, discussed below, pp 159-160.
8. [1992] 1 AC 310. Note also the English Court of Appeal's comments in *H v Home Office, The Times*, 7 May 1992.
9. (1967) 65 DLR (2d) 651, noted by J S Williams (1968) 46 Can BR 515; H J Glasbeek (1969) 47 Can BR 96. For similar cases see *Dietelbach v Public Trustee* (1973) 37 DLR (3d) 621; *Babineau v MacDonald (No 2)* (1975) 59 DLR (3d) 671; *Rowe Estate v Hanna* (1989) 71 Alta LR (2d) 136. Note also the effect of *Rhodes v Canadian National Railway* (1990) 75 DLR (4th) 248.
10. Note, however, Glasbeek, op cit, n 9 at 104 who is critical of this finding, arguing that "*nothing* could have been more readily foreseen than that nervous shock would be suffered by *this* plaintiff".
11. Reversing Sirois J (1965) 54 DLR (2d) 639 who awarded damages.
12. (1970) 125 CLR 383.

seeing at the scene of accident there disastrous and pitiful consequences for another man. I need express no opinion and wish to guard against it being thought that I express any opinion on what would be the result if the facts were significantly different. In particular I do not question decisions that nervous shock resulting simply from hearing distressing news does not sound in damages in the same way as does nervous shock from witnessing distressing events. If the sole cause of shock be what is told or read of some happening then I think it is correctly said that, unless there be an intention to cause a nervous shock, no action lies against either the bearer of the bad tidings or the person who caused the event of which they tell. There is no duty in law to break bad news gently or to do nothing which creates bad news.

That, however, seems to me remote from this case, and not to avail the appellant. No doubt the plaintiff's learning that the man who had been burnt had died added to his distress of mind: but it was not the sole or prime cause of it." [13]

Even Evatt J's now seemingly preferred dissent in *Chester v Council of the Municipality of Waverley* [14] stressed the need for plaintiff perception. While rejecting the majority decision to refuse relief on reasonable foreseeability grounds to a mother who suffered shock from witnessing the recovery of her dead son from a water-filled trench, his Honour considered that she could only succeed if her mental injury was due to:

"emotional distress caused by the circumstances existing from the moment when her search brought her to the trench up to the time when her child's body was removed therefrom. . . . [T]he plaintiff is not disentitled to recover merely because she came to the scene of the fatality after her child had fallen into the trench, provided that her shock and suffering were due in the main to what she realised from her own unaided senses during the period I have defined." [15]

Similar sentiments were expressed by Lush J in *Benson v Lee*: [16]

"[W]hat is, at the present time, required, is . . . a direct perception of some of the events which go to make up the accident as an entire event, and this includes seeing the immediate aftermath of the accident, even if, for example, the impact or explosion is neither seen nor heard." [17]

South African [18] and United States authority also upholds the traditional principle that there is no liability for shock caused by orally communicated distressing news. In Florida, for example, liability was not imposed where a mother learnt that her stillborn baby had been inadvertently sent through

13. Ibid at 407.
14. (1939) 62 CLR 1.
15. Ibid at 43. Note also *Bunyan v Jordan* (1936) 36 SR (NSW) 350 where Jordan CJ at 353 clearly assumed that shock must be perceived through the claimant's own sensory system.
16. [1972] VR 879.
17. Ibid at 880. Note also *Spencer v Associated Milk Services Pty Ltd and McNamara* [1968] Qd R 393 where Lucas J ruled that it was not reasonably foreseeable that a 17-year-old son would suffer emotional deterioration when told upon regaining consciousness of his parents' deaths in a car accident.
18. See *Waring & Gillow Ltd v Sherborne*, 1904 TS 340 where recovery was denied to a wife who suffered shock on receiving a report of her husband's death.

the hospital laundry,[19] and in Louisiana the same outcome was reached in relation to a hospital which told a woman that her comatose husband had been bitten by rats while lying in his bed.[20]

Breach of pre-existing duty

Despite these statements it is not accurate to assert that there have been no cases where shock-induced mental illness caused by third party communication has been compensated. The "told" rule against recovery is not absolute, an exception coming into play where there is a breach of a pre-existing duty owed to the plaintiff. The need for actual perception was disregarded in *Schneider v Eisovitch*[21] where the plaintiff was told, after regaining consciousness, of her husband's death in an accident in which they had both been involved, and suffered shock as a result. Rejecting the argument that the plaintiff could not recover because she sustained a solely communication-induced injury, Paull J pointed out that she had been owed a duty by the defendant driver not to cause her physical injury and that duty had been broken. It followed on the then prevailing *Re Polemis*[22] remoteness test that the defendant was liable for all direct consequences of his breach irrespective of their foreseeability. His Lordship said:

19. *Crenshaw v Sarasota County Public Hospital Board* (1985) 466 So 2d 427 (Fla).
20. *Lejeune v Rayne Branch Hospital* (1990) 556 So 2d 559 (La). See also *Burroughs v Jordan* (1970) 456 SW 2d 652 (Tenn); *Deboe v Horn* (1971) 94 Cal Rptr 77; *Schurk v Christensen* (1972) 497 P 2d 937 (Wash) (parents told that 15-year-old babysitter had sexually molested their five-year-old daughter); *Perlmutter v Whitney* (1975) 230 NW 2d 390 (Mich); *Gustafson v Faris* (1976) 241 NW 2d 208 (Mich); *Justus v Atchison* (1977) 565 P 2d 122; 139 Cal Rptr 97 (plaintiff fathers' shock did not result from witnessing deaths of their unborn foetuses because the "event was by its very nature hidden from [their] contemporaneous perception", but from being informed by their doctor); *Shelton v Russell Pipe & Foundry Co* (1978) 570 SW 2d 861 (Tenn); *Cortez v Macias* (1980) 167 Cal Rptr 905 (mother returned from paying her son's emergency room bill following treatment to be told by her husband that the child was dead); *Williams v Citizens Mutual Insurance Co* (1980) 290 NW 2d 76 (Mich); *Bernier v Board of County Road Commissioners* (1983) 581 F Supp 781 (mother learnt of accident to son two hours afterwards); *Nutter v Frisbie Memorial Hospital* (1984) 474 A 2d 584 (NH) (parents arrived at hospital shortly after death of child and were immediately advised of death); *Baas v Hoye* (1985) 766 F 2d 1190 (parent did not see child ingest improperly bottled medication); *Budavari v Barry* (1986) 222 Cal Rptr 446 (wife told of incurable lesions on husband's lungs); *H L O v Hossle* (1986) 381 NW 2d 641 (Ia) (parents told that their children had been sexually abused by neighbour); *De Los Santos v Saddlehill Inc* (1986) 511 A 2d 721 (NJ) (parents learnt that five-year-old daughter had been crushed to death in elevator); *Ledford v Delta Airlines Inc* (1987) 658 F Supp 540 (husband told of crash of plane on which his wife was passenger); *Burrus v Grange Mutual Companies* (1989) 545 NE 2d 83 (Ohio) (mother told of child's death in accident); *Martin By and Through Martin v United States* (1991) 779 F Supp 1242 (mother told that child abducted from day care centre and raped); *Christensen v Superior Court* (1991) 820 P 2d 181; 2 Cal Rptr 2d 79 (media or other secondhand reports insufficient for imposition of liability); *Hoover v Recreation Equipment Corporation* (1991) 792 F Supp 1484 (mother received telephone call informing her that son injured in playground accident). Note also the bizarre argument of the plaintiff in the Californian case of *Burke v Pan American World Airways Inc* (1980) 484 F Supp 850 who claimed to have suffered emotional injuries while at home in California through "extrasensory empathy" at the time her twin sister was killed in a plane crash in the Canary Islands. The court held that the plaintiff failed to state a cause of action. Despite her claim to have known at the moment of the crash that her sister had died, she did not know the circumstances until informed by third parties at a later date.
21. [1960] 2 QB 430, noted by H W Burnett (1960) 38 Can BR 615.
22. [1921] 3 KB 560.

"[O]nce a breach of duty is established the difference between seeing and hearing is immaterial. Hearing can be just as direct a consequence as seeing. The fact that, owing to unconsciousness . . . a period of time elapsed before the news was heard, makes no difference provided that the news was a consequence which flowed directly from the breach of duty towards the plaintiff. . . . The fact that the defendant by his negligence caused the death of the plaintiff's husband does not give the plaintiff a cause of action for the shock caused to her; but the plaintiff, having a cause of action for the negligence of the defendant, may add the consequences of shock caused by hearing of her husband's death."[23]

This reasoning was adopted in Australia in a case that was almost factually identical, even in the light of the *Wagon Mound (No 1)*[24] foreseeability test of remoteness which had superseded *Re Polemis*. In *Andrews v Williams*[25] the plaintiff, who had been driving and was rendered unconscious through a collision, was told a few days later of the death of her mother who had been a passenger. Delivering the judgment of the Victorian Supreme Court Winneke CJ stated:

"If nervous shock resulting from sight of the mother's death was, as we think it was, a reasonably foreseeable consequence of the [defendant's] negligent driving, we see no justification in logic or principle for saying that because the [plaintiff] did not become aware of the death for several days on account of unconsciousness or illness, the shock resulting therefrom was not likewise reasonably foreseeable. In our view, in such case the nervous shock . . . was just as much a reasonably foreseeable consequence of the [defendant's] negligent driving as shock resulting from sight of the death would itself have been."[26]

So too in *Kohn v State Government Insurance Commission*,[27] where a seriously injured teenage girl suffered psychiatric damage on being informed of her boyfriend's death in a car accident, Bray CJ was of the view that:

"It is now, I think, established that a plaintiff injured in an accident can recover damages for nervous shock and resultant physical or mental ill health caused by the death in the same accident of someone dear to him or her, even if that death is not directly witnessed or remembered by the plaintiff but only subsequently reported."[28]

23. [1960] 2 QB 430 at 441-442, noted by J A Jolowicz [1960] CLJ 156. See Heffey, op cit, n 4 at 206.
24. [1961] AC 388.
25. [1967] VR 831. This particular aspect of the means of communication issue does not appear to have directly arisen for consideration in Canada.
26. Ibid at 834. But note that two Queensland decisions denied recovery in similar circumstances: see *Shewan v Sellars (No 1)* [1963] QWN 19, where the plaintiff was told in hospital of the very serious injuries to his wife and child (who had been blinded and mentally incapacitated) and, blaming himself, began to suffer an anxiety neurosis; *Spencer v Associated Milk Services Pty Ltd and McNamara* [1968] Qd R 393.
27. (1976) 15 SASR 255.
28. Ibid at 256. See also *Hamlyn v Hann* [1967] SASR 387 per Mitchell J at 404 where the plaintiff, who though after the accident was sufficiently conscious to speak and to be able to hear his children crying, could not "put things together", was awarded $3,000 (in

A similar situation arose in British Columbia in *Kwok v British Columbia Ferry Corporation*.[29] The plaintiff, on vacation with his family, was at the helm of his pleasure craft when it collided with a ferry due, in the main, to the ferry captain's negligence. The plaintiff's boat capsized and when pulled from the water he was told that his wife and one of his three children had drowned, and that another was critically injured. Recovery was granted, no reference being made to the way he learnt of the deaths and injury.

In each of these cases the shock victim was injured in the same accident as the deceased and the question thus arises whether the involvement of the plaintiff in the accident is necessary to invoke the exception. Are non-participants equally able to recover for psychiatric injury caused entirely by the communication of bad news? Bray CJ left the question open in *Kohn v State Government Insurance Commission*,[30] although his comments in *Battista v Cooper*[31] suggest that he would not be prepared to extend recovery in this manner. But providing the criteria of proximity and reasonable foreseeability are satisfied, and there will be circumstances where they will be, it is submitted that there is no convincing argument against allowing recovery for shock caused solely by communication to a person not involved in the negligent activity in question. Some support for

28. *Continued*
   addition to the statutory solatium) for the shock and depression he suffered on learning a few days later that his wife and one of their children had perished; *Gannon v Gray* [1973] Qd R 411 per Williams J at 414; *Tsanaktsidis v Oulianoff* (1980) 24 SASR 500 per Mitchell J at 501. Note also *Regan v Harper* [1971] Qd R 191: the report does not make it clear whether the plaintiff in this case, who suffered relatively minor injuries, remained conscious and actually witnessed the injury to his wife and two children. However, given that he could only have become aware of the seriousness of the injuries to his family (in particular, the brain damage to the younger child) at a later date, compensation awarded to him for a severe psychic trauma can be regarded as within the principle enunciated in the cases above: see H Luntz, *Assessment of Damages for Personal Injury and Death* (3rd ed, 1990), 136-137. In *Richters v Motor Tyre Service Pty Ltd* [1972] Qd R 9 a woman developed a psychological reaction and morbid depression leading to suicide as a result of, inter alia, witnessing fatal injuries to her husband and father in an accident (in which she also received serious injuries) and learning of the father's death later. The case was not litigated as one of shock-related psychiatric damage and no point was taken that the knowledge that he had been killed was acquired from what she had learnt later, the whole of her anxiety state being compensable within her personal injury claim.
29. (1987) 20 BCLR (2d) 318. Note also *Apache Ready Mix Co v Creed* (1983) 653 SW 2d 79 (Tex).
30. (1976) 15 SASR 255 at 256-257. See also *Diakogiorgic v Anastasas* (unreported, Queensland SC, 4 Nov 1974, No 179 of 1972), noted (1975) 49 ALJ 188, where the plaintiff, although present at the accident scene, was uninvolved in the sense that she was not injured by the negligently driven vehicle which killed her husband and injured her two children as they tried to cross the road. She had been standing on the footpath and did not even see the accident, only becoming aware of it on hearing her daughter scream and not learning of her husband's death until the following day. Although on the facts she failed to recover for what was considered to be an abnormal grief reaction to her husband's death, nothing was said by Lucas J to suggest that, had there been evidence of psychiatric damage, her non-involvement coupled with the oral communication of bad news would have barred a claim. Note, however, that she was awarded $3,000 compensation for shock-induced harm caused by her presence at the scene, notwithstanding that she did not actually see the collision.
31. (1976) 14 SASR 225 at 230. Note, however, that this case was concerned with intentional rather than negligent wrongdoing. For discussion of this aspect of the decision see below, pp 287, 294-295.

this proposition may be found, albeit in a different context, in *Brown v Mount Barker Soldiers' Hospital*.[32] A hospitalised new mother resting in a ward was informed that her baby had suffered burns whilst in the children's nursery, that is, during a period when they had been separated. Resort to *Hambrook v Stokes Bros*[33] did not assist the defendant. Focusing on the hospital's duty to take proper medical care of child and mother, Piper J held for the plaintiff notwithstanding that she had not been present when the fire started:

"Here the defendant in taking charge of Mrs Brown as a patient assumed a care of her involving the need to avoid, so far as reasonably practicable, all things that might prejudice her health or comfort, or increase her need for exertion or care. It would be a breach of duty, actionable if followed by damage, to tell her untruly that her child had been burnt. As the truthfulness of the statement was owing to negligence, the truthfulness was no legal excuse for doing harm by telling her—it was a necessary consequence of the negligence that she had to be told."[34]

Whether this approach will be applied in other contexts such as road accidents remains to be seen but it seems illogical to draw such distinctions in the absence of any compelling reasons to do so.

Discontent with the traditional rule

Apart from inroads in the form of a parasitic recovery for communication-caused psychiatric injury on the basis of a pre-existing duty of care, there have been some notable expressions of discontent with the "unaided perception" limitation on liability. In contrast to Lord Wilberforce, Lord Bridge in *McLoughlin v O'Brian*[35] cautioned against an inflexible attitude towards claims by shock victims who were not present at the accident or its aftermath, alluding to the injustices that could result. His Lordship stated:

"[I]t seems to me inescapable that any attempt to define the limit of liability by requiring, in addition to reasonable foreseeability, that the plaintiff claiming damages for psychiatric illness should have witnessed the relevant accident, should have been present at or near the place where it happened, should have come upon its aftermath and thus have had some direct perception of it, as opposed to merely learning of it after the event, should be related in some particular degree to the accident victim—to draw a line by reference to any of these criteria must impose a largely arbitrary limit of liability. . . . [L]et me give [an example] to illustrate what injustice would be wrought by any such hard and fast lines of policy as have been suggested. . . . [C]onsider the

32. [1934] SASR 128, noted by S H Skipper (1934) 8 ALJ 286.
33. [1925] 1 KB 141.
34. [1934] SASR 128 at 130. Note also *Burgess v Superior Court* (1992) 831 P 2d 1197; 9 Cal Rptr 2d 615 (mother sued for negligent infliction of emotional distress as result of injury to baby during delivery) where the court allowed recovery on the basis that the mother was the "direct victim" of the hospital's negligence because the physician owed her a pre-existing duty.
35. [1983] 1 AC 410.

plaintiff who learned after the event of the relevant accident. Take the case of a mother who knows that her husband and children are staying in a certain hotel. She reads in her morning newspaper that it has been the scene of a disastrous fire. She sees in the paper a photograph of unidentifiable victims trapped on the top floor waving for help from the windows. She learns shortly afterwards that all her family have perished. She suffers an acute psychiatric illness. That her illness in these circumstances was a reasonably foreseeable consequence of the events resulting from the fire is undeniable. Yet, is the law to deny her damages as against a defendant whose negligence was responsible for the fire simply on the ground that an important link in the chain of causation of her psychiatric illness was supplied by her imagination of the agonies of mind and body in which her family died, rather than by direct perception of the event?''[36]

The necessity for a distinction between perception-produced and communication-produced shock and psychiatric illness has been questioned also by some members of the High Court in *Jaensch v Coffey*.[37] Whereas Brennan J stressed the necessity for perception-produced damage,[38] Gibbs CJ was reluctant to commit himself on this issue, reserving his opinion on whether shock must arise through the sight or sound of the event or its aftermath. The law, his Honour said, "must continue to proceed in this area step by cautious step".[39] Deane J, pointing out that the rule had not "enjoyed unqualified support"[40] in either England or Australia and citing *Schneider v Eisovitch*[41] and *Andrews v Williams*,[42] also viewed the issue as an open one. His Honour was sceptical of the logic behind the traditional attitudes, observing:

"It is somewhat difficult to discern an acceptable reason why a rule based on public policy should preclude recovery for psychiatric injury sustained by a wife and mother who is so devastated by being told on the telephone that her husband and children have all just been killed that she is unable to attend at the scene while permitting recovery for the reasonably, but perhaps less readily, foreseeable psychiatric injury sustained by a wife who attends at the scene of the accident or at its

36. Ibid at 442. The communication by writing of shocking news does not seem to have arisen on many occasions. For a rare example see *Barnes v Commonwealth* (1937) 37 SR (NSW) 511, discussed below, p 185, where shock was caused as a result of reading a letter stating that a husband had been admitted to a mental asylum. As Lord Bridge's example illustrates, psychiatric damage is just as likely to be suffered through this medium as any other. Suppose that a person asked to give a confidential reference writes an extremely unfavourable and grossly unfair report and negligently sends it to the subject of the reference rather than to its proper recipient. Any resultant psychiatric harm should be equally compensable.
37. (1984) 155 CLR 549.
38. Ibid at 567. In *Anderson v Smith* (1990) 101 FLR 34 at 49-50 Nader J observed that one may readily conceive of situations in which a vivid oral account of a traumatic event by a third party could produce shock. His Honour noted that "there is uncertainty as to whether shock induced by oral description would suffice", but preferred Brennan J's approach to Deane J's decision to leave the question open.
39. (1984) 155 CLR 549 at 555.
40. Ibid at 608.
41. [1960] 2 QB 430.
42. [1967] VR 831.

aftermath at the hospital when her husband has suffered serious but not fatal injuries."[43]

With respect, this reasoning is entirely convincing. The fact that trauma is orally induced should not be considered as trivialising its impact, or operate to defeat claims based on it.

Recognition of liability for communication-induced psychiatric damage

While the question of recoverability for shock and psychiatric illness induced solely by being told distressing news may be uncertain, there is no doubt that damage resulting from the combined effect of personal perception and third party communication is compensable. Psychiatric damage frequently comes about because of a number of contributing reasons and so long as hearing bad news is not the only one the plaintiff is not barred from relief. Deane J in *Jaensch v Coffey* confirmed this,[44] and the fact that aggravation of an existing psychiatric injury by being told of the deterioration or death of another will "neither preclude recovery nor require apportionment between different causes".[45]

Even before these careful reservations of opinion there were indications (apart from the emergence of the exception already dealt with[46]) that the traditional limitation on recovery may ultimately fade away. In *Fagan v Crimes Compensation Tribunal*,[47] an intentional wrongdoing case, the High Court drew no distinction, for criminal compensation purposes, between children who discovered their mother's murdered body and the

---

43. (1984) 155 CLR 549 at 608-609.
44. Ibid at 609. So did Dawson J at 613. See also *Hambrook v Stokes Bros* [1925] 1 KB 141 per Atkin LJ at 159; *Richters v Motor Tyre Service Pty Ltd* [1972] Qd R 9 per Wanstall ACJ at 16-17. The psychiatric damage in cases such as *Storm v Geeves* [1965] Tas SR 252, *Chadwick v British Railways Board* [1967] 1 WLR 912, *Benson v Lee* [1972] VR 879, *Cameron v Marcaccini* (1978) 87 DLR (3d) 442, *Butcher v Motor Accidents Board* (1984) *Victorian Motor Accidents Cases* 72-026 (CCH), *Kralj v McGrath* [1986] 1 All ER 54, *Chapman v Lear* (unreported, Queensland SC, 8 Apr 1988, No 3732 of 1984), *De Franceschi v Storrier* (1988) 85 ACTR 1, *Gibson v Trueba* (unreported, New South Wales SC, 2 Nov 1990, No 19749 of 1986), *Hevican v Ruane* [1991] 3 All ER 65 and *Mullally v Bus Eireann* (unreported, Irish HC, 13 June 1991) was caused by the combined impact of a report of a traumatic event and the subsequent observation of its aftermath. Contrast the much more restrictive attitude manifested in United States cases such as *Hewitt v Chadwick* (1988) 760 SW 2d 333 (Tex) where parents who learnt of an accident to their daughter and then saw her in hospital were adjudged to have no remedy, and *Benavides v County of Wilson* (1992) 955 F 2d 968 where (in a case of intentional infliction of emotional distress) it was held that the fact that a wife was told of her husband's paralysis from a fall in jail, before she saw him, disentitled her from recovering.
45. (1984) 155 CLR 549 at 609. See also *Mount Isa Mines Ltd v Pusey* (1970) 125 CLR 383 per Windeyer J at 407; *Kralj v McGrath* [1986] 1 All ER 54. It appears that this is the position even if the communication of bad news is the overwhelming factor leading to a psychiatric illness: see *Richards v Baker* [1943] SASR 245, where a mother recovered for injury caused by the initial shock of witnessing her son run down aggravated by the news of his subsequent death. Damages were assessed on the basis that the increased injury should be included notwithstanding that the severity of the plaintiff's illness was predominantly a result of the boy's death. Note, however, *Shewan v Sellars (No 1)* [1963] QWN 19 and Heffey, op cit, n 4 at 209.
46. See above, pp 156-159.
47. (1982) 150 CLR 666.

appellant, a child who did not see the body but was picked up from school by relatives rather than his mother, learning of her death later. Although their Honours agreed that tortious principles were inapplicable under the *Criminal Injuries Compensation Act* 1972 (Vic), Brennan J in particular was of the view that it was foreseeable, in the tortious sense, that the appellant would suffer "nervous shock". [48] The case may be interpreted as suggesting the presence of a duty owed to those who suffer nervous shock and psychiatric illness solely by hearing of the accident. [49]

Another decision of the early 1980s—though a rather odd one—which appears to give support to this proposition is *White v Butcher* [50] where parents of a teenage girl first heard of a serious accident to their daughter from a police officer who came to their house late one night. They went straight to the hospital, to find her lying unconscious. She did not recover consciousness for the next four days. Both parents suffered psychiatric injury as a result of these experiences. Though they did see her in hospital, Maxwell J appeared to accept without question that this harm stemmed from what they were told, even more so than from what they later saw. His Honour ruled that, once liability to the daughter was established, judgment should be entered for the parents in their actions, subject only to proper proof of "nervous shock". This laconic acceptance of the parents' case is puzzling, since a psychiatric damage claim brought by persons such as the parents in this case proceeds on very different principles from a personal injury action by the accident victim. Though the judgment nowhere so suggests, it is possible that the case was in fact brought as a statutory nervous shock claim, [51] under which liability to parents does not in any way depend on presence but merely on relationship. It is not easy to see why in New South Wales parents would prefer to claim under the common law. [52]

Concerns with traditionalism were also expressed in the post-*Jaensch v Coffey* [53] case of *Petrie v Dowling*. [54] Focusing on Deane J's reservations, Kneipp J, in a ground-breaking decision, ruled that in certain circumstances a plaintiff can recover for shock and psychiatric damage caused solely by what he or she has been told and not contributed to in any way by anything the plaintiff perceived. Although previously compensation had been awarded for nervous damage due to a combination of factors including the communication of bad news, [55] never before had a claimant clearly recovered for shock caused entirely by what was told to him or her. In this case the plaintiff's friends came to see her at work and informed her that

---

48. Ibid at 680. Note S Lebovici, "Observations on Children Who Have Witnessed the Violent Death of One of their Parents: A Contribution to the Study of Traumatization" (1974) 1 Int Rev Psychoanalysis 117; C P Malmquist, "Children Who Witness Parental Murder: Posttraumatic Aspects" (1986) 25 J Am Acad Child Psychiatry 320.
49. It is true, however, that the shock also resulted from a more direct experience in that his mother failed to collect him from school. See P Handford "Shock and Policy: McLoughlin v O'Brian" (1983) 15 UWALR 398 at 408.
50. (Unreported, New South Wales SC, 13 Oct 1982, Nos 9576, 9577 and 9578 of 1981).
51. Under s 4 of the *Law Reform (Miscellaneous) Provisions Act* 1944 (NSW).
52. On statutory causes of action for psychiatric damage see below, Chapter 11.
53. (1984) 155 CLR 549.
54. [1992] 1 Qd R 284.
55. See above, p 161.

her daughter had been knocked from her bicycle and hospitalised with gravel rash and concussion. On arriving at the hospital she quipped, trying to make light of the situation, "she isn't dead, is she?" to which a nurse replied "I'm afraid so". Kneipp J found for the plaintiff, considering that:

> "in an appropriate case it is sufficient that it be proved that shock and consequent illness follows on the receipt of distressing news. Of course, a decision in any particular case must depend on the circumstances. In the present case the plaintiff attended at the hospital, no doubt distressed at the fact that her daughter had been in an accident but in the belief that she had not sustained serious injury, only to be told bluntly that her daughter had died. In these circumstances . . . the plaintiff is entitled to recover."[56]

The reference to the way the plaintiff was told about the death may indicate that the mode of communication is an important consideration to be taken into account in determining if the facts ground recovery. If this was Kneipp J's intention, it is submitted that future courts should disregard such factors. Irrespective of whether a plaintiff is informed callously or without compassion or has bad news broken gently and with care, the manner in which the information is conveyed should be seen as immaterial. The vital point is that once it has been accepted that, on principle, psychiatric injury caused solely by what is told is capable of being compensated, the precise nature that the communication took is irrelevant if such damage has in fact been suffered as a result.

At least three other recent cases, each decided in a different country, lend support to the proposition that damages may be granted for shock-induced illness resulting purely from the receipt of distressing news.[57] The difference between these cases, certainly the first two, and *Petrie v Dowling* is that, in contrast to Kneipp J's carefully articulated analysis of the novelty of "told only" recovery, the courts seem to have failed to appreciate the significance of their decisions which were reached with no discussion of the

---

56. [1992] 1 Qd R 284 at 286-287.
57. It is not obvious from the judgment in *Mellor v Moran* (1985) 2 MVR 461, where a young child recovered for psychiatric illness on the death of her mother in a car accident, what the injury-inducing stimulus was. Presumably the child was not at the scene or aftermath and learnt of her mother's death only by what she was told later but the matter is not free from doubt. In any event, both Brennan and Deane JJ's comments in *Jaensch v Coffey* (1984) 155 CLR 549 were ignored. See also *Swan v Williams (Demolition) Pty Ltd* (1987) 9 NSWLR 172 where the plaintiff appears to have been informed of, rather than at the scene or aftermath of, his wife's and her parents' deaths when a 630kg sandstone block crushed their car. However an admission of liability prevented the examination of the limitations on recovery. Moreover it is unclear whether the husband's claim was based on s 4 of the *Law Reform (Miscellaneous Provisions) Act* 1944 (NSW), under which the means of communication is unimportant: see below, pp 168-169. Another New South Wales case, *Budget Rent-a-Car Systems Pty Ltd v Kemp* (unreported, New South Wales CA, 21 Dec 1984, CA No 7 of 1984), is also equivocal on the communication issue. A husband suing "at common law" who was told of his wife's death recovered for resultant mental harm, no mention of s 4 of the 1944 Act being made by McHugh JA. Note also *Bassanese v Martin* (1982) 31 SASR 461 where Zelling J interpreted *McLoughlin v O'Brian* [1983] 1 AC 410 as making it irrelevant that the plaintiff was not present when her husband was stabbed by the jealous lover of his mistress and suffered shock through hearing of the incident. This analysis, however, takes no account of the aftermath doctrine as extended by their Lordships in that case: see above, pp 137-138.

issues involved.[58] In *Heighington v The Queen in Right of Ontario*[59] the plaintiffs, who became aware only through having been told that their homes had been built on land contaminated with radioactive waste, were granted compensation for their psychiatric illnesses. In the New South Wales case of *X and Y v Pal*[60] a specialist gynaecologist and obstetrician negligently failed to screen a mother-to-be for syphilis before the birth of her first baby which died a month later. She was advised that there was no reason why she should not become pregnant again. Her second child was born dysmorphic and mentally retarded and tests after the birth revealed that both child and mother were suffering from syphilis, and that the mother had been infected at some time prior to her first pregnancy. When told these facts, the mother became distraught, was deeply shocked and suffered psychiatric harm. Although attention was chiefly devoted to the claim made on behalf of the baby, the Court of Appeal awarded damages to the mother for shock-related mental injury suffered as a consequence of the child being born with syphilis without examining in any detail the authorities on this area or even alluding to the means of communication debate. Perhaps the strongest of the three supportive authorities is the Supreme Court of Nebraska's very recent decision in *Haselhorst v State*.[61] While express discussion of the sufficiency of purely oral communication was absent here also, the court did address the corollary issue of contemporaneous perception of trauma. An action was brought by the parents of a foster child against, inter alia, the Department of Social Services alleging that they had suffered psychiatric problems in the form of enduring adjustment disorders arising out of the negligent placement with them of a known violent and unstable 15-year-old boy who physically and sexually abused the couple's four younger children. In a decision which runs against the general trend in the United States,[62] the majority considered it immaterial that the parents had not witnessed or heard the violation of their children and, significantly for our present purposes, in upholding the imposition of liability implied that their acquisition of knowledge of it solely through the reports of third parties was not fatal to the psychiatric injury claims. What was important was the fact that the parents had suffered and would continue to suffer from significant mental damage requiring intensive therapy, not the way they had come to suffer it.

Wilks v Haines[63] too, while it resists construction as authority supportive of liability for "told only" mental damage, is worthy of consideration in this context. The plaintiff, who was a dormitory supervisor

---

58. Note also *Prince v Pittston Co* (1974) 63 FRD 28, noted (1975) 63 Geo LJ 1179, where the defendant's motion for summary judgment was dismissed in a case where 30 plaintiffs claimed damages for emotional distress caused by hearing of a flood disaster in the valley where they lived. They had been absent at the time of the disaster. The court noted that none of the valley's residents could be denied recovery as a matter of law solely on this ground. Following the denial of summary judgment the parties announced a settlement. For a similar procedural ruling see *Cook v General Cable Corporation* (1989) 728 F Supp 38.
59. (1987) 41 DLR (4th) 208.
60. (1991) 23 NSWLR 26.
61. (1992) 485 NW 2d 180 (Neb).
62. See above, p 156, n 20.
63. (1991) Aust Torts Rep 81-078.

in a home for intellectually handicapped children, suffered shock and resultant psychiatric injury when two work colleagues were murdered and a third injured by an intruder. She appears to have been denied recovery not because her mental injury was due to being told about her colleagues' fate, but because it stemmed from a realisation that it should have been her. Loveday J gave no indication that, if shock is caused as a result of what happens to another, the fact that it is induced by communication only will operate to bar relief.

There have been some English first instance judges also prepared to row their "puisne sculling boat across [the] strong tide"[64] of judicial sentiment rejecting liability for psychiatric damage which is entirely communication-caused. In *Hevican v Ruane*[65] where the plaintiff's psychological injury took the form of a gradual realisation coming to him in stages that his son—"the apple of his eye"—was dead, brought about through the communication by others of the situation, Mantell J found for the plaintiff. His Lordship stated:

> "It would seem . . . that by reference to general principles [of negligence] alone there is no reason why a plaintiff who sustains a mental shock as a predictable result of learning of a loved one's death or injury and in consequence becomes ill either in the mind . . . or in the body . . . for example by suffering a heart attack, should not recover damages against a defendant whose negligent act caused the death or injury."[66]

Similarly in *Ravenscroft v Rederiaktiebφlaget Transatlantic*[67] Ward J awarded £16,500 for a prolonged depressive condition brought about when a husband told his wife that their son had been crushed to death by a shuttle wagon while working on a ship's cargo deck. Imagining the state of the body the husband had refused to allow the plaintiff to see their deceased son. The judge considered that the wife's absence from the accident scene or its aftermath and thus the lack of direct sensory perception did not serve to bar her claim, there being no public policy consideration preventing recovery.[68]

However, *Ravenscroft v Rederiaktiebφlaget Transatlantic* was later reversed by the English Court of Appeal[69] as a result of the disapproval of the decision expressed by the House of Lords in *Alcock v Chief Constable of South Yorkshire Police*,[70] in which the courts at all levels were generally unsympathetic to such deviations from traditionalism. Hidden J rejected the claim of a sister who learned indirectly of her brother's death without

---

64. *Ravenscroft v Rederiaktiebφlaget Transatlantic* [1991] 3 All ER 73 per Ward J at 87.
65. [1991] 3 All ER 65.
66. Ibid at 71.
67. [1991] 3 All ER 73.
68. Unfortunately, his Lordship reached this conclusion through an extended use of the notion of sensory impact (as to which see *Jaensch v Coffey* (1984) 155 CLR 549 per Brennan J at 565-567, discussed below, pp 192-193). Adopting a view of "hearing" a traumatic event different from the conventional understanding of that term as utilised in cases such as *Bourhill v Young* [1943] AC 92, Ward J at 78 considered listening to bad news an insult to that sense and the "sight" of an empty son-less home equally impacting on the mother's sense of vision.
69. [1992] 2 All ER 470n.
70. [1992] 1 AC 310.

having directly perceived the traumatic event in question or its aftermath. All members of the English Court of Appeal in this case refused to indorse Ward and Mantell JJ's extensions, focusing on Lord Wilberforce's insistence on direct sensory perception, rather than communication-caused shock, in *McLoughlin v O'Brian*.[71] In contrast to Kneipp J's approach in *Petrie v Dowling*,[72] Parker LJ said:

"A person who informs a parent of a victim of his death or multiple injuries cannot be held liable for obvious reasons and the wrongdoer cannot in my view be held liable for psychiatric illness resulting from what the parent is told. In so holding I respectfully differ from the decision of Ward J. . . . It is, moreover, to be noted that in *McLoughlin v O'Brian* [1983] 1 AC 410 the House of Lords proceeded on the basis that liability resulted from what the plaintiff had seen on arrival in the hospital on being told of the accident, not on the information of the accident which had led to her presence there."[73]

The House of Lords[74] also rebuked attempts to compensate shock victims whose psychological injuries stem from being informed of, reading or hearing about a traumatic incident and expressed "serious doubts" as to the correctness of the first instance decisions in *Ravenscroft v Rederiaktiebølaget Transatlantic*[75] and *Hevican v Ruane*.[76] In the light of a perceived (we would argue wrongly) lack of good policy reasons for change, their Lordships unanimously adhered to Lord Wilberforce's philosophy rather than incorporating the flexibility campaigned for by Lord Bridge,[77] categorising psychiatric damage sustained in the absence of direct visual or aural perception as non-actionable.

Not only is persistence with this distinction illogical, it is unjustified in the light of current medical knowledge. As Deane J observed in *Jaensch v Coffey*:

"The most important explanation of nervous shock resulting from injury to another is the existence of a close, constructive and loving relationship, with that person (a 'close relative') and . . . it is largely immaterial whether the close relative is at the scene of the accident or how he or she learns of it."[78]

71. [1983] 1 AC 410 at 422-423.
72. [1992] 1 Qd R 284.
73. *Alcock v Chief Constable of South Yorkshire Police* [1992] 1 AC 310 at 363. See also Stocker LJ at 379 and Nolan LJ at 386 who expressed similar views.
74. [1992] 1 AC 310 per Lord Keith at 398, per Lord Ackner at 400, per Lord Oliver at 416, 418, per Lord Jauncey at 423. Note also recent cases involving the King's Cross underground station fire in London and the Herald of Free Enterprise sinking at Zeebrugge, where relatives suffered psychiatric injury as a result of being told of the deaths of loved ones: see *Singh v London Underground Ltd* (unreported, QBD, 24 Apr 1990); *Crocker v P & O European Ferries (Dover) Ltd* (unreported, QBD, 3 Dec 1990). The judgments deal with preliminary procedural issues. In the former case the court indicated that to find the defendants liable would require an extension of the principles in *McLoughlin v O'Brian* [1983] 1 AC 410.
75. [1991] 3 All ER 73.
76. [1991] 3 All ER 65.
77. *McLoughlin v O'Brian* [1983] 1 AC 410 at 442.
78. (1984) 155 CLR 549 at 600. See also D J Leibson, "Recovery of Damages for Emotional Distress Caused by Physical Injury to Another" (1976-1977) 15 *Journal of Family Law* 163 at 196; H Teff, "Liability for Negligently Inflicted Nervous Shock" (1983) 99 LQR

The traditional position has been based on the premise that nervous shock suffered by direct insult to the sensory system is somehow more impacting than that suffered on being told of distressing news. This may be true in many cases, but it will not always be so, as Lord Bridge's example in *McLoughlin v O'Brian*[79] illustrates. It is conceivable that the impact on the nervous system of being told of particularly debilitating injuries, especially those which by their nature may occur without the spilling of blood or the breaking of bones, can be as great as (if not greater than) direct perception through attendance at the accident scene. For example, a parent's nightmare on learning at the hospital of their son's permanent quadriplegia as a result of a swimming pool accident may well be more intense than discovery of the injured child at the edge of the pool. Even Lord Oliver, a proponent of the "direct perception" theory, has conceded, in a heavily policy-influenced judgment, that:

> "The traumatic effect on . . . a mother on the death of her child is as readily foreseeable in a case where the circumstances are described to her by an eyewitness at the inquest as it is in a case where she learns of it at a hospital immediately after the event. . . . [Moreover] the news brought by a policeman hours after the event may be as sudden and unexpected to the recipient as the occurrence of the event is to the spectator present at the scene."[80]

Trindade has suggested that there should be recovery in "told" cases only if there is a close tie between the shock victim and the person killed, injured or imperilled.[81] In all other situations he argues that traditionalism should prevail and perception of the accident or its aftermath should remain a prerequisite to recovery. We would go further. In appropriate circumstances even a person not in any such close relationship should recover for "recognisable psychiatric illness" brought on solely by what is communicated to him or her. In all likelihood this situation will seldom arise, but if it is the case that on principle bystanders are not to be automatically barred from recovery and shock caused entirely by communication is compensable, this further extension must follow. So long as it is proved on the balance of probabilities that the claimant has in fact suffered a "recognisable psychiatric illness", the absence of a close relationship, or direct perception, should not operate to leave him or her without relief. Moreover, a strict application of the "told" rule would exclude compensation in cases where there is no accident or immediate

78. *Continued*
    100 at 107 who comments: "In several cases it is assumed as beyond argument that the psychic impact of the victim's injuries [is] more intense for a plaintiff who was at the scene than for one who heard or read about them later. Yet this is typically true only of the primary reactions [momentary fright etc], not of the fundamental and enduring secondary ones [psychic injury], which are more strongly correlated with closeness of relationship."
79. [1983] 1 AC 410 at 442. See also the examples given by F A Trindade, "The Principles Governing the Recovery of Damages for Negligently Caused Nervous Shock" [1986] CLJ 476 at 491-493.
80. *Alcock v Chief Constable of South Yorkshire Police* [1992] 1 AC 310 at 411. Note also *Hinz v Berry* [1970] 2 QB 40 per Lord Denning MR at 43, suggesting that the plaintiff would have suffered some damage if her husband had been killed in an accident even though she was 50 miles away.
81. Trindade, op cit, n 79 at 493.

aftermath to attend. Imagine, for example, the effect on the partner of a spouse of learning that the spouse has contracted the AIDS virus. Is the partner to be denied recovery because he or she was not present at the time of a careless screening of blood which was later transfused, or at the scene of an adulterous liaison?[82] (Even if present at these events the partner would more than likely not appreciate that a tortious act involving a breach of a duty of care owed to him or her was being committed.) Or suppose a couple learns that a hospital has negligently permitted their newborn baby to be taken home by third parties under the mistaken belief that it was the third parties' child,[83] or has negligently failed to prevent their baby being abducted.[84] And what if a body cannot ever be recovered, say where a person is lost overboard on a fishing trip far from land, or is completely destroyed, for example in an industrial accident, or for that matter is hidden by the tortfeasor?[85] Seeking refuge in the aftermath doctrine cannot achieve justice in such cases. Those who are visually or aurally impaired are also unfairly prejudiced by the traditional restriction on the means of communication. Is the blind and deaf parent who is present at the scene of an accident to his or her child to be denied recovery for shock and psychiatric damage suffered on learning about it later from a friend, merely through being incapable of perceiving such an event in the way the majority of the population does?

Judicial retreat to the sanctity of public policy arguments to deny the pragmatic and logical expansion of liability in this context is an unimpressive tactic and serves only to stunt the maturation of the common law. Fears of limitless liability are greatly exaggerated. Nor, as Mantell J has observed, would awarding damages in these cases leave the door open to fraud because:

> "To sustain a claim based on nervous shock, no matter what the circumstances in which the shock was received, a plaintiff would be bound to submit himself or herself over a protracted period to the close scrutiny of psychiatrists well able to detect humbug."[86]

Significantly, in New South Wales,[87] the Australian Capital Territory[88] and the Northern Territory,[89] where the ambit of liability for "mental or nervous shock" has been extended by statute, the legislature had no qualms

82. In *Homer v Leng* (1992) 599 A 2d 1193 (Md) it was held that a husband had no claim for intentional infliction of emotional distress against a psychiatrist who seduced his wife because the husband was not present when the seduction occurred!

83. This occurred in *Carter v Lake Wales Hospital Association* (1968) 213 So 2d 898 (Fla). See also *Espinosa v Beverley Hospital* (1952) 249 P 2d 843 (Cal) where a mother who was given the wrong baby at hospital failed to recover for consequent mental anguish because she had not suffered actual physical harm as a result of the defendant's want of care.

84. In *Johnson v Jamaica Hospital* (1984) 467 NE 2d 502 (NY) the abducted baby was returned four and a half months later. Incredibly, one of the bases on which the court denied recovery to the parents was that they had not been within the "zone of danger" at the time of the abduction!

85. Evatt J in *Chester v Council of the Municipality of Waverley* (1939) 62 CLR 1 at 35 opined that the fact that a body is never recovered should not allow a tortfeasor to escape liability.

86. *Hevican v Ruane* [1991] 3 All ER 65 at 71.

87. *Law Reform (Miscellaneous Provisions) Act* 1944 (NSW), s 4(1).

88. *Law Reform (Miscellaneous Provisions) Act* 1955 (ACT), s 24.

89. *Law Reform (Miscellaneous Provisions) Act* 1956 (NT), s 25.

about permitting close relatives to recover even though they were not present at the scene of the accident. South Australia has recently introduced more limited legislation[90] but even there such claimants have similar rights. Under the older statutes it is quite clear that parents and spouses (defined to include step-parents, grandparents, and persons in loco parentis, and in New South Wales, cohabitees[91]) can recover for shock caused on being informed that a relative has been killed, injured or put in peril. In *State Rail Authority of New South Wales v Sharp*[92] the daughter of the plaintiffs was killed in the Granville train disaster in Sydney. It was not until the next day they were informed of her death but this presented no obstacle to their claim for relief under the New South Wales statute. The contrast between the readiness with which the court accepted this plea and the problems encountered by courts contending with the common law "told" rule is marked. The Court of Appeal found it unnecessary even to enter the means of communication debate.[93] More recent examples include the recovery by a young mother under the New South Wales provision for extreme grief reaction to the drowning of her three-year-old son in an effluent water storage tank even though she did not witness the accident and learnt of it through a police officer.[94] Likewise, a number of civil law jurisdictions have adopted the rule that shock and psychiatric illness caused by being told of an accident to another is recoverable.[95]

The inescapable conclusion is that claims of this nature are within "the reasonable area for the imposition of liability".[96] If a plaintiff has suffered a compensable type of injury due to the defendant's negligent breach of a duty owed to him or her the plaintiff must recover irrespective of whether the particular facts surrounding the loss can be pigeon-holed into traditional, and it is submitted outdated, categories. The justifiability of allowing recovery in circumstances where there is no direct sensory perception was advocated by Goodhart as long ago as 1953:

90. *Wrongs Act* 1936 (SA), s 35a(1)(c); see also *Motor Accidents Act* 1988 (NSW), s 77.
91. *Law Reform (Miscellaneous Provisions) Act* 1944 (NSW), s 4(5); *Law Reform (Miscellaneous Provisions) Act* 1955 (ACT), s 22; *Law Reform (Miscellaneous Provisions) Act* 1956 (NT), s 23.
92. [1981] 1 NSWLR 240. Note that liability was admitted.
93. Nor was any concern over this issue articulated by the court when granting damages under the Act in similar circumstances in *Smee v Tibbetts* (1953) 53 SR (NSW) 391.
94. *Smith v Email Ltd* (unreported, New South Wales SC, 14 Mar 1986, No CLD S16572 of 1982); see also *Worboys v Hamill* (unreported, New South Wales SC, 3 Feb 1988, No 11216 of 1984); *Manufacturers Mutual Insurance Ltd v Hooper* (unreported, New South Wales CA, 6 May 1988, CA No 222 of 1987); *Reitsma v Government Insurance Office of New South Wales* (unreported, New South Wales SC, 31 Mar 1989, No 13879 of 1985).
95. See J G Fleming, "Distant Shock in Germany (And Elsewhere)" (1972) 20 AJCL 485 dealing, inter alia, with the German Supreme Court case, (1971) BGHZ, NJW 1883, in which the plaintiff suffered an allegedly severe and lasting depression on hearing the news of her husband's sudden death in an accident. See also LG Hildersheim (1970) VersR 720 (no recovery for being told that car damaged in accident); LG Hamburg (1969) NJW 615 (no liability for shock suffered by plaintiff when told that police investigating close relative). Note also B S Markesinis, *A Comparative Introduction to the German Law of Torts* (2nd ed, 1990), 34-35.
96. *Alcock v Chief Constable of South Yorkshire Police* [1992] 1 AC 310 per Lord Oliver at 411.

"It has been argued that if recovery were permitted in these circumstances, then there would be a great number of fabricated cases, and that it is dangerous to open the door too wide. It is exceedingly doubtful whether this is true. If it were true, it would hardly be a justifiable ground for denying a right to recover to persons who had genuinely suffered in such a way. The reason for denying recovery in these circumstances is, I believe, a more rational one. It is based on the ground that an ordinary person who hears about an accident will not have the same violent physical reaction as one who has actually witnessed it. I may read in the newspaper a detailed account of an accident, but this will obviously not have the same effect on me as witnessing the accident at first hand. The ground for excluding liability in these circumstances is therefore based on ordinary experience. But even here it would be dangerous to state the rule in too categorical a manner because there may be special circumstances which may make it reasonably foreseeable that mere repetition will cause such a shock."[97]

Psychiatric damage via television and radio

As discussed in the previous section of this chapter, the law is still grappling with the question of whether communication of the news of an accident through a third party, as opposed to being near and perceiving the event through one's own unaided senses, is sufficient. But the 20th century has brought with it legal complications unimaginable to courts dealing with nervous shock claims in the *Coultas*[98] era. Technology has advanced to such a degree that new and previously unforeseen means of communicating distressing and shocking news have become commonplace. Though news may be communicated orally and face to face, or in writing, it may now also be imparted by telephone or radio. In addition, the plaintiff may see the disaster on television, either broadcast live or on recorded news pictures. It was inevitable, therefore, that the courts would have to review the traditionally restrictive rules denying relief in the absence of direct perception and adjudicate upon the acceptability of these new means of information transfer.

Live broadcasts

Lord Wilberforce in *McLoughlin v O'Brian*, in holding that the shock must come through sight or hearing of the event or its immediate aftermath, speculated whether some equivalent of sight or hearing, such as simultaneous television, would be sufficient.[99] As Hidden J said in *Alcock v Chief Constable of South Yorkshire Police*, these words have proved to be tragically prophetic.[100] The events which took place at Hillsborough at

97. See Goodhart, op cit, n 4 at 25.
98. *Victorian Railways Commissioner v Coultas* (1888) 13 App Cas 222.
99. [1983] 1 AC 410 at 423.
100. [1992] 1 AC 310 at 335. Note also *Singh v London Underground Ltd* (unreported, QBD, 24 Apr 1990) where the plaintiff suffered psychiatric illness as a result of seeing scenes of the King's Cross underground station fire on television, knowing that her family were likely to be involved, and being told of their deaths the next day. Refusing a request for trial by jury, the court intimated that to allow the plaintiff to recover for this illness would require an extension of the principles of *McLoughlin v O'Brian* [1983] 1 AC 410.

the FA Cup semi-final between Liverpool and Nottingham Forest were broadcast live to many parts of the country,[101] and nine of the 16 first instance plaintiffs suffered psychiatric illness through seeing these events on television as they took place, knowing that their loved ones were in the Leppings Lane terraces.[102] The issue thus presented for decision was one which had not been raised in any previous case in any Commonwealth jurisdiction—whether the plaintiffs could recover for shock and consequent psychiatric harm sustained through the medium of television. The potential for this problem to arise has existed since the advent of live outside broadcasts.[103] It grows greater as television technology advances.

> "It is . . . increasingly foreseeable that the broadcast media will, with ever-increasing efficiency and speed, arrive at the scene of a catastrophic event and will broadcast coverage of the event in progress, or, as in the case of the recent space shuttle disaster, that the media will broadcast a catastrophe inadvertently during routine coverage of a news event."[104]

Live television broadcasts are different from the other means of communication referred to above. In the words of Stocker LJ in the English Court of Appeal:

> "[I]f the relevant television broadcast performed no function in relation to the plaintiff other than communicating the fact that an accident had occurred at a place at which the plaintiff knew that his relative was, it would be a mere communication of that fact and would place the plaintiff in a similar position to that in which he would have been had the information been communicated to him by any other media, oral or telephonic. . . . [but] [i]t is unlikely that any television broadcast would do no more than communicate the fact of the accident or disaster."[105]

101. The match was not to be broadcast live, but highlights were to be shown later. However, events at any ground where there was some significant event would be shown live on the BBC afternoon sports programme "Grandstand": see *Alcock v Chief Constable of South Yorkshire Police* [1992] 1 AC 310 per Parker LJ at 352.

102. There was another plaintiff who saw the events live on television in a coach at the ground, but Hidden J did not treat this as a television case. There was no appeal to the Court of Appeal against his decision with respect to this plaintiff: see above, p 145. Of the remaining plaintiffs, four were present at the ground, and two (whose cases are dealt with below, pp 179-181) heard television and radio reports of the tragedy. Two of the four plaintiffs present at the ground and six of the nine who saw the events on television proceeded with appeals to the House of Lords, together with the two who suffered shock through hearing television and radio reports.

103. The BBC Charter of 1927 gave the BBC the right to have its own reporters at the scene of important events. The first sports outside broadcasts, both in England and Australia, date from the 1920s: see J Arlott, "The Story of Cricket on the Air", in B Johnston (ed), *Armchair Cricket 1968* (1968), 9 at 10-11.

104. K K Andrews, "The Next Best thing to Being There?: Foreseeability of Media-Assisted Bystanders" (1987) 17 Sw UL Rev 65 at 81-82. The reference is to the ill-fated Challenger space shuttle flight in 1986, in which seven astronauts met their deaths as the result of a mishap during take-off, events watched on live television by millions. An earlier example is the assassination of United States President John F Kennedy in Dallas, Texas, in November 1963. The motorcade in which the President was riding was being televised. It was surely foreseeable that relatives or certain others watching these events might suffer psychiatric injury.

105. *Alcock v Chief Constable of South Yorkshire Police* [1992] 1 AC 310 at 379.

The viewer watching at home can see and (through the effects microphone) hear what is happening. Is this the same as being there, so that the principles of the "presence" cases apply?[106] Hidden J thought so, and awarded damages to those television-watching plaintiffs who were within the recognised degrees of relationship to the trauma victims.[107] The Court of Appeal disagreed.[108] The House of Lords concurred in the result reached by the Court of Appeal, though on rather different grounds.[109]

Hidden J analysed in some detail the differences between the way in which an event is seen by an eyewitness and a watcher of television:

> "The eyewitness receives images at the back of his eye of events that are taking place immediately before him in his presence. The watcher of television does not. For the eyewitness those images are seen as life size, for the television viewer they are not. The eyewitness can change those images by altering his field of vision, by the turn of a head or the movement of his body by, for instance, moving closer to the scene. The watcher of television is unable to do that, for whichever way he moves, the images on the screen will be the same, albeit seen at a different angle. The eyewitness is seeing something which is taking place actually where he is. The television watcher is enhancing his sight by 'borrowing' the images collected by the lens of a camera somewhere else. That camera lens, metaphorically, transports him from his actual physical position to the different location of the camera, and allows him to receive at the back of his eyes the images he would receive were he standing in the position of the camera. He may, in fact, metaphorically be slightly nearer the camera when one makes allowance for the power to focus. In a sense his metaphorical feet are mid-way between the camera and the image.
>
> His is a similar position to that of the watcher through binoculars, or a telescope, whose metaphorical feet have been moved closer to the object than his actual feet, and who is seeing a picture which he could not possibly receive from his actual position. I accept at once that in the case of the watcher through binoculars, or a telescope, it may be said that it is only the detail of what he is seeing which he could not see from his actual position. That detail, however, may disclose to his sight something which he could not see without the binoculars, such as the concealed figure of a man. Hence, binoculars, like television, may allow a person to see something in a distant position which he could not have seen with his own unaided eyesight. . . .
>
> Thus the television watcher in those circumstances is aware that he is augmenting his own eyesight by the lens of a camera in a distant position, but that his eyes are receiving, through the intervention of that camera lens, images of what is actually happening as he sees them."[110]

106. See generally Andrews, op cit, n 104.
107. *Alcock v Chief Constable of South Yorkshire Police* [1992] 1 AC 310 at 340-344.
108. Ibid per Parker LJ at 361-363, per Stocker LJ at 379-380, per Nolan LJ at 385-387.
109. Ibid per Lord Keith at 398, per Lord Ackner at 405, per Lord Oliver at 417, per Lord Jauncey at 423.
110. Ibid at 341-342.

As his Lordship pointed out, the picture seen by a television watcher is determined by third parties—camera operators and producers—and accompanied by a commentary which may provide additional information not apparent from the picture. However, for Hidden J it was the visual image which was all-important: "It is what is fed to the eyes which makes the instant effect upon the emotions, and the lasting effect upon the memory."[111] The defendant knew that the match would be televised and could foresee that live pictures might be shown in circumstances such as those which happened. Watchers on television, viewing the disaster, were just as likely to suffer psychiatric harm through fear for the safety of loved ones as those looking on from elsewhere in the ground. Hidden J therefore concluded that observation through simultaneous television of the disaster scenes at Hillsborough was sufficient to satisfy the test of proximity of time and space.[112]

The Court of Appeal took a very different view, and rejected the claims of all the television-watching plaintiffs. Their arguments seem to be characterised by a determination to hold, for policy reasons, that those who suffered shock and mental injury through viewing on television should not recover, even though both Parker and Stocker LJJ accepted that it was foreseeable that the scenes at Hillsborough would be broadcast both live and as recorded news items, and that among the millions watching would be relatives of those in the Leppings Lane terraces.[113] Parker LJ argued that the television watcher actually gained a better appreciation of what was happening than a viewer at the match:

"The mother in the West Stand sees only that which she can see through her own eyes from her position in that Stand. The watcher of television sees what the cameras and producer choose between them to broadcast. They may, and probably will, move from one part of the scene to another which seem best to convey the increasing horror of what was taking place. Zoom lenses will be used, not to record and send out pictures of mangled corpses or dreadfully injured persons, but simply to demonstrate to the viewer more clearly what was happening than could be appreciated by an actual watcher. A watcher from the far end of the North Stand would, for example, see and appreciate far less of what was happening than a television viewer 60 miles away or perhaps even hundreds or thousands of miles away. Such a watcher might not appreciate that there was anything more than the crowd trouble which regrettably occurs all too often at football matches, whereas the television viewer would at an early stage realise the true position."[114]

In addition Stocker LJ expressed the view that:

"No person present can view events more or less simultaneously from several different viewpoints. The fact that the television transmission does so (there were at least four cameras in different locations at Hillsborough) in itself requires some form of editorial or selective

111. Ibid at 343.
112. Ibid.
113. Ibid per Parker LJ at 362, per Stocker LJ at 379.
114. Ibid at 362.

process in a decision which cameras be operated at any given moment. The broadcast is likely to, and in this case did, include commentary which may itself be emotive. The 'zoom' lens enables an incident to be viewed in close-up, even though individual victims are excluded from such close-ups.''[115]

One cannot but agree that the camera often gives a better view than that enjoyed by the spectator at the match—we are all better informed about a doubtful LBW or a borderline offside decision when in front of our television screens than if we are at the ground, a good way removed from the incident and perhaps viewing from the wrong angle—but surely this is an argument *in favour* of recovery and not against. Vivid colour pictures through technically advanced zoom lenses coupled with incisive commentary from an experienced commentator will have a greater impact on the mind than perception from a distance through one's own unaided senses. Indeed, it can be argued that the likelihood of psychiatric harm might even be increased by feelings of helplessness and frustration at not being there and the inability to render assistance to loved ones.[116]

The Court of Appeal's other arguments are, with respect, equally unconvincing. Parker LJ, assuming that the conveying of information by television was the same as other cases of communication by a third party, suggested that if a duty was owed in such circumstances the reporter could be liable for causing psychiatric harm[117]—but this surely confuses the position of the communicator and the person responsible for the original negligence.[118] Both Parker and Stocker LJJ were concerned that the television broadcast might be seen all over the world, so enormously enlarging the time and space limitation,[119] but this is nothing more than a re-run of the hackneyed "floodgates" argument, which did not impress Hidden J.[120] As he pointed out, it is only in cases where injury by shock is foreseeable—and only where the viewer is within the necessary degree of relationship—that recovery will be allowed.

Nolan LJ was a little more encouraging than the other members of the Court of Appeal. He said that he would not exclude the possibility in principle of a duty of care extending to the viewers of a television programme.[121] He cited as an example a publicity-seeking organisation which made arrangements for a party of children to go up in a balloon, and for the event to be televised so their parents could watch. If through the organisers' carelessness the balloon crashed, in Nolan LJ's opinion it would be hard to deny that they were under a duty not to cause psychiatric injury to the parents. Nolan LJ evidently regarded this case as different from the

115. Ibid at 379.
116. L Lomax, "Closing the Floodgates" (1991) 141 NLJ 664.
117. *Alcock v Chief Constable of South Yorkshire Police* [1992] 1 AC 310 at 363.
118. As to liability for the communication of bad news, see below, pp 183-191.
119. *Alcock v Chief Constable of South Yorkshire Police* [1992] 1 AC 310 per Parker LJ at 362, per Stocker LJ at 379.
120. Ibid at 343. Nor were such arguments received with enthusiasm by the House of Lords in *McLoughlin v O'Brian* [1983] 1 AC 410 per Lord Wilberforce at 421, per Lord Edmund-Davies at 424-425, per Lord Russell at 429, per Lord Scarman at 431, per Lord Bridge at 442.
121. *Alcock v Chief Constable of South Yorkshire Police* [1992] 1 AC 310 at 386.

one before him, in that it was arranged for the purpose of being televised. In his view, in *Alcock v Chief Constable of South Yorkshire Police* "the element of immediate and horrifying impact on the viewer does not seem . . . to have been established either as being reasonably foreseeable or as having happened". [122] Whilst his Lordship's preparedness to countenance recovery in certain circumstances is to be commended, his focus on purpose seems of questionable significance when assessing issues of foreseeability. By approaching the problem in this manner the situations where recovery will be permitted will be unnecessarily limited.

Nolan LJ's judgment, and his balloon example, seem to be the source of the rather different reasoning on the basis of which the House of Lords dismissed the appeals of those who suffered shock and injury through watching the live television broadcasts. The House of Lords was not concerned with the technical differences between the watcher at the ground and the watcher on television. Only Lord Jauncey referred to these arguments, and not at any length. [123] Nor did concerns about opening the floodgates feature as strongly in their judgments in this context as they did in the Court of Appeal's reasoning. The major point, one made in all four main judgments, was that the broadcast scenes did not depict the suffering of recognisable individuals and that it would have been contrary to the broadcasting code of ethics to do so: *what* is seen is now the crucial consideration. [124] In the words of Lord Keith:

> "[T]he viewing of these scenes cannot be equiparated with the viewer being within 'sight or hearing of the event or of its immediate aftermath', to use the words of Lord Wilberforce [1983] 1 AC 410 at 423B, nor can the scenes reasonably be regarded as giving rise to shock, in the sense of a sudden assault on the nervous system. They were capable of giving rise to anxiety for the safety of relatives known or believed to be present in the area affected by the crush, and undoubtedly did so, but that is very different from seeing the fate of the relative or his condition shortly after the event. The viewing of the television scenes did not create the necessary degree of proximity." [125]

Lord Oliver pointed out that, because the transmitted image did not portray the suffering of particular persons, it was not the sole basis for the psychiatric injury of the viewers:

> "As I read the evidence, the shock in each case arose not from the original impact of the transmitted image which did not, as has been pointed out, depict the suffering of recognisable individuals. These images provided no doubt the matrix for imagined consequences giving rise to grave concern and worry, followed by a dawning consciousness over an extended period that the imagined consequence had occurred, finally confirmed by news of the death and, in some cases, subsequent visual identification of the victim. The trauma is created in part by such confirmation and in part by the linking in the mind of the plaintiff of

122. Ibid.
123. Ibid at 423.
124. Ibid per Lord Keith at 398, per Lord Ackner at 405, per Lord Oliver at 417, per Lord Jauncey at 423.
125. Ibid at 398.

that confirmation to the previously absorbed image. To extend the notion of proximity in cases of immediately created nervous shock to this more elongated and, to some extent, retrospective process may seem a logical analogical development. But, as I shall endeavour to show, the law in this area is not wholly logical and whilst having every sympathy with the plaintiffs, whose suffering is not in doubt and is not to be underrated, I cannot for my part see any pressing reason of policy for taking this further step along a road which must ultimately lead to virtually limitless liability. . . . [A]ny further widening of the area of potential liability to cater for the expanded and expanding range of the media of communication ought, in my view, to be undertaken rather by Parliament, with full opportunity for public debate and representation, than by the process of judicial extrapolation." [126]

Arguably, on one interpretation of his Lordship's words he would be prepared to countenance recovery where viewing television results in an immediate, as opposed to a delayed, shock. If his objection lies not with the medium of television per se, but rather with the nature of its effect in particular instances on particular individuals, this focus is highly debatable. [127] It is not clear that this is what Lord Oliver intended to say, but his combined discussion of the means of communication and the current need for sudden impact leaves the matter in some doubt.

Despite their unwillingness to concede that those who viewed the scenes on television were owed a duty of care in the particular circumstances of the case, their Lordships did make the encouraging suggestion that there will be cases where, in the words of Lord Oliver, "the element of visual perception may be provided by witnessing the actual injury to the primary victim on simultaneous television". [128] Lords Ackner and Oliver specifically affirmed Nolan LJ's example of an accident occurring during the broadcasting of a balloon flight, [129] on the basis that in such a case the pictures would convey the suffering of known and recognisable individuals. [130] Lord Ackner suggested that there were many other such situations in which the impact of simultaneous television pictures would be as great, if not greater, than the actual sight of the accident. [131] His Lordship would, for instance, presumably look with favour upon a claim by a viewer such as the wife of a motor-racing driver who is watching the race on television and sees him crash at high speed into a concrete retainer.

---

126. Ibid at 417.
127. The issue of sudden versus gradual impact is critically discussed below, Chapter 8.
128. *Alcock v Chief Constable of South Yorkshire Police* [1992] 1 AC 310 at 417.
129. Ibid per Lord Ackner at 405, per Lord Oliver at 417. Lord Jauncey at 423 expressly refrained from commenting on Nolan LJ's statement.
130. Shock-induced illness caused by observation through binoculars or telescopes, instanced by Hidden J, was not expressly excluded by their Lordships, and it cannot be argued that it was ruled out by implication. Certainly, if harm to known individuals is perceived through binoculars or a telescope, as for example where a bird watcher walking through hills near his home looks back through his binoculars and sees his wife run over by a car, recovery of damages should be governed by exactly the same rules as if the occurrence had been seen with the naked eye.
131. *Alcock v Chief Constable of South Yorkshire Police* [1992] 1 AC 310 per Lord Ackner at 405. In contrast to Nolan LJ neither Lord Ackner nor Lord Oliver employed the concept of purpose in relation to the television issue as a reason for allowing or denying recovery.

Though the decision was not cited to their Lordships, it is interesting to note that their attitude to the cases of those who suffered emotional injury through viewing the live television broadcast mirrors the approach taken by the Supreme Court of California in a leading United States decision. In *Scherr v Las Vegas Hilton*,[132] the plaintiff claimed damages for emotional distress suffered while watching a live television news broadcast of a fire at the defendants' hotel, where her husband was staying. The husband was injured in the fire, but the broadcast only showed the outside of the burning hotel and included no view of any injured or endangered people. The court held that the defendants were not under any liability. It was said that:

> "the decisive question in this case is whether the plaintiff, through whatever medium, received a sudden and severe shock by *actually* and *contemporaneously witnessing* not just the fire but the *infliction of injuries* upon her husband."[133]

In *Alcock v Chief Constable of South Yorkshire Police*, Lord Ackner suggested that had scenes showing the sufferings of recognisable individuals been broadcast, contrary to the code of ethics, this would have constituted a novus actus interveniens breaking the chain of causation between the defendant's alleged breach of duty and the psychiatric illness suffered by the plaintiffs.[134] This argument was accepted by the trial court in *Scherr v Las Vegas Hilton*, but the Californian Supreme Court, which viewed the intervention of the news media as a "red herring",[135] did not agree that it represented any breaking of the causal link. Stocker LJ in the Court of Appeal in *Alcock v Chief Constable of South Yorkshire Police*[136] made a somewhat similar point by suggesting, rather enigmatically, that the activities of the camera operator, producers and commentator constituted a novus actus interveniens. However, given that the broadcast was foreseeable, these persons were all doing exactly what they could be expected to do and what it was their job to do. The attitude of the Californian Supreme Court seems to be an appropriate response to Stocker LJ's suggestion.

If the claims of the television-watching plaintiffs are to be dismissed, then the grounds for doing so adopted by the House of Lords are much to be preferred to those of the Court of Appeal. Nonetheless, there are considerable difficulties with them. First, they rest on the basis that the suffering of recognisable individuals was not depicted and that to do so would be contrary to the broadcasting code of ethics. It is not easy to see how there could be any *guarantee* that such pictures might not be shown, at least inadvertently. Moreover, there was evidence that at least some of the plaintiffs saw particular individuals. Stephen Jones saw bodies and believed them to be dead, and Maureen Mullaney actually saw her sons in a section of the crowd where there were casualties, though fortunately, as it turned out, they survived without serious injury.[137]

---

132. (1985) 214 Cal Rptr 393. Note the factually similar example given by Lord Bridge in *McLoughlin v O'Brian* [1983] 1 AC 410 at 442.
133. (1985) 214 Cal Rptr 393 at 394-395.
134. [1992] 1 AC 310 at 405. Interestingly, counsel for the plaintiffs conceded this point.
135. (1985) 214 Cal Rptr 393 at 395.
136. [1992] 1 AC 310 at 380.
137. Ibid at 386.

More fundamentally, if the reason for rejecting the claims of the plaintiffs who suffered psychiatric injury through watching the scenes on television is that they did not see injuries to recognisable individuals, but only generalised scenes of the overcrowded terraces and unfolding chaos, causing worry and anxiety for the safety of people *known* to be involved but not causing shock by communicating the fate of particular individuals, how is the position of such plaintiffs different from that of those who were present elsewhere in the ground? Some of the judges appreciated this problem, none more clearly than Lord Oliver, who, discussing the cases of Brian Harrison and Robert Alcock, said:

> "[A]lthough both were present at the ground and saw scenes which were obviously distressing and such as to cause grave worry and concern, their perception of the actual consequences of the disaster to those to whom they were related was again gradual."[138]

On this basis he ruled that the necessary proximity was lacking in their cases also.[139] However, all the other judges in the House of Lords accepted that those plaintiffs present at the ground could have recovered if they had satisfied the relationship criteria.[140] Parker LJ in the Court of Appeal also pointed out that most of those present at the ground would see and appreciate less of what was happening than those watching on television,[141] and that Brian Harrison, the only successful plaintiff at first instance who was at the ground, did not witness the death of his brothers.[142] The other Court of Appeal judges were content to hold that it was sufficient for such plaintiffs to be present at the scene or its immediate aftermath.[143] It was Hidden J who explained the seeming contradiction inherent in these various opinions.[144] He said that the law originally required both presence at the scene and sight of the accident, but this was gradually relaxed so as to extend to presence near the scene without actual sight of the accident. The acceptance of the aftermath doctrine constituted a further relaxation.

If, then, the law is content to accept that presence at the scene, without actual sight of the accident, satisfies the proximity of time and space, it is hard to maintain that television viewers, who are also in a sense "present" at the scene, cannot recover unless they have actual sight of the harm suffered by a particular loved one. The House of Lords' approach artificially separates the way trauma is perceived from the closeness of the bond between the parties and seems to ignore the power of the television picture and the state of the police's knowledge. Given that they knew for a positive fact that television cameras were taking pictures of the match into houses all over the country, it was foreseeable that many people, including the friends and relatives of spectators in the crowd, would see the

138. Ibid at 417.
139. Ibid.
140. Ibid per Lord Keith at 398, per Lord Ackner at 405-406, per Lord Jauncey at 424. Lord Ackner, however, in an earlier part of his judgment treats the case of Robert Alcock, who was present at the ground, as an aftermath case turning on the time of identification of the body: ibid at 404-405.
141. Ibid at 362.
142. Ibid at 357.
143. Ibid per Stocker LJ at 379, per Nolan LJ at 386.
144. Ibid at 340.

broadcast—as the judges at all levels accepted. If the feelings of desperate anxiety and dread foreboding of the likely consequences for known individuals known to be at the game of what was taking place before their eyes are enough to cause those present in different parts of the crowd to suffer shock and psychiatric injury, even without exact knowledge of those consequences, the position of those watching the panic and desperation on television can be no different. The television viewers were just as much aware of and involved in what was happening as if they were actually there at the match.

Recorded broadcasts

Two plaintiffs suffered psychiatric injury through hearing the news on radio and seeing recorded television pictures of the tragedy. It appears that at least in one case, that of Catherine Jones who lost a brother, it was the television news coverage that was effectively the cause of the harm, but this was the culmination of a process of discovery which began with stories this plaintiff heard while out shopping and was fuelled by hearing radio reports. The other plaintiff, Joseph Kehoe whose grandson and son-in-law were killed, first heard the news on radio and later saw recorded pictures on television. [145] Hidden J rejected the claims of both plaintiffs on the ground that they were not within the requisite proximity of time and space. [146] This rejection was confirmed by the Court of Appeal[147] and by the House of Lords. [148] Even if it be accepted (as it was by Hidden J, but not by the Court of Appeal or the House of Lords) that those who viewed the live transmission could be regarded as being present, these plaintiffs did not fall into that category. Nor could they be considered as within the aftermath.

American cases have reached a similar result. In *Saunders v Air-Florida Inc*[149] the plaintiff asserted that he had suffered emotional shock when he saw film on television of a plane striking the car in which his son was crossing a bridge over the Potomac river, killing him. The court ruled that the father's injuries were too remote and unforeseeable to be actionable because the news coverage had not been live, but recorded. The court said that even if he had been able to see contemporaneous transmissions of the accident it was highly doubtful that he would have been able to discern before impact that the car on the bridge contained his son. In *Gain v Carroll*

145. Ibid per Hidden J at 339-340, per Parker LJ at 354. Note that the plaintiff in *Rhodes v Canadian National Railway* (1990) 75 DLR (4th) 248 first heard news of the train accident in which her son died in a radio report. Although her claim was denied, significantly it was not because of this fact. Note also that the successful applicant in *Dixon v Criminal Injuries Compensation Board* (1988) 216 APR 271 (NS), discussed below, pp 180-181, first learnt of her son's murder from the radio.

146. *Alcock v Chief Constable of South Yorkshire Police* [1992] 1 AC 310 at 340.

147. Ibid per Stocker LJ at 380, per Nolan LJ at 386. Parker LJ makes no specific mention of these plaintiffs.

148. The House of Lords judgments do not deal with these cases in any detail. Lords Keith, Ackner and Oliver make no separate mention of them. Lord Jauncey commented: "If a claimant watching a simultaneous television broadcast does not satisfy the requirements of proximity it follows that a claimant who listens to the wireless or sees a subsequent television recording falls even shorter of the requirement.": ibid at 423.

149. (1983) 558 F Supp 1233.

Mill Co Inc[150] members of the family of a person killed in an accident claimed damages for emotional injury suffered when they learnt of the occurrence through viewing recorded news pictures on television. Liability was denied on the ground that the plaintiffs were not present either at the accident or at the aftermath. The court said that mental distress where the plaintiffs were never present was "unforeseeable as a matter of law".[151]

But just as information can be effectively, accurately and graphically communicated in writing or by word of mouth, it can be so communicated by news broadcasts on television and radio. If, in the circumstances of the case, it is foreseeable that plaintiffs who hear of a tragedy by such means will suffer psychiatric injury as a result, there should be no bar to recovery. In this, as in many other cases of communication-induced shock, a claim should be theoretically possible if damage does in fact eventuate. It is the sustaining of compensable loss and not the medium by which it was brought about that the common law should regard as crucial. On the facts of the Hillsborough case, it could surely be contemplated that those who heard on radio or television news broadcasts that many people had been killed would be in great fear for the safety of loved ones known to be there and might suffer psychiatric injury as a result. As Hidden J said, "[i]t was not merely reasonably foreseeable, it was a pound to a penny"[152] that all over Liverpool television sets would be switched on and watched by people anxiously awaiting the latest news of the match. No doubt there were also many listening on radio. The horror of events can be graphically conveyed by television pictures, whether recorded or live. Radio descriptions can be equally effective in giving the listener a mental picture of events which are taking or have taken place. The two plaintiffs who suffered psychiatric injury through hearing the news on radio and viewing recorded pictures on television should have been able to recover damages; their cases are exactly the same as the other cases of communication-induced shock discussed above. In these, as in every other case discussed so far, what matters is whether psychiatric injury is foreseeable in the circumstances. The existence of a close relationship is probably the most powerful factor in such a finding, but neither the existence of such a relationship, nor presence at the accident or its aftermath, nor any other factor, should be regarded as an essential precondition to liability, if the foreseeability criterion is satisfied.

Some evidence in favour of these contentions is provided by a recent Canadian case, *Dixon v Criminal Injuries Compensation Board*.[153] A

---

150. (1990) 787 P 2d 553 (Wash).
151. In *Ledford v Delta Airlines Inc* (1987) 658 F Supp 540 the defendants were held to be under no liability to a plaintiff who saw recorded news pictures of an air crash involving a plane on which his wife had been a passenger, having previously learnt of the crash through other sources. Note also *Saxton v McDonnell Douglas Aircraft Co* (1977) 428 F Supp 1047 where it was held that the defendants, manufacturers of a DC10 aircraft which crashed in Paris in 1974, killing 346 people, were not liable for emotional distress suffered by a woman as a result of the television, radio and newspaper publicity about the accident, in which her son and daughter-in-law were killed, and her resultant suicide; *Christensen v Superior Court* (1991) 820 P 2d 181; 2 Cal Rptr 2d 79 where media or other secondhand reports about psychologically devastating events were held to be an insufficient basis for the imposition of liability.
152. *Alcock v Chief Constable of South Yorkshire Police* [1992] 1 AC 310 at 344.
153. (1988) 216 APR 271 (NS).

mother saw a television news item about the murder of someone whom she believed, correctly as it turned out, to be her son. As a result she suffered a major debilitating depression and made a claim for criminal injuries compensation. The Appeal Division of the Nova Scotia Supreme Court held that she was a person "injured" by the crime within the meaning of s 6 of the *Compensation for Victims of Crime Act* 1975 (NS) and was entitled to relief. This conclusion was reached with the aid of a detailed review of the case law on tortiously induced psychiatric damage. The court said that the mere fact that the plaintiff was not present at the murder or at its immediate aftermath was not fatal to her claim, the Act imposing no limits of time and space. Granted, this case involves the interpretation of a statutory provision, and also an intentional wrong; but the readiness of the judges to accept that it is appropriate to award compensation for psychiatric damage inflicted through a television broadcast is striking. It is reminiscent of the attitude displayed to nervous shock statutes by the Australian courts which seem unperturbed by issues which have bedevilled the courts in other jurisdictions.[154] Each of these statutory approaches to compensation for shock-induced harm offers an impressive contrast to the present state of the common law.

Psychiatric damage via telephone

The telephone, revolutionary in the late 19th century, has by the late 20th century become the standard means by which people communicate with each other when they are not close enough to talk face to face. As such, it is the quickest way of communicating news, pleasant or unpleasant. It is therefore not surprising that there are cases in which plaintiffs have suffered psychiatric damage as a result of news of the death or injury to a loved one being communicated by telephone.[155]

In some cases, the telephone communication is merely the prelude to closer involvement nearer the scene of the accident. In *Orman v Harrington*,[156] for example, in the words of Mullighan J, on the night Kerry Harrington was involved in a car accident, "the telephone rang with the message dreaded by all parents". Kerry's mother visited her badly injured daughter in hospital the next day, and the accident caused her to suffer anxiety, distress and shock. Liability for this damage was denied on the ground that it did not amount to recognisable psychiatric harm as required by the law. In *Jinks v Cardwell*[157] a woman was summoned by telephone to hospital to be informed that her husband, a mental patient, had drowned in a bath. The plaintiff recovered for the emotional harm she

154. See above, pp 168-169, below, pp 239-245.
155. Note also the possibility that one may hear an accident happen over the telephone and so in a sense be present, in a not dissimilar way to watching a live television broadcast. In *Hickey v National League of Professional Baseball Clubs* (1991) 565 NYS 2d 65 the plaintiff's fiancé, a baseball umpire, had a heart attack when talking to her over the telephone. Her claim for emotional distress against his employers, based on the allegation that the attack had been caused by the punishing schedule imposed on him, was ruled out on the ground of lack of contemporaneous observance.
156. (Unreported, South Australian SC, 30 Apr 1990, No 296 of 1990).
157. (1987) 39 CCLT 168, reversed in part on other grounds, sub nom *Jinks v Abraham* (unreported, Ontario CA, 23 June 1989, Doc Nos CA 181/87, 195/87).

suffered, which was exacerbated by the fact that the doctor suggested that her husband had committed suicide. [158]

A different issue is whether there is liability for psychiatric damage sustained solely as the result of bad news communicated by telephone. [159] This has not arisen in Australia, England or Canada, but it has in the United States. In *Kelley v Kokua Sales & Supply Ltd*, [160] the court denied recovery to the estate of a man who died of a heart attack in California immediately after hearing by telephone of the deaths of his daughter and granddaughter and the serious injury of another daughter in a car accident in Hawaii, on the ground that he was not located within a reasonable distance of the scene of the accident. The same reasoning was employed to reach a similar decision in the subsequent case of *Cohen v McDonnell Douglas Corporation*. [161] The plaintiff heard on radio of a plane crash. Knowing that his brother was on the plane, he telephoned his mother in Massachusetts to give her the tragic news. The mother experienced chest pains and died of a heart attack two days later, but the court held that "at all pertinent times Nellie Cohen was more than 1,000 miles from the scene of the crash", and that "the manner in which she learned of her son's death precludes the imposition of liability." [162]

Another Hawaiian case, six years after *Kelley v Kokua*, takes a different attitude. In *Campbell v Animal Quarantine Station*, [163] a telephone call informed the plaintiffs of the death of their dog "Princess" as a result of the defendant's negligence in transporting her in an unventilated van on a hot day. The six plaintiffs all suffered emotional distress, damage which was compensable under Hawaiian law. [164] Even though the family learnt of the accident by telephone and were never present at the scene, the Supreme Court of Hawaii found the proximity requirement satisfied. The need for close geographical location imposed by the court in *Kelley v Kokua* posed no problem since "plaintiffs and their dog were [both] located within Honolulu." [165] Although this case may raise a few eyebrows, in so far as there was a lack of emphasis placed on the telephonic communication of the news the decision is refreshingly positive. As the court impliedly recognised, development of the law of psychiatric damage should not be hindered by an undue concern about the ways shock can come about. Whether it be as a result of having been there, by telling someone face to face, through writing, by telegraph or facsimile, on television, on radio or by telephone really should make no difference to the likely success of a claim for

---

158. See also *Brown v Hubar* (1974) 45 DLR (3d) 664; *Chapman v Lear* (unreported, Queensland SC, 8 Apr 1988, No 3732 of 1984); *Butcher v Motor Accidents Board* (1984) *Victorian Motor Accidents Cases* 72-026 (CCH); *Mazzagatti v Everingham* (1986) 516 A 2d 672 (Pa); *Mullally v Bus Eireann* (unreported, Irish HC, 13 June 1991).

159. This is to be distinguished from liability for the negligent *conveying* of bad news, on which see below, pp 183-191.

160. (1975) 532 P 2d 673 (Haw).

161. (1983) 450 NE 2d 581 (Mass).

162. Ibid at 589. Note also *Hoover v Recreation Equipment Corporation* (1991) 792 F Supp 1484 (mother informed by telephone that child injured by falling off slide in school playground).

163. (1981) 632 P 2d 1066 (Haw). See A T Kido & E Quintal, "Campbell v Animal Quarantine Station: Negligent Infliction of Mental Distress" (1982) 4 U Haw L Rev 207.

164. See above, p 48.

165. (1981) 632 P 2d 1066 at 1069.

psychiatric damage medically proved on the balance of probabilities to have been induced by the negligence of the tortfeasor. The law, like technology, must move with the times.

Liability for communication of bad news

It is clear that if information is wilfully conveyed to a person with the actual or imputed intention to cause nervous shock, and physical or mental illness does in fact ensue, the conveyer will be held responsible at law. [166] What has not been clarified is whether an action will lie in negligence if information is communicated to another carelessly, rather than intentionally, and that other suffers nervous shock and psychiatric damage as a result. [167] Can there, in other words, be tortious liability for breaking bad news badly? This situation is to be distinguished from *Hedley Byrne* [168] liability for negligent statements which contemplates financial harm suffered through *reliance* on the statement. The potential cause of action under discussion involves psychiatric harm suffered by virtue of the fact that the statement was *made* and not because it was acted upon. [169]

English courts have not, as yet, shed any direct light on the question of the existence of a duty not to cause nervous shock and psychiatric injury by a negligent statement. [170] The only hints we get are some obiter comments by Lord Denning MR and a throwaway line by Parker LJ. In *D v National Society for the Prevention of Cruelty to Children* [171] the Master of the Rolls expressed the view that, while he could "understand" the imposition of liability in the intentional shock cases, it would be "a big step forward—or backward—to extend it to a statement which is made honestly in good faith". [172] His Lordship reasoned:

> "Many a person has occasion to investigate a complaint. It may be an employer or a police officer. Someone may report to him that goods have been stolen and that he believes that a man named AB is the thief. The employer or police officer sees the man AB and tells him that he is suspected. He is so shocked that he has a nervous breakdown. Has he cause of action against the employer or police officer on the ground

166. See the discussion of *Wilkinson v Downton* [1897] 2 QB 57 and intentional wrongdoing below, pp 283-292.
167. In *Wilkinson v Downton* [1897] 2 QB 57, where the plaintiff suffered shock as a result of being told a false story that her husband had had an accident, Wright J at 59 expressly held that the defendant's conduct was so plainly calculated to produce a harmful effect that an intention to produce such an effect ought to be imputed to him. His Lordship refused to regard the shock to the plaintiff merely as a reasonably foreseeable consequence of the defendant's actions and was not prepared to hold that the defendant was merely reckless. In his opinion, the harm could be regarded as intentionally (ie distinct from negligently) caused. No guidance can therefore be gleaned from the case with respect to this particular issue.
168. *Hedley Byrne & Co v Heller & Partners* [1964] AC 465.
169. The courts have acknowledged that these situations are different: see eg *Guay v Sun Publishing Co* [1953] 4 DLR 577 per Kerwin J at 579-582, per Estey J at 583-585, per Cartwright J (Rinfret CJC concurring) at 609-610; but compare Locke J at 603.
170. Although *De Freville v Dill* (1927) 96 LJKB 1056, which concerned a doctor who negligently certified the plaintiff to be insane, causing her to be detained in a mental home, is closely related to this issue.
171. [1978] AC 171.
172. Ibid at 188-189.

that he conducted the inquiry negligently? The question only has to be posed to see what an extension this would be."[173]

Contrastingly, in *Alcock v Chief Constable of South Yorkshire Police*[174] Parker LJ, having assumed that the conveying of information by television was akin to other cases of third party communication, suggested that if a duty was owed in such circumstances an action could lie against the reporter for causing psychiatric harm. Although his Lordship appears, with respect, in that passage of his judgment to have confused the position of the commentator with the party responsible for the original negligent act or omission, his comment does indicate that the notion of communicator liability for communication-caused psychiatric injury is not objectionable to at least one English judge. This is as far as we get with the English cases. One must turn to the Australian, New Zealand and Canadian authorities to assist in the determination of where the "bearer of bad tidings" stands in the psychiatric damage equation.

The traditional focus of the common law on direct physical perception led Windeyer J of the High Court of Australia to state obiter in *Mount Isa Mines v Pusey*:

> "If the sole cause of shock be what is told or read of some happening then I think it is correctly said that, unless there be an intention to cause a nervous shock, no action lies against either the bearer of the bad tidings or the person who caused the event of which they tell. There is no duty in law to break bad news gently or to do nothing which creates bad news."[175]

In this passage, perhaps the leading general statement of the law on this particular issue, his Honour drew no distinction based on the truth or falsity of the information conveyed. As regards untrue statements, no action of this kind could initially be maintained, at least in Australia. In *Blakeney v Pegus (No 2)*[176] there was a mix-up by a country telegraph operator who mistakenly sent a telegram from Murwillumbah addressed to Walter Black, Yamba and containing the message "James very ill would like to see you" to W Blakeney, Iluka. As fate would have it, Mr Blakeney also had a son named James working near Murwillumbah and he and his wife suffered an anxiety reaction on its receipt, Mr Blakeney in addition incurring expense in embarking on a hastily organised journey to see his son. Although he was stopped when the defendant realised her mistake, his wife's health deteriorated to the extent that she had to be sent to Sydney for treatment. While Martin CJ (with whom Faucett and Innes JJ agreed) was prepared to compensate the husband for the expenses incurred in preparing to visit his son and in treating his wife, he refused in the absence of fraud or contract between the parties to attribute responsibility in law for the consequences of a negligent misdelivery of the telegram: "[N]o erroneous statement is actionable unless it is intentionally false. . . . For mere negligence no action will lie."[177]

173. Ibid at 189.
174. [1992] 1 AC 310 at 363.
175. (1970) 125 CLR 383 at 407.
176. (1885) 6 NSWR 223.
177. Ibid at 231-232.

Subsequent Australian authorities have suggested, however, that in appropriate circumstances, liability may lie for psychiatric damage arising from distressing false information negligently communicated. The plaintiff's husband in *Barnes v Commonwealth*[178] was a pensioner. The defendant, by its servants, sent the plaintiff a letter quoting her husband's pension number and informing her that he had been admitted to a mental hospital. This was untrue, but on reading the correspondence the plaintiff suffered nervous shock and emotional distress, requiring expensive nursing and medical treatment. The Full Court of the New South Wales Supreme Court held that shock to the plaintiff was foreseeable as a result of the communication of such a statement and that the defendants therefore owed a duty to ensure that the information communicated was accurate. The court followed its own decision in *Bunyan v Jordan*[179] which, in general, accepted that an action would lie wherever shock to a normal person was a reasonably foreseeable result of negligent conduct. As Davidson J stated:

"[I]f a person doing an official act, as in the present case, recognised, as he must have done, that he was communicating some serious information which might possibly affect the recipient's feelings strongly, surely he owed some duty to that person to take care that the information which he was communicating was correct."[180]

Stephen J was in substantial agreement although he framed his analysis slightly differently, expressing the view that:

"[T]he defendant is legally responsible if he owes a general duty to the plaintiff not to convey incorrect information, and there is a breach of that duty. In such a case, it may be unnecessary to show a realisation of the harmful nature of the information. . . . [T]he defendant may be responsible if there is a specific duty to take care not to convey incorrect information arising from the special circumstances of the case."[181]

His Honour concluded that there was no general duty of care on the facts but that there was a specific one arising from the relationship between the parties making it reasonable that responsibility be placed on the defendant and under which the conveyer must have realised the capacity of the information which he was entrusted to convey to injure the plaintiff psychologically.

Like their Australian counterparts the Canadian judiciary has only had to face this particular aspect of psychiatric damage law on isolated occasions. In *Guay v Sun Publishing Co*[182] a majority of the Supreme Court ruled, in contrast to the court in *Barnes v Commonwealth*, that a newspaper was not responsible in law for shock caused to a wife from its having published a false story that her estranged husband and their three

---

178. (1937) 37 SR (NSW) 511.
179. (1936) 36 SR (NSW) 350, affirmed by the High Court (1937) 57 CLR 1.
180. (1937) 37 SR (NSW) 511 at 515.
181. Ibid at 516.
182. [1953] 4 DLR 577. See M M McIntyre, "A Novel Assault on the Principle of No Liability for Innocent Misrepresentation" (1953) 31 Can BR 770. Note also Lord Denning MR's comments in *D v National Society for the Prevention of Cruelty to Children* [1978] AC 171 at 188-189.

children had been killed in a car accident. The report had not come from any recognised news service, its authenticity had not been checked, and the defendant was unable to say from where it had received the information. Although the newspaper was found to have been negligent, the plaintiff failed, interestingly the majority articulating three different grounds. Estey J's verdict of non-liability was based on what he saw as the absence of physical harm resulting from the emotional distress suffered on reading the story (a point not taken by any other judge). He was not prepared to say that there could never be liability for shock caused by a negligent statement.[183] Kerwin J considered that no tortious duty was owed on ordinary *Donoghue v Stevenson*[184] neighbourhood principles regardless of what damage ensued[185]—a conclusion of questionable validity in the light of the appreciation of the courts in *McLoughlin v O'Brian*,[186] *Jaensch v Coffey*[187] and *Alcock v Chief Constable of South Yorkshire Police*[188] that shock-induced psychiatric harm is foreseeable to those who merely learn of the results of, rather than see, traumatic incidents. Distinguishing the case from wilful conduct such as that exhibited in *Wilkinson v Downton*,[189] Locke J opined that even where there was evidence that the plaintiff suffered compensable psychiatric damage, no cause of action would lie in the absence of fraud, deceit, malice or breach of any fiduciary or contractual relationship.[190] In contrast to Estey J, Cartwright J (Rinfret CJC concurring) interpreted the expert testimony as evidencing that physical damage and not just mental distress had been suffered by the plaintiff, and unlike Kerwin J was prepared to hold the defendant liable on *Donoghue v Stevenson* principles for the negligent communication of bad news.[191] It was, his Honour said, entirely foreseeable that a person in the plaintiff's position would suffer shock on reading a report of this nature. With the demise of the *Dulieu v White & Sons*[192] limitation that shock must be caused by fear of injury to oneself, there was no reason for declining to recognise a duty on the facts. Referring to *Hambrook v Stokes Bros*[193] he stated:

> "I cannot distinguish in principle between liability for nervous shock to a mother by carelessly allowing a truck to run away and so to cause her to think that it will injure her children and liability for nervous shock caused to her by carelessly communicating a false statement to her which will cause her to believe that all her children have met a violent death. Indeed, in my opinion the probability of injurious shock to the claimant would be more readily foreseen in the latter instance than in the former."[194]

183. Ibid at 587-589.
184. [1932] AC 562.
185. Ibid at 582.
186. [1983] 1 AC 410.
187. (1984) 155 CLR 549.
188. [1992] 1 AC 310.
189. [1897] 2 QB 57.
190. [1953] 4 DLR 577 at 603.
191. Ibid at 612-613.
192. [1901] 2 KB 669.
193. [1925] 1 KB 141.
194. [1953] 4 DLR 577 at 612-613.

As Cartwright J observed, the only distinction between this case and *Wilkinson v Downton* was the lack of wilfulness—a difference of little importance in relation to the question of the appropriateness of the imposition in principle of tort liability for careless communication. In the light of Estey J's lone stance on the insufficiency of evidence point and the fact that Kerwin J's reasoning must now be read as extremely suspect in the light of the general principles enunciated in the three leading psychiatric damage cases, it is arguable that *Guay v Sun Publishing Co* may not be inconsistent with the recognition of a tortious duty to prevent causing shock-induced psychiatric harm through careless statements.

Significantly, in the recent Ontario case of *Jinks v Cardwell*,[195] McRae J awarded compensation to a wife who suffered physical and emotional distress caused by a doctor's negligent communication of information which was in the main false. Mr Jinks suffered from a severe form of mental illness and was admitted from time to time to the defendant's psychiatric hospital. One morning he wandered from his ward and locked himself in a bathroom. By the time the door was forced open he had drowned in the bath with severe scalding from the still-running tap. A doctor concerned with how this would look for the hospital contacted the plaintiff and, with no justification for saying so, informed her that her husband had "committed suicide in the bathtub". This report was true only in so far as the husband was in fact dead. As the judge pointed out, the doctor's words were at best negligent and at worst callous and unfeeling. Without any reference to *Guay v Sun Publishing Co* compensation was awarded for the widow's trauma. The New York Court of Appeals took a similar approach in *Johnson v State*,[196] holding a hospital liable to the daughter of a patient for emotional harm suffered as a result of its false advice that her mother had died. Where there were objective physical manifestations evidencing emotional disruption due to negligent misinformation the court considered that relief was appropriate.[197] It is very difficult to find fault with this reasoning. One can appreciate, for example, the potential for shock-induced psychiatric harm on being informed that one has tested positive for AIDS only to be told later (perhaps much later) that a mistake has been made. To hold the negligent communicator of such shattering news responsible for ensuing mental disorder is entirely congruous.

The information in all these cases was, as noted, negligently false (as distinct from wilfully false) but there will be cases where distressing

195. (1987) 39 CCLT 168.
196. (1975) 334 NE 2d 590 (NY).
197. See also *Molien v Kaiser Foundation Hospitals* (1980) 616 P 2d 813; 167 Cal Rptr 831 (dealt with above, pp 48-49) where liability was imposed for a negligent diagnosis of syphilis which led to the break-up of the plaintiff's marriage and consequent mental trauma. Note the cases on the negligent transmission of telegraph messages cited above, p 49, n 187. Contrast *Hoard v Shawnee Mission Medical Center* (1983) 662 P 2d 1214 (Kan) where parents were mistakenly notified that their daughter had died whereas in fact she was in a critical condition at another hospital. The retention of the "impact rule" in Kansas (as to which see above, pp 11-12) prevented the imposition of liability. Compare also *Jacobs v Horton Memorial Hospital* (1987) 515 NYS 2d 281 where a wife failed to recover for the misdiagnosis that her husband had pancreatic cancer and the unfavourable prognosis that he had only six months to live.

information which is true is communicated in a particularly uncaring or callous manner. The question thus arises whether in analysing communicator liability any distinction should be drawn in principle based on the nature of the negligently conveyed bad news. It has been suggested that there can be no liability for the insensitive or heartless announcement of true bad news. During the drafting of the *Restatement of Torts Second* Prosser referred to the famous exchange: "Are you the widow Murphy?", "My name is Murphy, but I'm no widow", "The hell you ain't" as a case where there would be no liability.[198] Other scholars disagree. Winfield and Jolowicz argue that liability may be appropriately imposed where the impact of the news is needlessly exacerbated,[199] and Walker has gone so far as to express the view that a person communicating a report might be liable if he or she does not take reasonable care to break the news as gently as possible, citing the example where a village policeman charged to tell a woman that her husband had been killed, does so using the words: "Mrs McKenzie, your man's dead."[200] *Brown v Mount Barker Soldiers' Hospital*[201] provides some authority for the proposition that where shock results from being told of bad news, liability can, in principle, be imposed upon the carrier of it in both situations. There the defendant hospital negligently burnt a newborn baby out of sight of the mother who suffered shock when told of her child's injury.[202] Holding that the hospital owed the mother a duty of care Piper J concluded:

"Here the defendant in taking charge of Mrs Brown as a patient assumed a care of her involving the need to avoid, so far as reasonably practicable, all things that might prejudice her health or comfort, or increase her need for exertion or care. It would be a breach of duty, actionable if followed by damage, to tell her untruly that her child had been burnt. As the truthfulness of the statement was owing to negligence, the truthfulness was no legal excuse for doing harm by telling her—it was a necessary consequence of the negligence that she had to be told."[203]

Thus, we have a recognition that irrespective of the veracity of the information liability can in theory lie for its negligent communication. True, the weight of the case may arguably be weakened to some extent by the presence of a pre-existing duty of care owed to Mrs Brown on her admission as a hospital patient, but in an area of law where authorities are scarce it may well ultimately play an important role in the formulation of doctrine.

No other contemporary Australian authority has dealt with this question directly but comments by Kneipp J in *Petrie v Dowling*[204] suggest, at least

---

198. (1957) *Proceedings of the American Law Institute* 292. Note however that there was liability in *Price v Yellow Pine Paper Mill Co* (1922) 240 SW 588 (Tex) where the defendant brought a badly injured man home and abruptly delivered him to his pregnant wife.
199. W V H Rogers, *Winfield and Jolowicz on Tort* (13th ed, 1989), 110.
200. D M Walker, *The Law of Delict in Scotland* (2nd ed, 1981), 678.
201. [1934] SASR 128.
202. The evidence suggested that the shock did not stem from having to help care for the child's injuries later on.
203. [1934] SASR 128 at 130.
204. [1992] 1 Qd R 284.

on one interpretation, that liability may lie for the negligent communication of true bad news. There a woman arrived at a hospital believing, on the basis of information conveyed to her earlier by two friends, that her daughter had suffered only minor injuries from a fall from her bicycle, to be told "bluntly" by the nurse that she was dead. In what amounts to a very significant decision for the development of psychiatric damage law, his Honour awarded damages to the mother for psychiatric injury solely on the basis of what she was told at the hospital. What is important, however, for our immediate purposes is not that liability was imposed upon the negligent driver responsible for the girl's fall, but the possibility of an action lying against the nurse as the conveyer of the news of her death. Such a claim was not pleaded by the plaintiff or referred to by Kneipp J directly but his focus on the manner and language adopted by the bearer of bad tidings, albeit by way of an aside, may indicate a preparedness to impose such liability should the situation arise. Consider *Thomas v Corrective Services Commission of New South Wales*[205] where parents of a prisoner in Parramatta Gaol murdered by another prisoner were informed of his death by the Commission in "an extraordinarily callous and uncaring and reprehensible manner". Their claim for psychiatric damage caused by the death of their son due to negligence in the operation of the prison system was unsuccessful. A claim against the Commission in its capacity as communicator of the news might have met with a better fate.[206]

In New Zealand liability has been imposed even though the information in question was true. In *Furniss v Fitchett*[207] the Supreme Court allowed a plaintiff to succeed in an action against her doctor for nervous shock caused by his negligent disclosure of his opinion as to her mental stability. Without any foundation the plaintiff had told the defendant that her husband was insane and that he was doping and mistreating her, specifically that he was cruel and violent towards her. Understandably, domestic relations deteriorated and the anxiety resulting from these delusions affected the husband's health. He wanted to be separated from the plaintiff, if only temporarily, and tried to have the defendant certify her, something which he declined to do. Eventually, with the knowledge that it was to be provided to the husband's legal advisers, the defendant gave him a certificate describing her behaviour and expressing the opinion that the plaintiff was exhibiting signs of paranoia and was in need of psychiatric treatment. The defendant was aware that if the certificate's contents were disclosed to the plaintiff it would be harmful to her and he placed no limitations on the use of it, declining even to mark it "confidential". The plaintiff continued to

---

205. (Unreported, New South Wales CA, 20 Dec 1989, CA Nos 81 and 82 of 1983).
206. Note the suggestion in *White v Butcher* (unreported, New South Wales SC, 13 Oct 1982, Nos 9576, 9577 and 9578 of 1981) that the news of an accident to a teenage girl was announced to her parents "in somewhat dramatic terms", which may have been an element in the court's decision to award damages to the parents. Note also the claim in *Miller v Royal Derwent Hospital Board of Management* (unreported, Tasmanian SC, 29 May 1992, No 282 of 1988) that psychiatric damage suffered by a nurse following the death of a patient in her care may have been partly due to the breaking of the news to her. Zeeman J at 17 seems to lend this some support, although the major alleged cause of the harm she suffered was the failure to provide post-trauma counselling. His Honour ruled against the plaintiff on foreseeability and causation grounds.
207. [1958] NZLR 396.

consult with the defendant for the next year, first learning of the certificate's existence when in subsequent separation and maintenance proceedings instituted by her it was produced in cross-examination. She suffered shock as a result and sought relief. The jury having returned a verdict for the plaintiff, the defendant appealed and Barrowclough CJ applying the principles of *Donoghue v Stevenson*[208] accepted that a duty of care could be owed in respect of nervous shock caused by the communication of bad news.[209] On the facts it was entirely foreseeable that if the plaintiff was confronted with such a certificate it would do her psychological harm and clear that it would be so disclosed at some stage.[210] Although he did not decide the matter, his Honour went so far as to opine that, apart from any question of libel or slander, a duty of care may be owed by every "professional man", and indeed, by a person outside the professions in respect of what he or she writes or says of another if that other thereby suffers personal harm.[211] It was recognised, however, that there is a marked distinction between, for example, doctors and other persons, for though in certain circumstances a doctor may be able to foresee that a statement if made by him or her would be likely to cause psychiatric harm, the man in the street who has no medical knowledge might never be expected to foresee such a result.[212]

This was not the first time New Zealand courts had shown a preference for such an approach. Support for this type of shock liability can also be found in *Stevenson v Basham*.[213] Although the facts of the case were analogous to the *Dulieu v White & Sons*[214] line of cases in that the plaintiff feared for her own safety as a result of the defendant's threats to burn her and her husband out of their house if they did not surrender it, and concerned the intentional infliction of mental distress, Herdman J did recognise that as an alternative to liability under *Wilkinson v Downton*[215] there could be liability in negligence for shock caused by a statement.[216]

The potential liability for the negligent communication of true bad news is very significant for those (such as doctors, nurses, firemen and police) whose unpleasant duties all too frequently include having to deliver distressing news to friends, relatives and loved ones of accident victims, and for that matter, to accident victims themselves. A police officer considering

208. [1932] AC 562.
209. [1958] NZLR 396 at 403 His Honour said that any contractual, moral, professional or ethical duties owed by the defendant to the plaintiff were irrelevant to the question whether a tortious duty was owed.
210. Ibid at 404.
211. *Note Lawton v BOC Transhield* [1987] ICR 7 where Tudor Evans J recognised that the defendant employers owed a duty of care to the plaintiff to ensure that the opinions contained in their reference were based on accurate facts, even though the law of defamation is available to deal with false statements causing injury to reputation. The case does not involve psychiatric damage: counsel for the plaintiff in opening the case indicated that he would apply for leave to amend the statement of claim to allege that the plaintiff had suffered such damage due to the difficulty of finding employment, but did not do so.
212. Ibid at 403-404.
213. [1922] NZLR 225.
214. [1901] 2 KB 669.
215. [1897] 2 QB 57.
216. [1922] NZLR 225 at 228-229.

Walker's example noted above may have some justification in retorting "how else could the officer have announced the news of the death?" The same might be said of the nurse in *Petrie v Dowling*[217] who, when asked by the mother "she isn't dead, is she?", replied "I'm afraid so." Having said this, it is submitted that if shock-induced psychiatric damage is foreseeable and does in fact eventuate through the negligent communication of distressing information, it cannot make any difference in the attribution of legal responsibility that the information happened to be correct. It is foreseeability, not falsity, that matters. Even if the conveying of untrue bad news is arguably somehow more morally reprehensible, there will be occasions when it is entirely appropriate to impose liability for the manner in which true bad news is imparted. The court's distaste for mendacity could be reflected in the damages awarded rather than the confinement of liability to situations where falsehood is present. Moreover, the courts should resist any temptation to limit liability for the negligent communication of true bad news by the introduction of the same sorts of arbitrary restrictions that have thwarted the sensible development of other aspects of the law governing psychiatric damage.

It follows that nothing turns on whether the statement (true or false) is negligently communicated orally or in writing. Barrowclough CJ recognised this in *Furniss v Fitchett*: "[T]here seems to be no ground for drawing a distinction between what is said and what is written."[218] Shock may foreseeably be caused through reading a report or through hearing it. It is true, however, that establishing that shock to a particular reader of a newspaper or magazine item circulated to the general population is reasonably foreseeable is more difficult than showing this in relation to the recipient of a letter, but once this has been shown there is no reason in logic or principle to deny liability. In certain circumstances, therefore, we would argue that it is appropriate for liability to be imposed both on the party responsible for the original accident and on the conveyer of news of the circumstances and results of the original want of care.

217. [1992] 1 Qd R 284.
218. [1958] NZLR 396 at 403.

8

THE NEED FOR SUDDEN IMPACT

The traditional rule

The question arises whether it is a prerequisite to recovery that a tort victim suffering from a recognisable psychiatric illness must have become so afflicted as a result of a sudden impact to the senses. Is it sufficient that there has been a gradual onset of mental injury or an accumulation of circumstances which, although individually harmless, are a sufficient hazard to health in combination to lead to a deterioration in psychiatric and emotional well-being? In other words, is it the recognisability of the species of damage sustained or the way it was sustained that is crucial, or are these factors equally important?

Brennan J's words in *Jaensch v Coffey*[1] indicate that it is here causative issues arise and that there is a need to isolate and focus on the damage-inducing phenomenon. His Honour stressed that recovery may be had for psychiatric illness only where it results from nervous shock (or physical injury negligently inflicted) stating:

"Psychiatric illness caused in other ways attracts no damages, though it is reasonably foreseeable that psychiatric illness might be a consequence of the defendant's carelessness."[2]

"Shock" was defined as:

"the sudden sensory perception—that is, by seeing, hearing or touching—of a person, thing or event, which is so distressing that the perception of the phenomenon affronts or insults the plaintiff's mind and causes a recognisable psychiatric illness. A psychiatric illness induced by mere knowledge of a distressing fact is not compensable; perception by the plaintiff of the distressing phenomenon is essential."[3]

So, on this view, there must be a recognisable psychiatric illness and, in the absence of negligently inflicted physical damage, it must have been induced by a sudden shock to the plaintiff's sensory system. Brennan J proffered two examples where these elements would be lacking and thus where recovery would be denied:

"The spouse who has been worn down by caring for a tortiously injured husband or wife and who suffers psychiatric illness as a result goes without compensation; a parent made distraught by the wayward conduct of a brain-damaged child and who suffers psychiatric illness as a result has no claim against the tortfeasor liable to the child."[4]

1. (1984) 155 CLR 549.
2. Ibid at 565.
3. Ibid at 567.
4. Ibid at 565.

Deane J made similar comments:

"It would seem reasonably clear that the requisite duty relationship will not . . . exist in a case where mere psychiatric injury results from subsequent contact, away from the scene of the accident and its aftermath, with a person suffering from the effects of the accident. An example of psychiatric injury suffered as a result of such post-accident contact is that which may result from the contact involved in the nursing or care of a close relative during a period subsequent to immediate post-accident treatment."[5]

This type of non-compensable situation is illustrated by the pre-*Jaensch v Coffey* case of *Pratt and Goldsmith v Pratt*[6] where the Full Court of the Victorian Supreme Court denied relief to a mother who suffered mental illness through caring for her daughter and seeing her in the years that followed the accident. As Adam and Crockett JJ explained:

"[A]lthough the seriousness of the daughter's injuries was immediately known and their irreparable nature appreciated soon afterwards, it was only after the passage of some weeks, if not months, that a medically recognisable condition of some mental origin affected the mother, and perhaps more importantly, . . . it was only after a similarly substantial period that there first occurred the events that were causally connected with the mother's subsequent neurasthenic condition."[7]

Similarly, in *Anderson v Smith*[8] the plaintiff's daughter was brain-damaged as a result of a near-drowning. In an action for psychiatric damage against the pool owners (the plaintiff's mother and father[9]) recovery was denied on the ground that there was no evidence to suggest that the plaintiff's "phobic anxiety depression disorder" was caused by a sudden shock to her sensory system. As in *Jaensch v Coffey*,[10] the plaintiff was not near the pool at the time of the accident, having gone to a hotel with friends for a drink, and witnessed nothing capable of inducing a psychological disorder when she arrived there later, the unconscious child having been plucked from the water and taken to hospital. Nor, the medical evidence revealed, was her illness the result of a shock on hearing the oral description of what had happened to her daughter. Rather, Nader J considered that the "insurmountable barrier" to relief faced by the plaintiff was that her psychiatric syndrome was caused by a 15-month prolonged

5. Ibid at 606.
6. [1975] VR 378.
7. Ibid at 382. Note that even if caring friends and relatives, such as the mother in this case, incur expense in rendering voluntary services it is the plaintiff and not the carers who may recover compensation under the principle in *Donnelly v Joyce* [1974] QB 454 and *Griffiths v Kerkemeyer* (1977) 139 CLR 161, discussed above, pp 92-93.
8. (1990) 101 FLR 34.
9. It was the defendant grandmother who was negligent in that she failed to close a back door properly, so that the 14-month-old child was able to leave the house and fall into the swimming pool in the yard. (It was conceded that no case had been made out against the plaintiff's father.) Interestingly, the grandmother was called as a witness for the plaintiff. This is explicable by the fact that she was covered by insurance, though this will often be lacking in cases involving injuries on private property due to a failure to supervise: see H Luntz, "Torts" in R Baxt & G Kewley (eds), *Annual Survey of Australian Law* (1990), 117 at 125.
10. (1984) 155 CLR 549.

contact with her daughter in hospital between the date of the accident and the child's death due to septicaemia, chest infection and diminished cough reflex.[11] A number of stressful events occurred during that period, commencing with her being informed by police in the hotel that there had been an accident at her mother's home, what she was later told about her daughter's prospects, the sight of the daughter, her understanding of the gravity of the situation, her continued daily caring for a considerable period, viewing the daughter day after day in hospital, her eventual death and the quashing of the plaintiff's false hopes and expectations for a recovery.

The same sentiments have been expressed where the harm complained of does not in fact appear to have developed to such an extent as to be classified as a psychiatric disorder. This is evident from *Andrewartha v Andrewartha*[12] where the plaintiff's wife was rendered a quadriplegic as the result of a car accident negligently caused by the defendant. Following her eight-month stay in hospital, the husband decided that rather than institutionalise his wife he would care for her at home with the assistance of two live-in housekeepers and visiting nursing attendants. Sadly, however, the wife remained unresponsive to care and uncommunicative, displaying no interest in the husband. Over the years this took its toll on him. He claimed and recovered at first instance damages for, inter alia, distress and the gradual development of psychological depression as a result of the constant care of his wife and the stress, sadness and loneliness associated with it. The Full Court of the South Australian Supreme Court ruled, following *Jaensch v Coffey*,[13] that recovery in negligence for depressive illness was contrary to authority and was not open on the pleadings in any event. As White J pointed out, referring to the remarks of Deane J quoted above, if the plaintiff's contention was accepted it would mean that:

> "all defendants who cause harm to victims living with sisters or friends in a close, loving relationship should contemplate that the victim's close relations and friends may become, in the long term, proportionately distressed and even psychiatrically ill after caring for the victim for a long time".[14]

Thus, in Australia a firm line has been drawn between the sudden shock cases and the cases of gradual onset of subsequent psychiatric illness through constant contact with, and care of, a badly injured victim.

The plaintiff in the Canadian case of *Beecham v Hughes*[15] was injured in two separate accidents in two years, the first of which also involved his de facto wife. He sought compensation for psychiatric injury in the form of reactive depression arising out of his wife's injuries. The medical evidence indicated, however, that the depression was not caused by the shock of either accident or the sight of the severe injuries sustained by his wife in the first accident. Rejecting the claim on the basis of an absence of causal proximity, the British Columbia Court of Appeal stressed that the

---

11. Note that the plaintiff was awarded $10,000 for solatium pursuant to s 10(3)(f) of the *Compensation (Fatal Injuries) Act* 1974 (NT).
12. (1987) 44 SASR 1.
13. (1984) 155 CLR 549.
14. (1987) 44 SASR 1 at 4.
15. (1988) 52 DLR (4th) 625. Note also *Cameron v Marcaccini* (1978) 87 DLR (3d) 442.

plaintiff's loss stemmed from intervening events in his life, namely his inability to "accept the fact that his wife [would] not again be the person she was before the [first] accident".[16] It was the continuing and debilitating effect of viewing his wife in a state utterly unlike her pre-accident condition which served as a constant reminder of what they had lost and eroded the plaintiff's emotional fibre. Their Honours took a similar attitude in *Rhodes v Canadian National Railway*[17] where the facts did not involve post-accident care and counsel of a loved one, but the gradual realisation that someone close to the shock victim had died. They emphasised the need for shock and psychiatric injury to be sustained through a direct impact upon the senses by some event fraught with terror or horror. The disturbance of the plaintiff's mental equilibrium was an indirect consequence of the effect of the defendant's negligence on her son. Over a period of several days, the plaintiff gradually became convinced that her son had died in a train crash in Alberta, receiving little co-operation from the authorities in her attempts to discover the truth about his fate, including directing her to the wrong crash site and memorial service. It was held that indirect psychiatric damage of this nature stemming from her reaction to the consequences for her son of the tortfeasor's want of care did not sound in damages.

The English courts have also recognised the need to differentiate between immediate trauma-induced psychiatric harm and "delayed shock". This was recently affirmed in *Alcock v Chief Constable of South Yorkshire Police*[18] where the Law Lords stressed that in all the previous cases the injuries for which damages were claimed arose from sudden or unexpected shock rather than through the process of accumulation. While the facts of the prior authorities bear out their statements (for example, no English cases contemplated the enduring care situation), until the express reference made by the House of Lords, judicial comment on this requirement was notably absent in England. It appears to have always been assumed to be a necessary prerequisite to liability.

No distinction has been drawn by the courts between the different bases for sudden and unexpected shock. It does not appear to matter, for example, whether the shock victim's mind was agitated by horror (as will be the case in most rescuer claims[19]) or fright or terror (suffered, for example, where an accident is narrowly averted[20]) so long as the stimuli in

16. (1988) 52 DLR (4th) 625 per Taggart JA at 664 (Carrothers JA concurring). See also Lambert JA at 667.
17. (1990) 75 DLR (4th) 248 per Macfarlane JA at 251, per Wallace JA at 264-265, per Southin JA at 272-273, per Taylor JA (Wood JA concurring) at 297.
18. [1992] 1 AC 310 per Lord Keith at 396, per Lord Ackner at 401, per Lord Oliver at 416-417.
19. See eg *Chadwick v British Railways Board* [1967] 1 WLR 912; *Mount Isa Mines Ltd v Pusey* (1970) 125 CLR 383; *Wigg v British Railways Board, The Times*, 4 Feb 1986. Note also *Fenn v City of Peterborough* (1976) 73 DLR (3d) 177. It is foreseeable, however, that in addition to or instead of feeling horrified by what he or she witnesses, a rescuer may suffer shock and psychiatric injury through fear of the danger of physical injury to himself or herself or to fellow-rescuers in attempting to assist at the accident scene.
20. See eg the "near miss" cases of *Dooley v Cammell Laird & Co Ltd* [1951] 1 Lloyd's Rep 271; *King v Phillips* [1953] 1 QB 429; *Galt v British Railways Board* (1983) 133 NLJ 870; and the older authorities where the plaintiff suffers shock through fear of harm to himself or herself, best illustrated by *Dulieu v White & Sons* [1901] 2 KB 669.

question had an instantaneous rather than a progressive effect.[21] It is the result of a traumatic event, namely the nature of its impact on the human psyche, rather than the reason for the nervous response that is important.

Primary victim's condition contributing to the continuing effect of the initial shock

Although worry or anxiety for the condition of a seriously injured loved one (for example, a brain-damaged child) and any psychiatric illness resulting from continued association are not compensable, the primary victim's condition may contribute to the continuing effect of any initial shock to the nervous system which a plaintiff suffered at the time of the injury or within a sufficiently short time thereafter.[22] The distinction is an important one. This was emphasised by Miles CJ in *De Franceschi v Storrier*[23] where the daughter and two of the three sons of the plaintiff were seriously injured by a wayward driver whilst they were waiting for their school bus. It was approximately five years before it was known that the daughter would survive the accident with the consequence that the plaintiff's psychological disorder sustained as a result of her initial shock was prolonged, or to put it another way, its harmful effect was continued. During that period she was never able to take an "emotional break" from the trauma. The continuing psychiatric consequences would, the Chief Justice ruled, be compensable up to the point where they transmuted into irrecoverable natural parental concern. The drawing of the line between the compensable results of nervous shock and the uncompensable natural concern was recognised as a necessary, albeit highly artificial, exercise. Whilst the necessity to do this may, on one view, be debatable,[24] the case does reinforce the notion that, on the present law, in the absence of an initial sudden and dramatic impact a plaintiff will be denied relief for any mental damage he or she sustains. But once there is medical evidence of such harm damages may be collected for persisting or increasingly debilitating psychiatric harm that comes about due to the ensuing poor

---

21. See eg *Rhodes v Canadian National Railway* (1990) 75 DLR (4th) 248.
22. This is to be distinguished from the situation which arose in *McLaren v Bradstreet* (1969) 113 SJ 471 where the victims' recovery from shock-related complaints was retarded by the neurotic condition of their mother (not the primary victim). She encouraged constant discussion about the consequences of their accident and produced a morbid atmosphere in the home which prevented the natural healing process taking place. The English Court of Appeal refused to take this into account, Widgery LJ saying that the tortfeasor had to take the plaintiff as he found him but not the plaintiff's family.
23. (1988) 85 ACTR 1. Note also *White v Butcher* (unreported, New South Wales SC, 13 Oct 1982, Nos 9576, 9577 and 9578 of 1981) where the trauma suffered by parents as a result of an accident to their teenage daughter was greatly aggravated by her post-accident behaviour—"she acted as if she were from time to time two or three different people", and would often be violent and use abusive language to her parents; *Government Insurance Office of New South Wales v Maroulis* (unreported, New South Wales CA, 6 Apr 1990, CA No 274 and 275 of 1988) where the psychiatric damage suffered by the plaintiff was greatly exacerbated by the experience of living with her injured husband after the accident; and the slightly different case of *Richards v Baker* [1943] SASR 245 where a mother, who was compensated for the shock of witnessing injury to her child, was granted an additional sum for the aggravation of her condition as a consequence of his subsequent death.
24. On the compensation for grief issue see above, pp 43-51, 56-58.

condition of the primary accident victim—as the latter's health fails to improve or deteriorates, so may the former's, with a consequent effect on the compensation award.[25]

The same issue arose in England in *S v Distillers Co (Biochemicals) Ltd*[26] where a mother who took thalidomide during pregnancy recovered damages for the shock and resultant psychiatric damage caused by her son being born without arms. Hinchcliffe J held that the daily reminder involved in caring for the boy could increase the damages for the shock of the birth of a deformed child. The outcome would have been different if the shock and psychiatric harm had only developed over a period of time as the full consequences of the calamity were brought home to the plaintiff.[27] In *Whitmore v Euroways Express Coaches Ltd*[28] also, the plaintiff recovered £2,000 for both the immediate and the continuing "shock" (which lasted for eight weeks) suffered as a consequence of her husband's injuries in a coach accident in France and their continuing debilitating effects.[29] In a recent Irish case, *Mullally v Bus Eireann*,[30] the sight of the prolonged suffering of her son, who received terrible head injuries in a bus accident and died nine months later, in the eyes of the court was clearly a factor which aggravated the psychiatric damage suffered by the plaintiff as a result of viewing the hospital aftermath. A Scottish court, however, has refused to award damages for the retardation of the process of recovery from an initial assault on the nervous system. In *Wood v Miller*[31] a woman who sustained physical injury in a motorcycle accident in which her husband was involved averred that as a result of the likelihood of her husband suffering from the effects of his injuries for an indefinite period, her nervous anxiety condition would continue, with a consequent adverse effect on her health. Lord Wheatley saw no difference between this situation and one where a wife is shocked *after* an accident upon ascertaining the nature and extent of her husband's injuries. Accordingly, his Lordship viewed the continuing complaint as irrelevant. It is submitted that the fact that shock is suffered at the time of the accident, rather than later, does make these instances significantly distinct and that the approach of the Australian, English and Irish courts is to be preferred.

The key to these cases is the continuation or aggravation of the shock victim's condition (following the initial impact to the nervous system) caused by constant contact with a badly injured or incapacitated relative. Where the accident victim is dead there is no room for such a claim,

25. Consider the fact situation in *Kwok v British Columbia Ferry Corporation* (1987) 20 BCLR (2d) 318 where a severely shocked and traumatised father, having already lost his wife and one child in a boating accident, had to make the "wrenching" decision, after a two-day bedside vigil, to discontinue life support and allow a second child to die.
26. [1969] 3 All ER 1412.
27. But compare *Kralj v McGrath* [1986] 1 All ER 54, discussed below, pp 203-204, where shock occurred gradually rather than in one initial impact.
28. *The Times*, 4 May 1984. Note that this case is controversial in that Comyn J was moved to award compensation for "shock" which was "ordinary" in nature rather than "psychiatric". On the nature of the damage required to sustain a claim, see above, pp 14-21.
29. Note also *Malcolm v Broadhurst* [1970] 3 All ER 508 where a woman's (pre-existing) nervous disorder was aggravated by her husband's injuries sustained in the same car accident and their effect upon him.
30. (Unreported, Irish HC, 13 June 1991).
31. 1958 SLT (Notes) 49.

however distressing the problem of adjusting to a new life without him or her may be.[32] In *Schneider v Eisovitch*[33] a woman learnt upon regaining consciousness of her husband's death in a car accident in which she was also injured. She recovered for psychiatric damage caused by the shock of the accident itself which resulted in the physical injuries to herself and the shock of the discovery in hospital that her husband was dead. But she recovered nothing for her subsequent neurotic state attributable to continuing mental stress, tension and the strain of having to adjust her life after his death. The ensuing mental condition and neurodermatitis was not part of the shock caused by the death of her husband, although it continued to contribute to that condition. Similarly, in *Hinz v Berry*[34] only one of five factors identified as having contributed to the plaintiff's prolonged and severely depressed state was compensable, namely the original shock of witnessing the accident which claimed her husband's life and injured her children. Relief could not be had for grief and sorrow, anxiety about the welfare of the injured children, the financial stress of losing a breadwinner or the difficulties of adjusting to a new life as these were injury-contributing problems which surfaced after the initial shocking trauma.[35]

Expert medical testimony is not always cut and dried. Evidence may often be equivocal as to the precise cause of the psychiatric condition, especially in the permanent care situation. Such was the case in *Spence v Percy*[36] where a mother suffered psychiatric damage after the death of her daughter who had lain in a comatose state for three years as a result of a motor accident. The question arose whether the plaintiff's injury had been caused by the sudden shock of hearing about her daughter's death or as a result of a build-up of the tension and stress occasioned by the constant care required during the previous three years combined with an inability to adjust to the emptiness of life that the death of a child brings. Derrington J at first instance held that there had been a sufficiently sudden perception to ground recovery. Though on appeal his decision to award damages of $36,000 was reversed due to an absence of the requisite degree of proximity,[37] the Full Court of the Queensland Supreme Court was divided on the question whether the mother's mental illness was a direct result of the impact of learning of the death, de Jersey J concluding it was, Williams J that it was not and Shepherdson J not deciding. There was evidence that the plaintiff had suffered some shock caused by the initial sight of her daughter three years previously, but the claim was limited to that suffered after her death. Thus, it was unnecessary to consider whether a separate claim distinct from the consequences of the death could be maintained. Apart from illustrating the often inconclusive and conflicting nature of medical evidence and the difficulty of always accurately pinpointing the injury-inducing factors, the case serves as a good reminder that it must always be determined exactly what the plaintiff is claiming

32. But see *Bagley v North Herts Health Authority* (1986) 136 NLJ 1014 where Simon Brown J took into account the continuing nature of a psychiatric condition in assessing damages for negligence resulting in a stillbirth.
33. [1960] 2 QB 430.
34. [1970] 2 QB 40.
35. See the comments of Lord Denning MR at 42 and Lord Pearson at 44.
36. (1990) Aust Torts Rep 81-039 (Derrington J); (1991) Aust Torts Rep 81-116 (FC).
37. See above, pp 139-140.

for—illness from an initial shocking event or illness suffered as the severity and gravity of the event dawned on them later.

Undesirable consequences of the sudden impact requirement

The prevailing need for a sudden jolt to the sensory system was confirmed by the New South Wales Court of Appeal in *Campbelltown City Council v Mackay*.[38] Of greater significance, however, is the way the case highlights the undesirable consequences of the requirement and its inability to accommodate the vast number of complex psychiatric illnesses. A young married couple sued a local council, two engineers and a contractor for, inter alia, psychiatric damage allegedly suffered as a result of the deterioration of their "dream home" in the form of cracking and displacement. After the plaintiffs moved out, a demolition order was issued, the wife gave birth to a stillborn child, developed a psychiatric illness and the marriage broke down. Subsequently, the husband also developed a psychiatric illness. As well as awarding damages for the collapse of their home and consequential loss, Smart J granted relief for the plaintiffs' psychiatric injury on the basis that they had suffered mental illness as a result of the sudden perception of property damage.[39] In an appeal confined to the latter aspect, the Court of Appeal disagreed with Smart J's finding but upheld the award on the ground that compensation for vexation, distress and inconvenience suffered as a result of the property damage could be supported.

The court was clearly unimpressed by the plaintiff's contention that the injury-inducing phenomenon was the perception that severe structural damage had occurred to their home. They had undoubtedly suffered a recognisable psychiatric illness but not as a result of one isolated shocking incident. In truth, the psychiatric conditions of the claimants were the result of a combination of factors and not of the perception of property damage. McHugh JA (with whom Kirby P and Samuels JA agreed) stated:

"In an action for nervous shock it is not enough, as Brennan J pointed out in *Jaensch v Coffey*, that the psychiatric illness was the foreseeable result of the defendant's conduct. The illness must be the result of a shock caused by the perception of a phenomenon for which the defendant is responsible. Here the shock-inducing phenomenon was the stillbirth operating on a mind which had already been subjected to much worry, fear and stress as the result of the 'collapse' of the house. What is missing from the present case is any evidence that prior to the stillbirth [the wife] was suffering from any psychiatric condition. Indeed, the evidence establishes that notwithstanding the pressures and stresses she was able to cope. . . . In my opinion the evidence shows that the severe depressive disorder was the result of the stillbirth and that, although the 'collapse' of the house was a contributing factor,

38. (1989) 15 NSWLR 501. Note, however, that the respondents' concession that success in this claim depended upon proving that the psychiatric damage resulted from a sudden affront to their psyches, coupled with the comments in *Jaensch v Coffey* (1984) 155 CLR 549, prevented the court from thoroughly reviewing the boundaries of liability for psychiatric damage in this context.
39. For discussion of mental harm suffered as a result of property damage see below, pp 208-212.

that phenomenon did not produce a shock which brought on a psychiatric illness."[40]

A similar finding was reached in relation to the husband. Kirby P was particularly sceptical of the plaintiff's artificial attempts to blame the movement of their home on a particular night for their entire course of psychological problems. His Honour was critical of the stagnant state of the law in this context which forces claimants to try to "squeeze their claims into outmoded formulae".[41] Its artificialities, he said, pressure expert witnesses to "distort opinions on what they may feel to be legitimate claims out of deference to outmoded formulations of the legal basis of entitlement to recovery".[42] It seems certain that Kirby P, at least, were he free to do so, would eliminate this requirement as not being fundamental to the cause of action.

Moreover, from a medical perspective, the "shock" element is inappropriate to deal with the nature of psychiatric disorders. It will operate to exclude many deserving claims. As his Honour pointed out:

"[P]sychiatric injury . . . is very unlikely to result from the single impact upon the psyche of the claimant of an isolated event. Since the tort of nervous shock was fashioned, there have been substantial advances in the understanding of human psychology. It is highly artificial to imprison the legal cause of action for psychiatric injury in an outmoded scientific view about the nature of its origins. The causes of action at common law should, in my opinion, be released from subservience to 19th century science. . . . [P]sychological injury is a . . . complex process. It is rarely (if ever) explicable as the result of an isolated 'shock'."[43]

The initial reaction to traumatic stimulus is automatic and instinctive, commonly taking the form of fear, grief or anger and varying in intensity depending upon the stimulus and individual concerned. As noted,[44] on the present law damages do not sound for these responses. Nor can one recover for instant and initial shock, only psychiatric illness generated as a result, despite the inaccurately and imprecisely named category of claim. It is subsequent, more lasting and health-threatening human responses like neuroses which are compensable under the "nervous shock" label.[45] It will be extremely rare that this type of reaction will be triggered by the initial transient sensations normally experienced when trauma is perceived. Rather, mental damage of this sort commonly occurs as a result of a later

40. Ibid at 509.
41. Ibid at 503.
42. Ibid at 503-504. Note *Bassanese v Martin* (1982) 31 SASR 461 where it was recognised that although the plaintiff's depressive illness was consequent upon her adulterous husband's murder by a jealous suitor of his mistress, it was also due in part to causes existing prior to that sudden and impacting shock. She had long been emotionally fragile due to severe epilepsy and intellectual deterioration. Although a defendant must take the victim as he or she finds him or her (see the discussion below, pp 229-238), the court rejected attempts to present as matters justifying an award of damages symptoms which were present prior to the husband's death. Compare also *Chapman v Lear* (unreported, Queensland SC, 8 Apr 1988, No 3732 of 1984), discussed below, p 229.
43. (1989) 15 NSWLR 501 at 503.
44. See above, pp 14-18.
45. See above, pp 14-42.

realisation of the true severity or consequences of the trauma or a continued inability to cope with the situation in question. As one commentator has observed, "the consensus of modern medical opinion is that lasting [and compensable] damage does not occur in 'normal' individuals as a result of emotional shock, however severe".[46] Significantly, even in *Jaensch v Coffey*[47] itself the wife did not exhibit any psychiatric complaints until about a week after the second visit to the hospital to view her injured husband when she realised that he could actually die. Similarly, in *Mount Isa Mines Ltd v Pusey*[48] the plaintiff's rare schizophrenic reaction to seeing two fellow workmen horribly burnt did not manifest itself until approximately four weeks later.[49] If the enduring and compensable psychic impact does not normally result from a momentary dramatic event it is therefore inappropriate to insist on an immediate and significant consequence such as a "sudden sensory perception" as a prerequisite to recovery. Such insistence, in the absence of a change in the law barring relief for transient emotions like grief, sorrow, anger or an initial shock, will mean that plaintiffs with recognisable psychiatric illnesses will more often than not go uncompensated.[50]

Psychiatric harm in combination with physical damage

The only hope for relief for persons suffering neuroses caused by something other than a sudden shock to the senses (that is, the overwhelming majority of sufferers of this type) is if, in addition to sustaining mental injury, they have had the misfortune of sustaining bodily injury or incurring damage to property. In an action for physical injury a plaintiff is entitled to recover for consequential psychiatric illness without the need to establish that it was the result of a shock caused by the sudden perception of some phenomenon for which the defendant is responsible. It is sufficient that the mental condition is the reasonably foreseeable result of the defendant's negligence. The same is true of an action for damage to property.[51] As the New South Wales Court of Appeal confirmed in *Campbelltown City Council v Mackay*,[52] the plaintiff is entitled to recover for personal damage (including psychiatric illness) which is the reasonably foreseeable result of the defendant's negligent damage of that property. But as McHugh JA has noted:

"Proof that mental illness is the reasonably foreseeable result of negligent damage to property may often be more difficult to establish

---

46. See J Havard, "Reasonable Foresight of Nervous Shock" (1956) 19 MLR 478 at 482. Note also H Teff, "Liability for Negligently Inflicted Nervous Shock" (1983) 99 LQR 100 at 106-108; Comment, "Negligently Inflicted Mental Distress: The Case for an Independent Tort" (1971) 59 Geo LJ 1237 at 1248-1253.
47. (1984) 155 CLR 549.
48. (1970) 125 CLR 383.
49. Contrast *Young v Burgoyne* (1981) 122 DLR (3d) 330 where the Nova Scotia Supreme Court declined to award damages to a woman who did not sustain psychiatric injury until nine months after an "emotional upset". The language adopted by the court does not make it clear whether this was regarded as a sudden shock to her sensory system.
50. See Teff, op cit, n 46 at 108.
51. See eg *Campbelltown City Council v Mackay* (1989) 15 NSWLR 501 per McHugh JA at 511; *Perry v Sidney Phillips & Son* [1982] 1 WLR 1297; *Brickhill v Cooke* [1984] 3 NSWLR 396.
52. (1989) 15 NSWLR 501.

than proof that it is the reasonably foreseeable result of the negligent infliction of personal injury. But the same principles of causation and remoteness apply whether the cause of action in tort is for damage to property or harm to person."[53]

The greater restrictions placed on recovery in non-consequential psychiatric injury cases appear to have gone uncriticised. Not only does the result of this general division seem to lack a certain logic; as *Campbelltown City Council v Mackay* illustrates, the common law has reached the anomalous position where in a consequential psychiatric damage action it recognises the mental damage claims of those whose property has gradually deteriorated and rejects claims based on the gradual worsening of the health of a relative. Nader J in *Anderson v Smith* could see no foundation or policy reason for a stricter control mechanism in the latter type of case, viewing it as unreasonable:

> "for the law to vest the artificial (created by positive law) relationship of property to owner with a greater capacity for the infliction of compensable injury to the owner than the natural relationship of infant to mother has for the infliction of such injury to the mother".[54]

His Honour urged the law to take another "cautious step"[55] and to allow recovery for the gradual onset of psychiatric illness thereby putting parents of injured infant children on the same footing at least as owners of property who sue for consequential damage. It is submitted that higher courts should heed his call.

Liability in the absence of sudden impact

Although, on the present law, he refused to countenance compensation for those who have had no contact with an accident or its immediate aftermath, but who have suffered mental harm through subsequent constant social contact with an accident victim, Deane J in *Jaensch v Coffey*[56] suggested that it was not beyond the realms of possibility that the common law in Australia may develop such that recovery in this type of situation is possible. Tentative inroads have been made in this area by courts in some other jurisdictions. Significantly, some American States have recognised that the requirement of a sudden shocking event is an unwarranted restriction on mental damage suits. In *Ochoa v Superior Court (Santa Clara County)*,[57] the parents of a young boy in the custody of juvenile hall (a custodial institution for juvenile offenders) who died from

---

53. Ibid at 511.
54. (1990) 101 FLR 34 at 51.
55. A reference to *Jaensch v Coffey* (1984) 155 CLR 549 per Gibbs CJ at 555: "The law must continue to proceed in this area step by cautious step" Windeyer J in *Mount Isa Mines Ltd v Pusey* (1970) 125 CLR 383 at 403 used similar language.
56. (1984) 155 CLR 549 at 602-604.
57. (1985) 703 P 2d 1; 216 Cal Rptr 661. See N Quay-Smith, "The Negligent Infliction of Emotional Distress: A Critical Analysis of Various Approaches to the Tort in the Light of Ochoa v Superior Court" (1986) 19 Ind L Rev 809; E McFadden, "Ochoa v Superior Court: One Step Forward and Two Steps Back for Bystander Tort Law?" (1986) 21 Tort & Ins LJ 672; P R Bernal, "Dillon to Ochoa: The Elusive Foreseeability of Emotional Distress" (1987) 27 Santa Clara L Rev 91. Note also *Thing v La Chusa* (1989) 771 P 2d 814; 257 Cal Rptr 98 (dealt with above, pp 13, 147) at 824-825 where the Supreme Court of California referred to the case in this context without disapproval.

bilateral pneumonia due to a lack of adequate medical treatment alleged that they had suffered severe mental distress as a result of the defendant's medical neglect. They did not actually see their son's death, nor was it sudden, the boy having died after being extremely ill for four days. The Supreme Court of California considered that the sudden impact rule:

> "arbitrarily limits liability when there is a high degree of foreseeability of shock to the plaintiff and the shock flows from an abnormal event, and, as such, unduly frustrates the goal of compensation—the very purpose which the cause of action was meant to further".[58]

There are also some recent indications that the Canadian courts may deviate from the traditional common law requirement. Although in the British Columbia Court of Appeal decision in *Beecham v Hughes*[59] Taggart JA (Carrothers JA concurring) quoted at length from Brennan J's judgment in *Jaensch v Coffey*[60] stressing the need for a shock-inducing event, significantly Lambert JA stated emphatically:

> "I do not consider that there is any one key which opens the door to a simple and straightforward answer. . . . [T]he psychological injury does not have to arise from a specific 'shock'. There is no single question which solves the problem. There is no single limiting factor other than the composite answer."[61]

Again, in the New Zealand case of *Rowe v Cleary*,[62] a wife recovered damages in tort from a solicitor who had been sued for professional negligence by her husband. The delays caused by the defendant's incompetence, and the growing realisation that the financial stability of herself and her family was in danger, caused her to suffer a decline in mental health for which she required medical treatment. It was held that the defendant owed her an independent duty in tort. It seems clear that the damage to her health was gradual, rather than the result of a sudden event.

Similar steps have been taken by some first instance English judges, although unfortunately, the latest appellate pronouncements have retraced this advancement. In *Kralj v McGrath*[63] the plaintiff was admitted to hospital to give birth to twin boys, the first birth going smoothly. Complications arose, however, with respect to the second twin, Daniel. He was in a transverse position and the defendant obstetrician elected, inter alia, without anaesthetising Mrs Kralj, to perform an episiotomy[64] and to put his arm inside her in an attempt to manipulate the baby's position,

---

58. (1985) 703 P 2d 1 (Cal) at 7. But note the previous line of contrary authority: eg *Jansen v Children's Hospital Medical Center of East Bay* (1973) 106 Cal Rptr 883; *Hair v County of Monterey* (1975) 119 Cal Rptr 639; *Mobaldi v Regents of University of California* (1976) 127 Cal Rptr 720; *Justus v Atchison* (1977) 565 P 2d 122; 139 Cal Rptr 97; *Nazaroff v Superior Court* (1978) 145 Cal Rptr 657. Other States had taken a similar stance: see eg *Sim's Crane Service Inc v Reliance Insurance Co* (1981) 514 F Supp 1033; *Wilson v Galt* (1983) 668 P 2d 1104 (NM); *Wisniewski v Johns-Manville Corporation* (1987) 812 F 2d 81.
59. (1988) 52 DLR (4th) 625 at 651-652.
60. (1984) 155 CLR 549 at 565.
61. (1988) 52 DLR (4th) 625 at 665.
62. [1980] NZ Recent Law 71.
63. [1986] 1 All ER 54. See N Grace, "Doctors, Damages and Nervous Shock" (1986) 2 PN 46.
64. A surgical incision of the vulvar orifice for obstetrical purposes.

causing her to suffer excruciating pain. A caesarian section was ultimately performed and Daniel was born in an extremely debilitated state, suffering brain damage found to have been caused after the birth of the first twin, and subsequently died. The plaintiff successfully claimed damages from the doctor for the "nervous shock" caused by the consequences of what happened to Daniel. What is special about this case, which was concerned mainly with aggravated damages, is that the plaintiff's state was not caused by any immediate impact,[65] or fear of impact, to the plaintiff or her son but accrued after the labour, gradually over a period of eight weeks before his death, as a result of the fear and concern of watching him slowly die.[66] More recently in *Hevican v Ruane*[67] Mantell J was prepared to move the boundaries of psychiatric damage law forward to permit recovery for damage to the psyche arising from a series of cumulative incidents rather than one isolated sudden and nerve-racking event. The plaintiff's son was killed whilst a passenger in a school bus when it collided with a truck as a result of the bus driver's negligence. He brought an action against the driver's estate for damages for his nervous shock in the form of continued reactive depression. The case is significant in that the plaintiff recovered notwithstanding that the shock took the form of a gradual realisation in stages that his son was dead. Specifically, the father suffered a recognisable psychiatric illness as a predictable result of the cumulative effect of learning some time after the accident that his son was involved, being told later that his son had been killed and viewing his body, "not disfigured in any way", in the mortuary at the local hospital. Relief was granted even though the father was not present at the immediate aftermath of the collision and it was not foreseeable that the nervous shock suffered would result in continuing psychological illness. Mantell J opined:

> "It would seem . . . that by reference to general principles [of negligence] alone there is no reason why a plaintiff who sustains a mental shock as a predictable result of learning of a loved one's death or injury and in consequence becomes ill either in the mind . . . or in the body . . . for example by suffering a heart attack, should not recover damages against a defendant whose negligent act caused the death or injury."[68]

In *Ravenscroft v Rederiaktiebölaget Transatlantic*,[69] in a judgment subsequently reversed by the Court of Appeal,[70] Ward J, having expressed some reservations with Brennan J's words, stated:

> "If, as we are urged to do by *Attia v British Gas*, we cease to use the inaccurate and misleading expression 'nervous shock', then I see no reason why some notion of shock, especially one which is not to be

---

65. Although there was physical impact to Mrs Kralj in that the defendant inserted his arm into her vagina, the "nervous shock" did not stem from this.
66. Note also *Bagley v North Herts Health Authority* (1986) 136 NLJ 1014 where a woman suffered psychiatric illness arising from the birth of her stillborn child due to a hospital's failure to perform blood tests during pregnancy when it was known that she suffered from blood incompatibility and to intervene by caesarian section to ensure an early delivery.
67. [1991] 3 All ER 65.
68. Ibid at 71.
69. [1991] 3 All ER 73.
70. [1992] 2 All ER 470n.

understood in terms of 'recognisable psychiatric illness', is to be reintroduced as an element in the chain of causation.''[71]

Nolan LJ in *Alcock v Chief Constable of South Yorkshire Police*[72] would have none of this, however. Although he acknowledged that certain psychiatric illnesses could manifest themselves gradually, these particular varieties of mental harm were presently uncompensable in an action for nervous shock unaccompanied by physical or property damage. Rejecting the cumulative approach, his Lordship stated:

"[T]o my mind the expression 'nervous shock' . . . connotes a reaction to an immediate and horrifying impact. I have no doubt that the kinds of psychiatric illness to which nervous shock may give rise could equally be brought about by an accumulation of more gradual assaults upon the nervous system, but the law as it stands does not appear to me to provide for the latter category."[73]

It should. Regrettably, however, the House of Lords confirmed that dilution of the common law's insistence on a violent agitation of the mind will not be tolerated in England. Refusing to countenance psychiatric injury stemming from a dawning consciousness over an extended period as founding a claim in damages, their Lordships reinforced the need to identify a sudden rather than gradual assault on the nervous system.[74] Lord Oliver considered that:

"Grief, sorrow, deprivation and the necessity for caring for loved ones who have suffered injury or misfortune must, I think, be considered as ordinary and inevitable incidents of life which, regardless of individual susceptibilities, must be sustained without compensation. It would be inaccurate and hurtful to suggest that grief is made any the less real or deprivation more tolerable by a more gradual realisation, but to extend liability to cover [psychiatric] injury in such cases would be to extend the law in a direction for which there is no pressing policy need and in which there is no logical stopping point."[75]

With respect, this is unconvincing. Once again, it appears that groundless fears of uncontrolled liability have prevented desirable and long overdue modifications of principle. No basis other than policy is advanced for the veto of this particular variety of mental illness. Apart from encouraging claim distortion and being medically too imprecise to cater for the vast majority of psychiatric abnormalities, it seems obvious that a person may suffer as much of an emotional and psychological disturbance from seeing (or learning of) a loved one's deterioration or slow death as from seeing him or her killed or injured suddenly and unexpectedly, or coming upon the aftermath. Indeed, there is a strong argument for saying that helplessly witnessing another die a protracted or agonising death, or withering away from disease or injury, will give rise to a far more severe nervous

71. [1991] 3 All ER 73 at 77-78.
72. [1992] 1 AC 310.
73. Ibid at 387.
74. [1992] 1 AC 310 per Lord Keith at 398, per Lord Ackner at 401, per Lord Oliver at 411, 416-417.
75. Ibid at 416.

reaction.[76] Relatives of cancer or AIDS victims would no doubt testify to this. Moreover, the requirement that a sensory impacting shock be present is, in truth, totally superfluous to a claim for "nervous shock". A plaintiff recovers in these situations not for a shock to the system but for particular medical consequences of that shock, that is, any "recognisable psychiatric illness" that results.[77] Once a causal link between the defendant's actions and the plaintiff's injury is proved, the precise nature of the injury-producing phenomenon is immaterial and should be recognised as such. Not only where psychiatric damage results from a gradual accrual of shock, but also where mental distress (which on one view rightly does not sound in damages) leads to or transmutes into recognisable psychiatric damage, that damage should be compensable. That it started life as grief, sorrow, worry or anger is not to the point.[78] The unnecessary "shock" requirement stems, no doubt, from the inaccurate and misleading language of this category of claim.[79] If the present artificialities and imprecise terminology were cast aside, the true basis of this controversial species of negligence claim, as well as those concepts irrelevant to a successful suit, could be better appreciated. If the courts elect to continue to insist upon the existence of an isolated and sudden "shock" it is submitted that, at the very least, this must, for the reasons articulated above,[80] be extended to include all forms of shock whether arising from physical perception and direct impact upon the senses or not.

76. As A L Goodhart stated in his article, "Emotional Shock and the Unimaginative Taxicab Driver" (1953) 69 LQR 347 at 352, with reference to the comments of Denning LJ in King v Phillips [1953] 1 QB 429: "[I]t is not immediately obvious why a mother should receive less of a shock when she sees her child being slowly run over than when it is done rapidly."
77. See eg the use of the consequential sense of "nervous shock" in Mount Isa Mines Ltd v Pusey (1970) 125 CLR 383 per Windeyer J at 394-395 and Brennan and Deane JJ's careful choice of words in Jaensch v Coffey (1984) 155 CLR 549.
78. For a case where it was held that a child's grief at the death of her mother had developed into depression amounting to a psychiatric illness see Mellor v Moran (1985) 2 MVR 461. Note also Mitchell v Clancy [1960] Qd R 62, affirmed by the High Court [1960] Qd R 532, where worry over ability to support a family after a serious arm injury led to a nervous condition and in turn to a duodenal ulcer requiring surgery; Palamara v Fragameni (unreported, Western Australian SC, 13 Oct 1983, No 89 of 1983). See above, pp 21-24.
79. The crudeness of the expression "nervous shock" has been lamented by both commentators and courts: see above, pp 14-15, and also Teff, op cit, n 46 at 107; F A Trindade, "The Principles Governing the Recovery of Damages for Negligently Caused Nervous Shock" [1986] CLJ 476 at 476-477.
80. See discussion of the means of communication above, pp 153-183.

9

THE SOURCE OF THE SHOCK

Shock caused otherwise than as the result of an accident to another

Introduction

The vast majority of actions for compensation for psychiatric illness concern damage suffered as a result of the perception of the death of or injury or peril to a person other than the claimant, usually a loved one. The question arises whether recovery is, or should be, barred in other situations, for example where mental damage is brought about by the perception of physical danger to the plaintiff, or damage to the plaintiff's property, as a result of a negligently caused traumatic event.

According to Deane J in *Jaensch v Coffey* liability for shock-induced psychiatric damage will not arise unless:

> "the reasonably foreseeable psychiatric injury was sustained as a result of the death, injury or peril of someone other than the person whose carelessness is alleged to have caused the injury".[1]

However, this limitation is not one which should necessarily be imposed in all cases. "It is highly artificial to imprison the legal cause of action for psychiatric injury in an outmoded scientific view about the nature of its origins."[2]

Fear of death or injury to oneself

It is clear that Deane J is not outlawing recovery where the plaintiff himself or herself is placed in danger through the defendant's negligence and suffers a nervous disorder as a consequence.[3] From the standpoints of logic and policy there is no sound reason why, it having been medically proved that the plaintiff suffered a "recognisable psychiatric illness" and that it was sustained as a result of the defendant's negligence, relief should be any more difficult to obtain in a two party psychiatric injury case than

1. (1984) 155 CLR 549 at 604. See in addition his Honour's comments at 602. Dawson J at 612 also acknowledged, albeit tentatively, the existence of the limitation on liability referred to by Deane J.
2. *Campbelltown City Council v Mackay* (1989) 15 NSWLR 501 per Kirby P at 503.
3. See F A Trindade, "The Principles Governing the Recovery of Damages for Negligently Caused Nervous Shock" [1986] CLJ 476 at 481-482. It is inconceivable that a court would entertain a claim brought by a person who suffers shock-related psychiatric damage as the result of an accident due entirely to his or her own fault. A driver, for example, who due to a lack of care killed a pedestrian and then attempted to sue the deceased for shock caused by the body smashing through the windscreen as a result of the impact would, no doubt, receive short shrift from Commonwealth courts: note *Devereux v Allstate Insurance Co* (1990) 557 So 2d 1091 (La).

in the more usual three party scenario.[4] There is no reported case where it has been suggested that the courts would not entertain a cause of action in such circumstances. On the contrary, not only will the fact that a shock victim feared physical injury or death whilst within the "danger zone" not preclude recovery, it was at one stage a prerequisite in order to establish a cause of action. As noted,[5] in the old case of *Dulieu v White & Sons*[6] Kennedy J imposed the restriction that shock had to be suffered through reasonable fear of injury or death to the plaintiff personally. The formula stated by Deane J owes its origin to the rejection of this limitation in *Hambrook v Stokes Bros.*[7] There the English Court of Appeal made it clear that Mrs Hambrook could recover even though her shock was caused by fear for the safety of her children and not herself.[8] Although the "Kennedy limitation" has now been completely eroded,[9] it remains clear that shock and psychiatric illness from the perception of a personal predicament does not bar or reduce the prospects of compensation.

Damage to property

Until very recently the question whether it is possible to recover for psychiatric injury stemming from damage to property had not been settled in either England or Australia. That such damage might be remediable had been signalled in the peculiar case of *Owens v Liverpool Corporation*[10] where a hearse in a funeral parade was negligently damaged by the defendant's tram driver and mourners present recovered compensation for emotional shock and psychological damage caused by witnessing the overturning of the coffin and concern that it and its contents might fall from the hearse. Controversially (at least for that time) MacKinnon LJ went so far as to express the view that recovery may be allowed for shock and related apprehension for the safety of pets.[11] *Attia v British Gas Plc*[12] put the matter beyond doubt. There the plaintiff had engaged the defendants to instal central heating in her home, and as she returned to the house she saw smoke pouring from the roof. The fire extensively damaged the house and its contents. These events caused the plaintiff to suffer a psychiatric illness. Her claim for property damage was settled, but she also

---

4. Two party psychiatric injury cases will, of course, be "near-miss" cases, otherwise there would be no need to raise the issue of liability for shock at all, shock consequent on physical injury being subsumed in the personal injury action.
5. See above, pp 3-4.
6. [1901] 2 KB 669 at 675.
7. [1925] 1 KB 141 per Bankes LJ at 151, per Atkin LJ at 157-158 (but note Sargant LJ's comments at 162).
8. Sargant LJ, who dissented in *Hambrook v Stokes Bros* [1925] 1 KB 141 at 163-164 wondered whether the principle indorsed by the majority in that case—the three party situation—should extend to cases where no injury to the third party in fact occurred, but this qualification has never been adopted.
9. See above, pp 4-5.
10. [1939] 1 KB 394 at 399-400.
11. Ibid at 399. This places in some doubt the correctness of the decision in *Davies v Bennison* (1927) 22 Tas LR 52 where the plaintiff, who was shocked on seeing the defendant shoot her cat, failed to recover: see Nicholls CJ at 54. Note also P G Heffey, "The Negligent Infliction of Nervous Shock in Road and Industrial Accidents" (1974) 48 ALJ 196, 240 at 204.
12. [1988] QB 304.

claimed damages for her illness. The defendants pleaded that there could be no liability unless the shock was caused by fear for the safety of another, rather than through injury to property. This was tried as a preliminary issue. The English Court of Appeal unanimously rejected the defendant's contention, refusing to recognise any policy rule that there could be no liability for shock caused by witnessing damage to property. It is difficult to dissent from Bingham LJ's words:

"Suppose, for example, that a scholar's life's work of research or composition were destroyed before his eyes as a result of a defendant's careless conduct, causing the scholar to suffer reasonably foreseeable psychiatric damage.[13] Or suppose that a householder returned home to find that his most cherished possessions had been destroyed through the carelessness of an intruder in starting a fire or leaving a tap running, thereby causing reasonably foreseeable psychiatric damage to the owner. I do not think a legal principle which forebade recovery in these circumstances could be supported."[14]

Whether such damage was in fact foreseeable was a matter which would have to be decided at the trial in the light of all the circumstances. One factor which influenced the Court of Appeal was that if the property damage claim had not been settled the plaintiff could have recovered for her shock as consequential damage. A somewhat similar case is *Campbelltown City Council v Mackay*.[15] Smart J at first instance awarded damages, inter alia, for psychiatric injury suffered as a result of the gradual decay of the plaintiffs' house which was ultimately condemned as unsafe for human habitation. On appeal compensation was given for vexation, worry and distress consequent upon this determination.[16] The New South Wales Court of Appeal did not expressly rule out the possibility of recovery for psychiatric injury caused by the perception of property damage,[16a] although in their view on the facts the plaintiffs' mental disorders were not induced by a single sudden perception of property damage but by a combination of other events. Claims for emotional or mental stress consequent on damage to property are not to be confused with actions for property-based psychiatric illness. The two are conceptually distinct. The limits on recovery for damage to the mind posed in the latter, such as the need to prove a recognisable psychiatric injury, are absent in claims for the former.[17] The significance of the difference between them can be appreciated from the fact the settlement of a claim for property damage (as in *Attia v British Gas Plc*[18]) operates to convert what would otherwise be a

13. To modernise his Lordship's example, imagine the likely psychiatric upheaval if, due to the negligence of a computer software manufacturer, a doctoral thesis, after three or four years' work, were wiped from a student's computer a few days before its submission.
14. [1988] QB 304 at 320.
15. (1989) 15 NSWLR 501.
16. Note also *Pibworth v Bevan M Roberts Pty Ltd* (unreported, South Australian SC, 28 May 1992, No 770 of 1986) where damages were granted for post-traumatic stress disorder stemming from the destruction by fire of the plaintiff's home.
16a. The defendants accepted that had psychiatric injury been caused by the sudden shock of damage to the home (eg by its immediate rather than gradual collapse) they would have been liable.
17. See above, pp 201-202.
18. [1988] QB 304. Note that the successful property claim in *Campbelltown City Council v Mackay* (1989) 15 NSWLR 501 was not appealed against.

relatively uncontroversial action for consequential damage into a "pure" psychiatric damage claim with all its attendant prerequisites to relief.[19]

North American courts have, on occasion, also touched on the question of recovery for property damage-related shock. A majority of the Supreme Court of Nebraska in *Rasmussen v Benson*[20] were prepared to grant relief to a dairy farmer who suffered nervous shock (leading to cardiac decompensation and his eventual death) after his cows were poisoned through feeding on bran contaminated with arsenic. The defendant, intending to kill grasshoppers, had placed the poison in a sack of bran. He had forgotten about both the grasshoppers and the lethal levels of arsenic and sold the bran to the plaintiff at a farm sale. Significantly, in addition to distress from the loss of his entire business, the plaintiff's emotional injuries were viewed as having been due in part to concern for his customers who had consumed milk from the affected stock.[21] A more recent case from Texas is *Shade v City of Dallas*[22] where the negligence of a municipal authority caused a sewage backup in the plaintiff's home. Raw sewage erupted in his bathroom and flooded the whole house, the odour lingering even after it was cleared, and the dampness causing mould to grow throughout. The plaintiff recovered for the mental anguish of having to live with this situation. In the Nova Scotia case of *Horne v New Glasgow*[23] a truck careered out of control down a hill and crashed into the plaintiff's house, stopping within a few feet of her in the living room. Although suffering no physical injury through the impact of the accident itself, she was shocked through a combination of extreme worry about her elderly parents who had been upstairs at the relevant time, and about the fate of her badly damaged home. McQuarrie J was not moved to deny her recovery on the basis that her psychological injury was caused partly by the perception of damage to property and the belief that her home had been destroyed.[24] Nor is there, in either case, any indication that the damages

19. Recent restrictions of the ambit of negligence in England raise the question whether tort actions for defective building will remain a feasible avenue of redress in Australia: see *D & F Estates Ltd v Church Commissioners for England* [1989] AC 177; *Murphy v Brentwood District Council* [1991] 1 AC 398; *Department of the Environment v Thomas Bates & Son Ltd* [1991] 1 AC 499; see above, pp 77-78.

20. (1938) 280 NW 890 (Neb). Mr Rasmussen himself commenced this action, but at his death it was revived and continued by his wife as administratrix of his estate.

21. No consideration was made of fear of possible damage to the plaintiff from drinking the milk himself. In other American cases the courts have refused to countenance recovery in this type of situation: see eg *Buchanan v Stout* (1908) 108 NYS 38 (plaintiff saw pet cat mangled by defendant's dog); *Furlan v Rayan Photo Works* (1939) 12 NYS 2d 921 (recovery denied for mental distress caused by negligent mutilation of mother's picture); *Blanchard v Reliable Transfer Co* (1944) 32 SE 2d 420 (Ga) (plaintiff, while in bed at home, heard ambulance he owned crash); *Aronoff v Baltimore Transit Co* (1951) 80 A 2d 13 (Md) (plaintiff's truck loaded with plate glass run into by streetcar); *Fournell v Usher Pest Control Co* (1981) 305 NW 2d 605 (Neb) (distress resulting from failure to discover termite damage to home); *Smith v Clough* (1990) 796 P 2d 592 (Nev) (plaintiffs, while gardening in back yard, heard car crash into front of house); *Broadfoot v Aaron Rents Inc* (1991) 409 SE 2d 870 (Ga) (plaintiff's restaurant damaged by falling bricks).

22. (1991) 819 SW 2d 578 (Tex).

23. [1954] 1 DLR 832, noted by W R Lederman (1954) 32 Can BR 325.

24. [1954] 1 DLR 832 at 840. Whilst the fear for the safety of her parents was canvassed, once again it seems that little attention was focused on the claimant's immediate fear for her own life.

awarded reflected (or attempted to reflect) only the non-property related shock injuries. More recently, in *Heighington v The Queen in Right of Ontario*,[25] Holland J held that damages for psychiatric illness caused by shock and emotional distress were recoverable by persons who learnt that, unbeknown to them, they had been occupying residences built on land contaminated with radioactive waste.

Even South Africa, which resisted the modernisation of nervous shock law for many years, has contemplated that psychiatric damage arising from fear of, or damage to, one's property is properly the subject of liability for lack of due care. The incredible case of *Masiba v Constantia Insurance Co Ltd*[26] is illustrative. The deceased, his wife (the first plaintiff), their three-and-a-half-year-old daughter, her playmate of similar age and the first plaintiff's 18-year-old niece were travelling in a car driven by the deceased. The car stalled as it approached a bridge over a railway line and the deceased, the plaintiff and the niece got out to push it, leaving the two children inside. Four men offered their assistance, one of whom then assaulted the deceased intending to steal his watch. The first plaintiff, who was on the opposite side of the car, raced to his aid only to be struck by an oncoming car insured by the first defendant. The assailant having fled, the deceased went to help her. But while he was assisting her a third car insured by the second defendant struck the rear of their stationary car (still containing the two young children). The impact propelled the car forward across the road where it stopped against the side of the bridge. Crying "my children", the deceased started towards the car, but suffered a stroke due to his (not surprisingly) elevated blood pressure from which he died three days later. The first plaintiff sued the first and second defendants on behalf of herself and her children (one of whom, having come of age, became the second plaintiff) for loss of their breadwinner's support.[27] In examining whether liability for the death followed from the finding that the second driver's negligence had caused the collision, Berman AJ in the Cape Provincial Division ruled that although it may not have been reasonably foreseeable that the stationary car might contain children (although it is clear that his Lordship inclined to this view), it was reasonably foreseeable that the owner of the car might be among bystanders clearly visible and that he might well suffer "considerable shock" at seeing his property, that is, his car, badly damaged. Even a threat of injury to a chattel could suffice to ground liability for shock-induced injury if the other essential elements of liability were present.[28]

The recognition of liability for property-related psychiatric harm brings with it the questions whether the property must be owned by the shock claimant and tangible in nature. The former is inextricably interwoven with the relationship issue and has not yet been judicially addressed,[29] but if

25. (1987) 41 DLR (4th) 208.
26. 1982 (4) SA 333 (C).
27. Due to an absence of sufficient proof of the first driver's negligence all claims against the first defendant were dismissed.
28. 1982 (4) SA 333 (C) at 342-343. Note the comments of J M Burchell (1982) *Annual Survey of South African Law*, 176-180.
29. In *O'Sullivan v Williams* [1992] 3 All ER 385 an excavator toppled off a passing trailer and wrote off a car parked outside the plaintiff's home. The car belonged to her boyfriend but she had the right to use it on a regular basis. The County Court judge rejected her

nervous harm be foreseeable there seems no reason why compensation should not be had for injury resulting from damage (or anticipated damage) to the property of a family member, friend or even a bystander. Consider *Campbelltown City Council v Mackay*:[30] it so happened that the plaintiffs were joint owners of the home. Had this not been the case the claim of the spouse who had no property right would presumably have failed, notwithstanding that his or her reaction was as predictable as that of the spouse whose name appeared on the title deeds. The question of the nature of the property is more difficult, but again, once the other prerequisites to liability are present, nothing should turn on whether, for example, the property in question is a car or house, a Ming vase or Stradivarius violin, or an intellectual property right.[31] Nor should the market value of property have any bearing on the issue of liability. The destruction of or damage to commercially valueless but highly treasured or sentimental property is as likely (perhaps more likely) to trigger psychiatric injury as harm to something which could have been sold for a great sum.[32]

Miscellaneous cases

There are other cases which show that shock can be suffered in circumstances not involving a near-accident to the plaintiff or an accident or anticipated accident to another. For example, in *Barnes v Commonwealth*[33] a plaintiff recovered damages for shock caused by a negligently false statement that her husband had been detained in a mental hospital.[34] In *Al-Kandari v J R Brown & Co*[35] a firm of solicitors who negligently allowed a Kuwaiti husband to regain possession of his confiscated passport in circumstances where he was likely to remove his children to Kuwait against the will of his English wife were held liable to her for psychiatric injury resulting from the kidnapping of the children, which was effectuated by ambushing the wife and leaving her bound, gagged and imprisoned in a van. In the United States in *Rowe v Bennett*[36]

29. *Continued*
    claim for psychiatric injury consequent on the damage to the car, but it is clear that had such harm been found to exist liability would not have been denied on the ground that she was not the owner. The psychiatric injury claim was not appealed to the English Court of Appeal, but it would have upheld a claim based on inconvenience, even though the plaintiff was the bailee and not the bailor, had the defendant not already settled with the bailor.
30. (1989) 15 NSWLR 501.
31. Consider, for example, the anguish and shock of an author who wakes one morning to find his book being sold under an assistant's name on the local newspaper stand a few weeks before he was ready to submit the final version to a publisher, or a horticulturist who has devoted years and invested large sums of money in an attempt to produce a unique flower or fruit who discovers her secrets being used to make others rich. Relief granted for any sort of psychiatric harm that arises in these kinds of situations is as justified as that awarded in the more usual accident-related shock cases.
32. Note *Devin v United Services Auto Association* (1992) 8 Cal Rptr 2d 263 where it was stated that negligence which causes only monetary harm does not support an award of emotional distress damages.
33. (1937) 37 SR (NSW) 511.
34. A negligence equivalent of *Wilkinson v Downton* [1897] 2 QB 57. Note also *Bielitski v Obadiak* (1922) 65 DLR 627. See below, p 286.
35. [1988] QB 665.
36. (1986) 514 A 2d 803 (Me).

damages were awarded against an analyst who was counselling the plaintiff over difficulties in her lesbian relationship and who caused the plaintiff emotional distress by herself forming a liaison with her companion.[37] *Vince v Cripps Bakery Pty Ltd*[38] was a case in which a man developed a phobia after realising that he had eaten bread containing a dead mouse. (Mrs Donoghue, of course, did something very similar in a cafe in Paisley some years earlier, but the manufacturer principle in *Donoghue v Stevenson*[39] assumed that she suffered injury as a result of having drunk ginger beer containing the remains of a snail, rather than through shock at having done so.) Caring institutions have been found responsible for psychiatric damage suffered by persons in their care. A nursing home, for example, was held liable in negligence in *Doe v Woodbridge Nursing Pavillion*[40] when a housekeeper raped a patient who suffered post-traumatic stress disorder as a result. In *Mallon v Monklands District Council*[41] psychiatric illness in the form of reactive depression arose from a period of being housed in a refuge for teenagers and a homeless unit. Similar harm developed in *McMullin v F W Woolworth Co Ltd*[42] due to anxiety over two young children infected with a disease akin to typhoid fever as a result of salmonella bacteria transmitted from pet turtles purchased in the defendant's store. A mother sued and recovered in *S v Distillers Co (Biochemicals) Ltd*[43] from the biochemical company responsible for the marketing of the tragically defective drug thalidomide for the "permanent" emotional shock and resultant psychological damage brought about by the trauma and heartbreak of seeing her child born "misshapen and deformed". The daily reminder involved in the mother's care was viewed as possibly aggravating the shock resulting from the birth itself. Two recent Australian cases involve psychiatric damage suffered by public servants. The plaintiff in *Gillespie v Commonwealth*[44] suffered a "panic attack" and anxiety state after being posted to a new embassy in

37. Note also *Marlene F v Affiliated Psychiatric Medical Clinic Inc* (1989) 770 P 2d 278; 257 Cal Rptr 98 (psychologist molested children of plaintiff who was also a patient); *Corgan v Muehling* (1991) 574 NE 2d 602 (Ill) (psychiatrist held liable when he had sexual intercourse with plaintiff under guise of therapy, as a result of which plaintiff forced to undergo further intensive psychotherapy).
38. (1984) Aust Torts Rep 80-668. See also *Young v J D Coates Pty Ltd* (unreported, New South Wales CA, 5 Oct 1990, CA No 171 of 1988) where the plaintiff developed a phobia after eating poisoned apricot kernels. Two similar Canadian cases are *Curll v Robin Hood Multifoods Ltd* (1974) 56 DLR (3d) 129 where the plaintiff was shocked by discovering a partly decomposed mouse in a bag of flour and *Taylor v Weston Bakeries* (1976) 1 CCLT 158 where the shock arose from finding metal and blue mould in bread. See also *Sullivan v H P Hood & Sons* (1960) 168 NE 2d 80 (Mass) (dead mouse in milk); *Way v Tampa Coca Cola Bottling Co* (1972) 260 So 2d 288 (Fla) (plaintiff sucked on rat in bottle of soft drink); *Ford v ALDI Inc* (1992) 832 SW 2d 1 (Mo) (insect in spinach). Note *Ellington v Coca Cola Bottling Co of Tulsa Inc* (1986) 717 P 2d 109 (Okl) where the claimant perceived what she thought was a worm in her drink, but which was in fact a piece of confectionery.
39. [1932] AC 562.
40. (Unreported, Cook County Circuit, Ill, 15 Jan 1992). We thank Professor David Partlett for drawing our attention to this case.
41. 1986 SLT 347.
42. (1974) 9 NBR (2d) 214. Note that the claimant, their mother, failed on the facts.
43. [1969] 3 All ER 1412. Note also *Bagley v North Herts Health Authority* (1986) 136 NLJ 1014; *Kralj v McGrath* [1986] 1 All ER 54; *X and Y v Pal* (1991) 23 NSWLR 26.
44. (1991) 104 ACTR 1.

Venezuela, as a result of conditions there. It was held that the duty of an employer to an employee required that any officer posted to Caracas be given some preparation beyond that appropriate to less stressful posts, but on the facts the defendant had complied with this obligation. In *Wodrow v Commonwealth*[45] the plaintiff, an engineer in the Commonwealth public service, suffered a chronic anxiety neurosis as a result of the treatment he received at the hands of the defendants, and specifically in a minute criticising his failure to prepare a report on the "Fast Frigates Project" according to instructions given, and his work generally over a substantial period. A United States employment example is provided by *Ford v NCNB Corporation*[46] where the negligent loss of a deposit by a bank caused the depositor (who had placed the deposit for his employer) to lose his job. He recovered damages for emotional distress, in spite of the absence of actual or threatened physical contact.

A recent Tasmanian case falling into this diverse category is especially significant in view of the importance now attached to the provision of post-trauma counselling for all those involved in accidents, including witnesses and relief workers. In *Miller v Royal Derwent Hospital Board of Management*[47] a nurse on night duty placed a six-year-old epileptic, who had wet his bed, in a chair, strapping him in with a velcro strap for his own protection. After she went off duty, she was telephoned with the tragic news that the boy had died through moving lower down in the chair and strangling himself on the strap. She was asked to come into the hospital for an interview with the police. The hospital provided no psychiatric counselling, either at that time or afterwards. It is probable that she suffered psychiatric injury immediately on hearing the news, but the failure to provide professional counselling exacerbated it. Zeeman J highlighted the special nature of the case in the following passage:

> "[T]he case is different from the reported cases of nervous shock in that it is not suggested that the initial shock was the product of the defendants' negligence. Rather it is suggested that the plaintiff having suffered nervous shock, the defendants were in breach of their duty of care to the plaintiff in not taking interventional steps which would have prevented that nervous shock leading to mental illness or which would at least have minimised the injurious effect of that nervous shock."[48]

His Honour held that the plaintiff had failed to establish either that this kind of injury was foreseeable in the circumstances of the case, or that the relevant requirements of causation were satisfied.[49] However, there is a clear implication that a duty of care existed and that liability would have arisen had these hurdles been overcome.

These disparate examples serve as a reminder that the scope for psychiatric damage suits is now much wider than was once thought. As we edge towards the 21st century and the common law becomes more comfortable with damage to the mind, we will see the transformation of the

45. (Unreported, Australian Capital Territory SC, 13 Dec 1991, No SC 1 of 1984).
46. (1991) 408 SE 2d 738 (NC).
47. (Unreported, Tasmanian SC, 29 May 1992, No 282 of 1988).
48. Ibid at 17.
49. See above, pp 68-73, 86-88.

structure of negligence claims to incorporate pleas for relief for psychiatric harm in more and more situations where previously legal advisers might not have considered them a feasible option.

Shock caused as the result of an accident to another—variations on the traditional theme

There are cases—and interestingly they are, in the main, Australian cases—in which an accident to another is the essential cause of shock, and yet the facts do not fit Deane J's formula. One possible situation is where the plaintiff's shock arises as the result of the defendant negligently killing, injuring or endangering *himself* or *herself*. Alternatively, the defendant may negligently kill, injure or endanger a third party, and the plaintiff's shock may stem not from fear for the safety of that third party, but from the realisation of what the defendant has or might have done, or that if the circumstances had been different the plaintiff himself or herself might have been in that third party's position. Additionally, psychiatric injury may occur as a result of the mistaken belief that a third party has been harmed, and may be no less impacting than the mental effects of accidents that have in fact occurred. These more unusual situations have occurred in the case law and are considered in turn below.

Shock caused by death, injury or peril to the tortfeasor

The various Australian State Supreme Courts have adopted a very restrictive stance on this particular issue, refusing to entertain any modification of the traditional focus on accident victims other than those whose carelessness led or contributed to their predicament. In *Harrison v State Government Insurance Office*,[50] the plaintiff was a passenger in a car driven by her husband which was involved in an accident due entirely to the husband's carelessness. He died as a result of injuries sustained, the plaintiff suffering minor injuries and subsequently psychiatric damage caused by the trauma of the accident and her husband's death. The wife brought an action against her deceased husband's statutory insurer. Although recovery for psychiatric injury was ultimately allowed on the basis that it was impossible to separate the shock caused by the death from that caused by the trauma of the accident itself, Vasta J of the Supreme Court of Queensland, following Deane J in *Jaensch v Coffey*,[51] ruled that there could be no relief at common law in respect of shock-induced damage caused by physical injury to, or death of, a party responsible for his or her own misfortune. This was so notwithstanding that nervous shock and subsequent illness was a reasonably foreseeable consequence of the husband's death. Some support for this questionable position may also be found in *Dwyer v Dwyer*[52] and *Kohn v State Government Insurance*

50. (1985) Aust Torts Rep 80-723.
51. (1984) 155 CLR 549 at 602, 604, quoted above, p 207.
52. (1969) 90 WN (Pt 2) (NSW) 86 per Wallace P at 88 (Asprey and Mason JJ agreeing). His Honour ruled that a wife owes no duty to her husband not to injure herself. Note, however, *Klug v Motor Accidents Insurance Board* (1991) Aust Torts Rep 81-134, where Zeeman J rejected this as a basis for denying relief for psychiatric damage caused by the death of the tortfeasor.

Commission[53] where Bray CJ considered that "a man or his representatives can hardly be legally responsible for the injurious effect of his own death".[54] The latter case involved the assessment of damages against the statutory insurers of two deceased tortfeasors, the death of one of whom had caused psychiatric damage to the plaintiff (who had also suffered physical injuries). No request was made to Bray CJ to draw a distinction between the defendants as to the quantum of compensation recoverable,[55] thus relegating his Honour's comments to the status of obiter dicta.

This conservative approach was mirrored in the Supreme Court of Tasmania by Zeeman J in *Klug v Motor Accidents Insurance Board*.[56] There the plaintiff was a passenger in a car driven by his de facto wife, when due to her negligence they crashed. She was killed and the plaintiff injured. Compensation for the plaintiff's pathologically grief-stricken condition was refused, inter alia, on the basis that a duty of care did not arise because the injury in question resulted from the death of the negligent party. In this case, unlike *Harrison v State Government Insurance Office*, the psychiatric disorder was clearly not caused by the occurrence of the accident itself, and thus the difficult issue of apportionment between different causes of psychiatric damage was avoided.[57] Significantly, there were indications that, freed from the constraints of precedent, Zeeman J would allow recovery in this type of situation provided the legal prerequisites for liability exist. However, in the absence of any case permitting recovery for psychiatric injury due solely to the death, injury or imperilment of the defendant, his Honour felt compelled to accept that the issue was governed by what he viewed as the policy limitation referred to by Deane J. He did say, however, that as a matter of principle it may be thought that such plaintiffs ought not to be denied relief merely on this basis and, and echoing Deane J, that the common law may ultimately develop to recognise liability in these circumstances.[58]

The defendant in *Rowe v McCartney*[59] also caused serious injuries to himself as a result of his negligent driving of the plaintiff's high powered vehicle with which he was unfamiliar. The case is unusual in that the plaintiff passenger, who was also physically injured, incurred a depressive

53. (1976) 15 SASR 255.
54. Ibid at 256.
55. There was an agreement between the insurers that the same damages were to be awarded in respect of the liability of each of the drivers involved. The absence of such an agreement would, in the light of the position adopted by his Honour, have necessitated a complex adjustment.
56. (1991) Aust Torts Rep 81-134.
57. The psychiatric injury suffered by the plaintiff was sustained either as a result of a feeling of guilt at having let the deceased drive (which was not compensable: see below, pp 21-24, 217), or as a result of the death of the deceased, or both.
58. (1991) Aust Torts Rep 81-134 at 69,274. See *Jaensch v Coffey* (1984) 155 CLR 549 per Deane J at 602. If Zeeman J had granted recovery in this case, a question would have arisen as to the extent to which this represented an infringement of the principle in *Baker v Bolton* (1808) 1 Camp 493; 170 ER 1033 that "in a civil court the death of a human being could not be complained of as an injury", or the *Fatal Accidents Act* 1934 (Tas) under which damages have been interpreted as restricted to pecuniary losses: see above, p 97.
59. [1976] 2 NSWLR 72.

neurosis neither from the perception of her own injuries nor from witnessing or hearing of the defendant's quadriplegia, but from a sense of guilt at having given him permission to drive, aggravated by the fact that the defendant could not recover for his injuries. She failed in her claim for psychiatric damage on the ground that although shock was a reasonably foreseeable consequence of the defendant's negligence, the type of damage she sustained (that is, guilt-induced depressive neurosis) was not.[60] Although it was not alluded to by the New South Wales Court of Appeal, presumably, on the present state of the law, her claim was equally unsustainable because it stemmed from actual physical injury to the defendant responsible for his own predicament rather than physical injury to the plaintiff herself or a third party. The decision was followed in *Klug v Motor Accidents Insurance Board*,[61] Zeeman J ruling that in so far as the plaintiff's pathological grief-stricken condition was the result of his irrational feeling of guilt at having let his wife drive on the day in question, it was not compensable, and that even if the injury was not caused by this, relief was denied because damage did not result from the death of someone other than the careless party.

The basis for this limitation remains obscure. It may be bound up in the nebulous concept of proximity,[62] or stem from pure public policy considerations, or both. Taking a provisional view, Deane J in *Jaensch v Coffey* expressed a preference for the former:

> "[I]t is unnecessary to determine whether [this limitation] is properly to be seen as part of the requirement of proximity of relationship or as constituting some other and special controlling rule based on policy considerations. As at present advised, I am inclined to see [it] as [a] necessary [criterion] of the existence of the requisite proximity of relationship in the sense that, for policy reasons, the relationship will not be adjudged as being 'so' close 'as' to give rise to a duty of care unless [it] be satisfied."[63]

Whatever the true basis for this restriction, it is submitted that it is unwarranted and must be lifted. Why should there be no recovery if a

---

60. See the comments of Moffitt P at 75-76 and Samuels JA at 89-90. Samuels JA held that in addition she failed for want of a causative link between the defendant's negligent driving and her neurosis. Glass JA dissented, opining that it was sufficient in establishing liability that some kind of mental upheaval was reasonably foreseeable, and declined to further qualify or "penetrate" the "type of injury" criterion in the way the majority did. See also *Duwyn v Kaprielian* (1978) 94 DLR (3d) 424 where a parked car containing a four-month-old boy and his grandmother was driven into. No one in the car was physically injured. The boy's mother, who had been shopping nearby, arrived to find a great commotion about her car, heard her son screaming and immediately feared the worst. Psychiatric damage claims were brought against the negligent driver by both the boy (who was particularly disturbed by the incident) and his mother. Applying the test of foreseeability the Ontario Court of Appeal allowed the boy's claim but denied that of the mother, whose emotional damage had been caused by guilt feelings for not having been with her son at the time of the accident. Her shock was rooted in an experience earlier in life when, due to her carelessness, her baby brother had been injured.
61. (1991) Aust Torts Rep 81-134 at 69,271.
62. See N J Mullany, "Proximity, Policy and Procrastination" (1992) 9 Aust Bar Rev 80.
63. (1984) 155 CLR 549 at 604-605. But see *Klug v Motor Accidents Insurance Board* (1991) Aust Torts Rep 81-134 where Zeeman J discusses this restriction in terms of policy considerations. Lords Oliver and Ackner (less explicitly) did likewise in *Alcock v Chief Constable of South Yorkshire Police* [1992] 1 AC 310: see below, pp 219-220.

"recognisable psychiatric illness" is suffered due to the perception of the defendant killing, injuring or placing himself or herself in peril through his or her own carelessness? So long as the nervous injury is genuine and the defendant has caused or contributed to its onset through his or her negligence it should make no difference whether the defendant's carelessness harmed or could have harmed a third party or the defendant himself or herself directly.[64] Consider the situation where a speeding, intoxicated, and helmet-less motorcyclist loses control of his machine, careering head first into a lamp post lining a busy Sydney footpath. He sustains horrific head and facial injuries, remains fully conscious and experiences excruciating agony. For what reason should a pedestrian who witnesses the carnage closehand, viewing the bloody aftermath and hearing the screams of pain, be refused compensation for any "recognisable psychiatric illness" that affects him or her as a result of this emotionally crippling experience?[65] One is reminded also of the dramatic televised suicide by a United States politician not so long ago. Why should relief be denied to viewers who, with no forewarning, witness a distraught man place a gun in his mouth and blow his brains onto the rear wall of his office in all television's technicolour brilliance if they are psychologically damaged as a result of the scene?[66] Well-worn cries of a tidal wave of suits do not wash. Floodgates arguments are rarely, if ever, satisfactory, serving only to illustrate a paucity of reason.[67] Leaving aside for the moment the debate over the medium of communication of the traumatic event,[68] once the danger of a feigned or imagined claim is dispelled by medical evidence there is no logical or convincing public policy argument for preventing a shock action against the estate of such a man by those watchers whose nervous stability has been violated. The fact that there may be a considerable number of persons affected in this manner is not to the point. Defendants must be made to accept full responsibility, including full legal liability for

64. Although rescue cases normally involve three parties, it seems clear that a person injured as a result of his or her own negligence also owes a duty of care to a rescuer not to cause physical loss. In *Chapman v Hearse* (1961) 106 CLR 112, B, a doctor, was killed by C's negligent driving when aiding another motorist, A, who had negligently injured himself. It was held that A owed a duty to B and that C could recover contribution from A. Note also *Harrison v British Railways Board* [1981] 3 All ER 679. Similarly, in *Horsley v MacLaren* (1972) 22 DLR (3d) 545, A fell overboard from a yacht due to his own negligence and B was drowned trying to save him. Though the court was not called upon to decide the issue, it seems that A would have been liable to B. If, instead of being fatally injured or suffering bodily harm, a rescuer suffers mental damage, should he or she be treated any differently than in the more usual three party situation where recovery for psychiatric illness is allowed? (See above, pp 108-111.) It is submitted that no such distinction should be drawn.

65. Note *R v Criminal Injuries Compensation Board; Ex parte Webb* [1986] QB 184 per Watkins LJ at 196: "The trespasser who commits suicide on the railway may well be in breach of a duty of care owed to the driver of and the passengers on the train; his action may result in the driver suffering from depression and in passengers being injured." See also the example given by Trindade, op cit, n 3 at 481-482.

66. It should make no difference in this situation that the act in question was intentional rather than negligent. On the intentional infliction of psychiatric harm, see below, Chapter 14.

67. Note the short shrift they received in eg *McLoughlin v O'Brian* [1983] 1 AC 410: see above, p 174, n 120. See also H Teff, "Liability for Negligently Inflicted Nervous Shock" (1983) 99 LQR 100 at 111-112.

68. Above, pp 153-183.

all loss caused or contributed to by their failures. What is needed is an authoritative statement that recovery extends to cases where the plaintiff's psychiatric illness results from the actual or anticipated death or injury of the defendant himself or herself. At the very least, there should be no categorical bar in relation to claims of this nature.

At least one Law Lord has appreciated the illogicality of an unqualified denial of relief in this situation. Although the question of liability on the part of an injured tortfeasor or his or her estate for psychiatric injury caused to another as a result of a self-inflicted death, injury or imperilment did not fall to be determined in *Alcock v Chief Constable of South Yorkshire Police*, interestingly Lords Ackner and Oliver alluded to it.[69] Lord Oliver was clearly unimpressed by the inflexible and restrictive approach. No English case has squarely raised this issue, but significantly Lord Robertson in *Bourhill v Young's Executor*[70] did not view with favour the suggestion that a negligent window-cleaner who loses his grip and falls from a height, impaling himself on spiked railings, would be liable for the shock-induced psychiatric harm occasioned to a pregnant woman observing the scene from the window of her house on the opposite side of the street. It was perhaps on this basis that Lord Oliver predicted that policy considerations would lead an English court to adopt the Deane formula should the facts before it demand a ruling on the issue.[71] That said, his Lordship's further comments, uttered obiter, do offer some hope for the kind of doctrinal development and accommodation referred to by Zeeman J in *Klug v Motor Accidents Insurance Board*.[72] Reference was made to the insurmountable difficulties that the exclusory approach brings with respect to the application of defences to shock claims. Complications would ensue, for example, if an accident, although not solely caused as a result of the primary victim's lack of care, is materially contributed to by it. As Lord Oliver said:

> "If, for instance, the primary victim is himself 75 per cent responsible for the accident, it would be a curious and wholly unfair situation if the plaintiff were enabled to recover damages for his or her traumatic injury from the person responsible only in a minor degree whilst he in turn remained unable to recover any contribution from the person primarily responsible since the latter's negligence vis-à-vis the plaintiff would not even have been tortious."[73]

In addition to this specific concern, his Lordship was troubled with the restriction at a more general level. He considered it fundamentally flawed from the standpoints of principle and logic:

> "[T]he limitation must be based upon policy rather than upon logic for the suffering and shock of a wife or mother at witnessing the death of her husband or son is just as immediate, just as great and just as foreseeable whether the accident be due to the victim's own or to another's negligence and if the claim is based, as it must be, on the

69. [1992] 1 AC 310 per Lord Ackner at 401, per Lord Oliver at 418.
70. 1941 SC 395 at 399.
71. [1992] 1 AC 310 at 418. Surprisingly, no mention was made of any of the other Australian cases in point.
72. (1991) Aust Torts Rep 81-134 at 69,274.
73. [1992] 1 AC 310 at 418.

combination of proximity and foreseeability, there is certainly no logical reason why a remedy should be denied in such a case. . . . Take, for instance, the case of a mother who suffers shock and psychiatric injury through witnessing the death of her son when he negligently walks in front of an oncoming motor car. If liability is to be denied in such a case such denial can only be because the policy of the law forbids such a claim, for it is difficult to visualise a greater proximity or a greater degree of foreseeability."[74]

As noted above, we would suggest that the boundaries of the duty of care owed by all persons in their actions to third parties should not be erected so as to automatically exclude claims of this nature and that there are, as well as no reasons of principle or logic, no sound policy arguments for their exclusion. Significantly, Lord Oliver does not even particularise the policy he sees as militating against these claims. This arbitrary limitation cannot, it is submitted, be convincingly defended on any ground.

Shock caused by anxiety for the tortfeasor's position

Are the prospects of recovery diminished in the slightly different situation where a person suffers psychiatric damage due only to a concern about what the tortfeasor has or might have done because of his or her failure to take care rather than concern for a third party victim of that failure? Normally anxiety of this nature is absent because the parties to the action are unknown to each other, but it is feasible that a claimant may be psychologically injured through worrying about a defendant, particularly if they are related. Apprehension-induced mental injury of this sort appears to have been sustained by the plaintiff in *Stergiou v Stergiou*.[75] She was a rear seat passenger in a car driven by her husband, the defendant, which, due to his negligence, struck a cyclist at an intersection. The accident was very minor in nature leaving the cyclist with no significant physical injuries. However, the plaintiff claimed that at the material time she thought the cyclist had been killed, and suffered nervous shock due to anxiety that her husband may have been responsible for someone's death.[76] Although on the facts the wife failed in her claim, Gallop J of the Supreme Court of the Australian Capital Territory did not rule out the possibility that liability could arise in this situation. What if the plaintiff's concern for the tortfeasor extends to a fear of the unpleasant consequences which might befall him or her as a result of his or her carelessness? A wife may, for example, worry not only that her husband has killed another, but that he may lose his licence, have to stand trial, be fined and/or imprisoned and that such ordeals will place enormous financial burdens on them both. It is unclear from the facts in *Stergiou v Stergiou* whether the plaintiff's "fright and anxiety" that her husband might have killed the cyclist included fear and worry of the consequences likely to follow from this, but there

74. Ibid.
75. (1987) Aust Torts Rep 80-082.
76. It is not absolutely clear from the transcript whether the wife was worried that a third party may have been killed or solely by the fact that her husband may have been a killer. It appears most likely, however, that the latter consideration was the source of her concern.

seems no reason why a line ought to be drawn against recovery in these circumstances. Again, once the true basis of recovery in a claim for nervous shock is appreciated, that is, compensation for "recognisable psychiatric illness", it becomes evident that the nature of the particular injury-inducing phenomenon is unimportant. Provided the emotional response of plaintiffs in either of these circumstances is intensified to a degree exceeding that commonly experienced in distressing situations and to the point where it is psychologically debilitating,[77] it is submitted that these kinds of nervous shock claims should be as maintainable as a claim involving the perception of the death of, or injury to, the plaintiff's relatives. In truth, it should make no difference to the likelihood of success at common law whether the facts reveal a two or three (or more) party interaction. Nor should it matter whether, in a two party situation, the psychiatric damage is caused through the perception of the death, injury or imperilment of the defendant, concern over the results of the defendant's negligence or worry over what the future holds for him or her.

Shock caused by the realisation of what may have happened to the plaintiff

So too, there seems no logical or sound policy reason why recovery should be refused where the plaintiff suffers nervous shock and resulting mental damage not from the perception of the death, injury or imperilment of a loved one or of the plaintiff's own injuries or peril, but from the realisation of what might have happened to him or her. This is the "lucky escape" or "close call" situation, but it differs from the "near miss" cases[78] in that here the plaintiff suffers shock not from the perception of a narrow avoidance of death or injury to another but from the realisation of his or her own good fortune and what might have been. The unique case of *Wilks v Haines*[79] reveals just this type of injury-producing stimulus. There the plaintiff was a dormitory supervisor in a school for handicapped children. Although rostered for night duty on a particular evening she organised a switch with a colleague so that she was not on duty that night. During the early hours of her free evening a crazed intruder broke in and murdered two of the three supervisors on duty and injured the third. When told of the attack the plaintiff claimed that she suffered nervous shock, not because of the death of and injury to her workmates, but as a result of it having dawned upon her that had she not altered her schedule she would have suffered a similar fate. Although the proceedings were ultimately struck out some interesting comments were made by Loveday J. Focus was again (mis)placed on the cause of the mental disorder. Alluding to the unusual nature of the action, his Honour opined that, as a matter of policy, the "proper stopping place" for recovery for nervous shock was short of the circumstances in this case, convinced that appellate courts would be of the same view. Why, one might ask, if the requisite criterion necessary to give rise to a duty of care were present and the plaintiff did in fact genuinely

---

77. On the evidence this was not the case in *Stergiou v Stergiou* (1987) Aust Torts Rep 80-082.
78. See eg *Dooley v Cammell Laird & Co Ltd* [1951] 1 Lloyd's Rep 271: *King v Phillips* [1953] 1 QB 429; *Galt v British Railways Board* (1983) 133 NLJ 870.
79. (1991) Aust Torts Rep 81-078.

suffer a compensable injury due to the defendant's carelessness? Significantly, the nature of the policy dictating this result was not articulated. It is our view that prevailing social circumstances and public attitudes do not suggest that the line be drawn here. The courts must break free completely of the shackles of traditionalism and extreme over-caution as well as the persisting scepticism surrounding claims of this nature. What difference does it make whether the catalyst for the development of psychological disorders was the shock of learning of the fate of others or the realisation of one's own lucky escape from similar misfortune? Irrelevant distinctions of this nature must not be allowed to hinder the development of sound and consistent principle in this context. Loveday J recognised as much by refusing to regard the "it could have been me" type of shock as an absolute bar to recovery, rather viewing it as adding "another dimension to the application of the foreseeability and/or the proximity test".[80]

Shock caused by imagined harm to a third party

In all the varied situations so far dealt with, there actually was an accident to another which affected the plaintiff's mind. But psychiatric harm is dependent upon what the sufferer *believes* has happened, not what has in fact taken place. Shock victims who genuinely and honestly believe that they have killed or injured another are for all intents and purposes in the same position as if the imagined facts were true. A North Carolina court was confronted with this issue in *Williamson v Bennett*.[81] The plaintiff's car collided with that of the defendant. The plaintiff mistook the sound of the collision as indicating that she had run over a small child on a bicycle,[82] an assumption no doubt attributable to a similar accident involving her brother-in-law a month earlier being in the forefront of her mind. Her mental condition deteriorated markedly as a result. In a strained application of the then-prevalent zone of danger rule, the court held that her psychic conversion reaction was uncompensable because it was caused by concern for the safety of another.[83] Nothing turned on the fact that the source of the complaint had been imaginary. Even if one concedes that the zone of danger rule is, or once was, a sound approach to cases where there actually was an accident perceived by a bystander, to apply it to the scenario under examination is misguided. This issue aside, and assuming that any

80. Ibid at 68,657.
81. (1960) 112 SE 2d 48 (NC). See Comment, "Negligence and the Infliction of Emotional Harm: A Reappraisal of the Nervous Shock Cases" (1968) 35 U Chi L Rev 512.
82. Contrast *Stergiou v Stergiou* (1987) Aust Torts Rep 80-082 where the wife made a mistake as to the *severity* of the harm inflicted by her husband on a cyclist, as distinct from its existence. Note also the slightly different situation that arose in *English v Cory Sand & Ballast Co* (unreported, QBD, 21 Mar 1985) where a driver whose dumper truck fell into a quarry mistakenly thought his passenger was dead and developed a permanent reactive depression. He recovered damages. Unlike Mrs Stergiou, he also suffered personal injury in the accident.
83. See the similar reasoning in *Kaufman v Miller* (1967) 414 SW 2d 164 (Tex) where evidence was led that the plaintiff's conversion reaction neurosis suffered in a minor collision was linked to a very serious accident two years beforehand when his truck had jack-knifed and started a fire which killed three people. Realising that he had been unable to avoid another accident, he became neurotic.

problems presented by special susceptibility to mental harm could have been overcome, there should have been no barriers to her suit. Provided that mistaken belief can be proved to be genuine and honestly held, and causative of psychiatric injury, these types of case should be treated the same as any other.

Other possible situations

The circumstances discussed above do not exhaust the possible instances where psychiatric injury may be inflicted through tortious conduct. The instances reviewed under the second and third headings, like the standard bystander case, involve the reaction of an observer to an injury inflicted on another by the tortfeasor. It is however perfectly possible to have a situation where there is another link in the chain of causation. For example, one bystander may suffer psychiatric damage at the sight of the collapse of another bystander as a result of viewing the initial accident. The Pennsylvania case of *Scarf v Koltof*[84] comes very close to this situation. A husband was struck by a negligent motorist as he crossed the street. His wife, who was nearby, but not in any personal danger, saw the accident and suffered a heart attack from which she died two months later. The husband sued for damages not only for his own injuries but also for the fatal injury to his wife, bringing both a wrongful death action and a claim on behalf of her estate. The Pennsylvania Superior Court used the "zone of danger" limitation to deny liability for the wife's injuries, but proceeded to try the husband's own action. So far as can be ascertained from the report, the husband's claim did not include any allegation of shock damage. But what if, in a scene reminiscent of the fifth act of *Romeo and Juliet*, he had recovered consciousness only to see his wife in a state of collapse, and suffered nervous injury himself in consequence? The issue would be whether a tortfeasor can be expected to foresee that if he negligently injures A and thereby causes psychiatric damage to a bystander, B, another bystander might suffer a similar injury through seeing what happened to B. Such a situation should not be beyond the limits of foreseeability. Theoretically it should make no difference if the second bystander, as in the postulated situation based on *Scarf v Koltof*, was in fact the original accident victim, except that a court otherwise disinclined to allow recovery may invoke the doctrine of consequential damage and the principles espoused in cases such as *Schneider v Eisovitch*.[85]

---

84. (1976) 363 A 2d 1276 (Pa).
85. [1960] 2 QB 430: see above, pp 156-159.

10

THE SUSCEPTIBLE PLAINTIFF

The rule

It is not uncommon for defendants facing psychiatric damage claims to protest that the claimant has no cause of action because he or she is possessed of so unusual a character or disposition as to be of abnormal mental personality. Do those victims of negligently inflicted psychiatric damage who are particularly susceptible to psychiatric illness as a result of some pre-existing defect in their emotional make-up face any greater hurdles to recovery than plaintiffs of ordinary disposition?

Irrespective of whether the claimant is particularly sensitive or robust the start position in assessing liability for shock is identical, namely reasonable foreseeability of injury as a result of the tortfeasor's negligent breach of duty.[1] Clearly, there can be no recovery if this criterion is absent. In determining this question reference has been made to the hypothetical person of ordinary resilience and "phlegm" rather than to those possessed of greater or less fortitude than the general population. In *Bourhill v Young*[2] Lords Wright and Porter were clearly of the view that it would be unreasonable to expect defendants to bear in mind the extraordinarily sensitive victim. There the plaintiff, who was a woman in the latter stages of pregnancy, suffered nervous shock and subsequently gave birth to a stillborn child after hearing a collision involving a motorcyclist who was killed. Lord Wright stated:

> "What is now being considered is the question of liability, and this, I think, in a question whether there is a duty owing to members of the public who come within the ambit of the act, must generally depend on a normal standard of susceptibility. . . . It is here, as elsewhere, a question of what the hypothetical reasonable man, viewing the position, I suppose ex post facto, would say it was proper to foresee. What danger of particular infirmity that would include must depend on all the circumstances, but generally, I think, a reasonably normal condition, if medical evidence is capable of defining it, would be the standard. The test of a plaintiff's extraordinary susceptibility, if unknown to the defendant, would in effect make him an insurer."[3]

Similarly, Lord Porter considered:

> "It is not every emotional disturbance or every shock which should have been foreseen. The driver of a car or vehicle, even though careless, is entitled to assume that the ordinary frequenter of the streets has sufficient fortitude to endure such incidents as may from time to

1. See above, pp 64-73.
2. [1943] AC 92.
3. Ibid at 110.

224

time be expected to occur in them, including the noise of a collision and the sight of injury to others, and is not to be considered negligent towards one who does not possess the customary phlegm."[4]

In *Jaensch v Coffey*[5] Brennan J also opined that this threshold enquiry is based on normal standards of susceptibility. His Honour stated:

"[R]easonable foreseeability is an objective criterion of duty, and a general standard of susceptibility must be postulated. . . . Some general guidelines apply. The first guideline is this: the question 'whether there is a duty owing to members of the public who come within the ambit of the act, must generally depend on a normal standard of susceptibility'. . . . Unless a plaintiff's extraordinary susceptibility to psychiatric illness induced by shock is known to the defendant, the existence of a duty of care owed to the plaintiff is to be determined upon the assumption that he is of a normal standard of susceptibility."[6]

Gibbs CJ simply proceeded on the basis that shock-induced psychiatric injury "is not recoverable unless an ordinary person of normal fortitude in the position of the plaintiff would have suffered some shock".[7]

Significantly, in assessing whether some species of psychiatric illness are predictable, the existence of any special circumstance likely to render a shock-inducing event particularly emotionally damaging, such as a blood relationship between an accident victim and an observer, is to be taken into account. Brennan J has offered this guideline stating:

4. Ibid at 117. The same view has long been held in the United States: see *Spade v Lynn & B Rail Co* (1897) 47 NE 88 (Mass) per Allen J at 89: "Not only the transportation of passengers and the running of trains, but the general conduct of business and of the ordinary affairs of life, must be done on the assumption that persons who are liable to be affected thereby are not peculiarly sensitive, and are of ordinary physical and mental strength. If, for example, a traveller is sick or infirm, delicate in health, specially nervous or emotional, liable to be upset by slight causes, and therefore requiring precautions which are not usual or practicable for travelling in general, notice should be given, so that, if reasonably practicable, arrangements may be made accordingly, and extra care be observed. But as a general rule a carrier of passengers is not bound to anticipate or to guard against an injurious result which would only happen to a person of peculiar sensitiveness." This statement was quoted by Phillimore J in *Dulieu v White & Sons* [1901] 2 KB 669 at 685-686, who added: "Aliter in this case, where the plaintiff is not a passenger or a traveller." For more recent affirmations see eg *Williamson v Bennett* (1960) 112 SE 2d 48 (NC); *Kaufman v Miller* (1967) 414 SW 2d 164 (Tex). Note also Lord Hunter's words in *Currie v Wardrop*, 1927 SC 538 at 550: "As regards an occurrence . . . at a football match, it might, I think, there be perfectly truly said that any person with nerves of insufficient strength to witness such a contest had better stay at home and not go to the field at all."
5. (1984) 155 CLR 549.
6. Ibid at 568.
7. Ibid at 556. Note that the respondent in this case had, before her marriage, led an unhappy and deprived life, suffering abuse as a child. By reason of these events she was more than usually dependent on both her husband and the stability of her marriage, with the consequence that she had an exceptional predisposition to "neurotic upset, anxiety and depression". However, the trial judge held that her predisposition was controlled and that she was a person of normal fortitude. That finding made it right, the High Court ruled, to infer that the threshold inquiry had been established. See Deane J's comments at 609-610.

"[I]f it is reasonably foreseeable that the phenomenon might be perceived by a person or class of persons for whom it has a special significance—for example, the parent of a child injured in a road accident who comes upon the scene—the question whether it is reasonably foreseeable that the perception of the phenomenon by that person or a member of that class might induce a psychiatric illness must be decided in the light of the heightened susceptibility which the special significance of the phenomenon would be expected to produce."[8]

On the "ordinary phlegm" view, where "normal" folk would not foreseeably have suffered harm the unusually sensitive victim has no prospect of recovery unless it can be shown that the defendant knew or ought to have known of his or her sensitivity.[9] Imposing liability where there is evidence of special knowledge alerting the tortfeasor to the secondary victim's particular susceptibility is justifiable since accountability flows from the application of the "reasonable man" test to the particular defendant's circumstances, including the circumstances of his or her knowledge. It must be remembered that in this situation the relevant threshold test is the foreseeability of psychiatric injury to the *plaintiff* (or a person in *his or her* position), not the foreseeability of harm to the average citizen. The defendant will, however, seldom be possessed of such knowledge, with the result that actionable negligence will rarely arise where persons of a normal nervous resolve would have remained unaffected by the defendant's actions. In *Miller v Royal Derwent Hospital Board of Management*[10] Zeeman J, in considering the liability of a hospital authority to a nurse for psychiatric damage alleged to have been caused by failure to provide professional counselling following the death of a patient which the nurse had unwittingly brought about, referred to aspects of the plaintiff's personal history which might have suggested that she was a person particularly vulnerable to traumatic events. However he held that since the defendants were ignorant of this, the duty owed to the plaintiff was to be determined on the basis that she was a person of normal susceptibility.

Problems

Judging liability by reference to the standard of a reasonable person of ordinary firmness is problematic in a number of respects. It has been questioned, for example, whether injury to unusually susceptible plaintiffs is always unforeseeable. It may not, in particular circumstances, be unreasonable to demand that persons keep those with peculiar emotional sensitivities in mind. The likelihood of the presence of a pregnant and therefore particularly sensitive woman, for example, in the vicinity of the

8. Ibid at 568-569. See also *Miller v Royal Derwent Hospital Board of Management* (unreported, Tasmanian SC, 29 May 1992, No 282 of 1988) per Zeeman J at 17.
9. See *Bourhill v Young* [1943] AC 92 per Lord Wright at 110; *Jaensch v Coffey* (1984) 155 CLR 549 per Brennan J at 568; *Mount Isa Mines Ltd v Pusey* (1970) 125 CLR 383 per Windeyer J at 406-407. Note also *Bunyan v Jordan* (1936) 36 SR (NSW) 350 per Jordan CJ at 355-356 and P G Heffey, "The Negligent Infliction of Nervous Shock in Road and Industrial Accidents" (1974) 48 ALJ 196, 240 at 245.
10. (Unreported, Tasmanian SC, 29 May 1992, No 282 of 1988).

tortfeasor's act or its aftermath is high.[11] So too is the possibility of the presence of those vulnerable persons recovering from some personal loss, traumatic experience or grieving in relation to some previous matter. The point is that it is not inevitably correct to catalogue scenarios of this nature as beyond the bounds of reasonable foresight.

It is the inherent difficulty of determining what is to be viewed as a "normal standard of susceptibility" which raises the most concern with a rule which often operates to deny relief to supersensitive persons. In truth, there is a widely varying threshold of individual tolerance to psychiatric disturbance. Lord Wright himself acknowledged the vagueness of the test, ruling out a more precise definition for fear of undesirable limitations,[12] a somewhat ironic rationale given the insurmountable obstacle to recovery this standard can present for the special claimant. The artificial distinction necessitated by this test has not gone unnoticed either in England or Australia. In *Chadwick v British Railways Board*,[13] a rescue case involving a rail disaster, Waller J stressed that:

"The community is not formed of normal citizens, with all those who are less susceptible or more susceptible to stress to be regarded as extraordinary. There is an infinite variety of creatures, all with varying susceptibilities."[14]

Although the susceptibility issue did not arise on the facts, Windeyer J in *Mount Isa Mines Ltd v Pusey*[15] was also moved to emphasise that:

11. Indeed in *Bourhill v Young's Executor*, 1941 SC 395 at 438 Aitchison LJC described it as "almost . . . an obvious fact". See also *Mann Boudoir Car Co v Dupre* (1893) 54 F 646 per McCormick J at 652: "This theory . . . would require every pregnant woman to refrain from travel"; *Watt v Rama* [1972] VR 353 per Winneke CJ and Pape J at 360; Heffey, op cit, n 9 at 241-242. Note *Haley v London Electricity Board* [1965] AC 778 where the plaintiff, who was blind, suffered injury through falling into a trench in the street which had been excavated by the defendants. The Board had taken precautions sufficient to protect ordinary sighted passers-by, but they were inadequate to ensure the safety of blind people. The House of Lords held that the number of blind people going about the streets of London alone (there were over 7,300 blind people registered in the London area) was sufficient to require the defendants to have them in contemplation and to take appropriate precautions.
12. *Bourhill v Young* [1943] AC 92 at 110.
13. [1967] 1 WLR 912.
14. Ibid at 922. The problem of drawing this line is also illustrated by *Cook v Swinfen* [1967] 1 WLR 457 where a plaintiff prone to breakdowns suffered nervous shock when, owing to her solicitor's negligence, divorce proceedings did not progress as expected. The English Court of Appeal considered such deterioration in health to be an unforeseeable consequence of the defendant's failure, treating the plaintiff as particularly susceptible to nervous shock. Similarly, in *Duwyn v Kaprielian* (1978) 94 DLR (3d) 424 a mother's shock and extreme hysterical reaction at coming upon an accident scene involving her screaming young son (who was in fact physically unharmed) was not viewed as reasonably foreseeable. It could be attributed to a particular hypersensitivity to emotional upset stemming from an earlier traumatic experience involving injury to her two-year-old brother. For an example of a case where the court drew the line in favour of the plaintiff see *Dooley v Cammell Laird & Co Ltd* [1951] 1 Lloyd's Rep 271: Donovan J viewed the existence of pre-accident neurasthenia, which was worsened and accelerated by the accident, as irrelevant to the question of liability (although it did bear on the assessment of damages issue: see below, p 273).
15. (1970) 125 CLR 383.

"The idea of a man of normal emotional fibre, as distinct from a man sensitive, susceptible and more easily disturbed emotionally and mentally, is I think imprecise and scientifically inexact. . . .

However, I need say no more about the position of persons prone to suffer shock, for the present plaintiff is not such a person. I wish only to guard myself for the future by saying that, as at present advised, I am not convinced that the defendant in cases of this sort can escape liability simply by showing that, unknown to him, a person who has suffered harm was easily harmed." [16]

His Honour did, however, qualify his views, conceding the possibility that public policy may in some circumstances dictate a refusal of relief for supersensitive sufferers. Leaving the question open, Windeyer J stated:

"What I have said relates only to cases such as the present, industrial actions—or to road accidents, resulting from negligence. I do not doubt that in some other situations the policy of the law prevents a man being liable for nervous shock suffered by susceptible persons. That is because men are not expected to go about their lawful occasions in such a way that they will not disturb the peace of mind of persons easily upset, unless in particular cases they were aware, or should have been aware, of the frailty and susceptibility of a 'neighbour'." [17]

The delicate nature of the classification task left to the courts is compounded by the uncertainty as to whether the hypothetical "normal" citizen is possessed of any of the particularities of the claimant in question. Do, for example, the courts look to the emotional disposition of the ordinary child or elderly pensioner if the victim of psychiatric injury is among these classes? Or is it the case that such plaintiffs will always be viewed as being of particular susceptibility and therefore more unlikely to recover? It is submitted that the former view must prevail and the circumstances of the individual claimant must be considered if the "ordinary phlegm" approach is utilised. This appears to have been the attitude of the Ontario Court of Appeal in *Duwyn v Kaprielian* [18] which considered that a four-month-old plaintiff could not, on the basis of his young age alone, be categorised as abnormally sensitive. Some support for this approach may also be gleaned from Vasta J's focus in *Mellor v Moran* [19] on the fact that the death of the plaintiff child's mother occurred "when [she] was at an age when children are particularly vulnerable" and his rejection of the contention that damages for psychiatric harm to children should be lower than those awarded to adults because a child is, on one view, more emotionally resilient than an adult.

Despite the reservations raised by some judges and the difficulties of distinction associated with the utilisation of the normally robust person test as a standard for the determination of the existence of a duty of care, this approach has prevailed in both England and Australia. In *Brice v Brown* [20] the plaintiff had had a hysterical personality disorder since early childhood,

16. Ibid at 405-406. Note also Barwick CJ's comments at 390.
17. Ibid at 406-407.
18. (1978) 94 DLR (3d) 424 per Morden JA at 439-440.
19. (1985) 2 MVR 461 at 462-463.
20. [1984] 1 All ER 997, noted by C Gearty [1984] CLJ 238.

but this manifested itself only rarely, enabling her to lead a happy and socially accepted life. Things changed when a taxi in which she and her daughter were passengers collided with a bus. This caused her mental state to worsen considerably, leading to bizarre behaviour including attempts to commit suicide and pleading with people to cut her head off, periodically disappearing for weeks on end (when she probably behaved like a prostitute), spending most of her time in one room, eating food left out for her by her family and urinating on the floor. Stuart-Smith J held that she was entitled to damages in respect of all the consequences of the accident, but only on the basis that in the circumstances the defendant should have foreseen psychiatric injury to her, classifying the plaintiff for this purpose as a person of normal disposition and phlegm. [21] This attitude was confirmed recently in Queensland in *Chapman v Lear*. [22] There a Vietnam veteran predisposed to psychiatric illness as a result of a permanent post-traumatic stress disorder due to his war experiences suffered a psychological disturbance and severe personality upheaval after being told of his son's accident and seeing him in a post-operative state in hospital. Although the son ultimately recovered without any ill effects, the plaintiff was awarded $15,000 for the shock-induced aggravation of his personality disorder. [23] Williams J accepted the statements made in *Jaensch v Coffey*, [24] ruling that, given the existence of the father-son relationship, it was reasonably foreseeable by the defendant that some psychiatric injury to an ordinary person in the plaintiff's position would result as a consequence of his negligent infliction of injury to the boy.

The talem qualem rule

At first glance, the normal susceptibility standard appears irreconcilable with the long established principle of negligence that a tortfeasor must take his or her victim talem qualem—that is, the wrongdoer must take the injured party as he or she finds him or her. [25] The locus classicus for this

---

21. Ibid at 1006-7. See also eg *McLoughlin v O'Brian* [1983] 1 AC 410 per Lord Russell at 429, per Lord Bridge at 436-437; *Attia v British Gas Plc* [1988] QB 304 per Dillon LJ at 311 (where the plaintiff was assumed to be, for the purposes of the determination of a preliminary issue, of normal disposition).
22. (Unreported, Queensland SC, 8 Apr 1988, No 3732 of 1984). But see *Petrie v Dowling* [1992] 1 Qd R 284 at 287 where Kneipp J was of the view that, in contrast to the English courts, the High Court could not be said to have finally decided that proof that the plaintiff is of normal fortitude is a condition of recovery. With respect, it is submitted that the better view is that their Honours' statements in *Jaensch v Coffey* (1984) 155 CLR 549 do in fact identify this as a prerequisite to relief, save where the plaintiff's special susceptibilities are known: see above, pp 225-226.
23. The court noted that other events subsequent to the accident would have contributed to the aggravation of the plaintiff's condition, eg his daughter's fall from her bicycle causing a blood clot requiring neurosurgery, but these had occurred subsequent to the commencement of proceedings and in any event the plaintiff subconsciously attributed all his disabilities to his son's accident. Williams J rejected the contention that the accident to the boy was responsible for a nervous breakdown suffered three years later. The medical evidence revealed that the aggravation of his disorder caused by the son's accident would have dissipated by that time and that the later breakdown was entirely due to his combat service.
24. (1984) 155 CLR 549 per Brennan J at 568-569, quoted above, p 226.
25. See the concern expressed by Windeyer J in *Mount Isa Mines Ltd v Pusey* (1970) 125 CLR 383 at 406 at the apparent conflict between limiting actions to those possessed of normal mental makeup and the eggshell skull rule.

rule is the judgment of Kennedy J in *Dulieu v White & Sons*.[26] His Lordship stated:

"If a man is negligently run over or otherwise negligently injured in his body, it is no answer to the sufferer's claim for damages that he would have suffered less injury, or no injury at all, if he had not had an unusually thin skull or an unusually weak heart."[27]

These seemingly conflicting concepts do however lie comfortably side by side. It is clear that a claim for nervous shock is not actionable until the plaintiff incurs psychiatric damage caused, or contributed to, by the tortfeasor as a result of a breach of a duty or duties owed by him or her to the plaintiff. Only once this has been proved is the defendant bound to take the victim as he or she finds him or her. As Johnson JA stated in the Canadian case of *Pollard v Makarchuk*, "susceptibility to injury of a particular type creates no liability where liability does not otherwise exist."[28]

In establishing the necessary causal link it must be borne in mind that the doctrine comes into operation only where the defendant's carelessness aggravates or triggers the plaintiff's vulnerability so as to produce the shock-induced injury. Where the psychiatric damage itself pre-exists the initial wrong it cannot be attributed to the tortfeasor.[29] Nor can he or she be liable in respect of the aggravation of the plaintiff's injury if the negligent conduct merely accelerated rather than caused it.[30] With respect to the duty of care component of liability, the criterion of reasonable foreseeability is of particular importance in this context. If it is reasonably foreseeable that persons of normal emotional character in the plaintiff's position would be mentally injured by the defendant's action, recovery will not be denied because the plaintiff in question has suffered a greater loss due to his or her less than ordinary nervous fortitude. Thus, although the "thin skull" rule cannot operate to avoid or override the initial requirement of foreseeability of actionable damage, it can operate to extend liability to

26. [1901] 2 KB 669. See also *Smith v Leech Brain & Co Ltd* [1962] 2 QB 405; *Beavis v Apthorpe* (1962) 80 WN (NSW) 852; *Robinson v Post Office* [1974] 1 WLR 1176; *Nader v Urban Transit Authority of New South Wales* (1985) 2 NSWLR 501. The *Wagon Mound (No 1)* [1961] AC 388 remoteness test in no way displaces this principle. See generally A M Linden, "Down with Foreseeability! Of Thin Skulls and Rescuers" (1969) 47 Can BR 545; P J Rowe, "The Demise of the Thin Skull Rule?" (1977) 40 MLR 377. The leading United States authority is *Vosburg v Putney* (1891) 50 NW 403 (Wis). For a recent discussion see the judgment of Posner J in *Stoleson v United States* (1983) 708 F 2d 1217, especially at 1220-3.
27. [1901] 2 KB 669 at 679. See also eg *Chester v Council of the Municipality of Waverley* (1939) 62 CLR 1 per Latham CJ at 9, per Evatt J at 26. For a United States perspective see *Purcell v St Paul City Rail Co* (1892) 50 NW 1034 (Minn); *Sloane v Southern California Rail Co* (1896) 44 P 320 (Cal).
28. (1958) 16 DLR (2d) 225 at 230. See also *Bourhill v Young* [1943] AC 92 at 109-110 where Lord Wright remarked, after adverting to certain forms of hypersensitivity, "these questions go to 'culpability', not 'compensation' "; *Bester v Commercial Union Versekeringsmaatskappy van SA Bpk*, 1973 (1) SA 769 (A) per Botha JA at 779; *Masiba v Constantia Insurance Co Ltd*, 1982 (4) SA 333 (C) per Berman JA at 342.
29. *Jobling v Associated Dairies* [1982] AC 794.
30. *Cutler v Vauxhall Motors Ltd* [1971] 1 QB 418; *Zumeris v Testa* [1972] VR 839. Where the pre-existing tendency would inevitably have affected the plaintiff, the defendant is liable only for the acceleration. In most cases, however, the tortfeasor will have made certain what was merely hypothetical, thereby entitling the plaintiff to relief.

embrace the additional and unforeseen aggravated sequels of the foreseeable injury that are attributable to the secondary victim's vulnerability. In *Chester v Council of the Municipality of Waverley*,[31] Evatt J, in a strong dissent, stated:

> "A duty to take care to avoid injuring a person who has some peculiar physical or nervous weakness may be brought into existence where the special circumstances are known to the defendant. But where a class or group may be endangered by carelessness, the defendant's sphere of duty can seldom be contracted by denying a duty to weak and nervous members of the group."[32]

Deane J in *Jaensch v Coffey* has confirmed the fact that the psychiatric injury sustained by a tort victim:

> "may have been more likely or more severe in [the plaintiff's] case than in the case of a person of a different disposition does not absolve the defendant of liability in negligence in respect of it".[33]

Thus, it was held irrelevant in *Chapman v Lear*[34] that the plaintiff father and war veteran was more vulnerable to stress and that his reaction to his son's trauma was magnified to a greater degree than could have been anticipated. Canadian,[35]

31. (1939) 62 CLR 1.
32. Ibid at 27. Significantly Lord Bridge in *McLoughlin v O'Brian* [1983] 1 AC 410 at 439 found his Honour's reasoning "wholly convincing". Deane J in *Jaensch v Coffey* (1984) 155 CLR 549 at 590-591 said that it was "plainly to be preferred to that of the majority". Similarly, Hidden J in *Alcock v Chief Constable of South Yorkshire Police* [1992] 1 AC 310 at 328 thought it a "powerful . . . and totally convincing judgment".
33. (1984) 155 CLR 549 at 610. See also Heffey, op cit, n 9 at 241. Nor, for example, could the tortfeasor successfully assert that liability for the cost of psychiatric treatment should be halved on the basis that a normal individual, being mentally and emotionally more robust than the plaintiff, would have been cured in half the time: see P Q R Boberg (1973) *Annual Survey of South African Law*, 139.
34. (Unreported, Queensland SC, 8 Apr 1988, No 3732 of 1984). Note also *Bassanese v Martin* (1982) 31 SASR 461 where the plaintiff's depressive illness, although consequent on her husband's death, was due in part to pre-existing causes stemming from severe epilepsy and intellectual deterioration. Liability was admitted in this case, the issue turning on the assessment of damages.
35. See eg *Curll v Robin Hood Multifoods Ltd* (1974) 56 DLR (3d) 129 per Cowan CJTD at 131-132; *Krahn v Rawlings* (1977) 77 DLR (3d) 542 per MacKinnon JA at 544; *Bower v Mohawk Oil Co Ltd* (1986) 48 Sask R 1 per Hrabinsky J at 2-3; *Dickens v Thompson* (1990) 81 Sask R 133 per Wedge J at 137-138; *Campbell v Varanese* (1991) 279 APR 104 (NS) per Chipman JA at 119; *Bechard v Haliburton Estate* (1991) 84 DLR (4th) 668 per Griffiths JA at 681. Note also *Young v Burgoyne* (1981) 122 DLR (3d) 330 and *Beaulieu v Sutherland* (1986) 35 CCLT 237 where the plaintiffs had a history of emotional instability, in the latter case compounded by marital problems and a passive-dependent personality, but on the facts failed to establish conclusively that they had suffered psychiatric damage. Contrast, however, *Brown v Hubar* (1974) 45 DLR (3d) 664 where Grant J, in determining the duty of care issue, focused on the plaintiff's background (he had fought in wars, seen many of his friends killed and wounded and was convalescing from a heart attack when he learnt of his daughter's death) rather than first examining whether shock-induced psychiatric injury was foreseeable to persons of normal emotional disposition. Cormier CJQBD in *McMullin v F W Woolworth Co Ltd* (1974) 9 NBR (2d) 214 also seemed to concentrate on the plaintiff's pre-existing anxiety depression due to separation from her sailor husband when analysing her claim for shock caused by the bacterial infection of her children from pet turtles bought in the defendant's store. Approaching psychiatric damage cases from the question of plaintiff sensitivity is contrary to general principles of negligence.

United States,[36] Scottish,[37] South African[38] and English courts have also taken this path. Stuart-Smith J in *Brice v Brown*,[39] for example, agreed that it is immaterial "that a completely normal person would not have suffered the consequences that the plaintiff in fact suffered".[40] Similarly in *Galt v British Railways Board*[41] Tudor Evans J ruled that a train driver who feared he was going to strike two men on the track in front of him was entitled to recover for increased damage caused by his pre-existing symptomless condition which predisposed him to myocardial infarction (a heart attack).[42] As MacKinnon LJ remarked in the odd case of *Owens v Liverpool Corporation*,[43] where mourners at a funeral were shocked by the possibility of the corpse of a relative falling from a hearse onto the road in front of them, although a person of normal fortitude:

36. See eg *Alexander v Knight* (1962) 177 A 2d 142 (Pa); *Lockwood v McCaskill* (1964) 138 SE 2d 541 (NC); *Thomas v United States* (1964) 327 F 2d 379; *Steinhauser v Hertz Corporation* (1970) 421 F 2d 1169; *Martinez v Teague* (1981) 631 P 2d 1314 (NM); *Stoleson v United States* (1983) 708 F 2d 1217 (plaintiff with "dynamite heart" claimed for weekend chest pains allegedly stemming from her work in an ammunition plant; it was held that the illness was psychosomatic and that no causal connection was established); *Lancaster v Norfolk & Western Rail Co* (1985) 773 F 2d 807 (worker with latent schizophrenic personality who had been threatened with a broomstick by one supervisor, sexually assaulted by a second and almost hit with a sledgehammer by a third, became schizophrenic when threatened with a pickaxe by a fourth).
37. See eg *Gilligan v Robb*, 1910 SC 856 where a young boy set a dog upon a cow which was frightened and rushed into a house, severely shocking the plaintiff who was with her three-week-old baby; *Walker v Pitlochry*, 1930 SC 565 per Lord Mackay at 569; *Graham v Paterson*, 1938 SC 119 per Lord Mackay at 131; *Bourhill v Young* [1943] AC 92.
38. See eg *Bester v Commercial Union Versekeringsmaatskappy van SA Bpk*, 1973 (1) SA 769 (A); *Boswell v Minister of Police*, 1978 (3) SA 268 (E) (note that this case involved intentional infliction of shock, discussed below, p 286); *Masiba v Constantia Insurance Co Ltd*, 1982 (4) SA 333 (C) where the shock victim's pre-existing hypertension so greatly increased the extent of the harm produced by seeing a car containing his two young children roll towards the side of a bridge that he suffered a stroke and died three days later in hospital.
39. [1984] 1 All ER 997 at 1007.
40. See also *Mason v Campbell* (unreported, QBD, 7 Nov 1988) where as a result of being attacked and bitten by an Alsatian dog the plaintiff, who was mentally and physically disabled, developed a significant phobia about Alsatian dogs. This was said to be a terrifying incident for a man such as the plaintiff.
41. (1983) 133 NLJ 870.
42. See also *Malcolm v Broadhurst* [1970] 3 All ER 508 where the plaintiff's pre-existing nervous condition was aggravated by her husband's physical and mental injuries (eg changed personality and behaviour) sustained in the same accident. She was entitled to compensation for her disability because exacerbation of her nervous susceptibility was a foreseeable consequence of serious injury to her husband through the defendant's carelessness. Note also *Ibrahim (A Minor) v Muhammad* (unreported, QBD, 21 May 1984) where the psychiatric illness suffered by a father as a result of witnessing a negligent circumcision on his son was aggravated by a pre-existing psychiatric condition. (Compare the Canadian cases of *McMullin v F W Woolworth Co Ltd* (1974) 9 NBR (2d) 214 and *Young v Burgoyne* (1981) 122 DLR (3d) 330 where claims by a relative of the primary victim for psychiatric damage based on the aggravation of an existing nervous condition were refused.) In *Behrens v Bertram Mills Circus Ltd* [1957] 2 QB 1 an elephant frightened by a dog knocked down a booth containing the plaintiff and his wife, both midgets in the defendant's circus. In an action for shock caused by his wife's serious injuries, evidence was led that married midgets are exceptionally dependent upon each other. Note *Kralj v McGrath* [1986] 1 All ER 54 where the more drastic psychiatric effect attributable to grief suffered by a woman following the death of her brain-damaged newborn son was compensable.
43. [1939] 1 KB 394.

"might readily be disbelieved if he alleged that such an incident . . .
had caused him . . . shock . . . [it] may be that the plaintiffs are of that
class which is peculiarly susceptible to the luxury of woe at a funeral
so as to be disastrously disturbed by an untoward accident to the
trappings of mourning. But one who is guilty of negligence to another
must put up with the idiosyncrasies of his victim that increase the
likelihood or extent of damage to him: it is no answer to a claim for
a fractured skull that its owner had an unusually fragile one."[44]

Can a plaintiff recover in the slightly different situation where physical
damage suffered has been exaggerated or magnified in severity as a result
of a particular susceptibility to psychiatric illness (for example, where
excessive anxiety over physical injuries increases their disabling effect)?[45]
In *Moricz v Grundel Boilermaking & Engineering Works*[46] the plaintiff
was incapacitated as a result of an anxiety neurosis concerning minor work-
related physical injuries. In the absence of intentional malingering
defendants will be held liable, as they were in this case, for loss stemming
from such neurotic conditions. Indeed, some judges have made even greater
sympathetic allowances for the subjective weaknesses of shock claimants,
going so far as to say that recovery will be permitted even if there is evidence
of conscious malingering provided it exists side by side with genuine
neurosis attributable to the injury in question.[47] A similar English case is
James v Woodall Duckham Construction Co Ltd.[48] The plaintiff
carpenter fell about 35 feet whilst at work due to the negligence of his
defendant employer. He suffered severe pain after the accident which the

44. Ibid at 400-401. Note also *Currie v Wardrop*, 1927 SC 538 per Lord Murray at 555. But
see *Bourhill v Young* [1943] AC 92 per Lord Wright at 110 and A L Goodhart (1944) 8
CLJ 265 at 271. Note also *Mortiboys v Skinner* [1952] 2 Lloyd's Rep 95 per Willmer J
at 103: "[I]f the person who is injured unhappily has poor powers of recuperation so
much the worse for the wrongdoer. Quite clearly, the victim who makes the poorer
recovery prima facie is entitled to larger damages than the happier victim who recovers
quickly."

45. The medical literature on this type of condition is voluminous. See, in particular,
Comment, "Accident Neurosis" (1961) 35 ALJ 206; H Miller, "Accident Neurosis"
(1961) 1 Brit Med J 919, 992, reprinted in (1963) 10 *Proceedings of the Medico-Legal
Society of Victoria* 264; A Samuels, "Damages in Personal Injury Cases: A Comparative
Law Colloqium Report" (1968) 17 ICLQ 443 at 463-466; N Parker, "Accident Neurosis"
(1970) Med J Aust 362; F Lawton, "A Judicial View of Traumatic Neurosis" (1979) 47
Medico-Legal Journal 6; R Kelly & B N Smith, "Post-Traumatic Neurosis: Another Myth
Discredited" (1981) 74 J R Soc Med 275; G Mendelson, "Not 'Cured by a Verdict'—
Effect of Legal Settlement on Compensation Claimants" (1982) Med J Aust 132;
W A R Thomson, "Accident Neurosis" (1982) 22 Med Sci Law 143; V E Weighill,
"Compensation Neurosis—A Review of the Literature" (1983) 27 *Journal of
Psychosomatic Research* 97; M J Tarsh & C Royston, "A Follow-up Study of Accident
Neurosis" (1985) 146 Br J Psy 18; R I Cohen & J M Pfeiffer, "Accident Neurosis
Revisited" (1987) 27 Med Sci Law 177; R I Cohen, "Post-traumatic Stress Disorder: Does
It Clear Up When the Litigation is Settled?" (1987) 37 Br J Hosp Med 485.

46. [1963] SASR 112. See Travers J's comments at 114 where he spoke of the claimant's
"unfortunate kind of defeatist personality". A similar Canadian case is *Bower v Mohawk
Oil Co Ltd* (1986) 48 Sask R 1.

47. See *Corporation of the City of Woodville v Balassone* [1968] SASR 147 per Bray CJ at
153, per Bright and Walters JJ at 154-155 where a workman was held to be entitled to
the continuation of workers' compensation payments; *Donjerkovic v Adelaide Steamship
Industries Pty Ltd* (1980) 24 SASR 347 per White J at 359.

48. [1969] 1 WLR 903.

medical evidence revealed could not be attributed to any physical cause but was due to anxiety over the incident, in particular the ensuing compensation claim. There was evidence that the plaintiff's suffering would continue until the action for damages was settled or determined by the court. Recovery was allowed, although in this case it was reduced because of a lengthy delay in commencing proceedings.[49] Of interest too is *Hoffmueller v Commonwealth*[50] where the defendant was also held responsible for the effect of its carelessness on the claimant's peculiar emotional make-up. There, a plaintiff's pre-existing obsessional personality disorder flared into a persistent severe post-accident psycho-neurotic condition requiring treatment for nine years until the trial. There was evidence that his predisposition made him vulnerable to upsets and neurotic breakdown but he had managed to live his life without treatment prior to the accident. In ordering a new trial to consider damages, the Supreme Court of New South Wales concluded, inter alia, that there was a causal link between the accident and the symptoms exhibited by the plaintiff and that mental illness was a foreseeable consequence of the collision. The British Columbia Court of Appeal in *Enge v Trerise*[51] was also prepared to award compensation to a 16-year-old girl who developed a schizophrenic condition revolving around a bad scar on her forehead that she suffered in a car accident. Following the accident she withdrew from society, suffered from acute depression and paranoia, heard "voices" and became abnormally preoccupied with her scar, drawing irrational conclusions about it including the belief that people thought it signified that she was sexually approachable. Ruling that this type of emotional disturbance was not too remote a consequence of the defendant's negligence, the court held that the scar precipitated her breakdown which was unlikely to have developed in its absence.[52]

There is some authority for the proposition that damages may also be recoverable where excessive worry about the pecuniary ramifications of physical injury and incapacity causes actual mental or further physical suffering. In *Mitchell v Clancy*[53] a serious arm injury caused the plaintiff such worry about his ability to support his family that he developed a

---

49. Note also *Roome v Smith Ltd* (unreported, English CA, 3 July 1956) (following fall, plaintiff, a potential hysteric from birth, suffered deep nervous hysteria); *Williams v Jones Balers* (unreported, Chester Assizes, 30 Nov 1964) (following accident, machine operator had "hysterical paralysis" of left hand—had impression that fingers sticking out of wrist and had to look at hand to know that it was there). Compare *O'Brien v E H Burgess Ltd* (unreported, English CA, 12 Nov 1953) (plaintiff developed anxiety neurosis after being hit on head by brick and would only undertake light work; Court of Appeal confirmed trial judge's finding that this was supervening neurosis attributable to a deficiency in the plaintiff's make-up and not to injury).
50. (1981) 54 FLR 48.
51. (1960) 26 DLR (2d) 529.
52. There was expert evidence that the plaintiff was suffering from a latent schizophrenic condition prior to the accident. Note also *Tamplin v Star Lumber & Supply Co* (1991) 824 P 2d 219 (Kan) where the jury was able to consider as an element of a mental damage claim the anguish a six-year-old plaintiff *might* suffer if she worried during her teenage years about the effects of the very serious physical injuries sustained when a 150 pound roll of vinyl flooring fell on her head.
53. [1960] Qd R 62, affirmed by the High Court [1960] Qd R 532.

nervous condition leading to a duodenal ulcer requiring surgery. Philip J considered that the damage arising in connection with the ulcer and the operation was not too remote a consequence of the negligence to be recoverable. The same outcome was reached in North Carolina in *Lockwood v McCaskill*[54] where a plaintiff predisposed to amnesia recovered for a severe memory blackout brought on by mental distress and financial worries after a car accident. Some courts, however, have expressed concern over the causation and foreseeability issues that this situation potentially raises—a New Zealand judge opining in *Marra v New Zealand Refrigerating Co Ltd*,[55] a workers' compensation case, that "a mental state cannot be said to result from an injury unless it is directly related to such injury [and it] is not enough if the mental state is caused by worry and anxiety over inability to work or over fear of the consequences of an injury".[56] It is submitted that the former view should prevail. So long as psychiatric harm eventuates, it should not matter whether it does so via this sort of indirect route. Anxiety about the financial consequences of physical injury is an entirely natural reaction to physical debilitation, and psychiatric illness stemming from this is clearly foreseeable.

Returning to the more usual situations where claimant susceptibility is in issue, provided that some recognised type of psychiatric illness is reasonably foreseeable as a result of the defendant's lack of care, it is no bar to recovery that the particular form of damage in fact suffered was not.[57] The courts do not insist on specificity of foresight allowing, in this situation, recovery for any form of psychiatric loss actually incurred. Not only is foresight of the medically precise name irrelevant, but so is the precise mental or psychological process or "precise events leading to the administration of shock".[58]

It has been suggested that the incidence of potential for psychiatric damage amongst the community is perhaps higher than that for physical injury or "thin skulls".[59] Demographic considerations aside, the two are treated the same in the eyes of the law. A number of authorities have recognised that rationally no distinction can be drawn between eggshell bodies and eggshell minds—the talem qualem rule applies to the psychiatric fallout from the accident in exactly the same way as it does to physical

54. (1964) 138 SE 2d 541 (NC).
55. [1963] NZLR 432.
56. Ibid per Dalglish J at 435. See also *Palamara v Fragameni* (unreported, Western Australian SC, 13 Oct 1983, No 89 of 1983) where the plaintiff's worry concerning his ability to support his family and his financial uncertainty produced a neurosis which increased his perception of his physical injuries. This mental condition was further aggravated by treatment (eg epidural injections) which caused new symptoms. Although Burt CJ left the question open whether the mental condition must be directly related to the original negligence, his Honour's words, on one reading, indicate a preference for the "direct" rule, worry and anxiety over the consequences of a physical injury being insufficient to ground a claim. On the question of foreseeability see *Bunyan v Jordan* (1937) 57 CLR 1 per Dixon J at 16.
57. See above, pp 71-72.
58. *Jaensch v Coffey* (1984) 155 CLR 549 per Brennan J at 563. See also *Brice v Brown* [1984] 1 All ER 997 per Stuart-Smith J at 1007; *Campbelltown City Council v Mackay* (1989) 15 NSWLR 501 per McHugh JA at 512.
59. *Young v J D Coates Pty Ltd* (unreported, New South Wales CA, 5 Oct 1990, CA No 171 of 1988) per Mahoney JA at 9.

injuries sustained therein.[60] In *Wyld v Bertram & Coates*,[61] a South Australian case, Bray CJ stated:

"I think that the man with the fractured eggshell skull not only gets damages for his loss, but full damages, without any discount for his greater potentiality to injury. . . . The predisposition is to be ignored; the inevitable operation of pre-existing causes is to be taken into account."[62]

In *Pipikos v Brown & Sons Pty Ltd*[63] his Honour repeated these sentiments, stating:

"I am unable to distinguish for the purpose in hand the case of a man with an eggshell skull who has an abnormal susceptibility to fracture of the skull from the case of a man with a psychiatric weakness who has an abnormal susceptibility to psychiatric damage."[64]

He continued:

"As I have said, I cannot distinguish between a predisposition to psychiatric harm and a predisposition to physical harm. It seems to me that the question is of even greater practical importance in the former case, since predispositions to physical harm are probably less common than predispositions to psychiatric harm. It may well be that all men have some psychic weakness susceptible to the right pressure at the right time in the right circumstances."[65]

Significantly however Bridge and Wells JJ were not prepared to extend the thin skull principle relevant in conventional physical medicine to the area of psychiatric medicine where (at least at that time) psychiatric knowledge was less developed, although they did not definitively decide the matter.[66]

60. *Campbell v Varanese* (1991) 279 APR 104 (NS) per Chipman JA at 119. See also *Bechard v Haliburton Estate* (1991) 84 DLR (4th) 668 per Griffiths JA at 681. In this case, although the plaintiff had no pre-existing mental instability, the Ontario Court of Appeal assumed that as a result of a car accident a post-traumatic stress disorder had been initiated in her which was then significantly exacerbated by witnessing a motorcyclist, who had been injured in the first accident, run over by a second vehicle as he lay helpless on the road. She was held entitled to recover damages for more extensive mental illness due to this "unusual susceptibility". Though it is extremely unlikely that a recognised trauma-induced disorder (as distinct from a normal emotional reaction) will in fact develop almost instantaneously, thereby immediately rendering a person vulnerable to subsequent stressors (see above, pp 27-30, 200-201, below, pp 312-313), the case does illustrate the indiscriminate operation of the talem qualem rule.
61. [1970] SASR 1.
62. Ibid at 5-6.
63. [1970] SASR 508.
64. Ibid at 514.
65. Ibid at 515. See also *Sobiecka v Blanton* [1960] Qd R 152 per Stanley J at 164; *Donjerkovic v Adelaide Steamship Industries Pty Ltd* (1980) 24 SASR 347 per White J at 358; *Hoffmueller v Commonwealth* (1981) 54 FLR 48 per Glass JA at 52. Note *Negretto v Sayers* [1963] SASR 313 and *Zumeris v Testa* [1972] VR 839. In the former case a susceptible plaintiff recovered for one nervous breakdown attributable to her being knocked down by a car, but failed in relation to a second which was considered to be a reaction to her giving birth. Her physical injuries had not been serious but, due to a pre-existing tendency to mental disorder, she developed a post-concussional psychosis and was admitted to a mental hospital, later discharged, then readmitted a year later on becoming pregnant. Chamberlain J considered that the eggshell skull rule was still good law and awarded damages for the period ending on the date when she was first discharged.
66. [1970] SASR 508 at 519-520.

But more recently in *Prakash v Malkog*[67] the South Australian Full Court unanimously approved the recognition by the trial judge that a pre-disposition to psychiatric harm should be reflected in an award of damages. The plaintiff's existing psychiatric illness was exacerbated for 12 months as the result of a motor vehicle accident. By then, medical treatment had returned him to a psychiatric condition compatible with his pre-accident state, although he was left more vulnerable to future exacerbations of that condition. A second accident again caused a worsening of his psychiatric condition for a three-month period, and increased vulnerability to future stress. He recovered damages from each defendant for the effects of the accidents on his mental condition, awards with which the Full Court refused to interfere.

Other courts have adopted a similar attitude. In *Tuckey v R & H Green & Silley Weir Ltd*[68] a comparatively minor injury to the plaintiff at work resulted in traumatic neurosis (for which the defendant admitted liability). The plaintiff was "a man of almost eggshell nervous disposition, and so a slight accident was capable of precipitating a neurotic condition".[69] In *Storm v Geeves*[70] a mother's history of neurosis increased the effect of the shock of seeing her daughter pinned beneath a truck but in light of the parent-child relationship did not render her magnified mental damage too remote. Similarly, in *Benson v Lee*[71] there was evidence that a mother informed of her child's involvement in an accident and who ran to the scene soon after and suffered shock had been prone to mental illness. Lush J, however, ruled that her abnormality was not so pronounced as to take it beyond the bounds of reasonable foresight,[72] considering that it should be treated in the same way as predisposition in physical injury cases. He stated:

> "Only reasons of policy can justify the adoption of a different rule in 'nervous shock' cases, and since [the decision in *Mount Isa Mines Ltd v Pusey*[73]] those reasons cannot be regarded as decisive. There may, however, be cases in which an unusual susceptibility is such as to take the consequences suffered by the plaintiff outside the boundaries of reasonable foresight."[74]

It is clear also that, as with personal injury claims,[75] the onus is on the defendant to lead evidence that the claimant was predisposed to the

---

67. (Unreported, South Australian SC, 6 June 1990, Nos 516 and 517 of 1989).
68. [1955] 2 Lloyd's Rep 619.
69. Ibid per Pearson J at 620. Note also *Bailey v Hain Steamship Co Ltd* [1956] 1 Lloyd's Rep 641.
70. [1965] Tas SR 252 per Burbury CJ at 268-269.
71. [1972] VR 879.
72. See also *Chadwick v British Railways Board* [1967] 1 WLR 912 where the fact that a rescuer had suffered psycho-neurotic symptoms 16 years before a rail disaster did not reveal anything in his personality to put him outside the contemplation of the reasonable man. He was not treated as a susceptible plaintiff.
73. (1970) 125 CLR 383.
74. [1972] VR 879 at 881. His Honour's words were adopted by Williams J in *Gannon v Gray* [1973] Qd R 411 at 414. See also *Love v Port of London Authority* [1959] 2 Lloyd's Rep 541 per Edmund Davies J at 545; *Sayers v Perrin (No 3)* [1966] Qd R 89 per Sheehy ACJ at 94-96; *Malcolm v Broadhurst* [1970] 3 All ER 508 per Geoffrey Lane J at 511; *Bishop v Arts & Letters Club of Toronto* (1978) 83 DLR (3d) 107.
75. See *Watts v Rake* (1960) 108 CLR 158; *Purkess v Crittenden* (1965) 114 CLR 164; *Pastras v Commonwealth* [1967] VR 161; *Edwards v Hourigan* [1968] Qd R 202.

psychiatric injury proved to have been caused by the defendant's breach of duty. This was emphasised by Gibbs CJ in *Jaensch v Coffey*[76] and recently reaffirmed in *Petrie v Dowling*.[77] There Kneipp J considered the fact that a mother (who suffered shock-related mental illness after learning her daughter had been knocked from her bicycle and killed by a car) had undergone electro-convulsive therapy whilst a teenager did not lead to the conclusion that she had displayed depressive tendencies rendering her prone to psychiatric damage.

76. (1984) 155 CLR 549 at 556.
77. [1992] 1 Qd R 284 at 287. See also *Mount Isa Mines Ltd v Pusey* (1970) 125 CLR 383 at 405-406; *Benson v Lee* [1972] VR 879 at 881; *Gannon v Gray* [1973] Qd R 411 at 414.

11

STATUTORY LIABILITY FOR PSYCHIATRIC DAMAGE

The Australian statutes

In contrast to England and most other jurisdictions where liability for psychiatric damage is exclusively a matter for the common law, in several Australian jurisdictions the common law has been supplemented by legislation. It is instructive to compare the position under these provisions with recent developments in the case law. The legislatures in these Australian jurisdictions have recognised the logic behind a more expansive approach, which may provide food for thought by other courts.

Liability for personal injury arising from "mental or nervous shock"

In 1944, to avoid the restrictive effects of the case law,[1] the New South Wales Parliament made statutory provision for personal injury arising from "mental or nervous shock". After providing that the plaintiff in a personal injury action "shall not be debarred from recovering damages merely because the injury complained of arose wholly or in part from mental or nervous shock",[2] the *Law Reform (Miscellaneous Provisions) Act* went on to provide that:

> "The liability of any person in respect of injury caused after the commencement of the Act by an act, neglect or default by which any other person is killed, injured or put in peril, shall extend to include liability for injury arising wholly or in part from mental or nervous shock sustained by:
>
> (a) a parent or the husband or wife of the person so killed, injured or put in peril; or

---

1. Particularly the decisions in *Chester v Council of the Municipality of Waverley* (1939) 62 CLR 1 and *Bourhill v Young* [1943] AC 92: see the second reading speech of Hon R R Downing, Minister for Justice, in the Legislative Council: *New South Wales Parliamentary Debates* (1944), Vol 176, 826, 829-831, 835-837 and *Swan v Williams (Demolition) Pty Ltd* (1987) 9 NSWLR 172 per Priestley JA at 192-193. Note also *McLoughlin v O'Brian* [1983] 1 AC 410 per Lord Bridge at 439, suggesting that the enactment of the New South Wales legislation was a response to the injustice of the common law.
2. *Law Reform (Miscellaneous Provisions) Act* 1944 (NSW), s 3. There are similar provisions in four other Australian jurisdictions: *Wrongs Act* 1958 (Vic), s 23; *Wrongs Act* 1936 (SA), s 8; *Law Reform (Miscellaneous Provisions) Act* 1955 (ACT), s 23; *Law Reform (Miscellaneous Provisions) Act* 1956 (NT), s 24. For an example of the application of these provisions see *Richards v Baker* [1943] SASR 245.

(b) any other member of the family of the person so killed, injured or put in peril where such person was killed, injured or put in peril within the sight or hearing of such member of the family."[3]

Similar provisions were enacted in the Australian Capital Territory in 1955 and in the Northern Territory in 1956.[4]

Just as the common law does, this legislation requires the plaintiff to prove that the defendant's negligence caused him or her to suffer "mental or nervous shock". As at common law,[5] damages are not awarded for mere grief or anguish.[6] The most important difference from general negligence liability is that the common law foreseeability test is replaced by a statutory formula.[7] In some cases the mere existence of a family relationship gives rise to the plaintiff's right to sue and in others that right depends on a combination of relationship and presence. The legislation assumes that injury by shock to a parent, husband or wife is not an unlikely consequence where a child, wife or husband has been killed, injured or otherwise endangered.[8]

There has been speculation as to whether the statute requires the proof of a breach of duty to the person killed, injured or put in peril as a condition of liability to the plaintiff.[9] However, the High Court of Australia in Scala v Mammolitti[10] has held that the statute creates a new duty of care owed to the plaintiff and that liability to the accident victim is immaterial.[11] Thus in cases where wives recovered under the statutory provisions for shock caused by the death of a family member, this was held to be a breach of an independent duty owed to the wife,[12] and husbands were therefore able to claim damages for medical expenses[13] and loss of

3. *Law Reform (Miscellaneous Provisions) Act* 1944 (NSW), s 4(1).
4. *Law Reform (Miscellaneous Provisions) Act* 1955 (ACT), s 24; *Law Reform (Miscellaneous Provisions) Act* 1956 (NT), s 25. For a general discussion of this legislation see P G Heffey, "The Negligent Infliction of Nervous Shock in Road and Industrial Accidents" (1974) 48 ALJ 196, 240 at 248-254. On the procedural provisions in the legislation see *Thiele v Batten* [1962] NSWR 1426. One interesting limitation on the scope of these provisions is that they only apply to actions in the higher courts, namely the Supreme and District Courts in New South Wales and the Supreme Courts in the Australian Capital Territory and the Northern Territory: see *Law Reform (Miscellaneous Provisions) Act* 1944 (NSW), s 4(4); *Law Reform (Miscellaneous Provisions) Act* 1955 (ACT), s 24(5); *Law Reform (Miscellaneous Provisions) Act* 1956 (NT), s 25(5).
5. See above, pp 14-18.
6. *Macpherson v Commissioner for Government Transport* (1959) 76 WN (NSW) 352; *De Franceschi v Storrier* (1988) 85 ACTR 1.
7. *Anderson v Liddy* (1949) 49 SR (NSW) 320 per Jordan CJ at 323; *Armytage v Commissioner for Government Transport* [1972] 1 NSWLR 331; *State Rail Authority of New South Wales v Sharp* [1981] 1 NSWLR 240.
8. See R P Balkin & J L R Davis, *Law of Torts* (1991), 257.
9. See the discussion by Heffey, op cit, n 4 at 251-253.
10. (1965) 114 CLR 153.
11. Note also *Mount Isa Mines Ltd v Pusey* (1970) 125 CLR 383 per Windeyer J at 408: "[L]iability for nervous shock, resulting from the sight of another person's injury or peril negligently caused, is not a by-product as it were of liability to that other person. The shock-producing event is a tort to the plaintiff."
12. Contrast, however, *Armytage v Commissioner for Government Transport* [1972] 1 NSWLR 331 per Brereton J at 339: "[T]he cause of action . . . is based, not on breach of the duty owed to the plaintiff, but on breach of a duty owed to the plaintiff's deceased spouse."
13. *Smee v Tibbetts* (1953) 53 SR (NSW) 391.

consortium.[14] Another consequence of this ruling as to duty is that any contributory negligence by the primary accident victim will not reduce the damages awarded to plaintiffs suing under the statute.[15]

The legislation contemplates the traditional situation of the bystander cases—that A by negligently killing, injuring or imperilling B has caused shock to B's relatives.[16] The statute does not deal with the older variety of nervous shock case where the plaintiff suffers psychiatric harm through fear of injury to himself or herself.[17] Nor does it have any application where B (or B's agent[18]) is responsible for causing his or her own death or injury. In these situations liability continues to be a matter for the common law.[19]

In situations where one person suffers psychiatric damage as the result of another being killed, injured or put in peril by a third party, varying views have been expressed as to whether the legislative provisions supersede the common law, or merely provide an additional cause of action.[20] Windeyer J in *Mount Isa Mines Ltd v Pusey*[21] provides some support for the former position. He said obiter that in New South Wales "it may be that . . . by reason of an expressio unius, it is only a member of the family who can sue for nervous shock caused by the sight of a tortious injury to someone else".[22] However, this appears to be a minority view. Kitto J in *Scala v Mammolitti*[23] said that the statute "lays down a general rule of liability as an addition to existing rules of liability", and there are other decisions which have taken this view.[24] The matter was discussed most

---

14. *State Rail Authority of New South Wales v Sharp* [1981] 1 NSWLR 240. Note that the husband also claimed damages under the statute.
15. See below, p 255.
16. Thus it had no application in *Stergiou v Stergiou* (1987) Aust Torts Rep 80-082, where there was no family relationship between the plaintiff and the accident victim. Note also the recent settlement of a claim at common law by a man who suffered a recognisable psychiatric illness as a result of seeing injuries to fellow-passengers in the Granville train disaster in Sydney: see "Granville Deal", *The Australian*, 18 Feb 1992, 6.
17. As typified by *Dulieu v White & Sons* [1901] 2 KB 669.
18. See *Ball v Winslett* [1958] SR (NSW) 149.
19. See above, pp 207-208, 215-220.
20. In some cases it appears that actions are brought at common law without liability under the statute ever being contemplated: see eg the mother's claim for shock-related mental injury in *X and Y v Pal* (1991) 23 NSWLR 26, discussed above, p 164. Note also *White v Butcher* (unreported, New South Wales SC, 13 Oct 1982, Nos 9576, 9577 and 9578 of 1981), discussed above, p 162, where it is impossible to tell from the judgment of Maxwell J whether the parents' action was founded on common law or statute; and *Budget Rent-a-Car Systems Pty Ltd v Van der Kemp* (unreported, New South Wales CA, 21 Dec 1984, CA No 7 of 1984) where although McHugh JA classified the claim as one brought at "common law" and did not allude to the Act, it is nevertheless unclear into which category the action fell.
21. (1970) 125 CLR 383.
22. Ibid at 408. See, however, C S Phegan (1971) 45 ALJ 428 at 430: "New South Wales lawyers may be surprised at his Honour's suggestion that a plaintiff in circumstances similar to those in [*Pusey's*] case may have no action in that State."
23. (1965) 114 CLR 153 at 157.
24. *Anderson v Liddy* (1949) 49 SR (NSW) 320; *Smee v Tibbetts* (1953) 53 SR (NSW) 391, noted by B Hill (1954) 1 Syd LR 412; *Rowe v McCartney* [1975] 1 NSWLR 544 per Sheppard J at 549; *Stergiou v Stergiou* (1987) Aust Torts Rep 80-082. In *Jaensch v Coffey* (1984) 155 CLR 549 at 611 Deane J referred to the statutory provisions but said that it was unnecessary to consider this issue. A similar stance was taken by Miles CJ in *De Franceschi v Storrier* (1988) 85 ACTR 1 at 2.

recently in *Wilks v Haines*,[25] where the court emphasised that there had been no authoritative decision on the question—probably because of the restrictive view taken in the past to actions for shock-caused injury. Though it was not necessary for him to decide the question, Loveday J adopted the view that the Act did not limit the common law, but that the two causes of action existed side by side.[26]

At the time when the statutes, and in particular the New South Wales statute, were passed, they represented a considerable advance on the common law. Since then, however, the boundaries of liability have been extended a good deal. In spite of this, the statutes still allow plaintiffs to recover in cases where this is not possible at common law.

This is most obvious in the case of the first category of plaintiffs under the statute. If a parent or husband or wife of the person killed, injured or put in peril suffers shock as a result of the accident, they can recover whether or not they were present at the accident or its aftermath. What matters is not how they learnt of the accident, but their relationship to the accident victim—the statute in effect presumes that certain close relatives may well suffer psychiatric damage consequent on the accident.[27] The importance of this provision is underlined by the interpretation section,[28] which makes it clear that "parent" covers not only natural parents but step-parents and grandparents and persons in loco parentis, and in New South Wales the terms "husband" and "wife" include those who live together on a "bona fide domestic basis" though not married to each other.[29] All this goes far beyond the common law. Some of the persons in this category are unlikely to be able to recover at common law—a grandfather, for example, was one of those denied recovery in *Alcock v Chief Constable of South Yorkshire Police*[30]—and all must satisfy the additional requirement of being present at the accident or its aftermath, at least if the cases recognising liability when the plaintiff suffers psychiatric injury through being told of the accident do not prevail.

The second statutory category, which deals with other family members, is more restrictive, because it requires that they should be within sight or hearing of the accident. There does not appear to be any way in which the words of the statute can be interpreted to include the aftermath of the accident, rather than the accident itself. The statute, after all, was enacted before the development of the aftermath doctrine. However the family members who may recover in such circumstances again include some who may be unable to recover at common law. According to the interpretation sections,[31] "member of the family" means a husband, wife, parent, child,

25. (1991) Aust Torts Rep 81-078 at 68,652-68,653.
26. The *New South Wales Parliamentary Debates* also support this interpretation, suggesting that unrelated bystanders, though not covered by the Bill, may be able to recover under the general law: *New South Wales Parliamentary Debates* (1944), Vol 175, 100.
27. See above, pp 168-169.
28. *Law Reform (Miscellaneous Provisions) Act* 1944 (NSW), s 4(5); *Law Reform (Miscellaneous Provisions) Act* 1955 (ACT), s 22; *Law Reform (Miscellaneous Provisions) Act* 1956 (NT), s 23.
29. *Law Reform (Miscellaneous Provisions) Act* 1944 (NSW), s 4(5).
30. [1992] 1 AC 310.
31. See above, n 28.

brother, sister, half-brother or half-sister. As has been seen, before the decision of the House of Lords in *Alcock v Chief Constable of South Yorkshire Police*[32] it seemed that the English courts restricted recovery to spouses, parents and children. The Court of Appeal decision in that case espoused that general philosophy, and Hidden J's attempt to extend the permitted categories to include brothers and sisters, following the example of the Tasmanian Full Court in *Storm v Geeves*,[33] was rejected. The House of Lords has now adopted a different approach, emphasising the importance of the individual relationship and abandoning arbitrary rules based on the category of relative. However, there is still a most important difference between this case, as representative of the current common law position, and the Australian statutes. Under the statutes, family members within the stated categories have an automatic right to recover for shock, if they are present at the scene of the accident to the relative. At common law, they can recover only if the relationship satisfies the criteria of very close love and affection specified by the House of Lords. Brian Harrison, who lost his brother, failed to satisfy these criteria. He would have recovered under the Australian statutes.

It appears that the only cases in which the common law would provide a remedy when the statutes would not are those involving non-relatives (such as workmates and rescuers[34]) and those where relatives (other than spouses and parents) are present at the aftermath, rather than the accident itself, or who learn of the accident from others in situations where the common law permits recovery.

Restrictions on recovery in motor accident cases

Legislative provisions of a rather different kind have recently been enacted in South Australia and New South Wales, as part of a programme of limiting liability in road accident cases.

In South Australia, a 1986 amendment to the *Wrongs Act* provides that:

"Notwithstanding any other law, where damages are to be assessed for or in respect of injury arising from a motor accident . . . no damages shall be awarded for mental or nervous shock except in favour of

(1) a person who is physically injured in the accident, who was the driver of or a passenger in or on a motor vehicle involved in the accident or who was, when the accident occurred, present at the scene of the accident; or

(2) a parent, spouse or child of a person killed, injured or endangered in the accident".[35]

32. [1992] 1 AC 310.
33. [1965] Tas SR 252.
34. For example, *Dooley v Cammell Laird & Co Ltd* [1951] 1 Lloyd's Rep 271; *Chadwick v British Railways Board* [1967] 1 WLR 912; *Mount Isa Mines Ltd v Pusey* (1970) 125 CLR 383; *Carlin v Helical Bar Ltd* (1970) 9 KIR 154; *Galt v British Railways Board* (1983) 133 NLJ 870; *Wigg v British Railways Board, The Times*, 4 Feb 1986.
35. *Wrongs Act* 1936 (SA), s 35a(1)(c). Note the attempt by the Special Magistrate in *Orman v Harrington* (unreported, South Australian SC, 30 Apr 1990, No 296 of 1990) to apply the section in that case even though it had not come into operation at the time of the accident. There are as yet no reported cases on s 35a(1)(c).

"Parent" is defined in the same way as in the legislative provisions referred to above, and "child" has a corresponding meaning.[36]

The New South Wales *Motor Accidents Act* 1988, which restored common law liability in road accident cases after it had been abolished by the *Transport Accidents Compensation Act* 1987, provides that:

> "No damages for psychological or psychiatric injury shall be awarded in respect of a motor accident except in favour of—
>
> (a) a person who suffered injury in the accident and who—
>
>> (i) was the driver of or a passenger in or on a vehicle involved in the accident; or
>>
>> (ii) was, when the accident occurred, present at the scene of the accident; or
>
> (b) a parent, spouse, brother, sister or child of the injured person or deceased person who, as a consequence of the injury to the injured person or the death of the deceased person, has suffered a demonstrable psychological or psychiatric injury and not merely a normal emotional or cultural grief reaction."[37]

As is the case under the New South Wales 1944 Act, "spouse" includes a de facto spouse.[38]

Like the more general provisions dealt with above, these enactments accept that certain close relatives may suffer psychiatric injury irrespective of whether they are present at the accident. But this category has been carefully limited, particularly so in South Australia where brothers and sisters who were not present at the scene of the accident are not included. Relatives apart, however, recovery for psychiatric injury is limited to persons who were physically injured in the accident whether as a driver of or passenger in a vehicle or as a pedestrian or other road user. No allowance is made in either statute for trauma victims unrelated to the injured parties who are present but physically uninjured. Thus a stranger bystander who observes, closehand but safely, the carnage of a car accident has no prospect of recovery for resultant mental damage under the statute law of these two States. Moreover, it is clear that, unlike the earlier provisions in New South Wales and the two Territories (according to the more generally accepted view), these provisions aim to restrict common law liability. However they only apply in cases of motor vehicle accidents. Many cases of psychiatric damage occur in other situations. Although there may be good policy reasons behind the desire to limit liability in road accident situations, creating an artificial difference in the ambit of psychiatric damage recovery seems very unsatisfactory. The position in South Australia seems particularly restrictive. In New South Wales, trauma victims still have the benefit of the extensions of the law provided by the 1944 Act, at least in non-road accident cases.

36. *Wrongs Act* 1936 (SA), s 3a.
37. *Motor Accidents Act* 1988 (NSW), s 77.
38. s 3(1).

Conclusions

On a number of occasions, judges in the House of Lords have urged the desirability of statutory reform along the lines of the 1944 Act in New South Wales and its equivalents in the Northern Territory and the Australian Capital Territory. In *McLoughlin v O'Brian* Lord Scarman said that there was a "powerful case" for enacting such legislation[39]—though his views were not shared by the other Law Lords, who saw judicial technique as an entirely appropriate way of extending the law and put this into practice.[40] Now, in *Alcock v Chief Constable of South Yorkshire Police*, Lord Ackner has noted that the statutes recognised that it was appropriate to extend significantly the categories of claimants,[41] and Lord Oliver has suggested that it would be preferable for the limits of liability for psychiatric damage to be determined by Parliament, with the full opportunity for public debate and representation which that process gives.[42] Suggestions as to the desirability of statutory reform are clearly worthy of note. However, we envisage considerable problems in converting into legislative form all the issues that have arisen in the case law governing liability for psychiatric damage. The existing Acts, for example, do not canvass matters such as relationship beyond the familial sphere, modern means of communicating distressing news and many other problematic areas dealt with in earlier chapters. This is not to suggest that the steps that have been taken are anything less than wholly worthwhile, merely that further, and we would say essential, modification would be difficult to implement. In the light of the continuing difficulties presented by the common law, the example of the statutory reforms in Australian jurisdictions and the enlightened attitude taken by the judges in those jurisdictions to questions of liability for psychiatric damage should be heeded. In dealing with issues not only of family relationship but also of proximity to the accident or its aftermath and means of communication of the shock-inducing event, the common law rules should not, as Australian judges have emphasised,[43] be any less liberal than the jurisprudence which has evolved under the statutes of New South Wales and the two Territories.

Criminal injuries compensation legislation

Although statutory intervention in the common law remedy for shock damage in the civil context has been confined to four Australian jurisdictions, legislation providing compensation for "mental or nervous

---

39. [1983] 1 AC 410 at 431. In the English Court of Appeal [1981] QB 599 both Stephenson LJ at 616 and Griffiths LJ at 624 also opined that reform was better left to Parliament.
40. See [1983] 1 AC 410 per Lord Wilberforce at 423, per Lord Edmund-Davies at 425, per Lord Russell at 429, per Lord Bridge at 443.
41. [1992] 1 AC 310 at 404.
42. Ibid at 417.
43. In *Jaensch v Coffey* (1984) 155 CLR 549 at 557 Murphy J said that the court should not adopt a view of public policy more restrictive than that adopted by the legislature in New South Wales, the Australian Capital Territory and the Northern Territory, and at 601 Deane J said that conscious alteration of the common law would be less discriminating than that effected by the legislation in these three jurisdictions.

shock" caused by criminal injuries can be found in many jurisdictions.[44] Such statutes generally provide that injury to the mind is compensable if it is directly attributable to a criminal offence.

It is beyond the scope of this work to examine these provisions in any detail. However, it should be noted that in a number of cases in which applications for compensation have been made, the applicants have suffered recognised psychiatric damage and the courts have had recourse to common law principles in determining entitlement.[45] Just as is the case under the Australian statutes dealing with negligently inflicted harm, restrictions that would have presented problems at common law have been readily overcome. In *Fagan v Crimes Compensation Tribunal*[46] for example, the Australian High Court was moved to award compensation to a young child for shock caused by hearing of his mother's murder. This trend is confirmed by analyses of compensation awards under such legislation in other countries.[47] In the Northern Irish case of *O'Dowd v Secretary of State for Northern Ireland*[48] two masked gunmen burst into a man's home, shot two of his sons and his brother dead and seriously injured him. Another son returned home to be met at the door by his mother, who had been in the house at the time but had not been shot. She told him what had happened and to fetch his uncle who lived about a mile away. The son returned with his uncle and two more of his brothers who had been at the uncle's house. All four entered to find the three bodies and the bleeding father. His three sons claimed compensation for psychiatric damage, as did a son of the uncle who had been in his own house three miles away at the time of the shooting and ran to the scene soon after he heard of the tragedy. They successfully appealed to the Northern Ireland Court of Appeal from the decision of Gibson J in the High Court denying the claims. Lord Lowry LCJ expressly rejected the contention that mental damage can only

44. Early models were the *Criminal Injuries Compensation Act* 1963 (NZ), now superseded by the *Accident Compensation Act* 1972 (NZ), and the British extra-statutory scheme of 1964, as to which see now Criminal Injuries Compensation Board, *Criminal Injuries Compensation Scheme* (1990), and see also *Criminal Injuries Compensation (NI) Order* 1988. For legislation in Australia see *Criminal Injuries Compensation Act* 1983 (ACT); *Victims Compensation Act* 1987 (NSW); *Crimes Compensation Act* 1982 (NT); *Criminal Code* (Qld), Ch LXVA; *Criminal Injuries Compensation Act* 1977 (SA); *Criminal Injuries Compensation Act* 1976 (Tas); *Criminal Injuries Compensation Act* 1972 (Vic); *Criminal Injuries Compensation Act* 1985 (WA). For legislation in Canada see *Criminal Injuries Compensation Act*, RSA 1980, c C-33; *Criminal Injury Compensation Act*, RSBC 1979, c 83; *Criminal Injuries Compensation Act*, RSM 1987, c C-305; *Compensation for Victims of Crime Act*, RSNB 1973, c C-14; *Criminal Injuries Compensation Act*, RSN 1990, c C-38; *Criminal Injuries Compensation Ordinance*, RONWT 1974, c C-23; *Compensation for Victims of Crime Act*, RSNS 1989, c 83; *Compensation for Victims of Crime Act*, RSO 1990, c 24; *Criminal Injuries Compensation Act*, RSS 1978, c C-47; *Compensation for Victims of Crime Act*, RSYT 1986, c 27. There is no legislation in Prince Edward Island.
45. See eg *Battista v Cooper* (1976) 14 SASR 225; *Fagan v Crimes Compensation Tribunal* (1982) 150 CLR 666; *Dixon v Criminal Injuries Compensation Board* (1988) 216 APR 271 (NS). It appears that many more cases of post-traumatic disorders are processed by criminal injuries compensation authorities than by the courts: see R J Bragg, "Post-Traumatic Stress Disorder" (1992) 136 SJ 674.
46. (1982) 150 CLR 666.
47. See D S Greer, "A Statutory Remedy for Nervous Shock?" (1986) 21 Ir Jur (ns) 57, dealing with claims under criminal injuries compensation legislation in Northern Ireland.
48. [1982] NI 210.

be considered directly attributable to a criminal offence if the applicant was present at the time of its commission and suffered injury through personal perception of it. The experience with such statutes, like that of the Australian jurisdictions which have nervous shock legislation, underlines the fact that the common law preoccupation with maintaining arbitrary barriers against the expansion of liability is unnecessary. Caution may be required in drawing direct analogies from the criminal injuries compensation experience because the conduct in question is intentional and because the fact that shock results from criminal conduct is obviously an important factor in favour of granting compensation. But these statutes nevertheless provide some support for the powerful argument which can be mounted on the evidence of the case law interpreting the Australian nervous shock statutes in favour of removing some of the common law impediments to more extended liability for psychiatric damage.

12

DEFENCES

Contributory negligence

The most frequently raised defence to a negligence claim is a plea that the plaintiff's own fault also contributed to the harm which he or she suffered. At common law the plaintiff's contributory negligence was a complete defence, in that even if he or she was only partially responsible for his or her own misfortune this had the effect of entirely absolving the defendant from liability. In the words of Lord Ellenborough CJ: "One person being in fault will not dispense with another's using ordinary care for himself."[1] After various judicial attempts to mitigate the severity of this rule, notably the invention of the doctrine of "last opportunity", according to which even if the plaintiff was contributorily negligent the defendant would retain entire responsibility if he or she had the last opportunity of avoiding the harm,[2] Parliament stepped in. Beginning in Canada in 1924,[3] statutes in all Commonwealth jurisdictions[4] introduced apportionment of

1. *Butterfield v Forrester* (1809) 11 East 60; 103 ER 926 at 927. This case involved a public nuisance on the highway; the plaintiff galloping at full speed on his horse collided with a pole placed across the highway by the defendant. Judgment for the defendant was upheld.
2. *Davies v Mann* (1842) 10 M & W 546; 152 ER 588 is the origin of this rule. Note also *Radley v London & North Western Railway Co* (1876) 1 App Cas 754. See generally M M MacIntyre, "The Rationale of Last Clear Chance" (1940) 53 Harv L Rev 1225; A L Goodhart, "The 'Last Opportunity' Rule" (1949) 65 LQR 237; G Williams, *Joint Torts and Contributory Negligence* (1950), 223-280. On the extension of the rule to "unconscious" and "constructive" last opportunity see *British Columbia Electric Railway Co v Loach* [1916] 1 AC 719; J G Fleming, *The Law of Torts* (8th ed, 1992), 271. For the status of the doctrine prior to the introduction of apportionment legislation see *Admiralty Commissioners v S S Volute* [1922] 1 AC 129; *Swadling v Cooper* [1931] AC 1; *Alford v Magee* (1953) 85 CLR 437.
3. *Contributory Negligence Act*, SO 1924, c 32.
4. See *Law Reform (Contributory Negligence) Act* 1945 (UK) (the model for most of the others, and applying also to Scotland, with minor modifications); *Law Reform (Miscellaneous Provisions) Act* 1955 (ACT), Pt V; *Law Reform (Miscellaneous Provisions) Act* 1965 (NSW), Pt III; *Law Reform (Miscellaneous Provisions) Act* 1956 (NT), Pt V; *Law Reform (Tortfeasors' Contribution, Contributory Negligence, and Division of Chattels) Act* 1952 (Qld), Pt III; *Wrongs Act* 1936 (SA), ss 27a-27b; *Tortfeasors and Contributory Negligence Act* 1954 (Tas), s 4; *Wrongs Act* 1958 (Vic), Pt V; *Law Reform (Contributory Negligence and Tortfeasors Contribution) Act* 1947 (WA), ss 4-6; *Contributory Negligence Act* 1947 (NZ); *Contributory Negligence Act*, RSA 1980, c C-23; *Negligence Act*, RSBC 1979, c 298; *Tortfeasors and Contributory Negligence Act*, RSM 1987, c T-90; *Contributory Negligence Act*, RSNB 1973, c C-19; *Contributory Negligence Act*, RSN 1990, c C-33; *Contributory Negligence Ordinance*, RONWT 1974, c C-13; *Contributory Negligence Act*, RSNS 1989, c 95; *Negligence Act*, RSO 1990, c N-1; *Contributory Negligence Act*, RSPEI 1988, c C-21; *Contributory Negligence Act*, RSS 1978, c C-31; *Contributory Negligence Act*, RSYT 1986, c 32; *Civil Liability Act* 1961 (Ire), s 34(1); *Apportionment of Damages Act* 1956 (SAfr).

responsibility in proportion to the degree of fault.[5] In the United States this move resulted from statutes in some jurisdictions and judicial decisions in others.[6]

Thus defendants, in order to reduce their liability for negligence, must show that the plaintiff was also negligent, and that this negligence contributed to the injury. In theory the standard of care for contributory negligence is the same as that for negligence generally, although because the issue is whether the plaintiff took reasonable care for his or her *own* safety, in practice the test may be somewhat different.[7] Moreover, there is no need to show that the plaintiff's negligence was in breach of a duty of care owed to the defendant.[8] Causation and remoteness issues enter into the question whether the plaintiff's negligence was contributory to the harm.[9] In a typical contributory negligence case, such as a motor vehicle collision, the plaintiff's carelessness contributes to the accident causing the damage, but it may simply cause or increase the damage suffered as a result of the

5. On the principles of apportionment see eg Fleming, op cit, n 2 at 271-281; D J Payne, "Reduction of Damages for Contributory Negligence" (1955) 18 MLR 344. As to its effect on the last opportunity rule, the better view holds that it obviates the principle: see eg *The Boy Andrew v The St Rognvald* [1948] AC 140 per Viscount Simon at 149; *Grant v Sun Shipping Co Ltd* [1948] AC 549 per Lord du Parcq at 563; *Davies v Swan Motor Co (Swansea) Ltd* [1949] 2 KB 291 per Denning LJ at 321-324; *Cork v Kirby Maclean Ltd* [1952] 2 All ER 402 per Denning LJ at 406; *Harvey v Road Haulage Executive* [1952] 1 KB 120 per Denning LJ at 126; *Stapley v Gypsum Mines Ltd* [1953] AC 663 per Lord Porter at 677; *Chisman v Electromation (Export)* (1969) 6 KIR 456 per Lord Denning MR at 458-459, per Edmund Davies LJ at 460; *Rouse v Squires* [1973] 1 QB 889 per Cairns LJ at 898, per MacKenna LJ at 900, per Buckley LJ at 902; *Lloyds Bank v Budd* [1982] RTR 80 per Lord Denning MR at 83; *Chapman v Hearse* (1961) 106 CLR 112 at 124; *Teubner v Humble* (1963) 108 CLR 491 per Windeyer J at 502; *March v E & M H Stramare Pty Ltd* (1991) 171 CLR 506 per Mason CJ at 512. See also the discussion in Fleming, op cit, n 2 at 277-278; A M Linden, *Canadian Tort Law* (4th ed, 1988), 434-436. But note the contrary view expressed in *Henley v Cameron* (1948) 65 TLR 17 per Asquith LJ at 20; ·*Stapley v Gypsum Mines Ltd* [1953] AC 663 per Asquith LJ at 687; *Sherman v Nymboida Collieries Pty Ltd* (1963) 109 CLR 580 per Windeyer J at 590-591. See also the different arguments advanced by G Williams, "The Law Reform (Contributory Negligence) Act 1945" (1946) 9 MLR 105; Goodhart, op cit, n 2; J A Redmond, "Limits to the Defence of Contributory Negligence" (1954) 28 ALJ 3; J A Redmond, "Fault and Apportionment Acts" (1957) 31 ALJ 520; J F Keeler, "Alford v Magee and the Apportionment Legislation" (1967) 41 ALJ 148.

6. See W P Keeton, *Prosser and Keeton on the Law of Torts* (5th ed, 1984), 468-474.

7. See *McHale v Watson* (1966) 115 CLR 199. Courts not uncommonly deem conduct to be negligent which they would be unprepared to label as contributorily negligent. For suggestions that the law should openly recognise that the standard of care in negligence and contributory negligence should be different see F James & J J Dickinson, "Accident Proneness and Accident Law" (1950) 63 Harv L Rev 769; F James, "The Qualities of the Reasonable Man" (1951) 16 Mo L Rev 1; R Parsons, "Negligence, Contributory Negligence and the Man who did not Ride the Bus to Clapham" (1957) 1 MULR 163.

8. See *H & C Grayson Ltd v Ellerman Line Ltd* [1920] AC 466 affirming [1919] 2 KB 514; *Lewis v Denye* [1939] 1 KB 540; *Ross v McQueen* [1947] NI 81; *Davies v Swan Motor Co (Swansea) Ltd* [1949] 2 KB 291; *Nance v British Columbia Electric Railway Co Ltd* [1951] AC 601; *Staveley Iron & Chemical Co Ltd v Jones* [1956] AC 627; *Rukavina v Incorporated Nominal Defendant* [1992] 1 VR 677.

9. See eg *Admiralty Commissioners v S S Volute* [1922] 1 AC 129; *Long v McLaughlin* [1927] 2 DLR 186; *Jones v Livox Quarries Ltd* [1952] 2 QB 608; *Gent-Diver v Neville* [1953] St R Qd 1; *Gittens v O'Brien* (1986) 4 MVR 27.

accident, as in cases involving failure to wear seatbelts or crash helmets. [10]
Another variety of case is where the plaintiff, without contributing to the
accident as such, is exposed to the risk of involvement by the position in
which he or she places himself or herself. [11]

In psychiatric damage cases, as in any other kind of negligence case, the
plaintiff's claim may be met by a plea of contributory negligence. [12] This
may occur where the harm suffered stems from fear for the plaintiff's own
safety (as in the older "nervous shock" cases [13]) if a near-accident results
from the combined negligence of both parties: the plaintiff who carelessly
steps off the kerb into the path of a negligent driver, or does not take proper
care in the driving of his or her own vehicle, may be viewed as having been
partly responsible for the psychiatric injury resulting from the fright of a
narrowly-averted disaster. An analogous example is *Shotter v R & H Green
& Silley Weir Ltd* [14] where a welder using an oxy-acetylene burner with a
defective rubber tube was injured by a flash of flame caused by escaping
gas, luckily avoiding causing a major explosion in a dockyard. Damages for
injuries including psycho-neurosis were reduced by half due to his
contributory negligence in not making a proper examination of the tubes
before commencing work that day. Similarly, claimants who suffer
psychiatric consequences through experiencing an accident or near-accident
to another may themselves be partially to blame. In *Kwok v British
Columbia Ferry Corporation*, [15] where the plaintiff and his family were on
vacation on board their pleasure boat, the plaintiff was partly responsible
for the collision with a ferry which attempted to overtake his boat. The
plaintiff's wife and two of his children died as a result of this tragedy, and
the plaintiff claimed not only for his own personal injury but also for
psychological damage caused by the loss of his family. Cumming J of the
British Columbia Supreme Court adjudged him to be one third to blame for
the accident and reduced his damages accordingly. In *Regan v Harper* [16]
the plaintiff, his wife and two daughters were all injured in a car accident
for which the plaintiff, who was driving, was held 10 per cent responsible.
His claim for the severe psychiatric trauma caused by witnessing the injuries
to his wife and daughters was reduced by the same proportion, though their
personal injury claims were unaffected. In some other cases contributory

10. See eg *Yuan v Farstad* (1967) 66 DLR (2d) 295; *Gagnon v Beaulieu* [1977] 1 WWR 702;
    Froom v Butcher [1976] QB 286 (seat belts); *O'Connell v Jackson* [1972] 1 QB 270 (crash
    helmets). Compare *Kirk v Nominal Defendant (Qld)* [1984] 1 Qd R 592 (protective
    clothing).
11. See eg *Davies v Swan Motor Co (Swansea) Ltd* [1949] 2 KB 291 (dustman riding on back
    of dustcart). Note also *Owens v Brimmell* [1977] QB 859, which beautifully illustrates the
    three kinds of contributory negligence mentioned in the text. The plaintiff failed to wear
    a seat belt, voluntarily allowed himself to be a passenger in a car driven by a drunken
    driver, and assisted the driver to reach this state by going out with him for an evening's
    drinking (during which each consumed about eight or nine pints of beer). See
    N P Gravells, "Three Heads of Contributory Negligence" (1977) 93 LQR 581.
12. See generally T I Bailey, "The Relevance of Defences to Accident Liability in Nervous
    Shock Cases" (1983) 3 Leg Stud 43.
13. Typified by *Dulieu v White & Sons* [1901] 2 KB 669.
14. [1951] 1 Lloyd's Rep 329. See also *Matei v McCrorie* (unreported, Victorian SC, 22 May
    1986, No 27 of 1985).
15. (1987) 20 BCLR (2d) 318.
16. [1971] Qd R 191.

negligence has been raised in argument but on the facts has not been established, as for example in *Klug v Motor Accidents Insurance Board*[17] where the plaintiff claimed for psychiatric injury resulting from the death of his de facto wife due to her own negligent driving. The defendant pleaded that the plaintiff, who was a passenger in the car, contributed to his own injuries by failing to wear a seatbelt, but the court held that the defendant failed to discharge the onus of proving on the balance of probabilities that the plaintiff had neglected to "belt up". There was again a plea of contributory negligence in *Beaulieu v Sutherland*,[18] where the plaintiff and her two friends were walking three abreast along a road at night when the defendant ran down and killed one of the friends, but given the court's finding that the plaintiff had not suffered a psychiatric illness, only anxiety and grief, it was not necessary to examine the contributory negligence issue. In other cases, any hint of contributory negligence that might be suggested by the facts is presumably negatived by the defendant's failure to raise any such defence, as for example in *Chester v Council of the Municipality of Waverley*,[19] where a mother allowed her seven-year-old son to go out and play in a street in which there was a trench filled with water unguarded by any protective fencing, or *Boardman v Sanderson*,[20] where a father left his eight-year-old son on the forecourt of a petrol station while he went into the adjoining office.[21]

The most interesting issue which arises in cases where psychiatric damage results from an accident to someone else is whether the secondary victim's claim is affected by contributory negligence on the part of the *primary* victim. This question goes to the heart of the contributory negligence defence, because back in the 19th century when the plea evolved as a shield to protect defendants against the rapid advance of negligence liability, the courts were originally prepared to hold that not only the plaintiff's own contributory negligence, but also that of others with whom he or she was associated, sufficed to bar the claim.[22] It was held that those who travelled as passengers on board vehicles could not recover against third parties because they were identified with the driver's negligence,[23] and that children injured while in the care of parents or guardians had no claim if the negligence of the person in whose charge they were was partially responsible for the injury.[24] Something of this doctrine of identification can be seen in *Victorian Railways Commissioner v Coultas*,[25] the original case denying liability for nervous shock. It seems that at one point the

---

17. (1991) Aust Torts Rep 81-134.
18. (1986) 35 CCLT 237.
19. (1939) 62 CLR 1.
20. [1964] 1 WLR 1317.
21. See also *Rowe v McCartney* [1975] 1 NSWLR 544, affirmed [1976] 2 NSWLR 72 (no suggestion that plaintiff guilty of contributory negligence in letting friend drive her powerful car); *Galt v British Railways Board* (1983) 133 NLJ 870 (no suggestion that train driver who just managed to avoid hitting two railwaymen on track was negligent).
22. See generally Fleming, op cit, n 2 at 287-290; M M MacIntyre, "The Rationale of Imputed Negligence" (1944) 5 UTLJ 368.
23. *Thorogood v Bryan* (1849) 8 CB 115; 137 ER 452.
24. *Waite v North Eastern Railway Co* (1858) 1 E B & E 719; 120 ER 679. See also *Russell v Jorgenson* (1909) 9 SR (NSW) 164.
25. (1888) 13 App Cas 222.

defendant intended to plead that James Coultas, who was driving the buggy across the level crossing when the train appeared, was guilty of contributory negligence in driving on when the gatekeeper directed him to go back. However Sir Richard Couch, giving judgment in the Privy Council, said that since the defendants did not move for a new trial they could not now contend that there was contributory negligence.[26] If this plea had been successfully raised, it would have defeated not only James Coultas' claim for medical expenses but also his wife's claim for shock, since as a passenger she would have been identified with his negligence. Gradually—no doubt against the background of liability insurance becoming more common and then in road accident and other situations compulsory[27]—the law whittled down the doctrine of identification. The fictional agency which was the basis of the passenger being identified with the driver's negligence was repudiated in *Mills v Armstrong: The Bernina.*[28] The identification of children with the negligence of their elders met its end in *Oliver v Birmingham & Midland Motor Omnibus Co*[29] where an agile grandfather jumped out of the way of a "Midland Red" bus but let go the hand of his four-year-old grandson who was struck by the bus and injured. Husbands and wives are not identified with the negligence of their spouses,[30] nor are principals with independent contractors,[31] or friends with each other.[32] The most important situation in which the doctrine of identification now operates is in master-servant cases—the employee's contributory negligence is imputed to the employer.[33] It also applies where a car owner allows someone else to drive the car for purposes in which the owner has an interest.[34] Though it has been suggested that the doctrine of identification should apply in all cases where there would be vicarious liability,[35] this does not seem justifiable, because the policy basis underlying vicarious liability is to transfer liability to a financially solvent defendant, and there is no similar policy justification requiring financially solvent plaintiffs to meet part of their own loss out of their own pockets.[36]

26. Ibid at 225.
27. Compulsory liability insurance for the owners and drivers of motor vehicles was introduced in New Zealand in 1928, Britain in 1930 and Australia between 1935 and 1944: see Fleming, op cit., n 2 at 398. Liability insurance is also mandatory in such circumstances in all Canadian jurisdictions: see Linden, op cit., n 5 at 596-597.
28. (1888) 13 App Cas 1. See also *Horning v Sycamore* [1935] NZLR 581; *Biggs v Woodhead* [1940] NZLR 108; *Blight v Warman* [1964] SASR 163. Note *France v Parkinson* [1954] 1 WLR 581 where it was held that the negligence of the driver of a hired car could not be imputed to the car's owner who was in the same position as a passenger.
29. [1933] 1 KB 35. See also *Hudson's Bay Co v Wyrzykowski* [1938] 3 DLR 1; *Kaplan v Canada Safeway Ltd* (1968) 68 DLR (2d) 627; *Ducharme v Davies* [1984] 1 WWR 699.
30. *Mallett v Dunn* [1949] 2 KB 180; *Drinkwater v Kimber* [1952] 2 QB 281.
31. *Morton v Douglas Homes Ltd* [1984] 2 NZLR 548 per Hardie Boys J at 581.
32. Ibid.
33. *Chaplin v Hawes* (1828) 3 C & P 554; 172 ER 543; *Carberry v Davies* [1968] 1 WLR 1103. See Fleming, op cit, n 2 at 287-288.
34. *Berrill v Road Haulage Executive* [1952] 2 Lloyd's Rep 490; *Lampert v Eastern National Omnibus Co* [1954] 1 WLR 647; *Pennell v O'Callaghan* [1954] VLR 320; *Manawatu County v Rowe* [1956] NZLR 78; *Doyle v Pick* [1965] WAR 95; *Milkovits v Federal Capital Press of Australia Pty Ltd* (1972) 20 FLR 311.
35. The so-called "both ways" test: see C O Gregory, "Vicarious Responsibility and Contributory Negligence" (1932) 41 Yale LJ 831.
36. See C D Baker, *Tort* (5th ed, 1991), 192-193.

This is the background against which we need to ask whether a claim for psychiatric damage should be affected in any way by the primary victim's contributory negligence. The point has already been made that in such circumstances the plaintiff must show a duty of care owed to himself or herself personally.[37] The claim is in no way a derivative claim. In the words of Lord Wright in *Bourhill v Young*:

"If, however, the appellant has a cause of action it is because of a wrong to herself. She cannot build on a wrong to someone else. Her interest, which was in her own bodily security, was of a different order from the interest of the owner of the car."[38]

On general principle, then, it would seem to follow that the contributory fault of the primary victim should not operate to reduce the damages of another who suffers psychiatric injury in consequence of the accident.

However, the two major authorities do not bear out this conclusion. In *Dillon v Legg*,[39] the leading United States decision on bystander recovery for psychiatric harm, the defendant ran down and killed a little girl who was crossing the road. The accident was witnessed by her mother and older sister, both of whom recovered damages for resulting emotional trauma—in the mother's case, despite being outside the zone of danger. According to Tobriner J:

"[D]efendant has interposed the defence that the contributory negligence of the mother, the sister and the child contributed to the accident. If any such defence is sustained and defendant found not liable for the death of the child because of the contributory negligence of the mother, sister or child, we do not believe that the mother or sister should recover for the emotional trauma which they allegedly suffered. In the absence of the primary liability of the tortfeasor for the death of the child, we see no ground for an independent and a secondary liability for claims for injuries by third parties. The basis for such claims must be adjudicated liability and fault of the defendant; that liability and fault must be the foundation for the tortfeasor's duty of due care to third parties who, as a consequence of such negligence, sustain emotional trauma."[40]

On the facts, no such defence was made out and the plaintiffs recovered damages. Much more recently, in *Alcock v Chief Constable of South Yorkshire Police*,[41] Lord Oliver likewise suggested that the contributory negligence of the primary victim should affect a secondary victim's claim:

"I can visualise great difficulty arising, if this be the law, where the accident, though not solely caused by the primary victim has been materially contributed to by his negligence. If, for instance, the primary victim is himself 75 per cent responsible for the accident, it would be a curious and wholly unfair situation if the plaintiff were enabled to recover damages for his or her traumatic injury from the person responsible only in a minor degree whilst he in turn remained

37. See above, pp 64-68.
38. [1943] AC 92 at 108.
39. (1968) 441 P 2d 912; 69 Cal Rptr 72.
40. Ibid at 916.
41. [1992] 1 AC 310.

unable to recover any contribution from the person primarily responsible since the latter's negligence vis-à-vis the plaintiff would not even have been tortious."[42]

These dicta are undeniably important but appear to be inconsistent with the general principle that a psychiatric damage victim's claim is independent of that of any other party involved. As regards *Dillon v Legg*, the case seems to rest on the fact that in California at that time contributory negligence was still a complete defence.[43] The defendant being in no way responsible in law for the accident, there was no basis for legal liability to secondary parties. Lord Oliver's dictum in *Alcock v Chief Constable of South Yorkshire Police* seems to be grounded on the non-liability of the primary victim to the plaintiff, so preventing the defendant from obtaining contribution. But it has been argued in an earlier chapter that it is wrong to rule out liability for psychiatric damage caused by another person negligently killing, injuring or endangering himself or herself.[44] If this argument is accepted, the basis of Lord Oliver's assertion disappears. The secondary victim would be able to recover in full for psychiatric injury and the tortfeasor sued would be able to claim contribution from the other.

It has to be admitted that there is little in the way of case law to justify the view contended for.[45] Some indirect support can be gleaned from a few decisions, however. In *Young v Burgoyne*,[46] where a father suffered psychiatric harm on arriving at the aftermath of an accident in which his daughter was badly injured, Hallett J held that the defendant was solely at fault, in spite of the fact that the daughter's injuries were caused by failure to wear a seatbelt, and were also contributed to by her intoxication. In *Harvey v Cairns*[47] a claim for emotional damage was made on behalf of a brother who witnessed his six-year-old sister's death under the wheels of a pickup truck. Lord Murray held that children of that age could be found guilty of contributory negligence and that she was two thirds to blame. The tenor of the judgment suggests that this would not have brought about a reduction in the brother's damages, but his Lordship found that no causal link between the accident and the brother's illness had been established. Courts have sometimes had occasion to rule more directly on this issue. In *White v Butcher*[48] parents who suffered psychiatric injury as a result of a serious accident to their daughter recovered damages unaffected by their daughter's contributory negligence. In the United States in *Meredith v Hanson*[49] a Washington court made a clear finding that a stepfather's

---

42. Ibid at 418.
43. See Keeton, op cit, n 6 at 471.
44. See above, pp 215-220.
45. In *McLoughlin v O'Brian* [1983] 1 AC 410 Lord Russell at 429 said that the court was "not concerned with any problem that might have been posed had the accident not been wholly attributable to the negligence of the defendants, but partly attributable to negligent driving by the injured son of the plaintiff". Again the issue was not raised in *Mount Isa Mines Ltd v Pusey* (1970) 125 CLR 383, even though there seemed to be potential for it: the two electricians rescued by the plaintiff were, it seems, partly responsible for the explosion in which they were injured.
46. (1981) 122 DLR (3d) 330.
47. 1989 SLT 107.
48. (Unreported, New South Wales SC, 13 Oct 1982, Nos 9576, 9577 and 9578 of 1981).
49. (1985) 697 P2d 602 (Wash).

contributory fault could not be imputed to his stepson who witnessed the accident to him and suffered emotional trauma in consequence.

The principle that the shock victim's claim should be recognised as independent of that of the accident victim, and that the latter's contributory negligence should be regarded as irrelevant, receives support from the case law on the statutory causes of action for "mental or nervous shock" found in some Australian jurisdictions.[50] Under these provisions it is clear law that the cause of action given to those who suffer shock consequent on accidents or near-accidents to another is in no way dependent on whether the defendant is liable to that other,[51] and it must follow that such a claim is unaffected by contributory negligence on the part of the accident victim.

There are other contexts in which the problem has arisen whether the contributory negligence of one tort victim will affect another's claim. As regards rescuers, the law is clear: the duty to the rescuer is independent of any duty owed to the endangered person,[52] and if the latter is guilty of contributory negligence the rescuer's damages would remain unaffected. In most jurisdictions, a different view prevails as regards Fatal Accidents Act actions. The contributory negligence of the deceased is generally held to reduce the damages that must be paid to the relatives.[53] This, it is true, is simply a consequence of the special position of such claims, which from the outset have been dependent on the condition that the deceased would have been able to sue had he or she survived.[54] Nevertheless, when New South Wales abandoned the rule that contributory negligence constituted a complete defence it recognised the importance of providing proper compensation for the deceased's relatives, who were in no way to blame for the loss of their breadwinner, by specifically enacting that the contributory negligence of the deceased should not in any way operate to reduce the damages of plaintiffs in wrongful death actions,[55] and in 1982 a similar reform was enacted in Victoria.[56] Other jurisdictions should follow this example. Turning to actions for loss of consortium and services, the courts both in Australia and in England again accepted the principle that contributory negligence on the part of the injured employee or family member did not diminish the damages recoverable by the employer, husband or parent bringing the action,[57] although three Australian

50. *Law Reform (Miscellaneous Provisions) Act* 1944 (NSW), s 4; *Law Reform (Miscellaneous Provisions) Act* 1955 (ACT), s 24; *Law Reform (Miscellaneous Provisions) Act* 1956 (NT), s 25. Note also *Wrongs Act* 1936 (SA), s 35a(1)(c); *Motor Accidents Act* 1988 (NSW), s 77. See above, Chapter 11.

51. See above, pp 240-241.

52. See *Videan v British Transport Commission* [1963] 2 QB 650 (no duty owed to endangered person because he was trespasser). Note also *Chapman v Hearse* (1961) 106 CLR 112 (endangered person's contributory negligence operated to reduce damages payable to his estate).

53. *Senior v Ward* (1859) 1 E & E 385; 120 ER 954; *Littley v Brooks* [1932] 2 DLR 386.

54. See eg *Fatal Accidents Act* 1976 (UK), s 1(1). For details of equivalent legislation in other jurisdictions see above, p 95, n 33.

55. *Law Reform (Miscellaneous Provisions) Act* 1965 (NSW), s 10(4), though this does not apply in road and work accidents.

56. *Wrongs Act* 1958 (Vic), s 26(4).

57. *Mallett v Dunn* [1949] 2 KB 180; *Curran v Young* (1965) 112 CLR 99. See also *Howard v Loney* [1956] Tas SR 57; *Lloyd v Lewis* [1963] VR 277; *Cook v Wright* [1967] NZLR 1034 per Wild CJ at 1037; *Lawrence v Slatcher* [1968] VR 337.

jurisdictions have a different rule enshrined in statute,[58] and Canada[59] and the United States[60] also favour a reduction of the damages. Finally, it seems likely that the duty as regards pre-natal injuries recognised by *Watt v Rama*[61] would be unaffected by the mother's contributory negligence. The contrary rule laid down by statute in England[62] has been severely criticised.[63]

The law on the effect of the contributory negligence of one plaintiff on the rights of another is thus complex and contains some anomalies. Nonetheless it is submitted that in psychiatric damage cases the primary victim's contributory negligence should not reduce the damages of a secondary victim who has suffered resulting mental harm. Dicta in leading cases to the contrary[64] are influenced by outdated ideas of contributory negligence or unnecessary limits on the scope of psychiatric damage recovery, and cannot stand against the clear trend in negligence law away from the identification of one plaintiff with the want of care of another.

Assumption of risk

Assumption of risk is the other major defence to negligence, though it is raised much less frequently and is not often successful, due to the difficulty in establishing the two stringent prerequisites of the plea: that the plaintiff had a pre-existing and comprehensive appreciation of the precise nature of the risk incurred, and that he or she freely and voluntarily elected to be

58. *Wrongs Act* 1936 (SA) s 27a(9); *Law Reform (Miscellaneous Provisions) Act* 1955 (ACT), s 17; *Law Reform (Miscellaneous Provisions) Act* 1956 (NT), s 18.
59. See *McLaughlin v Young* [1927] SCR 303; *Attorney-General of Canada v Jackson* [1946] 2 DLR 481; *Enridge v Copp* (1966) 57 DLR (2d) 239. Contrast *Macdonald v McNeil* [1953] 2 DLR 248.
60. See Keeton, op cit, n 6 at 937.
61. [1972] VR 353. See also *Duval v Seguin* (1972) 26 DLR (3d) 418; (1973) 40 DLR (3d) 666; *Pratt and Goldsmith v Pratt* [1975] VR 378; *Presley v Newport Hospital* (1976) 365 A 2d 748 (RI). For earlier authorities based mainly on civil law principles see *Montreal Tramways Co v Léveillé* [1933] 4 DLR 337; *Pinchin v Sanlam Insurance Co Ltd*, 1963 (2) SA 254 (W). Older authorities had ruled against the existence of such a duty: see *Walker v Great Northern Railway Co of Ireland* (1891) 28 LR Ir 69. Although it had been assumed in thalidomide cases (see eg *Distillers Co (Biochemicals) Ltd v Thompson* [1971] AC 458; *Whitehouse v Jordan* [1981] 1 WLR 246; and note also *McKay v Essex Area Health Authority* [1982] QB 1166 per Stephenson LJ at 1178) that a duty of care is owed to an unborn child at common law, It was not until *Burton v Islington Health Authority* [1992] 3 All ER 833 that this was actually decided by an appellate court in England. The births in both these cases occurred prior to the commencement of the *Congenital Disabilities (Civil Liability) Act* 1976 (UK) which pursuant to s 1(1) and (2) in certain circumstances confers a right of action on a child born disabled in respect of that "disability". See generally P F Cane, "Injuries to Unborn Children" (1977) 51 ALJ 704; P J Pace, "Civil Liability for Pre-Natal Injuries" (1977) 40 MLR 141. All the above cases involve negligence on the part of someone other than the mother. The first case in which the mother was held liable for negligence to her unborn child appears to be *Lynch v Lynch* (1991) Aust Torts Rep 81-117.
62. *Congenital Disabilities (Civil Liability) Act* 1976 (UK), s 1(7).
63. See Cane, op cit, n 61 at 716.
64. *Dillon v Legg* (1968) 441 P 2d 912; 69 Cal Rptr 72; *Alcock v Chief Constable of South Yorkshire Police* [1992] 1 AC 310; see above, pp 253-254.

exposed to the danger.[65] Only if this is shown to have been the case is the defendant absolved from all responsibility for the risk of harm. The defence used to be of major importance in a number of contexts, particularly employment situations,[66] but now has little role to play in that arena[67] and has been excluded in other areas also.[68] It has also suffered something of an identity crisis due to controversy as to whether it should be confined to cases where there is express agreement to assume the risk of harm,[69] and whether it is truly a defence or negates the breach of duty element in negligence.[70] Nonetheless, it can be invoked in a number of situations, particularly in cases involving participating in or watching sport,[71] or where passengers accept lifts from drunken drivers,[72] and in employer-

65. See D M Gordon, "Wrong Turns in the Volens Cases" (1945) 60 LQR 140; T Ingman, "A History of the Defence of Volenti Non Fit Injuria" [1981] JR 1.
66. See *Priestley v Fowler* (1837) 3 M & W 1; 150 ER 1030; *Thomas v Quartermaine* (1887) 18 QBD 685.
67. The decline began with *Smith v Charles Baker & Sons* [1891] AC 325. It was in this case that the House of Lords made it clear that the fact that a plaintiff knew of a danger and continued to expose himself or herself to it does not amount to consent to run the risk of injury at his or her own expense rather than that of the defendant.
68. In the United Kingdom, the defence has been excluded by statute in cases involving the liability of drivers of vehicles covered by compulsory insurance to passengers: see *Road Traffic Act* 1972 (UK), s 148(3). Further, in any case involving "business liability" where limitations are imposed on the effectiveness of clauses excluding or restricting liability for negligence, a person's agreement to or awareness of an exemption clause is not of itself to be taken as indicating the voluntary acceptance of any risk: see *Unfair Contract Terms Act* 1977 (UK), s 2(3) (which leaves open the possibility of a plea of contributory negligence).
69. For argument in favour of this view see eg F H Bohlen, "Voluntary Assumption of Risk" (1906) 20 Harv L Rev 14, 91; D J Payne, "Assumption of Risk in Negligence" (1957) 35 Can BR 350; J W Wade, "The Place of Assumption of Risk in the Law of Negligence" (1961) 22 La L Rev 5; F James, "Assumption of Risk: Unhappy Reincarnation" (1968) 78 Yale LJ 185; A J E Jaffey, "Volenti Non Fit Injuria" [1985] CLJ 87. For discussion of the issue see Fleming, op cit, n 2 at 291-298; Linden, op cit, n 5 at 449-452; Keeton, op cit, n 6 at 493-495. See also *Wooldridge v Sumner* [1963] 2 QB 43 per Diplock LJ at 69; *Nettleship v Weston* [1971] 2 QB 691 per Lord Denning MR at 702.
70. Support for the theory that it negates breach of duty is provided by the cases on participation in sport: see below, n 71, and on drunken drivers: see below, n 72. For discussion see Fleming, op cit, n 2 at 303-305; Linden, op cit at n 5, 448-449; Payne, op cit, n 69. See also *Jaensch v Coffey* (1984) 155 CLR 549 where Deane J at 604-605, in discussing "the limitations on the ordinary test of reasonable foreseeability in cases of mere psychiatric injury", referred to assumption of risk in this context. Though he said that it was unnecessary to decide the matter, he stated his opinion that it was not merely a defence but that absence of assumption of risk was a necessary criterion of proximity of relationship.
71. See eg *Ratcliffe v Whitehead* [1933] WWR 447; *Elliott v Amphitheatre Ltd* [1934] 3 WWR 225; *Payne v Maple Leaf Gardens Ltd* [1949] 1 DLR 369; *Murray v Harringay Arena Ltd* [1951] 2 KB 529; *Wooldridge v Sumner* [1963] 2 QB 43; *Agar v Canning* (1965) 54 WWR 302, affirmed (1966) 55 WWR 384; *Ellison v Rogers* [1968] 1 OR 501; *Simms v Leigh Rugby Football Club* [1969] 2 All ER 923; *Wilks v Cheltenham Homeguard Motor Cycle & Light Car Club* [1971] 1 WLR 668; *Hagerman v City of Niagara Falls* (1980) 114 DLR (3d) 184. Compare *Standfield v Uhr* [1964] Qd R 66 where the majority overturned a jury's verdict that a jockey had voluntarily accepted the risk of danger presented by the location of a tractor close to where the horses were to run. Note also J G Fleming, "Assumption of Risk—California Style" (1993) 1 Tort L Rev (forthcoming).
72. See eg *Dann v Hamilton* [1939] 1 KB 509; *Insurance Commissioner v Joyce* (1948) 77 CLR 39; *Roggenkamp v Bennett* (1950) 80 CLR 292; *Car & General Insurance Corporation Ltd v Seymour and Maloney* (1956) 2 DLR (2d) 369; *Miller v Decker* (1957) 9 DLR (2d) 1; *Lehnert v Stein* (1963) 36 DLR (2d) 159; *Sara v Government Insurance Office of New*

employee situations of an exceptional nature such as *Imperial Chemical Industries Ltd v Shatwell*,[73] where two brothers agreed to disobey company instructions and carry out detonations with short firing leads, with fatal results.

Judicial references to the assumption of risk doctrine in psychiatric damage cases are few and far between, though in *Dulieu v White & Sons*[74] Kennedy J suggested that there could be no question that a person who suffered nervous shock as a result of narrowly escaping being hit by a negligently driven vehicle was volens to such a risk merely by using the streets. (The mere suggestion sounds strange today—courts in the 1990s would never dream of deeming road users, by their mere presence, to have consented to the risk of injury.) In addition, in *Bassanese v Martin*[75] there is an intimation that the wife acquiesced in the husband committing adultery with another woman, although of course there is no question that she thereby consented to the risk of mental harm resulting from his being murdered by the woman's jealous lover. However, circumstances can be envisaged where a plea of volenti non fit injuria might be successful against a plaintiff who has suffered psychiatric harm. For example, it has been suggested that the claim of a mother who suffers traumatic injury from the shock of seeing her son killed in a speedway accident due to the negligence of another rider may be met by the assumption of risk defence.[76] Arguably, so may companions electing to participate together in potentially hazardous pastimes such as parachuting, hang-gliding, mountain-climbing or skiing.[77] Voluntary acceptance of the risk of injury in these situations conceivably includes the risk of physical and psychiatric illness through perception both of injury or danger to oneself and of the death, injury or imperilment of one's partner. Again, someone who accepts a lift from a drunken driver and suffers psychiatric harm on witnessing the injuries he or she incurs in an accident resulting from his or her unfitness to control the vehicle may not have a good cause of action. If one of the Shatwell brothers had not been injured in the explosion, but traumatised at viewing the death of the other, it again seems likely that a plea that the plaintiff was volens would have been upheld.

72. *Continued*
    South Wales (1968) 89 WN (NSW) 203; *Eid v Dumas* (1969) 5 DLR (3d) 561; *Walker v Watson* [1974] 2 NZLR 175; *Jeffries v Fisher* [1985] WAR 250; *Dube v Labar* (1986) 36 CCLT 105; *Spicer v Coppins* (1991) 56 SASR 175. Note also *Morris v Murray* [1991] 2 QB 6 where the English Court of Appeal held that the plea of volenti could be maintained where a passenger went on a flight with a drunken pilot. Contrast the more benevolent attitude shown to learner drivers where the volenti defence is generally not applied: see eg *Lovelace v Fossum* [1972] 2 WWR 161; *Cook v Cook* (1986) 162 CLR 376, rejecting the view of Lord Denning MR in *Nettleship v Weston* [1971] 2 QB 691 at 699-700.
73. [1965] AC 656. See P S Atiyah, "Causation, Contributory Negligence and Volenti Non Fit Injuria" (1965) 43 Can BR 609; R W M Dias, "Consent of Parties and Voluntas Legis" [1966] CLJ 75.
74. [1901] 2 KB 669 at 672.
75. (1982) 31 SASR 461.
76. See D M Walker, *The Law of Delict in Scotland* (2nd ed, 1981), 678.
77. But note *Rootes v Shelton* (1967) 116 CLR 383 (cross-over water-skiing); *Bondarenko v Sommers* (1968) 69 SR (NSW) 269 (hot-rodding on a country road).

Illegality

In general, the fact that the plaintiff is involved in an illegal activity at the time injury is suffered is no bar to recovery in tort.[78] According to Latham CJ in *Henwood v Metropolitan Transport Trust*:[79]

"The person who is injured in a motor accident may be a child playing truant from school, an employee who is absent from work in breach of his contract, a man who is loitering upon a road in breach of a by-law, or a burglar on his way to a professional engagement—but none of these facts is relevant for the purpose of deciding the existence or defining the content of the obligation of a motor driver not to injure them."[80]

It is different, however, when the injury arises out of an unlawful joint venture undertaken by plaintiff and defendant, though, as with the volenti defence, a major issue is whether the principle ex turpi causa non oritur actio is simply a ground of defence or negates a duty of care. The leading authorities, at least in Australia, incline towards the latter view.[81] What is clear is that the courts will generally refuse to recognise that one injured participant has a cause of action against the other.[82] This would apply to psychiatric damage just as much as to any other form of harm. Thus, building on the standard example of the negligent safeblower who causes an explosion and injures another, if a third safeblower suffered psychiatric damage at the sight of the injury to his partner in crime, or in attempting to rescue him, there could surely be no available legal remedy. According

78. See however *Burns v Edman* [1970] 2 QB 541 (Fatal Accidents Act claim ruled out on ground that deceased was professional criminal); *Murphy v Culhane* [1977] QB 94 (person who attacks another in criminal affray may be debarred from suing).
79. (1938) 60 CLR 438 at 446. See also *Vancouver v Burchill* [1932] 4 DLR 200; *Green v Costello* [1961] NZLR 1010; *Andrews v Nominal Defendant* (1965) 66 SR (NSW) 85; *Westwood v Post Office* [1974] AC 1.
80. United States examples in psychiatric damage cases include *Meredith v Hanson* (1985) 697 P 2d 602 (Wash) where the defendant's defence that the plaintiff stepfather should not be granted recovery for emotional harm caused by the injury to his stepson on the ground that he had a criminal record and was therefore an unworthy stepfather was deservedly rejected, and *Caparco v Lambert* (1979) 402 A 2d 1180 (RI) where the court turned down the claim of a mother for psychiatric harm resulting from injury to her child when the child entered a neighbour's parked car and released the handbrake, but on the ground that she did not witness the injury, laying no stress on the fact that the child was trespassing.
81. See *Smith v Jenkins* (1970) 119 CLR 397; *Progress & Properties Ltd v Craft* (1976) 135 CLR 651; *Jackson v Harrison* (1978) 138 CLR 438; *Gala v Preston* (1991) 172 CLR 243: see N J Mullany, "Proximity, Policy and Procrastination" (1992) 9 Aust Bar Rev 80. See also *Ashton v Turner* [1981] QB 137 per Ewbank J at 146; *Kirkham v Chief Constable of the Greater Manchester Police* [1990] AC 282; *Pitts v Hunt* [1991] QB 24.
82. *Smith v Jenkins* (1970) 119 CLR 397; *Tomlinson v Harrison* [1972] 1 OR 670; *Tallow v Tailfeathers* [1973] 6 WWR 732; *Progress & Properties Ltd v Craft* (1976) 135 CLR 651; *Jackson v Harrison* (1978) 138 CLR 438; *Ashton v Turner* [1981] QB 137; *Mack v Enns* (1981) 17 CCLT 291; *Norberg v Wynrib* (1988) 44 CCLT 184, affirmed (1990) 66 DLR (4th) 553; *Gala v Preston* (1991) 172 CLR 243. See also *Canadian Cement LaFarge Ltd v B C Lightweight Aggregate Ltd* (1983) 24 CCLT 111. For general discussion see G H L Fridman, "The Wrongdoing Plaintiff" (1972) 18 McGill LJ 275; E J Weinrib, "Illegality as a Tort Defence" (1976) 26 UTLJ 28; W J Ford, "Tort and Illegality: The Ex Turpi Causa Defence in Negligence Law" (1977) 11 MULR 32, 164; J P Swanton, "Plaintiff a Wrongdoer: Joint Complicity in an Unlawful Exercise as a Defence to Negligence" (1981) 9 Syd LR 304.

to the cases[83] the same would apply if, as the result of the negligent driving of the getaway car, one criminal was injured and another suffered shock and resulting psychiatric harm. So too, there would have been no difference in outcome if the teenage plaintiff in *Gala v Preston*,[84] injured whilst joy-riding in a stolen car with his drunken mates, had been psychologically rather than physically incapacitated as a result of the wayward driving—both claims are equally unsustainable.

Limitation of actions

A rather different kind of defence is that the time allowed by law for the bringing of an action has expired before the issue of a writ. The limitation period in tort actions is traditionally six years in most jurisdictions,[85] but in some cases the Limitation Act provides a special shorter limitation period, typically three years, for personal injury cases.[86] The majority of limitation statutes also contain provisions to deal with cases in which it is not immediately apparent that injury has been suffered—again in some instances confined to personal injury.[87] In some instances, the period does

83. See *Ashton v Turner* [1981] QB 137; *Tomlinson v Harrison* [1972] 1 OR 670.
84. (1991) 172 CLR 243.
85. *Limitation Act* 1985 (ACT), s 11(1); *Limitation Act* 1969 (NSW), s 14(1)(b); *Limitation of Actions Act* 1974 (Qld), s 10(1)(a); *Limitation of Actions Act* 1936 (SA), s 35(c); *Limitation Act* 1974 (Tas), s 4(1)(a); *Limitation of Actions Act* 1958 (Vic), s 5(1)(a); *Limitation Act* 1980 (UK), s 2; *Statute of Limitations* 1957 (Ire), s 11(2)(a); *Limitation Act* 1950 (NZ), s 4(1)(a); *Limitation of Actions Act*, RSNB 1973, c L-8, s 9; *Limitation of Actions Act*, RSNS 1989, c 258, s 2(1)(e); *Statute of Limitations*, RSPEI 1988, c S-7, s 2(1)(g). In the Northern Territory the period is three years: *Limitation Act* 1981 (NT), s 12(1)(b). Alberta and British Columbia have a two year period: *Limitation of Actions Act*, RSA 1980, c L-15, s 51; *Limitation Act*, RSBC 1979, c 236, s 3(1). Western Australia, Manitoba, Newfoundland, North West Territories, Ontario, Saskatchewan and the Yukon Territory have various different periods: see *Limitation Act* 1935 (WA), s 38(1); *Limitation of Actions Act*, RSM 1987, c L-150, s 2(1); *Limitation of Personal Actions Act*, RSN 1990, c L-15, s 2; *Limitation of Actions Ordinance*, RONWT 1974, c L-6, s 3(1); *Limitations Act*, RSO 1990, c L-15, s 45(1); *Limitation of Actions Act*, RSS 1978, c L-15, s 3(1); *Limitations of Actions Act*, RSYT 1986, c 104, s 2(1). For Scotland, see the *Prescription and Limitation (Scotland) Act* 1973 (UK), s 6.
86. *Limitation Act* 1969 (NSW), s 18A; *Limitation of Actions Act* 1974 (Qld), s 11; *Limitation of Actions Act* 1936 (SA), s 36(1); *Limitation Act* 1974 (Tas), s 5(1); *Limitation Act* 1980 (UK), s 11; *Statute of Limitations* 1957 (Ire), s 11(2)(b). In New Zealand the period is two years: *Limitation Act* 1950 (NZ), s 4(7). In Canada, the period is also generally two years: see *Limitation Act*, RSM 1987, c L-150, s 2(1)(e); *Limitation of Actions Ordinance*, RONWT 1974, c L-6, s 3(1)(d); *Statute of Limitations*, RSPEI 1988, c S-7, s 2(1)(d); *Limitation of Actions Act*, RSS 1978, c L-15, s 3(1)(d); *Limitation of Actions Act*, RSYT 1986, c 104, s 2(1)(d) ("wounding or other injury to the person"); *Limitation of Actions Act*, RSNB 1973, c L-8, ss 4 (wounding), 5(1) (damages arising out of the operation, care or control of a motor vehicle); *Limitation of Actions Act*, RSNS 1989, c 258, ss 2(1)(d) (medical negligence), 2(1)(f) (injury occasioned by or arising out of the ownership, maintenance, operation or use of a motor vehicle). Note however that in Newfoundland and Ontario the period for "wounding" is four years: *Limitation of Personal Actions Act*, RSN 1990, c L-15, s 2(3); *Limitations Act*, RSO 1990, c L-15, s 45(1)(j).
87. Those confined to personal injury are: *Limitation Act* 1985 (ACT), s 36; *Limitation Act* 1969 (NSW), s 60C; *Limitation of Actions Act* 1974 (Qld), s 31; *Limitation Act* 1974 (Tas), s 5(3); *Limitation of Actions Act* 1958 (Vic), s 23A; *Limitation Act* 1980 (UK), s 11: see S Todd, *Limitation Periods in Personal Injury Claims* (1982); P J Davies, "Limitations of the Law of Limitation" (1982) 98 LQR 249. The Western Australian provision, *Limitation Act* 1935 (WA), s 38A, applies only to asbestos-related diseases: see

not begin to run until the plaintiff acquires the necessary knowledge; [88] in others the court is given a discretion to extend it. [89]

In relation to psychiatric damage cases, two issues arise in this context. The first is whether psychiatric damage, even though it is basically mental rather than physical, constitutes "personal injury" for the purposes of limitation provisions which are confined to this form of harm. The answer of course has a major effect on the position of psychiatric damage sufferers in determining how much time is available to them for bringing an action. Fortunately, the answer is reasonably straightforward. "Personal injury" under the statutes in question is generally defined as including any disease and any impairment of a person's physical or mental condition. [90]

The second issue is rather more complex. The limitation period in tort runs from the date a cause of action accrues, which in the case of a tort in which damage is a necessary element is the time at which damage is suffered. [91] This may be coincident with the time the breach of duty took place, but it may be much later. In the straightforward case involving physical injury the time at which damage is suffered is usually obvious (for example, one normally knows that an arm or leg has been cut or broken), but in other cases, and particularly in cases where the problem is the infliction of disease rather than injury, it gives rise to considerable difficulty, as is revealed by cases involving asbestosis, mesothelioma, silicosis and similar diseases where the problem is that the date of the disease's onset—through, for example, the inhalation of minute fibres or particles—is inherently unknowable. The leading case of *Cartledge v E Jopling & Sons* [92] suggested that there was a point in time, later than the exposure to such risks, at which the "secret onset" of the disease occurred, and that this was the point at which damage was suffered and the limitation

87. *Continued*
    P Handford, "Damages and Limitation Issues in Asbestos Cases" (1991) 21 UWALR 63. Those not so confined are: *Limitation Act* 1981 (NT), s 24; *Limitation of Actions Act* 1936 (SA), s 48; *Limitation Act*, RSBC 1979, c 236, s 6(3); *Limitation Act*, RSM 1987, c L-150, s 14(1); *Limitation of Actions Act*, RSNS 1979, c 258, s 3. Some jurisdictions also have special provisions allowing the extension of the limitation period in property damage cases: *Limitation Act* 1985 (ACT), s 40; *Latent Damage Act* 1986 (UK). See generally N J Mullany, "Limitation of Actions and Latent Damage—An Australian Perspective" (1991) 54 MLR 216; N J Mullany, "Reform of the Law of Latent Damage" (1991) 54 MLR 349; N J Mullany, "Limitation of Actions—Where Are We Now?" [1993] LMCLQ 34.
88. As is the case under the provisions in Queensland, Western Australia, the United Kingdom, British Columbia and Manitoba.
89. As is the case under the provisions in the Australian Capital Territory, New South Wales, Northern Territory, South Australia, Tasmania, Victoria and Nova Scotia.
90. See *Limitation Act* 1985 (ACT), s 8(1); *Limitation Act* 1969 (NSW), s 11(1); *Limitation Act* 1981 (NT), s 4(1); *Limitation of Actions Act* 1974 (Qld), s 5; *Limitation of Actions Act* 1936 (SA), s 36(2); *Limitation Act* 1974 (Tas), s 5(5); *Limitation of Actions Act* 1958 (Vic), s 3(1); *Limitation Act* 1980 (UK), s 38(1).
91. *Cartledge v E Jopling & Sons* [1963] AC 758; *Pirelli General Cable Works v Oscar Faber & Partners Ltd* [1983] 2 AC 1. See N J Mullany, "Limitation of Actions and Latent Damage—An Australian Perspective" (1991) 54 MLR 216; A McGee, *Limitation Periods* (1990), 61-70. Presumably, in actions under the principle of *Wilkinson v Downton* [1897] 2 QB 57 time runs from the onset of the "physical harm".
92. [1963] AC 758.

period would start to run,[93] but this does not make it any easier to measure the limitation period. In practice the problem is usually avoided by resort to the delaying or extending provisions referred to above.

In the psychiatric damage context, the issue is whether actionable damage is suffered at the time of the initial trauma or subsequently, when it becomes clear that the plaintiff has suffered the secondary reaction that constitutes a "recognisable psychiatric illness".[94] The latter alternative may present problems in pinpointing the date of accrual of the cause of action similar to those apparent in the disease cases;[95] yet, although there is no real authority on the point, rationally this must be the alternative the law adopts. If liability is dependent on proof of a recognisable psychiatric illness, the limitation period cannot begin to run until such damage is suffered. Initial and transient shock, then, will not start the clock. Nor will episodes of common emotional upset like normal grieving. This rule and the clinical nature of certain psychiatric complaints combine to create a potential for very long periods of grace. "Delayed shock" is not an uncommon phenomenon and post-traumatic stress disorder, for example, may not manifest itself for as long as 30 years after the traumatic event.[96] When in such a case the specified limitation period is then added a situation arises which runs contrary to one of the central policy aims of limitation law—that actions should have a finite life and not surface to haunt defendants years after their tortious conduct. Complications will arise, however, if the courts elect to include mental responses falling short of psychiatric disorder under the umbrella of actionable "shock". More than one murmuring has been made along these lines[97] and it remains to be seen if such an unorthodox view gains wider acceptance. But if the seriousness of the damage required to bring suit is decreased, some means will have to be devised of identifying the start date for limitation purposes. How this is to be done is not at present an easy question to answer.

93. See especially per Lord Pearce at 778-779. Note also J Stapleton, "The Gist of Negligence" (1988) 104 LQR 213, 389.
94. See above, pp 14-18.
95. With the issue ultimately turning on the burden of proof, on which see now *Pullen v Gutteridge, Haskins & Davey Pty Ltd* (unreported, Victorian SC, 9 June 1992, Nos 1256 of 1987 and 3111 of 1988), noted by N J Mullany (1993) 109 LQR (forthcoming).
96. See above, pp 37-38.
97. See above, pp 18-21.

13

ASSESSMENT OF DAMAGES

The principles of assessment

The common law has long awarded compensation for the mental repercussions of lesions to the body in the form of pain and suffering. Difficulties of assessment of this and other non-pecuniary damage are well known. A plaintiff cannot be compensated in the sense of achieving restitutio in integrum because the damage suffered is not quantifiable in monetary terms. No medium of exchange exists for freedom from physical and mental torment. Judges have repeatedly lamented the inadequacy of pecuniary relief for many of the components of personal injury awards and their forced arbitrary valuation of intangible but very real losses. As Lord Morris observed in *H West & Son Ltd v Shephard*:

> "A money award can be calculated so as to make good a financial loss. Money may be awarded so that something tangible may be procured to replace something else of like nature which has been destroyed or lost. But money cannot renew a physical frame that has been battered and shattered."[1]

Nor a mind that has malfunctioned through violation by traumatic stimuli.[2] Determination of reasonable compensation for psychiatric damage presents the ultimate nightmare for the judicial mind, especially where it is unaccompanied by physical impact on the patient's body. Indeed, concern about assessment complications was one of the contributory factors which thwarted a general recognition of liability for mental injury in the 19th century.[3] As Sir Gordon Willmer has said, in cases concerned with disturbances to the mind:

> "[W]e are in an area where the damages seem . . . to be even more than usually at large. It is practically impossible to find any signposts on the road; there is no tariff or pattern of awards in this class of case; and this makes it very difficult for any one judge to criticise another judge's estimate of what the damages ought to be."[4]

1. [1964] AC 326 at 346. In *Andrews v Grand & Toy Alberta Ltd* (1978) 83 DLR (3d) 452 Dickson J said at 475-476: "No money can provide true restitution. . . . Money is awarded because it will serve a useful function in making up for what has been lost in the only way possible, accepting that what has been lost is incapable of being replaced in any direct way." In *Arnold v Teno* (1978) 83 DLR (3d) 609 Spence J said at 638: "The award is not repairative: there can be no restoration of the lost function." For an analysis of the conceptual basis of such awards see A Ogus, "Damages for Lost Amenities: For a Foot, a Feeling or a Function?" (1972) 35 MLR 1.
2. See eg *B(A) v J(I)* (1991) 81 Alta LR (2d) 84 per Veit J at 91 commenting on the psychological and emotional injury caused to victims of sexual abuse, in this case the son and two daughters of the defendant.
3. See above, p 3.
4. *Hinz v Berry* [1970] 2 QB 40 at 46.

Of all the aspects of psychiatric damage law this is the one which we know least about. No clues can be gleaned from the oldest authorities given their reliance on jury assessment.[5] There is no thread linking the more modern cases, no commonality between awards,[6] no discernible process of damages calculation capable of extrapolation. All too often the question of damages for psychiatric harm is dealt with in a sentence or two with no indications given as to the reasoning which led to the figures decided on.[7] Guesswork, unfortunately a not uncommon means by which sums are arrived at under various heads of compensable loss in the personal injuries sphere, is the primary tool at the court's disposal in psychiatric damage cases. This has inevitably resulted in some instances in different judges taking radically differing views based on identical facts.[8] Sparsity of evidence compounds the unenviable difficulties presently faced by the

5. See eg *Byrne v Great Southern & Western Railway Co of Ireland* (unreported, CA of Ireland, Feb 1884); *Coultas v Victorian Railways Commissioner* (1886) 12 VLR 895; *Bell v Great Northern Railway Co of Ireland* (1890) 26 LR Ir 428; *Currie v Wardrop*, 1927 SC 538. The few modern jury cases can equally be ignored: see eg *Matei v McCrorie* (unreported, Victorian SC, 22 May 1986, No 27 of 1985). It is for this reason that reference to the American authorities is also unhelpful.

6. Some awards have been almost nominal in nature: see eg *Boardman v Sanderson* [1964] 1 WLR 1317 where the English Court of Appeal upheld the trial judge's assessment of £75 for what was described as no "more than slight shock"; *Mallon v Monklands District Council*, 1986 SLT 347 where £100 was granted for a "minor" psychiatric illness. Others have been quite substantial: see eg *Budget Rent-a-Car Systems Pty Ltd v Van der Kemp* (unreported, New South Wales CA, 21 Dec 1984, CA No 7 of 1984) ($50,000); *English v Cory Sand & Ballast Co* (unreported, QBD, 21 Mar 1985) (£17,500); *Smith v Email Ltd* (unreported, New South Wales SC, 14 Mar 1986, No CLD S 16572 of 1982) ($40,000); *Kwok v British Columbia Ferry Corporation* (1987) 20 BCLR (2d) 318 ($40,000); *De Franceschi v Storrier* (1988) 85 ACTR 1 ($25,000); *Worboys v Hamill* (unreported, New South Wales SC, 3 Feb 1988, No 11216 of 1984) ($35,000); *Cattanach v Abbott's Packaging Ltd* (unreported, English CA, 8 May 1989) (£18,000); *Bechard v Haliburton Estate* (1991) 84 DLR (4th) 668 ($50,000); *Wheatley v Cunningham* (unreported, QBD, 11 Dec 1991) (£10,000); *Mullally v Bus Eireann* (unreported, Irish HC, 13 June 1991) (£35,000). See *Tom v Pudovkin* (unreported, New South Wales CA, 27 Mar 1992, No 4098 of 1990) where a global sum of $200,000 general damages was upheld, the "principal amount" of which related to mental repercussions of trauma.

7. This is true both of the earlier cases: see eg *Owens v Liverpool Corporation* [1939] 1 KB 394, and the later cases in all jurisdictions: see eg *Chadwick v British Railways Board* [1967] 1 WLR 912; *Cameron v Marcaccini* (1978) 87 DLR (3d) 442; *Vince v Cripps Bakery Pty Ltd* (1984) Aust Torts Rep 80-668; *Mallon v Monklands District Council*, 1986 SLT 347, where Lord Jauncey at 349 considered himself able only to take "a very broad axe" to the question of assessment for a minor psychiatric disorder in the form of reactive depression, awarding £100; *Kwok v British Columbia Ferry Corporation* (1987) 20 BCLR(2d) 318; *Jinks v Cardwell* (1987) 39 CCLT 168; *McDermott v Ramadanovic Estate* (1988) 27 BCLR (2d) 45; *Reitsma v Government Insurance Office of New South Wales* (unreported, New South Wales SC, 31 Mar 1989, No 13879 of 1985); *Barrett v Short* (unreported, New South Wales SC, 12 Apr 1989, No 14685 of 1984), where $15,000 was awarded without elucidation to a wife who saw her husband fall to his death from a balcony at the defendant's surprise birthday party; *Carswell v British Railways Board*, 1991 SLT 73; *Petrie v Dowling* [1992] 1 Qd R 284; *Pibworth v Bevan M Roberts Pty Ltd* (unreported, South Australian SC, 28 May 1992, No 770 of 1986).

8. Compare eg Samuels JA's decision in *Swan v Williams (Demolition) Pty Ltd* (1987) 9 NSWLR 172 to uphold a nominal award of $400 to a man whose wife and in-laws had been crushed to death in their car by a falling sandstone block, with Priestley and McHugh JJA's valuation of his psychiatric complaint at $10,000. This discrepancy can be attributed to the divergent conclusions reached as to the nature of the damage suffered.

judiciary.[9] The formulation of guiding principle is hindered by the fact that very often the question of assessment is never reached, because liability for psychiatric damage is tried as a preliminary issue[10] or not imposed at trial,[11] or not analysed in any detail due to prior agreements as to quantum should an attribution of responsibility be made.[12] If the court is

9. See eg *X and Y v Pal* (1991) 23 NSWLR 26. In this case a mother was deeply shocked on discovering that her baby daughter was born with syphilis and the revelation that she was also infected. She developed a severe and acute depressive disorder for which she sought psychiatric counsel. The court was mindful of the need to separate this from the upset she experienced due to the fact that the child was also dysmorphic, brain damaged and epileptic, the reaction to the syphilis being the sole subject of this aspect of her negligence claim against her physicians. As the main issues before the court were causative ones, namely whether the baby's brain problems were attributable to the syphilitic infection, there was little evidence presented concerning the plaintiff's reaction to her daughter's condition. This prompted Clarke JA at 59 to give serious consideration to referring this issue for a new trial, fearful that adequate compensation could not be afforded on the evidence available. However, with no guarantee that such action would significantly advance her claim, and with a view to sparing the plaintiff further grief, his Honour proceeded based on the "limited materials" before him to assess her loss at $15,000, a figure he openly equated with a "rough guess" and one he knew would bring complaints from both sides. Crude guesswork, he felt, was the only way to "achieve broad justice". See also *Rice v Falzon* (unreported, New South Wales SC, 1 May 1987, No CLD S 17366 of 1981) where the paucity of evidence of mental damage led McInerney J to restrict the award to a "modest" $7,500.
10. See eg *Marshall v Lionel Enterprises Inc* (1971) 25 DLR (3d) 141; *Attia v British Gas Plc* [1988] 1 QB 304.
11. On some occasions the court first assesses damages without extended discussion subject to liability which it ultimately does not impose: see eg *King v Phillips* [1952] 2 All ER 459 where McNair J arrived at a figure of £100 but then gave judgment for the defendant. In other cases courts of first instance have after lengthy consideration denied a claim for psychiatric damage only to tack on at the end of the judgment, almost by way of an afterthought, the amount they would have awarded had they reached the contrary conclusion: see eg *Anderson v Smith* (1990) 101 FLR 34 where Nader J "in an effort to save the appellate court from having to remit the matter for assessment of damages" indicated, without any elaboration whatsoever of the means by which he arrived at such a figure, that he would have assessed damages at $40,000; *Rowe v McCartney* [1975] 1 NSWLR 544 per Sheppard J at 550 who indicated that if he had been in error in refusing this type of relief a further $10,000 should be added to the personal injuries award made. In *Al-Kandari v J R Brown & Co* [1987] QB 514 the parties had at the outset requested the assessment of damages irrespective of the decision as to liability. French J awarded, again without elucidation, £5,000 for the plaintiff's "physical injuries, shock and false imprisonment" and £15,000 for the "psychiatric consequences" of her ordeal of being bound, gagged and kept in a van by her estranged husband's accomplices while he kidnapped their children and took them to Kuwait. Although the ruling on liability was reversed, no interference was made with this assessment by the English Court of Appeal even though it was considered high: see [1988] QB 665. Note also *Spence v Percy* (1991) Aust Torts Rep 81-11 where, having allowed an appeal against liability for psychiatric illness consequent on hearing of the death of a permanently comatose child, the Full Court of the Queensland Supreme Court dismissed without discussion a cross-appeal against an award of $36,000, Williams J offering the only comment—that the sum was not "manifestly inadequate".
12. See eg *Turbyfield v Great Western Railway Co* (1937) 54 TLR 221 where, subject to liability, damages of £25 were agreed upon for the harm suffered by the twin sister of a girl killed by a negligently driven horse and dray; *Hevican v Ruane* [1991] 3 All ER 65 where "[t]hankfully" the parties agreed on a sum of £41,000. Note also *Ravenscroft v Rederiaktiebφlaget Transatlantic* [1991] 3 All ER 73 where at first instance the figure of £16,500 was settled on for a mother's psychiatric depressive reaction on learning of her son's death in an industrial accident. On appeal [1992] 2 All ER 470n the English Court of Appeal held that the defendants were not under any liability.

called on to assess damages, distinctions are seldom drawn between psychiatric illnesses incurred prior to trial and any likely continuing suffering,[13] technical medical language is not always precisely used,[14] and global damages figures are frequently not broken down, leaving in doubt the degree to which psychiatric damage or various loss components have been reflected in the sums awarded.[15] The most that one can do therefore when considering the question of assessment in this context is to cobble together the few strands of disparate argument which have surfaced in the authorities.[16]

Only very rarely have the principles governing the quantum of damages in psychiatric injury cases been considered at all, let alone in any detail. A rare example of a case dealing solely with the assessment issue is *Hinz v Berry*.[17] The only question before the English Court of Appeal was

13. See eg *De Franceschi v Storrier* (1988) 85 ACTR 1 where $25,000 was awarded with no indication as to the proportions reflecting past and inevitable future damage. Note also *Montgomery v Murphy* (1982) 136 DLR (3d) 525 per Galligan J at 532. For a rare example where an attribution to past and future injury was expressly made see *Morton v Wiseman*, 1989 SCLR 365.

14. In *Kherunisha Adatia v Air Canada, The Times*, 4 June 1992, for example, the English Court of Appeal were persuaded that despite referring to the "temporary or lasting psychiatric or psychological damage", "psychological reaction to trauma" and the like, Judge Harris QC at first instance could not be taken to have made an award for psychiatric injury per se. These statements were interpreted as having been included in an attempt to indicate the belief that the plaintiff was suffering from genuine pain (despite the absence of an organic cause) and was not a malingerer.

15. See eg *Whitmore v Euroways Express Coaches, The Times*, 4 May 1984 where apart from an award of £2,000 for the "ordinary shock" of seeing her husband injured and the continuing effect of those injuries, a wife was given a separate sum for the shock suffered on her own account but this was merged into the award of £4,500 general damages; *Bagley v North Herts Health Authority* (1986) 136 NLJ 1014 where Simon Brown J arrived at "an overall figure [of £18,000] . . . intended to reflect all the recoverable aspects of loss and [his] recognition that in certain respects they interact and possibly even overlap"; *Smith v Email Ltd* (unreported, New South Wales SC, 14 Mar 1986, No CLD S 16572 of 1982); *Chapman v Lear* (unreported, Queensland SC, 8 Apr 1988, No 3732 of 1984) where no breakdown of $15,000 awarded for three years of aggravation of the plaintiff's pre-existing personality disorder was attempted; *De Franceschi v Storrier* (1988) 85 ACTR 1; *Morton v Wiseman*, 1989 SCLR 365 where the view was expressed that psychological injury could not be considered in isolation from physical injury, £25,000 being awarded to compensate both types of damage; *Tom v Pudovkin* (unreported, New South Wales CA, 27 Mar 1992, No 4098 of 1990) where the only indication of the size of the psychiatric component in the very significant global award of $200,000 was that it comprised the "principal amount". Not all courts have lapsed into this mode of assessment: compare *Pucci v Reigate & Banstead District Council* (unreported, QBD, 21 Oct 1991) where Gower J split a general damages award for injuries suffered in a cycling accident into physical and psychiatric components

16. Obviously, as with any other personal injury claim, the duration of the injury will bear on the size of the award, whether this is expressly acknowledged or not. One principle that does appear settled is that once it is established as a medical fact that a mental disorder exists, damages may be awarded on the same principles as for any other injury: see eg *Liffen v Watson* [1940] 2 All ER 213 (allowance made for fact that by reason of the plaintiff's neurotic condition, she could not perform certain activities without experiencing pain); *Griffiths v R & H Green & Silley Weir Ltd* (1948) 81 LLLR 378 (allowance made for probable loss of wages for period during which plaintiff would suffer from hysteria and anxiety neurosis); *Bailey v British Transport Commission, The Times*, 29 Nov 1953 (railway worker was in train when two other trains collided with it, suffered no physical injury but developed neurosis which affected use of his legs; awarded compensation not far short of the amount he would have received had his legs been amputated).

17. [1970] 2 QB 40.

whether damages of £4,000 awarded at first instance to a woman who heard a crash and turned to discover that her husband and most of her eight children had been struck by a negligent driver were excessive. Although the sum was considered high no interference was made, their Lordships taking the view that the award was not a wholly erroneous estimation.[18] In reaching this decision it was made clear that some types of mental suffering would not be reflected in psychiatric damage awards. Specifically, Mrs Hinz was denied relief for the grief and sorrow of losing her husband, anxiety about the welfare of her injured children, financial stress resulting from the loss of the family breadwinner, and the strain of adjustment after the death of a spouse. It was only in relation to her morbid depressive state attributable to her presence at the accident scene that damages sounded. Compensation could not be obtained for the "whole of the mental anguish and suffering which [the plaintiff had] been enduring during the [previous] five or six years".[19] Herein lies the major difficulty with the question of relief for damage to the mind. How is the court to accomplish the task it has laboured itself with? The factors responsible for disruption to normal mental functioning are often inextricably linked—all of the factors mentioned above played a part in the development of Mrs Hinz's psychiatric condition.[20] Attempts to draw distinctions between the various ingredients and their significance, so as to reduce awards according to the extent that presently non-compensable factors contributed to the onset and duration of psychiatric illness, necessitates delving into what is often, in truth, a highly complex medical conundrum. Complications are inevitable whenever there is forced separation of different types of psychiatric damage on this basis or between psychiatric harm and emotional or mental distress or suffering. The arbitrariness and imprecise nature of the common law's methodology is illustrated by Lord Denning MR's suggested delineation technique:

18. Compare *Allen v Dando* [1977] CLY 738 where a father claimed for morbid depression suffered as a result of witnessing the death of his 11-year-old daughter in the back seat of the family car after a collision with a drunk driver and the vain attempts to resuscitate her. Reliance having been placed on *Hinz v Berry*, the defendant contended that that case was an exceptional one and not comparable with the situation at hand. Payne J held that while the facts before him were different, the English Court of Appeal's decision was relevant. The plaintiff was awarded £2,250 on the basis that the psychiatric damage in question was not as severe as that suffered by Mrs Hinz (who had suicidal tendencies and a potential need of ECT treatment) and there was evidence of considerable improvement, absence of insomnia, increased appetite and an active social life. These facts were considered to dictate a damages award considerably less than that approved in *Hinz v Berry*. Note also the interesting comparison of damages awards made in *Cattanach v Abbott's Packaging Ltd* (unreported, English CA, 8 May 1989) where £18,000 was awarded for pain and suffering in a case where an injury caused by a falling machine resulted in depression, neurosis and schizophrenia. The Court of Appeal held that the figure awarded by the trial judge was not so high as to warrant interference with it. The court referred for comparative purposes to the level of awards in earlier cases updated to 1989 values. *Hinz v Berry* (in which the £4,000 awarded was worth £28,000 on 1989 values) and *Brice v Brown* [1984] 1 All ER 997 (in which £22,500 paid in 1983 was now equal to £27,000-£27,500) were much more serious cases. By comparison the £600 granted in *Chadwick v British Railways Board* [1967] 1 WLR 912, dealt with below, p 272 would in 1989 be worth about £4,000.

19. [1970] 2 QB 40 per Lord Pearson at 45.

20. Ibid per Lord Pearson at 44. But note the discussion below, p 268.

"The way to do this is to estimate how much Mrs Hinz would have suffered if, for instance, her husband had been killed in an accident when she was 50 miles away: and compare it with what she is now, having suffered all the shock due to being present at the accident." [21]

The genesis of this approach can be traced to the judgment of Paull J in *Tregoning v Hill*[22] where a wife was granted £750 for the shock she suffered at seeing her husband struck and carried along by a car (the bicycle he had been riding having been caught up in the bumper), being turned over and over and finally left on the road some distance from her with a severe fracture of the skull from which he later died. The judge allowed recovery for the shock of seeing the incident, but denied a claim for depression suffered as a result of the accident and the deprivation of the husband's company. The view was expressed that there had to be a determination of the amount which represented the difference between the situation where the plaintiff had been at home and heard that her husband had been killed in a cycling accident and the situation where she actually witnessed the traumatic event.

In both these cases the need for direct physical perception was emphasised and it was clear that had psychiatric illness been suffered despite its absence no relief would have been forthcoming.[23] In *Hinz v Berry*, even if morbidity had developed as a result of the combination of presence at the scene and the other factors referred to above, it seems that the English Court of Appeal would have been unprepared to allow the award to stand. Lord Pearson said:

"If this factor [the shock of witnessing the traumatic event] had been merely one out of five and they had all been more or less equal in their effect, and there had been no special consequences attributable to this one, I would have thought the figure was much too high."[24]

In *Alcock v Chief Constable of South Yorkshire Police*[25] Lord Oliver flagged the case as a useful illustration of the "extreme difficulty" of separating the compensable damage arising from the presence of the claimant at the accident scene from the non-compensable consequences flowing from the simple fact that an accident has occurred. The same

21. Ibid at 43. This was described however as a "sensible test" by Holland J in *Fenn v City of Peterborough* (1976) 73 DLR (3d) 177 at 209.
22. *The Times*, 1 Mar 1965.
23. It is interesting to note that in *White v Butcher* (unreported, New South Wales SC, 13 Oct 1982, Nos 9576, 9577 and 9578 of 1981), where parents who did not witness the accident were granted recovery (as to which see above, p 162), the damages awarded were $10,000 to each parent. On this basis, the sum they would have recovered if they had witnessed the accident would have been considerable.
24. [1970] 2 QB 40 at 44. His Lordship went on to say at 45 that the element of witnessing the accident was the "sole cause of the added morbidity". Sir Gordon Willmer made a similar comment at 46. Earlier Lord Pearson suggested that all five elements referred to above contributed to Mrs Hinz's condition, but it appears that his Lordship meant to suggest that witnessing the accident was the crucial and primary cause, the other causes being insufficient to produce the depressive state: see P G Heffey, "The Negligent Infliction of Nervous Shock in Road and Industrial Accidents" (1974) 48 ALJ 196, 240 at 247.
25. [1992] 1 AC 310 at 413.

sentiments had been expressed by Rees J in *Carlin v Helical Bar Ltd*,[26] a case concerned only with the quantum of damages appropriate to award a 62-year-old crane operator who due to negligence and breach of statutory duty by his employer crushed a workmate to death between a steel stanchion and one of the supporting legs of the crane while it was in motion under his control. Referring to the "unusually difficult problem for any tribunal called upon to assess general damages" in this kind of case, his Lordship somehow arrived at the "fair sum" of £1,750. An argument could be mounted that a figure of say £2,000 more or £1,000 less would have been equally "fair" for, as Atiyah has pointed out, awards for such intangible losses "could be multiplied or divided by two overnight and they would be just as defensible or indefensible as they are today".[27] In *Storm v Geeves*,[28] a case five years prior to *Carlin v Helical Bar Ltd*, Burbury CJ, having satisfied himself that a mother's condition had "been brought about not merely from grief at the death of her child but substantially from the fact that she witnessed the immediate consequences of the accident and that she [could not] get the terrible picture of it out of her mind", described a £500 award to her as "moderately substantial" and granted a £2,000 award to her son for a "particularly severe reaction" to the trauma of seeing his sister killed. Such assessments are completely subjective in nature and it seems that in the absence of a tariff of damages for psychiatric disorders almost any sum awarded is unchallengeable. The New South Wales Court of Appeal has recently refused to interfere with a general damages award of $200,000, the "principal amount" of which related to the plaintiff's psychiatric problems following an accident where she and her sister were hit by a truck at a pedestrian crossing. Although it was a sum "at the very top of the permissible range", the large number of imponderables involved in its calculation dissuaded the court from disturbing the award.[29]

The separation test proposed by Lord Denning was referred to by Wanstall ACJ in *Richters v Motor Tyre Service Pty Ltd*[30] which involved a woman who was seriously injured in a car accident which killed her

---

26. (1970) 6 KIR 154.
27. P Cane, *Atiyah's Accidents, Compensation and the Law* (4th ed, 1987), 183. See also *Tuckey v R & H Green & Silley Weir Ltd* [1955] 2 Lloyd's Rep 619 per Pearson J at 630: "The real trouble in assessing damages in this case—I will say it quite frankly—is this: it is very easy to be very wrong either way. If one gives a very large sum, the man may recover in a very short time and go back to full work. On the other hand, if one gives a very small sum, the man may not recover and will lose a great deal of future wages, and suffer a great deal of pain and suffering, and the sum may be much too small. So in those circumstances one can only do one's best." Note also *Bailey v British Transport Commission, The Times*, 29 Nov 1953, where Barry J said how anybody could escape from this dilemma was "beyond comprehension".
28. [1965] Tas SR 252 at 267-269.
29. *Tom v Pudovkin* (unreported, New South Wales CA, 27 Mar 1992, No 4098 of 1990). See also the same court's refusal to alter a $15,000 general damages award for a phobia resulting from eating contaminated apricot kernels in *Young v J D Coates Pty Ltd* (unreported, New South Wales CA, 5 Oct 1990, CA No 171 of 1988). But note *Budget Rent-a-Car Systems Pty Ltd v Van der Kemp* (unreported, New South Wales CA, 21 Dec 1984, CA No 7 of 1984) where the court reduced an award from $80,000 to $50,000, and the reduction of a "manifestly excessive" jury award of $75,000 to $25,000 by the Full Court of Victoria in *Matei v McCrorie* (unreported, Victorian SC, 22 May 1986, No 27 of 1985).
30. [1972] Qd R 9.

husband and father-in-law and who became so psychologically depressed that she committed suicide two years later. In a claim brought by the executor of her estate three concurrent causes of the depression and suicide were identified: (1) the horror of her involvement in the collision; (2) the suffering attributable to her physical injuries; and (3) the shock of her husband's injuries and his death in the ambulance on the way to the hospital. It was felt that the comparison advocated by Lord Denning was not essential because in contrast to that case the three causative factors were all compensable.[31] The court's chief concern was the need to separate the shock of the injury to and death of the husband from the wife's natural grief and sorrow. It was made clear that following *Hinz v Berry* relief was being granted for the morbidity due to witnessing events as distinct from the emotional upheaval which would have been suffered if the plaintiff had merely heard later of her husband's death. Because it was the shock of witnessing events (and not grief alone) which "tipped the balance" and drove the wife to her psychiatric state, the "whole degree" of her mental condition was compensable.[32]

In *De Franceschi v Storrier*[33] Miles CJ considered the calculation of damages awardable to an Italian mother for the shock-induced psychiatric harm suffered as a result of her reaction to the injuries to her three children in an accident at a bus stop, particularly her brain-damaged daughter whose life was in jeopardy for five years, a "difficult task".[34] A distinction had to be drawn between the worry and anxiety for an injured child and contribution of the child's condition to the continuing effect of the initial shock suffered at the time of the mishap:

> "It is a highly artificial exercise to try and separate out those elements in [the plaintiff's] condition which relate to the nervous shock and those which relate merely to a natural concern for the children . . . but the exercise has to be undertaken. I think that uncompensable natural concern will at some stage displace the effects of nervous shock, if it has not already begun to do so, so that eventually the effect of the nervous shock will be minimal. That is not to say that the plaintiff will regain her pre-accident health and disposition, but simply to take the

31. Note *Montgomery v Murphy* (1982) 136 DLR (3d) 525 per Galligan J at 531 who referred to the "exceedingly difficult" task of applying his Lordship's test to the facts before him because the plaintiff's depression had been contributed to by three different factors: his perceived disability as a result of a back injury sustained in a car accident, the vision of his wife being run down and killed in the same accident, and grief and sorrow at the loss of his wife.
32. Note also *Frank v Cox* (1988) 213 APR 370 (NS) per Kelly J at 379-380.
33. (1985) 85 ACTR 1.
34. This was an action brought under s 24(1) of the *Law Reform (Miscellaneous Provisions) Act* 1955 (ACT), on which see above, pp 239-243. Miles CJ at 2 said that, as the injuries to the children occurred whilst the plaintiff was at home and the children at their school bus stop, it was open to serious question whether the injuries to them occurred within the "sight or hearing" of the plaintiff under s 24(1), but since the negligent driver admitted liability for the psychiatric consequences to the plaintiff it was unnecessary to discuss this issue. His Honour, however, appears to have overlooked the point that under the statute an action by a parent for "mental or nervous shock" does not have to be sustained within the parent's sight or hearing.

view that her condition will be due to normal and natural concern for the welfare of her children."[35]

Some judges have conceded defeat. In *Harrison v State Government Insurance Office*[36] the court considered it a "meaningless and unrealistic exercise" to attempt to distinguish between the proportion of the plaintiff's psychiatric illness brought on by concern for her husband (the negligent party responsible for the car accident in which he lost his life and the plaintiff was injured) and that attributable to the emotional trauma of being a passenger in a vehicle involved in an accident. Significantly, even the consultant psychiatrist called by the first defendant (SGIO) was unable to make such a determination. Notwithstanding that he was of the opinion that, if launched separately, her claim would have failed (based on the rule that reasonably foreseeable psychiatric harm must be sustained as a result of the death of, or injury or peril to, someone other than the tortfeasor[37]), Vasta J felt that "good sense" warranted granting the not insubstantial sum of $20,000[38] for psychiatric illness as a result of the trauma caused by virtue of the plaintiff's concern for her careless husband.

As has already been noted, the discussion of assessment in *Hinz v Berry* proceeded on the basis that presence at the accident scene was essential for recovery. But as indicated in a previous chapter, it is now clear that psychiatric harm suffered as a result of a combination of seeing trauma and being told of it subsequently is compensable.[39] Indeed there is some authority that total absence of direct physical perception is not fatal to a claim.[40] *Schneider v Eisovitch*[41] sheds some light on how damages are to be assessed in the former situation. It will be recalled that the plaintiff and her husband while travelling in France were involved in a car accident which killed the husband and rendered the plaintiff unconscious. Upon coming to, the plaintiff was informed of her husband's death and suffered shock leading, inter alia, to recurring attacks of neurodermatitis. The mental condition leading to the skin complaint was attributable to three factors: (1) the shock of the accident itself which resulted in physical injuries to the

---

35. (1985) 85 ACTR 1 at 8. For consideration of a similar situation see *White v Butcher* (unreported, New South Wales SC, 13 Oct 1982, Nos 9576, 9577 and 9578 of 1981). Note also the comments of Finlay J in *Smith v Email Ltd* (unreported, New South Wales SC, 14 Mar 1986, No CLD S 16572 of 1982) at 9.
36. (1985) Aust Torts Rep 80-723.
37. On the issue of the source of the shock in this particular context see above, pp 215-220.
38. Compare this with the $5,000 awarded for pain and suffering, loss of amenities and special damages associated with her minor physical injuries.
39. See above, p 161. Note also *Kohn v State Government Insurance Commission* (1976) 15 SASR 255 per Bray CJ at 257: "I think that the . . . defendant is responsible for all the consequences of the accident, including the plaintiff's mental and psychological ill health and instability, and that there need be no attempt to sever that part of those consequences which was caused by the report of the death of [her boyfriend] from that part of it which was caused by her own physical injuries." General damages were assessed at $77,500.
40. *Petrie v Dowling* [1992] 1 Qd R 284; *Wilks v Haines* (1991) Aust Torts Rep 81-078; *Hevican v Ruane* [1991] 3 All ER 65; *Ravenscroft v Rederiaktiebφlaget Transatlantic* [1991] 3 All ER 73, which was subsequently reversed by the English Court of Appeal [1992] 2 All ER 470n. Note also *Heighington v The Queen in Right of Ontario* (1987) 41 DLR (4th) 208 and *X and Y v Pal* (1991) 23 NSWLR 26, where however the issues were not discussed in detail.
41. [1960] 2 QB 430.

plaintiff; (2) the shock of discovering in hospital that her husband had been killed in the same accident; and (3) the continuing mental stress and strain of having to adjust to life without her partner. Paull J had no doubts as to the recoverability of the first of these and the non-recoverability of the last. After some consideration he concluded that the second was also allowable. The question of appropriate relief prompted his Lordship to say that it "is extremely difficult to divide up the consequences of the shock; one cannot hope to achieve more than a very rough and ready division".[42] Awarding £400 for the consequences of the shock, Paull J indicated that had he found against the plaintiff on the means of communication issue that sum would have been reduced to £125, and that if he had found in her favour in relation to the whole of the mental condition and neurodermatitis it would have been increased to £850. So in the result recovery was allowed for less than half of the plaintiff's mental injury because the remainder could be attributed to the burden of adjusting to a life alone—a presently non-compensable element. In the factually similar case of *Andrews v Williams*[43] the Supreme Court of Victoria applied the English authority, upholding a ruling of the trial judge in which he stated:

> "I will, of course, direct the jury that the injury to be taken into account in this regard comprises the mental and nervous condition resulting from the shock to the plaintiff of her mother being killed in the circumstances and that she cannot be compensated for the mother's death in any other respects."[44]

It appears that damages for shock-induced harm consequent upon the perception of a traumatic event may be aggravated by the subsequent and causally connected death of the primary victim. In *Richards v Baker*[45] a mother whose shock condition had been caused by witnessing her son run down and severely injured was considered, albeit after some hesitation, entitled to an additional sum for the aggravation of her disorder as a result of his death later that evening. Even the daily reminder of injuries to a loved one, for example through nursing care, may aggravate the damages for shock previously suffered on their infliction.[46] What is presently unclear is to what extent, if at all, the subsequent death of or physical injury to a psychiatrically disturbed claimant from causes *unconnected* with the negligence responsible for his or her mental condition affects the damages awarded for it. In *Chadwick v British Railways Board*[47] an action brought by a middle-aged man who became psychoneurotic from his experiences as a rescuer at the Lewisham train tragedy was continued by his wife as administratrix of his estate on his subsequent and unrelated death. In assessing general damages at £600, Waller J gave no indication whether he had been influenced in any respect by the death. Principles which emerge from cases on other kinds of damage suggest that death due to unconnected

42. Ibid at 442.
43. [1967] VR 831.
44. Ibid at 832. Damages of $24,657 were not altered.
45. [1943] SASR 245.
46. See eg *S v Distillers Co (Biochemicals) Ltd* [1969] 3 All ER 1412 where a mother's daily task of caring for her thalidomide child aggravated the award granted for the shock of the birth itself. Note also *Kralj v McGrath* [1986] 1 All ER 54.
47. [1967] 1 WLR 912.

causes reduces the size of awards, because it shortens the length of time over which the plaintiff's suffering endures.[48] This may apply also to awards for mental damage.

It was shown earlier that special susceptibility to psychiatric damage is not relevant to the question of liability. If normal members of the community would have suffered harm, the tortfeasor will not escape liability on the basis that the victim of his or her carelessness happened to suffer a particularly severe form of injury due to pre-existing fragility or "eggshell" mental stability.[49] That this may, however, be relevant when it comes to the assessment of compensation is apparent from *Dooley v Cammell Laird & Co Ltd*[50] where the plaintiff's pre-accident neurasthenia[51] (which had been aggravated and accelerated in its course by a crane accident leaving him "a permanently broken up old man") led to the reduction of damages by two thirds.[52] The issue remains unsettled, other courts having refused to reduce the damages for which the defendant is liable consequent on the plaintiff's pre-existing fragile psyche.[53] Another factor which may operate to reduce the damages awarded is refusal to undergo medical treatment for a psychiatric condition. In *Marcroft v Scruttons Ltd*[54] the plaintiff, who developed severe anxiety neurosis and depression following a minor accident, refused to follow his doctor's advice to undergo treatment at a mental hospital. His damages were reduced on the basis that his refusal was unreasonable, and the assessment was based on what his condition would have been had the treatment been successful, as on the facts was likely.

Assertions that damages in respect of physical injuries to children tend generally to be lower than in cases concerning adults because a child is

48. See eg *Jobling v Associated Dairies Ltd* [1982] AC 794.
49. See above, pp 229-238.
50. [1951] 1 Lloyds Rep 271. See *Smith v Email Ltd* (unreported, New South Wales SC, 14 Mar 1986, No CLD S 16572 of 1982) where a mother's general damages of $40,000 under s 4 of the *Law Reform (Miscellaneous Provisions) Act* 1944 (NSW) for "nervous shock" suffered when she was told that her three-year-old son had drowned in an effluent waste storage tank were not reduced despite the fact that her childhood background predisposed her to emotional illnesses in adult life. Compare also *Brice v Brown* [1984] 1 All ER 997 per Stuart Smith J at 1007 where damages were assessed at £22,500 without any reference to reduction due to the plaintiff's pre-existing and long-standing hysterical personality disorder. She was entitled to relief for the full extent of the shock suffered whilst a passenger with her daughter in a taxi which collided with a bus.
51. Neurasthenia is an indefinite term used to denote a number of conditions in which there is a functional (as opposed to organic) disturbance of the nervous system, combined with marked depression of the vital forces and a tendency to rapid exhaustion, due usually to prolonged or excessive expenditure of physical and/or mental energy; nervous exhaustion characterised by abnormal fatigue. The term was first employed in 1869 in America by Dr George Miller Beard in his *Practical Treatise on Nervous Exhaustion (Neurasthenia)* to describe a syndrome of mental and physical fatigue, poor appetite, insomnia, irritability, poor concentration and headache in the absence of specific disease. It came to be used in an expanded sense and was discussed at length in many textbooks of the late 19th and early 20th century: see D Gelder et al, *Oxford Textbook of Psychiatry* (2nd ed, 1989), 159.
52. See also *Wilson v Peisley* (1975) 7 ALR 571; *Malec v J C Hutton Pty Ltd* (1990) 169 CLR 638.
53. Interestingly, it is a term retained in the WHO's *International Classification of Diseases* (revised 10th ed) notwithstanding that it is now rarely used in the United Kingdom and the United States.
54. [1954] 1 Lloyd's Rep 395.

naturally more resilient, and that therefore a similar approach should be adopted in mental injury cases, are likely to receive short shrift from the courts. Although the considerations which lead judges to quantify particular psychiatric losses in particular ways remain very much a mystery, what is clear is that any such general method of assessment is avoided. As has been pointed out, there may be situations where mental trauma experienced in childhood which is comparatively mild by adult standards may have serious lasting effects in later life.[55]

A clear distinction has to be drawn between awards for psychiatric injury and those made pursuant to statutory solatium provisions.[56] The latter attempt to compensate close relatives for bereavement, anguish, grief and the destruction of the intangible interests in the life of a deceased loved one, including loss of companionship or moral comfort, rather than for a precise medical condition.[57] Although it is true that certain emotional states encompassed in solatium awards such as grief can develop into illnesses of a recognised psychiatric nature,[58] the two categories of relief are distinct[59] and sums granted may differ greatly, particularly in the light of the modest limits imposed upon the legislative awards.[60] The decision to compensate

55. See *Mellor v Moran* (1985) 2 MVR 461 per Vasta J at 462-463. In this case there was expert evidence that because the child plaintiff had had one severe episode of depression (her mother had been killed in a car accident when she was about nine), the likelihood of her developing a depressive disorder in the future should similar stress strike was increased. Damages were assessed at $5,000.

56. See *Wrongs Act 1936* (SA), ss 23a-23c; *Compensation (Fatal Injuries) Act 1974* (NT), s 10; *Fatal Accidents Act 1976* (UK) s 1A, as inserted by the *Administration of Justice Act 1982* (UK), s 3; *Fatal Accidents Act*, RSA 1980, c F-5, s 8(1); *Civil Liability Act 1961* (Ire), s 49.

57. Note that in Scotland the law always permitted the award of damages for non-pecuniary loss to relatives in fatal accident cases: see *Eisten v North British Railway* (1870) 8 M 980. This award was referred to as solatium and it is from this usage that the references to statutory awards for solatium derive. Damages for injuries causing death in Scotland are now governed by the *Damages (Scotland) Act 1976* (UK). Awards of solatium are abolished and in their place claimants are entitled to a "loss of society" award for their non-pecuniary losses: see s 1(4). As to the level of such awards see *Dingwall v Walter Alexander & Sons (Midland) Ltd*, 1981 SLT 313 and the recent discussion in *Jarvie v Sharp*, 1992 SLT 350. Under current Scottish practice damages in personal injury cases for non-pecuniary or "personal" loss are described as "solatium" and damages for pecuniary loss as "patrimonial".

58. See eg *Mellor v Moran* (1985) 2 MVR 461.

59. See eg *Richards v Baker* [1943] SASR 245 per Mayo J at 251; *Hamlyn v Hann* [1967] SASR 387 per Mitchell J at 403; *Bassanese v Martin* [1982] SASR 461 per Zelling J at 463, 465 466; *Rowe Estate v Hanna* (1989) 71 Alta LR (2d) 136 per Forsyth J at 141; *Alcock v Chief Constable of South Yorkshire Police* [1992] 1 AC 310 per Lord Oliver at 409-410. Note also *Andrewartha v Andrewartha* (1987) 44 SASR 1.

60. See eg *Bassanese v Martin* (1982) 31 SASR 461 at 466 where Zelling J awarded $10,000 to a widow for a depressive mental illness due in part to her husband's murder by the jealous lover of his mistress and in addition, on the basis that "[p]eople grieve for bad husbands as well as for good", the maximum amount allowable for solatium under the South Australian provision, namely $4,200. In *Richards v Baker* [1943] SASR 245 Mayo J awarded a mother £1,300 for "injury from mental and nevous shock" and £170 for solatium out of a possible £300 limit, the original statutory ceiling for parents of an infant in that State. Compare this with *Hamlyn v Hann* [1967] SASR 387 where Mitchell J gave a husband $3,000 for enduring three years of the same type of psychiatric condition caused by the deaths of his wife and child in a car accident in addition to the $1,400 awarded at first instance as solatium for the death of the wife and $1,000 for the death of the child, again the maximum amounts at that time.

for either loss should have no bearing therefore on the question whether to award damages for the other or upon the issue of size of the prospective award. Similarly, in psychiatric injury cases there is no necessary or standard correlation between damages awarded for this kind of loss and those awarded for other types of non-pecuniary harm such as inconvenience, vexation, worry or distress. It may well be that on the facts the two sums are comparable,[61] but attempts to formulate general statements as to whether relief for the former is likely to be greater or smaller than that for the latter have been labelled as "profitless".[62] The two kinds of mental state bear no relationship to each other save than by way of coincidence. Impacts on the mind take a variety of forms and affect people in a variety of different ways and to different degrees. All types of loss must therefore be judged on an individual and independent basis. However, whilst awards for different species and intensities of mental disturbance are to be separately and individually considered, this does not mean that reference to some predetermined yardstick regulating adequate compensatory levels for the various psychiatric complaints would be inappropriate or would not greatly assist courts in their current dilemmas. It is to this issue that we now turn.

A tariff for psychiatric injury

The inherent difficulties involved in assessing all forms of non-pecuniary loss can never be eradicated. Lord Denning MR once considered the problems insoluble.[63] Monetary relief will never be capable of "compensating" psychiatrically disturbed trauma victims for the disruption to their lives. To this extent any award made for this kind of mental harm will always be arbitrary and artificial. What is possible however is to provide for a comprehensive scheme designed to better promote consistency, uniformity and fairness between psychiatric damage cases as well as encouraging rehabilitation and settlement negotiations. At the very least a judicial tariff should be developed for damage to the mind in the same way that one has developed in relation to physical injuries. English,[64]

61. For example in *Campbelltown City Council v Mackay* (1989) 15 NSWLR 501 the New South Wales Court of Appeal considered that although an award made by Smart J at first instance for psychiatric illness alleged to have been caused by structural damage to a house could not be upheld, the sum awarded was appropriate to compensate the home-owners for their vexation, worry, distress and inconvenience. There is, however, no mention of the actual amount granted, although it does appear to have been more than $800.
62. Ibid per Samuels J at 505.
63. *Ward v James* [1966] 1 QB 273 at 296.
64. See eg *Bird v Cocking & Sons Ltd* [1951] 2 TLR 1260; *Rushton v National Coal Board* [1953] 1 QB 495; *Waldon v War Office* [1956] 1 All ER 108; *Bastow v Bagley & Co Ltd* [1961] 3 All ER 1101; *Morey v Woodfield* [1963] 3 All ER 533; *Hennell v Ranaboldo* [1963] 3 All ER 684; *H West & Son Ltd v Shephard* [1964] AC 326; *Jag Singh (An Infant) v Toong Fong Omnibus Co Ltd* [1964] 3 All ER 925; *Hodges v Harland & Wolff Ltd* [1965] 1 All ER 1086; *Naylor v Yorkshire Electricity Board* [1968] AC 529; *Jones v Griffith* [1969] 2 All ER 1015; *Thomas v British Railways Board* [1978] QB 912; *Walker v John McLean & Sons Ltd* [1979] 2 All ER 965; *Pickett v British Rail Engineering Ltd* [1980] AC 136; *Lim Poh Choo v Camden & Islington Area Health Authority* [1980] AC 174; *Croke (An Infant) v Wiseman* [1981] 3 All ER 852; *Wright v British Railways Board* [1983] 2 AC 773; *Chan Wai Tong v Li Ping Sum* [1985] AC 446. Note also Cane, op cit n 27 at 187-192.

Scottish,[65] Irish,[66] Canadian,[67] New Zealand,[68] Hong Kong,[69] and Malaysian[70] courts have long recognised the justification of some sort of comparison of prior awards when deciding questions of quantum and indications are that, despite the Australian High Court's repeated opposition to the utilisation of a tariff scheme to aid judges in this task,[71] the divergence between the position in that country and the other Commonwealth jurisdictions is narrowing.[72]

It is submitted that justice would be best served, and perhaps more importantly seen to be best served, by the introduction of a legislative scheme incorporating two related but different strategies which, although mooted separately in the past as potential aids in the assessment of non-pecuniary loss, have not been considered in combination. There should be a statutory guideline of average figures for loss of specified faculties, injuries and illnesses, including those of a mental nature, coupled with an

65. See eg *Allan v Scott*, 1972 SC 59; *McGregor v Websters Executors*, 1972 SLT 29. Note also *MacShannon v Rockware Glass Ltd* [1978] AC 795.
66. See eg *Doherty v Bowaters Irish Wallboard Mills Ltd* [1968] IR 277.
67. See eg *Walton v Todoruk* (1967) 66 DLR (2d) 556.
68. See eg *Gray v Deakin* [1965] NZLR 234.
69. The Hong Kong Court of Appeal in *Lee Ting-lam v Leung Kam-ming* [1980] HKLR 657 laid down general guidelines as to the amount of damages which should be awarded for various categories of injuries. See also *Law Sai-leung v Ho Chai-man* (unreported, Hong Kong CA, 6 Feb 1985) and the Privy Council's discussion of these guidelines in *Chan Wai Tong v Li Ping Sum* [1985] AC 446.
70. *Liong Thoo v Sawiyah* [1982] 1 MLJ 286. Note P F Rhodes, "Accident Compensation Reforms: England, Hong Kong and Malaysia" (1986) 16 HKLJ 8 at 9-11.
71. The view that no two personal injury cases are truly comparable and the consequent rejection of the relevance of a tariff approach was advanced for the first time by Windeyer, Menzies and Kitto JJ three decades ago: see *Braunack v Kuchel* (unreported, High Court, 23 Nov 1960, No A18 of 1960), noted (1964) 35 ALJ 296. The High Court has consistently favoured this reasoning and in 1968 emphatically rejected the suggestion that it adopt the contrary approach in *Planet Fisheries Pty Ltd v La Rosa* (1968) 119 CLR 118 per Barwick CJ, Kitto and Menzies JJ at 124-125. See also *Thatcher v Charles* (1961) 104 CLR 57 per Windeyer J at 71-72; *Bresatz v Przibilla* (1962) 108 CLR 541 per Windeyer J at 548; *Halley v Chudleigh* [1963] ALR 616 per Windeyer J at 619; *O'Brien v Dunsdon* (1965) 39 ALJR 78 per Barwick CJ, Kitto and Taylor JJ at 78; *Arthur Robinson (Grafton) Pty Ltd v Carter* (1968) 122 CLR 649 per Barwick CJ at 656-657; *Papanayiotou v Heath* [1970] ALR 105 per Windeyer J at 110-112.
72. Indeed the various publications setting out comparative tables and details of sums awarded (eg *CCH Australian Torts Reporter; Australian Legal Monthly Digest; Australian Current Law*) are premised on the basis that a comparable approach has prevailed in Australia. Hutley JA in *Vaughan v Calvert* (unreported, New South Wales CA, 28 July 1977, CA No 10 of 1977) stated that it was "beyond [his] understanding" how a judge could perform his function in the manner laid down by the High Court. See also *Hirsch v Bennett* [1969] SASR 493; *Joyce v Pioneer Tourist Coaches Pty Ltd* [1969] SASR 501; *Paroczy v Cook* (1971) 2 SASR 14; *Donelan v IND* [1973] VR 490; *Hall v Tarlinton* (1978) 19 ALR 501; *Matijevic v Khoury* (unreported, New South Wales CA, 26 Apr 1978, CA No 400 of 1977); *Bellingham v Dykes* (unreported, New South Wales CA, 22 Aug 1983, CA No 311 of 1982); *Gibb v Shaw* (1984) Aust Torts Rep 80-536; *Moran v McMahon* (1985) 3 NSWLR 700; *St Margaret's Hospital for Women (Sydney) v McKibbon* (1987) Aust Torts Rep 80-130; *Packer v Cameron* (1990) Aust Torts Rep 81-007; *CSR Ltd v Bouwhuis* (unreported, New South Wales CA, 23 Aug 1991, No 40434 of 1991). Ironically, there are dicta of the High Court itself which acknowledge that justice "in the abstract" demands "some sort of consistency in awards": see *Faulkner v Keffalinos* (1970) 45 ALJR 80 per Windeyer J at 82. See also H Luntz, *Assessment of Damages for Personal Injury and Death* (3rd ed, 1990), 166-168.

upper total limit on non-pecuniary awards.[73] Specifically, the various recognised neuroses, psychoses, and psycho-neuroses should be listed based on the American Psychiatric Association's *Diagnostic and Statistical Manual of Mental Disorders* (DSM-III-R) or the World Health Organisation's *International Classification of Diseases* (ICD) (revised 10th ed).[74] Differences between listed guides would reflect the relative seriousness of the various mental disorders. The figure specified for paranoid schizophrenia, for example, would obviously be greater than that suggested as adequate compensation for mild anxiety states. Duration of impact of disturbance would also be a factor, incurable cases and those likely to require intensive therapy for years after trial warranting higher awards than instances of disorders dissipating after a few weeks. Reference to a comprehensive legislative tariff of this kind (with an overriding ceiling) would remove some of the subjectivity of psychiatric damage awards and enable judges to strive openly to treat like cases in a like manner.

It is not suggested that the sums specified for the various forms of psychiatric damage be determinative for every judgment in every case. Rather the tariff should be structured to operate merely to provide the courts with a workable guide without imposing an undesirable rigidity on judicial discretion.[75] The figures should be geared to the cost of living and increased annually to offset inflationary pressures.[76] Each specified figure

73. This strategy is examined in greater detail in N J Mullany, "A New Approach to Compensation For Non-Pecuniary Loss in Australia" (1990) 17 MULR 714. There are a number of possible bases upon which the tariff could be formulated but the use of average figures seems the most appropriate. This was the provisional view of the English Law Commission: see *Personal Injury Litigation—Assessment of Damages: Working Paper No 41* (1971), 53. Note also *Report on Personal Injury Litigation—Assessment of Damages: No 56* (1973), 11; *Report of the Royal Commission on Civil Liability and Compensation for Personal Injury* (Cmnd 7054, 1978) 88-91 (Pearson Report): see Mullany at 729-730.

74. See above, pp 33-34.

75. The scheme could be structured to accommodate those jurisdictions which still provide for jury assessment of personal injury awards such as Victoria, New South Wales (in relation to non-motor accident cases) and Scotland (in the Court of Session) by making it incumbent on the courts to inform jurors of the statutory guide. The communication would not, as Lord Denning MR suggested in *Ward v James* [1966] 1 QB 273 at 301-303, defeat the purpose of having a jury. On the contrary, it would promote the objective of securing a fair, reasonable and just result by ensuring that neither party is prejudiced by a verdict based on ignorance of damage caused by psychiatric disorder. This view receives support from recent calls by the English Court of Appeal in *Sutcliffe v Pressdram* [1991] QB 153 for judicial guidance to assist jurors to appreciate the real value of large sums. Their Lordships have indicated that they see no danger in inviting juries notionally to weigh any sum they have in mind by reference to the financial implications of such a sum. Significantly, the majority of the Australian High Court in *Coyne v Citizens Finance Ltd* (1991) 172 CLR 211 indorsed this suggestion, going even further to indicate that providing the jury's autonomy is emphasised, it may be prudent for judges to indicate an appropriate damage range: see N J Mullany, "Interfering with Jury Damage Verdicts" (1992) 9 Aust Bar Rev 168. These practices would dramatically reduce the risk of awards being set aside on appeal thereby avoiding the inconvenience, expense, delay and anxiety of retrials: see Mullany, op cit, n 73 at 728.

76. There are numerous dicta recognising the need to take into account the fall in the value of money when comparing cases: see eg *Lee Transport Co Ltd v Watson* (1940) 64 CLR 1; *Taylor v O'Connor* [1971] AC 115; *Mitchell v Mulholland (No 2)* [1972] 1 QB 65; *Taylor v Bristol Omnibus Co* [1975] 1 WLR 1054; *Sharman v Evans* (1977) 138 CLR 563; *Lim Poh Choo v Camden & Islington Area Health Authority* [1980] AC 174; *Todorovic*

would represent the most appropriate sum to compensate the average plaintiff in an ordinary case for a particular condition and its effect upon him or her. It would not, as some have suggested,[77] detract from the principle that judges evaluate the individual case. On the contrary, it would allow the courts to analyse the circumstances of each plaintiff's claim and to determine whether the compensation awarded should be above or below the average and by how much. Judicial discretion in this context would thereby be maintained. The claimant would bear the burden of adducing evidence to demonstrate that the damage to him or her justified an award more than the specified norm and the defendant of proving that the claim merited less than that amount. Thus, the truly exceptional case would not be doomed to undercompensation. Nor would the legislative isolation of this form of non-pecuniary loss operate to reduce the significance of, or effectively abolish, the other elements of present awards. The difference between the total sum allowable (the upper limit) and the highest amount on the tariff for the most severe type of psychiatric disorder would provide sufficient scope for the courts to compensate trauma victims adequately for the other types of non-pecuniary damage.[78] The proposed scheme would, for this reason, also accommodate any overlap between the various subheads without prejudicing claimants. Not only would the tariff provide guidelines for the courts in their calculations (something that members of the judiciary have recognised would be of great assistance in this difficult task[79]) but importantly, it would also be conducive to a speedy resolution of settlement proceedings. Given the small number of disputes argued before courts of law, particularly those of a psychiatric nature, a guide that aids advisers in reaching agreement on the appropriate amount of damages outside that forum is to be especially welcomed.

Whilst it would be relatively easy to devise a helpful norm for "simple" losses such as that of an arm or eye, it is true that this task would prove more difficult in relation to complex psychiatric injuries, and would be exacerbated by the fact that psychiatric conditions afflict individuals to varying degrees of severity. There may be cases where psychiatrists cannot agree as to the proper classification of certain symptoms, or the appropriate level of compensation. However, as the English Law Commission has observed,[80] the problem of complex injuries and illnesses is not insurmountable and, it is suggested, does not warrant the abandonment of

76. *Continued*
    v Waller (1981) 150 CLR 402; *Lindal v Lindal* (1982) 129 DLR (3d) 263. Any legislative scheme introduced would need to have an inbuilt mechanism to compensate for annual reductions in the purchasing power of the amounts initially specified. Note J G Fleming, "The Impact of Inflation on Tort Compensation" (1978) 26 AJCL 51.
77. See the English Law Commission's comments on the English Bar Council's opposition in its *Report on Personal Injury Litigation—Assessment of Damages: No 56* (1973), 11.
78. Although the proposed scheme would, in the Australian and Canadian context, accommodate awards for loss of life expectancy, the variance between the maximum total amount awardable and the highest listed tariff for faculty loss would need to be slightly reduced in England, Wales and Northern Ireland to take account of the abolition of this kind of loss as a head of damage by s 1(1) of the *Administration of Justice Act* 1982 (UK).
79. See eg *Naylor v Yorkshire Electricity Board* [1968] AC 529 per Lord Devlin at 550 (dealing with damages for loss of expectation of life).
80. *Report on Personal Injury Litigation—Assessment of Damages: No 56* (1973), 11.

the legislative tariff approach. It would need to be made clear that in the case of multiple conditions the tariff does not operate cumulatively and that, with reference to the listed figures, the damage in question is to be analysed as a whole.[81] Any judgment made would be based upon the most appropriate tariff figure after consideration of the closeness of its relationship with the particular damage sustained.

The question arises as to who or which body ought to determine the list of norms. The formation of a multifaceted body designed to attract input from a wide cross-section of persons interested in the issue of mental disturbance would be more appropriate and prove more fruitful than simply relying upon parliamentarians and government departments to fix what they consider as the most desirable scale. One attractive option would be to convene conferences attended by judges, expert legal practitioners, leading academics and lay experts (including psychiatrists, psychologists, economists, and representatives from associations and persons conversant with the problems faced by the mentally disturbed) to debate the question of the most appropriate figures.[82] Medical information as to the relative seriousness of the identified conditions and their disruptive effects would be particularly important in order to differentiate between sums listed. Discussions would need to include considerations of not only the amount necessary to provide adequate compensation for victims of specified kinds of psychiatric damage, but also the wider ramifications of any decisions made. As evidenced by the United States experience,[83] for example, the undesirable effects on insurance premiums which flow from large court awards would have to be borne in mind to protect against the average figures being set at too high a level.[84]

Although it came to no final conclusion upon the desirability of a tariff system in its 1971 working paper on the assessment of damages in personal injuries litigation,[85] the English Law Commission ultimately rejected its

81. See English Law Commission, *Personal Injury Litigation—Assessment of Damages: Working Paper No 41* (1971), 52.
82. There is precedent for this in the form of judges' conferences on sentencing in criminal cases. The English Law Commission favoured this type of informed discussion in its *Report on Personal Injury Litigation—Assessment of Damages: No 56* (1973), 79-80. The proposed forum is to be distinguished from damage tribunals, the setting up of which was disapproved of by both the Commission and the earlier Winn Committee Report: see *Report of the Committee on Personal Injuries Litigation* (Cmnd 3691, 1968) 114-116. The Commission's rejection of this latter strategy was based largely upon the unsatisfactory operation of the Western Australian Third Party Claims Tribunal which was established by the *Motor Vehicle (Third Party Insurance) Act* 1967 (WA) and disbanded soon after.
83. See United States Department of Justice, *Report of the Tort Policy Working Group on the Causes, Extent and Policy Implications of the Current Crisis in Insurance Availability and Affordability* (1986); G L Priest, "The Current Insurance Crisis and Modern Tort Law" (1987) 96 Yale LJ 1521. Note J F Keeler, "The Crises of Liability Insurance" (1988) 1 Ins LJ 182.
84. Note *Heaps v Perrite Ltd* [1937] 2 All ER 60 per Greer LJ at 61; *Hately v Allport* (1953) 54 SR (NSW) 17 per Street CJ at 22; *Fletcher v Autocar & Transporters Ltd* [1968] 2 QB 322 per Lord Denning MR at 335-336; *Lim Poh Choo v Camden & Islington Area Health Authority* [1979] QB 196 per Lord Denning MR at 217 (but see [1980] AC 174 per Lord Scarman at 187). See also the discussion of the overall limits imposed in Canada below, p 281.
85. See *Personal Injury Litigation—Assessment of Damages: Working Paper No 41* (1971), 54.

legislative adoption.[86] It appeared to do so, not on the basis of sound legal justifications, but rather because of an "absence of any real enthusiasm for this innovation".[87] With respect, this is a dubious basis for any recommendation relating to law reform. The benefits of legislative guidance in the context of the assessment of non-pecuniary damage, and particularly in relation to that of a psychiatric nature, would go a long way to relieving judges of the onerous burden they presently face and ensuring that all plaintiffs and defendants are treated equally before the courts. Irrespective of public and legal sentiment or apathy on particular proposals, this is, and must always remain, the primary objective of every legal system.

Turning to the question of an overriding limit on the amount of damages recoverable,[88] given that compensation for psychiatric harm is not technically possible, setting damages at some "comfort" level designed to provide the injured person with a "reasonable solace for his misfortune"[89] makes sense, provided that the ceiling is regularly reviewed to ensure that they remain appropriate despite the effects of inflation. To do so could not, it is suggested, be said to operate to undercompensate individuals by depriving them of something to which they were entitled. The primary benefit of the introduction of maximum total limits of non-pecuniary awards is the advancement of the objectives of uniformity, consistency and fairness as between parties and certainty in the measure of damages. While retaining flexibility in the assessment of the individual subheads of non-pecuniary damage, such limitations avoid the possibility of extravagant awards and the consequent burden imposed on society through increased insurance premiums,[90] and ensure that barriers to rehabilitation are lifted by removing the incentive for victims to "dwell on their misfortune" in the hope of securing a large award. It is natural for victims to believe that if they appear to be adjusting to their loss this will minimise its severity in the eyes of the court with the result of a reduced payout. An upper limit would encourage a plaintiff to "get his life back in order and to look to the future".[91] Moreover, the reduction of a potential windfall is likely to discourage litigation and encourage settlement negotiations.[92]

86. *Report on Personal Injury Litigation—Assessment of Damages: No 56* (1973), 11. The Pearson Report at 88-89 also rejected a legislative tariff to control awards.
87. Ibid.
88. See Mullany, op cit, n 73 at 717-727.
89. *Andrews v Grand & Toy Alberta Ltd* (1978) 83 DLR (3d) 452 per Dickson J at 476. "Solace" in this context does not mean sympathy, but refers to those physical arrangements which can be made to make an injured person's life more bearable. See also Ogus, op cit, n 1 at 15.
90. See S M Waddams, "Compensation for Non-Pecuniary Loss: Is There a Case for Legislative Intervention?" (1985) 63 Can BR 734 at 736; Mullany, op cit, n 73 at 718; above, p 279, n 83.
91. See Law Reform Commission of British Columbia, *Report on Compensation for Non-Pecuniary Loss: LRC 76* (1984), 18. Courts frequently hear evidence that the plaintiff's mental condition will not improve or heal until after the trial has been concluded or damages claims settled: see eg *Griffiths v R & H Green & Silley Weir Ltd* (1948) 81 LLLR 378 per Birkett J at 381; *Tuckey v R & H Green & Silley Weir Ltd* [1955] 2 Lloyd's Rep 619 per Pearson J at 630-631; *James v Woodall Duckham Construction Co Ltd* [1969] 1 WLR 903; *Chrysler Australia Ltd v Skrypek* (1975) 10 SASR 569; *McLoughlin v O'Brian* [1981] QB 599 per Griffiths LJ at 624.
92. See F C Hutley, "Appeals within the Judicial Hierarchy and the Effect of Judicial Doctrine on Such Appeals in Australia and England" (1976) 7 Syd LR 317 at 333.

The advantages flowing from the imposition of some ceiling were recognised in 1978 by the Supreme Court of Canada in a series of cases known collectively as the "trilogy".[93] The adoption of an upper limit in England has also been urged in several cases.[94] Although the House of Lords has indicated that this is a matter which should be addressed through legislation,[95] the Court of Appeal has recently set down as a guideline a figure of £75,000 for non-pecuniary damages for the average case of tetraplegia with no complications.[96] The possibility of a maximum limit set at five times the average annual industrial earnings (about £20,000 in 1977) was discussed by the members of the 1978 United Kingdom Royal Commission on Civil Liability and Compensation for Personal Injury. Whilst they were equally divided on the appropriateness of restrictions of this nature, all were in agreement that some form of control on awards should exist.[97]

If one accepts the arguments for the justification for some form of ceiling on awards under this head of damages, it remains to be considered whether the judiciary, or Parliament advised by those who have special knowledge, is in the best position to formulate the extent of changes of this nature. It is suggested that whilst it probably cannot be asserted that judicial intervention in this matter usurps the role of the legislature, the parliamentary forum is better suited than the courtroom to the undertaking of thorough research into all the repercussions of such a policy-orientated reform. As Stephen J observed in *Pennant Hills Restaurants Pty Ltd v Barrell Insurances Pty Ltd*, "[i]t is no part of the judicial function to depress the level of awards on policy grounds: the courts have no mandate to entertain any such policy."[98] Again input from medical experts and

---

93. *Andrews v Grand & Toy Alberta Ltd* (1978) 83 DLR (3d) 452; *Arnold v Teno* (1978) 83 DLR (3d) 609; *Thornton v Board of School Trustees of School District No 57 (Prince George)* (1978) 83 DLR (3d) 480. Damages for this kind of loss, it was said, should be moderate and in order to achieve uniformity a "rough upper limit" was imposed at $100,000 adjusted for inflation (now approximately twice this amount) in cases involving two quadriplegic plaintiffs and one brain-damaged plaintiff: see B Feldthusen & K McNair, "General Damages in Personal Injury Suits: The Supreme Court's Trilogy" (1978) 28 UTLJ 381, 416. All three decisions were elaborated upon and explained by the Supreme Court in *Lindal v Lindal* (1982) 129 DLR (3d) 263: see E Veitch, "The Implications of Lindal" (1982) 28 McGill LJ 116.

94. See eg *Lim Poh Choo v Camden v Islington Area Health Authority* [1979] QB 196; *Croke (An Infant) v Wiseman* [1981] 3 All ER 852.

95. *Lim Poh Choo v Camden & Islington Area Health Authority* [1980] AC 174 per Lord Scarman at 183.

96. *Housecroft v Burnett* [1986] 1 All ER 332. *Dorland's Illustrated Medical Dictionary* (26th ed, 1981), 1352 defines "tetraplegia" as the "paralysis of all four extremities". An uncomplicated case is one where the victim is not in pain, is fully aware of his or her disability, has the capacity to see, speak and hear but requires assistance with bodily functions and has a life expectancy of 25 years. The Irish Supreme Court has suggested that there be a maximum award of £150,000 for general damages in quadriplegic cases where the victim is fully conscious of his or her plight: see *Sinnott v Quinnsworth Ltd* [1984] ILRM 523. Note also Widgery LJ's comments in *Jones v Griffith* [1969] 2 All ER 1015 at 1019-20 in relation to awards for epilepsy.

97. See the Pearson Report at 90-91.

98. (1981) 145 CLR 625 at 660. Note also *Morgans v Launchbury* [1973] AC 127; *D & F Estates Ltd v Church Commissioners for England* [1989] AC 177. Legislative rather than judicial reform has been preferred in New Zealand (see the *Accident Compensation Act* 1972 (NZ) as consolidated and revised by the *Accident Compensation Act* 1982 (NZ), s 78)

interest groups would be essential to clarify what constitutes adequate compensation for this type of damage.

98. *Continued*
and the majority of American States. The ceiling strategy was first adopted in Australia in South Australia in 1940 in relation to the solatium payable on death claims to spouses or to the parents of young children. In recent years various Australian jurisdictions have enacted legislation placing upper limits on specified heads of damages in relation to specified types of claim. They are characterised by their narrow scope and particularity of operation which is usually restricted to the motor vehicle and industrial spheres: see Mullany, op cit, n 73 at 720-727.

14

INTENTIONAL ACTS

So far, we have spoken exclusively of psychiatric damage resulting from negligence; but shock and consequent psychiatric damage are just as likely to result from deliberate wrongdoing, both where such wrongdoing is aimed at the plaintiff and where it is directed at third parties. Here, an action based on the principle of *Wilkinson v Downton*[1] offers an alternative to an action in negligence.

Wilkinson v Downton liability

The case

Wilkinson v Downton is one of those instances in which the origins of a new tort can be precisely located in a particular decision.[2] The defendant, Downton, entered the "Albion" public house in St Paul's Road, London, and told the landlady, Mrs Lavinia Wilkinson, that her husband Thomas (who that day had gone to a race meeting in Harlow) had on the return journey been injured in a road accident and was lying at "The Elms" in Leytonstone with both legs broken, and that he desired someone to come and fetch him home. Downton was a regular customer, and Mrs Wilkinson believed his story, even though her husband had told her that he intended to return home by train. She sent her son and a servant by train to Leytonstone, with pillows and rugs, but only when they arrived at "The Elms" was it discovered that the whole thing was a practical joke. Mr Wilkinson arrived home safely at midnight, having returned by train as he said he would. Downton's actions caused Mrs Wilkinson to suffer a severe shock. She was seriously ill for some time, to the point where at one time her life and sanity were threatened, and her hair turned white.[3] She and her husband brought an action against Downton in the High Court, alleging that the words had been falsely, fraudulently and maliciously spoken with intent to aggrieve, injure and annoy. Mrs Wilkinson claimed damages for mental anguish and resulting illness and her husband claimed for medical expenses and loss of services. Downton pleaded that he had no intention to injure, and that the damages were too remote. The jury, in

1. [1897] 2 QB 57. See generally P R Handford, "Wilkinson v Downton and Acts Calculated to Cause Physical Harm" (1985) 16 UWALR 31; F A Trindade, "The Intentional Infliction of Purely Mental Distress" (1986) 6 OJLS 219. For the position in South Africa see J M Potgeiter, "Delictual Liability for Intentional Infliction of Emotional Distress in South African Law?" (1976) 17 *Codicillus* 11; S K Parmanand, "Intentional Infliction of Emotional Distress—A Neglected Delict" (1984) 101 SALJ 171.
2. Some other examples are deceit: *Pasley v Freeman* (1789) 3 TR 51; 100 ER 450 and inducing breach of contract: *Lumley v Gye* (1853) 2 E & B 216; 118 ER 749.
3. Some of these facts are taken from the fuller report of *Wilkinson v Downton* in (1897) 66 LJQB 493.

answer to various questions put to them, decided that Downton had spoken the words and meant them to be heard and acted on, and that they were believed and acted on; that they were, to his knowledge, false; and that they caused Mrs Wilkinson to suffer shock and resultant illness. They assessed the damages as £100 for this, plus a small sum for the wasted train fares to Leytonstone.

Wright J held that it was appropriate to recover the cost of the train fare in the tort of deceit since it resulted from acting on the false statement. The shock damages, however, could not be subsumed under the same cause of action.

> "I am not sure that this would not be an extension of that doctrine, the real ground of which appears to be that a person who makes a false statement intended to be acted on must make good the damage naturally resulting from its being acted on. Here there is no injuria of that kind. I think, however, that the verdict may be supported upon another ground. The defendant has, as I assume for the moment, wilfully done an act calculated to cause physical harm to the plaintiff—that is to say, to infringe her legal right to personal safety, and has in fact thereby caused physical harm to her. That proposition without more appears to me to state a good cause of action, there being no justification alleged for the act. This wilful injuria is in law malicious, although no malicious purpose to cause the harm which was caused nor any motive of spite is imputed to the defendant."[4]

He went on to hold that the assumptions made in this proposition were justified.

Thus, the proposition which is at the centre of *Wilkinson v Downton* is that doing an act calculated to cause physical harm is actionable if physical harm results. This is a potentially wide-ranging proposition capable of drawing together many instances involving the intentional causing of harm to the person[5]—though not, perhaps, those based on purely dignitary interests such as assault and some cases of battery and false imprisonment.[6] Nowhere does Wright J limit the principle to the

---

4. [1897] 2 QB 57 at 58-59.
5. See the discussion of this issue in Handford, op cit, n 1 at 34-38. Note in particular the attempt of the High Court of Australia in *Beaudesert Shire Council v Smith* (1969) 120 CLR 145 to develop a general principle (derived from the old action on the case) to govern liability for all intentional harm, physical or non-physical—a principle not adopted in any other case and rejected by the Privy Council, the House of Lords and the New Zealand Court of Appeal: see *Dunlop v Woollahra Municipal Council* [1982] AC 158; *Lonrho Ltd v Shell Petroleum Co Ltd (No 2)* [1982] AC 173; *Van Camp Chocolates Ltd v Aulsebrooks Ltd* [1984] 1 NZLR 354; G Dworkin & A Harari, "The Beaudesert Decision—Raising the Ghost of an Action upon the Case" (1967) 40 ALJ 296, 347; G Dworkin, "Intentionally Causing Economic Loss—Beaudesert Shire Council v Smith Revisited" (1974) 1 Mon ULR 4; R J Sadler, "Whither Beaudesert Shire Council v Smith?" (1984) 58 ALJ 38. Note also the development of the "prima facie tort" doctrine in the United States: see *Restatement of Torts Second*, §870; M D Forkosch, "An Analysis of the 'Prima Facie Tort' Cause of Action" (1957) 42 Cornell LQ 465, under which a defendant may be liable for harm caused intentionally even where no specific intentional tort applies. This doctrine is based on a suggestion of Sir Frederick Pollock: see F Pollock, *Torts* (1887), 21, and a dictum of Bowen LJ in *Skinner & Co v Shew & Co* [1893] 1 Ch 413 at 422, and was first adopted by Holmes J in *Aikens v Wisconsin* (1904) 195 US 194.
6. See above, p 46, n 157.

intentional causing of shock. It is significant, however, that the cases in which *Wilkinson v Downton* has been followed and applied all involve shock and shock-related injuries.

The development of this action has run parallel with the growth of liability in negligence for psychiatric damage. The same arguments—for example, that the damage was too remote—were raised against recognising liability, and overcome.[7] Confirmation of the close links between the two causes of action is provided by the frequent citation of negligence authorities in the *Wilkinson v Downton* cases.[8]

Subsequent cases

The only English case which has followed *Wilkinson v Downton* is *Janvier v Sweeney*.[9] The defendants were private detectives, and one instructed the other to masquerade as a Scotland Yard detective in order to obtain some letters from the plaintiff, whose fiancé was an interned German. The second defendant told the plaintiff that she was wanted by them for corresponding with a German spy. As a result of this the plaintiff suffered shock and became ill. The English Court of Appeal held that the defendants were liable in accordance with the principle of *Wilkinson v Downton*. In Scotland, *Wilkinson v Downton* was adopted in *A v B's Trustees*,[10] where a lodger committed suicide by slashing his throat with a razor in his landlady's bathroom, which caused shock and injury to the health of the landlady and her daughter when they came upon the scene.[11] In New Zealand, *Wilkinson v Downton* was again followed in *Stevenson v*

7. The issue of remoteness of damage is dealt with in *Wilkinson v Downton* [1897] 2 QB 57 per Wright J at 60; *A v B's Trustees* (1906) 13 SLT 830 per Lord Johnston at 830; *Janvier v Sweeney* [1919] 2 KB 316 per Bankes LJ at 323-324, per Duke LJ at 327; *Stevenson v Basham* [1922] NZLR 225 per Herdman J at 231-232; *Bielitski v Obadiak* (1922) 65 DLR 627 per Lamont JA at 632-633, per Turgeon JA at 635-636; *Purdy v Woznesensky* [1937] 2 WWR 116 per Mackenzie JA at 122-123. The increase in medical and scientific knowledge since 1888 is referred to in *Purdy v Woznesensky* per Mackenzie JA at 122, per Gordon JA at 126.

8. Thus eg *Bell v Great Northern Railway Co of Ireland* (1890) 26 LR Ir 428 was relied on in *A v B's Trustees* (1906) 13 SLT 830 and *Stevenson v Basham* [1922] NZLR 225; *Dulieu v White & Sons* [1901] 2 KB 669 in *Stevenson v Basham, Janvier v Sweeney* [1919] 2 KB 316, *Bielitski v Obadiak* (1922) 65 DLR 627 and *Purdy v Woznesensky* [1937] 2 WWR 116; *and Hambrook v Stokes Bros* [1925] 1 KB 141 in *Purdy v Woznesensky*.

9. [1919] 2 KB 316. Note also *D v National Society for the Prevention of Cruelty to Children* [1978] AC 171 per Lord Denning MR at 188-189.

10. (1906) 13 SLT 830.

11. The court could not see the precise ground of action and suggested breach of contract. In a subsequent case involving similar facts, *Anderson v McCrae* (1930) 47 Sh Ct Rep 287, the court rejected breach of contract on the ground that damage such as this was too remote a consequence. They distinguished *Wilkinson v Downton* on the not very convincing ground that it was based on implied malice. Note also *Stedman v Henderson* (1923) 40 Sh Ct Rep 8, where the defendant was held liable for violent language and abuse causing fright and consequent illness, although *Wilkinson v Downton* was not in fact cited. An English case with very similar facts to *A v B's Trustees* is *Re Drake* [1945] 1 All ER 576 where a fireman suffered shock and consequent nervous disability when he found his company officer hanging dead in the storeroom at the fire station. For the purposes of compensation under wartime emergency legislation it was held that the injury arose out of and in the course of the plaintiff's duties, and the court remitted it to a tribunal to determine whether the injury was purely mental or physical.

Basham,[12] where a wife suffered shock and a miscarriage on hearing their landlord threatening her husband to burn them out of their house if they did not give up possession.[13] A South African case which relies on *Wilkinson v Downton* is *Els v Bruce*,[14] where the defendant threatened to have the plaintiff's husband arrested unless she paid him some money, causing injury to the plaintiff's health. More recently in *Boswell v Minister of Police*,[15] where the claimant suffered shock when a policeman told her that her nephew (to whom she was close) had been shot dead by police, it was held, adopting a principle closely related to *Wilkinson v Downton* (which was not cited), that a person who deliberately frightens or shocks another cannot be heard to say that he or she could not foresee the natural consequences of his or her act.[16]

Canadian courts have also recognised liability for the intentional infliction of shock and psychiatric damage.[17] In *Bielitski v Obadiak*[18] the defendant circulated a false report that Steve Bielitski had hanged himself from a telegraph pole, and the report in due course reached Bielitski's mother, who suffered a violent shock and became ill. *Wilkinson v Downton* was followed and the defendant was held liable on the assumption that he must have intended the report to reach the plaintiff. In *Purdy v Woznesensky*[19] the plaintiff and her husband were together at a local dance when the defendant, a neighbour who was still resentful of the fact that he had earlier been sued by the husband for breach of an agreement to deliver cattle, assaulted him in her presence, knocking him to the floor and causing her to think that he was dead. In consequence she became mentally ill. Again the defendant was held liable under *Wilkinson v Downton*.[20] More recently, in *Rahemtulla v Vanfed Credit Union*,[21] the summary dismissal of an employee wrongfully accused of taking money was held to give rise to liability under this principle. In consequence the plaintiff suffered depression accompanied by signs of physical illness. The court found the defendant's conduct "flagrant and outrageous",[22] and calculated to cause the profound distress experienced by the plaintiff. In *Timmermans v Buelow*[23] the plaintiff's landlord, in an attempt to evict the plaintiff from his apartment, threatened to "bring some guys over", as a result of which the plaintiff "would be in the hospital". The plaintiff was

---

12. [1922] NZLR 225.
13. The court held that the case could be treated either as a case of intentional conduct under *Wilkinson v Downton* or as one of negligence.
14. 1922 EDL 295.
15. 1978 (3) SA 268 (E).
16. Unlike *Els v Bruce*, which was brought under the actio injuriarum (which deals with interests of personality), *Boswell v Minister of Police* was an action under the lex Aquilia (which covers interests of substance). This made little difference to the principle on which liability was based, but limited the scope of the damages awarded.
17. See eg *Abramzik v Brenner* (1967) 65 DLR (2d) 651 per Culliton CJS at 654.
18. (1922) 65 DLR 627.
19. [1937] 2 WWR 116.
20. See also *Campagne v Hoffman* (unreported, Saskatchewan SC, 19 Mar 1959), noted in I Goldsmith, *Damages for Personal Injury and Death in Canada 1958-1972* (1974), No 277, a case with identical facts.
21. (1984) 29 CCLT 78.
22. Ibid at 95.
23. (1984) 38 CCLT 136.

already prone to panic attacks, as the defendant knew, and as a result of these threats (even though in the end they were not carried out) his mental condition progressively worsened. Catzman J, without mentioning *Wilkinson v Downton* by name, held the defendant liable for the intentional infliction of nervous shock.[24]

Wilkinson v Downton has been applied in three Australian cases. In *Johnson v Commonwealth*[25] the plaintiff suffered mental anguish and consequent ill-health as a result of acts done to her husband. The defendants wrongfully entered the plaintiff's house, assaulted her husband in her presence, and then carried him off to prison, where they kept him for some considerable time. The plaintiff recovered damages under *Wilkinson v Downton* and also for loss of consortium.[26] *Bunyan v Jordan*[27] also recognised the *Wilkinson v Downton* principle, but held that there was no liability on the facts. The plaintiff allegedly overheard the defendant threaten to kill himself and then heard a shot being fired, but it was held that her shock and her resulting neurasthenia (a state of nervous exhaustion) were not results that could reasonably be expected to follow in the circumstances.[28] The most recent Australian case recognising the *Wilkinson v Downton* principle is *Battista v Cooper*.[29] This was an application for criminal injuries compensation by the widow and three children of a man who was shot and killed in the presence of his wife during an armed hold-up. The applicants claimed that they had suffered shock and emotional distress as a result of the deceased's death. The South Australian Full Court held that it was not only the direct victim of the crime who could claim under the compensation legislation. All those who would have had an action for common law damages should be eligible. This holding focused the court's attention on the rights in tort of the four claimants, an issue on which it was appropriate to apply the rules relating to intentional wrongdoing. On the basis of the principle in *Wilkinson v Downton*, all four applicants were awarded compensation.

Requirements of the cause of action

This line of cases makes it possible to provide some elaboration of the basic prerequisites of this type of liability, namely that there be a wilful act

24. The principle indorsed in this case was referred to in *Frame v Smith* (1987) 42 DLR (4th) 81 and *Hasenclever v Hoskins* (1988) 47 CCLT 225, but not applied on the facts because no "visible or provable illness" had been shown to exist. In *Frame v Smith* the Supreme Court of Canada overruled *Cant v Cant* (1984) 49 OR (2d) 25, in which a county court judge had held that *Wilkinson v Downton* could be used in the context of a family dispute concerning custody and access to children.
25. (1927) 27 SR (NSW) 133.
26. On this ground the case was later overruled by *Wright v Cedzich* (1930) 43 CLR 493, which held that the action for loss of consortium did not lie in favour of a wife.
27. (1937) 57 CLR 1.
28. See Latham CJ at 11-12. The distinguishing facts were: (1) the person injured was not the person to whom the words were spoken—they were not even spoken in her presence but merely overheard; (2) the acts of the defendant could not, in the circumstances, be said to have been calculated or likely to cause harm to any normal person; (3) there was no intention to cause harm to the plaintiff.
29. (1976) 14 SASR 225. The principle was referred to, but not applied, in *Nichevich v Fullin* (unreported, Western Australian SC, 18 July 1990, Appeal No 181 of 1989); *Wodrow v Commonwealth* (unreported, Australian Capital Territory SC, 13 Dec 1991, No SC1 of 1984).

calculated to cause physical harm and that physical harm result. Without exception, in the cases outlined above the physical harm has taken the form of "nervous shock"—the "recognised psychiatric illness" which is now the preferred appellation in negligence cases. [30] Throughout this work we have been at pains to distinguish between physical harm sustained by impact and psychiatric damage, which is an injury to the mind rather than the body. However the *Wilkinson v Downton* cases generally reproduce the language of Wright J and refer to the psychiatric injury suffered by plaintiffs as "physical harm". On a number of occasions in this chapter it has been necessary to do likewise. In such instances the reservations stated above need to be borne in mind.

That the tortfeasor's act is required to be wilful, rather than merely careless, shows that this is an intentional tort and not one based on negligence. However, in tort recklessness is usually grouped with intention, and the notion of wilful conduct is presumably wide enough to include recklessness as well as intention. According to the American *Restatement of Torts Second*, conduct is intentional when the actor either desires to cause particular consequences or knows that they are certain or substantially certain to result from the act. [31] Recklessness denotes that, though the consequences of the act are less than substantially certain the risk of them occurring is greater than the mere foreseeability of consequences that characterises negligent conduct. [32] It is clear that recklessness is sufficient to ground liability under *Wilkinson v Downton*. According to Culliton CJS in *Abramzik v Brenner*: [33]

> "There can be no doubt but that an action will lie for the wilful infliction of shock, or a reckless disregard as to whether or not shock will ensue from the act committed." [34]

The requirement that the defendant's act be "calculated" to cause this harm has given rise to some difficulty. [35] "Calculated" seems to mean something between "intended" and "foreseeably likely". The meaning cannot be so restricted as to require that the defendant should have intended the physical harm to occur, because in *Wilkinson v Downton* itself the defendant only intended to play a practical joke and seemingly did not either desire or realise that more serious consequences would follow. On the other hand, it is necessary for the physical harm to be something more than merely foreseeable, because otherwise it will be difficult, perhaps impossible, to distinguish the *Wilkinson v Downton* principle from liability in negligence. [36] The Restatement probably provides the best indication of the meaning of the word: instead of "calculated", it uses the words

---

30. See above, pp 14-18. Note in particular *Rahemtulla v Vanfed Credit Union* (1984) 29 CCLT 78 per McLachin J at 95, requiring that the defendant's conduct cause the plaintiff to suffer a "visible and provable illness".
31. *Restatement of Torts Second*, §8A.
32. Ibid, §500.
33. (1967) 65 DLR (2d) 651 at 654.
34. See also *Rahemtulla v Vanfed Credit Union* (1984) 29 CCLT 78 per McLachin J at 94.
35. On this see L Vold, "Tort Recovery for Intentional Infliction of Mental Distress" (1939) 18 Neb L Bull 222 at 238. See also J Irvine's annotation to *Timmermans v Buelow* (1984) 38 CCLT 136 at 139-140.
36. See below, pp 290-292.

"intended or likely".[37] In *Wilkinson v Downton*, Wright J said that one question was "whether the defendant's act was so plainly calculated to produce some effect of the kind which was produced that an intention to produce it ought to be imputed",[38] and it may thus be that in *Wilkinson v Downton* itself the defendant intended to cause physical harm in the sense that while he had no desire to bring about the harmful consequences they were substantially certain to follow. Other cases, such as *Stevenson v Basham*,[39] in which the court expressly referred to the defendant's conduct as reckless, are perhaps cases in which the defendant's conduct was likely, rather than intended, to cause physical harm.

Although there is potential for some of the limitations imposed in the cases on negligently caused psychiatric injury to have an impact in the context of the intentional infliction of mental harm,[40] others such as the requirements as to relationship are seemingly not present. As regards the conduct which precipitates the physical harm, it may take any form. Statements predominate in the cases—lies, as in *Wilkinson v Downton* itself,[41] or threats, as in *Janvier v Sweeney*.[42] But some have involved other forms of behaviour, such as the suicide in *A v B's Trustees*.[43] What matters is not the kind of conduct but its likely effect on the plaintiff. The defendant's motive may vary from the desire to play a practical joke to the opposite extreme—Duke LJ in *Janvier v Sweeney*[44] referred to this case as "a much stronger case than *Wilkinson v Downton*" for precisely this reason. The principle of special sensitivity is recognised—if the defendant knows that the plaintiff is specially susceptible, his or her conduct may be viewed as calculated to cause harm to that particular plaintiff although it would not affect a person of ordinary firmness.[45] The physical harm must be caused by the defendant's act,[46] and it must not be too remote.[47]

37. See in particular *Restatement of Torts*, §46 and *Restatement of Torts Second*, §312, which both set out a cause of action for the intentional infliction of emotional distress which results in physical harm.
38. [1897] 2 QB 57 at 59. See also *Boswell v Minister for Police*, 1978 (3) SA 268 (E) per Kannemeyer J at 274.
39. [1922] NZLR 225 at 229.
40. See below, pp 294-295. This has already occurred in the United States context: see below, pp 302-303.
41. See also *Bielitski v Obadiak* (1922) 65 DLR 627; *Boswell v Minister of Police*, 1978 (3) SA 268 (E).
42. [1919] 2 KB 316. See also *Stevenson v Basham* [1922] NZLR 225; *Els v Bruce*, 1922 EDL 295; *Timmermans v Buelow* (1984) 38 CCLT 136.
43. (1906) 13 SLT 830. Note also the American case of *Nelson v Crawford* (1899) 81 NW 335 (Mich) where the defendant dressed up as a ghost to frighten the plaintiff. There was no liability on the facts because the shock suffered by the plaintiff was due to her special susceptibility and the defendant, a "harmless lunatic", had no intention to frighten her.
44. [1919] 2 KB 316 at 326.
45. See *Els v Bruce*, 1922 EDL 295 where the plaintiff was in a "delicate state of health"; *Timmermans v Buelow* (1984) 38 CCLT 136 where the defendant knew that the plaintiff was subject to "panic attacks". Note also *Bunyan v Jordan* (1937) 57 CLR 1 per Latham CJ at 14.
46. See *Bielitski v Obadiak* (1922) 65 DLR 627, where it was argued that, since the defendant's tale had reached the plaintiff through repetition by others, there was no liability on the basis that the intervening acts had broken the chain of causation. The court held that in such a situation there was a responsibility to break the bad news to relatives, and so the story was as certain to reach the plaintiff as if the defendant had told her himself. Haultain CJS, however, dissented from the majority on this ground.
47. See Wright J's discussion of remoteness in *Wilkinson v Downton* [1897] 2 QB 57 at 59-61.

Whither Wilkinson v Downton?

One of the major points of interest about the *Wilkinson v Downton* principle is that it has been applied in comparatively few cases. There are only three major cases since the Second World War in which it has been invoked—two 1984 Canadian cases,[48] and one Australian case in which it was adopted in the context of a claim for criminal injuries compensation.[49] It may well be a dying cause of action. In stark contrast, actions in negligence for shock-induced psychiatric harm have made major strides since that point in time. Is it possible that negligence is doing the work once done by *Wilkinson v Downton*—that Wright J's formulation of his principle in terms of intention was purely a device to evade the restrictions of *Victorian Railways Commissioner v Coultas*,[50] and since that case has long disappeared into the past actions which involve an element of deliberate conduct can more easily be based on failure to comply with the standard set by a reasonable man? There is some substance in this argument. Indeed, one can go further and suggest that a cause of action based on intention, however potentially useful it might have been in other contexts, was never appropriate for the facts in *Wilkinson v Downton*.

The argument for the *Wilkinson v Downton* action being distinct from the tort of negligence is that the cases based on this principle *do* involve the intentional or reckless causing of shock, in that the defendant intends to cause, or is reckless as to, the immediate consequences—fright or horror— and that the physical harm which results can be regarded as intended or likely, rather than as merely foreseeable. This distinction is clearly made in *Battista v Cooper*,[51] where the court stressed that the harm suffered by the wife and children of a man killed during an armed hold-up was to be regarded as intentionally caused. A distinction between *Wilkinson v Downton* and negligence is also supported by cases such as *Bunyan v Jordan*[52] and *Stevenson v Basham*,[53] in which the plaintiffs relied on them as alternatives. In *Bunyan v Jordan* the New South Wales Full Supreme Court rejected a claim based on negligence and the High Court of Australia rejected the *Wilkinson v Downton* claim, but in *Stevenson v Basham* the New Zealand Supreme Court held that the plaintiff was entitled to recover under either principle. Thus, there is certainly scope for argument that the two principles, though closely related,[54] are distinct.

Some commentators have questioned this. Goodhart, for example, says of *Wilkinson v Downton*:

48. *Rahemtulla v Vanfed Credit Union* (1984) 29 CCLT 78; *Timmermans v Buelow* (1984) 38 CCLT 136.
49. *Battista v Cooper* (1976) 14 SASR 225.
50. (1888) 13 App Cas 222.
51. (1976) 14 SASR 225 per Bray CJ at 230.
52. (1937) 57 CLR 1.
53. [1922] NZLR 225.
54. See *D v National Society for the Prevention of Cruelty to Children* [1978] AC 171, a case mainly concerned with Crown privilege, in which Lord Denning MR assumed that the cause of action would fall under *Wilkinson v Downton*, if it existed at all, whereas the other two judges assumed that it would be an action in negligence. Note also *Purdy v Woznesensky* [1937] 2 WWR 116 per Mackenzie JA at 119-120 where the language of the two actions appears to have been mixed: see below, pp 295-296.

"The physical harm was intended only in a limited sense—the acts were intentional, but there was no evidence that the defendant intended the plaintiff to become ill."[55]

If the physical harm cannot be regarded as more than foreseeable, then it can be argued that there is really no difference between the *Wilkinson v Downton* principle and negligence. Another writer says:

"The principle on which the case was decided gives rise to difficulty. The main trouble is with the words 'calculated to cause'. If these words mean no more than that harm was foreseeably likely as a result of the act or statement, there is great difficulty in distinguishing the *Wilkinson v Downton* . . . principle from negligence. If the words mean more than foreseeable, such as certain or substantially certain, there is difficulty with the case itself since nervous shock, as distinct from mental distress, though a foreseeable result of the news imparted to the plaintiff, was hardly a certain or a substantially certain result. Only if the case is interpreted in this way, however, does it seem that the principle can have a separate existence independent of the tort of negligence."[56]

One way of testing these arguments is to inquire whether *Wilkinson v Downton*, had it arisen at the present day, could have been accommodated within the principles of negligence. At the time the case was decided, the major obstacle in the path of such a decision was *Victorian Railways Commissioner v Coultas*,[57] but that case has long been overruled.[58] Certainly, there is extensive liability in negligence for acts causing shock and psychiatric injury, but *Wilkinson v Downton* itself, and some of the other cases, involve shock caused by a statement. Liability in negligence for statements has expanded considerably since the fundamentally important case of *Hedley Byrne & Co v Heller & Partners*[59] but, as has been pointed out,[60] this body of precedent involves harm suffered through *reliance* on the statement. In *Wilkinson v Downton* the harm was suffered because the statement was *made*, and negligence liability based on reliance is just as inappropriate for the shock damage in *Wilkinson v Downton* as was the tort of deceit on which the plaintiffs sought to rely. There are however some cases which suggest that there is a duty not to cause shock by a negligent statement. *Stevenson v Basham*[61] supports such a suggestion, as do the cases holding that there is liability for the negligent communication of bad news.[62] There thus seems no reason why the defendant in *Wilkinson v Downton* could not have been held liable in negligence. If the shock to Mrs Wilkinson is regarded as no more than a foreseeable consequence of Downton's conduct, negligence is the only appropriate cause of action.

55. A L Goodhart (1944) 7 MLR 87 at 87-88 (book review of P H Winfield, *Textbook of the Law of Tort* (2nd ed, 1943)).
56. C D Baker, *Tort* (5th ed, 1991), 29-30.
57. (1888) 13 App Cas 222.
58. See above, pp 2-3.
59. [1964] AC 465.
60. See above, p 183.
61. [1922] NZLR 225.
62. See above, pp 183-191.

Wright J, however, specifically held that an intention to produce some effect of the kind which was produced ought to be imputed to him, [63] in this way avoiding the problem of the *Coultas* decision. [64] He was not prepared to regard the harm as merely a foreseeable consequence. In his opinion it had to be classified as intentionally inflicted. It is on this, and on this alone, that the appropriateness of the *Wilkinson v Downton* principle for the facts of the case must rest.

Liability to secondary victims of intentional acts

Earlier chapters [65] have stressed the importance of the decision in *Hambrook v Stokes Bros* [66] which recognised that there could be liability in negligence for shock suffered by someone other than the primary accident victim. Prior to this, all the cases involved plaintiffs who suffered shock through fear for their own safety, because they were within the "zone of danger" created by the defendant's negligence. *Hambrook v Stokes Bros* was the catalyst for the recognition of liability to a wide range of secondary parties who suffer psychiatric damage as a consequence of the original act of negligence. The gradual extension of this liability, through avenues such as relationship, aftermath and different means of communication, has been documented in the foregoing pages. Nowhere is the importance of this distinction between primary and secondary psychiatric damage victims stated more clearly than in the judgment of Lord Oliver in *Alcock v Chief Constable of South Yorkshire Police*. [67]

What is the position of such secondary parties when the original act is intentional rather than negligent? In principle, if there is liability when the initial act is negligent there should be liability in such a case, either under *Wilkinson v Downton* or in negligence. Acts of intentional violence are prone to leave a trail of shock victims in their wake. A single such act may be seen by one other person or by many. As an example of the former situation, in *Mahnke v Moore* [68] the father of the plaintiff, a five-year-old girl, blew her mother's skull to pieces in her presence and kept the body in the house with them for six days. He then committed suicide by shooting himself with a shotgun, thereby causing masses of blood to lodge upon his daughter's face and clothing. She sued the executrix of her father's estate in tort for shock, mental anguish and permanent nervous and physical injuries. A similar action could be contemplated in a case of rape, for example where a mother is sexually assaulted in the presence of her children, [69] or where a person is traumatised by the thought of the rape of

63. [1897] 2 QB 57 at 59.
64. Alternatively, as his Lordship was not bound by decisions of the Privy Council he could have simply held that the case did not even apply in relation to negligence, as the court in *Dulieu v White & Sons* [1901] 2 KB 669 did four years later.
65. See above, pp 4-5, 134-136, 153.
66. [1925] 1 KB 141.
67. [1992] 1 AC 310 at 406-411: see above, pp 99-101.
68. (1951) 77 A 2d 923 (Md). Note C P Malmquist, "Psychiatric Aspects of Familicide" (1980) 8 Bull Am Acad Psy Law 221; R S Pynoos & S Eth, "Familicide" (1984) 40 *Journal of Social Issues* 87.
69. See *Anon* (unreported, Criminal Injuries Compensation Board, 19 June 1992), noted in (1992) 142 NLJ 1415.

a loved one even if they did not witness it.[70] Illustrations of the latter situation are provided by a recent instance in Western Australia where a rejected boyfriend stabbed to death the 15-year-old girl who was the object of his affections in a classroom in front of other students, many of whom suffered shock and required intensive post-trauma counselling, and a Queensland case where criminal injuries compensation was awarded to a 27-year-old legal secretary for post-traumatic stress disorder resulting from a distressing incident on her wedding day when a gunman opened fire on the wedding car, narrowly missing the bride herself and wounding the chauffeur and a bridesmaid.[71] Where there are multiple acts of violence there are likely to be many trauma victims also. In the last few years there have been many instances where a person has gone berserk and killed or wounded large numbers of people, usually ending by committing suicide. Among recent instances, in England in August 1987 Michael Ryan rampaged through the streets of Hungerford, killing 16 people and wounding 11 others.[72] In France in July 1989, Christian Dornier, a French farmer, killed 14 people in a village near the Swiss border. In Canada in December 1989, Marc Lepine shot dead 14 young women at the University of Montreal. In New Zealand in November 1990, David Gray shot fourteen people in the South Island town of Aramoana.[73] In Australia, as recently as August 1991, Wade Frankum plunged a knife into a girl seated next to him at a café in Strathfield, New South Wales, and then shot another six people in the adjacent shopping centre, finally ordering a car driver to give him a lift and shooting himself in her presence.[74] In the United States, even more recently, in October 1991, George Hennard shot 22 people in the unfortunately named town of Killeen in Texas before shooting himself.[75]

70. As in *T v State of South Australia and Bridge* (unreported, South Australian SC, 19 June 1992, No 67 of 1992). The victims themselves will have a civil cause of action for assault and battery, as for example in *B(A) v J(I)* (1991) 81 Alta LR (2d) 84 where three children sued their father for sexual assaults and recovered damages. Another possibility would be a claim for criminal injuries compensation, as to which see above, pp 245-247.
71. *Re Kelley and Criminal Code of Queensland* (unreported, Queensland SC, 26 Feb 1992, No 363 of 1991).
72. *Jackson* (unreported, Criminal Injuries Compensation Board, 18 May 1989) was a claim for criminal injuries compensation by one of the victims who suffered post-traumatic stress disorder as a result of being shot by Ryan and seeing him shoot his mother, her husband, his workmate and a police officer. Note also *Re W* (unreported, Criminal Injuries Compensation Board, 21 Jan 1991) where a woman police officer recovered compensation for post-traumatic stress disorder suffered as a result of being caught in a terrorist bomb attack which caused the death of close colleagues.
73. Other recent instances in New Zealand include the murder of six members of the Schlaeper family in Paerata in May 1992, and the slaying of seven people by Raymond Ratima at Masterton in June of the same year.
74. Other recent occurrences in Australia include the shooting of seven people dead and the wounding of 19 others by Julian Knight in Hoddle St, Melbourne in August 1987, the gunning down of eight people by Frank Vitkovic in an office block in Queen St in the same city three months later and the rampage across the Kimberley and Northern Territory by Josef Schwab who killed five people in 1987 before police shot him. The latest example is the killing of five people in three New South Wales central coast towns in October 1992 by Malcolm George Baker.
75. This is only one of many United States examples. In 1984 James Huberty killed 21 people in a McDonald's restaurant in California. In August 1991 nine Thai Buddhists were murdered in their temple in Phoenix, Arizona. In November 1991 a Chinese student at the University of Iowa whose dissertation failed to win an award shot five people, including the successful candidate and faculty members who reviewed the thesis.

In each case, a number of people, relatives and others, witnessed the incidents. Though it cannot be suggested that the killers in these instances intended to cause psychiatric damage to anyone, it would seem that they were at least reckless as to the consequences of their actions as regards third parties and should be under some civil liability if sued. The potential for multiple claims for psychiatric injury is as great, if not greater, in such situations as in disasters caused by negligence, such as the Hillsborough case.

The *Wilkinson v Downton* principle is capable of application where shock is suffered by people other than the primary victim of the defendant's wrongful act. In *Stevenson v Basham*[76] a wife, lying in bed in another room, overheard a threat made to her husband to burn their house down. In *Johnson v Commonwealth*[77] the plaintiff suffered shock when the defendants entered her house, assaulted her husband in her presence and arrested him. In *Purdy v Woznesensky*[78] again the plaintiff's husband was assaulted in her presence, and the plaintiff suffered shock, thinking that her husband had been killed. In each case the defendant was held liable to the plaintiff under the theory of *Wilkinson v Downton*.[79]

If compared with negligence-based liability, these are straightforward cases. The relationship between husband and wife is one of the obvious cases in which the law has always recognised a right to recover, and now presumes it; and each plaintiff was present and saw the occurrence. But is the *Wilkinson v Downton* principle capable of extending to more distant relationships, including those outside the immediate family, or to mere bystanders, or aftermath cases, or any of the other situations dealt with in earlier chapters? Strong indications that it is are given by *Battista v Cooper*.[80] This case recognised that the wife and children of a murdered man had a cause of action under *Wilkinson v Downton*, on the basis that the defendant's action was calculated to cause physical harm, in the form of shock, to them. It is especially noteworthy that those who recovered compensation, and could have successfully sued, included not only the wife of the victim, who was present at the time of the shooting, but his three children who, it appears, were not present but learned subsequently of the tragedy, some of them, at least, seeing their father admitted to hospital.[81] Bray CJ, delivering the judgment of the court, was clearly of the view that the scope of shock liability flowing from an intentional act was at least as wide as in negligence:

76. [1922] NZLR 225.
77. (1927) 27 SR (NSW) 133.
78. [1937] 2 WWR 116.
79. This is recognised by §46(2) of the *Restatement of Torts Second* in respect of the United States tort of outrage developed from *Wilkinson v Downton*: see below, pp 297-304. It provides: "Where [extreme and outrageous] conduct is directed at a third person, the actor is subject to liability if he intentionally or recklessly causes severe emotional distress (a) to a member of such person's immediate family who is present at the time, whether or not such distress results in bodliy harm, or (b) to any other person who is present at the time, if such distress results in bodily harm."
80. (1976) 14 SASR 225.
81. Another instance would be the effect of rape or sexual assault on those not present at the time of the offence, as for example if the mother of the children sexually assaulted by their father in *B(A) v J(I)* (1991) 81 Alta LR (2d) 84 had suffered traumatic injury as a result.

"[T]here is no reason for restricting the category of plaintiffs who can recover for physical injury from an intentional tort to those who could recover in the same circumstances if the tort were a negligent one, and every reason, in my opinion, for widening it. It is natural to expect much more lasting and serious emotional damage from the murder of a husband or father than from his death by being run down in the street. There is a discussion of this question in Fleming on *Torts* 4th ed (1971), at 32-35, and, with respect, I agree with what the learned author says. Certainly the intended consequences of a tort can never be too remote. And if intended consequences as to A produce unintended consequences as to B, I think that B can still recover if his connection with A is not too remote. The Canadian and New Zealand cases cited in Fleming support this proposition. A defendant who knowingly spread a false rumour that the plaintiff's son had committed suicide was held liable for nervous shock to her upon the rumour reaching her: *Bielitzki v Obadisk* [sic]. A defendant, who made a threat to the plaintiff's husband inside the house that she and her husband were occupying to burn it down, the threat being overheard by her when she was in a bedroom where she was lying and when she was pregnant at the time, was held liable for the nervous shock she sustained. It is true that he knew that she was there: *Stevenson v Basham*. In *Janvier v Sweeney* the defendants during the 1914-1918 war threatened the plaintiff, a French citizen engaged to a German, with internment. They were private detectives and their object was to induce her to hand over to them letters in the possession of her employers for the purpose, presumably, of a divorce suit. The shock caused her actual physical injury and she suffered damages. Supposing she had reported to her German fiancé what had happened and he had sustained physical injury from shock also. Could he not have recovered? I think he could.

In my opinion, an intentional tortfeasor is liable, not only for the injury caused directly to his victim, but to [sic] the injury indirectly caused to those connected with his victim or those witnessing the injury to the victim."[82]

It should not be forgotten, however, that those who are secondarily affected by deliberate wrongdoing have an alternative cause of action in negligence, on the basis that the harm which they suffer is a foreseeable consequence of the defendant's conduct. Sometimes the difference between the two causes of action is not clearly perceived. Mackenzie JA of the Saskatchewan Court of Appeal in *Purdy v Woznesensky*, for example, in describing liability under *Wilkinson v Downton* appears to have lapsed into the language of negligence:

"[I]t seems to me that the defendant must be presumed as a reasonable man to know of the vital concern which a wife instinctively feels for the safety of her husband and the serious physical reactions which an attack upon him threatening injuries to his person would in all likelihood produce in her. Hence I think he should have foreseen that by causing her to witness such a sudden and violent assault as he made

82. (1976) 14 SASR 225 at 230-231.

upon her husband he would probably upset her nervous system in such a way as to cause her some physical harm even if she were in fact, as she appeared to be at the time, in a healthy condition of body and mind. An intention to produce such an effect must therefore be imputed to him. It follows that by thus disregarding her legal right to maintain the safety and integrity of her person he committed a breach of duty towards her. Such I take to be the result of the authorities."[83]

However, in *Stevenson v Basham*,[84] Herdman J set out in unambiguous terms the two possible remedies, and other cases are consistent with a negligence action being available independently of a remedy based on intention. In *Bassanese v Martin*[85] a wife was awarded damages in negligence for a depressive illness consequent on the death of her husband, who was visiting the house of another woman to commit adultery when he was stabbed by that woman's jealous lover. It is noteworthy that the plaintiff was, of course, not present to see the occurrence.[86] In the United States, for many years, secondary victims of intentional wrongdoing have had the choice of recovery in negligence as an alternative to intention-based liability.[87] The earliest case recognising such liability is *Hill v Kimball*[88] in which the plaintiff suffered shock and a resultant miscarriage when the defendant assaulted two negro servants in the plaintiff's presence. This case antedates both *Wilkinson v Downton* and most of the case law on liability for negligent acts causing psychiatric damage. The continuing potentiality of this principle is attested to by *Ledger v Tippitt*[89] where the plaintiff was beside her de facto husband in their car when he was stabbed to death. The court held that a negligence claim could proceed.

Thus, those who suffer psychiatric injury as a result of acts directed at third parties have available remedies both in negligence and in an intention-based tort, provided the necessary preconditions are met. In the massacres described earlier the perpetrators could well be liable not only to actions at

83. [1937] 2 WWR 116 at 119-120.
84. [1922] NZLR 225.
85. (1982) 31 SASR 461. Liability was admitted. Zelling J was unimpressed with the pleadings, which failed to make clear the basis on which the defendant would have been liable to the husband. He speculated that the plaintiff's shock might, as much as anything, have been due to the activity in which the husband had been engaged when he met his death.
86. Note also *Fagan v Crimes Compensation Tribunal* (1982) 150 CLR 666, a claim for criminal injuries compensation on behalf of a child who suffered shock when told of his mother's murder. The High Court made it clear that compensation could be claimed by those who had a cause of action for "nervous shock" at common law, although the right to compensation was not necessarily limited to such cases.
87. This action is recognised by §312 of the *Restatement of Torts Second*, which reads: "If the actor intentionally and unreasonably subjects another to emotional distress which he should recognise as likely to result in illness or other bodily harm, he is subject to liability to the other for an illness or other bodily harm of which the distress is a legal cause, (a) although the actor has no intention of inflicting such harm, and (b) irrespective of whether the act is directed against the other or a third person." See also W P Keeton, *Prosser and Keeton on the Law of Torts* (5th ed, 1984), 65-66; J E Hallen, "Damages for Physical Injuries Resulting from Fright or Shock" (1933) 19 Va L Rev 253.
88. (1890) 13 SW 59 (Tex). See J E Hallen, "Hill v Kimball—A Milepost in the Law" (1933) 12 Tex L Rev 1. Note also *Watson v Dilts* (1902) 89 NW 1068 (Ia); *Jeppsen v Jensen* (1916) 155 P 429 (Utah); *Rogers v Williard* (1920) 223 SW 15 (Ark); *Duncan v Donnell* (1928) 12 SW 2d 811 (Tex).
89. (1985) 210 Cal Rptr 814.

the suit of the victims (or their estates or relatives) but also to bystanders and others who suffer psychiatric damage through witnessing the slaughter or its aftermath.

The possible extension of Wilkinson v Downton to purely mental distress

The law in the United States has long recognised a cause of action precisely the same as *Wilkinson v Downton*.[90] The earliest case appears to be *Hickey v Welch*,[91] decided four years after *Wilkinson v Downton*, in which relations between neighbours were at a low ebb, and the defendant's activities, which included abusing the plaintiffs, piling up earth around their water closet so that they could not use it, and brandishing a pistol when they tried to do so, aggravated the plaintiff's neurasthenia and caused serious injury to her health. Though there was a technical assault, the Missouri court chose to base liability on a general rule that where the defendant intentionally caused the plaintiff to suffer mental anguish which resulted in some proved nervous illness, an action lay. In the words of Goode J:

> "The ancient superstition which found the proximate cause of mental and nervous diseases in diabolical possession, was scarcely more ridiculous than the theory that when an ailment of that kind follows a great fright, due to another's tortious act, the fright and not the tort is the proximate cause of the injury. Such diseases, like all others, have their origin in a physical lesion, not a metaphysical state."[92]

Many subsequent cases also recognised this principle.[93]

However, American law did not stand still at this point. Round about 1930, United States courts began to grant recovery for the intentional causing of mental distress even though there was no consequent psychiatric illness and no likelihood of it.[94] No doubt the courts were beginning to

90. See Keeton, op cit, n 87 at 54-56; *Restatement of Torts Second*, §§46-48 and comments; Annotation, "Modern Status of Intentional Infliction of Mental Distress as Independent Tort: 'Outrage' " (1985) 38 ALR 4th 998. On the development of this tort see C Magruder, "Mental and Emotional Disturbance in the Law of Torts" (1936) 49 Harv L Rev 1033; F V Harper & M C McNeely, "A Re-examination of the Basis of Liability for Emotional Distress" [1938] Wis L Rev 426; W L Prosser, "Intentional Infliction of Mental Suffering—A New Tort" (1939) 37 Mich L Rev 874; Vold, op cit, n 35; W L Prosser, "Insult and Outrage" (1956) 44 Cal L Rev 40; P R Handford, "Intentional Infliction of Mental Suffering—Analysis of the Growth of a Tort" (1979) 8 Anglo-Am LR 1. For more recent discussion see W H Theis, "The Intentional Infliction of Emotional Distress: A Need for Limits on Liability" (1977) 27 De Paul L Rev 275; D Givelber, "The Right to Minimum Social Decency and the Limits of Evenhandedness: Intentional Infliction of Emotional Distress by Outrageous Conduct" (1982) 82 Col L Rev 42; W H Pedrick, "Intentional Infliction: Should Section 46 be Revised?" (1985) 13 Pepperdine L Rev 1.
91. (1901) 91 Mo App 4.
92. Ibid at 10.
93. See eg *Voss v Bolzenius* (1910) 128 SW 1 (Mo); *Kurpgeweit v Kirby* (1910) 129 NW 177 (Neb); *Goddard v Watters* (1914) 82 SE 304 (Ga); *Nickerson v Hodges* (1920) 84 So 37 (La); *Johnson v Sampson* (1926) 208 NW 814 (Minn); *Great Atlantic & Pacific Tea Co v Roch* (1930) 153 A 22 (Md).
94. The first such case is *Wilson v Wilkins* (1930) 25 SW 2d 428 (Ark), but note *Kurpgeweit v Kirby* (1910) 129 NW 177 (Neb) where recovery was allowed for mental distress without physical consequences, though in fact there was also a technical battery. See also *Barnett*

wonder why the physical harm requirement should be all important, since the defendant usually had no actual intention to cause it. In *Barnett v Collection Service Co*[95] for example, the court stated:

"The rule seems to be well-established where the act is wilful or malicious, as distinguished from being merely negligent, that recovery may be had for mental pain, though no physical injury results. . . . In this case the jury could well find that appellants exceeded their legal rights, and that they wilfully and intentionally sought to produce mental pain and anguish in the appellee, and that the natural result of said acts was to produce such mental pain and anguish."[96]

When the original *Restatement of Torts* appeared in 1936 it did not recognise this principle, confining liability to cases where a wilful act was intended or likely to produce bodily harm, and bodily harm resulted.[97] For some years cases in States which had not already recognised the wider principle tended not to go beyond the Restatement,[98] but before long it became clear that the Restatement was out of date, and in 1948 it was modified to recognise liability for purely mental distress caused intentionally.[99] The *Restatement of Torts Second* in 1965 indorsed the position adopted in 1948, holding that there is liability if a person, by extreme and outrageous conduct, intentionally or recklessly causes severe emotional distress to another.[100] There is now no need for consequent physical harm or the likelihood thereof. Practically all States have now accepted this proposition,[101] and the case law multiplies every year.[102] As

94. *Continued*
    v Collection Service Co (1932) 242 NW 25 (Ia); *La Salle Extension University v Fogarty* (1934) 253 NW 424 (Neb); *Erwin v Milligan* (1934) 67 SW 2d 592 (Ark); *Personal Finance Co v Loggins* (1935) 179 SE 162 (Ga); *Stephens v Waits* (1936) 184 SE 781 (Ga); *Spiegel v Evergreen Cemetery Co* (1936) 186 A 585 (NJ); *Interstate Life & Accident Co v Brewer* (1937) 193 SE 459 (Ga); *Aetna Life Insurance Co v Burton* (1938) 12 NE 2d 360 (Ind).
95. (1932) 242 NW 25 (Ia).
96. Ibid at 28.
97. *Restatement of Torts*, §§46 and 47A (1936).
98. See especially *Clark v Associated Retail Credit Men* (1939) 105 F 2d 62. Note also *Kirby v Jules Chain Stores Corporation* (1936) 188 SE 625 (NC); *People's Finance & Thrift Co v Harwell* (1938) 82 P 2d 494 (Okl); *Brown v Crawford* (1943) 177 SW 2d 1 (Ky); *Blakeley v Shortal's Estate* (1945) 20 NW 2d 28 (Ia); *Toler v Cassinelli* (1947) 41 SE 2d 672 (WVa); *Emden v Vitz* (1948) 198 P 2d 696 (Cal); *Digsby v Carroll Baking Co* (1948) 47 SE 2d 203 (Ga); *Richardson v Pridmore* (1950) 217 P 2d 113 (Cal); *Mahnke v Moore* (1951) 77 A 2d 923 (Md); *Fraser v Morrison* (1952) 39 Haw 370; *Urban v Hartford Gas Co* (1952) 93 A 2d 292 (Conn).
99. *Restatement of Torts, Supplement*, §46 (1948).
100. The first important case to adopt this principle was *State Rubbish Collectors Association v Siliznoff* (1952) 240 P 2d 282 (Cal). Other leading cases dealing in detail with the elements of the tort as outlined in §46 of the *Restatement of Torts Second* include *Halio v Lurie* (1961) 222 NYS 2d 759; *Alsteen v Gehl* (1963) 124 NW 2d 312 (Wis); *Fletcher v Western National Life Insurance Co* (1970) 89 Cal Rptr 78; *Harris v Jones* (1977) 380 A 2d 611 (Md); *MBM Co Inc v Counce* (1980) 596 SW 2d 681 (Ark); *American Road Service Co v Inmon* (1981) 344 So 2d 361 (Ala); *Yeager v Local Union 20, Teamsters, Chauffeurs, Warehousemen & Helpers of America* (1983) 453 NE 2d 666 (Ohio); *Watte v Edgar Maeyens Jr MD PC* (1992) 828 P 2d 479 (Or).
101. The only exceptions are Indiana and Rhode Island, where the action is not recognised, Florida, where there appears to be a conflict in the case law, and Texas, where the physical harm requirement is retained. There appear to be no cases on this issue in New Hampshire. See generally Annotation, op cit, n 90.
102. A Westlaw search of State and federal cases revealed that, in a ten-year period ending in 1989, there were 602 cases adopting the principle of §46 of the *Restatement of Torts*

is clear from the above formulation, recklessness as well as intentional conduct is sufficient: persons who perpetrate acts with reckless disregard of the high probability that emotional stress will occur do not escape liability.[103] The standard of "extreme and outrageous conduct" is the major control device limiting liability[104]—indeed the cause of action is now sometimes referred to as the tort of "outrage". Liability exists only where the conduct is so outrageous in character and so extreme in degree as to go beyond all possible bounds of decency and to be regarded as utterly intolerable in a civilised society.[105] The distress inflicted must be "so severe that no reasonable man could be expected to endure it".[106]

The tort covers a wide variety of situations.[107] The comments to the Restatement Second mention several broad categories which can be identified, including cases where the plaintiff, to the defendant's knowledge, is specially vulnerable,[108] as well as a more general group of

102. *Continued*
    Second: see X E Acosta, "The Tort of 'Outrageous Conduct' in New Mexico: Intentional Infliction of Emotional Harm without Physical Injury" (1989) 19 N Mex L Rev 425 at 434-435.
103. For the *Restatement* definitions of intention and recklessness see above, p 288. For examples of recklessness in this context see *Blakeley v Shortal's Estate* (1945) 20 NW 2d 28 (Ia) (defendant committed suicide in plaintiff's kitchen, knowing there was a high degree of probability she would find him); *Fletcher v Western National Life Insurance Co* (1970) 89 Cal Rptr 78; *Christensen v Superior Court* (1991) 820 P 2d 181; 2 Cal Rptr 2d 79. Contrast *Taylor v Vallelunga* (1959) 339 P 2d 910 (Cal) (attackers who beat a man while his daughter watched from hiding place were not liable to her because they did not know she was there, but had they known of her presence and her relationship to the man being beaten she would have succeeded). *Alsteen v. Gehl* (1963) 124 NW 2d 312 (Wis) would limit liability to intentional conduct, but it is out of line with the other authorities cited above on this point.
104. It is on this basis that the tort must be distinguished from liability for "insult" which was recognised as attaching to carriers, hotels, telegraph companies and certain other public utilities from the mid-19th century onwards: see Keeton, op cit, n 87 at 57-60; J W Wade, "Tort Liability for Abusive and Insulting Language" (1950) 4 Vand L Rev 63; P R Handford, "Tort Liability for Threatening and Insulting Words" (1976) 54 Can BR 563. For the distinction between insult and outrage see eg *Wallace v Shoreham Hotel Corporation* (1946) 49 A 2d 81 (DC); *Slocum v Food Fair Stores of Florida* (1958) 100 So 2d 396 (Fla); *Browning v Slenderella Systems of Seattle* (1959) 341 P 2d 859 (Wash); *Mitran v Williamson* (1960) 197 NYS 2d 689.
105. See *Restatement of Torts Second*, §46, comment (d); for general comment on this test see also *Rockhill v Pollard* (1971) 485 P 2d 28 (Or), suggesting that the standard should be worked out on a case-by-case basis. There is a plethora of authorities applying the standard to particular fact situations.
106. See *Restatement of Torts Second*, §46, comment (j). A North Carolina court has recently suggested that the element of severe mental distress means an emotional or mental disorder, or any other type of severe and disabling emotional or mental condition, which may be generally recognised and diagnosed by professionals trained to do so: see *Waddle v Sparks* (1992) 414 SE 2d 22 (NC).
107. See Keeton, op cit, n 87 at 54-56.
108. See eg *Nickerson v Hodges* (1920) 84 So 37 (La) (old lady obsessed with buried pot of gold; pot of stones planted, "found" and opened in public); *Great Atlantic & Pacific Tea Co v Roch* (1930) 153 A 2d 22 (Md) (defendant, knowing of the plaintiff's rat phobia, baked loaf of bread for him containing gory rat); *Delta Finance Co v Ganakas* (1956) 91 SE 2d 383 (Ga) (children); *Vargas v Ruggiero* (1961) 17 Cal Rptr 568 (pregnant woman); *Korbin v Berlin* (1965) 177 So 2d 551 (Fla) (children being vilified by mother); *Alcorn v Anbro Engineering Inc* (1970) 468 P 2d 216; 86 Cal Rptr 88 (negro called "goddam nigger" and dismissed by employer): *Wollersheim v Church of Scientology* (1989) 260 Cal Rptr 331 (church subjecting plaintiff to personal encounter discussions,

situations where the parties were previously strangers,[109] or where the case does not obviously fall into any other category.[110] A particularly important class of case is where the mental distress is caused by the abuse of a position or relationship. There are decisions in which the tort has been invoked against lawyers,[111] doctors and hospitals,[112] banks,[113] police,[114]

108. *Continued*
causing him to lose all contact with his family); *Williams v Voljavec* (1992) 415 SE 2d 31 (Ga) (doctor vented anger against patient when aware of her potentially fragile physical condition).

109. For example, threats: *Wilson v Wilkins* (1930) 25 SW 2d 428 (Ark); *Ruiz v Bertolotti* (1962) 236 NYS 2d 854; *Dickens v Puryear* (1981) 276 SE 2d 325 (NC); offensive acts or statements: *Halio v Lurie* (1961) 222 NYS 2d 759; *Young v Stensrude* (1984) 664 SW 2d 263 (Mo); *Ruple v Brooks* (1984) 352 NW 2d 652 (SD) (obscene telephone calls); *Wilson v Pearce* (1992) 412 SE 2d 148 (NC); isolated acts: *Golden v Dungan* (1971) 97 Cal Rptr 577 (writ served at midnight in loud and boisterous manner); *Womack v Eldridge* (1974) 210 SE 2d 145 (Va) (entering home and taking pictures for use in child molestation case); *Weisman v Weisman* (1985) 485 NYS 2d 568 (damaging windows of home leaving family without protection from severe cold); *Miller v National Broadcasting Co* (1986) 232 Cal Rptr 668 (filming dying man); course of conduct: *Guillory v Godfrey* (1955) 286 P 2d 474 (Cal) (preventing customers using restaurant which employed negro cook); *Tate v Canonica* (1960) 5 Cal Rptr 28 (repeated attempts to ruin business); *Mitran v Williamson* (1960) 197 NYS 2d 689 (soliciting sexual intercourse, sending obscene photographs); *Spackman v Good* (1966) 54 Cal Rptr 78 (defendant's permissive approach to sex lives of two children in his care alleged to have caused them to suffer "sex trauma"; on facts causation not proved); *Sheltra v Smith* (1978) 392 A 2d 431 (Vt) (preventing contact between plaintiff and daughter); *Kramer v Downey* (1989) 680 SW 2d 554 (Tex) (ex-lover of married man followed him around daily for several years).

110. See eg *Stump v Gates* (1991) 777 F Supp 808 (inadequate investigation by coroner, as a result of which he concluded that death was suicide and not murder); *Re Hanford Nuclear Reservation Litigation* (1991) 780 F Supp 1551 (property owners and residents of area surrounding nuclear reservation had claim in respect of present and threatened future injuries from storage and release of hazardous substances); *Rotondo v Reeves* (1992) 583 NYS 2d 739 (coroner mistakenly identified remains of pet rabbit as those of child); *Vance v Chandler* (1992) 597 NE 2d 233 (Ill) (plaintiff's daughter and former husband participated in conspiracy to have her murdered).

111. See eg *McDaniel v Gile* (1991) 281 Cal Rptr 242 (attorney withholding legal services when sexual favours not granted by client); *Perez v Kirk & Carrigan* (1991) 822 SW 2d 261 (Tex) (truck driver involved in fatal school bus accident claimed against attorney who disclosed prejudicial statement made in confidence which led to criminal proceedings being taken against driver).

112. See eg *Rockhill v Pollard* (1971) 485 P 2d 28 (Or); *De Cicco v Trinidad Area Health Association* (1977) 573 P 2d 559 (Col); *Chuy v Philadelphia Eagles Football Club* (1979) 595 F 2d 1265 (football club's doctor); *Roberts v Saylor* (1981) 637 P 2d 1175 (Kan); *Lucchesi v Frederic N Stimmell MD Ltd* (1986) 716 P 2d 1013 (Ariz) (concealing details surrounding breech birth and simultaneous decapitation of baby due to tugging on child's hip area after mother's cervix had contracted); *Kirker v Orange County* (1988) 519 So 2d 682 (Fla) (doctor removed eyes of drowned three-year-old child, after mother had expressly refused permission to do so); *Sanchez v Orozco* (1991) 578 NYS 2d 145 (psychiatrist persuaded patient to have sexual relations with him, made numerous harrassing telephone calls when patient terminated relationship); *Highfill v Baptist Hospital Inc* (1991) 819 SW 2d 436 (Tenn) (nurse hugged husband of woman who had just had a hysterectomy, sexually battering him, and taunted the patient that she could take her husband away from her; no liability on facts).

113. See eg *Ledbetter v Brown City Savings Bank* (1985) 368 NW 2d 257 (Mich); *Etchart v Bank One, Columbus NA* (1991) 773 F Supp 239 (credit card issuer).

114. See eg *Savage v Boies* (1954) 272 P 2d 249 (Ariz) (policeman told plaintiff that husband had been involved in accident to get her to hospital to be certified as insane); *Craft v Rice* (1984) 671 SW 2d 247 (Ky) (harassment by sheriff); *McCray v Holt* (1991) 777

school and university authorities[115] and trade unions,[116] but the most significant cases are those in which employers have been held liable for extreme attempts to cause employees to leave their jobs,[117] landlords held liable for harassing their tenants[118] in an attempt to evict them and insurance adjusters[119] and debt collectors[120] held liable for hounding

114. *Continued*
F Supp 945 (police abused deaf passenger in car physically and sexually, threw her property around, and kept other occupants in police car with heater turned on during afternoon of extremely hot day).

115. See eg *Johnson v Sampson* (1926) 208 NW 814 (Minn) (schoolgirl accused of immorality, forced to make false confession); *Blair v Union Free School District* (1971) 324 NYS 2d 222 (school divulged information given in confidence by student); *Goldfarb v Baker* (1977) 547 SW 2d 567 (Tenn); *Waldon v Covington* (1980) 415 A 2d 1070 (DC) (no liability on facts); *Russell v Salve Regina College* (1986) 649 F Supp 341 (nursing student persistently accused of being overweight).

116. See eg *State Rubbish Collectors Association v Siliznoff* (1952) 240 P 2d 282 (Cal) (union forced plaintiff to become member by threatening to beat him up, destroy his truck and put him out of business); *Yeager v Local Union 20, Teamsters, Chauffeurs, Warehousemen & Helpers of America* (1983) 453 NE 2d 666 (Ohio).

117. See eg *Alcorn v Anbro Engineering Inc* (1970) 468 P 2d 216; 86 Cal Rptr 88 (see above, p 299, n 108); *Agis v Howard Johnson Co* (1976) 355 NE 2d 315 (Mass); *Harris v Jones* (1977) 380 A 2d 611 (Md); *Contreras v Crown Zellerbach Corporation* (1977) 565 P 2d 1173 (Wash); *Harless v First National Bank in Fairmont* (1978) 246 SE 2d 270 (WVa); *MBM Co Inc v Counce* (1980) 596 SW 2d 681 (Ark); *Hall v May Department Stores Co* (1981) 637 P 2d 126 (Or); *Hubbard v United Press International Inc* (1983) 330 NW 2d 428 (Minn); *Howard University v Best* (1984) 484 A 2d 958 (DC); *Tandy Corporation v Bone* (1984) 678 SW 2d 312 (Kan); *Ford v Revlon Inc* (1987) 734 P 2d 580 (Ariz); *Anderson v Chatham* (1989) 379 SE 2d 793 (Ga); *Crump v P & C Food Markets Inc* (1990) 576 A 2d 441 (Vt). Note also *Loe v Town of Thomaston* (1991) 600 A 2d 1090 (Me). See R Austin, "Employer Abuse, Worker Resistance and the Tort of Intentional Infliction of Emotional Distress" (1988) 41 Stan L Rev 1.

118. See eg *Hickey v Welch* (1901) 91 Mo App 4; *Emden v Vitz* (1948) 198 P 2d 696 (Cal); *Ivey v Davis* (1950) 59 SE 2d 256 (Ga); *Scheman v Schlein* (1962) 231 NYS 2d 548; *Kaufman v Abramson* (1966) 363 F 2d 865; *Newby v Alto Riviera Apartments* (1976) 131 Cal Rptr 547; *Warren v June's Mobile Home Village & Sales Inc* (1976) 239 NW 2d 380 (Mich); *Brewer v Ervin* (1979) 660 P 2d 398 (Or); *James v Saltsman* (1984) 472 NYS 2d 129; *Latremore v Latremore* (1990) 54 A 2d 626 (Me) (liability of son who was parents' landlord); *LaCoure v LaCoure* (1991) 820 SW 2d 228 (Tex); *Brown v Hamilton* (1992) 601 A 2d 1074 (DC). See S E Keller, "Does the Roof Have to Cave In?: The Landlord-Tenant Power Relationship and the Intentional Infliction of Emotional Distress" (1988) 9 Cardozo L Rev 1663.

119. See eg *Fletcher v Western National Life Insurance Co* (1970) 89 Cal Rptr 78; *Eckenrode v Life of America Insurance Co* (1972) 470 F 2d 1; *Amsden v Grimmell Mutual Reinsurance Co* (1972) 203 NW 2d 252 (Ia); *Gruenberg v Aetna Insurance Co* (1973) 510 P 2d 1032; 108 Cal Rptr 480; *Agarwal v Johnson* (1979) 603 P 2d 58; 160 Cal Rptr 141; *Boyle v Wenk* (1979) 392 NE 2d 1053 (Mass); *Young v Hartford Accident & Indemnity Co* (1985) 492 A 2d 1270 (Md); *Tidelands Auto Club v Walters* (1985) 699 SW 2d 939 (Tex); *Atkinson v Farley* (1988) 431 NW 2d 95 (Mich).

120. See eg *Barnett v Collection Service Co* (1932) 242 NW 25 (Ia); *La Salle Extension University v Fogarty* (1934) 253 NW 424 (Neb); *Duty v General Finance Co* (1954) 273 SW 2d 64 (Tex); *Warrem v Parrish* (1969) 436 SW 2d 670 (Mo) (garage proprietor refused to lower car from lift until plaintiff paid); *George v Jordan Marsh Co* (1971) 268 NW 2d 915 (Mass); *Bennett v City National Bank & Trust Co* (1976) 549 P 2d 393 (Okl); *Moorehead v J C Penney Co* (1977) 555 SW 2d 713 (Tenn) (harassment by computer which continued to send out notices even though store admitted mistake); *Ford Motor Co v Sheehan* (1979) 373 So 2d 956 (Fla); *Ailetcher v Beneficial Finance* (1981) 632 P 2d 1071 (Haw); *Chedester v Stecker* (1982) 643 P 2d 532 (Haw); *Lawrence v Starford* (1983) 655 SW 2d 927 (Tenn) (threat by veterinarian to kill dog unless bill paid); *Bundran v Superior Court of City of Ventura* (1983) 193 Cal Rptr 671; *Venes v Professional Service*

creditors, or persons whom they believe to be creditors, in an attempt to collect debts. The latter instance is now regarded in a few States as a separate tort in itself.[121] The cases on mishandling of dead bodies, originally an independent development,[122] are now recognised as another variety of outrageous conduct,[123] and the tort has also been used in cases involving racial[124] and sexual[125] discrimination. The Restatement Second specifically mentions cases where secondary parties are affected by acts principally directed against others, as for example in a case[126] where an intoxicated defendant in the plaintiff's presence threatened to murder the plaintiff's husband and then carried out his threat. The plaintiff recovered for intentional infliction of emotional distress, the court holding that the defendant's conduct was intentional with regard to her.[127] All the common situations in negligence cases involving secondary parties have their equivalents in "outrage" cases, and here the limitations which United States courts have placed on liability for negligence have sometimes been

120. *Continued*
  Bureau Inc (1984) 353 NW 2d 671 (Minn); *Bell v Dixie Furniture Co* (1985) 329 SE 2d 431 (SC). See R M Berger, "The Bill Collector and the Law" (1968) 17 De Paul L Rev 327; P H Hubbard, "Recovery for Creditor Harassment" (1968) 46 Tex L Rev 950; M M Greenfield, "Coercive Collection Tactics—An Analysis of the Interests and the Remedies" [1972] Wash ULQ 1.
121. See eg *Moore v Savage* (1962) 359 SW 2d 95 (Tex); *Boudreaux v Allstate Finance Corporation* (1968) 217 So 2d 439 (La); *Southwestern Bell Telephone Co v Wilson* (1988) 768 SW 2d 755 (Tex) ($1,500,000 damages). On legislative remedies for unreasonable collection efforts see Givelber, op cit, n 90 at 65, n 114.
122. See *Larson v Chase* (1891) 50 NW 238 (Minn); *Gadbury v Bleitz* (1925) 233 P 2d 299 (Wash); *Boyle v Chandler* (1927) 138 A 273 (Del).
123. See eg *Spiegel v Evergreen Cemetery Co* (1936) 186 A 585 (NJ); *Stephens v Waits* (1936) 184 SE 781 (Ga); *Papieves v Lawrence* (1970) 203 A 2d 118 (Pa); *Swanson v Swanson* (1970) 257 NE 2d 194 (Ill); *Meyer v Noffger* (1976) 241 NW 2d 911 (Ia); *Golston v Lincoln Cemetery* (1978) 573 SW 2d 700 (Mo); *Whitehair v Highland Memory Gardens Inc* (1985) 327 SE 2d 438 (WVa); *Rubin v Matthews International Corporation* (1986) 503 A 2d 694 (Me); *Kirker v Orange County* (1988) 519 So 2d 682 (Fla); *Christensen v Superior Court* (1991) 820 P 2d 181; 2 Cal Rptr 2d 79 (no liability on facts).
124. See eg *Ruiz v Bertolotti* (1962) 236 NYS 2d 854; *Flamm v Van Nierop* (1968) 291 NYS 2d 189; *Alcorn v Anbro Engineering* (1970) 468 P 2d 216 (Cal); *Contreras v Crown Zellerbach Corporation* (1977) 565 P 2d 1173 (Wash); *Ledsinger v Burmeister* (1982) 318 NW 2d 558 (Mich); *Patterson v McLean Credit Union* (1986) 805 F 2d 1143; *Mumphrey v James River Co Inc* (1991) 777 F Supp 1458; *Littlefield v McGuffey* (1992) 954 F 2d 1337. However, mere discrimination without aggravating circumstances will not amount to outrageous conduct: *Browning v Slenderella Systems of Seattle* (1959) 341 P 2d 859 (Wash). See J E Duda, "Damages for Mental Suffering in Discrimination Cases" (1966) 15 Clev Mar L Rev 1.
125. See eg *Stewart v Thomas* (1982) 538 F Supp 891; *Hogan v Forsyth Country Club* (1986) 340 SE 2d 116 (NC).
126. *Knierim v Izzo* (1961) 174 NE 2d 157 (Ill). For other examples see *Grimsby v Samson* (1975) 530 P 2d 291 (Wash); *Bowman v Sears Roebuck & Co* (1976) 369 A 2d 754 (Pa); *Courtney v Courtney* (1991) 413 SE 2d 418 (WVa) (husband intentionally inflicted emotional distress on son when assaulted wife in son's presence). Note also *Strickland v Deaconess Hospital* (1987) 735 P 2d 74 (Wash) (holding that the class of family members entitled to sue consists of those entitled to bring wrongful death actions).
127. Here liability based on intention under §46 of the *Restatement of Torts Second* operates as an alternative to liability based on negligence under §312: see above, p 296, n 87. A third theory espouses the criminal law doctrine of transferred intent: see *Lambert v Brewster* (1924) 125 SE 244 (WVa); Comment, "Application of Transferred Intent to Cases of Intentional Infliction of Emotional Distress" (1983) 15 Pac LJ 147.

carried over into the area of intentional mental harm. Examples include cases where recovery was denied because the plaintiff was present only at the aftermath of the occurrence of the tort,[128] or was only told of what happened.[129] The volatility of this tort is shown by recent suggestions that it might apply in a host of diverse situations, including kidnapping of children by non-custodial parents and other family disputes,[130] divorce proceedings,[131] discriminatory speech,[132] combating the mass media[133]

128. See eg *Exxon Corporation v Tidwell* (1991) 816 SW 2d 455 (Tex) (service station cashier shot during armed robbery, mother unable to recover because arrived minutes after shooting).
129. See eg *Benavides v County of Wilson* (1992) 955 F 2d 968 (wife of prisoner paralysed as result of fall in cell, and left for 18 hours before medical care provided, had no claim because told by authorities what had happened before she saw her husband).
130. See eg *Smith v Smith* (1982) 640 SW 2d 490 (Mo); *Goode v Goode* (1982) 415 So 2d 321 (La); *Bhama v Bhama* (1988) 425 NW 2d 733 (Mich). See C W Cole, "Intentional Infliction of Emotional Distress among Family Members" (1984) 61 Denver LJ 553; Comment, "Intentional Infliction of Emotional Distress: Recovery of Damages for Victims of Parental Kidnapping" [1984] S Ill ULJ 145; C D Bargamian, "Intentional Infliction of Emotional Distress in the Child Custody Context: Proposed Guidelines" (1989) 36 Wayne L Rev 125. Note also the unsuccessful allegations of intentional infliction of emotional distress in the form of "AIDS-phobia" in *Doe v Doe* (1987) 519 NYS 2d 595, in an attempt to reintroduce issues of fault into the question of property distribution on divorce.
131. A Texas court refused to recognise intentional infliction of emotional distress as a cause of action in a divorce suit in *Chiles v Chiles* (1989) 779 SW 2d 127 (Tex) (wife after suffering husband's drinking and physical and verbal abuse, had nervous breakdown when she found him naked on floor of his office with secretary). For criticism of the decision see D Pfeuffer, "Chiles v Chiles: Divorce, Torts and Scandal—Texas Style" (1990) 42 Baylor L Rev 309, arguing that actions for this tort separate from divorce proceedings should be allowable. In *Ruprecht v Ruprecht* (1991) 599 A 2d 604 (NJ) a New Jersey court held that one spouse could sue another for intentional infliction of mental distress, but on the facts an 11-year adulterous affair did not constitute outrageous conduct.
132. See eg *Wiggs v Courshon* (1973) 355 F Supp 206; *Bailey v Binyon* (1984) 583 F Supp 923 (racist harassment); *Dominguez v Stone* (1981) 638 P 2d 423 (NM); *Gomez v Hug* (1982) 645 P 2d 916 (Kan) (ethnic harassment); *Samms v Eccles* (1961) 358 P 2d 344 (Utah); *Monge v Superior Court* (1986) 222 Cal Rptr 64 (sexual harassment by computer messages); *Swentek v USAIR Inc* (1987) 830 F 2d 552 (air hostess told: "I wish I were a coat so that I could wrap myself around your big tits"); *Hall v Gus Construction Co* (1988) 842 F 2d 1010; *Pavilon v Kaferly* (1990) 561 NE 2d 1245 (Ill) (requests for dates, sex, threats of rape and of telling parents). See B A Wolman, "Verbal Sexual Harassment on the Job as Intentional Infliction of Emotional Distress" (1988) 17 Cap U L Rev 245; Comment, "Relief for Health-Related Injury in Sexual Harassment Cases" (1990) 6 J Contemp Health L & Policy 171; J C Love, "Discriminatory Speech and the Tort of Intentional Infliction of Emotional Distress" (1990) 47 Wash & Lee L Rev 123; O C Dark, "Racial Insults: Keep Thy Tongue from Evil" (1990) 24 Suffolk U L Rev 559; D Goldberger, "Sources of Judicial Reluctance to Use Psychic Harm as a Basis for Suppressing Racist, Sexist and Ethnically Offensive Speech" (1991) 56 Brooklyn L Rev 1165.
133. See eg *Galella v Onassis* (1973) 487 F 2d 986 (press hounding of Jacqueline Onassis); *Vescovo v New Way Enterprises* (1976) 130 Cal Rptr 86; *Morgan By and Through Morgan v Celender* (1992) 780 F Supp 307 (article giving unauthorised details and picture of victim of sexual abuse; no liability on facts). See T C Mead, "Suing Media for Emotional Distress: A Multi-Method Analysis of Tort Law Evolution" (1983) 23 Washburn LJ 24; R E Drechsel, "Intentional Infliction of Emotional Distress: New Tort Liability for Mass Media" (1984-1985) 89 Dick L Rev 339; M D Sherer, "Photojournalism and the Infliction of Emotional Distress" (1986) 8 Com & L 27. Note also R E Drechsel, "Negligent Infliction of Emotional Distress: New Tort Problem for the Mass Media" (1985) 12 Pepperdine L Rev 889.

including the use of parody advertising,[134] and the activities of spiritual counsellors.[135] There seems no reason why children who have been physically or sexually abused would not also be able to sue for the tort of intentional infliction of emotional distress in addition to traditional torts. The extension of this cause of action to pure mental distress is paralleled in a number of United States jurisdictions by a similar extension of negligence liability.[136]

Is a similar extension in Commonwealth jurisdictions possible? The case for such an extension has been argued in the periodical literature.[137] It has been suggested that, in substance, the courts already recognise a cause of action for the intentional infliction of mental distress, and that in requiring physical harm they are resorting to the fiction of imputing an intention to cause physical injury or psychiatric damage in order to allow the defendant to recover damages, though in fact the only intention was to cause mental or emotional distress.[138] Though there is no decision ruling out such an extension, and though the kinds of situations dealt with by the United States case law also occur elsewhere, the development of liability for purely mental distress caused intentionally seems on balance unlikely. The situations dealt with by the American cases are generally resolved in some other way. Some, such as harassment by landlords[139] or debt collectors,[140] are covered by criminal penalties, and it is noteworthy that some of these statutes use a

134. See *Falwell v Flynt* (1986) 797 F 2d 1270 where Hustler Magazine was held liable for a parody advertisement in which television evangelist Jerry Falwell was depicted describing his "first time" (with Campari, a well-known alcoholic drink) in a back garden shed with his mother. For comment see eg M Maney, "Falwell v Flynt: First Amendment Protection of Satirical Speech" (1987) 39 Baylor L Rev 313; S Kirkpatrick, "Falwell v Flynt: Intentional Infliction of Emotional Distress as a Threat to Free Speech" (1987) 81 Nw U L Rev 993; H D Lester, "Did Falwell Hustle Hustler? Allowing Public Figures to Recover Emotional Distress Damages for Non-libelous Satire" (1987) 44 Wash & Lee L Rev 1381. On appeal sub nom *Hustler Magazines Inc v Falwell* (1987) 108 S Ct 876 the United States Supreme Court reversed the decision on First Amendment grounds: see eg B C Farnam, "Free Speech and Freedom from Speech: Hustler Magazine v Falwell, the New York Times Actual Malice Standard and Intentional Infliction of Emotional Distress" (1988) 63 Ind LJ 877; R A Smolla, "Emotional Distress and the First Amendment: An Analysis of Hustler v Falwell" (1988) 20 Ariz St LJ 423; P A Le Bel, "Emotional Distress, the First Amendment, and 'This Kind of Speech': A Heretical Perspective on Hustler Magazine v Falwell" (1989) 60 U Col L Rev 315.
135. See eg *Lewis v Holy Spirit Association for the Unification of World Christianity* (1983) 589 F Supp 10 (action by former member of church of Rev Sun Myung Moon alleging indoctrination and brainwashing); *Nally v Grace Community Church* (1985) 204 Cal Rptr 303 (parents allowed to pursue suit against church and clergy for son's suicide); *Murphy v I S K Congregation of New England Inc* (1991) 571 NE 2d 340 (Mass) (Hare Krishna liable for intentional infliction of emotional distress through influence on minor and effect of this on mother); *George v International Society for Krishna Consciousness of California* (1992) 4 Cal Rptr 2d 473 (religious group enticed teenager to leave parents' custody and concealed his whereabouts); L W Brooks, "Intentional Infliction of Emotional Distress by Spiritual Counsellors: Can Outrageous Conduct be 'Free Exercise'?" (1986) 84 Mich L Rev 1296.
136. See above, pp 48-49.
137. Handford, op cit, n 1 at 56-63; Trindade, op cit, n 1. Note also H J Glasbeek, "Outraged Dignity—Do We Need a New Tort?" (1968) 6 Alta LR 77.
138. Trindade, op cit, n 1 at 221-222.
139. See eg *Residential Tenancies Act* 1978 (SA), s 47; *Rent Act* 1965 (UK), s 30, now replaced by *Protection from Eviction Act* 1977 (UK), s 1.
140. *Trade Practices Act* 1974 (Cth), s 60; *Administration of Justice Act* 1970 (UK), s 40(1).

formula reminiscent of *Wilkinson v Downton* by referring to conduct calculated to subject people to alarm, distress or humiliation. If some recognised tort is committed, or (as regards harassment by landlords) if there is a breach of the covenant of quiet enjoyment, damages or an injunction may be obtained, but otherwise there are no civil remedies available in such situations. [141] In *Perera v Vandiyar* [142] the landlord cut off his tenant's gas and electricity, forcing the tenant to leave. The county court judge suggested that there should be a tort of "eviction" but the English Court of Appeal refused to indorse this view. More recently, in *McCall v Abelesz* [143] the English Court of Appeal again refused to recognise a tort remedy for harassment of tenants. There was no argument in these cases for an extension of the *Wilkinson v Downton* principle along United States lines. [144] There are Scottish and Canadian authorities which give some recognition to a liability for intentional interference with dead bodies, [145] but none elsewhere. Relief for the distress caused by intentional wrongdoing may also be indirectly provided by an award of exemplary damages, although the professed purpose of such an award is to punish the defendant for wrongdoing which can be described as wanton or outrageous—a "contumelious disregard of the plaintiff's rights". [146] In England, such damages are now much restricted in scope, applying only in particular cases identified by the House of Lords, [147] but these restrictions have not been adopted in Australia, [148] where exemplary damages continue to be available over a wide spectrum of torts involving intentional acts or omissions, [149] or

141. On harassment of debtors see B Kercher, "Debt Collection Harassment in Australia" (1979) 5 Mon ULR 87, 204; Report of the (UK) Committee on the Enforcement of Judgment Debts (Cmnd 3909, 1969) paras 1232-4. N Fricker, "Harassment as a Tort" (1992) 142 NLJ 247 makes a more general suggestion for the recognition of a tort remedy for harassment.

142. [1953] 1 WLR 672.

143. [1976] QB 585.

144. Note that in *Jennison v Baker* [1972] 2 QB 52 (action for injunction against landlord) Salmon LJ described the defendant's conduct as "outrageous", unconsciously echoing the United States test of liability.

145. See eg *Pollok v Workman* (1900) 2 F 354; *Conway v Dalziel* (1901) 3 F 918; *Hughes v Robertson*, 1913 SC 394; *Philipps v Montreal General Hospital* (1908) 33 Que SC 483; *Edmonds v Armstrong Funeral Home* [1931] 1 DLR 676.

146. *Uren v John Fairfax & Sons Pty Ltd* (1966) 117 CLR 118 per McTiernan J at 122, per Taylor J at 129, per Windeyer J at 153-154. According to Windeyer J, the phrase goes back at least to the first edition of *Salmond on Torts* in 1907.

147. See *Rookes v Barnard* [1964] AC 1129 per Lord Devlin at 1226; *Cassell & Co Ltd v Broome* [1972] AC 1027. Note also *Bradford City Metropolitan Council v Arora* [1991] 2 QB 507; *A B v South West Water Services Ltd, The Independent*, 15 May 1992. See generally G H L Fridman, "Punitive Damages in Tort" (1970) 48 Can BR 371; H McGregor, "In Defence of Lord Devlin" (1971) 34 MLR 520; J Stone, "Double Count and Double Talk: The End of Exemplary Damages?" (1972) 46 ALJ 311; R W Hodgin & E Veitch, "Punitive Damages—Reassessed" (1972) 21 ICLQ 119; J McMahon, "Exemplary Damages: A Useful Weapon in the Legal Armoury" (1988) 18 Vic U Wellington LR 35; P R Ghandhi, "Exemplary Damages in the English Law of Tort" (1990) 10 Leg Stud 182.

148. See *Uren v John Fairfax & Sons Pty Ltd* (1966) 117 CLR 118; *Australian Consolidated Press Ltd v Uren* [1969] 1 AC 590; *Lamb v Cotogno* (1987) 164 CLR 1 at 7-8; *Coloca v BP Australia Ltd* [1992] 2 VR 441.

149. For example, battery: see *Fontin v Katapodis* (1962) 108 CLR 177; *Johnstone v Stewart* [1968] SASR 142; *Pearce v Hallett* [1969] SASR 423; *Watts v Leitch* [1973] Tas SR 16; *Costi v Minister of Education* (1973) 5 SASR 328; *McIntosh v Webster* (1980) 30 ACTR

elsewhere.[150] In Australia, in fact, the courts have recently exhibited a preparedness to extend such damages outside the area of intentional wrongs and into cases involving road and work accidents.[151] Conceptually, exemplary damages, which are punitive, must be distinguished from damages which are sometimes referred to as "aggravated"—damages given for hurt feelings as part of the compensatory award.[152] Such damages, as already described,[153] are awarded mainly, though not only, in intentional torts.

What is the reason for the failure of common law systems outside the United States to develop this kind of liability?[154] One reason, perhaps, is reluctance to give direct protection to personality interests—a reluctance also exemplified by the failure to develop a cause of action for invasion of privacy[155] and the abolition of torts involving interference with family

149. *Continued*
　　19; *Downham v Bellette* (1986) Aust Torts Rep 80-038; *Henry v Thompson* [1989] 2 Qd R 412; trespass to chattels: see *Dymocks Book Arcade Ltd v McCarthy* [1966] 2 NSWR 411; *Healing Sales Pty Ltd v Inglis Electrix Pty Ltd* (1968) 121 CLR 584; trespass to land: see *Pollock v Volpato* [1973] 1 NSWLR 653; *XL Petroleum (NSW) Pty Ltd v Caltex Oil (Australia) Pty Ltd* (1985) 155 CLR 448; *Lincoln Hunt Australia Pty Ltd v Willesee* (1986) 4 NSWLR 457; nuisance: see *Willoughby Municipal Council v Halstead* (1916) 22 CLR 352; *Commonwealth v Murray* (1988) Aust Torts Rep 80-207; libel: see *Uren v John Fairfax & Sons Pty Ltd* (1966) 117 CLR 118; malicious prosecution: see *Brooke v Grimpel* (1987) Aust Torts Rep 80-108; deceit: see *Broken Hill Pty Co Ltd v Fisher* (1984) 38 SASR 50; *Musca v Astle Corporation Pty Ltd* (1988) 80 ALR 251; unlawful interference with trade or business: see *Ansett Transport Industries (Operations) Pty Ltd v Australian Federation of Air Pilots* [1991] 2 VR 636; conspiracy: see *Williams v Hursey* (1959) 103 CLR 30; *S S C & B Lintas New Zealand Ltd v Murphy* (1986) Aust Torts Rep 80-008; inducing breach of contract: see *Whitfeld v De Lauret & Co Ltd* (1920) 29 CLR 71.
150. For example, New Zealand: see *Fogg v McKnight* [1968] NZLR 330; *Taylor v Beere* [1982] 1 NZLR 81; *Donselaar v Donselaar* [1982] 1 NZLR 97; *Auckland City Council v Blundell* [1986] 1 NZLR 732; *Shattock v Devlin* [1990] 2 NZLR 88; McMahon, op cit, n 147. Whether Canadian courts will follow *Rookes v Barnard* [1964] AC 1129 is still a matter of dispute: see G H L Fridman, *The Law of Torts in Canada* (1989), Vol 1, 80; *Vorvis v Insurance Corporation of British Columbia* (1989) 58 DLR (4th) 193; note also Fridman, op cit, n 147; D L Hawley, "Punitive and Aggravated Damages in Canada" (1980) 18 Alta LR 485.
151. See *Lamb v Cotogno* (1987) 164 CLR 1 (action for unintentional trespass); *Midalco Pty Ltd v Rabenalt* [1989] VR 461; *Coloca v BP Australia Ltd* [1992] 2 VR 441 (action in negligence).
152. Though prior to *Rookes v Barnard* [1964] AC 1129 there was a degree of confusion between them: see *Uren v John Fairfax & Sons Pty Ltd* (1966) 117 CLR 118 per Windeyer J at 149 and *Cassell & Co Ltd v Broome* [1972] AC 1027 per Lord Hailsham LC at 1069-74 discussing the confusion surrounding the use of the terms "punitive", "aggravated", "retributory", "vindictive" and "exemplary". As a practical matter it may be important to keep the two awards separate, even in Australia where exemplary damages have not been restricted in scope: see *XL Petroleum (NSW) Pty Ltd v Caltex Oil (Australia) Pty Ltd* (1985) 155 CLR 448; *Lamb v Cotogno* (1987) 164 CLR 1; *Henry v Thompson* [1989] 2 Qd R 412; but note *Johnstone v Stewart* [1968] SASR 142 where Bray CJ considered it inappropriate to make separate awards and fixed a single lump sum having taken both elements into account; *Cassell & Co Ltd v Broome* per Lord Hailsham LC at 1074; *Attorney-General of St Christopher, Nevis and Anguilla v Reynolds* [1980] AC 637.
153. See above, pp 45-47.
154. In many civil law jurisdictions compensation for intentionally caused mental distress, and indeed also for such injury caused negligently, is an established category of relief: see above, pp 57-58.
155. See eg *Victoria Park Racing & Recreation Grounds Co v Taylor* (1937) 58 CLR 479; *Tolley v J S Fry & Sons* [1931] AC 333.

relationships, such as seduction, enticement and harbouring.[156] Another reason is the effect of the number of cases coming before the United States courts. As the preceding discussion demonstrates, in Commonwealth countries there have been only a few *Wilkinson v Downton* cases whereas in the United States there have been a vast number, especially over the last decade. Once the courts accepted this liability as an established fact, there was considerable pressure to extend it. A contributory factor is the existence of the *Restatement of Torts Second*, drafted mainly by academic lawyers, which has had a great influence on the courts. There is no real equivalent elsewhere. A further, more pragmatic, reason is that Commonwealth judges tend to be more conservative and ruled by precedent than their American brothers,[157] though one cannot ignore major doctrinal developments of recent years, particularly in the High Court of Australia[158] and the House of Lords.[159] The large number of American jurisdictions helps here, since precedents in other States can always be found by judges who wish to depart from the restriction of their own case law. An allied reason may be an unwillingness on the part of legal advisers to advise their clients to base their claims on such a cause of action.[160] Thus, though the United States developments are without doubt closely related to *Wilkinson v Downton* liability,[161] and cases invoking this principle address some of the fact situations covered by the American tort,[162] the likelihood of extension to cases where there is no resultant psychiatric illness appears remote.

---

156. *Family Law Act* 1975 (Cth), s 120; *Wrongs Act* 1936 (SA), ss 35-36; *Law Reform (Miscellaneous Provisions) Act* 1970 (UK), s 5; *Domestic Actions Act* 1975 (NZ), s 4(1); Family Proceedings Act 1980 (NZ), s 190. On the position in Canada see C Davies, *Family Law in Canada* (1984), 88-89.

157. See L Brittan, "The Right of Privacy in England and the United States" (1963) 37 Tul L Rev 235, reaching a similar conclusion on the right to privacy.

158. See eg *Zecevic v Director of Public Prosecutions for Victoria* (1987) 162 CLR 645; *Oceanic Sun Line Special Shipping Co Inc v Fay* (1988) 165 CLR 197; *Trident General Insurance Co Ltd v McNiece Bros Pty Ltd* (1988) 165 CLR 107. Note B Horrigan, "Towards a Jurisprudence of High Court Overruling" (1992) 66 ALJ 199.

159. See eg *R v Shivpuri* [1987] AC 1; *R v Howe* [1987] AC 417; *Murphy v Brentwood District Council* [1991] AC 398. Note J W Harris, "Murphy Makes It Eight—Overruling Comes to Negligence" (1991) 11 OJLS 416.

160. See Trindade, op cit, n 1 at 223.

161. See the references to United States case law in *Rahemtulla v Vanfed Credit Union* (1984) 29 CCLT 78 per McLachin J at 94-95.

162. For example, landlords: *Stevenson v Basham* [1922] NZLR 225; *Timmermans v Buelow* (1984) 38 CCLT 136; employers: *Rahemtulla v Vanfed Credit Union* (1984) 29 CCLT 78.

15

CONCLUSION

The analysis in this work has served to illustrate the reluctance with which the courts have recognised the individual's interest in mental tranquillity and the influence of underlying concerns that continue to cultivate undue judicial caution and foster the imposition of inappropriate doctrinal restrictions on recovery. Considerable (but highly selective) advancements have been made in psychiatric damage law since claims of that nature first emerged and were unceremoniously dismissed, but they have been piecemeal and slow in coming. Despite its history and movements forward, this area of the common law remains very far from the position it ought to be in. Indeed, in terms of doctrinal maturation, psychiatric damage law is still, after over a century, to some degree in its embryonic stages. The relatively recent sophistication of this branch of medical science provides part of the explanation for the immaturity of the law, but the more telling reason is society's failure to appreciate, or refusal to admit, that serious disruption to peace of mind is no less worthy of community and legal support than physical injury to the body, even given that priorities in accident compensation require careful thought in the face of limited resources. As Lord Oliver said in *Alcock v Chief Constable of South Yorkshire Police*:

"There is . . . nothing unusual or peculiar in the recognition by the law that compensatable injury may be caused just as much by a direct assault upon the mind or the nervous system as by direct physical contact with the body. This is no more than the natural and inevitable result of the growing appreciation by modern medical science of recognisable causal connections between shock to the nervous system and physical or psychiatric illness. Cases in which damages are claimed for directly inflicted injuries of this nature may present greater difficulties of proof but they are not, in their essential elements, any different from cases where the damages claimed arise from direct physical injury and they present no very difficult problems of analysis where the plaintiff has himself been directly involved in the accident from which the injury is said to arise. In such a case he can be properly said to be the primary victim of the defendant's negligence and the fact that the injury which he sustains is inflicted through the medium of an assault on the nerves or senses does not serve to differentiate the case, except possibly in the degree of evidentiary difficulty, from a case of direct physical injury."[1]

Damage to the psyche has throughout history provoked apprehension, induced a sense of uncertainty and been shrouded in ignorance. People have

1. [1992] 1 AC 310 at 406-407.

always feared what they do not understand and been sceptical of that which they cannot "verify" by sight. As Birkett J observed:

> "I quite recognise that when we are in this field, it is a very difficult one for laymen to understand. When witnesses speak about a man suffering from an anxiety neurosis—and I suppose that none of us is quite immune from anxiety in these days—but when people speak of anxiety neurosis when a man is not suffering organically but has hysteria, the ordinary, sound, healthy man is apt to look upon that with a little disdain or a little suspicion and to treat it sometimes rather lightly and to say: 'Well, if you have a little courage or determination you can overcome it. If you have a little will-power to go back to work and confront the difficulty, that would overcome it.' I say it is comparatively easy for healthy people to think and speak like that, but nobody who has undergone a very severe illness or, indeed, a slight illness can forget that people who are not in that happy state frequently look upon small matters as very important. They are fearful and nervous and apprehensive."[2]

The fact that an injury cannot always be seen by the naked eye does not mean that it is any less of a "real" injury than those which involve the breaking of bones, the spilling of blood, the scarring of tissue or "physical" pain. Indeed, on one view, the mental repercussions of trauma are more serious, more deserving of the law's attention than those of a physical nature. Mental conditions frequently persist long after organic injuries have disappeared. Broken bones knit, wounds heal often without scarring or permanent disability and those that do scar, although unsightly, leave less of a mark than scars on the mind. Physical pain usually subsides and often long before the psychological impact of distressing events disappears. The after-effects of trauma may never fully dissipate and may remain to haunt a person for the remainder of his or her life, forever eroding mental stability. A sailor, for example, involved in a collision between two warships during a training exercise, and suffering severe post-traumatic stress disorder, depression and acute anxiety attacks, was still being treated 20 years after the disaster.[3] Certainly, not every form of psychiatric abnormality will be permanent or even long-lasting and tragically there are physical conditions such as paraplegia and quadriplegia which remain with victims until death. But as a general observation, an injured mind is far more difficult to nurse back to health than an injured body and is arguably more debilitating and disruptive of a greater number of aspects of human existence.

Suspicions of malingering may explain why damages for post-traumatic psychiatric disorders are often substantially less than those for physical injury, despite the fact that the limitations on the sufferer's daily life caused through impact on the mind may actually be greater. Scientific and medical knowledge is equal to any difficulties of proof of the existence and extent of mental damage. Even if it is conceded that there is a possibility that a certain percentage of false claimants may slip undetected through the screening processes, this is an illegitimate basis for restricting the right to

2. *Griffiths v R & H Green & Silley Weir Ltd* (1948) 81 LLLR 378 at 380.
3. *Clark v Commonwealth* (unreported, Victorian SC, 24 Feb 1992, No 31 of 1985).

redress in deserving cases. As one American judge has said, "[d]oing away with an entire class of action solely because some may be tainted by mischief is like employing a cannon to kill a flea".[4] In the light of current psychological and psychiatric investigative techniques, the risk of fraud is minuscule.[5] One suspects it is easier to fake or magnify a bad back than a psychiatrically imbalanced mind.

In the same way that different values have been attached by some courts to the need to protect individuals and their personal property from harm and the need to protect economic interests,[6] a value judgment has been made as to the importance of shielding people from mental as opposed to physical injury. For all the recent judicial discussion, psychiatric damage has been and continues to be demoted to a secondary status behind damage of a physical nature by way of unnecessary and illogical constraints on liability. This is unjustified. The two kinds of personal harm should not be treated differently in terms of the rules governing responsibility at law.[7] The right to recover for psychiatric damage should not hinge on the relationship of the psychiatrically disturbed claimant to the primary victim or whether he or she was present at the accident or its aftermath, news of the distressing event was communicated by a third party or via modern media, the particular form of psychiatric complaint was shock-induced or developed rapidly or gradually, was lengthy in duration or short-lived or attributable to factors other than an accident to another or sensitivity to damage to the mind. That these types of issues in themselves have no legitimate function in the attribution of legal responsibility for psychiatric damage was recognised by Lawson and Markesinis ten years ago when, after a detailed comparative study of the contrasting approaches of civil and common law systems to liability for negligence, they reflected:

> One wonders . . . if the time has not come to say that if the plaintiff, as a result of the defendant's conduct, has suffered some kind of serious and 'recognisable psychiatric illness' he should be allowed to recover damages irrespective of his relationship with the victim, his physical position at the time of the accidents, or even his personal propensities towards such type of injury. Indeed, the law may be slowly moving in that direction."[8]

It may be, but "slowly" is the operative word. Those judges who have attempted to broaden the common law's outlook have seen much of their work undone. Relief has been refused at appellate level on the basis of illogical and irrational historical rhetoric. True it is that positive headway has been made in some respects, especially in certain jurisdictions, but many other sensible steps have not been taken, or if taken retraced. And with the

---

4. *Gates v Richardson* (1986) 719 P 2d 193 (Wyo) per Cardine J at 197.
5. Note *Dulieu v White & Sons* [1901] 2 KB 669 per Kennedy J at 681; *McLoughlin v O'Brian* [1983] 1 AC 410 per Lord Edmund-Davies at 425.
6. See eg *Murphy v Brentwood District Council* [1991] 1 AC 398 per Lord Oliver at 487. Note also *D & F Estates Ltd v Church Commissioners for England* [1989] AC 177; *Caparo Industries Plc v Dickman* [1990] 2 AC 605; *Department of the Environment v Thomas Bates & Son* [1991] 1 AC 499.
7. Compare eg *McLoughlin v O'Brian* [1983] 1 AC 410 per Lord Wilberforce at 421-422.
8. F H Lawson & B S Markesinis, *Tortious Liability for Unintentional Harm in the Common Law and the Civil Law* (1982), Vol 1, 47.

recent pronouncement by the House of Lords any momentum that may have been gathering speed has now almost certainly ground to a halt, at least in England—closer but still far short of the desirable mark.

We live in a rapidly developing world. Change is an integral component of 20th-century society and exposure to and digestion of new ideas, new technology and new knowledge seem almost part of everyday life now. If the law is to continue to play a fundamental role in the 21st century the courts cannot persist in ignoring the valuable contributions that can be made by other disciplines in the formulation and development of the common law. The barriers of precedent must be lowered in the interest of advancement rather than allowed to stagnate the law by suffocating fresh and innovative ideas. In 1983 Lord Bridge said that "this whole area of English law stands in urgent need of review"[9] and proceeded to redefine the ambit of the cause of action. The need for further and more radical change is long overdue. That every one of the claimants whose lives have been torn apart as a result of the horrific events at Hillsborough failed in attempts to extract some solace for their losses makes this abundantly clear. Although courts do sometimes make reference to the tragedy of the losses suffered by psychiatrically damaged plaintiffs and offer condolences in a sentence or two, one could be forgiven for thinking that they sometimes decide these matters without a complete appreciation of the utter destruction of the lives before them. We are not to be taken as suggesting that legal accountability should be attributed on the basis of sympathy— merely that relief should be awarded where there is no sound or convincing legal, policy, medical, scientific or commonsense ground for refusing it. Appellate courts are in a position to offer some comfort to and thereby assist persons whose minds have been traumatised by the negligent and therefore avoidable conduct of others and should not allow outdated reasoning to dictate results that confound rational thought.

The number of persons potentially at risk of suffering some form of psychiatric damage through perceiving or learning of a traumatic event can, in theory, greatly exceed the number of individuals physically harmed by the incident in question. For this reason fear of multiplicity of actions continues surreptitiously to impede the abandonment of unsound principle. It is an extremely poor reason for denying or limiting a remedy if the cause is a just one. As long ago as 1703, Holt CJ said in *Ashby v White*:

> "[I]t is no objection to say, that it will occasion multiplicity of actions; for if men will multiply injuries, actions must be multiplied too; for every man that is injured ought to have his recompense."[10]

This cause is very much a just one. Wherever the consequences of a wrong call for redress it is incumbent upon the courts to create precedent irrespective of the by-product of increased litigation. Tortfeasors must be made to take full responsibility for their actions or inactions including full legal liability for all kinds of loss caused by their substandard conduct. Negligently caused trauma-induced psychiatric damage is not an independent intervening cause but flows in uninterrupted sequence from the defendant's lack of care and is a harm for which his or her responsibility

9. *McLoughlin v O'Brian* [1983] 1 AC 410 at 431.
10. (1703) 2 Ld Raym 938; 92 ER 126 at 137.

to provide recompense does not diminish because of a potential frequency of occurrence. It is open to serious question, however, whether further liberalising of the law governing recovery for mental damage would in fact lead to the predicted increase in suits. The constituent elements of the tort of negligence and *Wilkinson v Downton*[11] liability impose sufficient limitations on recovery. In relation to the negligent infliction of psychiatric damage it should primarily be a question of proving the existence of such injury or illness, the reasonable foreseeability of that psychiatric harm— and it is here that the relationship between the parties, the claimant's location at the time of the trauma, the means of knowledge of it and other issues will be relevant—and establishing the causative link between the tortfeasor's conduct and the plaintiff's mental condition. It must be remembered that although "[a] defender is not liable for a consequence of a kind which is not foreseeable . . . it does not follow that he is liable for every consequence which a reasonable man could foresee".[12] Sound policy considerations may therefore, in certain circumstances, have a role to play,[13] but these must not be permitted to operate covertly and their influence on decision making must be expressly acknowledged by the courts. Differences in the strengths of various types of claims can be reflected in the quantum of damages awarded rather than leading to the automatic exclusion of some actions on the basis of the inability of an antiquated theory to accommodate them.

Verifying the presence of the first of the factors, that is, recognised psychiatric damage, is no mere formality—it is a considerable hurdle to surmount in itself.[14] The medical literature makes it clear that the mental equilibrium of most "normal" members of society will not be upset by traumatic stimuli, even those which are quite severe in nature.[15] As Mantell J has observed: "The kind of psychological illness which the plaintiff has had the misfortune to experience [in this case, continuing reactive depression] is a most unlikely consequence of hearing of the death of a loved one or, one suspects, of witnessing it either. . . . Indeed, on the statistical and medical evidence before me, psychiatric illness resulting from nervous shock . . . can be no more than the most remote of possibilities".[16] The mind is a remarkably resilient piece of machinery and it is only in the minority of individuals that actual psychiatric damage going beyond the typical emotional reactions experienced when confronted with stressors will be sustained. Secondary psychiatric responses are in truth

11. [1897] 2 QB 57.
12. *McKew v Holland & Hannen & Cubitts (Scotland) Ltd* [1969] 3 All ER 1621 per Lord Reid at 1623.
13. Take, for example, the situation where the spouse, parents or friends of a victim of a serial killer attempt to sue the police authorities for psychiatric injury suffered on learning of the death, alleging that due to want of care the perpetrator had remained at large and able to commit the murder, causing resultant mental damage to them, the secondary victims. Although this scenario is foreseeable, there would be disturbing implications if tort actions against the police were sanctioned for failing to prevent criminal conduct and the psychiatric consequences of it. Note *Hill v Chief Constable of West Yorkshire* [1989] AC 53.
14. See *McLoughlin v O'Brian* [1983] 1 AC 410 per Lord Bridge at 431.
15. See eg J Havard, "Reasonable Foresight of Nervous Shock" (1956) 19 MLR 478 at 482; above, pp 27-30, 200-201.
16. *Hevican v Ruane* [1991] 3 All ER 65 at 68-70.

relatively rare phenomena.[17] For example, one study examining the prevalence of post-traumatic stress disorder in the general United States population established a rate of 1 per cent for this condition.[18] This relatively low figure will have included a vast number of non-tortiously inflicted patients, making the proportion of cases relevant for our purposes even lower. There is no reason to suspect that the rate would be any higher in the other countries considered in this work. When the total sum of tort victims who have been caused to suffer the different types of recognised psychiatric conditions is tallied the number of potential claimants is, despite assertions to the contrary by some members of the judiciary, minimal. Even in the United States, where the law has evolved further in this area and where recovery is permitted for mental disturbances falling well short of psychiatric illness, according to one estimate, albeit now a little dated, only approximately 2 to 3 per cent of all torts are associated with psychiatric disability.[19]

Even if this figure has increased slightly in the last 20 years we are still talking of a proportionally limited number of cases, certainly not an amount that would warrant the imposition of the severe limiting devices currently operative. Moreover, pragmatic and personal considerations will convince a number of those who do manage to prove that they have suffered a compensable loss that it is better to refrain from instituting proceedings, leaving the courts to deal with a very small number of suits indeed. Apart, for example, from financial constraints, few persons relish the thought of a court appearance and in the context of psychiatric illness the prospect of reliving in minute detail the trauma of their loss in hostile surroundings will be particularly unnerving dissuading many sufferers from pursuing matters any further. Indeed, the stress and strain of such a "re-run" may well be medically inadvisable. Years pass before civil proceedings run their course and psychiatric sufferers may have only just managed to set their lives on track again. They may not wish to risk this often painstakingly slow and hard-won progress in courtroom battle. It is questionable too whether, in contrast to physical injury victims, sufferers of secondary mental disorders are really all that concerned with legal redress. This is not to say that such victims will seldom consider suing for the damage done to them, just that this is probably not priority number one in their broken lives. Although significant damages have on occasion been granted, the general trend of low awards dispels any suggestion of a flood of suits commenced in the hope of securing large financial windfalls. Further, and perhaps more debatably, there may be some truth in the speculation that where the primary and secondary victims are closely bonded, some individuals would consider litigation on their own behalf as

17. "[T]his case is unusual in the sense that unfortunately many people in the community lose loved ones in motor vehicle accidents. The grief which they suffer at the time in many cases, carry with them for the rest of their lives, rarely develops into an incapacitating psychiatric illness as has occurred in this case.": *Butcher v Motor Accidents Board* (1984) *Victorian Motor Accidents Cases* 72-026 (CCH) per Mr Higgins at 83,141.

18. J Helzer, "Post-Traumatic Stress Disorder in the General Population" (1987) 317 N Eng J Med 1630.

19. L F Sparr & J K Boehnlein, "Posttraumatic Stress Disorder in Tort Actions: Forensic Minefield" (1990) 18 Bull Am Acad Psy Law 283 at 286.

particularly inappropriate and distasteful, or perhaps even a kind of betrayal of or disrespect for the dead or injured loved one. [20]

Liberalisation will not see a deluge of psychiatric damage claims because most claimants will be unable to clear the still significant hurdles to relief. There has to date been a paucity of litigation in this area, [21] especially outside the United States, [22] and it is submitted that even if the law develops along the lines advocated in this work this will continue to be the case. Significantly, those Australian jurisdictions where statutory remedies have been introduced for certain plaintiffs who did not witness an accident or physical injuries have not been swamped by litigants. [23] The difference will be that the claims of those that do sue will be adjudicated upon according to more sensible doctrine and bearing the relevant medical literature and observations in mind. Denial will be based on sound legal and scientific reasoning rather than the perceived need to prevent trespass beyond artificially constructed boundaries.

Repeated reference has been made in the case law to the "good sense" of judges and their inherent ability to know where to draw the line of acceptability. [24] But, as Goodhart once noted, "the fact that a judge has good sense does not explain the grounds on which he has based his decision". [25] One hopes that if and when the question of the principles governing psychiatric damage law reaches the highest appellate levels in Australia and Canada, the many issues which have hitherto escaped detailed judicial scrutiny will be thoroughly investigated and both the precise reasons for the outcome of the cases before the courts and the scope of this special cause of action articulated. The necessity of taking the additional steps that the English judiciary have been unprepared to do must be recognised. Unfortunately, *Alcock v Chief Constable of South Yorkshire Police*, [26] although welcome in some respects such as the relationship issue, will stifle further, and we would say essential, development in the United Kingdom, probably for many years to come. But as Williams J in *Spence v Percy* has noted:

20. See H Teff, "Liability for Negligently Inflicted Nervous Shock" (1983) 99 LQR 100 at 112.
21. One informal survey of the major insurance companies in England suggested that the number of psychiatric damage claims did not rise significantly in the years immediately following *McLoughlin v O'Brian* [1983] 1 AC 410: see D S Greer, "A Statutory Remedy for Nervous Shock" (1986) 21 Ir Jur (ns) 57 at 77.
22. Even in litigation-preoccupied America *Dillon v Legg* (1968) 441 P 2d 912; 69 Cal Rptr 72 is said to have had a negligible impact on the insurance rates in California: see P A Bell, "The Bell Tolls: Toward Full Tort Recovery for Psychic Injury" (1984) 36 U Fla L Rev 333 at 366.
23. See *Law Reform (Miscellaneous Provisions) Act* 1944 (NSW), s 4(1); *Law Reform (Miscellaneous Provisions) Act* 1955 (ACT) s 24; *Law Reform (Miscellaneous Provisions) Act* 1956 (NT), s 25. Note also *Wrongs Act* 1936 (SA), s 35a(1)(c); *Motor Accidents Act* 1988 (NSW), s 77. See above, Chapter 11.
24. See eg *Bourhill v Young* [1943] AC 92 per Lord Wright at 110; *Marshall v Lionel Enterprises Inc* (1971) 25 DLR (3d) 141 per Haines J at 151; *McLoughlin v O'Brian* [1983] 2 AC 410 per Lord Bridge at 443; *Jaensch v Coffey* (1984) 155 CLR 549 per Brennan J at 571; *Attia v British Gas Plc* [1988] 1 QB 304 per Bingham LJ at 320-321.
25. (1971) 87 LQR 8 at 10.
26. [1992] 1 AC 310.

"Undoubtedly the last word has not yet been written on the scope of liability with respect to [psychiatric] injury and new factual situations coupled with new technology will cause appellate judges to review the limits of liability for such injury from time to time."[27]

At the first opportunity, the boundary stone must be moved again.

27. (1991) Aust Torts Rep 81-116 at 69,081.

INDEX

Accident neurosis, 233

Actio injuriarum—*see under* **South African law**

Acute stress reaction, 34, 40

Adrenalin secretion, 28-29

Adultery, damages for—*see under* **Domestic relations, torts affecting**

Aftermath
    accident, at scene of, 5-6, 136-137, 149
    communication, relationship to means of, 150-152
    generally, 5-6, 13, 83, **136-152**, 153, 159-160, 163, 179-180, 292
    history, 5-6, 136-139
    hospital, in, 6, 137-138, 142, 148-150
    identification of dead body, 141-143, 150
    lapse of time, substantial, 139-141, 151
    limits, 138-140, 143, 145-152
    medical negligence cases, in, 142
    no aftermath, cases where, 151, 168
    presence at scene of accident, relationship to, 144-145
    relationship of parties, relationship to, 151-152
    uncertainty as to outcome of accident, 140-142, 144, 151
    United States, in, 145-148
    victim coming to plaintiff, 149
    see also under **Statutory liability for psychiatric damage**

AIDS, 23, 168, 187, 206, 303

Anxiety states, 16, 29-31, 34, 39, 88-89, 116, 157, 193, 197, 214, 231, 233-235, 266, 273, 277, 309

Aquilian action—*see under* **South African law**

Assault
    generally, 8, 46, 59, 284, 293
    psychiatric damage caused by, 8

Assumption of risk
    compulsory insurance, and, 257
    drunken driver cases, 257-258
    employment cases, 257-258
    exemption clauses and, 257
    generally, **256-258**
    psychiatric damage cases, in, 258
    requirements for, 256-257
    scope of defence, 257
    sport cases, 257-258

Pre-existing duty
    liability for psychiatric damage where, 13, 61, 100, 147, 156-159, 188, 223
    person not involved in accident, to, 158-159
    see also **Direct victim**

Pre-impact mental distress, 6, 50-51

Pre-natal injury—*see under* **Negligence; Contributory negligence**

Presence, as element in recovery for psychiatric damage, 4-6, 12, 83, 134-136,
             142-143, 147-148, 153, 158-160, 172, 178-180, 192
    see also **Aftermath**

Prima facie tort, 284

Primary and secondary victims, 90-105, 292-297
    see also **Fear for safety of another, psychiatric damage caused by**
    see also under **Negligence**

Privacy, invasion of, 306-307

Property damage, psychiatric damage resulting from
    chattels, 211-212
    generally, 3, 61, 106, 164, 199, **208-212**
    intangible property, 211-212
    market value, property without, 212
    property owned by others, 211-212
    sudden impact, relationship to, 199-200, 209
    see also under **Mental distress**

Proximity—*see under* **Negligence; Duty of care**

Psychiatric damage
    contract, in—*see under* **Contract, damages for breach of, causing**
    duration, 17, 309
    extension of liability, arguments for
        generally, 308-315
        physical harm, compared with, 308, 310-311
        potential actions, number of, 311-312, 314
        rarity of secondary reactions, 312-313
    history of liability for, 1-7, 99
    "nervous shock", 14-15, 19
    reasons for denying recovery for
        assessment of damages, difficulty of, 2, 263
        causation, problem of proving, 2
        generally, 2-3, 11
        false claims, danger of, 2, 21, 39, 168, 170, 218, 309-310
        "floodgates" argument, 2, 119, 129-130, 168, 170, 174-176, 218,
            311-314
        insurance, 2
        medical ignorance, 2, 285, 309
        proof, difficulty of, 308-309
        remoteness, 285
    recognisable—*see* **Recognisable psychiatric damage, requirement of**
    severity, 18
    tort, as a, 59-60